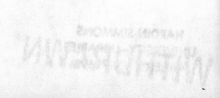

PRINCIPLES OF

2d edition

ECONOMICS

Ryan C. Amacher
Dean, College of Commerce
and Industry
Professor of Economics
Clemson University

Published by

HI5   **SOUTH-WESTERN PUBLISHING CO.**

CINCINNATI   WEST CHICAGO, ILL.   DALLAS   PELHAM MANOR, N.Y.   PALO ALTO, CALIF.

ISBN: 0-538-08150-3

Library of Congress Catalog Card Number: 81-85859

1 2 3 4 5 D 7 6 5 4 3

Printed in the United States of America

The second edition of a textbook is a learning experience for any author. I have had the good fortune of having very helpful and concerned users of the first edition on both the faculty and student sides of the podium. I hope the improvements in *Principles of Economics,* Second Edition, reflect their helpful comments.

My goal is not to make professional economists out of students. A common complaint in economics is that instructors and textbook authors often approach the principles course as if it were an initial step in receiving a Ph.D. This text is not intended to train professional economists, but to show the rich analysis that economic theory offers the policy analyst or adviser. In this sense, this is both a theory book and a policy book. Policy cannot be understood without theory, and theory without policy isn't too useful.

CHANGES IN THE SECOND EDITION

This second edition represents a substantial revision. Chapter 6, which examines the role of government as a taxing and spending agent, is a completely new chapter, as is Chapter 16 on supply-side economics. Other changes in this edition are as follows.

In Part 1, "Introduction to the Economic Approach," the first chapter gives a more complete introduction to what the student will learn and what types of questions are addressed in microeconomics and in macroeconomics.

In Part 2, "Money, Taxes, and National Income Accounting," the chapters on money have been expanded to give a more complete explanation of money stock expansion and to incorporate changes resulting from recent legal developments. Chapter 6, an entirely new chapter, details the workings of the governmental sector in the U.S. economy. The chapter on national income accounting has been substantially revised to present definitions and techniques in a more standard, and less detailed, fashion.

The seven chapters in Part 3, "Macroeconomics," have been extensively revised. The Keynesian model is presented in a more complete fashion which avoids repetitive explanations of ways to solve it. The discussion of rational expectations has been expanded. An entirely new chapter on supply-side economics has been added, with a section on Say's Law.

In Part 4, "The Basics of Microeconomics," only minor revisions have been undertaken. Policy applications of elasticity concepts have been expanded.

In Part 5, "The Organization of Product Markets," a section on product curves and the stages of production has been included.

In Part 6, "Factor Markets and Governmental Intervention," all statistical material has been updated and recent developments in labor union activity have been included. A discussion of the War on Poverty has been added.

In Part 7, "International Influences," the material on international trade in the Keynesian model has been moved to Part 3. The chapter on development economics has been streamlined and updated. The Polish Solidarity crisis is discussed.

In Part 8, "The Economics of Being an Economist," the material has been updated.

IMPORTANT FEATURES OF THE SECOND EDITION

The following features make this introductory text a unique product.

Organization

This book allows the student to see the power of economic analysis very quickly. After elementary tools are discussed, they are applied to a wide range of social policy questions.

The final chapter looks at what economists do, how much they are paid, how they are educated, and why students might major in economics. The chapter answers a host of questions that potential majors might have about economics as a career option. No other book on the market includes such a feature.

Important Economists, Economic Institutions, and Issues

Each chapter includes two insets featuring important economists, economic institutions, and relevant contemporary issues. The insets are closely related to the material in the chapter and highlight the way a particular theory was developed or how it is being applied to important problems.

References, Questions, and Reading Suggestions

Since one of the major goals of this book is to demonstrate the relevance of the economic way of thinking, numerous references that are intended to direct interested students to more information on particular subjects are included. The carefully selected *Suggestions for Further Reading* at the end of each chapter serve this same purpose. *Questions for Discussion* appear at the end of each chapter. These are intended to generate interest in the material that has been presented in the chapter. The questions can serve as a foundation for more in-depth understanding of policymaking. Suggested answers to all the questions appear in the instructor's manual.

Glossary

All terms that appear in boldface type and in the margins of the book are defined in the *Glossary*.

TEACHING AND STUDY AIDS

This book contains teaching and study aids. In addition, a study guide, an instructor's manual, a test bank, and transparency masters are available. The test bank and instructor's manual have been substantially revised and expanded for this second edition.

The Text

The appendix to Chapter 2 contains a review of the graphing techniques used in the text. Each text chapter begins with a set of *Learning Objectives*. Students can use these as a handy guide to areas which may require more work or as an aid to reviewing the subject matter. At the end of each chapter, there is a *Summary* which provides a useful review. *New Terms* are listed at the end of the chapter in the order in which they appear. All these new terms may be found in the *Glossary*. Each new term also appears in the margin on the page on which it first appears.

The Study Guide

The *Study Guide* has a chapter which corresponds to each chapter in the text (with the exception of the final chapter). Each study guide chapter includes:

1. Learning objectives for the chapter
2. A list of important terms and concepts
3. Completion questions based on the list of important terms and concepts
4. Problems requiring numerical or graphical solution
5. Multiple-choice questions
6. Short discussion questions
7. Complete answers to all questions in the study guide

Extensive classroom testing of the study guide has shown it to be an effective way for students to improve their understanding and performance.

The Instructor's Manual

The instructor's manual has a chapter corresponding to each chapter in the text (with the exception of the last). Each of these chapters include:

1. A short discussion of the purposes of the chapter
2. An outline based on the headings within the text chapters
3. The *Learning Objectives* as found in the text and study guide
4. A *Summary* of the chapter
5. The *New Terms* (with definitions used in the text) that appear in that chapter
6. Selected lecture notes that expand on chapter themes
7. Answers to all end-of-chapter questions

The Test Bank

A test bank is available to adopters. It consists of multiple-choice questions which have not been used in the study guide.

ACKNOWLEDGEMENTS

Any project as complex as this takes a number of dedicated and talented people to insure that it doesn't remain just another "book in progress." I am extremely grateful to those people. I especially wish to acknowledge the contributions of a co-author of the first edition, Richard James Sweeney, whose other commitments prevented his participation in this edition.

I also owe a significant debt of gratitude to the users of the first edition. It goes without saying that without them there would not be a second edition. But even more, many of these users, and other reviewers, provided encouragement and suggestions. In particular, I would like to thank the following individuals for their helpful comments:

Ogden Allsbrook, University of Georgia

Mohsen Bahmani, Michigan State University

Ted Ball, Consumnes River College

Jack Blicksilver, Georgia State University

James Boughton, Indiana University

Robert Bray, California State Polytechnic University

Paul Burgess, Arizona State University

Akram Chowdry, San Jose State University

Larry Davis, East Texas State University

Mark Evans, California State College

Bernard Feigenbaum, Washington University

Brother Edward Grinder, St. Vincent College

William Gunther, University of Alabama

W.W. Hall, University of North Carolina, Wilmington

Stephen Happel, Arizona State University

Bruce Harger, Lake Superior State College

Pershing Hill, University of Alaska

David Klingaman, Ohio University

Hannis Kvarin, Arizona State University

Dale Lehman, California State Polytechnic University

Albert Link, Auburn University

Adolph Mark, DePaul University

Paul McGouldrick, SUNY Binghamton

Michael Melvin, Arizona State University

Norman Miller, York College

Narayan Nargund, Allegheny College

Gerald Nickelsburg, University of Southern California

Paul DePippo, Glendale Community College

Rose Pfetterbaum, Mesa Community College

Beverly Schaeffer, Emory University

Edwin Stecher, University of San Diego

Donald Swanson, Indiana University Southeast

Suzanne Thomas, Fordham University

Holley Ulbrich, Clemson University

Lloyd Valentine, University of Cincinnati

Norman Walzer, Western Illinois University

Larry Wilson, Sandhills Community College

Frank Wert, Central State University

Joseph Zoric, University of Steubenville

As with the first edition, Jon Ozmun and James Pinto prepared the companion test bank and study guide. In this second edition, they participated more actively in planning the revision and, in some cases, drafting the revisions of some of the chapters. Their help in improving the quality of this book is greatly appreciated.

Finally, I would like to thank my wife, Susan, who wore the hats of secretary, editorial assistant, and quarterback for the second edition. Without her help the process would have been more rocky and less fun.

Ryan C. Amacher

CONTENTS

PART 1

Introduction to the Economic Approach

CHAPTER 1

Economics, Economic Issues, and Economic Methodology

Learning Objectives

After studying the materials found in this chapter, you should be able to do the following:

1. Understand why you should study economics.

2. Define economics and be able to make basic distinctions between microeconomics and macroeconomics.

3. Discuss many of the reasons why economists disagree with each other.

4. Evaluate the basic steps necessary for the development of an economic theory and the means for judging the validity of a theory.

5. Discuss the self-interest hypothesis and its importance to the study of economics.

6. Discuss the economic approach to problem solving.

In this introductory chapter we present a wide-range discussion of what economics is, the main problems in economics, the scientific method in economics, and some basic elements of the economic view of the world. Most importantly, we stress the economic way of thinking. This chapter ends with an introduction to some typical issues studied by economists.

WHY STUDY ECONOMICS?

Before we proceed, it is appropriate to address the question of why you should study economics. Many, perhaps most, of you are in an economics course and therefore reading this book because you are required to do so. Most probably, economics is a prerequisite at your college, whether you are an engineering, business, or liberal arts major. So, our first response to the question, "Why study economics?" could be that academicians believe that training in economics is a good foundation for almost all students. But this really doesn't answer the question; it simply avoids it. Therefore, we will offer you some better answers.

The fact that so many academicians from so many different disciplines think it is important to study economics offers a clue to why you, too, should study economics. Economics interacts with almost all other academic disciplines. It is intimately intertwined with current events, and it has a profound effect on political events, both domestically and internationally. The answer, then, is quite straightforward: You should study economics to better understand the profound effect that economic issues have on the world.

A second reason for studying economics is based on the effect that economic ideas and theories have on world leaders. Much of what political decision makers do is based on economic theory. As John Maynard Keynes, one of the most influential economists of all time, wrote:

> . . . the ideas of economists and political philosophers, both when they are right and when they are wrong, are more powerful than is commonly understood. Indeed, the world is ruled by little else. Practical men, who believe themselves to be quite exempt from any intellectual influences, are usually the slaves of some defunct economist. Madmen in authority, who hear voices in the air, are distilling their frenzy from some academic scribbler of a few years back.[1]

Thus, if we want to understand what politicians are advocating, be they great or mad, we must understand the economic theory upon which they are acting.

A third, and perhaps most important, reason for studying economics is that it allows us to better understand how the world and its people function. Economic theory is very useful in understanding behavior because it allows the person who understands it to develop models with predictive power. As Alfred Marshall (see Chapter 3 for a biographical sketch) wrote, "Economics is the study of mankind in the ordinary business of life."[2] Studying economics, then, can give powerful insights into human behavior.

Finally, economics is fun, and people who are trained in economics find rewarding jobs and careers. If you like to think in a logical fashion, you will enjoy studying economics. If you study hard and learn the material well, your efforts will pay off in the future. Now, can you think of better reasons for reading the rest of this book and for taking the economics course in which you are enrolled?

WHAT IS ECONOMICS?

For many of you, this is your first course in economics. Many people like to start studying a new subject with a definition of what it's about. You will have a much better idea of what economists do and what they think about by the time you finish this book, but if you want a definition of economics, here's one. *Economics* is the scientific study of people and their institutions from the point of view of how they go about producing and consuming goods and services, and how they face the problem of making choices in a world of scarce resources.

The study of economics is often divided into microeconomics and macroeconomics. *Microeconomics* looks at the interactions of producers and consumers in individual markets—say, for shoes—and the interactions between different markets—say, the market for steel and the market for aluminum. (*Micro* is a Greek prefix meaning small. This is in contrast to the Greek prefix *macro* which means large.)

economics The scientific study of people and their institutions from the point of view of how they go about producing and consuming goods and services and how they face the problem of making choices in a world of scarce resources.

microeconomics The study of individual market interactions. Microeconomics concentrates on the individual unit, the consumer, the firm, and the industry.

---

[1]William Breit and Roger L. Ransom, *The Academic Scribblers* (New York: Holt, Rinehart & Winston, CBS, Inc., 1971), p. viii.

[2]Alfred Marshall, *Principles of Economics* (8h ed.; Don Mills, Ontario: The Macmillan Co. of Canada, Ltd., 1920), p. 323.

macroeconomics   *The study of the economy as a whole. Macroeconomics is concerned with policy issues such as the level of employment and the overall price level.*

Macroeconomics studies the behavior of economy-wide figures, such as the gross national product—the value of final output that the economy produces in a given time period—as well as categories that cut across many markets, such as total employment in manufacturing industries or total exports.

In microeconomics, the most important tools are the ideas of demand and supply. They help to explain price and output in individual markets and how price and output in different markets are related. Macroeconomics deals with *aggregates,* numbers that are determined by adding across many markets. In microeconomics, we may look at the demand for the output of a single industry, such as bicycles. In macroeconomics, we look at the overall demand for the economy's total output of final goods for, say, a year. In the same way, microeconomics will look at the supply of bicycles, and macroeconomics looks at the economy's total supply of output of all final goods. Keep in mind, however, that microeconomics and macroeconomics are very much related.

DO ECONOMISTS EVER AGREE?

Economists argue about many issues. If you look at your daily newspaper or at weekly newsmagazines such as *Newsweek* or *Time,* it seems that many of the economic stories are about economists disagreeing over issues. However, you will see in the rest of this book that economists do agree on many issues. It's only natural that news stories play up disagreements, especially among experts. But we don't want to lie to you—there are a lot of disagreements in economics. Throughout this book, we want to talk about where economists agree and also where and why they disagree. It's not our job to sell you on one point of view. On every issue, we want to present the pros and cons, so you can begin to make up your own mind.

Perhaps the most pervasive reason why economists disagree is that since they are all human beings from different personal backgrounds, they have different value judgments. They will disagree on economic policy, because even if they use the same theory and the same facts (so that their conclusions are the same on what the impact of a particular policy will be), they will disagree on whether the net results are good or bad.

THEORY

theory   *A set of principles that can be used to make inferences about the world.*

economic approach   *A way of thinking about and analyzing problems that relies heavily on the basic tools of economic theory.*

Theory often suffers from bad press. It is sometimes viewed as abstract and useless, maybe even too hard. In part, the complaints are justified. Theory, for theory's sake, is a waste of time for most people. *Theory* is valuable, however, because it allows the development of a set of principles that can be used to untangle the web of different forces involved in social problems. Principles will then develop into a framework for thinking. We might call this way of thinking the *economic approach.* This approach will allow you to analyze and understand a wide range of social interactions.

All economists have the same tool kit of ideas to use on the particular problem they wish to analyze. In this book we present the basic tools in that kit which allow economists to approach problems in very similar ways.

Theorizing and the Scientific Method

The chapters to follow will develop the theoretical models of economic *science* so that you can use this science to develop operational hypotheses about the world and analyze a wide range of social policy problems. Science consists of appealing to facts in a systematic manner. The early scientists did little more than systematize and classify the facts that they uncovered. If you have taken an introductory course in botany or zoology, you are familiar with this methodology. Such an approach can very quickly lead to diminishing returns, unless your mind works like a giant filing cabinet. It is very easy to get lost and bogged down with facts, and unless you are preparing for an appearance on the College Bowl, this approach is not very appealing. As an alternative, economic theorists make assumptions that simplify a problem and then develop a theoretical model that will yield a **testable hypothesis.** This hypothesis can then be checked by appealing to the facts.

testable hypothesis   An inference from economic theory that can be subjected to empirical testing.

The role of theory is an important one in everything we do. Any interpretation we make about the environment around us has an implicit theory. Our senses receive information and we interpret that information. But how we interpret that information will affect the way we behave, and our interpretation will be based on a theory about the world which we have developed over time. These theories are, for most people, constantly being revised and improved. The only difference with the theory in this book and the theory that you use in your daily life is that we will make this theory explicit and examine its implications in detail.

As an example, we might develop a theory that leads to the hypothesis that if we hold supply constant and increase demand, price will rise. We could then examine actual situations in which this has happened and determine if price did rise. Such experiments often are referred to by economists as ***ceteris paribus*** experiments. The economist changes one variable in the theoretical model (demand, in this example) and then hypothesizes what will happen *ceteris paribus* or "holding everything else constant." In this example, if demand rises *ceteris paribus* (with all else held constant), it is hypothesized that price will rise. In many of the theoretical chapters that follow, we will venture into a never-never land that has been created by the assumptions we make. This never-never land could be compared to the frictionless world often assumed in physics courses.

ceteris paribus   A Latin term that means "holding everything else constant."

We plan to "tell it like [we think] it is," and here is the first point where there is disagreement among economists. This disagreement on the role of assumptions is the crux of an often bitter (and often not too valuable) debate between Paul Samuelson, of the Massachusetts Institute of Technology, and Milton Friedman, who was at the University of Chicago for many years. Both men are Nobel prizewinners in economics. The traditional view, taken by Samuelson, is that once a theory is proven to be logically correct, its usefulness can be tested by examining whether the assumptions it makes are realistic. Friedman disputes this view, arguing that the purpose of theory is to abstract from the unimportant aspects of reality, and the test of the theory is: Does it work? Does it describe what happens to the important aspects of reality? Although the debate has never been resolved, in part because it hinges on semantics, it offers some important points. Assumptions can fulfill very different roles. Some are fundamental to the analysis; others are not. Some simplify the problem and reduce it to manageable proportions. These fundamental and simplifying assumptions are the key to economic theorizing and policy analysis. They are valuable because they permit the economist to come to grips with the key element of a problem and then to explain the problem to noneconomists.

The Self-Interest Hypothesis

Perhaps our most basic assumption in economics is that people behave in a selfish, self-interested manner. This assumption is the foundation of many of our models. For consumers, it is referred to as *utility maximizing behavior;* for resource owners, it is referred to as *income* or *wealth maximization;* and for business firms, it is referred to as *profit maximization.*

self-interest   A basic assumption of economic theory that individual decision makers behave in a selfish manner; they do what is best for themselves.

    Self-interest, as a motivation factor, is often viewed as a cynical way of looking at the world. Much of what you may learn in philosophy or in theology is counter to this view. Many social reformers, such as Marx and Mao, and many experiments in socialism, such as the Fourier settlements in the United States and

The Nobel Prize for Economics

    The Nobel Committee, set up by the Swedish Royal Academy of Sciences, awarded the first Nobel Prize in 1901. It wasn't until 1969, however, that the first *Nobel Prize for Economics* was awarded. The Bank of Sweden funded the 1969 prize to celebrate its 300th anniversary.

    The emergence of economics into the Nobel Prize family of chemistry, physics, and medicine is proof that economics has far surpassed most other social sciences in the eyes of the world's scientific community. Receipt of a Nobel Prize is a high, and monetarily rewarding, honor for an economist.

    Fifty percent of the recipients have been Americans. This percentage is likely to grow since many of today's major economists are American.

    The following have been winners of the prize since 1969:

1969	Ragnar Frisch, Norway
	Jan Tinbergen, Netherlands
1970	Paul A. Samuelson, United States
1971	Simon Kuznets, United States
1972	Kenneth J. Arrow, United States
	Sir John R. Hicks, Great Britain
1973	Wassily Leontief, United States
1974	Gunnar Myrdal, Sweden
	Friedrich A. von Hayek, Great Britain
1975	Leonid V. Kantorovich, USSR
	Tjalling C. Koopmans, United States
1976	Milton Friedman, United States
1977	James E. Meade, Great Britain
	Bertil Ohlin, Sweden
1978	Herbert A. Simon, United States
1979	Sir Arthur Lewis, Great Britain
	Theodore Schultz, United States
1980	Lawrence R. Klein, United States
1981	James Tobin, United States

Milton Friedman *(1912–   )*

Paul A. Samuelson *(1915–   )*

Milton Friedman and *Paul A. Samuelson* are two of the best known contemporary economists. They both are recipients of the Nobel Prize in Economics—Samuelson in 1970 and Friedman in 1976. The two men represent polar extremes in their economic policy advice. Samuelson is a liberal activist who sees an important role for government in the modern industrial society. Friedman advocates a *laissez-faire* economic policy, arguing that the market economy operates very well and that the interventions Samuelson supports cause more harm than good. Samuelson represents the Eastern Establishment brand of economics, while Friedman represents the Chicago School. Friedman was recently quoted in *People* magazine as saying "There is no such thing as a free lunch. That is the sum of my economic theory. The rest is elaboration."

Samuelson, a professor at M.I.T., was awarded an A.B. degree from the University of Chicago and A.M. and Ph.D. degrees in economics from Harvard University. Samuelson's Ph.D. dissertation, *Foundations of*

Economic Analysis, written when he was only 23 years old, still ranks as a monumental work in the application of mathematics to neoclassical economics. Present day graduate students still study Samuelson's *Foundations.* Samuelson is largely responsible for making M.I.T.'s economics department one of the best in the country. After receiving his degree at Harvard, he took a job at M.I.T. and helped to attract what some people consider to be the leading graduate faculty in economics.

Friedman presently is retired from the University of Chicago, where he taught for 30 years, and is a Senior Research Fellow at the Hoover Institute at Stanford University. Friedman received a B.A. degree from Rutgers (where he took courses from Arthur Burns), an A.M. degree from the University of Chicago, and a Ph.D. degree from Columbia University. Friedman has published many articles and books, but his ideas are readily available in two books: *Essays in Positive Economics* (1953) and *Capitalism and Freedom* (1962).

the Cultural Revolution in China, have had an express goal or purpose—to make individuals respond to motivations that are higher than that of self-interest. However, our models are based on the premise that individuals are motivated by self-interest.

Economists using the self-interest assumption often think in a calculating way about things that have a highly emotional element. This leads to the caricature of economists as hard-hearted by those who are critical of the economic approach and the conclusions economists reach. Kenneth Boulding, professor of economics at the University of Colorado, in his presidential address to the American Economic Association, argued that this attack arises from the economist's neglect of the heroic.[3] While "economic man" may be a clod to some, Boulding argues that "heroic man" is a fool, and he wonders how economic institutions have survived so long given the fact that "economic man" is so unpopular.

It is important to keep in mind that the economist does not use the concept of self-interest to predict any one individual's behavior, but rather the economist uses the concept to predict group or average behavior. It is similar to the way insurance companies use attributes of certain groups to predict behavior. Insurance companies tend to grant lower auto rates to young female drivers than they do to young male drivers. This is because they predict that, as a class, young women have fewer accidents than do young men. This says nothing about how any individual young man or young woman will do relative to the group.

A SHORT GUIDE TO THE ECONOMIC APPROACH

We now turn to a short discussion of the basic elements of the economic approach. The list is not meant to be exhaustive, but rather introductory. Our list is not arranged in any particular order and, as usual in any listing, there is some redundancy. This is unavoidable and we hope the repetition will aid the cause of better understanding. If this guide seems difficult to understand, that's because it represents much of the material you will be exposed to in upcoming chapters.

positive (nonnormative) economics   A set of propositions about what is, rather than what ought to be.

normative economics   A set of propositions about what ought to be. Value judgements about the world.

1. Economic theory is *positive,* or *nonnormative;* that is, it consists of a set of refutable propositions about *what is* rather than individual *normative* value judgements about *what ought to be.* This simply means that economic theory strives to be scientific. This, however, is very difficult, because economics is a social science and the outcome of economic analysis can have important social significance. Keep in mind that theory isn't biased, but appliers of theory—in this case, economists—may be.

2. Economic theory cannot predict the future but can only explain the consequences of certain occurrences. Economic theory allows "if A then B" types of statements and does not predict the occurrence of A. This merely means that economic theory is not a crystal ball. Note that in this element and in the first element, there is a difference between economic theory and what

---

[3]By heroic, he means behavior as envisioned in novels, folk tales, and movies—where an individual rises to the occasion by making a supreme self-sacrifice.

economists do. Many economists, particularly macroeconomists, spend a great deal of time forecasting future conditions, and, to do this, they make use of economic theory, but the theory itself doesn't predict the future.

This last statement is confusing, but very important. Economic theory predicts behavior from certain events: If A happens, then B will happen. To forecast, an economist guesses the likelihood that A will occur, and then uses economic theory to predict the occurrence of B. Often, however, the forecasts are wrong. This doesn't mean that the economic theory was incorrect, but that the forecaster was incorrect in predicting the likelihood of A happening.

3. Economists tend to look at private market processes for solutions to social problems. This means that economists appreciate the freedom and efficiency inherent in decentralized processes. This should become clear as you study Chapter 3.

4. Economists spend a great deal of time clarifying options and making the *cost* of a given choice as clear as possible. This tendency to draw attention to the cost of various choices often makes the economist appear as an agitator, because the economist draws attention to the fact that some *good* things may be too costly. However, this important, but unpopular, element of economic thinking is essential, because economic theory always seeks to identify the costs that are associated with any action. This topic is discussed in the next chapter.

5. Economists are likely to recognize the opportunity for substitution among existing options. This proposition is closely related to the previous element. If we look at the costs of various projects and options, we see that some are superior to others. This belief is often unpopular among decision makers and bureaucrats in government and in industry who argue for certain options without considering substitutions.

6. A closely related point is that economists employ an incremental or *marginal analysis.* Economists equate at the margin.[4] This idea will become old hat as you proceed through the book. In essence, *marginalism* means that economists look at costs and benefits for small increases or decreases in projects.

marginalism A technique used to analyze problems in which the results of small changes in quantity are examined.

7. Economists tend to take an individualistic approach to social analysis; that is, they regard the decisions and behavior of individuals as an important influence on the formation of public policy and the organization of the economy. There are several reasons for this individualistic approach (which stands in stark contrast to some political science or sociological approaches to public policy). Perhaps most important, economists tend to view the individual unit as the one that is best suited for decision making.

8. Economic theory is applicable to all economic systems. The legal and political institutions among systems may differ, but the theory that is applied to these systems is the same. It is possible, then, for the economist to

---

[4]In this case, *marginal* means extra, or incremental, rather than inferior.

apply the tools, which historically have been extensively developed to analyze western market economies, to examine socialist economic relations and a wide variety of nonmarket behavior.

A MENU OF EXCITING TOPICS

You are about to begin studying what will prove to be one of the most exciting and worthwhile subjects in your formal education. Many of these important subjects will appear daily on the front pages of newspapers. Economics has come of age, and economic analysis offers insight on topics ranging from crime to inflation. To set the stage, we offer a few examples.

Macroeconomic Goals and Policies

The topics we study will be classified as macroeconomic and microeconomic, because we need to proceed in some orderly fashion. But keep in mind that almost all topics have both a macro and a micro element. Let's enumerate some topics that are primarily macro in nature.

Curing Inflation—The Goal of Price Stability. All countries aim to set price in such a way as to promote price stability. In the 1950s and early 1960s, prices were quite stable in the United States. Since the mid-1960s, however, inflation has become a topic about which you frequently read in the newspapers. Election campaigns have been built around inflation as a political problem. When studying macroeconomics, you will examine the causes and cures of inflation, and evaluate public policy aimed at promoting price stability.

Unemployment—Full Employment. Price stability and full employment are two of the most important macroeconomic goals. Therefore, in a course on macroeconomics, it is necessary to define unemployment and full employment, and then to examine their causes and cures. After studying macroeconomic theory, you will be able to evaluate proposed programs that are designed to cure unemployment.

Economic Growth. Almost everyone is in favor of economic growth. The advocacy of economic growth is understandable. If we define economic growth as producing a larger volume of goods and services, it becomes a means by which the poor can become better off, without taking income away from others. We examine the causes of economic growth and devote an entire chapter to special problems found in less developed countries.

Macroeconomic and Microeconomic Topics

Macroeconomic goals of full employment, price stability, and economic growth are laced with microeconomic considerations. To demonstrate the mixed macro-micro nature of most topics, consider the following.

Economic Security. The issue of economic security has many macroeconomic considerations, because inflation and unemployment are important aspects of economic security. Inflation decreases the value of retirement income and makes people uncertain about their future. The chance of becoming unemployed is a very serious concern for many Americans. There are also microeconomic dimensions to economic security. One important concern is the effect that programs designed to increase security will have on incentives. For instance, if we increase taxes to protect the old and unemployed, will we reduce the incentives of productive workers?

Environmental Standards. The question of environmental standards is primarily micro in nature, because generally the focus is on a particular market or industry. For example, how will the coal industry be affected by the requirements to return strip-mined land to its original condition? This concern also contains many macro considerations: Does environmental policy have an impact on economic growth by making it too costly to do business? Are we forcing the death of some United States industries? These, and other questions related to environmental policy, will become more clear to you as you study economics.

Defending the Dollar. We usually think of the theory and policy that concerns the value of currencies and intervention in exchange markets as both a micro and a macro issue. It is micro in the sense that we are examining a single market—the market for the currency in question. It is macro in the sense that many of the things that affected the demand for, and the supply of, a particular currency are determined by macroeconomic considerations. An entire chapter is devoted to the study of international economics.

Primarily Microeconomic Issues

Again, the following issues are primarily micro, but they have macro considerations.

Activity of Government. Every section of government has an effect on different parties. It creates benefits and costs to different groups of people, changing incentives and disincentives. As a result, all sorts of special interest groups arise. We are all members of various special interest groups, no matter how much we detest and deride such groups. Microeconomics presents a way of uncovering and sorting out the incentives created by governmental action in markets. After studying microeconomics, you will have a way of analyzing the incentives created by governmental policy.

Energy Policy. A good example of governmental activity is energy policy. You will learn in microeconomics how governmental policy created the energy crisis, and how efforts to solve it created all sorts of incentives and rewards that have far-reaching effects.

Labor Unions. Labor unions, like other institutions, have profound effects on markets. It is important to understand what gave rise to the birth of unions in the United States, and which forces have influenced their present status. In microeconomics, you will develop ways to analyze their influence and you will arrive at an informed decision about the worth of labor unions.

ISSUES—ISSUES—ISSUES

In short, the economic approach is a unique way of analyzing the world. Since it is a way of thinking in a logical sequence, and with a set of tools, it provides insight into an endless menu of issues.

CONFLICTS IN POLICIES

One of the frustrating things about public policy analysis is the possibility for conflict among goals. This is so obvious that it almost goes without saying. For example, goals of a clean environment run counter to the goals of promoting economic growth; increasing economic security can destroy incentives, thereby stifling productivity; and energy policy aimed at self-sufficiency may collide with environmental policy. The list of potential conflicts is endless. However, don't become frustrated and put your head in the sand. Economics and the economic approach to thinking allows the anticipation of these conflicts so that the wisest course of action can be selected. Economics uncovers alternative courses of action.

GETTING ON WITH IT

Economics is an exciting social science. The individual who understands the economic way of thinking will gain insight into an endless array of interesting questions. We wish you well. Let's get on with it!

SUMMARY

1. Economics is the scientific study of people and institutions from the point of view of how they produce and consume goods and services and face the problem of scarcity.

2. Microeconomics looks at the interactions of producers and consumers in individual markets.

3. Macroeconomics is the study of the economy as a whole, and is concerned with aggregates.

4. Economists often disagree, but they do agree on a large body of economic theory.

5. Economic theory is an abstract way of thinking that allows the development of principles, or tools, that can be used to study complex social issues.

6. The self-interest hypothesis is a very basic assumption of economic theory. Although economists recognize that economic behavior is a complex process, it is assumed in economics that human beings pursue their own self-interest.

7. The economic approach is positive, or nonnormative; it can't predict the future, but it can make statements of an if-A-then-B type.

8. Because of their individualistic approach, economists tend to look to the market to solve social problems. In analyzing problems, economists spend a great deal of time clarifying options and looking at costs. In examining possibilities for substitution, economists look at costs and benefits at the margin.

9. The menu of topics to which we can apply economic analysis is endless.

NEW TERMS

economics
microeconomics
macroeconomics
theory
economic approach
testable hypothesis

ceteris paribus
self-interest
positive (nonnormative) economics
normative economics
marginalism

QUESTIONS FOR DISCUSSION

1. Write four statements about the energy crisis (it doesn't matter if they are based on correct economic reasoning). Classify each statement as being positive or normative.

2. Do you think people exhibit behavior patterns that confirm the self-interest hypothesis? Does your own behavior confirm the self-interest hypothesis? Can you develop any theory based solely on this assumption?

3. Why do economists theorize rather than attempt to describe reality?

4. Do assumptions have to be realistic to work?

5. What is the difference between *theory that predicts* and *forecasting?*

SUGGESTIONS FOR FURTHER READING

Amacher, Ryan, Robert Tollison, and Thomas Willett. *The Economic Approach to Social Policy Questions.* Ithaca: Cornell University Press, 1976, Chapter 1.

Boulding, Kenneth. "Economics as a Moral Science?" *American Economic Review* (March, 1969).

Buchanan, James M. "Toward an Analysis of Closed Behavioral Systems." In James Buchanan and Robert Tollison (eds.), *Theory of Public Choice.* Ann Arbor: University of Michigan Press, 1972.

Friedman, Milton. *Essays in Positive Economics.* Chicago: University of Chicago Press, 1953, Chapter 1.

Samuelson, Paul. "Discussion—Problems of Methodology." *American Economic Review* (May, 1963).

Tullock, Gordon. "Economic Imperialism." In James Buchanan and Robert Tollison (eds.), *Theory of Public Choice.* Ann Arbor: University of Michigan Press, 1972.

CHAPTER 2

Scarcity, Choice, and Economic Problems

Learning Objectives

After studying the materials found in this chapter, you should be able to do the following:

1. Explain the relationship between scarcity, economizing, and choice.

2. Define and understand the concept of opportunity cost.

3. Use a production possibilities curve to show:
   (a) opportunity cost.
   (b) increasing opportunity cost.
   (c) economic growth.
   (d) unemployment of resources.

4. List the four basic microeconomic questions that must be addressed by every economic system.

5. Describe briefly how traditional, command, and market economies provide answers to the four basic microeconomic questions.

6. Explain why the institution of property rights is necessary for a properly functioning market economy.

7. Using a circular flow model, show the relationships inherent in a market economy.

8. List the four basic macroeconomic issues that confront every economic system.

scarcity *The fact that there are not sufficient resources to produce everything that individuals want.*

This chapter covers two main topics. First, in this world of finite resources, we have to face the fact of *scarcity.* Our wants and desires for economic goods are very great compared to our ability to satisfy them. This forces us to economize and to make choices among different desirable things. Second, in this process of choosing, every economy must face certain questions. Some of these questions are macroeconomic in nature: How do problems such as inflation and unemployment arise? What can be done to prevent these problems? When they arise, what can be done—and how costly will it be—to solve these problems? Other questions are microeconomic in nature: What will be produced, and in what quantities, and how? Who gets what share of the goods produced? We shall introduce all these questions in this chapter. The rest of the book answers them in detail.

SCARCITY

It should be clear to everyone that we live in a world of finite resources. The oil we use today, for example, is gone forever. Limited resources become a problem because they are combined with insatiable human wants.

Wants are said to be *insatiable* —unable to be satisfied—because no matter how much people have, they always want more of *some* goods. Of course, you may know some people who are perfectly content with what they have. However, if you questioned them carefully, you would probably find that they would like cleaner air, or more time to play tennis or golf, or maybe more income so that they could give it to less fortunate people. Thus, even if we find a few people who are exceptions to the assumption of insatiable wants, it's clear that we live in a world where most people have many unsatisfied wants. Since not all wants can be satisfied, individuals have to pick and choose among the possibilities open to them. In fact, every society is faced with the same problems of scarcity and choice.

Wants are insatiable and resources are scarce. This scarcity forces individuals to make choices. Individuals must *economize.* This simple fact is very important because without scarcity it would not be necessary to economize or to make decisions on the priority of wants. Thus, there would be no need to study economics. Every decision to produce or consume something means that we forego producing or consuming something else. For instance, the cost of engaging in some activity, say, going to a football game, includes an assessment of what is given up in order to participate in that activity. Economists use the term *opportunity cost* to denote such costs. One part of the cost of attending a football game is the price of the ticket. Another part of the cost is the most valuable alternative that you could have done during that three-hour time period. Suppose you would have studied for a test, but instead went to the game. In this instance, the opportunity cost (what you gave up in order to attend the game) could be viewed as the price of the ticket plus the difference in the test score that three more hours of study could have produced.

An interesting way of using the idea of opportunity cost was discussed several years ago when politicians were debating the volunteer army. Some politicians said we couldn't afford the volunteer army. Economists viewed this as a foolish statement. Take yourself as an example. If your two alternatives were to earn $10,000 selling insurance or to be drafted (or to volunteer) and earn $4,000, which would you do? Using the self-interest assumption, we predict that you would decide to sell insurance. In fact, the government would need to raise salaries to $10,001 to get you to volunteer (assuming you are indifferent to the other conditions of the two situations). This would cause the price of the volunteer army to increase. But what if you are drafted? You will earn $4,000, although by selling insurance you could have earned $10,000—your opportunity cost. If the government drafts you, it is taking $6,000 from you and giving it to all taxpayers in the sense that they now have to pay fewer taxes to raise an army. So actually you have been taxed $6,000 to raise an army. In this sense, the cost of the volunteer army is the same as the cost of a drafted army. The difference is that, in one instance, taxpayers have to pay the cost, and in the other instance, those drafted have to pay the cost. The draft, then, is a very discriminatory tax because it is a tax levied only on a small subset of the population; that is, young, healthy males. If society thinks each soldier costs only $4,000 per year, it will use more of them

insatiable wants   There can never be enough of everything to satisfy everyone's wants for all goods and services.

economize   Since wants are insatiable and resources are scarce, individuals must make choices; they must economize.

opportunity cost   Because of scarcity, every decision to consume or produce means that we forego consuming and producing something else.

than it will if it knows each is really costing $10,000. And, by thinking it is cheaper to use soldiers than it really is, society will rely more on soldiers and less on machines and equipment than if society knew the true cost of using soldiers.

THE PRODUCTION POSSIBILITIES CURVE

production possibilities curve
A graph which depicts the concept of opportunity cost by showing production trade-offs between two goods in a hypothetical economy.

production possibilities schedule
A tabular representation of the production possibilities curve.

One way of looking at scarcity and opportunity cost is to use the *production possibilities curve, PR,* as in Figure 2-1, and the *production possibilities schedule,* as in Table 2-1. To construct this first economic model, we must make a few simplifying assumptions. First, we must assume that the economy is working at maximum efficiency; that is, everyone who wants a job can find one, and business is producing exactly the right amount of output to meet demand (all resources are fully employed). Second, we must assume that there are only two kinds of output in the economy—guns and butter. Third, we must assume that society's

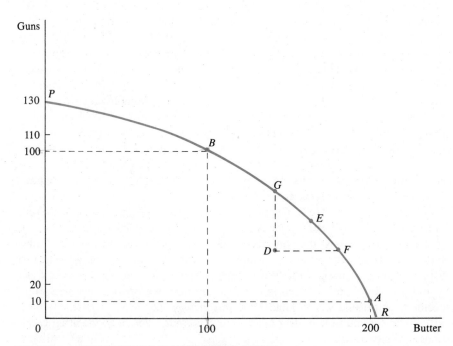

FIGURE 2-1   PRODUCTION POSSIBILITIES CURVE

A production possibilities curve plots combinations of two goods that can be produced with a given level of resources and technology. This production possibilities curve shows the possible combinations of guns and butter open to the economy. If 100 units of butter are produced, only 100 units of guns can be produced. If butter output is expanded to 200 units, the output of guns falls to only 10 units. This shows that the opportunity cost of getting more butter is the number of guns that have to be sacrificed. In addition, it can be seen that one more unit of butter requires a larger sacrifice of guns when butter output is 200 units than when only 100 units of butter are being produced. This shows increasing opportunity cost.

If the economy is inside the production possibilities curve at some point, such as point *D,* more of both goods could be produced, or the economy could produce more of one good without sacrificing any units of the other good.

TABLE 2-1   PRODUCTION POSSIBILITIES SCHEDULE

	Butter	Guns
	205	0
(A)	200	10
	194	20
	187	30
	179	40
	169	50
	158	60
	146	70
	133	80
	117	90
(B)	100	100
	77	110
	50	120
	0	130

resources can be shifted between the production of guns and butter. Fourth, we must assume that resources and technology are fixed. Table 2-1 shows combinations of guns and butter that the economy can choose to produce. Figure 2-1 shows that if we're at point *A,* the economy can produce 200 units of butter and 10 units of guns. If we're at point *B,* the economy can produce more guns, 100, but can only produce 100 units of butter. This illustrates an important economic fact—to get more of one good, you have to give up some of another good. This is the opportunity cost concept.

If society is at point *A,* we can get another gun by shifting resources from butter production to gun production. In the process, we must give up a small amount of butter. But if society is at point *B,* another gun requires a larger sacrifice of butter. This shows the principle of ***increasing opportunity costs*** —the more guns you have, the larger the sacrifice of butter required to get one more gun. Table 2-1 shows that at point *A,* 10 more guns cost 6 units of butter, but at point *B,* 10 more guns cost 23 units of butter. We have seen this phenomenon at work in wartime. As more war goods are demanded, civilian sacrifices become greater. This is because, initially, the economy uses labor that is relatively more productive at making guns and relatively less productive at making butter. As the switch to guns continues, however, the war economy takes people who are relatively less productive at making guns; although these people were productive at making butter. Butter production falls, therefore, because more resources are stripped away from butter for every extra gun, and these resources are increasingly the best the butter industry has to offer.

The production possibilities curve illustrates another very important point for macroeconomics. Suppose the economy is at point *D* in Figure 2-1, which is inside the production possibilities curve. This may result because of economic dislocations such as unemployed workers, factories, land, and machines. If we could get from point *D* to point *E,* we could have both more guns and more butter. If we went from point *D* to point *F,* we could have the same number of

increasing opportunity cost   As production of one good rises, larger and larger sacrifices of another are required.

guns but more butter, or if we went to point *G,* we could have more guns without giving up any butter. This principle again is demonstrated in wartime. If there are resources unemployed before a war starts, as there would be if the economy were in a depression, then the economy can produce more guns (for a while) without a sacrifice of butter. Cynics may say the war was useful in getting the resources employed. In any event, citizens didn't have to pay for the war in terms of less butter. One of the big issues in macroeconomics is to explain how the economy can end up inside the production possibilities curve at a point such as point *D.* Once we see how this can happen, an important question is: What can we do to keep this from happening, to avoid the idleness and waste of the unemployed resources? Perhaps even more important, if we end up at a point such as point *D,* what can we do to get back to the production possibilities curve? Investigation of questions such as these takes up much of this book.

Another macroeconomic issue that can be illustrated by the production possibilities curve involves economic growth. As labor becomes more skilled and productive, and as machines and plants embodying the latest technology come into use, the production possibilities curve shifts outward from the curve *PR* to the curve P_1R_1 in Figure 2-2. If the economy is initially at point *A* on *PR,* it is producing OD_1 units of butter and OC_1 units of guns. With the growth to P_1R_1, the economy can move to some production point, such as point *B,* where it produces both more butter (OD_2) and more guns (OC_2). Of course, the economy could produce the same amount of one good and more of the other (such as at

---

**FIGURE 2-2   SHIFTS OF THE PRODUCTION
                        POSSIBILITIES CURVE**

An outward shift of the production possibilities curve means that more of both goods can be produced. This represents economic growth. The shift in the production possibilities curve from *PR* to P_1R_1 means there is an increase in the economy's ability to satisfy human wants. Output of both goods could be increased, or society could have more of one good without sacrificing units of the other.

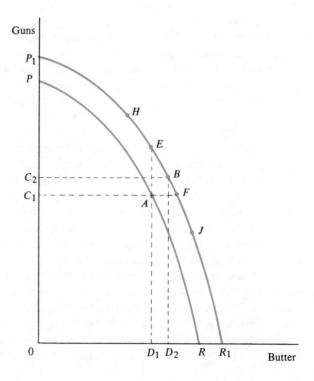

points E or F), or it could end up producing less of one good and more of the other (such as at points H or J). The important thing to notice is how the shift from PR to P_1R_1 has increased the economy's capacity to respond to human wants.

FUNDAMENTAL QUESTIONS

We saw in the previous section that the production possibility curve can be used to demonstrate macroeconomic concepts, such as unemployed resources and economic growth. The curve also can be used to demonstrate some microeconomic principles, such as the necessity of choosing a single point on the production possibility curve. In other words, how does an economy choose among the possible combinations of guns and butter? Which of the points in Figure 2-2 is best for a particular economy? This is the fundamental problem of economic scarcity. On the production possibility curve, scarcity is demonstrated by the necessity of choosing only one combination of guns and butter. We can't have everything; therefore, several fundamental questions arise.

Microeconomic Problems

The microeconomic questions can take many forms, but they can be reduced to four basic questions:

1. What is to be produced?

2. How much of each good or service is to be produced?

3. In what way, or how, are the goods and services to be produced?

4. Who will get the goods and services produced, and how much of each will each person get?

Each of these questions is addressed in every society, and microeconomic theory concentrates on the ways different types of economic organizations formulate answers to these questions.

Economists divide economic systems into three major groups—the *traditional economy,* the *planned (or command) economy,* and the *market economy.* Of course, no economy fits neatly into any one of these classification schemes because all economies are *mixed.* A mixed economy contains elements of traditional, planned, and market economies.

The traditional economy, sometimes called the subsistence economy, answers the fundamental questions by appeals to tradition. What is produced is what the young have been taught by their parents to hunt, to gather, or to plant. The techniques of production or how to produce are also passed on, often without change, from generation to generation. The amount of production is, of course, highly dependent on good fortune. The last question, concerning distribution, is also traditionally determined. If you have studied cultural anthropology, you know that such traditional societies often have rules on how the spoils of the hunt or the good harvest are to be divided. In a traditional society, the same goods and

traditional (or subsistence) economy   An economy in which fundamental questions are answered by appeals to tradition.

planned (or command) economy   An economy in which fundamental questions are answered through central command and control.

market economy   An economy in which fundamental questions are answered by the forces of supply and demand.

services are always produced year after year. Many of you may recognize that some elements of tradition exist even in societies as modern as our own. For example, there are still many small, rural communities almost untouched by the modern farming techniques of the past 50 years. In recent years, such life-styles and such techniques have even been pursued by some groups in our society as a better quality of life.

The planned economy answers the fundamental questions through planning or through central command and control. The decisions on what, how, and how much to produce are spelled out and documented. Detailed plans and orders are sent to producers, and these instructions carry the weight of law. A large part of the question of who gets what is determined in the same way, because planners determine wage rates and the amount of production of consumer goods. Such planning is the primary method of organization in the USSR and in other countries in Eastern Europe. Of course, in any economy people plan; that is, they think about the future and make preparations for it. Economists use the term *planned economy* to refer to one in which the government plays a large role in answering the production and consumption questions of the society. Most economists view this as quite different from the planning that goes on in an economy of decentralized decision making in markets.

Later in this book, we go into a detailed explanation of the benefits and costs of such economic organization. Centralized planning, however, exists in all economies, including our own. Washington-based bureaucrats determine, to some extent, what is produced and the manner in which it is produced. Governmental policies also affect the distribution of income and thus affect the determination of who gets what.

The third type of economic organization, which again operates in all economies, is the market.

The Market Resolution

The organizing principles in a market economy are the forces of supply and demand. The determination of what to produce is made by consumers, and the force of demand causes prices to go up for certain products when consumers desire more of them.

In a sense, consumers vote with their dollars. The result of this voting process determines what will be produced. Suppliers combine resources, determining how things are to be produced. Assuming suppliers are selfish and seek to maximize their profits, they tend to combine inputs to produce any good or service at the lowest possible cost. This determination depends on the prices of resources. Suppliers will use more of relatively abundant resources because they are relatively cheap. This, in turn, helps conserve the scarcer (more expensive) resources. The goods are then distributed to consumers who have the purchasing power to buy them. Those who have more purchasing power receive more goods and services. This purchasing power is in large part determined by the quantity and quality of the skills the individual sells—about 75 percent of the income in the United States is labor income. Those with high quality, scarce skills receive high salaries and can be more of a force in directing production. In a sense, these people have more votes. In other words, star basketball players with high quality, scarce basketball skills receive more for those skills than most of us receive for the market exchange of our less scarce, less valuable skills.

Adam Smith *(1723–1790)*

Adam Smith generally is recognized as the founder of modern economics. He was born in Kirkcaldy, Scotland, educated at the University of Glasgow and at Oxford, and eventually became professor and vice-rector at Glasgow. *The Wealth of Nations,* which he published in 1776, marked a break with previous economic thought. Smith stressed the role of individual self-interest in promoting overall welfare. In his view, the "invisible hand" of self-interest led people to act in socially desirable ways. Thus, you would know, for example, that when you arrive in a new city in the evening, you'll be able to buy breakfast in the morning because people who hope to make a profit will have restaurants and coffee shops open in the hope of attracting business.

Before Smith, people who wrote on economic issues often looked at things from the point of view of government and what government could and should do to run the economy in the national interest. Smith, however, argued that the role of government should be minimal—it should provide for the national defense, produce and regulate a money supply, and supply a system of laws with swift, efficient justice in the courts. Beyond these activities, private individuals pursuing their own gain would lead to efficiency in the economy; there was no need for government to intervene.

From Smith's time until the 1930s, economists tended to view the best economic role of government as minimal. With the Great Depression of the 1930s and the new school of Keynesian macroeconomics that arose, many economists began to take an opposite view of government.

Smith was not naive about the concept of self-interest. He realized that people can and will collude to take advantage of other people. He argued that whenever manufacturers of the same product get together, their thoughts rapidly turn to conspiring to raise prices and increase profits. He was opposed to this type of monopoly behavior and in particular thought that government should do nothing to encourage such practices. Many economists today argue that government regulatory agencies often contribute more to creating problems of monopoly than they do to regulating these problems. Examples offered are the Interstate Commerce Commission, which regulates interstate truckers, movers, railroads, barges, and so on, and the Civil Aeronautics Board, which regulates air fares and airline routes.

Opportunity cost also played a role in Smith's thinking. He raised the example of a village where people could hunt deer or beaver. As he pointed out, the cost of bagging one deer was the number of beaver that could have been trapped with the same time and trouble. The only true cost in economics is opportunity cost.

The market resolution is not without problems, but it does generate valuable information at low cost and passes only needed information on to consumers and producers. As an example, suppose that for some reason, say an earthquake closing some copper mines, the supply of copper is suddenly cut by one half. In a command economy, the central planners have to investigate, determine the possible effects of this shortage, and estimate how long it will last. They then have to notify all consumers of copper that they should use less of it. Instructions have to be sent to firms producing electric generators to command them to substitute other metals for copper.

Contrast this process to what occurs in a market system. When the mines close, copper prices rise. Consumers of copper know immediately that the price has gone up. They then search for cheaper substitutes. (All this happens very quickly with no need to process and send information.) The market has economized on the amount of costly information needed to make production and consumption decisions.

property rights   The legal right to a specific property. Markets and exchanges can occur only if individuals have property rights to goods, services, and labor.

The basic institution needed for the market resolution to work is the institution of **property rights.** Markets will function and exchange will occur only if individual buyers and sellers possess the property rights to the goods and services they exchange. If a market system is to function well, legal enforcement of property rights and freedom to exchange these rights are required. If the cost of protecting the property right becomes too high, the market process will break down. Suppose you were considering the purchase of a bicycle. Would you buy a bicycle if the probability is 95 percent that it will be stolen? Probably not. But what if you could reduce the probability of theft to one tenth of one percent with the purchase of a $5 lock? In this case, the cost of enforcing your property right probably isn't too high, so the market process works. What we need, then, is a legal system or other mechanism that works reasonably well in insuring the protection and exchange of property rights.

The Circular Flow Model

In Chapter 1, we discussed models and the fact that economists try to develop simple descriptions from which wider conclusions and inferences can be made. One model that often has been used to describe an economy—and a model that can point out some of the distinctions between macroeconomics and microeconomics—is the **circular flow of income.**

circular flow of income   The idea that the expenditures of one group are income for other groups, who in turn spend and produce income for others.

The first economist to describe such a flow was Francois Quesnay (1694–1774). Virtually every introductory textbook on economics begins with a discussion of the circular flow of income and its relation to a pure market economy.

product markets   Markets for the goods and services produced by firms or individuals.

In a pure market economy, we have two distinct markets in which firms interact with households. Figure 2-3 shows these markets. Households are purchasers of goods and services that firms produce, and there is a flow of dollars to firms in payment for these goods and services. The market in which these exchanges take place is referred to as the **product market** (also known as the output market or the goods and services market). Firms buy factors of production (inputs or resources) from households in order to produce the goods and services they sell to the households. The market in which these transactions take place is referred to as the **factor market** (also known as the input market or resource market). It gets this name because the firm is buying **factors of production.** These factors are **land, labor, capital,** and **entrepreneurship.** The price paid for land is **rent;** the price paid for labor services is **wages;** the price paid for using capital is **interest;** and the return to entrepreneurship is **profit.**

factor markets   Markets in which owners of factors of production sell these factors' services to producers or consumers.

factors of production   The land, labor, capital, and entrepreneurship that a firm uses to produce outputs.

In this simple circular flow model, all factors of production are owned by households and all goods are produced by firms. Quesnay saw such a system as a closed one, in which the flow would be continuous like the circular flow of blood in our bodies.

land   The factor of production that represents resources that are fixed or nonrenewable.

Keep in mind that this is a very simple model of the way a market economy operates. If we discuss some of the complications that make the model more realistic, we can see some of the economic problems to be studied in later chapters.

The first, and perhaps most obvious, shortcoming of this model is that it doesn't contain a governmental sector. We know that local, state, and federal governments produce, or cause the production of, goods ranging from schools and libraries to MX missiles. When you study microeconomics, much time is spent discussing how government affects the mix of things that are to be produced; and, when you study macroeconomics, much time is spent studying how government affects the amount of total production.

The second shortcoming to the simple model we drew in Figure 2-3 is that it shows factors being sold on factor markets and products being sold on product

labor The factor of production that represents the human element in the production process.

capital The durable, or long-lived, but depreciable, input in the production process. Machines, tools, and buildings are capital.

entrepreneurship The input that represents management, innovation, and risk-taking.

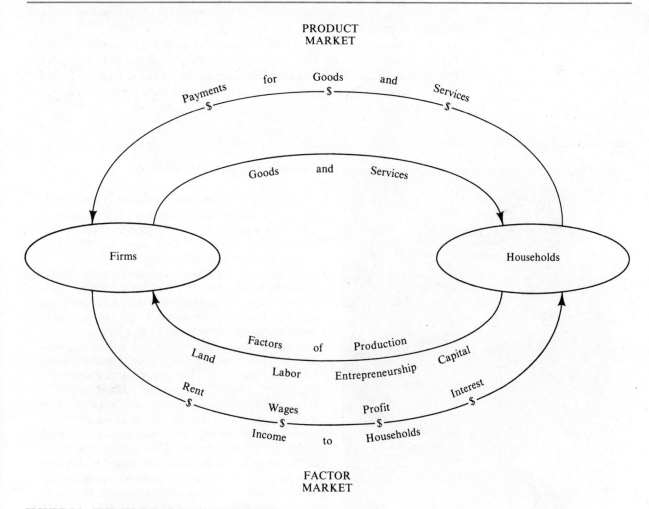

FIGURE 2-3 THE CIRCULAR FLOW OF INCOME
Households purchase goods and services and supply land, labor, capital, and entrepreneurship. Firms buy these factors of production and supply goods and services. In the product market, goods are exchanged; and in the factor market, factors of production (resources) are exchanged.

rent   The return to the land factor of production.

wages   The return to the labor factor of production.

interest   The return to the capital factor of production.

profit   The return to the entrepreneurship factor of production.

markets, but it doesn't go into detail on how product prices are determined or how the mix of products is selected by producing firms. It doesn't indicate how factor prices come about, how the firm determines which factors to purchase, or how those factors are combined to produce the goods it will sell. These questions are complicated, and they are just some of the questions in a market economy. They range from simple questions, such as why one product sells for a higher price than another, to extremely complex questions, such as how an entrepreneur might select the best way to combine 10,000 different resource components to produce an electric generator. These questions are primarily microeconomic in nature and constitute roughly half of a normal introductory course in economics.

A third complication we may add to the model is to relax the assumption that the flow of income to households (the bottom dollar flow in Figure 2-3) and the flow of payments to firms (the top dollar flow in Figure 2-3) are equal. It may be the case that they aren't equal; that there is a leak out of, or an injection into, this system. This could be caused by a number of factors which would make the flow increase or decrease in size. These are important questions that you will examine in great detail.

As you can see, this simple model of a market economy raises more questions than it answers. It is very valuable, however, because it allows us to organize our thoughts about the subject we are going to study. As we saw in Chapter 1, models are an important part of economic analysis because they permit more orderly thinking about the world.

Francois Quesnay *(1694–1774)*

Francois Quesnay was the leader of a school of economics known as Physiocracy. The Physiocrats were the first group of economic thinkers to be credited with a school of thought. They were also the first to engage in macroeconomic analysis.

The name *Physiocrats* comes from the French word *physiocrate,* which means "rule of nature." Physiocrats believed that economics was a natural order and that the cause of wealth could be discovered within that order. They believed that all wealth came from using nature. Farming, fishing, and mining were seen as productive industries. Thus, merchants were seen as parasites, because they consumed what farming, fishing, and mining produced, without producing something themselves. Quesnay, who was a physician (he was Louis XV's doctor), was inspired by William Harvey's discovery that blood circulated in the human body. This led him to develop the circular flow model of the macro economy, which was based on the view that the circulation of the macro economy was similar to the circulation of blood within the human body. And, like the loss of blood, the Physiocrats were concerned about any interruption to this flow.

Macroeconomic Problems

In addition to the fundamental microeconomic questions addressed above, there are major macroeconomic questions which must be answered by every society. These include:

1. Are resources being used fully, or does society have idle labor, land, plants, and equipment?

2. Is the general level of prices fairly stable, or is it rising due to inflation, or perhaps fluctuating violently?

3. Are the productive possibilities of society increasing over time, and how fast are they changing?

4. What can be done to improve the society's performance in some or all of the three categories above? And what will it cost to bring about improvement?

It appears that every industrialized, developed economy has to face macroeconomic problems from time to time. During the Great Depression of the 1930s, the United States faced severe unemployment and low rates of output, as did every other industrial country during this period. In the 1920s, Germany suffered astronomical inflation rates; goods that cost one German mark on the first day of the month would cost thousands of marks by the end of the month. The same sort of inflation also struck Austria and Hungary.

From 1955 to 1968, inflation in the United States averaged about 2.3 percent per year. But in the early and mid-1970s, inflation jumped in the United States, reaching 9.6 percent in 1974. Most other countries also faced inflation during this period. In 1976 Great Britain faced inflation in excess of 25 percent. Japan had inflation above 10 percent for several years during this period. Many countries with high inflation see prices rise and fall violently from month to month. Even Communist countries face the same kinds of problems.

Economic growth can be both a blessing and a curse in modern economies. During the 1960s, Japan's production grew by more than 10 percent per year, while America's production grew by about 3 percent annually and Great Britain's grew by only 1 percent per year. All these economies experienced economic growth, but the rate of growth varied significantly. The higher rate of growth in Japan meant the creation of many new jobs each year, making it easier for people to find employment. The lower growth rate in the United States and Great Britain made it harder for people to find jobs. Furthermore, the Japanese standard of living improved rapidly, though remaining below that of the United States. However, Japanese growth also caused environmental problems, such as traffic congestion and air and water pollution. Thus, a high rate of growth isn't always beneficial; it may create new, or more intense, problems or costs.

The Mixed Economy Resolution

In each of these instances, and in many others, society has to decide what to do about these macroeconomic problems. The choices are usually made by government bodies. These policies are often designed to aid the market economy. The goal of such policies is to leave economic decisions to the marketplace when it works well, but to intervene in the economy when the marketplace leads to unsatisfactory performance. On a macroeconomic level, a high rate of unemployment is an example of unsatisfactory results; on a microeconomic level, pollution caused by steel mills is an example of unsatisfactory results. In both instances, some people argue that a government body should step in to correct the unsatisfactory performance of the market. An economy which solves problems in this way is often referred to as a *mixed economy,* partly determined by market forces and aided by government policies to produce better overall results.

All noncommunist industrial nations are properly categorized as mixed economies. The mix varies between countries though. Governments are much more heavily involved in the economy in Sweden and Great Britain than in the United States and West Germany. People in different countries have different ideas on the proper mix for an economy. This is due, in part, to past experience. The unemployment suffered in Great Britain in the 1920s and 1930s made government full-employment policies quite important. The Netherlands is small and heavily engaged in international trade. It is, then, understandable that the Dutch government pays very close attention to international economic developments. Intervention in a mixed economy may not be for the purpose of improving macroeconomic performance. In the United States and elsewhere, governments intervene to try to handle microeconomic problems, such as monopoly power.

How the government intervenes in a mixed economy can differ within the same country from year to year. In the United States, we attempted to fight inflation by implementing different kinds of wage and price controls, lasting for different lengths of time, in the 1940s, 1950s, 1960s, and 1970s. We designed a variety of special tax incentives to increase investment in plants and equipment and to increase productivity and economic growth. Payments to the unemployed were introduced in the 1930s in an attempt to reduce their misery; and, from time to time, this program has been altered as lawmakers perceive new problems.

In the remainder of this book we will study economic theory and relate that theory to a mixed economy. For the most part (until the very end of the book), the mixed economy to which we refer is the economy of the United States. The economic theory that we develop, however, is universally applicable; it is the way in which different countries intervene and distort the market that is quite different.

SUMMARY

1. We live in a world of finite resources, but human wants are insatiable. This leads to a fundamental problem in economics—scarcity. We cannot have everything we want; therefore, we must economize and make choices.

2. The production possibilities schedule and curve illustrate the problem of scarcity. If society wants more butter, it must accept fewer guns.

3. The cost of an extra unit of butter is the number of guns that must be given up to get that unit of butter. This is defined as the opportunity cost of that unit of butter.

4. The more butter we have, the greater the number of guns we must sacrifice to get one more unit of butter. This is the principle of increasing opportunity costs.

5. If there are unemployed resources, then society is inside the production possibilities curve. We can have more of both guns and butter by employing these resources and moving to a point on the curve.

6. Every society must answer four basic economic questions: (1) What is to be produced? (2) How much of the good or service is to be produced? (3) In what way, or how, are the goods and services to be produced? (4) Who will get the goods and services produced, and how much of each will each person get? In one degree or another, every society partly relies on the market forces of demand and supply to answer these questions.

7. Each society also must face certain major economic questions: (1) Are resources standing idle, or are they fully employed? (2) Is the general level of prices fairly stable, or is it rising due to inflation, or perhaps changing violently? (3) Are the production possibilities of society changing over time, and how fast? (4) What can be done to improve performance in each of these categories, and what will it cost to bring about their improvement?

8. The circular flow diagram is a useful model of the interrelationships found in a market economy.

9. In different degrees, western industrial nations have tried to solve these problems by using a mixed economy, where the government intervenes in the marketplace in an attempt to improve economic performance.

NEW TERMS

scarcity
insatiable wants
economize
opportunity cost
production possibilities curve
production possibilities schedule
increasing opportunity cost
traditional (or subsistence) economy
planned (or command) economy
market economy
property rights
circular flow of income

product markets
factor markets
factors of production
land
labor
capital
entrepreneurship
rent
wages
interest
profit

QUESTIONS FOR DISCUSSION

1. Are wants insatiable?
2. How does scarcity force us to economize and make choices?
3. What is opportunity cost? What is increasing opportunity cost?
4. How is opportunity cost involved in the decision to spend Easter vacation skiing at Aspen instead of tanning at Fort Lauderdale?
5. What are some fundamental microeconomic questions that every society must answer?

6. Economists typically divide economic systems into three major groups. How do these groups deal with the problems raised in Question 5?
7. What are some basic macroeconomic problems with which every economy has to deal?
8. What is the mixed economy approach to handling macro problems?
9. What is the circular flow of income?
10. What is the difference between factor markets and product markets?

SUGGESTIONS FOR FURTHER READING

Economic Report of the President. Washington: U.S. Government Printing Office, yearly.
Herskovits, Melville J. *Economic Anthropology.* New York: W. W. Norton & Co., Inc., 1965.
Radford, R. A. "The Economic Organization of a P.O.W. Camp." *Economica* (November, 1945).

APPENDIX: WORKING WITH GRAPHS

Economic ideas, theories, and models are often expressed as relationships among variables. These relationships can be put into mathematical form, but we often express these relationships in graphical form. It is important to be comfortable with graphs because, while economics is not *about graphs,* graphs allow us to illustrate our theories and models in ways that make them easier to remember and apply to the real world. Remember that everything that can be said in graphs can also be said in words. Don't get hung up on graphs; if you can master their use it will make this book and the course you are taking much easier. It is also important not to memorize graphical relationships; understand them, don't memorize them. They are an aid to understanding the theory, not ends in themselves.

Relationship Between Variables

One of the most common ways to represent the relationship between two variables is through the use of a graph. A graph shows how the quantity of one variable changes when another changes. Table 2A-1 shows how much corn is produced on an acre of land as the rainfall is varied. We could graph this relationship. Before we do, however, we need to discuss graphs in general.

Figure 2A-1 depicts a typical graphing quadrant system. The vertical line is referred to as the *y-axis* and the horizontal line is referred to as the *x-axis.* The *x*-axis and *y*-axis divide the graph into four quadrants. The axes' point of intersection is the *origin.* The intersection represents zero value for both the *x* variable and the *y* variable. As you move upward from the origin, above the *x*-axis, the *y* variable takes on positive values. Below the *x*-axis, movement along the *y*-axis

TABLE 2A-1   RELATIONSHIPS BETWEEN VARIABLES

Rainfall in Inches/Month	Bushels of Corn/Acre
1	1
2	10
3	40
4	80
5	100
6	110
7	115
8	110
9	100
10	70

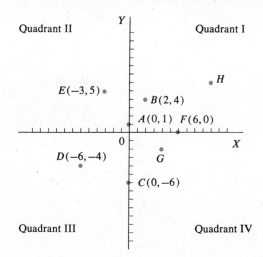

FIGURE 2A-1 QUADRANT SYSTEM
A quadrant system allows us to plot points in a horizontal and vertical dimension. The four quadrants represent combinations of positive and negative values in the two dimensions. Point *C*, for example, thus represents a zero *x* value and −6 *y* value.

represents negative values for the y variable. Likewise, as you move away from the origin along the x-axis to the right of the y-axis, positive values for the x variable are represented. Leftward movement from the origin represents negative values for the x variable.

You can now locate points on the graph. Each point has a *coordinate,* which is a pair of numbers, one representing the x value and one representing the y value. For example, point B on Figure 2A-1 represents the value 2 for the x variable and 4 for the y variable. The x value is always given first. For example, point E represents $x = -3$, $y = 5$. Can you give the coordinates of points G and H? The concept to keep in mind is that each point has a vertical and horizontal dimension.

In this book we will usually plot lines in Quadrant I. This is because most of the data from which we will plot our lines are positive. However, in some cases we are interested in relationships in the other quadrants.

Now we can plot the relationship between rainfall and corn which we listed in Table 2A-1. Figure 2A-2 plots the relationship with rainfall as the x variable and corn output as the y variable. You will note that we could represent the amount of rainfall and the production of corn by selecting almost any scale on the axis that we would want. The scale should be chosen to suit the problem. We can then connect the plotted points with a smooth curve to produce a graph. The value of the graph is that it gives you a visual picture of the mathematical relationship between the variables. In Figure 2A-2, we can easily see that as rainfall increases to 7 inches per month, corn output increases, and then more rain causes a decrease in output.

When plotting lines in economics we usually plot the dependent variable as the y variable and the independent variable as the x variable. In this case bushels of corn per acre is the dependent variable because it is a function of the independent variable, rainfall. Therefore, we plot the corn output on the y-axis. In economics there is one important exception to this principle. When we plot

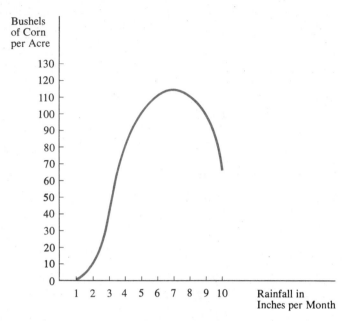

FIGURE 2A-2 · RAIN AND CORN OUTPUT

A graph usually is plotted with the dependent variable on the *y*-axis and the independent variable on the *x*-axis. This graph shows that as the independent variable——rainfall——increases, the dependent variable——corn output——increases and then decreases.

demand and supply curves, which you will be doing in Chapter 3, we plot price as the y variable and quantity as the x variable even though quantity is the dependent variable and price is the independent variable.

Slopes and Relationships Between Variables

When we are studying and describing graphs, it is often very convenient to consider the graph in terms of slopes. The *slope of a line* is the ratio of the change in the y value to the change in the x value. This is seen in Figure 2A-3, where the slope of line A is equal to $+\frac{1}{2}$ because the y value changes by one unit for each two-unit change in the x value. The slope of line B is $+5/3$, or $+1.67$. It is very important to keep track of the sign of the slope because the sign tells you the relationship between the two variables. If the variables move in the same direction, that is, if when y is increasing x is also increasing, we say we have a *positive relationship*. A slope with a positive sign designates a positive relationship. If, on the other hand, the variables move in opposite directions, we have an *inverse relationship*. An inverse relationship is one in which increases in the y variable result in decreases in the x variable, and vice versa. Such a relationship is graphed in Figure 2A-4. A line depicting an inverse relationship will have a negative slope.

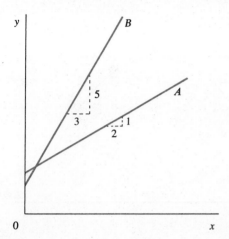

FIGURE 2A-3 POSITIVELY SLOPED LINES
The slope of a line is the ratio of the change in the *y* value to the change in the *x* value. A line sloping upward to the right indicates a positive slope. We say a positive slope represents a positive relationship between the variables; as one increases, the other increases.

Slopes of Curves

A straight line graph, like those in Figures 2A-3 and 2A-4, has the same slope along the entire line, but the slope of the curve varies along the curve. The *slope of a curve* is defined as the slope of the straight line tangent to the curve at that point. A *tangent line* is a line that touches a curve without crossing it. Calculating the slope of the curved line in Figure 2A-5 gives us a slope of $+1$ at point *A* and a slope of -1.5 at point *C*. The slope of the curve at point *B* is equal to 0. This is because changes in *x* occur but there are no changes in *y* on the straight line tangent to the curve at point *B*.

The 45° Line

A geometric construction that proves very useful in economic analysis is what economists refer to as the *45° line*. It is a straight line that cuts the origin of

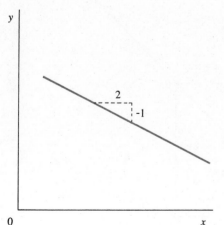

FIGURE 2A-4 NEGATIVELY SLOPED LINE
A negative slope represents an inverse relationship between the variables; as one of the variables increases, the other decreases.

FIGURE 2A-5 SLOPES OF CURVES

A curved graph has a slope that changes along the curve. The slope of the curve at any point is the slope of a straight line tangent to the curved line at that point.

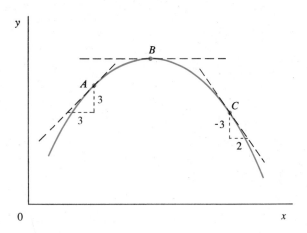

Quadrant I, dividing it into two sections at a 45° angle. If both axes are measured in the same units, the slope of this line will be 1.0. In other words, at any point on the line, the values of the x-axis and the y-axis will be equal. A 45° line is presented in Figure 2A-6.

Graphs Without Numbers

We have plotted graphs and calculated slopes of graphs using explicit relationships between variables. These relationships were explicit because there was a set

FIGURE 2A-6 THE 45° LINE

A 45° line drawn in the first quadrant has a slope of 1.0. If both axes are measured in the same units, the 45° line shows all points where the x-axis value and the y-axis value are equal.

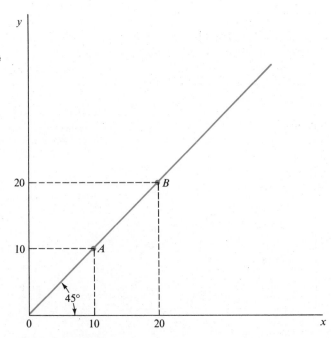

of numbers from which we actually plotted the graph. In economics, however, we sometimes plot graphs of theoretical concepts without having a set of numbers from which to plot the graph. In these cases the graph represents a conceptualization of an abstract principle we wish to depict. For example, we might theorize that there is a negative relationship between price and the quantity demanded of any good that people consume. If price is the y variable and quantity demanded the x variable, the relationship we have theorized would be expressed by a negatively sloped line similar to the one in Figure 2A-4. It doesn't matter that we don't have specific coordinates to plot; instead we have graphed an abstract idea. Much of the graphing in economics is of an abstract nature.

Supply and Demand: The Basics of Economic Analysis

Learning Objectives

After studying the materials found in this chapter, you should be able to do the following:

1. Define supply and demand and list the factors influencing each.

2. Demonstrate the concepts of supply and demand using the following:
   (a) words.
   (b) numbers or functions.
   (c) graphs.

3. Identify on a graph the differences between:
   (a) changes in demand and changes in the quantity demanded.
   (b) changes in the supply and changes in the quantity supplied.

4. Identify on a graph the excess quantity supplied or excess quantity demanded when the price is at other than the equilibrium price.

demand   The desire and ability to consume certain quantities at certain prices.

welfare economics   A branch of economics which evaluates the economic order from an ethical perspective.

The subject matter of this chapter is basic to the study of economics. Many economists contend that economics is 90 percent supply and demand analysis and that 10 percent is the study of what causes supply and demand to be what they are. To begin, it is essential to reemphasize that economists view *demands* as desires to consume at certain prices, not needs or wants that can be measured in some social or biological way. The concept of need is reserved for *welfare economics,* which evaluates the economic order from an ethical perspective, or for the realms of the biologist, the sociologist, and the cleric. In addition, for these needs and wants to be demands, they must be viewed as what people actually will do when confronted with different sets of prices. We are not talking about wishes but rather the actual consumption of specified amounts at certain prices.

DEMAND

When we talk about demand, we first need to isolate the factors that can affect the demand for a good or service. We generally focus on a few, namely:

1. The price of the good or service

2. The tastes of the group demanding the good

3. The size of the group

4. The income and wealth of the group

5. The prices of other goods and services

6. Expectations concerning *1* through *5* above

All things that affect demand work through one of these factors. The weather, for example, may affect the demand for beer by changing people's taste for beer. These factors become the *ceteris paribus* conditions we discussed in Chapter 1. We hold all but one factor constant and determine what happens when we change the factor under consideration.

The Law of Demand

Initially we want to focus on what happens when the price of a good or service changes relative to the prices of other goods and services. We focus on price and hold all the other factors that affect demand constant. We can then state the **law of demand:**

> The *quantity demanded* of a good or service is an inverse function of its price, *ceteris paribus.*

In other words, holding all else constant, consumers will purchase more of a good or service at a lower price; and as price rises, *ceteris paribus,* consumers will demand a smaller quantity of a good or service. It is important to note that we are saying *quantity demanded,* not demand, is a function of price. This allows us to make important distinctions.

We can now generate a hypothetical **demand schedule** for an individual. A demand schedule shows the quantity demanded at various prices. Such a schedule is created in Table 3-1. You will notice that there is a time dimension attached to the demand schedule. It wouldn't make any sense if we didn't know the time period under investigation; we need to talk about the demand for beer per day,

law of demand The quantity demanded of a good or service is an inverse function of its price, ceteris paribus.

demand schedule A tabular listing which shows the quantity demanded at various prices.

TABLE 3-1 FREDDY FOGHORN'S DEMAND FOR PABST BLUE RIBBON

Price per Can	Quantity Demanded per Day
50¢	1
40¢	7
30¢	13
20¢	19
10¢	25
5¢	28

Alfred Marshall *(1842–1924)*

Alfred Marshall is perhaps the most important modern economist and may be the most influential economist of all time, in large part because of the great number of students he influenced through his teaching and writing.

Marshall was the great synthesizer and expositor of the *neoclassical school of economics.* The neoclassical school consisted of a regeneration of much of classical economics after Karl Marx (and others) had criticized the errors in classical analysis. Most present day microeconomic theory can be directly traced to this neoclassical school of economic thought.

Born in London, Marshall came to the study of economics by a circuitous route. His father, William Marshall, was a strict disciplinarian who pushed brilliant Alfred to the point of mental and physical exhaustion after endlessly drilling him in Latin and Greek until midnight. Marshall was offered a scholarship at Oxford which would have led to the ministry. Instead, he enrolled at Cambridge to study mathematics. This was in part a rebellion against his father, who had forbidden him to study mathematics. Later, Marshall began to study political economy, but he made extensive use of mathematics in developing his economic theory.

After marrying a former student, Marshall returned to Cambridge. There he belonged to what he called "a small cultural society of great simplicity and distinction." At Cambridge, Marshall generated a tremendous impact on the economics profession. At first, this impact was felt primarily through his influence as a teacher of almost all the major British economists of the early twentieth century. Later, his book *Principles of Economics* (1890) influenced still larger numbers of students. Generations of economists learned economics from Marshall's *Principles.* In fact, if you had taken a course in economics before 1950, it is very probable that you would have studied from Marshall's book.

demand curve A graphical representation of a demand schedule showing the quantity demanded at various prices.

per week, per year, etc. Table 3-1 conforms to our law of demand and demonstrates that Freddy Foghorn demands larger quantities of Pabst Blue Ribbon beer at lower prices. We can now convert the demand schedule of Table 3-1 to a graphical representation which we call a *demand curve.* Such a curve is drawn in Figure 3-1. The demand curve is the line graph representing the demand schedule. When we draw a demand curve, we designate the *y*-axis as the price per unit variable and the *x*-axis as the quantity per time period variable.[1] It is important to always designate the quantity as quantity per unit of time. In drawing a hypothetical demand curve, this can be done by labeling the *x*-axis as *x/t,* meaning quantity of *x* per time period.

---

[1] If graphing the schedule is confusing, review the appendix to Chapter 2. We usually draw linear curves for convenience.

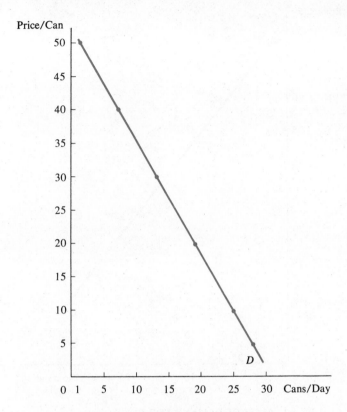

**FIGURE 3-1   FREDDY FOGHORN'S DEMAND FOR
                PABST BLUE RIBBON**
An individual's demand curve shows the quantity that the individual
will purchase at different prices.

Market Demand

We have now generated a demand schedule and a demand curve representing
Freddy Foghorn's demand for Pabst Blue Ribbon beer. This, however, is of little
interest unless we wish to examine only Freddy's behavior in isolation. We usually
are more concerned with the *market demand* curve for Pabst Blue Ribbon or even
the market demand curve for all beer. This market demand could be found by
adding all the individual demand schedules or by a horizontal geometric summation of all the individual demand curves. Figure 3-2 is a market demand curve
for beer. It tells us the total quantity demanded at various prices.

   As price changes in the market, the quantity demanded changes inversely.
In Figure 3-2, 13,000 cans of beer are purchased at a price of 35¢ per can. If price
falls to 20¢, the quantity demanded increases to 25,000 cans, or if price rises to
45¢, the quantity demanded decreases to 5,000 cans.

*market demand   The
summation of all the individual
consumer demand curves. A
market demand curve shows
what quantity will be demanded
by all consumers at various
prices.*

Changes in Demand

We will now see how the other factors affect the market demand for the commodity. To keep things simple, we will continue to use the beer example.

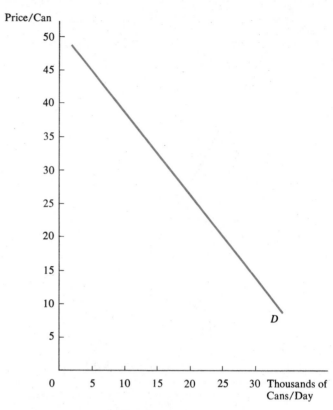

FIGURE 3-2   MARKET DEMAND FOR BEER
A market demand curve is a graphical depiction of how much will be purchased by the market at various prices. It is the aggregation of all the individual demand curves.

Suppose the tastes of the group change. The reason for a change in tastes is best left to a field like psychology. Let's just assume that people's tastes change in favor of beer; perhaps beer drinking has become more glamorous because famous people are beer guzzlers. Such a change in taste is reflected in Figure 3-3 as an ***increase in demand***. At every price, consumers demand a larger amount than before. The demand curve shifts from D to D_1. The opposite would have occurred if tastes changed away from beer. Such a change in tastes would cause a ***decrease in demand***, represented by a shift from D to D_2.

The market demand curve, as we saw earlier, is found by aggregating the individual demand curves. Consequently, if the number of individuals in the group (the size of the group) changes, market demand will change. In Figure 3-4, demand curve D_1 is the demand for bourbon in a state which has a 19-year-old age limit on drinking hard liquor. If the law is changed to allow 18-year-olds the right to drink liquor, the demand curve will shift from D to D_1 as in Figure 3-4. The size of the group has increased and, therefore, there has been an increase in the demand for the good. This means that more will be consumed at every price.

increase in demand   A shift in the demand curve indicating that at every price consumers demand a larger quantity than before.

decrease in demand   A shift in the demand curve indicating that at every price consumers demand a smaller quantity than before.

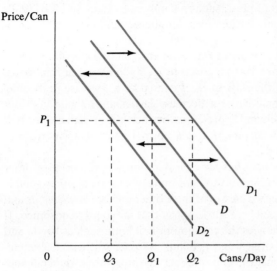

Price/Can

P_1

0   Q_3 Q_1 Q_2 Cans/Day

D_1

D

D_2

FIGURE 3-3 EFFECTS OF CHANGES IN TASTES ON THE DEMAND FOR BEER

Changes in tastes can cause a demand curve to shift. If the tastes of the group change in favor of the item, more will be demanded at every price and the curve will shift to the right, as from D to D_1. A change in tastes away from the good causes a shift to the left, as from D to D_2.

Conversely, if the size of the group decreases, there will be a decrease in demand. This would be depicted as a shift from D to D_2.

If income changes, we have similar shifts in demand, again represented geometrically by shifts in the demand curve. The first consideration in assessing the effect of income changes on demand is to determine if the good under consideration is a ***normal good*** or an ***inferior good*** . A normal good is one for which demand increases as income increases. Most goods are normal goods. It is very hard to think of goods that people collectively consume less of when their income increases. If this happens, we call such a good an inferior good. If we define goods quite narrowly, it is possible to identify some inferior goods. Con-

normal good   A good for which demand increases as income is increased.

inferior good   A good for which demand decreases as income increases.

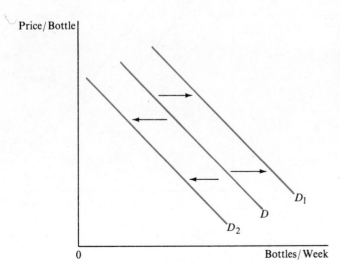

Price/Bottle

0   Bottles/Week

D_1

D

D_2

FIGURE 3-4 EFFECTS OF CHANGES IN GROUP SIZE

Changes in group size can cause a demand curve to shift. If more consumers enter a specific market, the demand curve will shift from D to D_1. A decline in group size will cause demand to decrease, as from D to D_2

sider, for example, poorer cuts of meat, such as hamburger. If, as an individual's income increases, the individual consumes less hamburger and more steak, hamburger is an inferior good and steak is a normal good, but meat or beef is still considered a normal good.[2] In terms of our geometric analysis, an increase in income causes demand in Figure 3-5 to increase to D_1 if good x is a normal good. If good x is an inferior good, the shift to D_1 is caused by a decrease in income. The opposite changes in income cause a decrease in demand. Again consider Figure 3-5. The decrease in demand represented by the shift in demand from D to D_2 represents a decrease in income if x is a normal good or an increase in income if x is an inferior good.

The fourth factor that we held out for consideration was the price of other goods and services. Here it is important to determine what type of other good is under consideration. There are two classes of these other goods, *complements* and *substitutes.* Complementary goods are those goods that are jointly consumed. If consuming goods together enhances the consumption of both, such as bacon and eggs, lox and bagels, or hamburgers and ketchup, we refer to them as complements. Substitute goods have just the opposite relationship. Rather than enhancing the consumption of the other good, substitute goods replace the consumption of it. Orange juice and grapefruit juice, Miller High Life and Pabst, and bacon and sausage would be examples of this type of relationship.

After we determine if goods are complements or substitutes, we can examine how changes in the price of one affect the other. Examine, for example, the demand for complementary good x (bagels), as represented in Figure 3-6. If the price of complementary good y (lox) goes up, the demand for bagels will decrease, shifting from D to D_2 in Figure 3-6. This is because consumers will now consume fewer lox, and thus fewer bagels, at every price. The opposite would occur if the

complements   Those goods that are jointly consumed. The consumption of one good enhances the consumption of the other good. Complements have a negative cross elasticity of demand.

substitutes   Goods that replace the consumption of other goods. Substitutes have a positive cross elasticity of demand.

FIGURE 3-5   EFFECTS OF CHANGES IN INCOME ON THE DEMAND FOR GOOD x

Income and changes in income affect the demand for a good. An increase in income causes the demand for a normal (inferior) good to increase (decrease), as depicted in the shift from D to D_1. A decrease in income causes the demand for a normal (inferior) good to decrease (increase), as depicted in the shift from D to D_2.

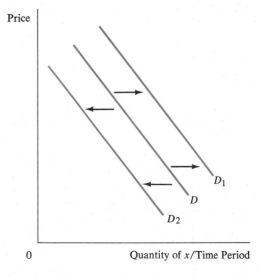

---

[2]Perhaps the best example of an inferior good is an outhouse. As a community's income rises, its demand for outhouses decreases.

Price

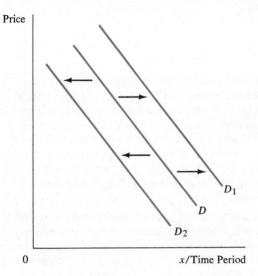

D_1

D

D_2

0   x/Time Period

FIGURE 3-6   THE PRICE OF OTHER GOODS AND THE DEMAND FOR x

Prices of related goods cause changes in the demand for the good under analysis. An increase (decrease) in the price of a substitute (complement) causes an increase in demand for the good, represented by the shift from D to D_1. A decrease (increase) in the price of a substitute (complement) will, for similar reasons, cause a decrease in demand for the good, as demonstrated by the shift from D to D_2.

price of good y (lox) fell. Consumers would now want to consume more lox, and thus more of good x (bagels), at each price. This would be geometrically depicted as a shift from D to D_1 in Figure 3-6.

Now consider what happens when we have a substitute relationship between the two goods. Good x (Miller High Life) and good y (Pabst) are substitutes and we can again use Figure 3-6. Curve D represents the demand for good x (Miller High Life). The price of good y (Pabst) now increases relative to the price of good x. This makes good x more attractive to consumers and at every price consumers will now demand more of good x. This is geometrically represented by the shift from D to D_1 in Figure 3-6. If instead the price of the substitute good y decreased relative to the price of good x, the opposite would happen. Consumers would now find good x less attractive and would desire less of it at each price as they shift consumption to good y. This is a decrease in demand for good x, represented by the shift from D to D_2 in Figure 3-6.

The last of the *ceteris paribus* factors that affect demand is **expectations.** If individuals expect demand to change in the future, they may take action now that brings that change into effect. For example, if you expect that the demand for automobiles will be so high next year that price will rise, you may take action to demand a car now to avoid the higher price. If enough people act on that same expectation, the price will be higher now because of the expectation. The same situation will, of course, hold for other factors. If you expect your income to be higher in the future, you may demand more goods now and expect to pay for them later.

expectations   Individual forecasts for the state of the future.

Expectations and the effect of expectations on demand are important in both microeconomics and macroeconomics. In microeconomics, expectations of events in certain markets are important. For example, if you expect drought conditions to affect the price of wheat next fall, you will adjust your behavior accordingly. If enough people agree with your expectations, the price of wheat will rise,

Billy Beer—A Collector's Item

Goods that are no longer being produced often increase in price as collectors bid against each other

for the already existing stock of goods. The price of these goods can often rise quickly on the basis of expectations of future prices.

One of the most recent products to take on value as a collector's item was *Billy Beer.* In 1977, Jimmy Carter's brother, Billy, and a Kentucky brewery marketed Billy Beer. The beer, as a brew, was a bust. Thus, it didn't sell and production stopped. In 1981, however, collectors got into the act. *Newsweek* reported that Bob Ayres, of Concord, California, advertised a six-pack for $2,400, and empty cans were selling for as much as $20 a can.

This phenomenon is not limited to Billy Beer. In some areas, stores have sprung up that specialize in selling empty beer cans. For instance, in Coultersville, California, there is a store that has over 3,000 different brands of empty beer cans. Some cans are from the old gold rush days and have sold for as much as $5,000.

This collecting mania has hit almost every type of product and industry. There are conventions for comic book collectors, baseball card collectors, duck decoy collectors, model train collectors, etc.

You probably could make a million if you could correctly predict the next collector's good to be produced.

---

affecting the market for wheat *before* the growing season is over. Similar effects can occur in the macro economy. If groups of consumers think that inflation will continue unabated, they will purchase as many goods as they can now to avoid the higher prices that inflation will later bring. If large numbers of people follow this behavior, they will bring about the very behavior that they expected.

We have seen that economists spend a lot of time distinguishing clearly between changes along a demand curve and changes (or shifts) of the curve itself. Changes along the curve are *changes in quantity demanded* caused solely by a change in the *price* of the good. Changes (or shifts) of the curve are *changes in demand* caused by changes in any of the *ceteris paribus* conditions.

SUPPLY

supply schedule A tabular listing which shows quantity supplied at various prices.

A *supply schedule* shows the quantity of goods offered for sale at a particular time and at a particular price. When we talk about *supply,* we need to isolate the factors that affect the supply of a good or service. When examining supply, we usually concentrate on four factors:

1. The price of the good

2. The price of the factors of production

3. The level of technology

4. Expectations

supply The quantity of goods offered for sale at a particular time or a particular place.

Everything that affects supply works through one of these factors. For example, if there is a natural disaster that affects society by destroying large amounts of capital, the price of that factor of production will rise.

We should be careful to avoid confusing the words *cost* and *price.* The cost of using a factor of production includes both price and productivity. Thus, the cost of a factor could rise even if its price remained the same if the productivity of the factor fell.

cost The value of the factors of production used by a firm in producing or distributing goods or services.

price The value, usually in money terms, for which goods and services are exchanged.

The (Not Quite) Law of Supply

Initially we will focus on what happens when the price of the good or service under consideration changes. We want to make this a *ceteris paribus* experiment by holding constant everything but the price of the good or service. We can thus state the *(not quite) law of supply.*

(not quite) law of supply The quantity supplied of a good or service is usually a positive function of price, ceteris paribus.

> The *quantity supplied* of a good or service is *usually* a positive function of price, *ceteris paribus.*

This means that, holding all else constant, suppliers will usually supply less of a good or service at lower prices; and as prices rise, the quantity supplied will increase. It is important to note that we are saying *quantity supplied* is a function of price. This distinction is important just as it was when we considered demand. But note we said *usually.* This is why we call it a "not quite" law. There are two exceptions to this relationship. The first is when there is no time to produce more units (for example, theater seats at a sold-out performance), or when a unique supplier no longer exists (for example, paintings by Picasso). The second exception occurs in certain areas of production where increased volume causes costs to fall.

We can now generate a hypothetical supply schedule for an individual supplier, which we will call a firm. A supply schedule shows the quantity supplied at various prices. Such a schedule is created in Table 3-2. You will notice that,

TABLE 3-2 SUZY SIZZLE'S SUPPLY OF LEMONADE

Price per Glass (Cents)	Quantity Supplied per Day
5	0
10	5
15	10
20	15
25	20
30	25

*supply curve   A graphical
representation of a supply
schedule showing the quantity
supplied at various prices.*

just as when we considered demand, there is a time element attached to the supply schedule. It wouldn't make sense to talk about supply without knowing the period of time. Table 3-2 conforms to our (not quite) law of supply and demonstrates that Suzy Sizzle supplies larger quantities of lemonade at higher prices. We can now convert the supply schedule of Table 3-2 to a graphical representation called a ***supply curve***. Such a curve is drawn in Figure 3-7. As when graphing demand, we put price per unit on the *y*-axis and quantity per time period on the *x*-axis. We generally draw supply curves as linear curves for convenience, and they usually are drawn with a positive price (*y*-axis) intercept, indicating that at some low price none of the commodity may be supplied.

Market Supply

*market supply   The summation
of all the individual firm supply
curves. A market supply curve
shows what quantity will be
supplied by all firms at various
prices.*

We now have generated a supply schedule and a supply curve depicting Suzy Sizzle's supply of lemonade. The ***market supply*** curve can be found by adding all the individual supply schedules or by a horizontal geometric summation of all the individual supply curves. Figure 3-8 is a market supply curve for lemonade. It tells us the total quantity supplied at various prices.

As price changes in the market, the quantity supplied changes as a positive function of this price change. In Figure 3-8, 5,000 glasses of lemonade are supplied at a price of 10¢ per glass. If price fell to 5¢, the quantity supplied would decrease to zero glasses, and if price rose to 20¢, the quantity supplied would

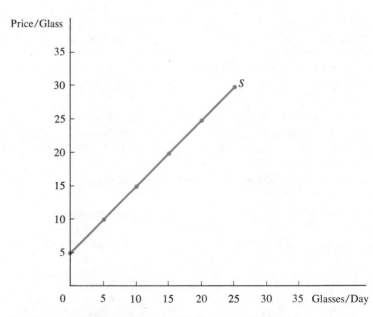

FIGURE 3-7   SUZY SIZZLE'S SUPPLY OF LEMONADE
A supply curve for an individual (or an individual firm) graphically depicts how much will be offered for sale at various prices.

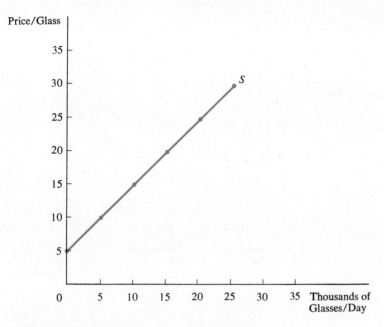

FIGURE 3-8   MARKET SUPPLY OF LEMONADE
A market supply curve is a graphical depiction of how much will be offered for sale at various prices. It is the aggregate of all the individual supply curves.

increase to 15,000 glasses. These changes occur because most producers are willing to sell more units if the price rises enough to cover the additional costs of production.

Changes in Supply

We can now see how other factors affect the market supply of a good or service. Suppose technology changes and this change has a positive effect. For instance, assume we are looking at the supply of beef and that agricultural researchers develop a very inexpensive pill which causes a young steer to double in weight rapidly. This technological advance will mean that more beef will be supplied at each price. There is an *increase in supply.* Such an increase in supply is represented in Figure 3-9 as the outward shift from S to S_1. A negative technological change will have the opposite effect. Suppose the government discovers that this drug, now in use for steer fattening, has harmful side effects on humans, and farmers are therefore prohibited from giving it to steers. This will mean that less beef will be supplied at each price. There will be a *decrease in supply,* and this decrease will be represented as a shift from S to S_2 in Figure 3-9.

Now consider changes in the prices of the factors of production. You remember from the previous chapter that these factors of production are land, labor, capital, and entrepreneurship. The price paid for the use of land is rent; the price paid for labor services is wages; the price paid for using capital is interest; and

increase in supply   A shift in the supply curve indicating that at every price a larger quantity will be supplied than before.

decrease in supply   A shift in the supply curve indicating that at every price suppliers will supply a smaller quantity than before.

**FIGURE 3-9   CHANGES IN TECHNOLOGY AND
            SUPPLY**

Changes in technology can cause the supply curve to shift. A positive change in technology would cause more to be supplied at each previous price. This increase in supply is represented by the shift from S to S_1. A negative change in technology causes the supply to decrease, as from S to S_2.

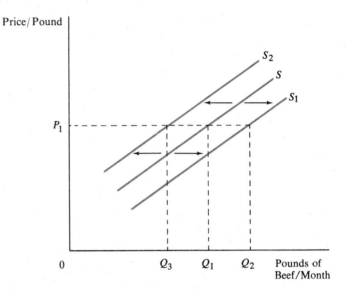

the return to entrepreneurship is profit. If the price of a factor, say, labor services, goes up, it will affect supply. It will mean that less of the good will be supplied at each price. That is to say, supply will decrease because the costs of production have gone up. Suppose that S in Figure 3-10 represents the market supply of beef. Assume the wage rate of meat cutters increases. This will mean less beef will be supplied at each price; supply will decrease. This is represented as a shift from S to S_2. Another way of looking at this is to see that before the increase in wages, amount OQ_1 was supplied at price OP_1. When S decreases to S_2 after wages go up, suppliers will only supply the old amount (OQ_1) at a higher price (OP_2).

The same principle holds for any factor of production: A rise in the price of a factor of production, *ceteris paribus,* causes a decrease in supply. This happens because the producer will now find the cost of supplying the same quantity has increased. We will thus find that after the price rise in a factor of production, less will be supplied at the old price or the same amount will be supplied at a higher price. This is graphically represented by a shift in the curve. The opposite is also true. Any decrease in the price of a factor of production will cause an increase in supply. Such an increase in supply is geometrically depicted as a shift from S to S_1 in Figure 3-10.

Expectations play an important role in supply. Changes in supply brought about by changing economic expectations are behind much of *supply-side economics* —a theory very popular in the administration of President Reagan. The idea is a simple one. If the business community sees the potential for costs to be lowered because of fewer government regulations, and the potential for greater profits through decreased taxes and faster depreciation, supply will increase. Supply-siders think this response will be very quick because expectations of an environment conducive to business are created. Figure 3-11 demonstrates such a supply-side response. Expectations change and, as a result, there is an increase in supply from S to S_1. The key to supply-side economics is how fast this change will occur.

supply-side economics   An economic theory which holds that if expectations of an environment conducive to business are created, business will see a potential for costs to be lowered, and supply will increase.

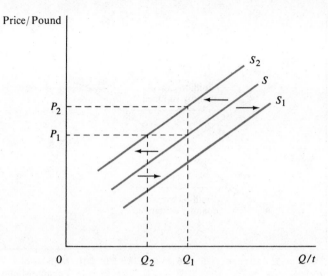

FIGURE 3-10   CHANGES IN THE PRICE OF FACTORS OF PRODUCTION AND SUPPLY

Increases and decreases in the prices of factors of production cause increases and decreases in supply. An increase in the price of a factor of production can cause a decrease in supply. Such a decrease is depicted by the shift from S to S_2. A decrease in the price of a factor of production can cause an increase in supply, as the shift from S to S_1 represents.

MARKET EQUILIBRIUM

We can now combine market supply and market demand schedules or curves for a good or service and determine the ***market equilibrium.*** The equilibrium is the price and quantity that will exist in the market if no impediments are placed on the free working of the market. To see how equilibrium comes about, examine Figure 3-12 and Table 3-3. In Figure 3-12, we have market demand and market supply curves for coffee corresponding to the supply and demand schedules in Table 3-3. Examine Table 3-3 first. At a price of $2.00 suppliers *want* to supply

market equilibrium   The price and quantity that will exist if no impediments are placed on the free working of the market.

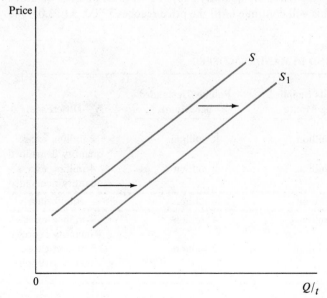

FIGURE 3-11   CHANGES IN EXPECTATIONS

A change in expectations can cause the supply curve to shift. An increase in supply from S to S_1 is brought about by positive expectations concerning the business environment.

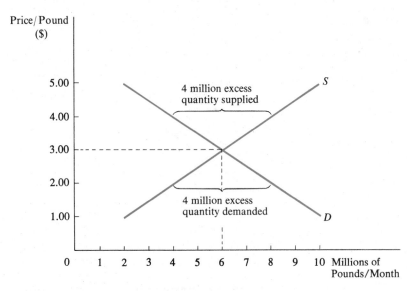

FIGURE 3-12   SUPPLY AND DEMAND OF COFFEE

The supply and demand curves produce an equilibrium. At equilibrium, the amount demanders wish to purchase is equal to the amount suppliers wish to sell. The price established at equilibrium is called the market clearing price because there are no frustrated purchasers or suppliers.

At $2.00 suppliers want to supply 4 million pounds of coffee and demanders *want* to purchase 8 million pounds. This is a difference of 4 million pounds. The quantity demanded exceeds the quantity supplied by 4 million pounds at a price of $2.00. This means that at $2.00 some consumers will be frustrated by not being able to purchase the desired amount. Since markets are free, some of these consumers will offer more and bid the price up. As the price rises, the quantity supplied will rise and the quantity demanded will fall. This will continue until the price reaches $3.00. At $3.00, the

TABLE 3-3   SUPPLY AND DEMAND OF COFFEE

Price per Pound	Pounds Supplied per Month	Pounds Demanded per Month	Difference
$1.00	2 million	10 million	8 million excess quantity demanded
$2.00	4 million	8 million	4 million excess quantity demanded
$3.00	6 million	6 million	equilibrium
$4.00	8 million	4 million	4 million excess quantity supplied
$5.00	10 million	2 million	8 million excess quantity supplied

amount consumers wish to purchase is exactly equal to the amount suppliers wish to sell. This is equilibrium. We also say that $3.00 is the **market clearing price.** It is the market clearing price because there are no frustrated purchasers or suppliers.

To see the same process from the other side of the market, assume a price higher than the market clearing price. At $4.00 per pound, suppliers offer 8 million pounds per month for sale. Consumers only wish to purchase 4 million pounds per month at a price of $4.00 per pound. We thus have an excess quantity supplied of 4 million pounds per month. Suppliers with unsold coffee will lower the price. As the price falls, the quantity supplied decreases and the quantity demanded increases. This continues until the equilibrium price of $3.00 is reached. This $3.00 price again clears the market.

You should understand that the point representing equilibrium price and equilibrium quantity is not the same thing as the point where the amount sold equals the amount bought. Quantities bought and sold are *always* equal. At $2.00 and $4.00, 4 million pounds per month were bought and sold. The key to equilibrium is that at the equilibrium price, the amount demanders *wish* to purchase is equal to the amount suppliers *wish* to sell.

Figure 3-12 demonstrates the same process. The equilibrium price is $3.00 and 6 million pounds per month are sold at equilibrium. At $4.00 there is an excess quantity supplied and price will fall, causing the quantity demanded to increase and the quantity supplied to decrease. The opposite happens at a price of $2.00 per pound.

A THEORY OF PRICE FORMATION

We have been using the law of demand and the (not quite) law of supply and have developed a very powerful theory of price formation in free markets. We have used the assertions that:

1. Demand curves always have a negative slope.

2. Supply curves almost always have a positive slope.

We have also generated a theory that says when the quantity demanded exceeds the quantity supplied ($QD > QS$), price will rise; when the quantity demanded is less than the quantity supplied ($QD < QS$), price will fall; and when the quantity demanded equals the quantity supplied ($QD = QS$), price will remain the same. We can now combine this theory with the possible *ceteris paribus* shifts to examine further the effects of various factors on free markets.

Changes in Demand and Supply

When changes occur in any of the other factors (our *ceteris paribus* conditions) that affect demand, we can trace out the effect on market equilibrium. Assume first that there is an increase in demand; that is, an upward or rightward shift of the entire curve. This increase in demand could be a result of: (1) an increase in income if this is a normal good (or a decrease in income if this is an inferior good);

(2) a change in tastes in favor of the good; (3) an increase in the price of a substitute; or (4) a decrease in the price of a complement. The increase in demand is geometrically represented by an outward shift in the demand curve from D to D_1, as drawn in Figure 3-13. The effect of this increase in demand is to cause the equilibrium price to rise from OP_e to OP_{e1}. This price increase causes the quantity supplied to increase to OQ_{e1}, the new equilibrium quantity. Consumers are now demanding a larger quantity of the good at every price than before the shift in demand.

Now consider a decrease in demand. A decrease in demand means that consumers will demand less of the good at every price. A decrease in demand would result from: (1) an increase in income if this is an inferior good (or a decrease in income if this is a normal good); (2) a change in tastes away from this good; (3) a decrease in the price of a substitute; or (4) an increase in the price of a complement. The decrease in demand can be geometrically represented by the leftward shift in the demand curve from D to D_2 in Figure 3-13. The decrease in demand causes equilibrium price to fall from OP_e to OP_{e2}. As a result of the decrease in price, the quantity supplied falls from OQ_e to OQ_{e2} and consumers are consuming OQ_{e2}.

Changes in the factors that affect supply cause changes in supply, which are represented by shifts in the supply curve. Consider first an increase in supply. This would be caused by a positive change in technology or a decrease in the price of a factor of production. The increase in supply would be represented by the outward shift in the supply curve, from S to S_1 in Figure 3-14. This increase in supply would cause the equilibrium price to fall from OP_e to OP_{e1}. The decrease in price would cause an increase in the quantity demanded from OQ_e to OQ_{e1}.

FIGURE 3-13   CHANGES IN DEMAND

An increase in demand from D to D_1 causes equilibrium price to rise from OP_e to OP_{e1} and the quantity supplied to increase from OQ_e to OQ_{e1}. A decrease in demand from D to D_2 causes the equilibrium price to fall from OP_e to OP_{e2} and the quantity supplied to fall from OQ_e to OQ_{e2}.

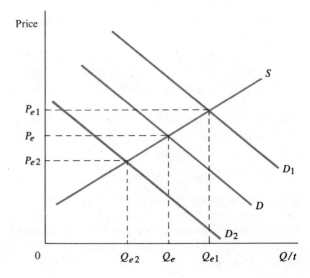

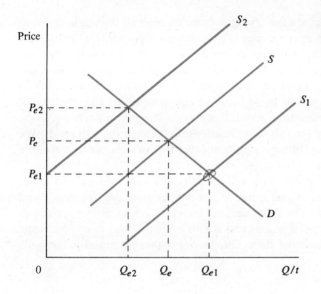

FIGURE 3-14   CHANGES IN SUPPLY

An increase in supply from S to S_1 causes equilibrium price to fall from OP_e to OP_{e1}, and the quantity demanded to increase from OQ_e to OQ_{e1}. A decrease in supply from S to S_2 causes price to rise from OP_e to OP_{e2} and the quantity demanded to fall from OQ_e to OQ_{e2}.

A decrease in supply would be geometrically represented by a shift in the supply curve in an inward direction. Such a decrease in supply could result from a negative change in technology or an increase in the price of a factor of production. This decrease in supply is represented by the shift of S to S_2 in Figure 3-14. This decrease in supply causes equilibrium price to rise from OP_e to OP_{e2}. This increase in price causes the quantity demanded to decrease from OQ_e to OQ_{e2}.

Shifts and Movements

We can now analyze some of today's economic problems in terms of simple supply and demand theory. Economists in government and business spend much of their time analyzing problems with these basic tools. Later we will examine a range of social problems in terms of basic supply and demand theory. As we proceed, you should keep in mind the difference between changes in demand and supply (that is, changes in the position of the curve, or shifts) and changes in quantity demanded and quantity supplied (that is, changes along the curve, or movements). The importance of this difference will become very clear as you attempt to untangle situations where you proceed through several changes in *ceteris paribus* conditions.[3] It is also important to realize that we are looking for

---

[3]To test yourself, work through these shifts. You need to determine the effect on price and quantity that changes in demand and supply have. For example, ask yourself, What is the effect on equilibrium of an increase in demand coupled with a decrease in supply?

the most salient effect and are not trying to trace through all the implications of a price change or change in *ceteris paribus* conditions. For example, if we know that the price of a substitute has gone up, we know that the demand for the good under consideration will increase. But the rise in price of the substitute good also means that real income (actual purchasing ability) has fallen. The effect of the decrease in real income would be to decrease the demand for the good under consideration. This decrease in demand, however, is insignificant relative to the change brought about by the substitute relationship between the two goods. We are primarily interested in the most significant response to a change in one of the *ceteris paribus* conditions.

One final word is in order. You will note that we have said nothing about what constitutes a fair or a just price. We are developing ***positive theory*** and simply predicting, for example, that if demand increases, *ceteris paribus,* price will rise and the quantity supplied will increase. This price rise may mean that some group can no longer afford the item. Our theory makes no moral judgements about this.

positive theory   A theory that leads to implications and a hypothesis about the consequences of certain actions. A positive theory makes no judgements about the moral correctness of these implications.

SUMMARY

1. Demand depends on the tastes of the consuming group, the incomes of that group, the prices of related goods, the price of the good or service in question, and the expectations concerning all these factors.

2. The law of demand states that the quantity demanded of a good or service is an inverse function of its price.

3. Changes in the price of a good affect the quantity demanded of that good; that is, a change or movement along the curve.

4. Changes in other factors that affect demand cause demand to either increase or decrease; that is, a shift in the position of the entire curve.

5. When income increases, the demand for a normal good will increase while the demand for an inferior good will decrease.

6. Two goods are complements when a price increase in one will cause a decrease in demand for the other. Similarly, goods are substitutes if an increase in price of one good causes an increase in demand for the second good.

7. Supply depends on the prices of the factors of

production, the level of technology, the price of the good or service being supplied, and expectations.

8. The (not quite) law of supply states that the quantity supplied of a good or service is usually a positive function of its price.

9. Changes in a good's price affect the quantity supplied of that good. Changes in other factors that affect supply cause supply to either increase or decrease. When the prices of factors of production increase, there will be a decrease in supply. A technological advance usually will cause supply to increase.

10. The market clearing price is the price at which the amount consumers wish to purchase is equal to the amount suppliers wish to sell.

NEW TERMS

demand
welfare economics
law of demand
demand schedule
demand curve
market demand
increase in demand
decrease in demand
normal good
inferior good
complements
substitutes
expectations

supply schedule
supply
cost
price
(not quite) law of supply
supply curve
market supply
increase in supply
decrease in supply
supply-side economics
market equilibrium
market clearing price
positive theory

QUESTIONS FOR DISCUSSION

1. How can expectations of economic conditions affect supply?

2. Does the fact that some people appear to buy more of some goods, such as mink coats or diamonds, as their price goes up negate the law of demand?

3. How can the belief in a change in the future availability of gasoline affect the demand for automobiles?

4. Pat, a professional student, failed principles of economics and decided to sell flowers on a street corner to make ends meet. A second flower seller established a business directly across the street from Pat. Pat, unconcerned, came up with the following hypothesis: When supply increases, demand will increase, and therefore I will be just as well-off now as I was before the second flower seller arrived. Did Pat deserve to fail economics? Why or why not?

5. A market clearing price is the price at which the amount sold equals the amount purchased. Is this correct?

6. List all the factors that can decrease demand or supply.

7. List all the factors that can increase demand or supply.

8. Why is it so important to distinguish changes in demand and changes in supply from changes in quantity demanded and changes in quantity supplied?

SUGGESTIONS FOR FURTHER READING

Ferguson, C. E., and S. Charles Maurice. *Economic Analysis*. Homewood, Ill.: Richard D. Irwin, 1978, Chapter 2.

Kamerschen, David R., and Lloyd M. Valentine. *Intermediate Microeconomic Theory,* 2d ed. Cincinnati: South-Western Publishing Co., 1981, Chapter 2.

PART 2

Money, Taxes, and National Income Accounting

CHAPTER 4

Money: What It Is, Where It Comes From, and Why We Use It

Learning Objectives

After studying the materials found in this chapter, you should be able to do the following:

1. Explain why money replaces barter and reciprocity as the preferred system of exchange when a society becomes more complex and specialized.

2. Distinguish among the following types of exchange systems:
   (a) barter.
   (b) reciprocity.
   (c) accounting.
   (d) money.

3. List the four functions of money and briefly discuss the meaning of each function.

4. Recognize the more important, desirable properties of money.

5. Define and contrast each of the following monetary terms:
   (a) bills of exchange.
   (b) bank notes.
   (c) greenbacks.
   (d) commodity money.
   (e) representative money.
   (f) certificates of deposit.
   (g) demand deposits.
   (h) time deposits.
   (i) NOW accounts.
   (j) ATS accounts.
   (k) M_1, M_2, M_3, L.

6. Explain why the early goldsmiths are considered the precursors of modern banking.

7. Explain why acceptability is the most important characteristic of any money.

money An item (thing) that people accept as payment for a good or service.

This chapter discusses why we use money and why it makes economic sense to do so. It also shows how money evolved over the centuries. Defining money is an important goal of this chapter. *Money* is an item (thing) that people accept as payment for a good or service. This definition draws attention to the major requirement of anything that is to serve as money: it must be acceptable to those who are exchanging on markets. Thus, anything that is acceptable has the potential to serve as money.

If you go into a store and buy a new pair of jeans, chances are you pay for them with small pieces of paper with green printing on them—Federal Reserve Notes. The paper by itself isn't very valuable, and the printing isn't artistic. But we know we can pass it on in stores, restaurants, and at the theatre. Other people are willing to take these pieces of paper from us because they know they can, in turn, spend the money and pass it on to someone else. If you believed that no one would take the money, you wouldn't be interested in having it. If everyone thought the money was worthless, no one would take it, and the money really would be worthless because it couldn't be used to buy anything.

This chapter deals with questions regarding the role of money and how and why we use it. We have to point out that at times, people did decide money—or at least some form of it—was worthless, and their beliefs made it worthless. This lack of confidence in money brought on the bank panics of the 1800s and the early 1900s in the United States. In these panics people tried to turn in their paper money for a commodity—gold. Chapter 5 discusses in more detail how the monetary system works in the United States and points out why such such panics aren't very likely today.

BARTER AND THE INVENTION OF MONEY

Your economics instructor works for a living by providing you with high quality teaching services. This is not merely because he or she is generous; rather, your instructor wants to get things in return—such things as housing, food, books, vacations, etc. Thus, although your instructor's teaching services are provided to one particular segment of society—you and your classmates—your instructor wants things from a very different part of society.

In societies that have few goods, trades can be carried out fairly easily. Certain tribes of pygmies in Zaire are hunters and use metal-tipped arrows and spears. They trade the ivory from their elephant hunts for needed metal and for some agricultural goods. Prices in such trades are not measured in money, but rather in "number of arrow tips per tusk." Money really is not needed here—people directly trade what they have for what they want. This type of direct trade of goods and services is called *barter.*

barter   Exchange of one good for another without intermediation of money.

Consider a barter economy in which a shoemaker desires to buy a duck for dinner. If the shoemaker goes to the market and the fowl merchant wishes to exchange a duck for a pair of shoes, all is well. But what if the fowl merchant isn't interested in shoes, and wants a shirt instead? The shoemaker then has to find an individual who wants to trade a shirt for a pair of shoes so that the duck can be purchased. Very rarely would the shoemaker find what was wanted on the first trade. This is because such trades require a *double coincidence of wants.* You have to want what I have and am willing to trade, and I have to want what you have and are willing to trade. In our example, the shoemaker wants a duck but the fowl merchant wants a shirt.

double coincidence of wants   In barter, the requirement that a trader find someone wanting to trade what the first trader wants for what the first trader has.

These complications mean that a complex society will have tremendous pressure and incentive to find an alternative to a barter system. The most common

The Subterranean Economy

Rural communities have bartered for years. Farmers have always helped one another, knowing that they would receive help when needed. A *subterranean,* or underground, economy in the United States is emerging. It entails a switch from cash transactions to barters. Spurred by high inflation and high taxes, bartering has recently become a major factor in the U.S. economy.

U.S. News & World Report reports that a dentist in California traded his dental services for a new floor covering from a carpet dealer. An auto company traded cars for a corporate jet. A Colorado woman traded homegrown vegetables for auto repairs from her neighbors.[1] Households, small businesses, and large corporations have all entered the subterranean economy.

One of the motivations behind the barter system is the avoidance of taxes. If you trade homegrown vegetables for car repairs, the mechanic doesn't show earned income. Similarly, your tax return does not reflect the payment you received for your vegetables, because it came in the form of a service.

Another reason for participating in barter exchanges is to avoid the use of money. If confidence in money declines due to inflation, people will engage in bartering to avoid the use of money. Some firms have been established to facilitate barter exchanges. These bartering exchange firms did $350 million in sales in 1981. However, these exchanges were not tax motivated, because the records that were kept created a paper trail that could have resulted in a tax liability. If these exchange firms keep records, then, and use concepts such as trade units, they essentially have created a new kind of money.

A recent study by Thomas Spitznas of Chemical Bank contends that 20 percent of New York City's transactions are underground. He estimates that New York City lost $465 million in taxes due to underground sales in fiscal 1981.[2]

[1]"As Barter Boom Keeps on Growing—," *U.S. News & World Report,* Vol. XCI, No. 12 (September 21, 1981), pp. 55–58.
[2]"Measuring New York's Underground Economy," *Business Week,* No. 2717 (December 7, 1981), p. 28.

solution is to use money. The use of money is extremely efficient because it saves on the transaction and search costs that are involved in bartering. A great deal of time is wasted in barter exchanges and the invention of money is one solution to the problem. There are, of course, others.

Tradition as an Alternative to Using Money

Another alternative to a barter system is a system of exchanges of goods and services based on a combination of tradition, family ties, and social customs. Some farming societies, existing into the twentieth century, depended on labor from outside the farming family at certain times of the year—for example, at harvest and planting time—and got this labor from others on the basis of tradition and feelings of obligation. Most often this involved reciprocal obligations, or the system worked on *reciprocity.* At one extreme, this was like the American frontier where neighbors came to help out at barn raisings. A participant could reasonably expect some sort of reciprocal behavior, either for a barn raising or for some other occasion that required good neighbor behavior, such as sickness, economic hard times, or death in the family. Frontier neighbors were keenly aware of who fulfilled their neighborly obligations and who did not.

reciprocity   A system of performing tasks and services for others in the expectation that others will recompense you by acting similarly.

It is easy to idealize simpler times when family custom and tradition ruled our lives much more completely than today. People felt more a part of their surroundings, and, when things worked out well, more at peace with themselves and their role in the world. But we must make no mistake about this. Any such society has to have ways to make sure people do what is expected of them and to punish those who don't live up to expectations or else the system will disintegrate, for there are always those who do not feel like fitting into a pattern, however ideal it may be to the average member of the society. Thus, when the system becomes very large and complex, when day-to-day needs are not met by repetitive dealings with people whom you see every day and to whom you are bound by recognized social and moral ties, some alternative system must be found.

A Bookkeeping Alternative to Using Money

To look at this problem, let us think of workers in a society producing a large pile of different kinds of goods during the year. People are allowed to take away part of the goods until all the goods are divided. If the only thing produced were bananas, however, the problem would be relatively simple. Some people, such as rulers or people who are thought to deserve special consideration—the elderly, for example—would take more than they produced, but this is just a redistribution of income such as happens in many societies, both market and nonmarket. The real problem is to ensure that, after these transfers of income, people get their fair share of a pile that is made up of literally hundreds of thousands of different goods.

In the distribution of goods, it is necessary to make sure that the prices of different goods make sense relative to one another. For example, if one banana was worth one color TV and vice versa, bananas would be clearly overpriced and color TVs underpriced in the United States. This problem can be solved by letting prices adjust relative to one another to make quantities demanded and supplied equal to each other, as discussed in Chapter 3. Even if prices of goods relative to each other make sense and produce equilibrium, there is still the problem of making sure the goods get to those who want them and can afford them; that is, to make sure that people have a way to claim the goods they want and to which they are entitled. In a town of 3,000 families, equilibrium may require 200 new color TVs per year. It is still necessary to see that the families who want the TVs get them. Of course, if the people who initially get the TVs really want coats, they can barter and perhaps end up with coats, but only after bearing the costs associated with barter.

We might suppose that everyone in the village is given credits in one central store where each good costs a certain number of credits. For example, a color TV might cost 100 credits, and a coat might cost 10 credits. Thus, when the 200 TVs are delivered to the village's central store, those families who want them pay the 100 credits per TV, and the families who want coats use up 10 credits per coat. However, having one central store can be quite inconvenient, even in a village of 3,000. You can imagine what would happen in a city the size of Moscow or Los Angeles. In addition, imagine the difficulties of running a single store that carries every good distributed in the town or city.

Thus, an alternative to the credit system we've been discussing is to have many different stores. This is more efficient than one store, but it is necessary to see that people don't use more credits than they have. For instance, if a family has a monthly income of 1,000 credits, what is to prevent it from spending 1,000 credits at each of ten different stores? There would have to be some sort of central bookkeeping to make sure that the family didn't spend more than its 1,000 credits —to make sure it didn't take more from society's pile than it was entitled to take. (This is one of the problems of credit cards in the much more sophisticated United States system of credit.) Of course, central bookkeeping is not a cheap task. Even with today's modern computers and rapid cross-continental communication in the United States, it still costs banks an average of 15 cents to transfer the funds from the person who writes a check to the person who receives it. These costs are much greater in societies that are less technologically sophisticated.

From this viewpoint, it is easy to see why the use of money offers a socially desirable and useful way to handle such problems. When we contribute to the pile of social production, we receive money for our contribution, and we use this money to claim portions of the pile. When a family buys a color TV, it pays, say, $600 for a particular model, and the appliance store has no need to feed this into a giant bookkeeping system that checks to see if the family has $600. If it pays the money, that's enough. The family might pay with a check, forcing the store to take the risk that the check will bounce. But even this is efficient compared to the system we described. Further, the family might pay with a store credit card. This is really a loan, such as banks make, and many stores make substantial profits by providing credit this way. Other stores accept Visa, MasterCard, or other bank credit cards in order to encourage people to buy there, and pay the banks or companies that issue the credit cards for the privilege of using their credit systems.

Problems with Money

Basically money has been invented and used because it is a low-cost way of facilitating the distribution of goods that a complex society produces and distributes to a varied and mobile population with a wide range of tastes. The use of money, however, can lead to many problems. As we mentioned above, any one person will accept it only because of the belief that others will accept it. If people begin to doubt money's acceptability, they won't take it, and money won't be acceptable. We will discuss some problems of this sort and how the United States has dealt with this problem in the next chapter.

inflation   A rise in the general level of prices, particularly an ongoing increase in prices rather than a single increase.

Another problem with money is *inflation,* or a rise in the general level of prices. If you find a summer job paying $3,000, you might think of this sum in terms of what it will buy at prices in effect at the beginning of the summer. However, if the general level of prices is subject to ups and downs, it will be hard for you to plan for the next school year. Inflation means money is worth less, so to stay even you need more money. If you can judge the inflation rate, say 5 percent over three months, you could make a deal with your employer to incorporate this into your salary. You bargain for a bit more than $3,000. But suppose you are wrong. If there is no inflation, you do well, but if there is 20 percent inflation, your employer does well and you do worse than expected.

If inflation becomes too serious and variable, people fall back on barter. Instead of making contracts in terms of money, they exchange their goods and services. The surgeon performs an operation on the bricklayer's daughter in return for a wall, rather than either of them relying on a money price for the other's services. Thus, the use of money is a device to make society operate more efficiently, but it can be subject to serious problems caused by changes in the general level of prices. Inflation is one of the major problems, along with unemployment, addressed in this book.

THE FUNCTIONS OF MONEY

Throughout history many items, sometimes even bizarre items, have served as money. Before we discuss the evolution of a particular item as money, let's review the desirable properties of money. In order to understand these properties, we need to examine the purpose that money serves. First, money is a *medium of exchange.* We use money to pay for hamburgers, sweaters, and oil changes. We receive money for our work and when we sell a car. The discussion on barter shows how efficient money is as a medium of exchange. Second, money is a *standard of value.* We compare the costs of two goods by asking how many dollars we would have to pay for each good. How do you compare apples and oranges? One way to judge their relative worth is to look at their prices in terms of dollars. If we did not have prices and money as a standard of value, we would have to keep track of the value of each good in terms of all other goods. We couldn't say an apple costs $.10 and then compare $.10 spent on an apple to the other things $.10 would buy. Instead, we would have to say that an apple costs 2/3 of an orange, 1/500 of a pair of shoes, or 1/5000 of an automobile. In fact, in a simple economy that consists of only 100 goods, one would have to worry about 4,950 prices without money. The invention of money as a standard of value reduces those 4,950 prices to 100 prices. Third, money is a *standard of debt* for use in making contracts that extend into the future. If you work for someone today, you may be paid one month from now. Instead of specifying payments in terms of one chicken, three gallons of gasoline, and so on, you almost always specify it in terms of dollars. In this way, money allows an economic link to the past and the future. This is much safer when the general level of prices is stable than when it is subject to uncertain changes. The same reasoning applies to borrowing or lending money. People will lend money that buys goods and services now, to be paid back in some way in the future. It is easier to specify a repayment in terms of money than to list a large number of goods. However, as we have seen above, using money for such purposes becomes less attractive the more unstable the general level of prices. Fourth, money serves as a *store of generalized purchasing power.* If we store our wealth in the form of automobiles, that works out well if we happen to need a car in the future. But, not knowing what will be needed in the future, we usually want to store wealth in a generalized form that has purchasing power for many kinds of goods. Money has this property beyond any

medium of exchange *Money in its function of facilitating the exchange of goods by allowing people to exchange their services for money and then exchange money for goods they want.*

standard of value *Money in its function of providing a standard in terms of which goods can be valued and thus readily compared with each other.*

standard of debt *Money in its function of allowing borrowers and lenders to specify how a debt can be repaid in a generalized form of purchasing power rather than in specific goods.*

store of generalized purchasing power *Money in its function of providing purchasing power in a general form that can be used to purchase any particular good the holder then desires.*

other store of wealth. In any town in the United States that has a pizza parlor, you can get a pepperoni pizza by using dollars. If you show the proprietor a $10,000 Treasury security that you own, that won't buy you a pizza—or a new fan belt for your car, or a bouquet of daisies.

These purposes or functions of money provide some standard for an ideal money. While no money has ever been created that has performed ideally, there has been a movement in this direction—slowly, haltingly, and with many reverses —in human history.

DESIRABLE PROPERTIES OF MONEY

Some desirable properties of money are stability of value, transferability, scarcity, portability, durability, homogeneity, divisibility, acceptability, and recognizability. *Stability of value* is of key importance in making people want to use money and accept it. General *transferability* also makes money more useful. For instance, some types of money in Africa in the early 1900s were used almost solely for paying a "bride price" to the father of the bride, and such money was only useful to a family with sons who had to find brides. *Scarcity* is a prime consideration. The general level of prices tends to increase directly with the availability of what is used as money. Money can be literally immovable, but still useful. However, *portability* increases its usefulness. At one point in Sweden's history, copper was principally used for money, and, as a result, the weight of the coins was great. One needed help carrying the coins. More recently, portable wealth has been a literal lifesaver to people who are getting out of countries in times of upheaval or who are fleeing from persecutions, such as those who fled Nazi Germany in the 1930s. *Durability* is important, particularly if it is hard to trade in old, used money for fresh money. In the United States, if a dollar bill becomes tattered, you can turn it in for a new one at a bank, which then turns it in to the Federal Reserve for a new bill. The tattered bill is destroyed. If you can't trade it in, the money may disappear from wear and tear. This is related to general *acceptability* and *recognizability.* To be useful, money must be acceptable, and people are more willing to accept payment if they know they have a genuine (not counterfeit) dollar. The Susan B. Anthony silver dollars that were introduced into circulation during the Carter administration failed, mainly because of the difficulty of recognizing them. They were so similar in size to the quarter that this similarity prevented quick and easy recognition. *Homogeneity* is also important. Imagine the problems if dollar bills came in four sizes and five colors. *Divisibility* was an important property of gold. These days we see divisibility in operation when we turn in a $10 bill at a bank for two $5 bills or ten $1 bills.

An enormous variety of goods, and even ideas, have been used to serve all or some of the four purposes we have listed for money. These various monies have had the desirable properties we listed in quite different degrees. The property of stability of value has been the most elusive. Many types of money, including the U.S. dollar, have suffered when their values changed erratically.

The variety of items used as money may seem incredible. They have ranged from axes to yarns. Milk has been used—a very nondurable item (but liquid). Cattle, slaves, and so on have been used, though they are neither very homogeneous nor divisible. Even cannons have been used as money, though they are not very portable. Various precious metals, such as gold and silver (and copper, as we mentioned, though it is not very rare) have been used, though they are subject to counterfeit by being combined with less expensive (base) metals and can be reduced in weight by clipping, chipping, or shaving. Governments, by the way, have been the worst abusers of coinage. It was not uncommon in the Middle Ages for a monarch to call in all the coins, melt them, add base metals, recast them, and redistribute twice as many coins. Thus, *debasement* made money very suspect. How much gold really was in a coin?

On the island of Yap, in the South Pacific's Caroline Islands, large stones with holes in them were used as money until well after World War II. They weren't portable or divisible, but they could not easily be counterfeited and had good stability of value. A new stone could be brought only from Palau or Guam

debasement of money The practice of reminting coins while adding base metals; thus, increasing the number of coins, driving up the prices of goods, and reducing the value of each coin.

Yap Island Money

Yap, one of the Caroline Islands, lies in the western Pacific Ocean north of the equator and the island of New Guinea, and east of the Philippines. The fame of Yap lies in its stone money, called *fei*, which was written up in the anthropological literature on economics in the first four decades of this century. The *fei* are large stones, more or less wheel-shaped, with holes in the center to allow them to be carried on poles. The stones range in size from one foot to eight feet in diameter.

The stones are individually quite valuable and constitute a significant part of the island's wealth. As you can imagine, the stones aren't used in everyday transactions. The usual mediums of exchange are tridacna shells, used for large transactions, and mother-of-pearl used for less grandiose transactions. Thus, the stones are used primarily as a store of value, a standard of value, and as a means of deferred payment rather than as a common medium of exchange. They are nonetheless usually thought of as money. The larger stones are well-known and can change hands without their location being changed. Indeed, even stones that are now under the sea maintain their value, and their ownership, though not location, can be changed.

The Yap experience with modern currencies illustrates why the stones retained their value and why some people accumulate gold today. The Spanish first claimed Yap, but after the defeat of Spain in the Spanish-American War, Yap was sold to Germany in 1899. After Germany's defeat in World War I, Yap was transferred as a League of Nations trust territory to Japan in 1920. After World War II, Yap was transferred as a United Nations trust territory to the United States in 1947. All these nations introduced their currencies to Yap. Upon the introduction of United States currency, a Yap chief offered, "First Spanish money no good, then German money no good, now Japanese money no good. Yap money always good!"[1]

---

[1]*Life* (April 25, 1949), p. 100.

by raft or canoe, and all this cost a certain amount of human time, trouble, and effort.

During World War II, prisoners of war held in German detention camps used cigarettes as money. They received cigarettes as part of their rations from the Red Cross and elsewhere. There were fewer cigarettes than people wanted to smoke, so they were traded for other goods. The demand for cigarettes was stable, and cigarettes were used by a substantial part of the population. The supply was well known, so cigarettes gradually became a recognized money with a fairly stable value. Toward the end of the month, before new cigarette rations arrived, many of the cigarettes had been smoked, and the price of a cigarette in terms of most other goods, such as chocolate bars, tended to rise. However, this rise was predictable and hence was not as damaging as unexpected general price changes.

In Great Britain, prices are sometimes quoted in guineas, though there is no coin or piece of paper that is a guinea. Rather, in the old pound sterling (before adoption of the decimal system in 1967), there were 20 shillings, and a guinea was simply 21 shillings. As a standard of value, the idea of a guinea works perfectly well, though not, of course, as a medium of exchange. In Babylon, grains of rice were used for paying taxes, though the rice never circulated as money in the way dollar bills do in the United States.

THE EVOLUTION OF OUR MONETARY SYSTEM

In the United States we often think of the money stock as coins and currency (quarters and $5 bills, for example) in the hands of the public, and also checking accounts (technically called demand deposits).

For many transactions, a check is simply more convenient and safe than using currency. If you buy a $50,000 house with a 20 percent down payment, you can either write a check for $10,000 or hand over that amount in cash. Carrying that much cash would obviously be a big risk. Furthermore, the seller might be a bit nervous that all the bills are genuine, while the only risk with a check (on the assumption that it won't bounce) is that the bank will cease business before it can be cashed. In the United States, this is a very minor risk because of federal government insurance on deposits at banks.[1] In fact, checking accounts have a total value of almost three times as great as the currency and coin holdings of the public, as Figure 4-1 shows. Thus, the bulk of the United States money supply is made up of entries in your checkbook and entries in the books of banks you deal with. When you write a check for $50 to the grocery store, your bank deducts that $50 from your account and adds it to the store's account; if the store has its account at a different bank, things are more complicated and involve settling up between the two banks. We will look at this in detail in Chapter 5. Our goal here is to show how monetary institutions evolved to give us the arrangements we have today.

---

[1] In 1933 the United States Government set up the Federal Deposit Insurance Corporation (FDIC) to guarantee bank deposits. Currently, deposits up to $100,000 by an individual in a covered bank are guaranteed. There is no chance of loss if the bank goes bankrupt, and usually the money can be obtained very quickly. Only a very small percentage of deposits are in banks not insured by the FDIC.

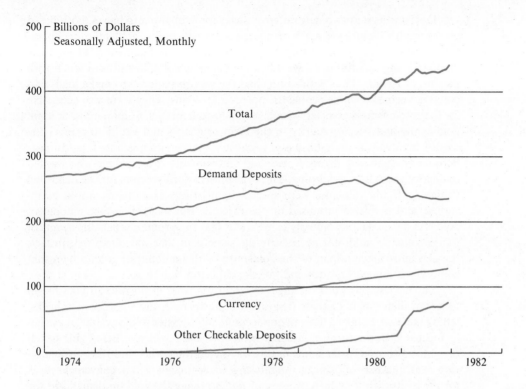

FIGURE 4-1 *M*₁ MONEY STOCK

Under the M_1 concept, the money stock equals checking accounts at banks (technically known as demand deposits) plus currency in the hands of the public, NOW and ATS balances at banks and thrift institutions, credit union share drafts, and demand deposits at thrift institutions. As Figure 4-1 shows, checking accounts now make up well over two thirds of the M_1 money stock. (Source: *Federal Reserve Chart Book* [February, 1982]).

Goldsmiths and the Rise of Banking

Modern banking is the result of three main needs (or demands) of society. First, some people want to borrow; this is what the ancient practice of moneylending is all about. Second, people want to hold their wealth in some form that is safe; recall our example of using a check rather than cash to make a down payment on a house. You are less likely to be robbed, there isn't the risk of counterfeit, and there are no coins to be possibly debased. Third, from the same example we can also see that the check is more convenient, at least for some transactions, than using cash. For all these reasons, ***goldsmiths*** began to play roles that are now associated with modern banks. They loaned money, they added to safety, and they increased convenience. Goldsmiths, or jewelers who specialize in working gold, have existed from the time society discovered gold, began to covet and hoard it, and became rich enough to have it worked. Jewelers have been found in almost all societies, and goldsmiths have been found in all societies where jewelers could and did use gold.

goldsmiths People who work gold. In their roles of accepting deposits and making loans, goldsmiths were the forerunners of banks.

Goldsmiths had two natural advantages for evolving into banks, both based on the wealth required to carry on a large-scale, substantial gold-smithing operation. First, keeping an inventory of gold for use in manufacturing gold products involved tying up substantial wealth and, of course, put goldsmiths in touch with persons of wealth. Thus, goldsmiths had the wealth required to make loans and could be seen as obvious people to approach for loans. They were also accessible for loans to business associates and even to customers such as monarchs. Second, goldsmiths had strong security in the form of guards and vaults to protect the wealth involved in their business. Because of these circumstances, goldsmiths both lent money and also accepted gold and valuables from people who wanted to deposit them for safekeeping. The goldsmiths issued receipts for the deposited valuables. If the valuables were specific items, these exact items would be returned, and it was so promised on the receipts. But when a specific amount of gold was deposited, it gradually came about that the promise was made to return that *amount* of gold, not necessarily the same gold that was deposited. In fact, the depositor made a loan to the goldsmith of this amount of gold, a loan that could be reclaimed "on demand" of the depositor.

note   Promise of payment.

The next step toward the modern bank was when depositors of gold began to assign their rights to these deposits to other people, just as we write checks, telling the bank to take $50 from our account and transfer it to, say, our physician or mechanic in the form of either deposits or cash payments. Being able to tell the goldsmith to transfer funds in this way saved the bother and risk of transferring large numbers of coins or weights of gold. A further step in convenience was for the goldsmith to issue a promise or *note* to repay the gold on demand to the bearer of the promise, whether or not the bearer was the initial depositor. In this way, the depositor could transfer the claim (or note) to the original deposit, and the receipt of the note was just like getting the gold and then depositing it with the goldsmith. If the receiver had faith in the goldsmith, this note was even better than receiving the gold, since it was safer. In the history of the United States, bank notes, or paper money issued by banks, were for a long time simply promises to pay a certain amount of gold. This was *redeemable paper money,* backed by gold. In 1933, President Roosevelt took the United States off the gold standard by not allowing bank notes to be redeemed for gold, and even forbidding U.S. residents to hold gold. (This prohibition was removed in 1975.)

redeemable paper money   Paper money that would be redeemed at face value in terms of some other money, usually precious metals.

Banks as Creators of Money

From all these elements came the main feature of modern banking: the creation of money. Goldsmiths lent out their own funds and took in deposits of other people's funds. Then, in the 1600s, goldsmiths began to lend out the funds of their depositors. Up until then, goldsmiths ran a system based on *100 percent reserves;* if they owed depositors 1,000 ounces of gold, they had 1,000 ounces in the vault. If one morning every depositor demanded every ounce owed, the gold was all there and could be paid out. However, goldsmiths noticed that depositors did not all ask for their deposits at the same time. Instead, some drew out their gold while others were depositing gold. This suggested that goldsmiths need not keep 100 percent reserves. Instead, they could lend, say, half of the gold that was on deposit and earn interest on these loans. After they lent some of this gold, the goldsmiths

100 percent reserves   Reserves equal to 100 percent of the obligations outstanding.

held only a fraction of the amount they owed, or they held only *fractional reserves.* Goldsmiths had people who came to them for loans, so this extra lending that used depositors' gold was easy enough to carry out and earned interest for the goldsmith. If the goldsmith lent out half of the gold that was deposited, there were 50 percent reserves. This made no difference to depositors as long as only a few of them wanted their gold at the same time. The important point to notice is that by lending some of the deposited gold, the goldsmith increased the money stock. For instance, if 100 ounces of gold were deposited, the goldsmith issued notes in this amount to the depositors. Then the goldsmith lent out 50 ounces. Thus, where there had been 100 ounces of gold outstanding, there were now notes (certificates of ownership) worth 100 ounces of gold plus 50 ounces of gold, for a total money supply of the equivalent of 150 ounces instead of 100 ounces of gold.

fractional reserves   Reserves equal to only a fraction of the total obligations outstanding.

Bank Services

Modern banks perform a large number of services and fulfill a large number of functions. Most will sell you traveler's checks, some will prepare your taxes, and some will even make your travel arrangements. Many will provide you with private deposit boxes in their vaults, some will pay your bills automatically or allow you to pay by using the telephone, and all will pay your bills as ordered by the checks you write. Some will even give you a watch or a blender for depositing certain amounts of money. Many of these services (but not all) are relatively new.

However, the major historical change in financial institutions was the start of money creation. The other activities of goldsmiths had gone on before. We noted that moneylending has long been with us, even if it is not quite the oldest profession. (Some might even hold that it is less honest than the oldest profession.) Further, there were *banks of deposit,* or so-called "giro" banks dating from the 1300s that took in precious metal, evaluated it, and promised to return metal of equal value. One main purpose of these banks of deposit was to take care of problems arising from the wide variety of different coins that had been minted in the world throughout the ages and the counterfeiting, clipping, and debasement that had taken place. But these banks never took on the role of lending more than was deposited with them. As for convenience, *bills of exchange* had long been used, probably in Roman times, but certainly quite extensively in the Middle Ages. A bill of exchange is essentially an order by one person to another, requiring the second person to give a certain payment to a third person. In more concrete terms, suppose someone in London owes you five ounces of gold. You can order the person in London to pay the five ounces to someone in Amsterdam to whom you owe this amount. Dating from the late Middle Ages, there were a number of reliable ways of executing bills of exchange.

banks of deposit   In the Middle Ages, organizations that took in precious metal, evaluated it, and promised to return metal of equal value.

bills of exchange   An order by one person to another, requiring the second person to give a certain payment to a third person.

Bank Notes, Checking Accounts, and Other Forms of Money

By the late 1700s, bank notes had become a substantial part of the money supply in England and many other countries. Such bank notes carried promises to give the bearer an amount of gold, stated on the note's face, on demand. Sometimes banks could not meet their obligations to redeem these notes, and these banks collapsed. In 1797, during the Napoleonic Wars, the government of Great Britain suspended gold payments for notes. Holders could no longer turn in notes and demand gold. England returned to gold payments, partially in 1816 and fully in 1821. During the United States Civil War (1861–1865), the federal government issued notes called *greenbacks* that were not redeemable in gold. The Confederate States of America also issued nonredeemable notes. When the war was going well for the federal forces, the greenbacks traded at close to their face value in gold, but traded for less when the war went badly. The Confederate notes became virtually worthless toward the end of the war, since too many had been issued, and it was becoming clear the Confederacy would lose and the notes couldn't be redeemed. It is still possible to buy confederate currency at some shops, but its only value is as a memento. This episode showed the possibility that bank notes, not redeemable in gold, could survive and be used, but also showed the importance of confidence of the people in the money. By the 1900s checking accounts were becoming more important than either gold or bank notes in the United States, and they again depended on confidence in the issuing banks for acceptability.

In the 1970s, banking practices changed significantly and many new types of accounts appeared. These accounts were largely the result of fewer regulatory barriers and of banks adapting computer techniques to monitor and more rapidly transfer funds. The suspension of interest rate ceilings in the early 1970s forced banks to bid more aggressively for large time deposits. This led to the development of *certificates of deposit (CDs),* which are long-term, high-value savings accounts. CDs are deposits with financial institutions that are for specific periods. They have a maturity and there is a penalty (often substantial) for early withdrawal.

NOW accounts and *ATS accounts* were created in the late 1970s and mushroomed with the passage of the Depository Institutions Deregulation and Monetary Control Act of 1980. NOW accounts (negotiable orders of withdrawal) are essentially demand deposits; checking accounts that pay interest. ATS accounts (automatic transfer system) are accounts that allow the individual to electronically transfer funds from one account to another, or to pay bills automatically.

THE ACCEPTABILITY OF MONEY

The important question of why money is or is not acceptable at any particular time is difficult to answer. If the money is also a commodity (such as gold), its value as a commodity sets its minimum value, and this would give it some general acceptability. If the money is not a commodity but is always redeemable in a commodity, the acceptability and value of the commodity transfers to that which represents it—the *representative money.* This was the case for gold-certificate and silver-certificate currencies. It was also true of bank deposits when they were redeemable in gold. The acceptability of representative money clearly depends on whether people believe it will be redeemable as promised.

Modern money, however, is normally neither a commodity nor redeemable in any specific commodity. What gives such money—called *fiat* or faith money —value and acceptability? One part of the answer is the legal institution called *legal tender*. The law says that certain things (currency and coin in the United States) are "legal tender for all debts, public and private." This means, for example, that governments must accept this designated category for the payment of taxes. Since such a large amount of taxes must be paid, this is a very important objective reason for people to be willing to accept legal tender in exchange for goods or services of real value. Even people who don't have to pay taxes can feel confident that this money will be of value and acceptable to others.

legal tender Money that must be accepted by private parties and governments in payment of debts and obligations.

The other important aspect of legal tender is that a debtor fulfills the obligation to repay a debt by offering legal tender money. The debt is not eliminated if the creditor refuses to accept legal tender, but the obligation to pay interest on the debt ceases at that time, and the debtor is not obliged to pay anything but legal tender. Since debt is so large in our economy, this is another very important objective reason for people to be willing to accept legal tender.

If you start to fear that the value of your money is in danger of being rapidly eroded by price increases, you will be tempted to switch some of your assets into land, buildings, fine art, rare coins, diamonds, or gold. These are real goods whose value rises when prices increase, and thus partly protect you against inflation. Hence, the fact that coin and currency are legal tender in the United States makes you more willing to hold money; but the amount you hold will depend on the outlook for the value of money. However, we don't want to stress the legal tender feature too much. Many forms of money that worked well and were acceptable were not legal tender. In fact, in the United States, currency is legal tender, but the major part of our money supply is accounted for by demand deposits which are not legal tender. The institution of legal tender enhances the acceptability of money, but is not necessary for it. We can imagine an inflation rate high enough that people abandon the use of currency and revert to barter, even though currency is legal tender.

ALTERNATIVE MONEY STOCK CONCEPTS

If you look at an older textbook, or even at the previous edition of this one, you will notice that the definition of the United States money supply has changed significantly. The change is a result of a Federal Reserve action, which in large part was motivated by the changing character of the way in which the public holds deposits. This change in the way the public banks is a result of the Depository Institutions Deregulation and Monetary Control Act of 1980. This Act removed legal distinctions among financial institutions and, as a result, changed the way in which the public was allowed to conduct its financial business.

The M_1 *money stock* is the amount of demand deposits at commercial banks plus currency, the traveler's checks of nonbank issuers, the NOW accounts, and ATS accounts. M_1 also includes credit union share drafts and demand deposits at mutual savings banks. To find the M_2 *money stock*, we add small-denomination time and savings deposits at all financial institutions to M_1. Time and savings deposits are those on which you earn interest and on which you cannot write a check. M_2 also includes *money market mutual fund* shares. Money market mutual fund shares are accounts which invest your deposit in the money market and on which you can write checks. The M_3 *money stock* is M_2 plus large time deposits and repurchase agreements. The footnote to Table 4-1 gives exact definitions of these money stock concepts.

M_1 *money stock* The amount of demand deposits at commercial banks plus currency, the traveler's checks of nonbank issuers, NOW accounts, and ATS accounts. It also includes credit union share drafts and demand deposits at mutual savings banks.

M_2 money stock   *The total of M_1 plus small-denomination time and savings deposits at all financial institutions plus minor entries.*

money market mutual funds Accounts which invest deposits in the money market and on which checks can be written.

M_3 money stock   *The total of M_2 plus large time deposits and repurchase agreements.*

near money   Assets that are relatively close and similar to the kinds of assets included in the money stock concept being considered.

In order to make some sense out of this whirl of *M*'s, let's compare M_1 and M_2. If you arbitrarily decide M_1 is the concept to use for measuring the money supply, you have to admit that savings and time deposits at banks are very good substitutes for checking accounts at the same banks. You usually cannot write checks on savings accounts, but even so, you could go to the bank, transfer funds from your savings to your checking account, and be in the same position as if the funds had been in the checking account all along. As compared to M_1 money we say these savings and time deposits are *near money;* they are close to what we call money. In fact, since most financial institutions now pay interest on checking accounts, there is very little difference between savings accounts and checking accounts.

Once you begin to think in terms of near money, you can easily see that whatever *M* concept you pick, there will always be some near money close to it. If you pick M_2, deposits at savings and loan associations are not very different from similar accounts at banks. Further, if you pick M_3 or *L,* which include large negotiable CDs, you would see that short-term U.S. government obligations, such as Treasury bills, are not too far removed from these negotiable CDs; there are active resale markets for these Treasury bills.

There seems to be no way to draw the line based just on logic, though people have tried. At one time, people argued that bank notes were not money—only

TABLE 4-1   MONEY STOCK MEASURES AND COMPONENTS

	1977 (Dec.)	1978 (Dec.)	Billions of Dollars 1979 (Dec.)	1980 (Dec.)	1981 (Oct.)
			Seasonally Adjusted		
Measures[1]					
1. M_1	336.4	364.2	390.5	415.6	433.0
2. M_2	1,296.4	1,404.2	1,525.2	1,669.4	1,798.8
3. M_3	1,462.5	1,625.9	1,775.6	1,965.1	2,143.3
4. *L*	1,722.7	1,936.8	2,151.7	2,378.4	n.a.
Components					
5. Currency	88.6	97.4	106.1	119.9	121.4
6. Demand Deposits	239.7	253.9	262.8	267.4	234.7
7. Savings Deposits	486.5	475.5	416.5	393.0	329.3
8. Small Time Deposits	453.8	533.3	652.7	756.8	841.1
9. Large Time Deposits	145.1	194.0	219.7	256.8	298.7

Source: *Federal Reserve Bulletin* (December, 1981).
[1]Composition of the money stock measures is as follows:
M_1:   Currency held by the public plus commercial bank demand deposits, traveler's checks of nonbank issuers, NOW and ATS account balances, credit union share draft accounts, and demand deposits at mutual savings banks.
M_2: M_1 plus savings and small-denomination time deposits at all depository institutions, overnight repurchase agreements at commercial banks, overnight Eurodollars, and money market mutual fund shares.
M_3: M_2 plus large-denomination time deposits at all depository institutions and term repurchase agreements at commercial banks and savings and loans.
L: M_3 plus other liquid assets.

gold was. Later, it was argued that bank notes and gold were money but checking deposits were not.

In Chapters 8, 12, and 13 you will see how changes in the money stock affect the general level of prices. But which money stock concept to use in studying these changes is not clear. As a result, economists often use different definitions and compare the results of their studies.

SUMMARY

1. We accept money because it can be passed on to people in exchange for other things we want. Money is desirable and useful only because it is accepted.

2. Barter is extremely costly and inefficient. A system of centralized stores or bookkeeping is too cumbersome and expensive to use. The use of money allows people to carry out their transactions economically.

3. There are problems associated with the use of money. For one thing, it must always be acceptable to people so they will take it in the belief that they can pass it on in exchange for what they want. Changes in the general level of prices, or inflation, can cause great hardship and uncertainty.

4. The functions of money include its use as a medium of exchange, standard of value, standard of debt, and store of generalized purchasing power.

5. Desirable properties for items used as money include stability of value, transferability, scarcity, portability, durability, homogeneity, divisibility, and recognizability.

6. A variety of items have been used as money such as axes, yarn, milk, cattle, cannons, slaves, gold, silver, paper notes, and cigarettes.

7. Banks developed from the lending activities of goldsmiths and their acceptance of deposits for safekeeping. Over time, the goldsmiths came to issue promises to return a certain amount of gold. These promises to pay evolved into bank notes.

8. When goldsmiths came to see that not all their deposits were withdrawn at once, they began to lend some of the gold deposited. This increased the money supply and was the forerunner of the modern bank's ability to create money.

9. Bank notes gradually became more important than gold; then checking accounts became more important than either. It is not necessary that bank money or checking accounts be redeemable in gold. For money to work well, it must simply be acceptable and useful. The institution of legal tender adds to money's acceptability.

10. There are several different money stock concepts used today in the United States and abroad. Whatever concept used, there will be close substitutes called near money. To draw the line between money and near money, we usually try to determine which money stock works best for the problem we are working on.

NEW TERMS

money
barter
double coincidence of wants
reciprocity

inflation
medium of exchange
standard of value
standard of debt

store of generalized purchasing power
debasement of money
goldsmiths
note
redeemable paper money
100 percent reserves
fractional reserves
banks of deposit
bills of exchange
greenbacks

certificates of deposit (CDs)
NOW accounts
ATS accounts
representative money
fiat money
legal tender
M_1
M_2
money market mutual funds
M_3
near money

QUESTIONS FOR DISCUSSION

1. Why is acceptability so important for what-ever is used as money?

2. Discuss some alternatives to using money, with attention to their drawbacks in a complex soci-ety such as ours.

3. Discuss some of the problems caused by changes in the general level of prices.

4. List and discuss some principal functions of money.

5. What are some desirable properties of money? Why are they desirable?

6. Why do checks sometimes have advan-tages over cash?

7. What are some of the needs that modern banking fulfills? How did banking arise from the ac-tivity of goldsmiths?

8. Why are there so many different concepts of the money stock? How might we choose among them?

9. How important is it that money be legal ten-der? What part of the U.S. money supply is legal tender?

SUGGESTIONS FOR FURTHER READING

Galbraith, John Kenneth. *Money: Whence It Came, Where It Went.* Boston: Houghton Mifflin, Co., 1975.

Goldfeld, Stephen, and Lester Chandler. *The Economics of Money and Banking,* 8h ed. New York: McGraw-Hill Book Co., 1981.

Herskovits, Melville J. *Economic Anthropology.* New York: W. W. Norton & Co., Inc., 1965.

Polanyi, K., M. Arensberg, and H. W. Pearson (eds.). *Trade and Market in the Early Empires.* New York: The Free Press, 1957.

Radford, R.A. "The Economic Organization of a P.O.W. Camp." *Economica* (November, 1945), pp. 189–201.

CHAPTER 5

Money Creation and the Federal Reserve System

Learning Objectives

After studying the materials found in this chapter, you should be able to do the following:

1. Explain how financial institutions create money.

2. List and discuss the three needs which led to the creation of the Federal Reserve System (the Fed).

3. Explain the structure of the Federal Reserve System.

4. Define the following terms important to an understanding of monetary policy:
   (a) reserve requirements.
   (b) legal reserves.
   (c) required reserves.
   (d) excess reserves.
   (e) discount rate.
   (f) open market operations.
   (g) currency drain.
   (h) money expansion multiplier.

5. Understand how the Fed influences interest rates, credit conditions, and the money supply through the manipulation of:
   (a) reserve requirements.
   (b) the discount rate.
   (c) open market operations.

6. Calculate the maximum possible change in demand deposits given by an initial reserve requirement (r) and:
   (a) the amount of an open market transaction.
   (b) a new reserve requirement.

7. Discuss the federal funds market and explain how the Fed influences the federal funds rate.

8. Explain how the Depository Institutions Deregulation and Monetary Control Act of 1980 affected financial institutions.

This chapter discusses the role of financial institutions in the creation of money and the role of the Federal Reserve System in regulating this money creation. The **_Federal Reserve System_** acts as a central bank to regulate financial institutions in the United States, as well as to influence interest rates, credit conditions, and the

Federal Reserve System The central bank and monetary authority of the United States.

Fed   Nickname of the Federal Reserve System.

supply of money. We will study how and why Congress set up the Federal Reserve System, or the *Fed*, as it is usually called. We will also discuss the tools the Fed can use to influence credit and money conditions, particularly how it can influence the amount of money commercial banks lend to their customers. Recent legal changes have had a significant effect on financial markets. Most of the differences between commercial banks and other financial institutions have been eliminated; thus, we now use the two terms interchangeably.

THE CREATION OF MONEY

In the previous chapter we saw how a goldsmith could increase the money supply by making loans against the gold others had deposited for safekeeping. This developed because the goldsmith discovered that on a given day, most depositors did not withdraw any of their gold. A fractional amount of reserves was all that was necessary to keep the goldsmith solvent. The way in which present day depository institutions create money is not radically different from the way in which the goldsmiths created money. Depository institutions lend multiples of their deposits, creating debt. This debt can serve as money. To see how this process works, begin by assuming a simple economy in which there is only one financial institution. We will call it the First Monopoly National Bank.

First Monopoly National Bank

To keep things simple, let's say you have just moved to a primitive economy that has not yet developed a banking system. Clam shells serve as the money supply in this country. You bring with you a T-account ledger and open the first and only bank in this country. You convince a local investor to join you. The investor puts up 100,000 clams. Table 5-1 represents the ledger you open.

Your first activities are to construct a building and to deposit the cash (clams) remaining after the building is built. These transactions are shown as Transaction *A* in Table 5-1. Your building costs 50,000 clams and you hold another 50,000 clams in cash. The net worth, or capital stock, of your bank is 100,000 clams. Your bank is now open for business.

Your first customer wants to borrow 100,000 clams to start a business exporting native artwork to the United States. Being a conservative banker, you want to hold at least 20 percent of your clams in reserve, so that if a depositor comes in to cash a check for clams or wants to withdraw clams, you will be able to satisfy

TABLE 5-1   LEDGER OF FIRST MONOPOLY NATIONAL BANK

	Assets		Liabilities	
Transaction *A*	Cash	50,000 clams	Capital Stock	100,000 clams
	Property	50,000 clams		
Transaction *B*	Loans	100,000 clams	Demand Deposits	100,000 clams
Transaction *C*	Loans	50,000 clams	Demand Deposits	50,000 clams

the request. You look at your liquidity and see you have reserves of 50,000 clams and no deposits against those reserves. You agree to grant the loan.

In granting the loan, your accounts are affected in two ways. First, you create a demand deposit of 100,000 clams for the customer. The customer can write checks on this account to begin the export business. At the same time you have created an asset for your bank. The would-be exporter has signed a note that he owes you 100,000 clams. These two transactions are depicted as Transaction *B* in Table 5-1.

In Transaction *B* you, the banker, have created new money by making the loan. Now you have 50,000 clams in cash against 100,000 clams in demand deposits. This is a reserve of 50 percent.

A second customer enters your bank and wants to borrow 50,000 clams to buy a house. You have more cash reserves than you need, so you grant the loan. Your loans increase by 50,000 clams and your demand deposits increase by 50,000 clams as in Transaction *C* in Table 5-1. You now have total demand deposits of 150,000 clams against cash reserves of 50,000 clams. Your reserves are now 33 percent of demand deposits, so you could expand your loans still more. The incentive to expand your loans is that the customer must pay you interest for the use of the money which you created.

The Money Multiplier

As a new banker, you may wonder what limits the amount of money you might create. The answer depends on two things: the initial amount of reserves (in the case of your bank it was 50,000 clams) and the reserve ratio you decide is safe (20 percent). The ***money expansion multiplier*** is the coefficient by which a bank can expand the money supply from a new deposit of money. This multiplier is the reciprocal of the percentage amount of reserves the bank desires to hold against deposits. The money multiplier is the reciprocal of the reserve ratio. In the case of your bank the *money multiplier* is 1/.2 or 5. You will reach your limit after granting loans worth 250,000 clams.

money expansion multiplier Shows the maximum increase in the money supply for a given increase in reserves.

A Multiple Bank Economy

Our example assumed that you were the only banker in this economy, and that the recipients of the checks drawn on your bank would deposit these checks in your bank, thereby opening new accounts. No deposit would ever leave your bank in this simple example. You, as a banker, would only move funds from one depositor's account to another's.

Suppose your neighbor sees you earning money on marks in a ledger and opens a competing bank. This competing bank adds a complication to our example, because the money you create may not remain in your bank. In other words, the exporter to whom you made the initial loan may write a check to a local artist for crafts and the artist may deposit the check in a competing bank. The competing bank would then present the check to your bank for payment.

There is an important economic phenomenon taking place when there is more than one bank. When a check drawn on one bank is deposited in another, it will result in a loss of reserves (and deposits) to the original bank. This loss of reserves will decrease the money expansion ability of the bank that loses reserves.

Conversely, the bank that receives a deposit of a check drawn on another bank will increase reserves and deposits. The receiving bank's ability to expand the money supply will increase. An important point emerges from these happenings in a multibank setting: regardless of the number of banks, the impact on the banks as a group is no different than the impact would be in a single bank system. In other words, the ability of a system of banks to expand the money supply is no greater than that of a single monopoly bank. As long as the money stays in the system, the money multiplier holds for the system. If the exporter received payment for the art from an importer in the United States, for instance, that new money in the system will cause the whole system to expand. If money leaves the system, say, because people decide to take payment in cash and hold the clams at home in the mattress, the ability of the system to expand will diminish.

We'll return to the ways in which money expansion and contraction occurs, but first we will explain the Federal Reserve System, so we can make the examples more realistic.

HISTORICAL BACKGROUND OF THE FEDERAL RESERVE SYSTEM

The Federal Reserve System was created because many voters and their representatives in Congress saw two needs: first, a need to regulate banks to prevent them from doing risky and unsound business; and second, a need to rescue sound banks that nevertheless were sometimes threatened by failure and bankruptcy. Later, a third goal of helping to promote a strong economy with high employment and a stable price level was established. This last goal, however, was not envisioned by the founders of the system.

bank panics **Sudden waves of fear that banks won't be able to pay off their depositors.**

The first two needs arose from the same conditions which caused the *bank panics* that periodically swept the United States in the 1800s and early 1900s. In these times, banks made loans by issuing their own bank notes (private paper currency), which they promised to redeem in gold. As we know from Chapter 4, they could not keep this promise if everyone tried to redeem the notes for gold at the same time. As long as all bank-note holders believed they could redeem their notes, only a small percentage were presented each day, and the demand for redemption in gold was easily met. However, some banks made far too many loans, as well as loans that were unsound in the sense that they were unlikely to be repaid. If a bank has $1 million in gold reserves, it may safely make loans and issue bank notes for, say, $10 million. But if $100 million is issued, it is much more likely that in any one day there will be a demand to turn in $1 million in notes for gold, thus wiping out the gold reserve. For every bank that followed such unsound practices, there usually came a day when people would present for redemption too many of the over-issued notes, and the bank's reserves would be so low that it could not redeem all the notes presented. When this happened to one bank, people naturally became worried about all banks and would try to redeem their notes. At the height of these bank panics, or *runs on banks,* many sound and prudent banks were unable to redeem the high proportion of their notes that could be presented in a single day. These banks failed, or closed, even though they were fundamentally sound. People who had their money in these

runs on banks **Attempts by large numbers of people to get their money all at once from the banks.**

banks lost it, and people who needed loans would, of course, not be able to get them from out-of-business banks. Even the banks that didn't fail had to retrench considerably because of the fear these panics caused.

A bank run could develop on a perfectly sound bank. All that was needed was a rumor of possible failure that was believed by enough people. The run could then wreck that bank. Many people saw that, to prevent sound banks from going under in a panic, a *lender of last resort* was needed. The purpose of such a lender would be to bail out sound banks during a run by lending them as much as they needed to meet the temporary demands put on them by depositors who were afraid of losing their money. When people realized that the sound banks could get funds from a lender of last resort, they would be less likely to panic; thus, runs would be less likely to occur in the first place and would be less severe when they did occur.

lender of last resort   A lender for banks that were sound but couldn't pay off sudden large demands during runs on banks.

During the nineteenth century, a number of private banks, and groups of private banks, tried to curb the unwise practices of other banks and also act as a lender of last resort. With the exception of the Suffolk Bank and its affiliated banks in New England, such attempts never worked very well. This was because the private banks lacked strong means of regulating other banks, and they weren't financially strong enough themselves to withstand major bank panics. A major bank, or group of banks, that was worried about possible overexpansion and unsound loan practices at, say, bank *A,* could exert pressure mainly by forcing bank *A* to redeem its notes in gold. That is, if some of bank *A*'s notes came to bank *B,* bank *B* could redeem them at bank *A* for gold. This drained gold at bank *A* and slowed down its note expansion. But this regulation stopped far short of the power to examine bank *A*'s books and lending practices and to force the bank to stop unsound lending practices. The Bank of the United States, located in Philadelphia (privately owned but chartered by the federal government), tried to play this role and also tried to serve as a lender of last resort. It went bankrupt in the panic of 1841.

The lesson seemed to be that only the federal government had the power to regulate banks sufficiently, as well as the financial resources to act as a lender of last resort. However, Americans fought political battles for over a century on the issue of giving these powers to the federal government. There were many reasons for this resistance. For one thing, it seemed to many that the power of regulation and the ability to act as a lender of last resort would be used to the benefit of rich and powerful bankers. The Bank of the United States, mentioned above, had originally been chartered by the federal government and had tried to restrain the excesses of other banks. Many people felt the Bank was simply using governmental power to benefit the Bank's owners, their friends, and business associates. The second and last charter of the Bank expired in 1836, and the Bank collapsed in 1841. Another reason for resistance was that two of the problems that government control could solve did not seem like problems to some voters. First, it was argued that if banks overextended their loans, the money supply growth would cause prices to rise. However, the people who wanted the loans—for example, farmers on the western frontier—looked upon the expansion of loans as a good thing.

Second, many people did not look upon rising prices as an evil, but as a good thing for them. They were in debt and had interest payments fixed in dollar terms that they had promised to make. In times of rising prices, they had increasing incomes with which to make their payments; but in times of falling prices, they had to make these dollar payments out of a falling income. To understand this, consider the case of people who buy an automobile in times of generally rising prices and wages. They borrow the money to pay for the automobile, and every month they make a fixed payment that eventually (after, say, 48 months) pays off the debt. As time goes on and prices, income, and wages all rise, these monthly payments come to seem less and less burdensome. You can well imagine the problems that might arise if prices, wages, and income generally started to fall instead of rise. This was what the debt-ridden farmers could easily foresee for themselves.

National Banking System Chartered and regulated national banks during the latter half of the nineteenth century; preceded the Federal Reserve System.

During the United States Civil War (1861-1865), the *National Banking System* was established, under which banks could receive charters from the federal government. A national bank charter is the formal permission from the federal government to incorporate and operate a bank. Banks which receive their charters from the federal government are called *national banks.* The alternative was a charter from one of the states, as had been the case before, which resulted in a *state bank.* National banks are chartered and regulated by the *Comptroller of the Currency* in the Department of the Treasury, and state banks are regulated by various banking agencies and commissions in the different states. However, in this system the various regulators lacked the power and the wisdom to effectively police banks and also to act effectively as lenders of last resort. Banking crises continued.

national banks Those banks that are chartered by the federal government and are subject to its rules and regulations, as opposed to state banks.

state banks Banks chartered and regulated by individual states, as opposed to national banks.

Finally, in the aftermath of the panic of 1907 and the recession that followed, Congress moved forward, and, after a series of compromises designed to quiet some of the fears of opponents, the Federal Reserve Act was passed in 1913. The Federal Reserve System commenced operation in November, 1914. The current structure of the System is that which was given to it in 1913. However, the actual work of the System is quite different from what the designers had in mind; experience has changed what people want of the System, and now the major issues facing the Fed involve the macro economy and how monetary policy will affect it.

Comptroller of the Currency Regulator of some aspects of national banks; grants charters to national banks.

STRUCTURE OF THE FEDERAL RESERVE SYSTEM

Federal Reserve districts The United States is divided into 12 Federal Reserve districts, each with its own district bank and board of directors.

In many details, the structure of the System reflects the fears people had and their attempts to prevent the fears from coming true. For example, the United States is divided into 12 *Federal Reserve districts,* each with its own Federal Reserve Bank (see Figure 5-1). The idea was to keep the people who run each Bank in closer touch with the people in their district than would be the case if all the power in the System were centralized in Washington, D.C., or in New York City. In addition, it was felt that each district would have the ability to experiment with different policies, allowing everyone to learn which strategies worked best. The latter idea never really worked out. The Board of Directors of each Federal Reserve Bank was to be composed in specified proportions of representatives of

*Board of Governors of the Federal Reserve System
●Federal Reserve Bank Cities

FIGURE 5-1   THE FEDERAL RESERVE SYSTEM
There are 12 Federal Reserve Districts, each with its own bank (and these banks have branches). The Board of Governors of the Federal Reserve System is located in Washington, D.C. (Source: *The United States Directory of Federal Regional Structure* [Washington: U.S. Government Printing Office, 1981], p. 127.

the banking industry, agriculture, and the general public. This was to prevent domination by any one group.[1]

National banks were required to belong to the Federal Reserve System and state-chartered banks were allowed to join. Only member banks could borrow from the Fed, and this was the main incentive for joining. These original requirements held until 1980, when the law was changed to place all financial institutions under the control of the Fed. We will later examine this 1980 law in detail. Since the 1980 Act, the differences between commercial banks and other financial institutions have been diminished. Therefore, we use the terms *banks* and *financial institutions* synonymously.

The need for some central control was also recognized in the 1913 Act, and a **Board of Governors** for the System as a whole was created. There are seven governors, with no more than one governor from any one of the 12 districts. For example, if there is a Board member whose home is in New York State, there cannot be another member from the 2d district.

Board of Governors   Central governing body of the Federal Reserve System.

---

[1]You can tell by looking at each bill issued by the Federal Reserve which Fed it came from. To the left of George Washington's picture on a dollar bill is a seal that gives the Fed district. The letter in the middle of the seal corresponds to the number that appears in all four corners. For example, a bill from Dallas will have a *K* in the seal and an 11 in each corner. This is because Dallas is the 11th Fed district (*K* is the 11th letter of the alphabet).

Carter Glass *(1858–1946)*

The mighty political storms of yesteryear are often soon forgotten, along with the politicians who played such large roles in them. Such is the case with the founding of the Federal Reserve System, and, in the sort of joke history often plays, the Fed is far different from what the political actors who created it envisioned. Among the major influences on the legislation creating the Fed was *Carter Glass.*

The panic of 1907, with its many bank closings, was something of a last straw after the considerable number of post-Civil War recessions and depressions. Congress formed a National Monetary Commission in 1908 (composed of senators and representatives) to "inquire into and report to Congress at the earliest date practicable, what changes are necessary or desirable in the monetary system of the United States. . . ." The Commission was very thorough, and didn't submit its final report until early 1912.

One of the main defects found by the Commission, and by many other observers, was that the monetary system had no reserve force or elasticity in times of strain. That is, no bank had the incentive to hold large excess reserves or the ability to create more reserves in times of crisis and panic. The Commission proposed a National Reserve Association as a way of pooling reserves, but one defect with this plan was that this would be essentially a voluntary association of banks run by banks. This sat poorly with those who worried about the power of banks (eastern banks, in particular) and those who generally opposed bigness in business.

However, the House Banking and Currency Committee, chaired by Carter Glass of Virginia, produced a bill that centralized reserves under the Federal Reserve System. The bill provided for a board appointed by the federal government, which diluted the influence of bankers in the System. All nationally chartered banks had to join the Fed. Member banks had to hold reserves as determined by the Fed, and the Fed could provide reserves to banks through the discount window. The Federal Reserve Act was passed in late 1913, and the Fed came into existence in 1914. It was in many ways a compromise, but, given the array of hostile forces in every direction, it was an impressive legislative achievement.

It is now quite clear that the reserves held with the Fed are not a hedge against panics but are rather a tool of monetary policy. The primary purpose of the Fed is not what its founders envisioned; i.e., providing elasticity and regulating banks. Rather, its purpose is the making of monetary policy. The Fed as it now stands would have had no chance of being created in 1913.

Carter Glass was born in Lynchburg, Virginia, in 1858 and entered the United States House of Representatives in 1902 after a career in publishing and Virginia politics. The Federal Reserve Act was his great achievement. He resigned from the House to serve as Woodrow Wilson's Secretary of the Treasury in 1919 and 1920 and was thus involved in the post-World War I treaty and financial negotiations at which John Maynard Keynes was a high British Treasury representative. In 1920 he was appointed to the United States Senate to fill a vacancy and subsequently remained in office in his own right until his death in 1946.

FEDERAL RESERVE SYSTEM TOOLS

In addition to certain powers to examine banks' books, scrutinize lending practices, and impose penalties, the Fed has, over the years, been granted three tools that have become very important in monetary policy, or the attempt to influence interest rates, credit conditions, and the money supply.

Reserve Requirements

First, the Fed sets *reserve requirements* for financial institutions. At the present time, *legal reserves* (items eligible for meeting the reserve requirement) consist of three categories of assets: the currency and coin the bank has on its premises, called *vault cash,* the funds member banks have on deposit with their district Federal Reserve Bank, and the deposits held by some categories of financial institutions at commercial banks. One of the reasons banks collapsed in runs or panics was that their reserves were too small or not readily available. The Fed now requires financial institutions to hold reserves equal to certain fractions of the different kinds of deposits they have. In practice, reserves now have nothing to do with safety from the point of view of people who put their funds in checking and savings accounts at the financial institution. This safety is provided by the Federal Deposit Insurance Corporation, up to a maximum of $100,000 per account.

To see why reserve requirements are not very important in providing protection for depositors, let us suppose banks have to hold reserves equal to 20 percent of their checking accounts, and, neglecting the existence of savings accounts, suppose a given financial institution has exactly the needed reserve level—say, deposits of $1,000,000 and reserves of $200,000. If people withdraw currency of $100,000 from their checking accounts (demand deposits), the bank will have only $100,000 left in reserves. However, with deposits now of $900,000, the bank is required to have $180,000 in reserves (20 percent of $900,000). This means that the bank now has only $100,000 left in reserves to meet any further withdrawals. Thus, it is $80,000 below the level the Fed requires it to hold and must make up these reserves or face fines by the Fed.

Clearly, if the Fed alters the reserve requirements, it will make banks either more or less willing to lend. With a given level of reserves, an increase in the requirement (say, from 20 percent to 25 percent) will create a reserve shortage and make bankers less willing to lend or buy securities. Reduction in the requirement (to, say, 15 percent) will make bankers more willing to make loans or buy securities.[2]

Federal Reserve Lending

One way to make up the shortage of reserves if depositors withdraw their funds is to borrow from the Fed. This opens the way for the Federal Reserve

reserve requirements *Requirements that certain percentages of Fed members' deposits be held as reserves.*

legal reserves *Those assets of banks that count as reserves; the actual amount of reserves versus the required amount.*

vault cash *Cash held in bank vaults.*

---

[2]Reserve requirements on the banks' demand deposits differ, based on the size of the bank, with larger banks having higher requirements (see Table 5-9 at the end of this chapter). Savings accounts and other accounts where funds are to be left on deposit for a specified time period are also subject to reserve requirements, and these differ with the size of the bank and how long the deposits must remain there. These differences merely complicate the analysis of this chapter without changing any fundamental point.

discount   A loan where the interest is taken in advance.

discounting   Taking the interest on a loan in advance.

rediscount   Using a discounted loan as collateral for borrowing, with the interest on this loan paid in advance.

discount window   The Fed is said to make loans to its members at the "discount window."

discount rate   The interest rate the Fed charges its members on loans it makes to them.

advances   Direct loans from the Fed to its members rather than discounts of member bank assets.

open market operations Purchases and sales of securities on the open market by the Fed.

Treasury bills   Shorter term Treasury securities which pay no interest; the investor earns a return by buying the bill at an amount less than the amount the Treasury pays when the bill matures.

Banks to exercise a second method of control that fits in with the notion of the central bank as a lender of last resort. A commercial bank borrows from the Fed by putting up some of its assets as backing or collateral for the loan. Only certain kinds of assets held by financial institutions are eligible to be put up to back the loan. The institution **discounts** such an asset with its district Bank. The term **discounting** refers to the method by which the Fed charges interest on the loan to the bank.

In lending to their own customers, financial institutions often lend at discount. This means that the interest on the loan is paid at the time the loan is granted rather than at the end of the loan period. For example, a firm might borrow $10,000 for one year at 10 percent. It would receive $9,000 as the proceeds of the loan, the lender keeping $1,000 as prepaid interest. This, of course, is a higher rate of interest than when the interest is paid at the end of the loan. (A 10 percent interest rate on $9,000 would involve the repayment of $9,900 as opposed to $10,000 in the discount case.) The bank could take a note for a loan like this to its Federal Reserve Bank and **rediscount** it. For example, a note might have a value of $10,000 in one month, and if the discount rate at the Federal Reserve Bank were 6 percent (or ½ of 1 percent per month), the financial institution could get $9,950 as the proceeds of the loan from the Federal Reserve Bank. The financial institution is selling the loan to the Fed.

Borrowing from the Fed is called using the **discount window.** The rate of interest charged on its loans is called the **discount rate,** and changing the discount rate is one of the tools of monetary policy. The higher the rate charged, of course, the less eager financial institutions are to borrow; the lower the rate, the more willing financial institutions are to increase reserves by borrowing. Financial institutions that behave badly can be denied use of the discount window, and if they borrow more than the Fed thinks is wise, they can be denied further discounts. The discount rate is almost always below other interest rates at which the financial institution could borrow.

Actually, it is current practice for financial institutions to obtain direct loans (called **advances**) from the Federal Reserve Banks rather than to discount the notes of its borrowing customers. The financial institution typically pledges U.S. government securities as collateral and pays interest at the stated discount rate.

Open Market Operations

The third, and most often used, tool of the Fed is **open market operations**. This refers to purchases and sales by the Fed of U.S. Treasury securities on the open market. These securities are **Treasury bills** (T-bills) with a maturity of one year or less. T-bills don't pay interest. Instead, the buyer earns a return by paying, say, $9,500 for a one-year T-bill that will pay $10,000 at the end of the year. This gives a return of an extra $500 and a yield of a little over 5.26 percent $\left(= \frac{\$500}{\$9,500} \times 100 \right)$. The Fed also operates in longer term Treasury obligations. We shall discuss open market operations in more detail later in this chapter, but we can show here how they work to change bank reserves. Suppose bank *A* has reserves of $1,000,000 that it holds in the form of deposits with the Fed. The Fed performs an open market operation by buying $100,000 worth of Treasury securities from bank *A*. The Fed now owns the Treasury securities and pays for them by writing on its books that bank *A* has $100,000 more deposits with the Fed. Thus, bank *A*'s reserves are now $1,100,000, up by the $100,000.

If the Fed buys the security not from a bank, but from a member of the nonbank public, the customer of bank *A* sells the securities to the Fed. We assume the customer would deposit the check received from the Fed in a commercial bank. The commercial bank would then deposit the check with the Fed, and the bank's deposits with the Fed would increase by the amount of the sale. In this example, then, regardless of who sells the securities, member bank reserves increase by the amount of the purchase if the Fed buys them. Conversely, open market sales by the Fed decrease reserves of member banks by the amount of the sale. The point is that, through open market operations, the Fed can directly affect the reserves of the member banks in the System. We will see how this works in much greater detail in the next section.

FEDERAL RESERVE SYSTEM TOOLS AND THE MONEY SUPPLY

We can see how these three tools affect the supply of money in the economy by using T-account ledgers that show banks' assets and liabilities. Table 5-2 shows that bank *A* has demand deposits outstanding of $1,000,000; these are liabilities, because bank *A* owes them to people. For the moment, let's neglect other kinds of deposits, such as savings deposits. People can demand that bank *A* make good on its liabilities and hand over $1,000,000 in cash, though the idea behind modern banking practices is that people are not expected to cash in all their deposits at the same time. On the asset side, the bank has holdings of loans and Treasury securities worth $800,000, and also $200,000 in reserves held in the form of deposits with the Fed. The bank earns interest on the $800,000 in loans and securities, but none on the $200,000 in reserves.

The Effects of Open Market Operations

Let's assume for the sake of simplicity that the level of required reserves is 20 percent of demand deposits. Then *required reserves,* or the amount of reserves that the Fed requires, is $200,000, the same amount of reserves the bank actually has, or its *legal reserves.* If the Fed now buys $100,000 in Treasury securities from

required reserves   The amount of reserves that a bank is required to hold on its various deposits.

TABLE 5-2   ASSETS AND LIABILITIES OF BANK *A*
(no excess reserves)

Assets		Liabilities	
Earning Assets (Loans and Treasury securities)	$800,000	Demand Deposits	$1,000,000
Reserves (Deposits with the Fed)	$200,000		

Nancy H. Teeters *(1930–   )*

Nancy H. Teeters is the first woman to serve on the seven-person Board of Governors of the Federal Reserve System. (The first Black, Andrew F. Brimmer, was appointed by President Lyndon Johnson in 1966. He is now a private consultant.) Appointed by President Carter in 1978, her term expires in 1984. Teeters did her undergraduate work at Oberlin College and her graduate work at the University of Michigan.

Her career has included many important economic positions in Washington. She was a staff economist at the Fed from 1957 through 1966, taking a year off in 1962 to serve on the staff of the Council of Economic Advisers in the Kennedy administration. She was at the Bureau of the Budget (now the Office of Management and Budget) from 1966 to 1970. Thereafter, she was at the Brookings Institution from 1970–1973, where she worked as one of the authors on the yearly volume, *Setting National Priorities,* Brookings's annual "counter-budget" that stands in comparison to the administration's budget. From 1974 until her appointment to the Board in 1978, Teeters was chief economist for the House Budget Committee, where she worked "to make the federal budget controllable."

Until recently, the chairperson of the Board of Governors had a great deal of control over the Board. However, with President Carter's appointment of G. William Miller as chairperson in 1978, the Board has seen more dissension. Thus, individual Board members such as Teeters now have more influence.

Teeters would be classified on the more liberal end of the political spectrum. However, her broad experience in Washington insures that she is less doctrinaire than is implied by labels such as liberal or conservative.

One of Teeters's greatest powers as a Board member is a seat on the Federal Open Market Committee (FOMC). All seven members of the Board are on the FOMC, along with five representatives of the district Banks. These representatives must be either presidents or vice-presidents of the Banks. The New York Fed is always represented on the FOMC, and the other representatives serve in rotation. Under the law authorizing the FOMC, the FOMC can make monetary policy independently of the president and Congress. However, what Congress gave, it can also take away, so FOMC members must be careful not to anger Congress or the administration too much.

---

earning assets *Assets that pay a return, as opposed to reserves held with the Fed that pay no return.*

excess reserves *Reserves held in excess of those that are required.*

bank *A* and pays with a check on itself—and that is the way the Fed always pays —bank *A* has the changes shown in Table 5-3. Its *earning assets,* loans and government securities, have fallen by $100,000, while its reserves have risen by $100,000. Its legal reserves are now $300,000 while its required reserves are still $200,000 since its demand deposits are unchanged. Its *excess reserves,* total reserves *minus* required reserves, are $100,000. Before the Fed purchase of Treasury securities, excess reserves were zero because legal and required reserves were both equal to $200,000.

This change in the composition of bank *A*'s assets is only the first round effect of the open market operation. What will bank *A* do with these excess reserves?

**TABLE 5-3   AN OPEN MARKET OPERATION AND ITS
EFFECTS ON BANK *A* IN THE FIRST
ROUND (excess reserves = $100,000)**

Assets		Liabilities	
Earning Assets (Loans and Treasury securities)	$700,000[1]	Demand Deposits	$1,000,000
Reserves (Deposits with the Fed)	$300,000[2]		

[1]$100,000 worth of Treasury securities was sold to the Fed.
[2]Reserves increase by $100,000 because of sales of Treasury securities to the Fed.

Very likely the bank will try to relend them. It now has only $700,000 in earning assets, since it has $100,000 less after the Fed buys the $100,000 in Treasury securities. We can imagine that when a customer asks for a $100,000 loan, it will be granted if the customer looks like a good risk. This is shown in Table 5-4 as an increase in both demand deposits of the borrower and the earning assets of the bank. The loan couldn't have been granted before, because the bank didn't have the reserves to support any new demand deposits. Further, we would not be surprised to find the bank just a little more eager to make loans on easier terms and without quite as much insistence on the borrower's being a first-rate credit risk.

The bank now has deposits of $1,100,000, required reserves of $220,000 (equal to 20 percent of $1,100,000), total reserves of $300,000, and excess reserves of $80,000. Why didn't bank *A* lend more money? Because the money could be expected to be withdrawn from the bank very soon. And, when deposits are withdrawn, reserves will decline by the same amount. The borrower usually does not take out a loan just to let the money sit idle in a checking account. The money is usually quickly spent. For instance, a builder will take out a loan to finance a new office building and will use the funds from the loan to pay for materials, for the services of construction workers, and so forth. The lesson for a single bank is clear. It can safely lend only the amount of its excess reserves because it can

**TABLE 5-4   BANK *A* EXPANDS ITS LOANS (excess
reserves = $80,000)**

Assets		Liabilities	
Earning Assets (Loans and Treasury securities)	$800,000[1]	Demand Deposits	$1,100,000[1]
Reserves (Deposits with the Fed)	$300,000		

[1]Bank *A* lends the borrower $100,000 by depositing this amount in the borrower's account at bank *A*. Earning assets rise by the $100,000 loan.

afford to lose these reserves and still satisfy its reserve requirement. As long as a bank only lends reserves that are in excess of its required reserves, it will be safe, even if all loaned funds leave the particular bank.

What happens to these funds that the builder pays out? A number of possibilities exist, but as we saw earlier the key point is that, for the banking system as a whole, it doesn't matter a great deal what happens to these funds. The extra reserves the Fed created will remain in the banking system until the Fed withdraws them (perhaps by an open market operation in the opposite direction). These extra reserves can be passed around from bank to bank but the only way the reserves can be removed from the system is by the Fed removing them.[3]

Suppose that everyone the builder pays deposits the checks they receive in bank *B*. Then, bank *A* finds the changes that Table 5-5 shows. Demand deposits fall by $100,000 as the builder spends the funds from the loan. The people the builder pays cash their checks and deposit the funds in bank *B*. Bank *A* loses $100,000 in reserves. This is a *reserve leakage* for bank *A*. However, someone has to end up holding these reserves; they cannot leave the banking system. Everyone receiving a check from the builder deposits the funds in bank *B*, which initially (we will assume) had liabilities and assets just like bank *A*'s in Table 5-2. Then, bank *B*'s liabilities and assets change, as in Table 5-6. Bank *B* now has demand deposits increased by $100,000, as well as $100,000 more in reserves. Notice that while bank *A*'s deposits have returned to their original level as shown in Table 5-2, bank *B*'s deposits are higher by $100,000, so the total in the system is still $100,000 above the level before the open market operation. Reserves also are $100,000 above their level before the open market operation.

Bank *B* will now likely expand its loans or purchase more securities. It has $100,000 of new deposits and of the new $100,000 in reserves, $20,000 are required reserves and $80,000 are excess reserves that can be loaned out to

reserve leakage   *When a bank makes a loan, it expects that some of the loan will eventually be deposited elsewhere, meaning its reserves will fall.*

TABLE 5-5   THE BUILDER PAYS PEOPLE WHO, IN TURN, WITHDRAW THEIR FUNDS FROM BANK *A*
(no excess reserves)

Assets		Liabilities	
Earning Assets (Loans and Treasury securities)	$800,000	Demand Deposits	$1,000,000[1]
Reserves (Deposits with the Fed)	$200,000[2]		

[1]When the builder pays people who withdraw the funds from bank *A*, deposits there fall by $100,000.
[2]When these people deposit their checks at bank *B*, bank *A* then owes bank *B* $100,000. The Fed reduces bank *A*'s reserves by $100,000 and increases bank *B*'s reserves by $100,000.

---

[3]This is not quite true. Certain actions by the Treasury, foreigners, and the public can reduce member bank reserves. We will neglect these for the moment, but will show their influence when we consider currency drains.

TABLE 5-6 A DEPOSIT INFLOW TO BANK B (excess reserves = $80,000)

Assets		Liabilities	
Earning Assets (Loans and Treasury securities)	$800,000	Demand Deposits	$1,100,000[1]
Reserves (Deposits with the Fed)	$300,000[1]		

[1]Deposits rise by $100,000 and the Fed transfers $100,000 from bank A's reserve account to bank B's reserve account.

customers. Of the $80,000 loaned, some will be spent in ways so that funds flow out of bank B, while some may not. From our discussion above, we know what will happen if all of the loan amount flows to another bank; that bank will have $80,000 more in reserves, $80,000 more in deposits, and can lend out its new excess reserves of $64,000 (80 percent of $80,000) if it chooses. Suppose the funds are all redeposited in bank B; for example, everyone who receives the funds is a depositor at bank B. Bank B then would still have $64,000 in excess reserves and could make further loans if it wished.

Maximum Expansion of the Money Supply Due to an Open Market Operation. We can set some limits on where this process will end. First, we must recognize that no one can force a bank to make loans from its pool of excess reserves. If there are no loan customers that look worthwhile to a bank, it can simply hold the reserves. Second, we can ask by how much the banking system as a whole can possibly expand its loans. From the example above, we know that any bank can expand its loans as long as it has excess reserves, and the banking system as a whole can expand loans as long as there are excess reserves in the system. Thus, expansion must stop only when there are no more excess reserves. Since the total of legal reserves in the financial system can only be changed by the Fed, the only way to eliminate excess reserves is by turning them into required reserves. In our example, every dollar of new demand deposits turns 20 cents of excess reserves into required reserves.

We can find the maximum amount by which the money supply can expand by using a little arithmetic. Suppose each bank wants to lend out any excess reserves (ER). Then, the process will stop only when there are no more excess reserves, or when all of the legal reserves (LR) have become required reserves (RR). If the reserve requirement ratio is r, the banks' required reserves are rD (where D = demand deposits). Thus, the banking system (and an individual bank) is fully loaned up when LR equal RR, or

$$LR = rD, \qquad (5\text{-}1)$$

and dividing both sides of equation (5-1) by r, we get

$$D = \frac{1}{r} LR. \qquad (5\text{-}2)$$

According to equation (5-2), demand deposits (D) can change only if r changes or LR changes. Since we are not changing r by open market operations,

$$\Delta D = \frac{1}{r} \Delta LR. \tag{5-3}$$

Thus, the change in demand deposits will be equal to the reciprocal of the reserve requirement ratio times the change in legal reserves. If open market purchases of \$100,000 take place, $\Delta LR = \$100,000$, and if $r = .20$, $\frac{1}{r} = 5$, and $\Delta D = 5 \cdot \$100,000 = \$500,000$. The money expansion multiplier is 5. As we have seen, the money expansion multiplier $\left(\frac{1}{r}\right)$ is the reciprocal of the reserve requirement ratio (r).

Expansion of deposits can occur only when excess reserves appear. By the definition of excess reserves as the difference between legal reserves and required reserves ($ER = LR - RR$), excess reserves can increase only when legal reserves increase or when required reserves decrease. Since $RR = rD$,

$$ER = LR - rD. \tag{5-4}$$

In the example of the open market purchase by the Federal Reserve, LR increased by the purchased amount. If the securities are sold by banks, RR remains fixed since neither r nor D changed. Thus, ER changes initially by the full amount of the open market operation. The money expansion occurs as banks increase their loans and investments so that D increases. As D increases, RR increases, decreasing ER. When D increases by 5 times the original increase in LR, excess reserves will be back to zero and no more lending and investing by the banks is possible. Table 5-7 depicts these cumulative effects as they work themselves through the banking system in the example we have been using.

A Currency Drain. The above calculations were made on the assumption that everyone deposited funds with some bank, or that there was no *currency drain* where some funds are held by the public in the form of currency and coin and not redeposited with banks. We can easily imagine other, more realistic cases involving a currency drain.

currency drain   An increase in currency holdings by the public causes a dollar-for-dollar decline in reserves available to the banking system.

For example, when bank A loaned \$100,000 to the builder, and the builder used this money to pay expenses, the people receiving the funds might have decided to hold \$10,000 in currency and deposit only \$90,000 in bank B. What would bank B's financial position look like in this case? We can figure that both deposits and reserves will rise by \$90,000. Required reserves rise by \$18,000 (equal to 20 percent of \$90,000). Thus, the excess reserves that bank B can lend are only \$72,000 in this case, not the \$80,000 we saw in Table 5-6. Currency drains will reduce the total amount by which any injection of reserves will allow the money supply to expand. Remember, we said before when there were no currency drains that the only way to eliminate excess reserves was to turn them into required reserves through expansion of demand deposits. Now we see there is another way. Excess reserves might be eliminated by expanding demand deposits and also through the siphoning of legal reserves out of banks through a currency drain. For every dollar of currency flowing into circulation, LR falls by one dollar, which means that \$5 of deposits have to be eliminated.

**TABLE 5-7   INCREASE IN MONEY SUPPLY AND
RESERVES WITH AN INITIAL OPEN
MARKET PURCHASE OF $100,000 OF U.S.
TREASURY SECURITIES AND A RESERVE
REQUIREMENT OF 20 PERCENT**

Bank	ΔD	ΔRR	Amount the Bank Lends
A		$ 0	$100,000
B	$100,000	20,000	80,000
C	80,000	16,000	64,000
D	64,000	12,800	51,200
E	51,200	10,240	40,960
.	.	.	.
.	.	.	.
.	.	.	.
.	.	.	.
.	.	.	.
.	.	.	.
All Other	.	.	0[2]
All Banks	$500,000[1]	$100,000[1]	$600,000

[1]Total of all banks.
[2]Excess reserves of each bank are zero *after* the loan is made and the borrower has spent the funds. Note that the money expansion multiplier, 5, is the reciprocal of the reserve requirement of $\frac{1}{5}$ (or 20 percent).

Open Market Sales of Securities. We have been considering the expansionary impact of open market purchases by the Fed. When the Fed purchased securities, it paid for these securities by increases in the member banks' reserves. An open market sale of securities will have exactly the opposite effect.

If the Fed wishes to contract the money supply or prevent financial institutions from expanding the money supply, it will offer to sell bonds to the member banks. Very small changes in the yield will make it extremely profitable for banks to purchase these securities so the Fed has no trouble finding eager buyers. When the Fed sells the securities, it accepts payment from the member financial institutions by decreasing the reserve account of that institution.

As a result of the purchase, the purchasing financial institution has experienced a decrease in its legal reserves. The money multiplier works on this reduction in reserves the same way in which it works on an expansion of reserves. The net result is that the ability of the money supply to be expanded has decreased and if banks are fully loaned up, there will be a decrease in the money supply.

Changing Reserve Requirements

Open market operations work on the quantity of demand deposits by changing legal reserves relative to required reserves, which changes the level of excess reserves. Changes in reserve requirements also work on demand deposits by changing excess reserves. The difference is that changes in reserve requirements leave legal reserves the same but cause changes in required reserves and thus in excess reserves.

To see this, return to bank A as we saw it in Table 5-2. Now, suppose the reserve requirement is reduced from 20 percent to 10 percent, giving the results in Table 5-8. Reserves are still $200,000, but required reserves have fallen to $100,000 and excess reserves have risen to $100,000. With these $100,000 in excess reserves, we expect bank A to expand its lending in much the same way as when an open market operation increased reserves. This expansion in demand deposits will be limited by exactly the same forces that worked in the case of an open market operation: the willingness of the banking system as a whole to lend as long as it holds excess reserves and the currency drain that moves reserves out of the banking system and into currency and coin as demand deposits expand. Notice that just as in the case of an open market operation, the excess reserves generated by a change in the reserve requirement are a hot potato that the banking system can pass around but can eliminate only by turning into required reserves.

We can set an upper limit to the expansion of demand deposits due to the reduction in the reserve requirement. It is important to remember that no amount of excess reserves can force a bank to lend, so a given increase in excess reserves could result in no change in demand deposits. Of course, if excess reserves are initially zero, an increase in the reserve requirement will make them negative and thus will cause a fall in demand deposits as banks are forced to contract. But if excess reserves are positive, an increase in the reserve requirement that reduces excess reserves but still leaves them positive may lead to no fall in demand deposits if the banks feel they would rather live with lower excess reserves than contract their business. At this point, we simply wish to find the maximum expansion in demand deposits due to a change in the reserve requirement. First, we need to find the new money multiplier.

We know that the money multiplier is the reciprocal of the reserve requirement $(1/r)$. The reserve requirement is now 10 percent, so the money multiplier is 10. Looking at Table 5-8, we see that Bank A has $200,000 in legal reserves and has required reserves of $100,000 for its $1,000,000 in deposits. Bank A therefore has $100,000 in excess reserves. The banking system can thus increase the money supply by $1,000,000 ($100,000 $\times$ 10), if there are no currency drains.

An increase in the reserve requirement works in the opposite way by generating negative excess reserves. Given zero excess reserves at the beginning and at

TABLE 5-8   CHANGE IN RESERVE REQUIREMENTS OF BANK A FROM 20 PERCENT TO 10 PERCENT (excess reserves = $100,000)[1]

Assets		Liabilities	
Earning Assets (Loans and Treasury securities)	$800,000	Demand Deposits	$1,000,000
Reserves (Deposits with the Fed)	$200,000[1]		

[1]The reduction of the reserve requirement to 10 percent reduces required reserves to only $100,000, leaving $100,000 in excess reserves.

the end of the process, demand deposits will decline by the amount of the new multiplier times the negative excess reserves. Our earlier example started with a reserve requirement of 20 percent, legal reserves of $20 billion, and deposits of $100 billion. Now assume the reserve requirement is raised to 25 percent. Required reserves at the moment the reserve requirement was raised would be .25($100 billion) = $25 billion. Excess reserves are now negative, because legal reserves were only $20 billion. Excess reserves of $-$5 billion can be eliminated or brought back to zero by the banks' decreasing their loans and security holdings, by the loan customers' paying off their debts to the banks, or by the banks' selling earning assets to the public. In each case, the demand deposits of the public are decreased. The amount by which demand deposits must decrease is the (new) multiplier of four times the excess reserves of $-5 billion, which gives a change in D of $-$20 billion.

Changing the Discount Rate

In the example just cited, where negative excess reserves were imposed on the banking system, we noted that banks would be forced to contract their deposits by selling their earning assets or eliminating loans. This is a very traumatic situation for both the banks and the banks' debtors. It takes time to make the necessary adjustments if the transition to the new conditions is to proceed without major bank and commercial failures or general panic. This is one important justification for the discount mechanism. With an open discount window, instead of immediately calling in loans and distress selling of securities, the banks can borrow from their district Federal Reserve Bank. What they borrow is deposits with the Federal Reserve, so an increase in Fed discounts means an increase in legal reserves. Since these discounts are loans the banks have to repay, they can be considered only a temporary expedient, and the banks will have to make the ultimate adjustment over time by reducing their earning assets.

There are many other, less dramatic circumstances when excess reserves would become negative if the banks were not able to avail themselves of the discount privilege. Each Federal Reserve Bank sets a discount rate at which the financial institutions of its district can borrow. The Board of Governors must approve the rate, so it usually turns out that the rates are the same in all the districts. Normally the discount rate is below market interest rates, so to keep banks from borrowing at low and lending at high rates, the Federal Reserve Banks ration the borrowing ability of the commercial banks, and banks are warned by Fed officials about abusing the discount privilege. The Fed frowns on excessive borrowing by the member banks, and since the Fed is the regulatory agency, this has some force.

Varying the discount rate is a tool of monetary policy in that raising the rate is viewed as a contractionary or discouraging act, while lowering the rate is viewed as an expansionary or encouraging act. There are two reasons cited for this belief. One is the view that an increase in the discount rate is a signal to banks that the Fed wants to cool down the economy, and when the rate is decreased it signifies the Fed's desire to accelerate the economy, with the banks encouraged to contribute to the process. More importantly, discount rate changes alter the profitability of borrowing. Raising the rate makes it more expensive to borrow, so banks would be expected to borrow less and hold larger excess reserves in order to avoid the prospect of having to borrow. A lower rate makes borrowing more profitable and encourages banks to hold fewer excess reserves since they would be less concerned about getting into situations where they would need to borrow from the Fed.

The Federal Funds Market

federal funds market   Where banks borrow and lend reserves.

federal funds rate   The interest rate charged in the federal funds market.

Banks can borrow reserves from each other as well as from the Fed. If bank *A* has excess reserves, it can lend some of these (for one day at a time) to bank *B*. These loans are between members of the Federal Reserve System and are said to be lent in the *federal funds market;* they are really switches in entries on the books at the Fed, transferring reserves from the account of one member who has lent to the other member who has borrowed. The rate charged is the *federal funds rate;* it is quoted on an annual basis, so if the rate is, say, 6 percent, it costs the borrowing bank (approximately) 1/365 of 6 percent for a one-day loan. Such loans can be renewed, but a bank can get its loaned funds back after any one day if it so desires.

The Fed does not directly set the federal funds rate, but it does play a large role in this market. The Fed sets a target band for federal funds, say, plus or minus ⅛ of 1 percent around 8 percent. If the federal funds rate drops to 7⅞ percent, the Fed sells Treasury securities and thus drains reserves from the banking system. As reserves fall relative to the demand for them, the federal funds rate is driven up. Similarly, if the rate rises to 8⅛ percent, the Fed buys Treasury securities and thus injects reserves into the system. This increases the supply of reserves relative to demand and will drive the federal funds rate back toward 8 percent. Many economists think that this method of controlling the federal funds rate plays a very important role in monetary policy and how well the policy works.

Other Tools of the Fed

moral suasion   Attempts by the Fed to convince banks to do what the Fed thinks is right.

The Fed has a number of other tools. For example, in the past it has set maximum rates that banks can pay on time and savings accounts. It can also set proportions of stock purchases that a buyer can finance with credit. Changes in these tools, however, are not used very frequently.

Further, the Fed can use *moral suasion,* or can try to persuade banks on moral grounds to behave in ways that please the Fed. For example, the Fed may think that the money stock is expanding too quickly and therefore urge banks not to make as many new loans in order to hold down the rate of money stock growth. The Fed regulates banks and controls their access to the discount window, so banks have to pay some attention to such pronouncements. However, it seems that not too much attention is paid, and open market operations are a more reliable way of controlling the money stock.

The Fed's Use of Its Tools

Changes in reserve requirements are not made very often and they certainly are not used on a day-to-day basis the way open market operations are used. The structure and the use of reserve requirements by the Federal Reserve have evolved over the history of the System. Originally requirements were fixed by law with no provision for variation. Banks were divided into three classes, determined mainly by the financial importance of the city in which the banks were located. After 1972 the classification of banks for reserve purposes was abandoned, and reserve requirements on demand deposits were set according to the volume of deposits in the bank. The legal changes made in 1980 set the reserve requirements shown in Table 5-9.

Changing reserve requirements is a rather crude instrument for monetary policy. The reason is that they are too powerful in their effect. Even a change of a fraction of 1 percent can have a very large (and somewhat uncertain) impact on the economy and can be very unsettling to the banks. For this reason, changes are not made frequently.

In contrast to the shortcomings of reserve requirement changes as a policy tool, open market operations represent a very flexible tool. The impact on reserves can be precisely determined, can be as large or small as desired, can be reversed if necessary, and can be done without any fanfare. As a result, the Fed depends most heavily on open market operations for monetary policy. Many economists feel that it is the only tool the Fed should use.

Open market operations are used daily. These operations are carried out by the *open market desk* at the Federal Reserve Bank of New York. This simply means there are people at the New York Fed who buy and sell Treasury securities through brokers in New York City. This is sensible, because New York is the financial center of the country. The open market desk, however, does not buy and sell on the basis of its own decision, but tries to carry out the overall directives it receives from the *Federal Open Market Committee (FOMC)*. The FOMC is composed of all seven members of the Board of Governors of the Federal Reserve System, plus the president of the Federal Reserve Bank of New York and the presidents of four other Federal Reserve District Banks, serving in rotation.

open market desk   The part of the Fed that engages in open market operations.

Federal Open Market Committee (FOMC)   Fed committee that sets general monetary policy.

TABLE 5-9   DEPOSITORY INSTITUTIONS RESERVE REQUIREMENTS OF THE FEDERAL RESERVE SYSTEM

Type of Deposit and Deposit Interval	Depository Institution Requirements After Implementation of the Monetary Control Act of 1980	
	Percent	**Effective Date**
Net Transaction Accounts		
$0–$25 million	3	11/13/80
Over $25 million	12	11/13/80
Nonpersonal Time Deposits by Original Maturity		
Less than 4 years	3	11/13/80
4 years or more	0	11/13/80
Eurocurrency Liabilities		
All types	3	11/13/80

Source: *Federal Reserve Bulletin* (Washington: Board of Governors of the Federal Reserve System, October, 1981), p. A8

Raising and lowering the discount rate is a relatively weak tool, and its impact is largely unpredictable, since the magnitude of the effect depends upon bankers' reaction to the changes. It is not a very flexible tool and if it is used too often, the signaling function would probably be lost. Many people are under the impression that the Federal Reserve sets the market interest rates, but the discount rate is the only rate the Fed sets directly. We will discuss later how the Fed has an indirect effect on the general level of market interest rates.

THE DEPOSITORY INSTITUTIONS DEREGULATION AND MONETARY CONTROL ACT OF 1980

In March, 1980, Congress passed the Deregulation and Monetary Control Act of 1980. This Act, which was divided into nine titles or sections, has had profound effects on financial institutions in the United States. It has substantially altered the rules that made financial institutions different and, as a result, speeded a trend toward similarity of operations. Since this Act is so far-reaching in its effects, it is worth examining some of its more important aspects.

Monetary Control

In Title I, Congress extended the Fed's control by putting all financial institutions under Fed requirements; previously only member banks were under the Fed's control. As a result, all commercial banks, savings banks, savings and loan associations, and credit unions are under the regulations of the Federal Reserve System. Thus, all financial institutions are now required to report to the Fed and to maintain reserves under the Fed's control. These reserve requirements are 3 percent for the first $25 million of deposits and from 8 to 14 percent for deposits over $25 million.

In addition, all financial institutions have been given access to the same Fed discounting and loan services. Similarly, all financial institutions now have access to check clearing, wire services, and settlement services at a charge (previously, these services were free to member banks).

Deregulation

Title II of the Act requires that all interest rate ceilings be phased out by 1986. The goal of this Title is to allow interest rates to be determined by market forces. This phasing out of interest rates ends a long history of interest regulation by the Fed. (*Regulation Q,* the law under which ceilings were placed on the interest rate that could be paid on certain kinds of deposits, caused banks great problems in attracting deposits. However, all controls will be lifted by 1986.)

Checking Account Equity

Title III of the Act allows all financial institutions to offer NOW accounts. Negotiable Order of Withdrawal accounts are checking accounts that pay interest on the transaction balance. These accounts are offered to all individuals and nonprofit organizations. This Title also allows banks to offer automatic transfers between savings and checking accounts, and allows credit unions to offer share drafts. In essence, it gives all financial institutions a mechanism to pay interest on checking account balances. This Title also increases the federal insurance on deposits from $40,000 to $100,000.

Savings and Loan Institutions

Title IV of the Act has greatly expanded the role of thrift institutions. It allows savings and loan institutions to invest in consumer loans, commercial paper, corporate debt, and money markets. This is a distinct change from the almost exclusive reliance they had on home mortgage loans and this change will affect the way in which homes are financed in the future. Before 1980, home buyers were subsidized by the fact that thrift institutions had no choice but to make home loans.

Other Titles

In the other titles of the Act, all state usury laws were preempted unless reinstated by April 1, 1983. Truth in lending laws were simplified to make them more understandable to consumers; burdensome banking laws were changed; federal regulations were simplified; and foreign takeovers of domestic banks were examined.

Effects on Financial Institutions

The Deregulation and Monetary Control Act of 1980 has had a profound effect on financial institutions. Banks have begun to offer NOW accounts, and financial institutions that never competed in the past, now actively court depositors' money. A likely outcome of this is that the number of different types of financial institutions will decline. For example, many services provided by credit unions were performed because credit unions existed in a noncompetitive market. However, credit unions will now have to compete or go out of business.

A second important impact of this law is that it should increase the ability of the Fed to control the money supply. After a transition period, the Fed will have more potential for control, because of the Fed's influence on all financial institutions.

SUMMARY

1. Financial institutions make loans which have the effect of expanding the money supply. The limitation on money expansion is determined by the reserves they must keep.

2. The Federal Reserve System was authorized in 1913 to help reduce the damage that the economy suffered because of bank panics and runs on banks in the nineteenth and early twentieth centuries. It was designed to serve as a regulator and lender of last resort to member commercial banks. The need for some institution to play both roles had long been noted, but many people opposed giving this much power to one agency, fearing that it would be dominated by big bankers and their associates.

3. There are 12 Federal Reserve districts in the United States, each with its own Bank. The central authority is the Board of Governors in Washington D.C. A main concern of the Fed is monetary policy; that is, policy which influences interest rates, credit conditions, and the money supply.

4. The Fed has three main tools it can use in implementing monetary policy: reserve requirements, open market operations, and lending through the Fed discount window at the discount rate.

5. Reserve requirements tell banks what reserves they must hold at the Fed as a fraction of their demand deposits.

6. Open market operations are purchases and sales of Treasury securities by the Fed.

7. Both reserve requirements and open market operations work by changing banks' excess reserves, which is the difference between legal reserves and required reserves. As excess reserves expand, the banks can increase their loans and thus the money supply. Reductions in excess reserves tend to force contractions of loans and the money supply.

8. Banks can borrow at the discount window to cushion reductions in reserves.

9. Both reserve requirements and the discount rate are changed infrequently.

10. Open market operations go on daily and are the main tool of the monetary policy of the Fed.

11. The Depository Institutions Deregulation and Monetary Control Act of 1980 made all financial institutions members of the Federal Reserve System and greatly diminished the distinctions between different types of financial institutions.

NEW TERMS

Federal Reserve System
Fed
money expansion multiplier
bank panics
runs on banks
lender of last resort
National Banking System
national banks
state banks
Comptroller of the Currency
Federal Reserve districts
Board of Governors
reserve requirements
legal reserves
vault cash
discount
discounting

rediscount
discount window
discount rate
advances
open market operations
Treasury bills
required reserves
earning assets
excess reserves
reserve leakage
currency drain
federal funds market
federal funds rate
moral suasion
open market desk
Federal Open Market Committee (FOMC)

QUESTIONS FOR DISCUSSION

1. How are banks and financial institutions different today than they were in 1979?

2. Why are there 12 Federal Reserve districts? Which district are you in? What is the Board of Governors?

3. What are the three main tools of the Fed?

4. Suppose the required reserve ratio is 20 percent. If an extra $2 billion in excess reserves are injected into the system through a Fed open market purchase of Treasury securities, by how much can

demand deposits rise? What would your answer be if the required reserve ratio was 10 percent? Does the quantity of demand deposits *have* to rise?

5. In the preceding problem, would it make a difference if the increase in excess reserves came about by the Fed's lowering the discount rate and thus inducing banks to borrow $2 billion?

6. Suppose reserves are $100 billion, the required reserve ratio is 20 percent, and banks are fully loaned up (that is, excess reserves are zero). Now reduce the required reserve ratio to 10 percent and suppose banks once again become fully loaned up. What is the new quantity of demand deposits? Do this problem again, but assume the required reserve ratio rises to 25 percent.

SUGGESTIONS FOR FURTHER READING

Chandler, Lester V. *Benjamin Strong, Central Banker.* Washington: Brookings Institution, 1958.

Galbraith, John Kenneth. *Money: Whence It Came, Where It Went.* Boston: Houghton Mifflin Co., 1975.

Modern Money Mechanics. Chicago: Federal Reserve Bank of Chicago.

"Special Project—Usury and Monetary Control Act of 1980." *Arizona State Law Journal,* Vol. 1981, No. 1, pp. 27–34.

CHAPTER 6

The Government Sector: Taxes and Spending

Learning Objectives

After studying the materials found in this chapter, you should be able to do the following:

1. Explain the basic justifications for government.

2. Explain and distinguish among the allocation, distributive, and stabilization functions of government.

3. Define Wagner's Law.

4. Discuss what government does in the United States.

5. List alternative ways of financing government activity.

6. Define the tax base.

7. Distinguish among income, wealth, and sales taxes.

8. Explain what constitutes a "good" tax.

9. Understand the Reagan Tax Cut.

10. Explain how regulation is similar to a tax on the economy.

fiscal federalism   The system of relationships that exists between various levels of government in the United States.

We often criticize government and the growth of government. Yet if a group of us were transplanted to an uninhabited island to start a new economy, one of the first things we probably would do would be to form a government. The reason for this is simple. We all belong to, contribute to, and expect certain things from government. Even Adam Smith (see his biography in Chapter 2) advocated government in a *laissez-faire* system of economy.

This chapter looks at the role of government in a market economy. In particular, it examines the size and scope of fiscal federalism in the United States. *Fiscal federalism* is the system of relationships that exists between various levels of government in the United States. After chronicling the growth of government in the United States, we will examine how we pay for it. We will look at the existing tax system and develop some ways to examine the tax structure. This chapter concludes with a review of the Reagan tax reform of 1981.

A BASIC GOVERNMENT

Even the most *laissez-faire* economists or libertarian politicians would not advocate a world without government. Most individuals would say that, at a minimum, a government must provide a money supply, national defense, and a system of law and order.

We discussed the reason for government control and maintenance of the money supply in the two previous chapters. Money facilitates trade. Thus, a medium of exchange is bound to evolve in a trading economy, and a set of governmental rules concerning money helps to insure its stability. Of course, inflation is evidence that government is not always successful in maintaining stability.

National defense is another justification for government. Some extreme pacifists dispute this, but most people see a need for it. All national governments spend some tax revenue on defense.

Law and order or, more specifically, the enforcement of a set of laws designed to insure property rights is also crucial to the survival of a market economy. If exchange is to take place, property rights must be enforced. When property rights break down, economic exchange breaks down. Consider a few examples. Buffalos slaughtered in the Old West went into near extinction. However, cattle, which are similar animals, did not face this problem. Why? Because buffalos were unowned; therefore, no one would get upset when one was shot. On the other hand, if a cow was shot, the ranchers would get upset and would probably send out a posse. Similarly, if you live near a lake, you know that every summer there is a battle between the people fishing and the water skiers over use of the lake. And why is this? Because no one has an enforceable property right.

One final example originates from a socialist country, which shows that the concept of enforceable property rights is not only a capitalistic phenomenon. Shortly after World War II, the Tito partisans ushered in an era of socialism-communism in Yugoslavia. There was to be no private ownership. Instead, the *people* would own the means of production. These were hard times in Yugoslavia and the people lacked the necessary fuel to heat their homes. Thus, the Yugoslavs decided to cut down their trees. Once this began, deforestation accelerated. If you didn't cut down your trees quickly, your neighbor would, and you wouldn't get any use out of your trees. The lesson is simple. People can't own a forest. The state has to own it, so property rights can be enforced. To summarize, then, even the most anti-government philosopher wouldn't make an argument for no government. We must have a money supply, national defense, and a system to enforce property rights; that is, law and order.

MODERN GOVERNMENT IN A MIXED ECONOMY

As we saw in Chapter 2, all economic systems are mixed. The U.S. economy is a market economy with a great deal of government intervention. We generally divide the economic functions of government in the United States into three categories: the allocation function; the distributive function; and the stabilization function.

Allocation Function

The **allocation function** is concerned with what should be produced. In Chapter 2 we reviewed the four fundamental questions faced by every economy: What

allocation function of government **The government's**

effect on the mix of goods and services that is produced.

should be produced? How much? How? and For whom? Thus, the allocation function is microeconomic, because it involves the government's alteration of the production mix. The justification for this government intervention is that the market solution would not be a correct one. Too much entertainment and not enough education would be produced. Therefore, government must provide more education. The allocation function is a justification for government to encourage the production of a menu of goods. Note that this is a normative function for government. If the government is altering the pattern of production, it is altering it from a pattern that was chosen by consumers.

It is sometimes argued that certain goods are **merit goods** and that the government should compel consumers to consume these goods in correct amounts. This argument is often put forward in defense of such goods as compulsory education and national health care. Many economists—in particular, free market economists—reject this argument on the grounds that the government is not any better (perhaps even worse) at judging what is a merit good than are consumers.

Other goods produced by government are called public goods. **Public goods** are goods that are nonrivals in consumption and for which the consumption is not excludable. The nonrivalrous quality means that if I consume the good, the good is still available for you to consume. If I consume an apple, it is gone, and none is left for you to consume. But if I consume a park, there are still plenty of trees, flowers, and paths left for you. The nonexcludability feature means that it is difficult (costly) to prevent people from consuming the good.

National defense is the prototypical public good. My consumption of protection from foreign enemies does not decrease the amount of protection left for you. Secondly, it is very difficult for the government to protect me and not to protect you. Since consumption is nonrivalrous and nonexcludable, consumers tend to **free ride** on the public. Free riding is the consumption of a public good without paying a fee. To avoid free riding, the government causes the good to be produced and forces us to pay through taxes.

merit goods   Goods that are considered inherently good and won't be consumed by individuals in great enough volume unless government supplies them; e.g., free education.

public goods   Goods for which the consumption is nonrivalrous and nonexcludable; e.g., national defense.

free ride   The consumption of a public good with avoidance of a fee. Since public goods are nonexcludable, people will attempt to free ride on their provision.

Distribution Function

The **distribution function of government** is also primarily microeconomic in nature. The distribution function involves the fourth fundamental question: Who gets the goods that are produced?

The arguments for a distribution function for government are based on the belief that the market does not produce a socially desirable distribution of income. In this case, the government should impose some forms of taxes and transfer payments on the economy to redistribute income.

distributive function of government   The government's involvement in changing the mix of incomes. This usually takes the form of transfers to the poor.

Stabilization Function

The **stabilization function of government** is to promote price stability and full employment. This is a macroeconomic proposition, which we will discuss in detail in future chapters.

Governments have almost always had allocational and distributional functions. However, it is only in recent history that stabilization has become a major governmental function. In the United States the stabilization function is a role

stabilization function of government   The government's involvement in promoting full employment and stable prices.

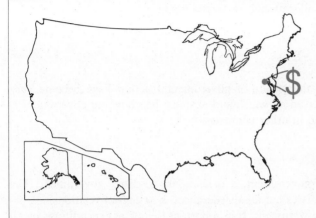

Tennessee	$1.35
Alabama	$1.32
South Dakota	$1.29
Maryland	$1.24
North Dakota	$1.23
Missouri	$1.22
Arkansas	$1.21
South Carolina	$1.20
Utah	$1.20
Idaho	$1.15
Washington	$1.14
Arizona	$1.13
Montana	$1.13
Florida	$1.11
Georgia	$1.11
Massachusetts	$1.11
Vermont	$1.11
West Virginia	$1.10
Kentucky	$1.07
Colorado	$1.02
Rhode Island	$1.02
Oklahoma	$1.01
California	$1.00
Nebraska	$1.00
North Carolina	$ .98
Connecticut	$ .97
Louisiana	$ .97
New Hampshire	$ .95
New York	$ .95
Kansas	$ .94
Pennsylvania	$ .93
Nevada	$ .90
Texas	$ .90
Delaware	$ .86
Minnesota	$ .86
Oregon	$ .85
Wyoming	$ .83
Iowa	$ .79
Ohio	$ .77
Illinois	$ .74
Indiana	$ .73
New Jersey	$ .71
Wisconsin	$ .71
Michigan	$ .68[1]

Fiscal Federalism: Who Gains, Who Loses

Fiscal federalism describes the relationship between governments in the United States. The federal government, state governments, city governments, and a host of other jurisdictions levy taxes and spend the money. In addition, the federal government collects taxes for the city and state governments, and returns the tax money collected at the federal level to state and local governments. This, in essence, sets up a competition between states, since some states receive more in revenue sharing and in federal spending than they pay in taxes.

The scorecard is presented here. California and Nebraska set the break-even point, as they received $1 in federal funds for every $1 in tax revenue sent to Washington. The states on the list which are above California and Nebraska did better, and the states that are listed below them did worse. New Mexico won the competition, while Michigan came in last.

This type of competition explains, in part, why government budgets tend to grow. Every government official tries to get more for the home state. This behavior on the part of all our representatives causes the budget, as a whole, to grow.

New Mexico	$1.72
Alaska	$1.58
Maine	$1.58
Mississippi	$1.48
Virginia	$1.42
Hawaii	$1.36

---

[1]"Do States Get Their Money Back?" *U.S. News & World Report,* Vol. XC, No. 23 (June 15, 1981), p. 12.

for only the federal government. State and local governments limit their activities to those areas that are allocational or distributional.

GOVERNMENTAL SIZE

Since government and the effects of governmental action have become very popular topics of conversation, we should examine just how big government is in the United States and in other countries.

Governmental Size in the United States

To measure the size of government, it is necessary to define government. The United States has what is called fiscal federalism, a system of relationships between various levels of government. It is important to look at expenditures by all levels of government to get an idea of the size of government in the United States. In 1980, all levels of government accounted for 33 percent of the gross national product.[1] Table 6-1 shows these and related figures on the growth of government. It is interesting to note that government grew very rapidly from 1940 to 1950 (the period of World War II) and from 1960–1970 (the period of the Vietnam War and the Great Society Programs of President Lyndon Johnson).

By carefully examining the numbers in Table 6-1, we can see that government in the United States grew at an uneven rate, but that the growth was continuous. This observation conforms to *Wagner's Law,* which is named for the German economist, Adolph Wagner. Wagner argued that economic growth, through

Wagner's Law A law named for Adolph Wagner, which states that in a democracy government will grow.

TABLE 6-1 GROWTH OF GOVERNMENT IN THE UNITED STATES

	1890	1929	1940	1950	1960	1970	1980
				Billions of Dollars			
Expenditures in Current Dollars	.08	10.3	18.4	61.0	136.4	313.4	869.0
Expenditures in 1972 Dollars	—	31.4	63.3	113.9	198.5	342.7	489.7
Per Capita Expenditures in 1972 Dollars	—	257.9	479.1	748.0	1098.7	1672.7	2197.9
				Percent			
Government Expenditures as a Percent of GNP	6.5	9.96	18.4	21.3	26.9	31.6	33.07

Source: *Economic Report of the President,* January, 1981.

---

[1]Some of the terms used in this chapter are developed and defined in detail in the following chapter.

industrialization, would produce political pressure for governmental expansion. His law seems to be borne out, as most democratic, industrialized countries have experienced a tendency toward growing governmental sectors.

What Government Does in the United States

Once the allocation function of government is established, we have generated an argument for government interference in an endless array of market decisions: Should tobacco be subsidized? Should it be prohibited? Should it be regulated?

Local and state governments spend large portions of their budgets on education and welfare. Figure 6-1 shows that in 1980, $.32 of each state and local government dollar was spent on education and $.18 was spent on welfare. Utilities and liquor stores were the next largest expenditure. The federal government spent the largest share of its budget on income security (transfer payments) and on national defense. Figure 6-1 also shows how the expenditure pattern of state and local governments changed over the last 20 years. Figure 6-2 shows how the federal government spent its budget in 1970 and 1980, and how the pattern changed over the last decade. An examination of Figures 6-1 and 6-2 on pages 104 and 105 permits a comparison of expenditure patterns of the federal government relative to state and local governments. Note the increased expenditure on programs to promote income redistribution at the federal level and the increased reliance on the federal government for revenue at the state and local levels.

Governmental Size in Other Market Economies

As we saw earlier, Wagner's Law predicted that governmental growth would accompany economic growth and industrialization. In every market economy, government spending, as a percent of GNP, has increased since 1950.

You should realize that the size of the governmental sector in the United States is not very different from that in other countries. The growth of government in the United States parallels the growth of government in other countries. This is not to say that the growth in the United States is inevitable or justified. However, it suggests that those who would like to blame the decline in productivity in the United States (relative to Germany and Japan) on burdens of government are ignoring the facts of the size of government worldwide.

HOW SHOULD WE FINANCE GOVERNMENT?

As we have seen, all levels of government spend money on a great number of programs and for very different reasons. In order to pay for these programs, the government must generate a flow of revenue. There are four ways government entities generate the cash flow to pay for expenditures.

State and local governments receive funds from the federal government. This *revenue sharing* is an integral part of fiscal federalism. Essentially, revenue sharing passes the task of collecting revenues on to a higher level of government.

revenue sharing   The sharing of tax revenue between governments. In the United States the direction of this sharing is usually from the federal government to state and local governments.

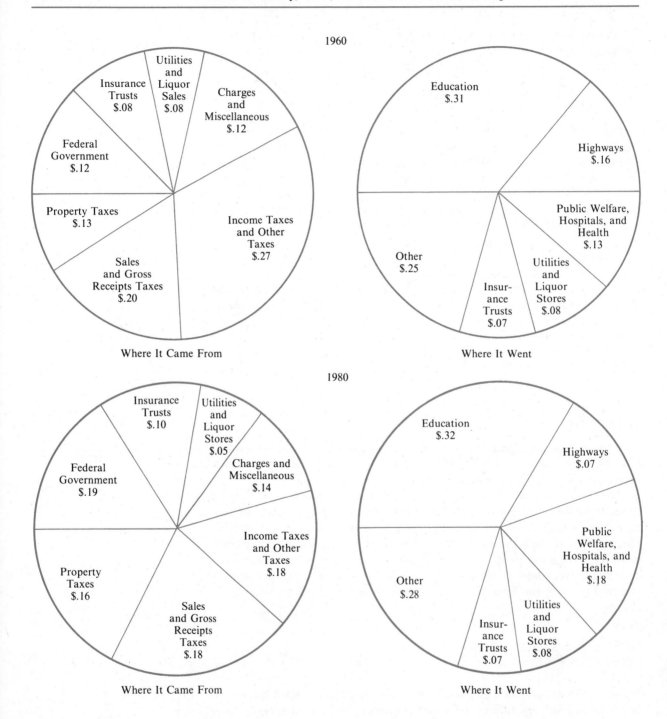

FIGURE 6-1   THE STATE AND LOCAL TAX DOLLAR

These graphs indicate the share of state and local revenues and expenditures by category. (Source: U.S. Department of Commerce, Bureau of the Census, *Statistical Abstract of the United States, 1980* [Washington: U.S. Government Printing Office, 1980].)

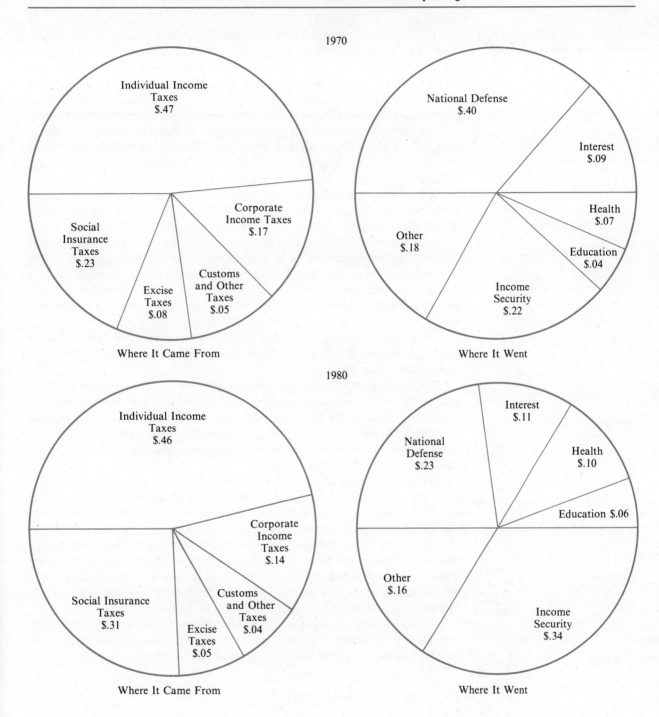

FIGURE 6-2 THE FEDERAL TAX DOLLAR

These graphs show how expenditures and revenues have changed from 1970 to 1980. (Source: U.S. Department of Commerce, Bureau of the Census, *Statistical Abstract of the United States, 1980* [Washington: U.S. Government Printing Office, 1980].)

user charge *A fee charged by a governmental unit to consumers of certain publicly supplied outputs.*

User charges are a second way governments generate revenue. A user charge is a fee that a government unit charges consumers. Such fees are limited to goods that are excludable. The nonexcludability characteristic of public goods makes it very difficult to charge user fees for these goods. But many government-supplied goods can be financed through user charges. Some economists argue that if users can be charged, governments should not interfere, because the free market will provide a solution. Examples of user charges can be found at all levels of government. Municipal golf courses and tennis courts charge for playing time. Some bridges and roads are financed by toll charges. At the federal level, a large share of the postal budget is financed through the sale of stamps.

A third way to finance government activity is through borrowing. The federal government is a prolific borrower of funds. The **national debt** and the federal deficits that contribute to this debt have been a political issue for years.

national debt *The debt of the U.S. federal government.*

It is important to distinguish between the national debt and governmental deficits. The budget should be in balance on a *yearly* basis, only if it makes economic sense to do so. There is nothing magic about a year. If annual budgets were in deficit some years and in surplus other years, we would have no national debt. Thus, national debt arises when we run *continuous* deficits in the federal budget.

There are numerous arguments against the national debt. Two of these arguments are heard frequently. One is mostly a political argument; the other makes sound economic sense.

The first argument is that the national debt is a burden passed on to future generations. Whether this argument is valid depends on how the borrowed resources are used. If the resources generated by the debt are used to put the unemployed to work, there is no real cost to society now nor in the future, because the debt expenditure has moved the economy from a position off the production possibilities curve toward the frontier.

If debt is increased in a period of full employment, no unemployed resources are put to work. In this case, debt finance chokes off capital formation and the economy does not grow as rapidly as it might have. As a result, there are fewer goods and services for future generations to consume.

The real burden of national debt comes from financing the debt. With a large debt, the Treasury must continually borrow money. This borrowing drives up interest rates and crowds other investors out of the market. As a result, there is less investment on the part of private industry. Productivity and economic growth will suffer as a result of this retarded private investment.

The fourth and last way the government generates revenue is through taxation. Most government revenue is generated through taxation, and economists spend a great deal of time studying the effects of taxation.

Principles of Taxation

There are two generally accepted principles of taxation, the *benefits principle* and the *ability to pay principle.*

The **benefits principle** is the idea that people should pay taxes in relation to the benefits they receive from governmental programs. The tax is really the fee or the price of the good being supplied by government. In practice, it is hard to apply the benefits principle. However, in a few cases, it has worked remarkably

benefits principle *People should pay taxes in relation to the benefits they receive from public programs.*

well. Highways, for example, have traditionally been financed by sales tax on gasoline. Since the benefits from roads accrue to motorists, it is appropriate to apply a benefits tax. Further, if you assume that the benefits accrue in proportion to usage, a proportional tax on gasoline would approximate the benefits received. Governments have built bridges, tunnels, and highways by charging users a toll on every trip.

The *ability to pay principle* is an argument for contribution based on economic capacity to pay. This is a difficult principle to apply, because it forces us to make some decisions about equity. We usually beg the issue by saying that the determination of a fair distribution of tax shares using the ability to pay principle will evolve from the political process. In effect, this means that what is obtained in the political forum is what we will accept as equitable.

ability to pay principle People should pay taxes in relation to their ability to pay such taxes.

The Tax Base

A tax can be levied on almost any base. Most taxes in the United States are levied on the economic bases of income, consumption, and wealth.

Income is the primary tax base of the federal government. Figure 6-2 shows that corporate and personal income taxes represented 60 percent of all revenues of the federal government in 1980. Income taxes are also an important source of state government revenues. Almost all states tax income; but as Figure 6-1 shows, the share of state tax revenue that comes from an income tax is much lower than it is at the federal level. State governments rely heavily on sales taxes, which are taxes on consumption. Figure 6-1 shows the degree to which states rely on sales taxes for their revenue. Local governments in the United States rely heavily on property taxes, which are taxes on wealth.

Historically, governments in the United States have divided the tax base. The federal government has taxed income, the state governments have taxed sales, and local governments have taxed property. Now states are beginning to tax income with increasing regularity, and local governments are beginning to increase their sales tax activity.

What Is a Good Tax?

Two of the most important yardsticks by which we evaluate tax structures are *equity* and *tax efficiency*. By *equity,* we mean the normative concept of fairness. By *efficiency,* we mean how the tax affects economic activity.

equity A measure of fairness.

tax efficiency A measure of how a tax affects economic efficiency.

Equity

The equity of a tax or tax structure is one of the most discussed topics in any political arena. Because equity is a normative concept, the answer to the question, "Is it fair?" will be different for different people. We must try to answer the question because, as economists, we will be asked to make recommendations. So, to help policymakers, we must develop some ways of describing a tax structure.

One of the most common ways to describe a tax structure is to discuss the progressiveness of the tax. A tax can be regressive, proportional, or progressive. A *regressive tax* is one that takes a smaller share (percentage) of your income as your income rises. In Table 6-2 we have three income earners. Column 2 gives

regressive tax A tax that takes a lower percentage of income as income rises.

TABLE 6-2   MEASURES OF TAX SHARE

	1 Income	2 Regressive Tax	3 Proportional Tax	4 Progressive Tax
Jones	$ 10,000	$ 500 = 5 percent	$ 500 = 5 percent	$ 500 = 5 percent
Smith	$ 80,000	$1,600 = 2 percent	$ 4,000 = 5 percent	$ 20,000 = 25 percent
Brown	$500,000	$5,000 = 1 percent	$25,000 = 5 percent	$250,000 = 50 percent

an example of a regressive tax. Jones pays a higher share of his income (5 percent) than does Brown, who pays only 1 percent of her income.

Sales taxes on food are generally thought to be regressive, because the proportion of an individual's budget spent on food declines as income rises. As a result, the tax paid on food declines as income rises. You should note that a regressive tax doesn't require the tax to decline in absolute dollars. Brown paid $5,000 and Jones paid $500, but Brown's tax, as a percentage of income, was lower. Many people feel that regressive taxes are unfair. In many states and cities, sales taxes on food and medicine have been lowered or done away with, because they are seen as inequitable.

proportional tax   *A tax that takes the same percentage of income as income rises.*

Proportional taxes are taxes that take the same percentage from each class of taxpayer. Column 3 of Table 6-2 shows a proportional tax of 5 percent. All individuals pay the same percentage share of income, but the dollar amount increases as income increases.

progressive tax   *A tax that takes a greater percentage of income as income rises.*

A **progressive tax** structure is one that takes a larger share of income from people as their income rises. Column 4 in Table 6-2 represents a progressive tax. The federal personal income tax in the United States is a steeply progressive tax with a maximum rate of 50 percent. Many people might argue that progressive taxes are more fair, but the difficulty lies in determining the appropriate degree of progressiveness.

bracket creep   *A situation that arises when individuals move into higher tax brackets as a result of inflation. Bracket creep can only occur in a progressive tax system.*

A serious problem that relates only to progressive taxes is what is known as **bracket creep.** Bracket creep occurs when inflation moves people into higher income tax brackets, even though their real incomes haven't increased. For example, assume that, over a given period of time, there has been 800 percent inflation. This means that an income of $80,000 now buys what could have previously been purchased for $10,000. According to Table 6-2, the tax rate on this income has risen from 5 percent to 25 percent, even though the individual has the same purchasing power as before the inflation. In other words, in a progressive tax structure, inflation generates more revenue for the government, because people creep into higher brackets even though they are not better off in terms of what their incomes will buy.

horizontal equity   *A situation that is achieved when all taxpayers in a certain economic category pay the same tax.*

vertical equity   *A situation that is achieved when taxpayers of different economic categories are treated differently.*

When we speak of equity, we often distinguish between vertical equity and horizontal equity. *Horizontal equity* in a tax structure is achieved when all taxpayers in a certain economic category pay the same tax. People with the same income pay the same income tax, and owners of similar houses pay similar property taxes. *Vertical equity* is achieved when individuals of different economic categories pay different taxes. Determination of the correct degree of difference involves a normative judgement of fairness that has to be determined in the political process.

Efficiency

To judge the efficiency of a tax, one has to look at the effect the tax has on the economic activity of the taxpayer. An ideal tax is one that is neutral. A **neutral tax** causes no distortion in economic activity. However, there is no such thing as a neutral tax, because all taxes create some distortion. Income taxes distort choices between work and leisure; sales taxes distort decisions concerned with goods to be consumed; and property taxes affect decisions on home location. A good tax—an efficient tax—is one that least distorts economic activity; in other words, a tax that significantly distorts economic behavior is a bad tax.

neutral tax   A tax that causes no distortion in economic activity.

Compliance, Administration, and Visibility

In addition to equity and efficiency, there are some other elements which we might use to judge a tax or a tax structure. Taxes should be visible and their compliance costs and administrative costs should be low.

To say that compliance costs should be low simply means that people have to cooperate. The United States tax structure requires a great deal of voluntarism. To be sure, if you cheat and defraud the Internal Revenue Service (IRS) you might go to jail, but this is a threat only because most people cooperate. If there were massive acts of uncooperative behavior, the IRS simply could not cope with the problems that would result.

When we say that administrative costs should be low, we are simply saying that we want to raise money for the government as efficiently as possible. Clearly, a tax that costs more to collect than is collected is a bad tax.

Taxes and Behavior

Taxes on beer in Thailand are driving Thais to drink hard liquor. In 1981, the Thai government slapped a heavy tax on beer. The price of a pint of beer rose to $1.75. This made the price of a pint of whiskey equal to the price of three beers. Thus, hundreds of Thais switched their alcohol consumption from beer to whiskey.

The director of the Boon Rawd Brewery, which is a major brewery in Thailand, reported that daily sales fell from 80,000 dozen cases to 40,000 dozen cases.

This example is drastic, but not unique. Taxes distort decision making. However, the key to a good tax or an ideal tax system is to select taxes that least distort decisions. All taxes distort behavior to some degree; but in general, the more specific a tax, the more it distorts behavior. This is because the more specific a tax is, the more it changes the price of one good relative to substitute products. In our example, tax on all alcoholic beverages would have distorted behavior less than would a tax on beer alone.

In the early days of the United States, tariffs were an important source of revenue, because they were easily collected. The tax collector merely had to audit the important ports such as New York, Boston, Charleston, and New Orleans to collect duty from cargo ships.

Visible taxes are those taxes that individuals are aware that they pay. If taxpayers are unaware of the tax, it will become easier for governments to raise money, and government officials may become less careful about how they spend it.

To give an example of visibility, consider the following proposition. Do you think federal personal income taxes would be the same if we had to write the government a check every week? At present, our taxes are withheld from our paychecks. However, if people started to think more in terms of their gross pay rather than their net pay, their income tax would become more visible. Thus, if we were reminded more often of the amount of taxes we pay, we would probably demand that they be reduced.

Alternative Forms of Taxation

There are some alternative ways that government at any level can tax individuals. In some circumstances, the government might directly appropriate goods or services in the economy. In the United States, governmental action to confiscate goods or services is used infrequently. Examples are the drafting of labor for jury duty rather than paying market wages for jurors; the military draft, when it is used; and the governmental right of *eminent domain*. Eminent domain allows government to buy land at prices other than the market price. This usually requires a condemnation proceeding and arguments by some governmental jurisdiction that the proceeding is in the public's interest.

eminent domain   *The right of governmental units to condemn certain land for use in the public interest.*

A recent innovation in alternative taxation has been state lotteries. In effect, the government is sponsoring gambling and is skimming some of the funds collected. These funds are then used to support governmental services. One of the criticisms of governmental lotteries is that they are regressive in their incidence.

THE REAGAN TAX CUT

The passage of the Economic Recovery Act of 1981 was a major victory for President Reagan. It is worthwhile to examine the Act in some detail, because its provisions are being phased in and will remain effective through 1987. The economic idea behind the Act is to reduce the disincentives that increasing taxes have created. Although this Act is described by many commentators as a major tax cut, it really is not. A more accurate description of the Act is that it mitigates tax increases that would have otherwise occurred. In other words, this cut merely offsets major tax increases that have been caused by bracket creep.

Individual Income Taxes

By 1984, the Act will cut individual income taxes by about 25 percent. Congress has decided that, beginning in 1984, individual tax brackets, the zero bracket amount, and the personal exemption should be indexed. This indexing will be based on the Consumer Price Index (CPI) which is discussed in detail in the next chapter. Such indexing will end bracket creep problems and put some limitation on the automatic increase in revenue that inflation produces. Table 6-3 compares tax rates in 1981 to those in following years.

In addition to the reduction in tax rates, the Reagan package has made other adjustments to personal income taxes. The maximum tax on investment income has been reduced from 70 percent to 50 percent. This has the effect of reducing the maximum effective rate on long-term capital gains from 28 percent to 20 percent, and is aimed at reducing disincentives to investment. As we saw earlier, high tax rates on unearned income discourage productive (i.e., income-generating) investments, and instead channel funds into tax shelters and items such as gold, jewelry, and art.

The Act has many other provisions aimed at reducing the personal tax bite. It allows those over age 55 to sell their homes tax-free; it provides a small tax break for charitable contributions by people who don't itemize their deductions; and it minimizes the marriage penalty. The marriage penalty is a quirk in the law that requires married couples who both earn incomes to pay more tax than two single wage earners with the same combined incomes.

Estate and Gift Taxes

Two major changes also have been made in the way estates and gifts are taxed. First, federal tax rates on large estates have been significantly reduced. The maximum tax on estates over $2.5 million is now 50 percent. Furthermore, as shown in Table 6-4, beginning in 1982 the unified credit and exemption equivalent

TABLE 6-3   NEW TAX RATES

		New Law		
Taxable Income	1981	1982	1983	1984
	%	%	%	%
0 to $ 3,400	0	0	0	0
$ 3,400 to $ 5,500	14	12	11	11
$ 5,500 to $ 7,600	16	14	13	12
$ 7,600 to $ 11,900	18	16	15	14
$ 11,900 to $ 16,000	21	19	17	16
$ 16,000 to $ 20,200	24	22	19	18
$ 20,200 to $ 24,600	28	25	23	22
$ 24,600 to $ 29,900	32	29	26	25
$ 29,900 to $ 35,200	37	33	30	28
$ 35,200 to $ 45,800	43	39	35	33
$ 45,800 to $ 60,000	49	44	40	38
$ 60,000 to $ 85,600	54	49	44	42
$ 85,600 to $109,400	59	50	48	45
$109,400 to $162,400	64	50	50	49
$162,400 to $215,400	68	50	50	50
$215,400 and over	70	50	50	50

TABLE 6-4   NEW ESTATE TAX LAWS

	Unified Credit	Exemption Equivalent
1982	$ 62,800	$225,000
1983	79,300	275,000
1984	96,300	325,000
1985	121,800	400,000
1986	155,800	500,000
1987	192,800	600,000

Source: *Estate and Gift Tax Changes Under 1981 Tax Law* (Chicago: Commerce Clearing House, Inc., 1981), p. 7.

increases and will continue to increase annually through 1987. The unified credit is an amount that is offset against lifetime taxable gifts. In 1987 the unified credit will reach $192,800 and there will be no tax, either estate or gift, on transfers totalling $600,000. Thus, the Act makes it much easier for individuals to pass wealth on to their heirs.

Business Taxes

The Economic Recovery Act of 1981 aims to create incentives for business to invest in more plant and equipment. This goal is accomplished by what is called *accelerated cost recovery system depreciation.* This allows business to deduct the cost of capital investment at a much faster pace. This type of tax treatment lowers the real cost of income-generating investment and makes it more economically attractive to invest. The goal is to increase investments in new plant and equipment in order to increase productivity.

THE COST OF REGULATION

We can measure how much government spends and how much it collects in taxes, but another cost of government is the cost of regulation. Presumably, every regulation has a benefit, or it wouldn't have a political constituency to promote it. However, every regulation also has a cost associated with it, and these costs are often ignored when we examine the size of government and look at the costs of government activity. When we look at the costs of government we tend to simplify by adding up tax collections and governmental borrowing. This simplification, however, causes us to overlook costs built into the price of products and services that are mandated or caused by government. Regulation has perhaps been the area where government has grown most rapidly in the last decade. Government has become intimately involved in promulgating standards and regulations in manufacturing. Consumer product regulation has become a major industry with individuals vying to be spokespersons for the public interest. Government has become a major manager of the environment and of job safety. None of these regulatory tasks of government are free of cost. The paperwork burden on industry is very costly and the cost of compliance is high. The problem is that it is very difficult to measure the costs of this type of governmental activity. Murray Weidenbaum, Chairman of President Reagan's Council of Economic Advisers, has done much work on the cost of regulation. Before coming to Washington he was at Washington University in St. Louis, where his research concentrated on the costs of regulation. He calculated that the cost of regulation in the U.S. economy was approximately $66 billion in 1976. Sixty-three billion dollars of this was the cost business incurred by complying with federal and state regulations.

SUMMARY

1. At a minimum, government must provide a money supply, national defense, and a system of law and order.

2. We generally divide the economic functions of government in the United States into three categories: the allocation function, the distributive function, and the stabilization function.

3. The allocation function is a justification for government to cause a menu of goods to be produced.

4. Public goods are goods that are nonrivalrous and nonexcludable in consumption.

5. The distributive function of government concerns changing the market distribution of income.

6. The stabilization function of government is to promote price stability and full employment.

7. Wagner's Law states that government will grow in a democracy.

8. State and local governments spend the greatest share of their revenue on education while the federal government has increasingly spent money on income redistribution.

9. Revenue sharing is the passing of tax revenue from higher to lower levels of government.

10. User charges are fees that governments charge for certain goods and services supplied.

11. It is often argued that the national debt is a burden to future generations. This is true only if debt finance crowds capital goods away from private firms.

12. Most governmental revenue is generated via taxation.

13. The benefits principle of taxation is that people should pay taxes in relation to the benefits they receive from governmental programs. The ability to pay principle of taxation is an argument for taxation based on economic capacity to pay.

14. Most taxes in the United States are levied on the economic bases of income, consumption, and wealth.

15. The equity of a tax is its fairness. The efficiency of a tax concerns its impact on people's economic decision making.

16. A tax can be regressive, proportional, or progressive. Bracket creep is the phenomenon in which individuals move into higher tax brackets because of inflation. It only happens when taxes are progressive.

17. Horizontal equity and vertical equity are measures for determining the fairness of taxes.

18. A neutral tax is a tax that causes no distortion in economic decision making.

19. Compliance, administration, and visibility are elements to consider in examining tax structures.

20. The Reagan Tax Cut mitigates tax increases that otherwise would have occurred.

21. Regulation is a cost of government activity that often is not measured or counted as a cost.

NEW TERMS

fiscal federalism
allocation function
merit goods
public goods
free ride
distributive function
stabilization function
Wagner's Law
revenue sharing
user charge
national debt
benefits principle

ability to pay principle
equity
tax efficiency
regressive tax
proportional tax
progressive tax
bracket creep
horizontal equity
vertical equity
neutral tax
eminent domain

QUESTIONS FOR DISCUSSION

1. What if the President drastically cut federal spending and revenue sharing? Could state and local governments fill the void and take over these programs? Why or why not?

2. Why do most economists prefer general taxes to specific taxes?

3. We generally use, as we did in this chapter, figures on the level of government spending as an indicator of what government does. What is wrong with this?

4. Is education a public good? Do you think education should be state supported? How does free education impact on the distribution of income?

SUGGESTIONS FOR FURTHER READING

Musgrave, Richard A., and Peggy B. Musgrave. *Public Finance in Theory and Practice.* New York: McGraw Hill Book Co., 1980.

Singer, Neil. *Public Microeconomics.* Boston: Little, Brown & Co., 1976.

Weidenbaum, Murray L. *Business, Government and the Public.* Englewood Cliffs, NJ: Prentice-Hall, Inc., 1981.

Measuring Economic Performance and National Income Accounting

Learning Objectives

After studying the materials found in this chapter, you should be able to do the following:

1. Distinguish between:
   (a) stocks and flows.
   (b) real and monetary disturbances.

2. Use the circular flow concept to explain how the various sectors of the macro economy are related.

3. Explain the purposes and uses of national income accounting.

4. Define and compute each of the national income accounts using both the expenditure and income approaches to find the totals.

5. Differentiate between gross and net national product and gross and net investment.

6. Explain why actual saving and investment must always equal one another in national income accounting.

7. Understand the role of price in determining real GNP in relation to GNP in dollar terms.

8. Be aware of the shortcomings of using GNP as a measure of economic welfare.

This introductory chapter contains few, if any, theoretical principles that will help you better understand the way the world works. Nevertheless, it is crucial to the study of macroeconomics, as it sets the foundation for a great deal of the theory that follows.

IMPORTANT CONCEPTS AND DEFINITIONS

To begin our study of macroeconomic theory, it is necessary to define various concepts and to discuss some of the definitions used in the measurement of economic performance. These concepts and definitions have precise meanings to the macro economist; it is important to be able to distinguish among them.

Stocks and Flows

stock variable   *An amount in existence as of a given point in time.*

A primary difference in economic quantities is that some are stocks of economic quantities and others are flows. An example of a ***stock variable*** is the number of apartments that exist today. These units are on hand, existing, there today. Notice that we put a date on this stock—today, in this example. A year from today, there will likely be more or fewer units, depending on how many apartment buildings are put up and how many are torn down. The number of new apartments built from January 1 of this year to December 31 is an example of a ***flow variable.*** It is something measured over a period of time. We must specify the length of the period—hour, day, month, quarter, year, decade—or we can be seriously misleading.

flow variable   *The rate at which consumption, production, sales, etc., take place between two points in time.*

What is the right interval to choose for looking at a flow? This depends on what question you are interested in, the nature of the flow you are looking at, and how expensive it is to collect information. The U.S. Census, which is taken every ten years, collects much economic information as well as tries to count the U.S. population. For indicating broad trends in the United States these data are probably good enough. But if you were a speculator in the wheat market, you would want day-to-day information on crop prospects, just as if you were operating a nuclear reactor, you would want very frequent readings on the core's temperature.

You know that new houses are built every year in your city and that some are torn down. If we take the number of new houses built this year and subtract the number destroyed, we have the *net* flow of houses; that is, the total number of new houses built is the *gross* flow of houses, and we subtract the number destroyed to find the *net* flow. The difference between gross and net flows can be quite large. Even if new houses are being built in your town, there may be more destroyed than built, so the net flow would be negative.

The flow obviously affects the stock. Suppose there are 1,000 houses on January 1 of this year—this is a stock figure as of a certain date. Suppose 200 new houses are built this year—the gross flow of new houses is 200 per year in this year. If 100 old houses are destroyed, the net flow is 100. At the end of the year, the stock of houses is 1,100—there were 1,000, but 200 new ones were built and 100 old ones were destroyed. The change in the stock of housing is equal to the net flow of new housing.

depreciation   *A reduction in the value or usefulness of an asset, such as a machine or factory, from one point in time to another.*

Another way to look at this relationship is to think about the ***depreciation*** of the stock of housing. The number of units destroyed is the depreciation. In our example, 100 units were lost through depreciation. If there were no new houses built, the stock at the end of the year would be 900. But we add the gross flow of new housing and get a year-end stock of 1,100. The net flow is the gross flow minus depreciation, so the year-end stock is the January 1 stock plus the net flow, or it is the January 1 stock minus depreciation plus the gross flow.

It is important to note that we are talking about averages. One house is not like every other house. If the 200 new houses are all very small and the 100 houses destroyed were the largest in town, it might be misleading to say the stock has increased by 100. Further, if the 200 new houses all have very small, inconvenient kitchens or fewer bathrooms than the destroyed houses, we would find the figure of a 100-house increase more misleading. (The people who produce our statistics try to adjust for some of these problems.) The point is that our figures are not perfect by any means, and we have to be aware of their shortcomings when using them. But we are far better off using the imperfect statistics than ignoring them completely.

Numbers of houses may be an important piece of information for certain purposes. For example, if we know the population of a community and the number of houses, we know the average number of people per house in that community. The quality of houses, however, is better reflected in their dollar values. If, for example, 500 houses worth $2½ million are lost through depreciation and 200 houses worth $10 million are built, the physical stock of houses has decreased, but the value and quality of the housing stock has increased.

The Circular Flow Again

The circular flow of income and product that we examined in Chapter 2 is depicted again in Figure 7-1. The figure is a model of the economy in its simplest

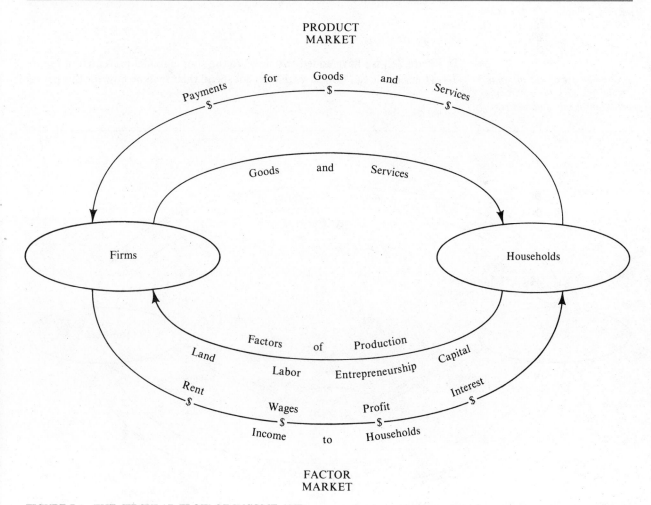

FIGURE 7-1   THE CIRCULAR FLOW OF INCOME AND PRODUCT

National income is the value of the flow of incomes received by households in the form of rent, wages, interest, and profit. National product is the value of the flow of goods and services produced.

form with only two sectors—households and firms. Keep in mind that the concepts in the circular flow model are flows rather than stocks.

Households are purchasers of goods and services and suppliers of factors of production. Firms are purchasers of factors of production and suppliers of goods and services. The monetary flow that accompanies the flow of goods to households is called payment for goods and services, and the monetary flow from firms to households is income to households.

national income (NI)   The sum of income payments to labor, land, capital, and entrepreneurship.

We can now expand our terminology to bring it closer to that used in macroeconomic theory. What we have labeled income to households we will now call **national income.** It is the value of all rent, wages, interest, and profit received by households. What we have labeled payments for goods and services we will now call national product. It is the value of all goods and services produced in the economy. In this model, national income and national product are equal, although they represent payments to different flows.

We must now complicate our simple economic model by adding other sectors and other activities to these sectors.

Savings and Investment

save   The act of not spending an income flow for a particular period on goods and services.

In Figure 7-2, we have added two flows to the simple model presented in Figure 7-1. Households can now *save;* that is, not spend their income flow for this period

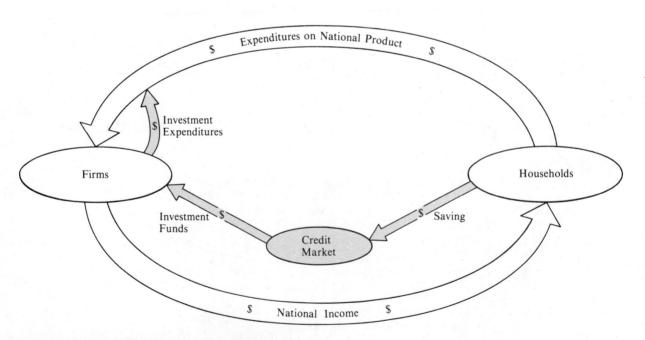

**FIGURE 7-2   THE CIRCULAR FLOW OF INCOME AND
PRODUCT WITH A CREDIT MARKET**

A credit market allows saving (nonconsumption) by households to be converted into investment funds for firms. These investment funds are then spent on goods and services produced by firms.

on goods and services. In addition, firms *invest* the flow of funds that households save. This investment can be of two different types—investment in plant and equipment, or investment in inventories. The exchange of funds takes place in the **credit market** which consists of financial institutions of all sorts channeling the savings of households to business firms that want to invest.

invest   When businesses buy (or produce) some real, tangible asset such as a machine, a factory, or a stock of inventories.

credit market   Financial institutions of all sorts that channel the savings of households to business firms that want to invest.

Government

Government buys goods and services produced by firms and also buys factors of production from households by paying rent, interest, wages, and profits. In addition, the government reduces household consumption by taxing the incomes of households. If government spends more than it taxes, thereby running a **deficit,** it must borrow needed funds on credit markets.

deficit   When government or an individual spends more than is taken in as income.

The government, then, enters the circular flow model at a number of points. It takes funds out of the stream by taxing households and by borrowing on credit markets. It adds to the flow by purchasing goods and services from firms. The effect of government on the circular flow is depicted in Figure 7-3.

Exports and Imports

A foreign sector changes the circular flow because households can now purchase goods and services from firms outside the country. These purchases from foreign

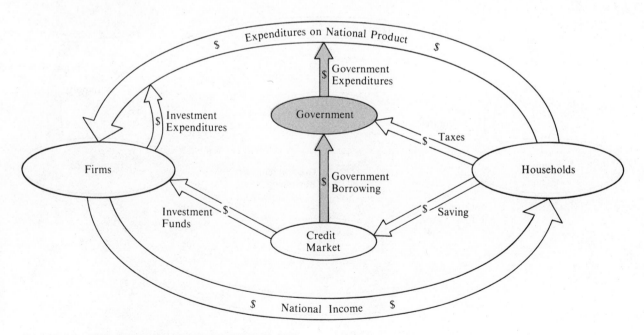

FIGURE 7-3   THE CIRCULAR FLOW OF INCOME AND PRODUCT WITH A CREDIT MARKET AND A GOVERNMENT

A government takes out of the circular flow of product by taxing households and borrowing on credit markets. It adds to the flow by buying goods and services from firms.

imports   Purchases from foreign firms.

exports   Goods and services sold to foreign buyers.

firms are called *imports. Exports* are those goods and services sold to foreign buyers. Imports are flows out of the system and exports are flows into the system. Figure 7-4 adds a foreign sector.

A MODEL OF THE MACRO ECONOMY

The circular flow diagram in Figure 7-4 is now a fairly complete one. It includes households, firms, a credit market, and a foreign sector.

Keep in mind that each sector in the model has flows associated with it. Some sectors, such as the foreign sector and the government sector, have flows out of and flows into the system. Some economists depict this model as a tank of water with a faucet running and the drain open. Flows out of the system—saving, taxes, and imports—are called *withdrawals* from the system. Flows into the system—investment, government spending, and exports—are called *injections.* If injections into the system exceed withdrawals out of the system, the size of the system will grow. If water flowing into the tank exceeds water flowing out of the drain, the level of water will rise. Likewise, if withdrawals exceed injections, the size of the system will decline; i.e., the level of water will decline. This is the most

withdrawals   Flows out of the circular flow model such as savings, taxes, and imports.

injections   Fresh spending in the circular flow of income; investment, government expenditures, and/or exports.

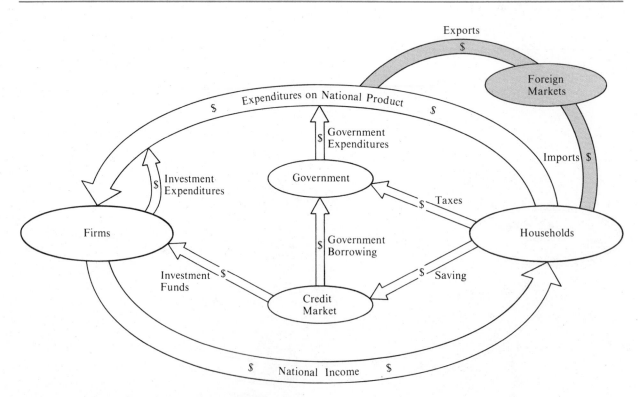

FIGURE 7-4   THE CIRCULAR FLOW OF INCOME AND
PRODUCT WITH A CREDIT MARKET,
GOVERNMENT, AND A FOREIGN
SECTOR

A foreign sector represents a subtraction from the flow when households import. It represents an addition when firms export.

elementary type of macroeconomic model. More complicated models are discussed in forthcoming chapters.

Aggregate Prices and Quantities

Consider the quantity of gasoline demanded at service stations and the price charged for it per gallon. This illustrates a simple and fundamental difference in variables in economics. Some are quantities—quarts, gallons, millions of tons, billions of barrels—and others are prices associated with units of these quantities —dollars per gallon, dollars per ton, dollars per barrel.

Suppose you filled your gas tank this morning. If we ask you what the price of gas is, you could have an easy answer: "I paid $1.00 per gallon this morning." But if you read in your newspaper that the price of gasoline has risen 1 cent per gallon from last month, you know it doesn't really mean that all last month you paid 99 cents per gallon and all this month you will pay $1.00. In fact, many times there is a station on another corner offering gas at a different price from the price you pay. During the month, the price of gas may change—sometimes it will fall, often it will rise. In different parts of the city and state, gas prices can vary greatly, and prices are often quite different in different parts of the country. The prices economists use are almost always averages. We use averages because it's too complicated to talk about all the different prices.

Macroeconomics uses average, or aggregate, prices, but these prices are much more general than "the" price of a gallon of gasoline. In macroeconomics, we talk about prices such as the cost of living, or we talk about general price indexes such as the *consumer price index (CPI)*. We'll talk about the construction and meaning of price indexes later. These represent the average price of a large number of goods. If the newspaper says that the CPI has gone up 5 percent since last year, the cost of what *you* bought may have gone up more or less than 5 percent. The change in the CPI is supposed to give us a picture of what happened to the average person. It is too complicated to try to analyze what has happened to each person, so we have to concentrate on the average to make any progress at all in understanding the problems of the entire economy.

consumer price index (CPI) An index showing changes in the average price of a basket of goods purchased by consumers.

The CPI refers to the price of an average or representative bundle of goods, so we have the same problem of averages when we talk about the output that corresponds to the CPI. The same *average* level of output of consumer goods can include more gasoline, or shirts, or bread, or anything else, and less of other commodities.

The economy produces much more than just consumer goods. It also produces investment goods. We are interested in this kind of output, too, because these investment goods can be used to produce more output in the future. Government spending on goods and services is a significant fraction of the total output of the economy. Total consumer spending, investment, government spending, and net foreign spending on final goods and services are the components that make up most of the *gross national product (GNP)*. Clearly, GNP is a broader aggregate than consumer goods, so any price index for GNP is going to be broader than the CPI. Because GNP is a broader aggregate than consumption goods, GNP could be going up while the average household is consuming fewer goods, because investment, or net foreign or government spending, might account for the rise in GNP. Therefore, we have to be careful in interpreting GNP movements.

gross national product (GNP) The total value of final goods and services produced in a given country over a given time period.

Real Vs. Monetary Disturbances

In macroeconomics we often distinguish real variables from monetary variables. The best way to see this distinction is to consider an historical example. In the mid-1920s, Germany suffered economic chaos. Prices rose by thousands of percentage points per month. Savings accounts, bonds, and many other investments that people held became worthless as prices rose. For example, a stamp cost 10 billion marks in 1923. A savings deposit of 100 marks in 1921 was worthless by 1923. But the same factories existed in 1923 as in 1921. The same railroads and cities were there, as were the same people with their skills. The country had been hit by a **monetary disturbance** or shock, but the productive capacity of the economy was left nearly intact. People who held their assets in real goods (real estate, gold, cars, diamonds, and so on) did not lose their wealth.

It was very different for Germany at the end of World War II in 1945. Many factories were destroyed, many people were dead (including many who would have been in the most productive parts of their lives), the country was conquered, the Russians occupied the eastern part of the country and detached it from the western part, and there were many refugees from the East. This was a **real disturbance** or shock—the economy was physically disrupted and the real productive apparatus of the economy was damaged.

These two different disturbances—one real, one monetary—illustrate an important distinction. When we speak of a real variable, whether it be output, capital stock, or some other variable, we are referring to a variable from which the effect of price changes has been eliminated. This contrasts with a monetary phenomenon or a nominal value that is affected by price changes.

monetary disturbance A change in monetary conditions that disturbs the economy but does not change the capital stock, labor supply, or productive capacity of the economy.

real disturbance A disturbance which affects some real aspect of the economy, and thus changes the productive capacity of the economy.

AGGREGATE DEMAND—AGGREGATE SUPPLY

We saw earlier that national income and national product are flow measures. National product is a measure of the goods and services sold, and national income is a measure of the incomes paid to factors of production. National income and national product are measures of different things, but they are equal in magnitude. The dollars spent on goods and services are equal to the dollars received by factors producing those goods and services.

Other terms that can be used to describe flows in the macro economy are aggregate demand and aggregate supply.

Aggregate demand is the total amount of goods and services demanded by all buyers in the economy. Aggregate supply is the total amount of goods and services available to purchasers. These definitions are quite similar to those of national income and national product. Aggregate supply and national product are the same thing. They are just two different names for the total of all goods and services produced in a given time period. Aggregate demand is similar to national income, because it is a measure of the planned expenditures of all income recipients.

We have now defined enough new terms to start examining how actual national income and national product numbers are determined.

In the United States, the *national income accounts* are compiled by the Department of Commerce. The accounts contain some of the most important statistics with which economists deal, such as gross national product.

national income accounts A system of accounting at the national level that focuses on overall output and income of the economy.

GROSS NATIONAL PRODUCT BY PRODUCING SECTOR

Table 7-1 shows gross national product by producing sector for the United States in 1981. The $2,628.9 billion for the business sector is the net sales of all business firms. The statisticians in the Department of Commerce who put together the national income account try to add up *net* sales and eliminate double counting. This means that all goods produced must be counted, but that they must be counted only once. We need to account for *final goods* or final sales and not *intermediate goods.* Intermediate goods are those that are sold to be further processed into final goods. For example, we would want to count the sale of flour to consumers in supermarkets, but would not want to count the sale of flour to bakers who intend to process that flour into bread. That flour will be counted in the GNP when the price of bread is added into the statistics.

final goods   Goods that do not have to be further processed for their final sale.

intermediate goods   Goods that are to be further processed before being sold as final goods.

Another source of GNP is the product of the government sector. We know that the product of the business sector in this account is its sales of final product, measured in dollars. How is the product originating in the government sector found? For the government sector, the value of the product is defined as equal to government's compensation of employees, or the wages and salaries paid to government workers. Government agencies at the local, state, and federal level hire employees to produce services. Since these services are not sold in the marketplace, it is difficult to place a value on them. Hence, they are valued at the wages and salaries paid to the people who produce the services. They may be worth more or less than this amount, depending on how useful people view the services provided.

TABLE 7-1   GROSS NATIONAL PRODUCT FOR THE UNITED STATES, 1981
(billions of dollars; by sectors that produce the GNP)

Gross National Product			$2,922.2
Business Sector[1]		$2,628.9	
Government Sector		293.3	
Federal	$ 90.0		
State and Local	203.3		

Source: *Economic Report of the President,* 1982.
[1]This figure includes the product originating in the "Households and Institutions" sector and in the "Rest of the World" sector ($97.7 billion and $54.0 billion, respectively, in 1981). For purposes of analysis, aggregating these into the business sector is convenient.

GROSS NATIONAL PRODUCT BY BUYING SECTOR

A key to understanding national income accounting is that, according to its definition, everything that is produced is also sold. If the business sector produces goods that it cannot sell to anyone else, these must be added to *business inventories,* and the changes in these inventories count as sales of the output to business.

Table 7-2 shows how GNP for 1981 was divided among the four possible sectors it could be sold to—the household, business, government, and foreign sectors.

business inventories   Stocks of goods held by business, from which it can make sales to meet demand.

The Household Sector

Sales to the household sector are called *consumption expenditures.* These are defined as final sales, so they all count as part of GNP. This consumption can be divided into various categories. *Consumer durable goods* are such things as refrigerators and washing machines, while *nondurables* are items that have a very short useful life, such as a loaf of bread. *Services* are things like movies, concerts, being waited on when you go out for dinner, or hiring a gardener. Services form a large part of total consumption.

consumption expenditures   Expenditures by the household sector on currently produced final output.

consumer durable goods   Goods that last, on average, a substantial length of time; for example, automobiles.

consumer nondurable goods   Goods that last, on average, only a short period of time; for example, bread.

The Business Sector

Business sector purchases of final output are called *gross private domestic investment.* This is investment before we have subtracted the capital goods that have worn out or become so obsolete they aren't worth using, and before we adjust for wear and tear on machines and factories. Thus, if the business sector buys 10,000 tractors during 1980 but has to scrap 1,000 old tractors that year, the *net* change in the number of tractors is 9,000. We might also want to say that some of the old tractors are so ineffective through depreciation that it is equivalent to having 500 fewer of them, so net investment would only be 8,500 tractors.

services   That part of consumption that is composed of such services as those provided by gardeners, service personnel at restaurants and hotels, and so forth.

gross private domestic investment   New capital equipment or inventories added to the domestic economy without adjusting for depreciation (thus, gross rather than net).

What about the words *private* and *domestic* in gross private domestic investment? The word *private* means that this investment was made by private people and/or firms, not by the *public* or government sector. (In contrast, government expenditures to build a dam or a new city hall are sometimes described as public investment.) The word *domestic* means that this investment was made in the

TABLE 7-2   GROSS NATIONAL PRODUCT FOR THE UNITED STATES, 1981
(billions of dollars; by sectors that buy the GNP)

Gross National Product		$2,922.2
Personal Consumption Expenditures	$1,858.1	
Gross Private Domestic Investment	450.6	
Government Purchases of Goods and Services	589.6	
Net Exports of Goods and Services	23.8	

Source: *Economic Report of the President,* 1982.

United States, not abroad. Investment abroad by Americans is termed *foreign investment.* Most of this investment was *fixed investment.* Fixed investment is for things such as factories, tractors, drill presses, and so on. Some investment, however, is for *changes in business inventories.* The national income accounts treat inventory changes as sales by businesses to other businesses or to themselves, and since these inventories aren't used up in the year, they are treated as final product, not intermediate product. Whatever businesses produce and don't sell to other sectors becomes part of inventory investment. This makes sure that the national income accounts balance. Every dollar of output that is produced has a buyer, because if no one else wants it, the national income accountants indicate that the business that produces it buys it to add to its own inventories.

foreign investment Investments by residents of one country in the economy of another.

fixed investment The part of investment that does not add to inventories.

Economic Meaning of Changes in Inventories. From an accounting viewpoint, everything produced is sold. From an economic viewpoint, the question is whether businesses are pleased by their changes in inventories. Businesses do, of course, desire some level of inventories. But holding inventories is not free. Accounting practices mean every dollar of output produced has a buyer, but businesses can still be unhappy if they have to buy inventory that they don't want (or sell inventory they do want). Business reactions to undesired inventory changes can have a powerful effect on production and employment. This happens as producers move to restore inventories to the desired level or cut back production to reduce inventories.

"Investment" Vs. Investing in Stocks and Bonds. One final point is that "investment" in national income accounting means that businesses buy (or produce) some real, tangible asset, such as a machine, a factory, or a stock of inventories. In everyday language, however, you might talk about "investing" in stocks or bonds. You are not using the word incorrectly, but this investment is not at all the same thing as investment as it is defined in the national income accounts. In fact, if a business uses some of its undistributed profits, say, to buy stock in another firm, this is also not investment in the national income accounting sense.

The Government Sector

You may be surprised to learn that state and local governments spend more than the federal government does. Out of the total expenditures of $590 billion, government mostly bought services from itself. These are the payments to government employees that we discussed earlier. Government produces these services, and national income accounting treats the services as then being sold to government. The rest of government spending is for items produced by other sectors, principally the business sector, but many things are bought abroad also. Some purchases are used up almost immediately, such as food for army mess halls. Other expenditures, such as for dams or highways, result in goods that will last for years. For this reason, government expenditures are often divided into *government consumption* and *government* (or *public*) *investment.*

The Foreign Sector

The final sector is the foreign sector. Consumption, investment, and government expenditures all include some imported goods, and we have to subtract imports and add exports to determine GNP. This gives us *net* exports of goods and services.

Adding Up

We can now add up the total spending by each group to find total GNP. We add spending by households or consumers (which we will designate as *C*), spending by business or investment (which we will designate as *I*), spending by government (which we will designate as *G*), and the surplus of exports over imports (which we will designate as [*X*−*M*]). We have now created this formula for GNP:

$$GNP = C + I + G + (X-M). \tag{7-1}$$

NATIONAL INCOME

We have seen where GNP comes from and who demands it. Now let's see where the money that is spent on output goes; that is, we want to look at the accounting concept of *national income*—the other side of the circular flow model.

The key to understanding national income is that it is defined so that all the income earned by the economy has to go to factors of production—land, labor, capital, and entrepreneurial skills. Thus, all national income must consist of rent, wages and salaries, interest, or profits (before the taxes that are paid by the factors on their incomes). In a very simple economy, all the value of production of final goods and services (GNP) would go as payments to factors of production. GNP and national income (NI) would be equal. However, our economy is not so simple. Our first step, then, is to show how (and why) we move from the figures for GNP to the figures for national income.

capital consumption allowances and adjustments (depreciation)
An entry in the national income accounts that reflects depreciation; equal to the difference between gross and net national product, and between gross and net private domestic investment.

net national product (NNP)
Equal to gross national product less capital consumption allowances and adjustments (depreciation).

net private domestic investment
Equal to gross private domestic investment less capital consumption allowances and adjustments (depreciation).

Table 7-3 shows that GNP minus *capital consumption allowances and adjustments* is equal to *net national product (NNP)*. The capital consumption allowances reflect the depreciation of capital that we talked about.[1] The total output of society is adjusted downward because some of the capital stock was used up in the production of the output. Using the same sort of reasoning, we define *net private domestic investment* as gross private domestic investment minus capital consumption allowances and adjustments. This allows us to write

$$NNP = C + I_n + G + (X-M), \tag{7-2}$$

where the I_n represents net, rather than gross, investment. The only difference between GNP and NNP is that we have used gross private domestic investment rather than net private domestic investment in determining GNP.

Next, we can adjust NNP to arrive at national income. If we reduce NNP by subtracting indirect business taxes and business transfer payments while add-

---

[1]These capital consumption allowances are more for purposes of determining the taxes of business than for providing a good estimate of depreciation. If tax laws allow business to overstate actual, economic depreciation and thus result in tax savings, business will naturally do it; it's legal. If tax laws don't allow a particular business to claim all its actual depreciation, then the capital consumption allowances will understate depreciation.

**TABLE 7-3   RELATION OF GROSS NATIONAL PRODUCT
(GNP), NET NATIONAL
PRODUCT (NNP), AND NATIONAL
INCOME (NI) IN 1981 (billions of dollars)**

GNP	$2,922.2
Less: Capital consumption allowances and adjustments	321.5
Equals NNP	$2,600.7
Less: Indirect business taxes and nontax liability, and business transfer payments[1]	262.0
Plus: Net subsidies and surplus of government enterprises	5.1
Equals NI	$2,343.7

Source: *Economic Report of the President,* 1982.
[1]This also includes a statistical discrepancy based on the fact that GNP is estimated from sales and NI from factor income. The discrepancy is the difference in estimates after the "plus" and "less" items are deducted from GNP.

ing the *net* subsidies to farmers, other businesses, and so forth, and the surpluses of government enterprises, we have that part of NNP that was earned by the factors of production. This is called *national income (NI).* We subtract indirect business taxes, such as license fees, because they were not earned by any factor of production, and we do the same with business transfer payments, such as private pension payments, bad debts, prizes in promotional contests, and so forth. But we have to add subsidies the government gives to shipping companies or to tobacco farmers, because these firms and their factors are paid even though the value of their output is less than their income. The surplus of government enterprises is subtracted from the subsidies, because this amount is not earned by any household owner of factors of production. The resulting figure is the *net* amount added to NNP.

As Table 7-4 shows, national income is made up of wage and salary income, income to proprietors (such as owners of small grocery stores, independent farmers, and other businesses that are not corporations), rental income, corporate profits, and net interest earnings. All of this income goes to households *except* for the part of corporate profits that business saves as undistributed profits and the taxes that business pays to the government.

We should note that a large part of rental income is *imputed;* that is, the national income accountants estimate how much it would have cost to rent owner-occupied houses and include this imputed value in national income. Rent that one business pays another will be netted out, of course, since this is a cost for an intermediate product. Net interest similarly nets out all payments of interest from one member of the household sector to another; for example, the interest you pay a relative for a loan to buy a used car is netted out.

Personal income (PI) is the income *received* by households (whether earned or not), whereas national income is the income *earned* by the household sector. To get from national income to personal income, we must subtract corporate taxes and undistributed corporate profits, since these are not paid to the house-

personal income (PI) Equals national income after the subtraction of corporate profits taxes and undistributed corporate profits and the addition of net transfer payments.

TABLE 7-4   NATIONAL INCOME BY TYPE OF INCOME, 1981
(billions of dollars)

National Income	$2,343.7
Wages and Supplements (including supplements and contributions to social insurance)	$1,771.7
Proprietor's Income	134.4
Rental Income of Persons	33.6
Corporate Profits	189.0
Net Interest	215.0

Source: *Economic Report of the President*, 1982.

transfer payments   *Income payments to households not based on services performed. Transfers can be made by any sector, but the most important in the national income accounts are business and government transfer payments.*

hold sector. In addition, we must add *transfer payments.* These include those business transfer payments, but much more importantly, they include government transfer payments, such as Social Security, unemployment compensation, Aid to Dependent Children, and other social welfare benefits. They also include interest payments on the national debt, since such payments are thought to be unrelated to current output. All these are called transfer payments, because national income accounting views them as just a transfer of spending power from one group of citizens to another and unrelated to current production. *Net* transfer payments are the difference between contributions of firms and employees to social insurance and the transfer benefits mentioned above.

    The household sector can use the resulting personal income in three principal ways: (1) it can pay personal taxes to various levels of government and make some nontax payments (including the income tax, licenses, fees, fines, and so on), though most often there is little choice in this matter; (2) it can spend the income on consumption goods; or (3) it can divert the funds to personal saving. A fourth use, but not so important, is personal transfers, such as sending money to relatives overseas or making interest payments to the business sector. The income that the household sector has after taxes is *disposable income.*

disposable income   *Equals personal income after subtracting personal taxes and nontax payments (such as license fees).*

    Thus, from the above discussion of the sources of personal income, and other payments to the government, we can write

$$PI = NI + \text{Net transfer payments} \qquad (7\text{-}3)$$
$$- \ (\text{Corporate saving} + \text{Corporate profit taxes}).$$

From the discussion of the uses of personal income, we can also write

$$PI = \text{Consumption} + \text{Personal saving} + \text{Personal taxes}. \qquad (7\text{-}4)$$

Rearranging equation (7-3) gives

$$NI + \text{Net transfer payments} \qquad (7\text{-}5)$$
$$= PI + (\text{Corporate saving} + \text{Corporate profit taxes}).$$

Then, substituting for PI from equation (7-4) into equation (7-5), we find

NI + Net transfer payments   (7-6)
    = Consumption + Personal saving + Personal taxes
    + (Corporate saving + Corporate profit taxes),

and, rearranging terms,

NI = Consumption + (Personal saving + Corporate saving)   (7-7)
    + (Personal taxes + Corporate profit taxes
    − Net Transfer payments).

In equation (7-7), we subtract net transfer payments from personal taxes and corporate profit taxes. This makes sense, because if a household pays $1,000 in taxes but receives $900 in Social Security income, the net tax burden is only $100. Equation (7-7) says that national income is either spent on consumption, used for net tax payments (business or household), or used for some form of saving (business or household). This is perfectly reasonable because, by definition, whatever income is not spent or paid in taxes has to be saved. Remember that consumption is defined as household expenditures on current output of final goods. If you buy an Old Master painting (or a used bicycle or car), then you have merely passed some of your income on to someone else, who must decide whether to spend it or save it.
    Let's now define

Taxes = (Personal taxes + Corporate profit taxes
        − Net transfer payments), which we will designate as T,

and let's define

Private saving = (Personal saving + Corporate saving), which we will
                designate as S.

Then, from equation (7-7),

$$NI = C + S + T.$$ (7-8)

To make matters a little simpler, let's suppose that there are no indirect business taxes and no nontax liabilities, no business transfer payments, and no net subsidy to government enterprises. Then, as we can see from Table 7-3, $NNP = NI$. Also,

$$NNP = C + I + G + (X - M).$$ (7-9)

Hence, combining equations (7-8) and (7-9), we have

$$C + I + G + (X - M) = C + S + T.$$ (7-10)

Subtracting "consumption" from each side of equation (7-10) gives

$$I + G + (X - M) = S + T.$$ (7-11)

If we move government expenditures to the right-hand side of equation (7-11), we have

$$I + (X - M) = S + T - G. \qquad (7\text{-}12)$$

net foreign investment **In the national income accounts, net foreign investment is equal to exports of goods and services minus imports. This difference equals the accumulation of domestically held foreign assets.**

National income accountants define net exports, the trade surplus, as equal to **net foreign investment** and also define taxes minus government expenditures as equal to **government saving.** This makes sense. If the United States exports $1 billion more than it imports, it acquires title to $1 billion of the rest of the world's goods and services. In other words, net exports have the same effect as investment in that the net amount owed to this country can either be used to buy capital goods (invest) in other countries, or more goods and services can be acquired from them in the future. Government saving is the amount taken in taxes less the amount spent by the government. This represents the freeing of resources to go to investment, just as much as personal saving does. Government saving is defined as equal to the budget *surplus,* which occurs when taxes are greater than spending. A negative budget surplus is a *deficit.* [2]

government saving **Equal to tax collections minus government expenditures; the government budget surplus (or, if negative, the deficit).**

"REAL" GNP AND THE GNP DEFLATOR

Suppose that in two different periods (say 1982 and 1983) the production of every single item stays the same—10,000 cars, 300 movies, 4,000 dorm meals—but every price doubles. GNP would then also double. But the total number of real goods produced in the two periods would be the same. Thus, to get an idea of what GNP would be without the effects of price changes, we often look at *real GNP.* This is called *deflated* GNP; that is, GNP adjusted to account for price level changes.

real gross national product **Gross national product adjusted for price level changes (inflation).**

GNP is found by taking the dollar value of final sales. *Real* GNP is found by adjusting nominal GNP for the increase that was due solely to changing prices. We can refer to real GNP as GNP measured in the dollars of some *base year* (in our example, 1982 dollars), or as GNP in constant dollars, meaning we have adjusted for price level changes. We often emphasize the fact that GNP is measured in current dollars by calling it *money* or *nominal GNP.*

base year **The year relative to which other years' prices, gross national products, etc., are measured.**

The nominal or money value of GNP is the total (or summation) of every good produced times its price. Thus, nominal GNP equals real GNP (number of units of output) times the average unit price. If we continue to let GNP represent nominal GNP, Y represent real GNP, and P represent average unit price or price level, then $GNP = PY$ and $P = \frac{GNP}{Y}$. If we multiply $\frac{GNP}{Y}$ by 100, the number that results is called the *GNP price deflator.*

money (nominal) gross national product **The value of gross national product in current dollars, as opposed to real gross national product.**

gross national product price deflator **Equals money gross national product divided by real gross national product. Used to measure how average prices of final goods have changed.**

In recent years, nominal GNP in the United States has increased significantly, but real GNP has grown slowly, or has even fallen. This is why it is so

---

[2]Note that this is the "government deficit on the national income accounting basis"; there are other bases, but this is the one most economists feel is of greatest importance. Note that the *federal* government deficit is the one most frequently referred to in the news articles you may see. Since state and local governments do not always have balanced budgets, the overall government deficit can differ from the federal deficit.

important to look at real GNP. Often the newspapers don't make it very clear whether they are talking about nominal GNP or real GNP, but as you see, it makes a big difference. It should be clear that the GNP price deflator is a *price index*—it depends on changes in prices as averaged over many industries.

price index   An index intended to show how the average price of a basket of goods changes.

THE CONSUMER PRICE INDEX, REAL WAGES, AND THE PRODUCER PRICE INDEX

GNP consists of consumption spending, investment spending, spending on net exports, and government purchases of goods and services. Since you are a consumer, you are probably much more interested in how the prices of consumer goods change than in how the price of cement mixers or the salaries of government bureaucrats change. Thus, you would want to look at an index that includes only consumer goods, a consumer price index (CPI). If the GNP deflator rises 10 percent, that's pretty bad inflation, but if the CPI rises 20 percent, that's even worse for consumers. The Bureau of Labor Statistics (BLS) in the Department of Labor publishes a CPI every month, and it keeps separate series for major cities in the United States and for various categories such as food, shoes, rent, and so on.

The BLS surveys stores and distributors to find the rates at which different goods' prices have risen; clothes may have gone up by 10 percent, rent by 5 percent, and restaurant meals by 6 percent. It then weights these changes by the importance of the goods in consumers' expenditures (where the consumer is taken as an average urban wage earner). The CPI may then be found to have changed by, say, 6 percent.

Of course, how well off you are depends on the income you receive as well as the prices you pay for the goods and services you buy. Since about 75 percent of the income in the United States is labor income, this issue is often discussed by comparing movements in the general level of wages with changes in the price level. For example, we could make up an index of wages *(W)*, with $W_{1982} = 100$. Suppose wages rise on the average by 5 percent. Then, $W_{1983} = 105$. If $CPI_{1982} = 100$ and $CPI_{1983} = 110$, we can divide W by P and multiply by 100 to find $\frac{W_{1982}}{P_{1982}} \times 100 = \frac{100}{100} \times 100 = 100$; and $\frac{W_{1983}}{P_{1983}} = \frac{105}{110} \times 100 = $ approximately 95. What this index, W/P, shows is how average wages have changed relative to average prices. In this case, money wages have risen by 5 percent but *real wages* (W/P) have fallen by about 5 percent.

real wages   An index of wages divided by a price index, showing how wage rate changes compare to price level changes.

If you think it over a minute, you have an interest in what happens to prices other than the CPI, even if you own no stocks and bonds. What happens to the prices of machines, oil, cotton, wheat, copper, and buildings will affect the business sector where most Americans earn their living, and consumer prices would be expected to reflect those price changes later. The *producer price index (PPI)* is an index for these types of prices that are of special interest to business. (The Bureau of Labor Statistics publishes the PPI as well as the CPI.)

Thus, we see that the GNP deflator, the CPI, and the PPI are all different. They usually move in similar, but not identical, ways.

producer price index (PPI)   An index showing changes in the average price of goods that are of particular interest to producers.

CPI: Confusing Price Index?

The *consumer price index* is the price index that receives the most media attention. Many people refer to the CPI as the cost of living. Millions of Americans are significantly affected by changes in the CPI, because they receive increases in income based on changes in the CPI. Social Security payments and many labor contracts have cost of living adjustments that are based on the CPI.

But what does the CPI measure? The CPI is a fixed quantity index. It measures price changes for a given market basket of goods that is judged to be average. In 1981 the market basket selected was a representative market basket for an average urban family in 1972–1973. The Bureau of Labor Statistics adjusts this basket every 10–12 years. This does not reflect the CPI for people who have different patterns of consumption than did the average urban family in 1972–1973. Most of us eat less meat and use less gasoline than we did a decade ago. Moreover, since the CPI uses a fixed basket of goods it does not account for the fact that consumers adjust their consumption patterns as prices change.

The effect that housing prices and interest rates have had on the CPI has created a political uproar. When interest rates rise, as they did in the late 1970s, the CPI is dramatically affected, because the housing component represents 46 percent of the market basket currently used. Critics argue that most people don't buy a home every period and that the housing component overstates the rate of inflation for this reason. Because of this political heat, new calculations will begin in 1983.

The political problems are obvious. A 1 percent increase in the CPI triggers $2 billion in extra federal spending. In addition, more than nine million workers have contracts pegged to the CPI.

The problem does not lie with the CPI. It lies with the use that has been made of the CPI. Any price index is an average of a selected basket of goods. Anyone who does not consume an identical basket will be either worse off or better off, depending on how his or her consumption pattern differs. If the price of meat rises, those who consume less meat than average (vegetarians) will be better off. Another example is that most retired people already own their own homes. When the CPI rises due to rising interest rates or rising home prices, Social Security payments rise, too, making those retired people who own their homes better off. Indeed, it is believed that the inflation of the late 1970s made Social Security recipients better off.

PROBLEMS WITH USING GNP STATISTICS

If California were not part of the United States, but instead were an independent nation, it would have one of the largest GNPs in the world. If you could work in Alaska and live in Mississippi, you would have a very high real income because Alaska has very high nominal wages and Mississippi has a very low cost of living. These two "if's" illustrate two common pitfalls in using GNP data to decide how well people are doing. You have to deflate GNP to find out how much it is in real terms. And you should divide it by the population to find it on *per capita* terms.

Deflating and figuring per capita GNP help make GNP more relevant, but that doesn't make it perfect. Another problem with GNP data is the distribution of income or product in the compared countries. It may be that a few individuals control most of the income and that the statistics give no indication of how an average citizen lives. GNP or national income measures market value of output, not quality of life or the well-being of citizens.

GNP accounts make no measures of the type of housing people live in. For example, by some per capita GNP measures, Sweden is better off than the United States. However, a substantial part of the Swedish population lives in the capital, Stockholm, and the majority there live in apartments. Of course, if you live in New York City, this may strike you as perfectly reasonable. If you live in an area where the majority of people live in large, single-family houses, this may seem unattractive, but per capita GNP comparisons between the United States and Sweden don't take this into account.

GNP measures all goods regardless of the reasons they are produced. After World War II, many families could afford to buy cars and move to the suburbs. Thus, central cities became more run-down as the middle class left, and smog became an eye-watering, life-threatening problem, due in part to increased driving. Production of more cars raised GNP, but how do we account for increased smog, congestion, and deteriorating cities? Production of anti-smog devices, which was necessitated by these problems, also increased GNP.

GNP statistics only measure goods that are produced and sold on a market. If Mrs. A. and Mrs. B., next-door neighbors, went to work for each other, cleaning each other's houses, cooking meals, caring for children, and so forth, the wages they paid each other would be counted as part of GNP, but the same things, if done in their own homes, would not be counted. Similarly, if you build a fence around your house your labor isn't counted, but the labor is counted if you pay to have it done.

Illegal activities are also not counted. Marijuana is a major cash crop in some parts of the country, yet it doesn't enter GNP figures in the United States. In countries where prostitution is legal, per capita GNP is higher than if it were illegal. Gambling is in the same category. These differences in what is counted and what isn't are very important when you try to compare the GNP of different countries.

There are also a number of problems with estimating statistics. The figures for the U.S. population can easily be off by 5 percent. Many statisticians think the 1980 census missed many Hispanic people, because those who had entered the country illegally were reluctant to cooperate. Thus, if statistics say per capita real GNP rose by one half of one percent, we can't be sure that it actually did. The increase may be due to a statistical error.

These comments all demonstrate that when you read an economic statistic, you should be a little suspicious of just what it means. When statistics show we're better (or worse) off than other people, remember that the statistics can be very misleading. The same is true of comparing current figures to those of past periods. Comparing the 1980s to the 1920s is like comparing apples and oranges. Furthermore, there are many rules of national income accounting that are outright silly, such as not counting a homemaker's work. As mentioned earlier, illegal activity

Simon Kuznets *(1901–   )*

Simon Kuznets, the Nobel prizewinner in economics in 1971, was born in Russia and received his education in the United States. He received his Ph.D. from Columbia University in 1926.

Kuznets taught at Harvard University, the University of Pennsylvania, and Johns Hopkins University. From 1926 through 1960, he was associated with the National Bureau of Economic Research (NBER). The NBER is a prestigious organization dedicated to empirical research on how economies function. Researchers there have a long tradition of collecting, organizing, and analyzing data; Kuznets made a distinguished contribution to that process.

When the conceptual framework for national income accounting was being formulated in Great Britain, the United States, and Sweden, Kuznets did not participate and apparently wasn't very interested. However, when he turned his attention in the early 1930s to gathering and analyzing data, he greatly expanded the possibilities for empirical work on the U.S. economy. He extended time series on the national income accounts back to the period immediately following the United States Civil War. Thus, we have a record of the U.S. economy from the time the country was a rather small, agricultural nation through its development into the world's industrial giant.

Kuznets's approach to compiling data blends skepticism about the accuracy of the data with the belief that it is worthwhile to use even inexact data if they have been compiled as exactly as possible. If the actual, exact value of GNP for a year is $2,000 billion, the collected data may show GNP higher or lower than this figure. These errors in estimates will be larger the less reliable the sources of the data are, the less carefully kept the records are, the less effort has been spent in trying to take good surveys, and so on. Kuznets is an acknowledged master at making estimates based on incomplete, fragmentary, and unreliable data. While he believes that it is better to do the best one can in gathering data and that it is more useful to have questionable data than none at all, he emphasizes that care has to be used in interpreting data that are imprecise and subject to quite possibly large errors. For example, if the true unemployment rate for this month is 6.5 percent of the civilian labor force, the estimate may well be 6.2 or 6.8 percent. Thus, changes of three tenths of a percent from month to month should be viewed with caution. In his well-known book, *On the Accuracy of Economic Observations* (2d ed., 1963), Oskar Morgenstern provides a wealth of evidence on the need for caution in relying too heavily on the exactness of data.

Kuznets also emphasizes that preconceived theory dictates the very choice of what data to collect and how to do so. Many of the concepts of Keynesian economic theory are rather close to the ideas behind national income accounting concepts (though the accounting system preceded the theory). This provides Keynesian economists with a wealth of data to use in their studies and ensures an ongoing demand for the output of the data-gathering teams.

is also left out of GNP statistics. The production and distribution of marijuana isn't counted, but beer and whiskey are. The lesson is to be careful with GNP statistics, because they are not precise measures of economic activity or well-being.

Even with all these problems of measurement, however, GNP growth is usually viewed as a good thing. Economic growth has made the average person far better off than 200 years ago. Growth offers one of the main avenues for the disadvantaged to escape and move up the economic ladder. An improved economy is one of the best things that can happen to sick cities. We shouldn't revel over every extra one tenth of 1 percent of real GNP growth, but we shouldn't lose sight of the fact that growth is vital to individual and national success.

It is difficult to dispute an argument that we may not be much better off today than in 1970. But if we look at the life of the average person in 1900, 1920, 1930, or 1940, we're clearly better off. There may have been a lot of good things about the "good old days," but few would choose to return to them. It would imply living without refrigerators, air conditioning, automobiles, and airplanes. Most nostalgia about the "good old days" forgets the standard of living improvements that economic growth has produced in the United States since 1900.

SUMMARY

1. Stocks are existing quantities of commodities. Flows are measurements of commodities over time.

2. The circular flow diagram can show the interrelationships between the various producing and consuming sectors in the economy.

3. A real shock to an economy is one that affects the actual physical stock or flow of goods. A monetary shock only affects the prices of goods and services.

4. GNP is the value of final output over a specific period.

5. GNP measures final output; no double counting is allowed. This output is bought by the household, business, government, and foreign sectors. It is important to remember that any output that business produces and cannot sell is counted as a purchase by business to increase inventory. Too much investment for inventories is undesirable.

6. It is tricky to use GNP statistics to make comparisons between a given country at different times or between two countries.

NEW TERMS

stock variable
flow variable
depreciation
national income (NI)
save
invest
credit market
deficit

imports
exports
withdrawals
injections
consumer price index (CPI)
gross national product (GNP)
monetary disturbance
real disturbance

national income accounts
final goods
intermediate goods
business inventories
consumption expenditures
consumer durable goods
consumer nondurable goods
services
gross private domestic investment
foreign investment
fixed investment
capital consumption allowances and adjustments
net national product (NNP)

net private domestic investment
personal income (PI)
transfer payments
disposable income
net foreign investment
government saving
real gross national product
base year
money (nominal) gross national product
gross national product price deflator
price index
real wages
producer price index (PPI)

QUESTIONS FOR DISCUSSION

1. What is double counting? final output? an intermediate product?

2. How do national income accountants place a value on the output of the government sector?

3. What do we mean when we say that everything produced is also sold?

4. Explain the meaning of gross private domestic investment.

5. How is the use of the word "investment" by national income accountants different from ordinary usage?

6. Why are we interested in *net* exports, rather than total exports, in national income accounting?

7. In general terms, how do we move from figures for GNP to figures for national income?

8. Discuss some of the problems of using GNP figures in making comparisons between countries or different time periods.

SUGGESTIONS FOR FURTHER READING

Dauten, Carl. A., and Lloyd M. Valentine. *Business Cycles and Forecasting,* 5h ed. Cincinnati: South-Western Publishing Co., 1978, Chapter 3.

McKenna, Joseph P. *Aggregate Economic Analysis,* 5h ed. Hinsdale, Ill.: The Dryden Press, 1977, Chapter 2.

Meyer, Lawrence H. *Macroeconomics: A Model Building Approach.* Cincinnati: South-Western Publishing Co., 1980, Chapter 2.

PART 3

Macroeconomics

CHAPTER 8

Classical Macroeconomics

Learning Objectives

After studying the materials found in this chapter, you should be able to do the following:

1. Explain the reasoning behind the quantity theory of money argument that increases in the money supply lead to increases in the level of prices.

2. Describe the major weaknesses of the quantity theory of money.

3. Discuss the contributions to the quantity theory of money made by:
   (a) David Hume.
   (b) David Ricardo.
   (c) Alfred Marshall.
   (d) Irving Fisher.

4. Explain how Say's Law led classical economists to conclude that the economy would not experience prolonged periods of overproduction or unemployment.

5. Discuss the importance of each of the following self-regulating markets in classical macroeconomic theory:
   (a) the credit market.
   (b) the product market.
   (c) the labor market.

6. Discuss and contrast the competing business cycle theories.

quantity theory of money The *dominant macroeconomic theory until the Keynesian revolution of the 1930s. It focused on the determination of the overall price level in the long run and viewed the quantity of money as the primary influence on the long-run price level.*

The study of macroeconomics usually starts with what is referred to as classical macroeconomics. Classical macroeconomics was the dominant system of economic thought during the 150 years preceding the 1930s. The foundation for classical macroeconomics is found in three ideas: the quantity theory of money, Say's Law, and the notion of self-regulating markets. The *quantity theory of money* represents the earliest ideas regarding the influence of the money supply on economic activity. Say's Law and the system of self-regulating markets led classical economists to conclude that prolonged periods of unemployment were impossible in a competitive market economy.

Classical macroeconomics is a good place to begin our study for a number of reasons. First, it represents the early economists' best efforts at developing a theoretical system to explain and predict economic activity on a national scale.

Second, it provided the background against which John Maynard Keynes, the great British economist, developed his revolutionary ideas. Third, each of the three parts of the classical foundation has renewed significance in the economic debates of the 1980s. The controversy over self-regulating markets is a key issue in the continuing debate betwen Keynesian and monetarist economists. The roots of current monetarist economic thought are found in the earlier quantity theory of money. Finally, what is now referred to as supply-side economics is in some ways a second generation application of Say's Law. Each of the ideas examined in this chapter will reappear in later chapters.

HISTORICAL BACKGROUND—THE INFLATION AFTER THE DISCOVERY OF THE NEW WORLD

Among the early writers on the quantity theory of money was the Scottish philosopher David Hume (1711–1776). Hume had great influence on another Scottish philosopher, Adam Smith, author of *The Wealth of Nations* (1776), which is usually cited as the starting point of modern economics. Hume was interested in a very practical problem—the inflation that followed the discovery of the New World.

Gold and silver were the principal money of Europe and the New World in the 1500s. They remained the principal money until the late 1700s in England and even later elsewhere. When the New World was discovered and claimed by several European nations, precious metals, which were abundant in the New World, were brought into Europe, principally by the Spaniards who seized the gold and silver of the Aztecs in Mexico and the Incas in Peru. The Spanish took both the precious metals and the mines from which they were produced. The Spaniards who initially acquired the gold and silver, mainly the Spanish monarchy, spent a large part of it. After this great increase in Spanish wealth, prices rose throughout Europe. To acquire goods and services that had been going to other people, the Spanish bid against other potential buyers and thus drove up the prices of the goods and services they sought. The purpose of the early writers on the quantity theory was to clarify the link between the inflow of money and rising prices, and to discuss in general terms the relationship they had uncovered between the stock of money and the general level of prices.

These early writers did not have present day economists' tools of demand and supply, but, as you can see, they were working toward modern theory. Figure 8-1 is similar to those we examined in our discussion of demand and supply in Chapter 3. It shows that the inflow of gold and silver caused the demand for, say, woolen goods, to rise relative to supply. An increase in income causes a rightward shift (increase) in the demand schedule. The Spanish were richer, so they demanded more woolen goods from both Spanish and British suppliers. Of course, the people who sold to the Spanish then had extra money, so they too demanded more goods. In this way, all demand curves for output tended to shift and prices in general rose. It didn't end there. People who supplied woolen goods found that the prices of goods they bought were also going up, and this meant their costs were rising. For example, the new, higher prices for wool and agricultural products induced more people to enter these industries, and their competition for land drove up the rent that the sheep owners had to pay for grazing land.

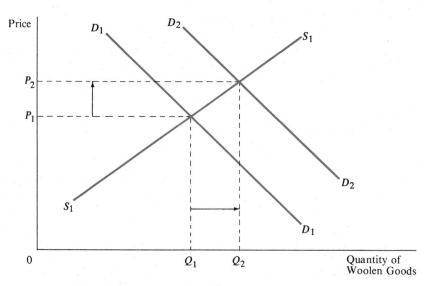

**FIGURE 8-1   AN INCREASE IN THE STOCK OF
MONEY SHIFTS THE DEMAND CURVE
FOR WOOLEN GOODS RIGHTWARD**

The gold and silver from the New World made Europeans richer, so they increased their demand for various goods, including woolen goods. This led to a rightward shift in demand, *not* just a movement along a demand curve. In response, price increased and so did the quantity supplied.

We show these increased costs in Figure 8-2 as a leftward shift in the supply curve. Remember, we learned previously that an increase in the price of inputs causes a leftward shift (decrease) of the supply schedule. For any quantity, price must be increased before people will supply that quantity, because costs have risen. For a given inflow of money, both demand and supply tend to shift up by the same amount, so price rises; but after both demand and supply adjust, equilibrium quantity remains the same as before. This is because the inflow of gold and silver did not change any of the underlying real resources of the economy or the technology or efficiency with which they were used. Hence, there seemed to be no reason why output would change once the economy adjusted fully.

As long as money was flowing into Europe, prices were destined to go on rising as demand increased and supply decreased. Since Spanish demand spilled out of Spain to England, Portugal, and elsewhere, the demand and supply curves in all these countries continued to shift. Thus, the money inflow to Spain led to increasing price levels throughout Europe.

Where would this price rise end? If the inflow of new money never stopped, the classical authors could see no end in the price rise. However, suppose the money inflow did end. Then, they argued, the increase in the price level would be in the same proportion as the increase in the stock of money. If the money stock is twice as large, prices would be twice as high. If the money stock is four times as large, prices would be four times as high. Of course, when we talk of

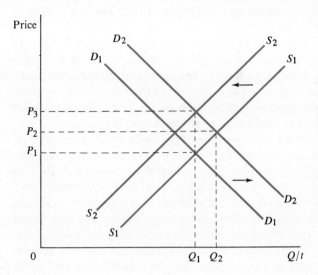

FIGURE 8-2 AN INFLOW OF MONEY SHIFTS THE DEMAND CURVE RIGHTWARD; EVENTUALLY THE SUPPLY CURVE SHIFTS TO THE LEFT

With the general increase in demand for goods, the average level of prices rises, as do the costs of suppliers, since they must now pay more for the inputs they use. This rise in costs shifts the supply curve to the left. In fact, the supply curve shifts left by the same amount that the demand curve shifts right, so that price rises to OP_3 instead of just OP_2, but equilibrium quantity ultimately returns to its equilibrium level (OQ_1), instead of rising permanently to OQ_2. Thus, when all prices and costs have adjusted (the supply curve has shifted as well as the demand curve), there is no change in output, but there is an increase in price.

general price level changes, we are also thinking of changes in the prices of factors of production. Thus, land prices and production costs rise, as do the wages of labor, in proportion to increases in the money supply. It should be kept in mind, however, that while the money stock was rising, other things may have happened that also influenced the price level. For example, the productivity of labor may have risen. This simply means that quantity theory predictions are *ceteris paribus* experiments.

The insight that the long-run level of prices is directly related to the money stock was a key achievement of the early quantity theory writers. It gives a precise answer to the question, How much will prices change? Prices change in the same proportion as the change in the money stock. However, a genuine weakness of the theory was that it could not predict how long it would take prices to change. Furthermore, we saw in Figure 8-1 that output goes up when demand increases. Figure 8-2 shows that when both demand and supply have shifted, price has risen, but in the long run output returns to the same level as before the new money came into the system. How much will output go up at the start? How long will it take output to settle back to its old level? The classical quantity theorists could not answer these questions with any of the precision with which they could predict the long-run price level. The quantity theory was much better at explaining long-run prices than it was at analyzing what happened to real variables, such as output or the length of time it takes to achieve the new long-run equilibrium price.

INFLATION AND THE NAPOLEONIC WARS

The quantity theory was initially developed to answer the question of what caused the inflation after the discovery and conquest of the New World. Another major development in this theory occurred between 1800 and 1820 and was associated with David Ricardo (1772–1823).

For most of the period between 1793 and 1815, Britain was involved in wars set off by the French Revolution of 1789. These Napoleonic wars were associated with a substantial rise in prices in Europe, including Britain. Historically, major wars are almost always accompanied by inflation. Production of war materials generates income without a corresponding increase in goods and services for domestic consumption. When purchasing power increases, but output does not, prices will rise. A debate arose in Britain over what to do about such inflation.

During this period in Britain, notes supplied by banks were an important part of the total money supply. Before the Napoleonic Wars, banks promised to redeem these notes in gold; that is, to exchange them for gold at face value. During the Wars, Britain went off the gold standard and bank notes could not be redeemed for gold. If a person borrowed money from a bank, the bank would simply hand over the loan amount in the form of its own bank notes. The question arose, How much money in the form of bank notes should the banks be allowed to issue from the perspective of getting inflation under control? One side of the debate argued that banks should issue enough money to meet the needs of trade.

Ricardo and others pointed out the dangers of this view. The amount of money required to meet the needs of trade depends on the price level. But the quantity theory says the price level depends on the money stock. If prices rise, the demand for loans will be higher. If this demand for loans is met, the extra bank notes that are loaned will make the money stock larger, and this will drive prices even higher than before. At these higher prices, the needs of trade will require more loans and an even larger money stock, resulting in an upward spiral of prices in which the stock of bank notes and the price level chase one another.

To break this spiral, the Bank of England (the central bank of Great Britain) could hold the money stock at a particular level. After a time, the price level will become proportionate to the money stock, according to the quantity theory. Of course, the theory could not specify how long this adjustment process would take, only what the long-run result for the general level of prices would be. The debate showed that controlling the price level depended on controlling the supply of money.

THE CAMBRIDGE *k*

We can now turn our attention to the more systematic and formal analysis of the factors affecting the price level. The quantity theorists believed that the main influences on the price level were the stock of money, the long-run equilibrium level of output, and the demand for money.

The dominant figure in English economics from about 1880 until his death in 1924 was Alfred Marshall of Cambridge University. Marshall developed an approach to the quantity theory referred to as the *Cambridge k.* He postulated that the public's demand for a stock of money (M^d) depends positively upon a country's income.[1] Marshall reasoned that if your income is higher, you will buy

Cambridge k   *The constant that relates a country's nominal income to the stock of money it desires to hold.*

---

[1] By "demand for money," Marshall was referring to peoples' desire to hold a portion of their income in a money form.

more things and will hold, on average, a larger stock of money. In line with Marshall's theory, M^d depends positively on GNP. Marshall realized that M^d would depend on other variables in addition to GNP. Some of these such as the structure of industry, payments habits, and the ease of transferring funds between checking and savings accounts are more or less fixed and do not have to be discussed in detail. Other variables that Marshall mentioned, such as wealth, are not explicitly considered in the theory even though they can change and are important. We might justify Marshall's neglect of wealth by arguing that the key relationship in his view was between M^d and GNP. To include other variables would obscure the relationship and make the theory more complicated.

A simple way of showing the positive relationship of M^d to GNP is to write it as a linear equation,

$$M^d = k \cdot GNP, \tag{8-1}$$

where k is constant. This way of looking at money demand led economists to define k as the fraction of a year's income (equal to some number of months' income) that people want to hold in the form of money balances. This would depend on their desire for the convenience of using money.

To focus more clearly on prices, let us use Y to represent real GNP, and let us define a price level, P, for the units of output in Y. In practice, we can use actual GNP statistics on real output as an expression for Y, and the GNP price deflator for P, but we should keep in mind the many difficulties and ambiguities associated with using GNP statistics. Thus we have,

$$GNP = P \cdot Y. \tag{8-2}$$

We can then use equation (8-2) to rewrite equation (8-1) as

$$M^d = k \cdot P \cdot Y. \tag{8-3}$$

Equation (8-3) shows that the public's demand for money depends upon the price level and the amount of real output. Marshall assumed that both k and Y were constants, while M^d and P were treated as variables. He believed that the economy was always at, or near, a full-employment level of real output. The concept of the full-employment level of output is an important one and one that will be used often in upcoming chapters. It refers to a level of GNP, or size of the economy, that is necessary to sustain full employment. At lower levels of output some people will be unemployed. This full-employment level of real output (Y) did not vary much over time (i.e., the economy did not experience rapid growth), and for all practical purposes, could be assumed to be constant for the time period under consideration.

In addition, Marshall clearly saw that the public had to hold whatever amount of money was being supplied. If the money supply (M^s) was $1,000, then collectively the public has to hold (demand) that $1,000. If a situation occurred where the public's demand for money was not equal to the money supply, the system would be in disequilibrium. Disequilibrium would cause changes in spending by individuals, which would result in a change in the price level (P). The changes in the price level would change the value of output $(P \cdot Y)$ so that the public would be satisfied to hold exactly the amount of money being supplied to the system. Thus, price level changes would assure that the equilibrium condition,

$$M^d = M^s,$$ (8-4)

would be satisfied. At equilibrium, since $M^d = M^s$, and since Y is assumed to be constant, we can rewrite equation (8-3) as

$$M^s = k \cdot P \cdot \bar{Y}$$ (8-5)

where the bar over Y indicates a constant full-employment level.

Let's look at an example to gain a better understanding of Marshall's analysis. Assume that the economy is at the full-employment level of real output with 500 units of output being produced ($\bar{Y} = 500$). Further, assume that people's desire to hold money balances is constant and equal to 25 percent of their annual income ($k = 0.25$). Finally, assume that the money supply is initially $1,000 ($M_1^s = \$1,000$) and that the annual value of output ($P \cdot \bar{Y}$) is such that the public is satisfied to hold $1,000 in money balances ($M^d = M^s$). We can then determine the initial price level (P_1) for the economy by rearranging equation (8-5) and solving for P_1:

$$P_1 = \frac{M_1^s}{k \cdot \bar{Y}}$$ (8-6)

$$P_1 = \frac{\$1,000}{(.25)(500)} = \frac{\$1,000}{125} = \$8.$$

The equilibrium price level is $8; that is, the price for each unit of output is $8 and the annual value of income and output is $4,000 ($8 \times 500$).

What would happen if, as a result of an influx of gold into the economy, the money supply doubled ($M_2^s = \$2,000$)? Using the new money supply ($M_2^s = \$2,000$) and solving equation (8-6) for the new price level (P_2), we would find that equilibrium would be reestablished when the new price level is $16:

$$P_2 = \frac{\$2,000}{(0.25)(500)} = \frac{\$2,000}{125} = \$16.$$

According to these calculations, a doubling of the money supply (from $1,000 to $2,000) would cause a doubling of the equilibrium price level from $8 to $16. Therefore, the annual value of income and output would also double to $8,000 ($16 \times 500$).

How and why do prices rise in response to increases in the money supply? Given an initial equilibrium ($M_1^d = M_1^s$), an increase in the money supply puts the public in the position of having more money than it wishes to hold ($M_1^d < M_2^s$), given the value of output, $P_1 Y$. Individuals who find themselves with more dollars than they wish to hold will increase their spending for other assets such as stocks and bonds or goods and services. But in doing so, they simply pass the extra dollars on to other individuals. These individuals pass the excess dollars on to others as they increase expenditures. While individuals can decrease their money holdings through spending, the public collectively cannot, and the excess dollars are passed from person to person. The increased spending, therefore, causes shifts in the demand schedules for assets and goods and services as in Figure 8-1. The resultant shortages cause price increases, which eventually result in leftward shifts of the supply curve and result in further price increases. You can review this process by re-examining Figures 8-1 and 8-2. At a higher price level, the value of output is increased and, therefore, the public's demand for money is also increased. Spending and responding of the excess money supply eventually drive up the value of output $(P \cdot Y)$ and, therefore, the public's demand for money, so that $M_2^d = M_2^s$. The economy is again in equilibrium. Thus, by spending the excess money balances and driving up prices, the public creates the conditions necessary for holding a larger money stock.

You should prove to yourself that a reduction of the money supply to half its original level would cause a decline in the equilibrium price level to half its original level. Marshall concluded that if one equilibrium situation was compared with another, the price level in the economy would change in direct proportion to the change in the money supply.

VELOCITY AND THE EQUATION OF EXCHANGE

Between the 1890s and 1930s, the greatest American economist was Irving Fisher (1867-1947) of Yale University. Among other topics, Fisher wrote on the theory of interest and capital, on mathematical economics, and on macroeconomics. Taking a somewhat different approach from Marshall's, Fisher arrived at the same conclusion, that in the long run, the price level changes in direct proportion to a change in the money stock.

To understand Fisher's approach, we begin with his concept of the *velocity of money*. *Velocity* is the number of times the average dollar is used per period. We can define this idea more precisely by considering the number of times the average dollar is spent in a given period to purchase GNP. We will continue to call real output Y and use P to refer to the price level associated with Y (i.e., P is the GNP deflator). Thus, $P \cdot Y$ is equal to GNP in dollar terms.

Velocity (V) is defined as GNP divided by the money stock, or

$$V = \frac{P \cdot Y}{M^s}.$$ (8-7)

If, for example, GNP or $(P \cdot Y)$ is $1,000 and M^s is $200, then V equals 5. The average dollar has to be spent five times during the period to purchase all the GNP the economy produces during the period.

If we multiply both sides of equation (8-7) by M^s, we get

$$M^s V = P \cdot Y,$$ (8-8)

which is the *equation of exchange.* This equation says that the number of dollars in the economy multiplied by the average turnover of dollars must equal money GNP. The equation of exchange is really an identity, meaning that it is true by definition. It is simply a rearrangement of the definition of the velocity of money

velocity of money The number of times the average dollar must "turn over" (be used) to purchase the period's final output (gross national product).

equation of exchange An identity stating that the money stock multiplied by velocity must equal the price level multiplied by real output.

Irving Fisher *(1867–1947)*

"His name will stand in history principally as the name of this country's greatest scientific economist," was what one observer wrote upon the death of *Irving Fisher*. Many economists would agree today. Yet Fisher managed in his lifetime to dim his reputation through enthusiasm for social reform, health faddism, and an ill-timed belief in the 1920s that prosperity was here to stay.

Fisher did his undergraduate work at Yale, specializing in mathematics. He also did graduate work at Yale in mathematics and social sciences and wrote an outstanding dissertation using mathematics to investigate the microeconomic theory of value and prices. Even before his dissertation was finished, Fisher was appointed to the Yale faculty, where he spent his entire academic career.

Fisher was a skilled mathematical economist in an age when most economists were innocent of mathematical knowledge and technique. Further, he had an empirical bent and tried to formulate his theories in terms of what one would expect to observe if they were valid as well as what one would expect to observe if they weren't. He also carried out empirical research in attempts to verify his theories. He was the founding president of the Econometric Society.

Fisher's most important work was on the theory of interest and capital. He questioned why there is a positive rate of interest on borrowed funds and what determines whether this rate is 2 percent or 10 percent per year. Among his achievements in this area was that Fisher clearly saw that the higher the rate of inflation, the higher the interest rate. Further, he investigated the meaning of income, wealth, and the capital stock, and he did pioneer work in explaining how they are determined. While capital and interest theory are notoriously difficult, it is notable that Fisher's writings are unusually clear and are designed to help the reader.

Fisher's other major work was on the role of money in the economy. He used the idea of velocity to show that in the long run the price level is proportionate to the money supply. He also believed, however, that money was a major influence on the fluctuations in the economy. He discussed such problems under the heading of "transition" from one long-run price level to a new one when the money stock was changed. While Fisher had many things to say about money, it is clear that he did not find a large number of followers; there was no coherent quantity theory view of how variables such as real output and unemployment are determined.

Fisher was not as honored as he might have been. His work was often a decade or two ahead of its time, and mathematical and quantitative work encountered resistance (though Fisher made only very slight use of these techniques in his books). Perhaps more importantly, he gained the reputation of being something of a crank. Fisher developed tuberculosis in 1898, a very serious and often deadly disease in those days. It took him three years to recover his health, and afterwards he was a crusader for good health, as well as other issues.

Fisher also was caught in the stock market crash of 1929. Worse yet, he had predicted not long before that the United States had reached a permanent plateau of prosperity. Nevertheless, in the years since the Depression, Fisher's reputation as a distinguished pioneer has grown.

(V). However, by making two assumptions, we can translate this equation into the quantity theory of money, and then use it to analyze the behavior of prices. Again, we assume that in long-run equilibrium, real output *(Y)* is at the full-employment level and is constant. We also assume that velocity, in the long run, is constant. In Fisher's view, velocity depends in large part on the technology of payments—i.e., the frequency of receipts and payments, the extent of the correspondence of timing between receipts and payments, the efficiency of transportation and communication systems, the degree of specialization and integration of industry, the population of the country and its habits of thrift, and the use of trade credit. For example, in an economy where almost all transactions must be paid for with cash, people hold a great deal more money than in an economy where credit is extended easily and bills need only be paid at the end of the month. Velocity, then, will change slowly over time as payments technology changes. When a trend toward change in payments technology begins, the long-run change in velocity can be predicted. For example, the introduction of credit cards and the way their use has been expanded mean velocity will rise as the demand for money decreases. While we cannot know how fast this will happen, we do know the general direction of the trend.

In any case, even though the long-run velocity changes over time, there is no reason to believe that in the long run, velocity changes *in response* to changes in M^s or *P*. Hence, when determining the price level in the long run, we can view *V* as a constant. Equation (8-8) makes it clear that an increase in velocity or in the money stock will cause the price level to rise in exactly the same proportion.

Fisher's version of the quantity theory of money tells us that in the long run,

$$M^s \cdot \bar{V} = P \cdot \bar{Y}. \tag{8-9}$$

The bars over *V* and *Y* indicate that these variables are now assumed to be constant. In Marshall's Cambridge *k* version of the quantity theory of money he told us that in the long run

$$M^s = k \cdot P \cdot \bar{Y}. \tag{8-5}$$

From equations (8-5) and (8-9), we can see that in the long run, velocity is the reciprocal of *k;* that is,

$$V = 1/k. \tag{8-10}$$

For example, if *V* equals 4, then $k = \frac{1}{4}$. Fisher approached the problem of what determines the price level by looking at what determines the payments technology of the economy, while Marshall discussed the problem in terms of the demand for money as a fraction of the economy's income. Both approaches give the same results, results very much like those of the early quantity theorists such as Hume and Ricardo.

DYNAMICS IN THE QUANTITY THEORY

According to the quantity theory, a doubling of the money supply leads in the long run to a doubling of the price level and no change in real income. Recall that this proposition is based on the assumption that there is no long-run equilibrium growth, that the demand for money (Marshall's version) or the velocity of money (Fisher's version) are unchanged, and that the increase in the money supply is a one-time unexpected change. But what happens to the price level and to output between the time the money supply changes and the time when P changes proportionately and output returns to its long-run equilibrium value? Perhaps the major shortcoming of the quantity theory was its inability to give precise or definite answers to questions about the transition from one equilibrium position to another.

The classical economists spent a good deal of time discussing what *might* happen on the transition path from one equilibrium to another, but they had little success in specifying exactly what *would* happen and at what time. Beyond this, they had no precise policy prescriptions or advice for government policymakers as to what could be done at various stages of adjustment in order to improve the behavior of the macro economy.

SAY'S LAW

The second part of the foundation of classical macroeconomics is based on the work of a French economist, Jean-Baptiste Say. In a disarmingly simple, yet profound analysis, Say presented a theoretical picture of how the market economy operated. Say's idea was based on the relationship between production, income, and spending. He argued that the creation of products for the market generated an amount of income equal to the value of the products produced. If businesses produced products with a value of $1,000, then they also created incomes equal to $1,000. Since the value of income was the same as the value of products, the production process had created the income necessary to purchase the products. Say further argued that people offered their labor or the product of their labor in order to earn income to use for consumption spending. Production generated income which was spent for production. This idea—supply (production) creates its own demand (spending for production)—became known as *Say's Law.*

Early classical economists contended that this analysis proved that a market economy would not be subject to severe or prolonged periods of overproduction. If you think about it, you may recognize a serious flaw in Say's reasoning: Does everyone spend their entire income? Obviously not. Many people save a portion of their income. Spending is less than the value of products to the extent that saving occurs. Insufficient spending causes overproduction, which in turn generates unemployment. Yet, Say's Law promised that severe, prolonged unemployment could not exist, because insufficient spending would never occur. This problem is depicted in Figure 8-3. Businesses produce $1,000 in products and generate $1,000 in incomes. But, individuals save a portion of their income, say $200, so spending is insufficient to purchase output. Unsold products cause a buildup of inventories, and businesses respond by decreasing production and employment. Thus, as a consequence of saving, unemployment results.

The classical economists found an answer to the potential problem created by saving. They concluded that no matter what amount of income was saved, it would be exactly offset by investment spending by business. To show this argument, we turn to the third part of the foundation of classical macroeconomics—the system of self-regulating markets.

Say's Law   Jean-Baptiste Say's theory which states that supply creates its own demand.

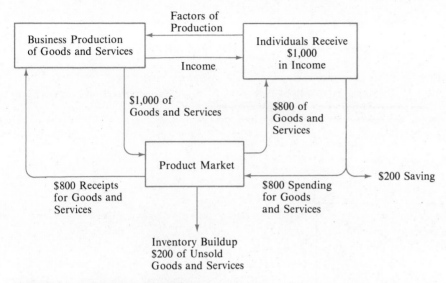

FIGURE 8-3 SAVING—A PROBLEM?

Businesses produce $1,000 in goods and services, and in doing so, generate $1,000 in incomes to the suppliers of factors of production. If $200 of this income is saved, then only $800 is spent for goods and services. As a result, $200 of goods and services are unsold, causing a buildup of inventories. In response to this inventory buildup, business output is reduced, resulting in reduced incomes and/or rising unemployment.

SELF-REGULATING MARKETS

Classical economists believed, on the basis of theory and experience, that full employment of resources in a capitalistic economy was virtually assured. The classical economists did not claim that the economic system *always* operated at a position of full employment. Occasional problems of overproduction and unemployment did occur. These problems were quickly eliminated by the ***self-regulating markets*** which comprise the capitalistic economic system. Thus, capitalism's system of self-regulating markets assured that Say's Law was valid and that prolonged periods of unemployment were impossible. A self-regulating market is one that quickly eliminates problems of shortages or surpluses through price changes. The three general markets which comprise the capitalistic economy are the money (or credit) market, the product market, and the labor market. Each was believed to be capable of self-regulation, and each played a vital role in the efficient functioning of the overall system.

self-regulating markets
Markets which quickly eliminate problems of shortage or surplus through price changes.

The Credit Market

The self-regulating credit market assured that saving would not destroy the validity of Say's Law. Through the credit market, income that was saved would flow into the hands of businesses, which would in turn spend it for investment purposes. A flexible interest rate would assure the equality between saving and investment spending. With the aid of Figure 8-4, we can develop this argument.

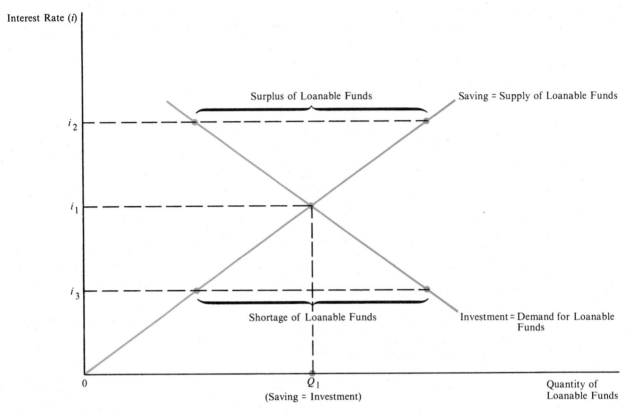

FIGURE 8-4 THE CREDIT MARKET (Classical View)
In the view of the classical economists, the interest rate would adjust to assure that the supply of and demand for loanable funds would be equal; that is, saving would be exactly offset by investment spending. Saving and investment are equal (Q_1) at i_1, the equilibrium interest rate. At higher interest rates (e.g., i_2), the surplus of loanable funds will put downward pressure on i. At lower rates (e.g., i_3), the shortage of loanable funds will drive i higher. Market forces will drive the interest rate to i_1.

In the classical view, the supply of credit (loanable funds) resulted from people's decisions to save, while the demand for credit (loanable funds) resulted from the desire by businesses to borrow for investment purposes.

The supply schedule has a positive slope to indicate that saving is directly related to the interest rate. This is based on the argument that people forego spending (save) only if there is an incentive to do so. The interest rate is the incentive for saving. When the interest rate rises, the incentive has increased, so the quantity of saving will increase. When the interest rate declines, the incentive to save declines, so the quantity of saving will decline.

The demand schedule has a familiar negative slope which indicates that the investment spending will increase when the interest rate declines, and decrease when the interest rate rises. This is because the interest rate is the price businesses pay to obtain credit. When the price is lower, businesses will demand more credit for investment; when the price is higher, they will demand less credit for investment.

According to classical economists, the credit market would establish an equilibrium interest rate which would equate the amount of saving and investment spending. This interest rate is shown as i_1 in Figure 8-4 and is determined by the intersection of the saving and investment schedules. At interest rates above equilibrium, such as i_2, the supply exceeds the demand for credit, and the surplus of saving relative to investment spending forces the interest rate downward to i_1. At interest rates below equilibrium, such as i_2, demand exceeds the supply of credit. This shortage causes the interest rate to be bid up to i_1. Suppose people suddenly became more thrifty; that is, the amount of saving increases at each interest rate. In this case, the saving schedule would shift to the right. The new equilibrium interest rate would be below i_1. Because the price of credit would be lower, the increase in saving would cause an increase in the amount of investment spending.

Jean-Baptiste Say *(1767–1832)*

The Physiocrats (see the biography of Francois Quesnay in Chapter 2) felt that interruptions in the circular flow model, caused by saving, would be damaging to the economy. *Jean-Baptiste Say* was critical of this argument. Say, a businessman turned academic, held a chair in political economy at the *Conservatoire des Arts et Metiers.* Say presented an alternative theory which stated that production caused prosperity.

Say's Law, which became the basis of classical macroeconomics, is a simple theory of markets. It contends that aggregate supply (GNP) will always equal aggregate demand (national income). Say maintained that the sum of all wages, profits, rents, and interest paid in manufacturing would be equal to the price of the goods produced and, therefore, would be sufficient to buy it; that is, the purchasing power in a system was always sufficient to purchase the goods produced. This is the foundation of Say's Law, which states that supply creates its own demand.

Say never argued that overproduction of certain goods and underproduction of others would not occur. But he believed these imbalances would be corrected by entrepreneurs seeking profits by satisfying consumer demands.

Supply-side economics, which gained popularity with the election of President Reagan, draws on Say's theory. Many supply-siders like to quote the following passage from Say:

"The encouragement of mere consumption is no benefit to commerce; for the difficulty lies in supplying the means, not in stimulating the desire of consumption; and we have seen production alone furnishes that means. It is the aim of good government to stimulate production; of bad government to encourage consumption."[1]

---

[1]Jean-Baptiste Say, *A Treatise on Political Economy* (Philadelphia: John Grigg, 1830).

In summary, flexible interest rates in the credit market would assure that saving could not exceed investment spending. A major oversight in Say's analysis had been corrected and classical economists could again claim that "supply creates its own demand."

The Product and Labor Markets

Classical economists argued that the product and labor markets operated in the same manner as the credit market; that is, flexible prices and wages would eliminate overproduction and unemployment.

The hypothetical market for straw hats, a popular consumer product during the 1920s, is shown in Figure 8-5. For the moment, ignore demand schedule, D_2, and consider only the initial supply and demand schedules, S_1 and D_1. Assume that the market is initially in equilibrium at price P_1 and quantity supplied is equal to quantity demanded at Q_1.

Now look at Figure 8-6, which shows the market for labor to produce straw hats. Again, ignore labor demand schedule D_{L2}, and consider only the initial labor supply and demand schedules, S_{L1} and D_{L1}. The labor supply and demand schedules have typically positive and negative slopes respectively. The positive slope of the labor supply schedule implies that the quantity of labor offered in the market increases as the wage rate increases. Casual observation and experience confirm this relationship. The negative slope of the labor demand schedule implies that businesses will employ more labor if the wage rate declines. This stems from the fact that the demand for labor is derived from the demand for the product that labor produces; in our example, straw hats. If more labor is employed, more straw hats will be produced. But to sell additional straw hats, their price must be reduced. Thus, firms can afford to profitably employ more labor only if the wage rate declines.

The labor market would initially be in equilibrium at wage rate W_1, with employment at L_1 (L_1 units of labor are required to produce Q_1 straw hats).

Now, suppose the demand for straw hats declines as shown by the shift from D_1 to D_2 in Figure 8-6. At price P_1, only Q_3 straw hats can be sold. This decline in the demand for straw hats causes a decrease in the demand for labor from

---

FIGURE 8-5   THE MARKET FOR STRAW HATS

Initially the market is in equilibrium at the intersection of S_1 and D_1 with price P_1 and quantity exchanged Q_1. A decrease in demand from D_1 to D_2 results in only Q_3 hats being sold at P_1. Falling wages in the labor market allow for price to be lowered to P_2. A new equilibrium is achieved at the intersection of S_1 and D_2 with price P_2 and quantity exchanged at Q_2.

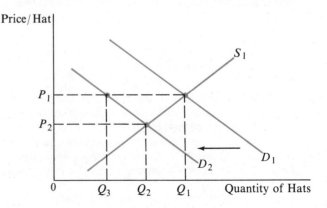

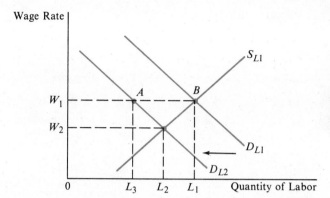

Wage Rate

W_1

W_2

0   L_3 L_2 L_1 Quantity of Labor

FIGURE 8-6   THE MARKET FOR LABOR TO PRODUCE STRAW HATS

Initially the market is in equilibrium at the intersection of S_{L1} and D_{L1}, with wage rate W_1 and L_1 units of labor employed. The labor demand schedule shifts left to D_{L2}, as a result of a decrease in the demand for straw hats. The result is unemployment of AB units of labor at wage rate W_1. Unemployed labor forces the wage rate down to W_2. A new equilibrium is achieved at the intersection of S_{L1} and D_{L2} with wage rate W_2 and L_2 units of labor employed.

D_{L1} to D_{L2}. With these changed conditions, unemployment of AB exists at wage rate W_1. According to classical economic theory, unemployment would be temporary. Unemployed workers would compete for existing jobs forcing down the wage rate. At a lower wage rate, production costs would decrease and the firm could profitably lower the price of straw hats. At a lower price, more hats could be produced and sold. As production increases, unemployment declines. The wage rate eventually falls to W_2 and the price of straw hats falls to P_2. The product market and labor market are once again in equilibrium. Flexible wage rates and prices have eliminated unemployment and overproduction.

Notice two things about the new equilibrium situation. First, fewer straw hats are being produced and sold at a lower price. Second, as a result, less labor is employed by the firm and labor is paid a lower wage rate. Where do the people previously employed in making straw hats go? To other firms or industries which are experiencing an increase in the demand for their products. Since underspending was impossible for the entire economy, decreases in the demand in one part of the system would be offset by increases in demand in another part.

Thus, the classical economists concluded, on the basis of their theories (verified by many decades of experience), that the capitalistic economy would self-regulate to full employment. Occasional problems would arise; but through flexible interest rates, prices, and wage rates, overproduction and unemployment would be eliminated. All that was required, claimed the classical economists, was patience; the system would automatically adjust.

THE BUSINESS CYCLE THEORISTS

The classical economists were not, of course, the only economists who discussed macroeconomic issues before the Keynesian revolution of the 1930s. In the 1800s and early 1900s, a number of economists put forward theories that attempted to explain the business cycle. **Business cycles** refer to the irregular ups and downs of business activity along the long-run trend line. Figure 8-7 shows an idealized business cycle starting with an upswing in activity leading to a peak, which is followed by a downturn in activity leading to a trough, or recession. Unlike

business cycle   Irregular ups and downs of business activity along general trend lines.

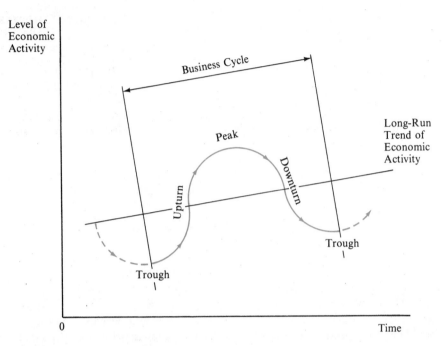

FIGURE 8-7   THE "IDEALIZED" BUSINESS CYCLE

This figure shows an idealized business cycle—tracing the level of economic activity over time. This business cycle is idealized because it shows the peak and trough being equal in magnitude, and the length of time of the upturn and downturn also being equal.

Figure 8-7, actual business cycles do not trace smooth curves over time, nor are upswings and downswings of equal magnitude in time or intensity.

It was clear to early observers that business or trade, meaning economic activity, had its ups and downs. But economic statistics were very sparse prior to the twentieth century. In fact, they were not very detailed nor systematic for the United States until 1929. Nevertheless, price statistics were available (for example, for food products such as wheat) and showed periods of high and low prices. Though there were no statistics available on national unemployment rates or rates of real GNP growth, it was clear that real activity showed periods of upturn and downturn. In some periods, factories were quite busy and most workers had jobs; in other periods, many factories were idle, many people were unemployed, and work was very hard to find.

Many economists thought they could see cycles in economic activity, suggesting the idea that upturns and downturns recurred periodically in a kind of natural rhythm. The variety of explanations offered for the business cycle is both impressive and bewildering.

Karl Marx was among the earliest contributors to business cycle theory. He believed that capitalism contained fatal flaws which would lead to unavoidable business cycles whose intensity would increase over time. Marx argued that capitalism's source of profits was the exploitation of labor. In order to increase profits, capitalists would continually search for ways to increase the exploitation of labor. Marx believed this process would lead to an increase in the amount of machinery used with labor in the production processes, ultimately throwing workers out of jobs. This would cause situations of growing unemployment and declining incomes. As incomes declined, spending would decline, and overproduction would result in gluts of products in the market. Competition among businesses would force product prices down, until the weakest capitalistic firms went bankrupt. These bankruptcies would signal that the trough of the cycle had been reached. The output of the surviving firms would not exceed the demand for output and an upswing would begin. Surviving firms would absorb the bankrupt firms, forcing their owners into the labor force and resulting in fewer firms of greater size and economic power. The drive by the surviving capitalistic firms to increase their profits would lead to a downturn in business activity as the process repeated itself.

Marx thought that each business cycle would be more severe and economically destructive than the previous one, and that unemployment would grow over time. Capitalism would finally fail when the size and strength of the unemployed labor force was sufficient to bring about a labor force revolt and economic takeover.

Most early business cycle theorists, however, did not go so far as to predict the downfall of the capitalistic economic system. One of the most unique explanations of business cycles was the *sunspot theory,* which was developed by the English economist William Stanley Jevons. According to this theory, the occurrence of unusually severe radioactive storms on the surface of the sun, referred to as sunspots, were highly correlated with business cycles. Jevons argued that the weather patterns on earth were strongly influenced by the activity on the sun's surface. Weather obviously was a primary influence on the agricultural sector of capitalistic economies, and would produce similar patterns of activity throughout the economy. Therefore, he concluded that sunspots caused business cycles!

sunspot theory A theory which states that business cycles are closely related to activity on the surface of the sun, or sunspots.

The Austrian economist Joseph Schumpeter, who taught at Harvard University from the 1930s until his death in 1950, explained the business cycle (in part) by waves of innovations that stimulated new activity, followed by periods of economic slowdown when the economic possibilities of the innovations had been exhausted. In such periods, inefficient firms were weeded out through bankruptcy, and in this way the economy was actually strengthened. Some economists were convinced that business downturns were caused by people hoarding their money (or refusing to spend their money) and suggested that, to remedy this problem, a tax on money was needed to reduce the incentive to hold it.

None of these business cycle theorists attracted a large following of believers. The failure of any one theory to become the main theory was due in large part to the fact that none of them could give more precise predictions about the cycle than could classical macroeconomic theory. Further, statistics simply did not exist that could be used to examine the competitive theories in order to determine which were useful and which were not, which had some predictive power and which were quite wrong.

Thus, as the world approached the Great Depression of the 1930s, classical macroeconomic theory was the most important way of understanding macroeconomic problems, but it was not precisely developed. Both classical macroeconomic theory and many competing business cycle theories were, however, quite weak in providing explanations of the time path of such fluctuations. Most importantly, macroeconomics, at this point, offered little guidance that was widely accepted among economists about what might be done to alleviate these macroeconomic problems.

SUMMARY

1. Classical macroeconomic theory was developed during the 150 years prior to the Great Depression. Its foundation consists of (1) the quantity theory of money, (2) Say's Law, and (3) the system of self-regulating markets.

2. Early classical economists worked on the practical problem of explaining how the inflow of money (gold and silver) from the New World led to rising prices in Europe. David Ricardo used the quantity theory of money to help analyze inflation during the Napoleonic Wars and to develop policy to provide price stability.

3. The conclusions of Hume, Ricardo, and others were that (1) in the long run, prices would be proportionate to the money stock and (2) the stock of money had to be controlled to provide price stability.

4. Alfred Marshall extended the quantity theory of money analysis by introducing the idea of the demand for money. He concluded that the public wanted to hold some fraction of its income in the form of money and referred to the fraction as the Cambridge k. The economy would only be in equilibrium when the public's demand for money was equal to the amount of money being supplied.

5. Irving Fisher contributed to the quantity theory of money through his studies on the velocity of money—the ratio of total economic activity to the money supply. Both Fisher and Marshall reached the same general conclusion as a result of their research—that in the long run, the real output of the economy would depend only on real factors such as the amount and productivity of labor and capital. Long-run real output was independent of the money stock or price level. They supported the earlier conclusion that in the long run, prices would be proportionate to the money stock.

6. The quantity theory of money was useful for comparing one long-run equilibrium situation with another. Its weakness was that it offered no help to economists in explaining the fluctuations in output and price that occurred when the economy was in disequilibrium.

7. Jean-Baptiste Say argued that overproduction was impossible in a capitalistic economy, because the production of output generated an equivalent amount of income. The idea that supply creates its own demand became Say's Law.

8. Classical economists believed that capitalism was comprised of a system of self-regulating markets. Flexible interest rates, prices, and wages would automatically alleviate temporary problems in the credit, product, and labor markets. The system of self-regulating markets plus Say's Law led classical economists to conclude that the capitalist economy could not suffer prolonged or severe periods of unemployment. Temporary problems would be eliminated by the automatic response of the markets.

9. The history of capitalistic economic activity shows an irregular pattern. These fluctuations in economic activity became known as business cycles. Early theories put forth to explain these business cycles included: (1) the theory of labor exploitation by Marx; (2) Schumpeter's innovation theory; (3) Jevons's sunspot theory; and several others.

10. As the world's capitalistic economies entered the 1930s, no single theory was yet available which could explain the short-run behavior of business activity.

NEW TERMS

quantity theory of money
Cambridge k
velocity of money
equation of exchange

Say's Law
self-regulating markets
business cycle
sunspot theory

QUESTIONS FOR DISCUSSION

1. Use graphical analysis to show how an influx of precious metals from the New World would raise the price level in Europe. Would the level of prices stop rising if the influx went on forever?

2. Why might you be skeptical about allowing the stock of money to be determined by the needs of trade?

3. If $k = ¼$, long-run real output or income equals 2,000 units, and the stock of money is $100,000, what is the price level in the long run? What happens to the long-run price level if the demand for money increases and k rises to ½?

4. If V equals 6, long-run real output or income equals 2,000 units, and the stock of money is $200,000, what is the long-run price level? Discuss the effect on V due to a change in the price level.

5. Explain Say's Law of "supply creates its own demand." How was this idea used to argue that underproduction was impossible?

6. Use graphical analysis to show how an increase in saving will cause the interest rate to decline.

7. Use graphical analysis to show how an increase in the demand for a product will result in an increase in employment and the wage rate in the labor market for that product.

SUGGESTIONS FOR FURTHER READING

Fisher, Irving. *The Purchasing Power of Money,* 2d ed. Fairfield, N.J.: Augustus M. Kelley, Pubs., 1922.
Kamerschen, David R. *Money and Banking,* 7h ed. Cincinnati: South-Western Publishing Co., 1980.
Marshall, Alfred. *Money, Credit, and Commerce.* Fairfield, N.J.: Augustus M. Kelley, Pubs., 1923.
Robertson, Dennis. *Money.* New York: Cambridge University Press, 1959.

The Keynesian Revolution

After studying the materials found in this chapter, you should be able to do the following:

1. Outline the macroeconomic history of the United States since the Civil War.

2. Contrast the behavior of prices in pre-World War II recessions with those in post-1950 recessions.

3. Discuss the Great Depression (1929–1941), the stock market crash of 1929, and subsequent bank failures.

4. Explain how the Roosevelt administration attempted to deal with the Great Depression.

5. Outline the life of John Maynard Keynes and his contributions to economics.

6. Discuss Keynes's criticism of classical macroeconomic theory.

7. Describe Keynesian economics, including the theories that are used to explain consumer and business investment spending, as well as the cause of the Great Depression.

Great Depression *The severe downturn in real U.S. economic activity from 1929 to 1941.*

This chapter examines some historical fluctuations of the American economy in order to show the range of experiences that the economy has encountered and to give a basis for comparison with more recent developments. Perhaps the worst contraction ever experienced by the United States and the world was the *Great Depression,* which began in 1929 and finally ended after our entry into World War II in 1941.

This chapter also looks at John Maynard Keynes's criticism of classical macroeconomic theory. Keynes argued that flaws existed in the classical theory and that it was logically possible for the economy to experience severe, prolonged periods of overproduction and unemployment. Keynes's views became the basis for the Keynesian Revolution. His ideas held a dominant position in macroeconomic theory and policymaking from 1936 to 1979.

U.S. ECONOMIC HISTORY OVER THE PAST 100 YEARS

The U.S. economy experienced 27 recessions between the end of the Civil War and 1982. Thus, on the average, a recession has occurred in the United States every four and one-half years. Economists define a *recession* as a decline in real GNP which lasts two quarters (six months) or longer. The 1929–1933 recession was so severe it was given a special name, *depression.* President Harry Truman once said that when your neighbor is out of work, that's a recession; but when you lose your job, that's a depression.

In each recession, people suffered unemployment, inability to get credit, and losses of their homes, farms, savings, and businesses. The earlier recessions were often associated with banking panics or were started by them.

Figure 9-1 shows that in the period from the end of the Civil War in 1865 until 1900, wholesale prices in the United States had a downward trend, though the decline was clearly not steady.[1] At present, we worry a great deal about rising prices, or inflation, so you might think that these falling prices would have been greeted as a good thing. This, however, was not the view of most farmers and other debtors. They were in debt for their equipment, seed, livestock, and land (after almost all good homestead land had been claimed). The payments they had to make on these debts were fixed in dollars, but the prices they received for their farm products were falling, making it ever more difficult for them to meet the payments on the debts. This is one reason why people in the western areas of the United States were enthusiastic about including silver in the U.S. money supply along with gold. This would have increased the money supply by combining the stocks of the two metals, and even though most farmers had never heard of the quantity theory, they realized this increase in the money supply would raise prices or at least help curtail falling prices. This policy of *bimetallism* was not adopted in the United States, though the Democratic candidate for president, William Jennings Bryan, almost won the election in 1896 by making bimetallism one of his main proposals. People in favor of "sound money" were able to stop this monetary plan, as well as others that were quite farfetched.[2]

Furthermore, reform plans relied mainly on monetary changes, in part because of the association of banking panics with business downturns. We have seen that the panic of 1907 and the recession that followed it prodded Congress to

recession *A decline in real GNP which lasts two quarters or longer.*

bimetallism *The use of both gold and silver as parts of the money stock.*

---

[1] Figure 9-1 is drawn on a ratio or semilog scale. By ratio scale, we mean that equal movements up the vertical axis represent equal *percentage* changes in the producer price index (PPI). For example, the distance from 50 to 100 is the same as that from 100 to 200; both are 100 percent increases in the PPI. This effect is achieved by plotting the natural logarithm (or log) of the PPI on the vertical axis. Since time is measured in years on the horizontal axis rather than in log of years, this is said to be a semilog scale rather than a double-log scale. An important property of a ratio or semilog chart is that the slope of the curve is equal to the percentage rate of change in the variable. In particular, this allows us to visually compare changes at different times. For example, wholesale price inflation is the percentage rate of change of the PPI; from Figure 9-1, we can see that inflation was very sharp during the Civil War (1861–1865) and World War I (the United States entered in 1917 and the war ended in late 1918), but was not as rapid in World War II (the United States entered the war in late 1941 and the war ended in 1945).

[2] The bimetallic standard was used in the United States from the early 1800s until 1878, when it was abandoned and replaced by the gold standard.

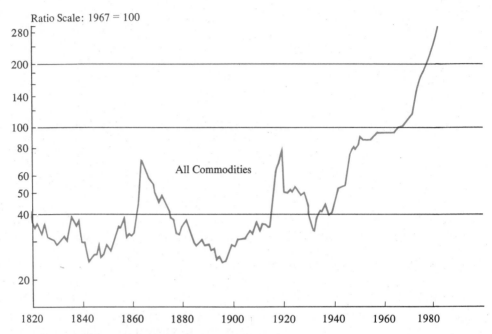

Ratio Scale: 1967 = 100

FIGURE 9-1   WHOLESALE PRICES IN THE UNITED
STATES, 1820–1981

From the end of the Civil War in 1865 until almost 1900, wholesale prices in the United States tended
to fall, though by no means steadily. From the start of the Great Depression in 1929 until 1933, prices
fell sharply. During wars, prices tend to rise rapidly, such as happened during the Civil War
(1861–1865), World War I (1917–1918), and World War II (1941–1945). (Source: *Historical Chart
Book,* Board of Governors of the Federal Reserve System.)

create the Federal Reserve System. But recall that the Fed was not designed to
put any schemes such as bimetallism into practice or to use policy to fight
recessions. Rather, it was supposed to regulate banks and serve as a lender of last
resort in an effort to avoid the waves of panics and bank failures that had occurred
throughout U.S. history. It was only after the Keynesian revolution that people
began to believe the government could and should use fiscal and monetary policy
to curb ups and downs in the economy.

Figure 9-2 uses the index of industrial production to illustrate some of the
ups and downs the economy has experienced.[3] We can easily see the large reduction in industrial production in 1920 and 1921 in the recession that followed
World War I. There was a much more extensive slide in industrial production
between 1929 and 1933, as the Great Depression reached its depths. Also, we can
see a sharp contraction in 1938 as the recovery from the Depression was inter-
rupted by a sharp setback.

---

[3]The industrial production index measures the nation's manufacturing, mining, and utilities output.
    As compared with real GNP, or GNP in constant dollars, industrial production leaves out farms
    and the service sector, which includes such things as the services of physicians, gardeners,
    salespeople, and other workers who do not produce physical outputs of goods.

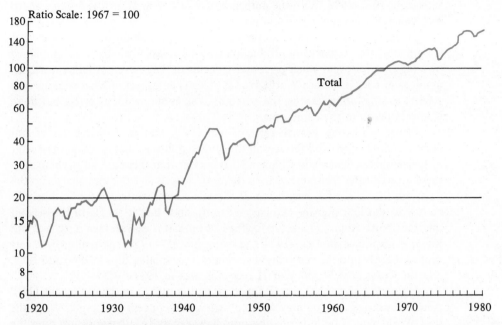

FIGURE 9-2   INDUSTRIAL PRODUCTION IN THE UNITED STATES, 1919–1980

Industrial production (the output of factories, mines, and utilities) has risen over time in the United States. However, there have been occasional sharp setbacks. The worst contraction occurred at the start of the Great Depression from 1929 to 1933. There also tend to be contractions after wars, such as occurred after World Wars I and II. In comparing Figures 9-1 and 9-2, we note that before World War II, contractions in output tended to be accompanied by declines in the price level. In the post-World War II period, prices have often kept on rising during contractions, a phenomenon which has been labeled *stagflation.* (Source: *Historical Chart Book,* Board of Governors of the Federal Reserve System.)

With the coming of World War II, industrial production began a rapid rise as the country prepared for a strong war effort. After World War II came a reduction of some magnitude in industrial production. This was only natural as the economy shifted from the production of war goods to the production of civilian goods. For example, no civilian automobiles were produced in the United States from 1942 until after the war, at which time automakers switched from making tanks and other military hardware back to civilian production. The United States experienced more minor ups and downs in the 1950s, and there was a period of fairly steady growth from 1961–1968. The ups and downs resumed with the recession of 1969–1970, with the most severe downturn in 1973–1975.

Wholesale prices tell a crucially different story in the post-World War II period. In the aftermath of World War I, there was a fall in prices from the levels reached in wartime. This fall accompanied the sharp contraction in industrial production. Then there was a sharp and prolonged fall in prices between 1929 and 1933 during the worst of the Great Depression. Wholesale prices fell by about a third between 1929 and 1933. As the economy's production began to recover after 1933, prices also began to rise, but, as with production, there was a sharp

stagflation   A stagnant economy, combining recession or low economic growth with inflation.

setback in 1937–1938. With the outbreak of World War II, prices began a sharp rise, which is the usual pattern in wartime in almost every country. However, in comparing changes in prices and production in the years since World War II, it is noticeable that setbacks in production have been less likely to be accompanied by a fall in prices, and when prices have declined, they have not fallen nearly as much as in periods before World War II. This is an aspect of what some people refer to as ***stagflation;*** that is, the economy is stagnant or not growing, but there is also inflation at the same time.

Figure 9-3 shows growth rates of real GNP; that is, growth rates of real output of final goods and services in the United States economy. (You may want to review these concepts in Chapter 7.) It is clear that there are large changes in these growth rates from one year to the next, as well as from one quarter to the next, but this is not too surprising. If there is a hard winter, output is likely to be low in the first quarter (January–March), and then it spurts in the second quarter (April–June) to make up for the lost time. It is easy, however, to pick out major disruptions. In 1953–1954 and again in 1957–1958, the real growth rate dipped sharply into the negative range. There were smaller dips in 1960 and 1969, and the worst post-World War II recession was in 1973–1975.

Figure 9-4 shows the record for the inflation rate as measured by the GNP price deflator (again, you may want to review this concept in Chapter 7). In the post-World War II period, inflation rates have generally fallen at or just after the declines in real GNP growth rates that we noted—1953–1954, 1957–1958, 1960, 1969, and 1973–1975. But notice that the declines are not always very large and do not last long, and often the inflation rates remain positive—this is particularly noticeable in 1960, 1969, 1974, and 1975. Thus, the price level has continued to rise even in the face of recessions. This is a very different pattern from the one we saw before World War II. And this troublesome problem of stagflation is one that economic policymakers continue to face in the 1980s.

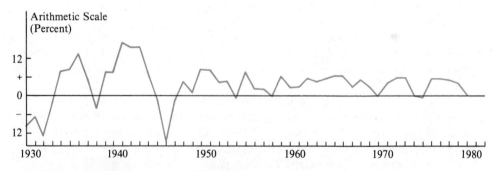

FIGURE 9-3   REAL GNP ANNUAL GROWTH RATE, 1947–1980

Growth rates of real gross national product (GNP in constant dollars) show a good deal of variation from one quarter of the year to the next, as well as from one year to the next. Nevertheless, it is easy to pick out the recessions where output fell (growth rates were negative). The most severe post-World War II recession was 1973–1975. (Source: *Historical Chart Book,* Board of Governors of the Federal Reserve System.)

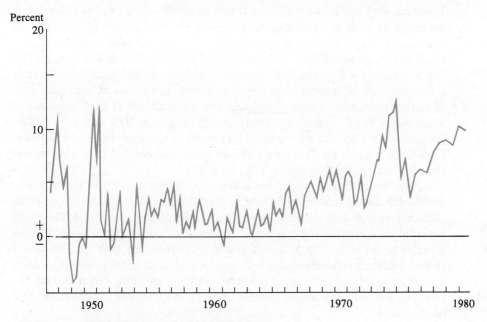

Percent

FIGURE 9-4   INFLATION RATE AS MEASURED BY
THE IMPLICIT PRICE DEFLATOR FOR
GNP, 1947–1980

As real growth rates (Figure 9-3) have varied greatly from one year to the next, so have inflation rates. In comparing Figures 9-3 and 9-4, note that inflation has often continued (remained positive) during post-World War II recessions and has fallen only slightly (if at all) during these recessions. (Source: *Historical Chart Book,* Board of Governors of the Federal Reserve System.)

The dominant macroeconomic theory from 1936 to 1979, Keynesian economics, was originally fashioned to deal with the problems of the Great Depression of the 1930s, which we shall now take up.

THE GREAT DEPRESSION—1929–1941

One of the major disasters of the twentieth century was the Great Depression. It produced great human hardship and led to some far-reaching changes in the U.S. economy, particularly in the role of government in the economy. It also led to a revolution in economic theory and policymaking which has come to be known as the Keynesian revolution.

What exists now may seem normal, natural, and usual to those who have known no other circumstances. Government expenditures on goods and services now account for over 33 percent of GNP, taxes (federal, state, and local) are over 32 percent of GNP, and the Social Security System is well-established. Congress regularly debates inflation, real growth, and various government expenditures and tax proposals, and the Fed regularly adjusts monetary policy. In 1929, things were far different. Government expenditures were only about 8 percent of GNP.

There was no Social Security System; it arrived in 1935. There was no government medical plan such as Medicare; the first such plan was established in 1966. In most people's minds, government taxation and spending policies were not supposed to be used to stabilize the economy, but to balance the federal budget. The Fed's monetary policy was not supposed to stabilize output growth and prices; it was supposed to prevent bank panics by acting as a lender of last resort and, of course, to regulate banks. There was also no insurance of bank deposits, so when banks failed, depositors simply lost their money. The changes in these systems since 1929 can be traced in large part to the experience of the Great Depression and to the Keynesian theory that took command of economists' thinking during the Depression.

After World War I, there was a brief but sharp recession as the economy switched from war-related production to peacetime production. This is a frequent pattern if war has used a significant portion of an economy's resources. The 1920s provided prosperity for the majority of Americans, though farmers began to have troubles in the mid-1920s with falling prices for their products. As Figure 9-2 shows, industrial production rose during the decade (except for a relatively minor slowdown in 1923–1924). Other countries were not so lucky. Great Britain, for example, suffered high unemployment and depressed output in the second half of the 1920s.

stock market crash *The large, swift fall of the U.S. stock market in October, 1929.*

In August, 1929, industrial production in the United States turned down and began the long plunge that finally ended in 1933 (see Figure 9-2). This was two months before the famous *stock market crash* of October, 1929. It is not true that the crash caused the Depression. The economy had begun to slide downward before the crash. But there is no doubt that the crash badly scared people and made them reluctant to put their funds in financial assets that appeared risky, such as stocks and corporate bonds. This reaction made it more difficult for business to obtain funds. Figure 9-5 shows the Dow-Jones average of 30 industrial stocks' prices on the New York Stock Exchange. The fall in the average stock price between 1929 and 1932 is clearly the worst ever experienced in the United States. Every sector of the economy was frightened, and people were afraid to take chances.

It is not hard to understand this fear. Figure 9-2 depicted the rapid drop in industrial production between 1929 and 1933; Figure 9-6 shows the great rise in the rate of unemployment. In addition, banks were once again failing.[4] Between 1929 and 1933, the number of commercial banks in the United States fell by one third. More than a fifth of all banks had to suspend operations because of financial difficulties, and these banks held nearly one tenth of the volume of deposits. Few depositors ever recovered any of the funds they lost. No wonder people were frightened of financial institutions, for their jobs, and for the prospects of the economy and the country.

Things were no better abroad. The Depression affected every European country. Banks failed and the European financial system was badly shaken. The United States and European countries began to raise tariffs, put quotas on imports, and take other antitrade measures as each country tried to stimulate its

---

[4]See Milton Friedman and Anna Schwartz, *A Monetary History of the United States, 1867–1960* (Princeton, N.J.: Princeton University Press, 1963), Chapter 7.

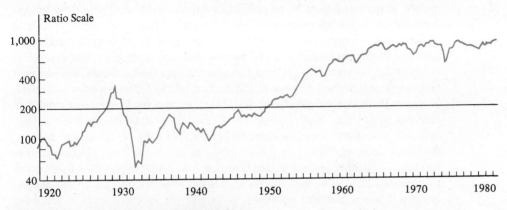

**FIGURE 9-5   DOW-JONES PRICE INDEX OF 30
INDUSTRIAL STOCKS, 1919–1980**

The stock market is represented here by the Dow-Jones price index of 30 industrial stocks. Clearly, the stock market has had a great many ups and downs. Perhaps the most impressive rise was in the 1920s, ending with the crash of October, 1929, and the long slide down through 1932. This caused a great deal of fear among investors in financial markets and made it quite difficult for businesses to raise funds. (Source: *Historical Chart Book*, Board of Governors of the Federal Reserve System.)

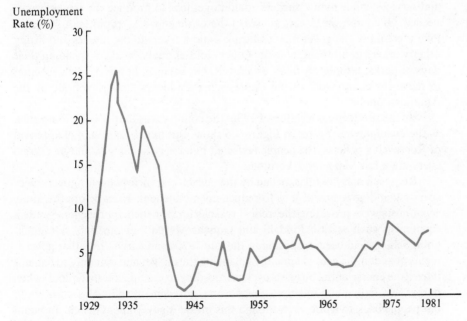

**FIGURE 9-6   UNEMPLOYMENT RATES IN THE
UNITED STATES AS A PERCENTAGE OF
THE CIVILIAN LABOR FORCE, 1929–1981**

Unemployment rates soared with the onset of the Great Depression. By 1933, almost one quarter of the labor force was without a job. Many of those still employed were working less than full time. Unemployment continued to be severe until the onset of World War II when war production needs dictated almost complete employment of the civilian labor force. (Source: *Economic Report of the President*, various issues; and *Survey of Current Business*, various issues.)

exports to provide jobs at home and cut its imports to preserve jobs from foreign competition. Trade fell drastically. The follow-up of this policy will be discussed in detail in the coming chapter on international trade. The misery of the Depression and the fear it inspired helped lead to political changes. In January, 1933, Adolf Hitler became Chancellor of Germany. In the United States, disillusioned voters rejected Herbert Hoover in the election of 1932. The Socialist candidate, Norman Thomas, received almost 900,000 votes, and the Communist candidate received more than 100,000 votes. The Democratic candidate, Franklin Roosevelt, was inaugurated as president in March, 1933. In his inaugural address, Roosevelt declared, "The only thing we have to fear is fear itself." In fact, neither Roosevelt nor other leaders of free countries had concrete plans for fighting the Depression. Though he had run on a platform of balancing the federal budget, Roosevelt was a practical politician, willing to try various tactics to solve the pressing problems of the economy. One plan the administration tried was to put people back to work by employing them on government projects such as constructing dams and public buildings, putting in sewers and streets, and so forth. Naturally, the jobless who found work on these projects were pleased, not only because they were making money, but also because they had regained the dignity of having worthwhile work and providing for their families. There seemed to be no harm and much good in such projects. Jobless workers were once again providing things people could use. One of the most disturbing aspects of the Depression was the terrible paradox of many people living in great need of goods and services, while many workers couldn't get jobs to produce the things people needed. Of course, there were abuses of these "make work" projects. A standard joke was told of the government's hiring some workers to dig ditches and hiring other workers to fill them in again. Others told of public workers spending their days in parks, leaning on rakes or shovels. On balance, however, such schemes to move the country out of the Depression were looked upon favorably by the American public.

By the presidential election of 1936, the country was hardly back to normal, as the unemployment rates in Figure 9-6 show. But in a definite sign of approval of Roosevelt's policies, the people reelected him overwhelmingly, and he carried every state but Maine and Vermont.

Roosevelt and his advisers had by then developed their plans for government spending and government jobs to reduce unemployment. Even before this time, economists were providing theoretical reasons for just such approaches. Swedish economists such as Erik Lindahl and Gunnar Myrdal,[5] members of the Stockholm School, had been proposing in the late 1920s and early 1930s that governments abandon the goal of annually balancing the budget and aim only to balance it over the course of the business cycle. According to the Stockholm School, when output was falling and unemployment rising, government should spend more to put people back to work, even though this meant a government deficit. In boom times, the government could run a surplus by cutting back on its projects, thus cooling off the boom. Only over the entire course of a business cycle, then, would

---

[5]Myrdal was awarded the Nobel Prize in Economics in 1974. His early work in macroeconomics was noted in the award as well as his later work in sociology and development economics.

the government budget be balanced. This was the idea of government *stabilization policy,* or, particularly, *countercyclical policy.*

Much more influential than the Stockholm School was a book that came out in 1936, the year of Roosevelt's reelection. That book was *The General Theory of Employment, Interest, and Money,* by John Maynard Keynes. At that time, the Depression in the United States was to last over five more years before it would end by U.S. entry into World War II. Recovery from the Depression was already progressing in Great Britain (and in some other countries, including Nazi Germany). It is not true that Keynes, his theories, or his followers had much influence on either the British or U.S. recovery. However, the Depression convinced many people that the Keynesian theory was right and that it provided sound guidelines for economic policymaking.

THE DEMISE OF CLASSICAL MACROECONOMICS

Keynes's *General Theory* started the Keynesian revolution that overthrew the classical macroeconomic theory. For convenience and simplicity, we will not always separate the original ideas of Keynes from those of his followers. Instead, we will use the expression "Keynesian" to include both Keynes's arguments and those of later writers.

Three things must occur in order for an existing theory to be overturned as the most acceptable explanation of a particular economic experience. First, the theory must be demonstrated to be inconsistent with experience. Second, the theory must be shown to be based on faulty assumptions or reasoning. Third, a new and better explanation must be developed which is consistent with experience. Classical macroeconomic theory was the dominant economic theory as the Great Depression began. However, the severity and the length of the Great Depression demonstrated to many economists that this theoretical view of how capitalism worked was inconsistent with experience. Classical macroeconomic theory concluded that severe and prolonged periods of unemployment were unlikely. It also concluded that problems of unemployment in individual markets would be eliminated quickly through the automatic adjustment of wages and prices. Patience and the absence of government intervention were all that was required in order for the capitalistic economy to automatically readjust to full employment. After several years of economic depression, and with no relief in sight, economists could no longer accept classical macroeconomic theory. The theory was inconsistent with experience and the experience was very painful. Keynes showed the faults of classical macroeconomic theory and developed a superior explanation of economic activity, thus hastening the demise of the old ideas.

KEYNES'S CRITICISM OF CLASSICAL MACROECONOMICS

In *The General Theory,* Keynes expressed disagreement with each major aspect of classical macroeconomics: the quantity theory of money, Say's Law, and the theory of self-regulating markets.

stabilization policy
Government policy designed to stabilize the macro economy and smooth out its fluctuations.

countercylical policy
Government policy designed to offset the cyclical fluctuations of the macro economy.

Depression Era Soup Line

The Depression brought severe economic hardships to a large portion of the U.S. population. Real output fell by more than one third, and unemployment rose to almost 25 percent of the work force in the depths of the Depression. People who had jobs were worried they would lose them, and many of these jobs were reduced to a part-time basis in order to spread the work.

People were affected beyond the economic hardships. America seemed to have lost its bright promise. People who had worked hard all their lives, who had saved and planned for the future, and who had believed in the work ethic found themselves wiped out—losing their homes, businesses, jobs—through no fault of their own. Retired people found their stocks and bonds virtually worthless, and their bank accounts van-

ished in bank failures. Many people's self-image and status depend on their jobs, on their successes in the workaday world, and on their ability to provide for their families. The Depression sowed doubt and fear among those who lost their jobs and those in danger of losing theirs. When Franklin D. Roosevelt, in his first inaugural address, said, "The only thing we have to fear is fear itself," he was talking about the social, spiritual, and moral crisis in America as well as its economic problems.

The suffering during the Depression was not eased by such programs as unemployment insurance, welfare, Social Security, Medicare, etc., that we have today; these programs were in large part inspired by the experience of the Depression. In 1933, people out of work had to rely primarily on private charity and relief from state and local governments. These governments faced hard times themselves. Many municipal governments couldn't pay their debts and were in a poor position to help their residents. In addition, many people felt ashamed to take handouts from charity or the government, such as receiving food from soup lines.

The problems facing the country seemed clear. People had to be put back to work and, in the meantime, had to be given help. Beyond this, policies had to be adopted to insure that the Great Depression would never happen again. When people did suffer hard times, there should be programs to aid them as a matter of "right," so they needn't feel ashamed. To put people back to work, Roosevelt and his advisers experimented with government hiring programs. This policy was the forerunner of the popular view today that government should be the employer of last resort for people who can't find jobs elsewhere. Social welfare programs were introduced such as Old Age and Survivors Insurance and Aid to Dependent Children. Some proposals of the 1930s, such as national health insurance, are still being debated. Within the economics profession, the Depression and the resulting policies of the Roosevelt administration set the stage for the ascendency of the Keynesian revolution.

John Maynard Keynes *(1883–1946)*

John Maynard Keynes was from an academic family that was economically well off. His father, John Neville Keynes, was a well-known economist who taught at Cambridge. Born in Cambridge, England, the younger Keynes grew up in an atmosphere of witty, well-educated people who were passionately interested in the government policy issues of the day. All his life, Keynes was apparently able to dominate any group by his intelligence, conversation, and personality.

Keynes divided his life between teaching at Cambridge and active involvement in government and business affairs. Keynes went to the British Treasury, where he rose rapidly during World War I. In fact, Keynes was a member of the British delegation to the Versailles Peace Conference in 1919 that drafted and signed the peace treaty ending World War I. He was disillusioned by the negotiations at Versailles, and the peace treaty imposed on the losers, particularly the harsh conditions imposed on Germany. He wrote a book, *The Economic Consequences of the Peace,* that argued against the punishing economic conditions imposed on Germany on the grounds that they would lead to more trouble with that country in the future than would a fairer, less harsh treaty. This book ruined Keynes's career at the Treasury. He returned to Cambridge and turned to business, where he made a great deal of money in the financial markets. He also managed funds for Cambridge, to the University's great benefit.

Keynes was a principal member of the Bloomsbury Group, which included such literary people as Lytton Strachey, author of *Eminent Victorians,* and Leonard and Virginia Woolf. Keynes married a ballerina and was well-known for his interest and taste in the arts and literature. He wrote essays on policy topics and biographical essays on many people, including economists. He also wrote a small book on the theory of probability.

In the midst of all this activity, he kept up his work on macroeconomics. During the 1920s, he wrote the two-volume *Treatise on Money,* which was published in 1930, after the beginning of the Great Depression. The *Treatise* was basically a quantity theory approach to macro problems in the spirit of Keynes's teacher, Alfred Marshall. By the time the *Treatise* was published, Keynes was very dissatisfied with this approach and had begun what he called his "long struggle" to see macro questions in a different perspective from the quantity theory approach he had been taught. The new view Keynes was working toward was contained in his *General Theory of Employment, Interest, and Money* (1936). *The General Theory* was designed to do many things and answer many questions but aimed particularly to determine how economies had fallen into the Great Depression and how they could get out of it.

Keynes and the Quantity Theory of Money

The quantity theory of money was useful in describing the long-run movement of the economy from one equilibrium situation to another. It was based on the assumption that k and V were stable; yet Depression experience showed otherwise. Figure 9-7 shows that the velocity of money (and therefore k) was not stable during the Great Depression. The decrease in V during this period meant that k was increasing (remember that in equilibrium $V = 1/k$). An increase in k meant that society's demand for money, relative to GNP, was increasing. The quantity theory of money had no explanation for this sudden increase in the demand for money implied by the sharp drop in V.

Addressing the first weakness of the quantity theory of money, Keynes suggested that a theory which explained only the long-run view was not acceptable. He pointed out that we live in the short run and ". . . in the long run we're all dead!" Keynes set about developing a theory which could explain short-run economic activity and make policy recommendations to make the short run better.

Concerning the instability of V, k, and the demand for money, Keynes built on the work of his teacher, Alfred Marshall. Keynes reasoned that the demand for money was strongly influenced by factors other than the level of GNP. He

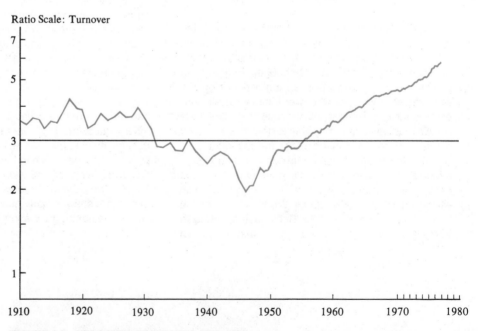

FIGURE 9-7 VELOCITY OF MONEY, 1910–1978

The velocity of money is equal to GNP divided by the money stock. At the start of the Depression, velocity fell sharply. Quantity theorists had no generally acceptable explanation for this. Instead, the quantity theory concentrated on long-run developments for the price level, and for this purpose assumed velocity was constant. (Source: *Historical Chart Book*, Board of Governors of the Federal Reserve System.)

acknowledged the transactions demand for money, but argued that people also want to hold money as a hedge against the uncertain yields on securities, such as stocks and bonds. He called this the *speculative motive* for holding money. Keynes reasoned that when expected yields on securities were high, people would prefer to hold more of their wealth in securities and less in money. If expected yields on securities were low, the opposite would be true; that is, people would avoid securities and hold more wealth in the form of money. We will examine this idea in greater detail in Chapter 12, when we discuss the modern quantity theory of money.

speculative motive The factor that makes people want to hold money as a hedge against the uncertain yields on securities.

Following this line of reasoning, Keynes was able to show that the expected yields on securities had a strong influence on the demand for money. If expected yields declined, then M^d would increase even if GNP were stable or declining. Thus, the increase in k and the decline in V during the depression could be explained by including the expected yields on securities as an important influence on the demand for money. Keynes extended this analysis to reach the conclusion that monetary policy was neither a strong nor a reliable tool for implementing economic policy. He favored using government expenditures and taxes for conducting economic policy.

Keynes on Say's Law

Keynes was particularly critical of the classical macroeconomic view of the credit market. In Chapter 8, we presented the idea that in the credit market, the interest rate would automatically adjust to equate savings by households, and investment spending by businesses. If saving was exactly offset by investment spending, Say's Law would hold true and overproduction would be impossible. Keynes argued that while saving and investment decisions were influenced by the interest rate, other influences were important, too, and could keep the interest rate from serving its vital function of equating saving and investment spending.

For example, Keynes identified the following noninterest rate motives for saving by individuals: (1) to build a reserve against unforeseen events; (2) for retirement; (3) for an increased standard of living; (4) to gain economic independence; (5) to build a reserve for speculative purposes; (6) to leave an inheritance; and (7) to satisfy greed.[6] These motives, he argued, generate saving regardless of the level of the interest rate.

Looking at business investment decisions, Keynes again concluded that the interest rate was only one factor to be considered. He argued that investment spending would take place only if business decision makers could expect to make a profit. While the cost of financing—the interest rate—was an important consideration in the business decision to invest, it was not the only consideration. Based on their expectation of the rate of profit for a given investment project, businesses would often borrow when interest rates were high and refuse to borrow when interest rates were low. Thus, Keynes would say that the classical economists were wrong about the causes of saving and investment. Given that both saving and investment respond strongly to influences other than the interest rate, Keynes

---

[6]J.M. Keynes, *The General Theory of Employment, Interest, and Money* (1936, reprint ed.; New York: Cambridge University Press, 1973), Chapter 9.

concluded that saving *could* exceed investment spending, making Say's Law invalid. Thus, prolonged, severe overproduction and unemployment were possible in a capitalistic economy.

Keynes on Self-Regulating Markets

Keynes also argued that neither the product nor labor markets could be counted on to adjust quickly and automatically to eliminate unemployment and overproduction. According to the classical macroeconomic theory, declining demand in individual markets would result in overproduction and unemployment. These problems would be eliminated as the unemployed workers competed for existing jobs and drove down wage rates. To the firm, these falling wage rates resulted in decreasing costs of production. With lower costs, the firm could lower prices and consequently increase sales. This would eliminate overproduction and lead to increased employment of labor.

Keynesians stressed that the existence of market power in the form of labor unions and large corporations would keep the markets from reaching their competitive equilibrium situations. First, in the face of rising unemployment, labor unions would fight to keep wage rates from declining as they attempted to protect their employed constituency. Because labor unions influenced the labor market, wage rates could not completely respond to the force of unemployment. Without declining wage rates, businesses could not profitably lower their prices. Second, in the face of overproduction, large corporations would choose to cut production levels rather than lower their prices and risk becoming involved in cutthroat price competition. Thus, Keynesians concluded that in a mature, capitalistic economic system, prices and wages were *sticky downward*. Without downward price and wage flexibility, the automatic adjustments in the individual product and labor markets were impossible.

sticky downward *The downward inflexibility of prices and wages.*

In summary, Keynes questioned both the stability of the demand for money and the general usefulness of the quantity theory of money. He argued that Say's Law was invalid and that prolonged periods of overproduction and unemployment *were* possible. Furthermore, no automatic mechanisms could be counted on to bring the economy out of a business downturn. Keynes believed that it was quite possible for the economy to become trapped in an equilibrium position with widespread unemployment. This, he concluded, was what had happened during the 1930s. Furthermore, only government intervention could bring the free enterprise economy out of the Great Depression.

KEYNESIAN ECONOMIC THEORY

During the Great Depression, the American economy was mired in a situation of severe unemployment. As we have seen, unemployment, on a national scale, was not dealt with in classical macroeconomic theory. In developing an alternative theory, Keynes and his followers raised the important question of, How is the level of employment determined in a capitalistic economy? They knew that if employment could be explained, then unemployment could be, too. In attempting to identify the cause of employment, Keynesians reasoned as follows:

1. The level of employment is determined in the business sector and is directly related to the level of production.

2. In a modern capitalistic economy, the level of business production will be determined by the amount of spending to purchase business products. Businesses will adjust their level of production to accommodate the demand for their products. Put simply, "Supply adjusts to demand." This is in contrast to Say's Law, "Supply creates its own demand."

3. Since employment depends on production and production responds to spending, the level of employment in a capitalistic economy is ultimately determined by the level of spending (or demand) in the economy.

Using this simple but logical analysis, the cause of high national levels of unemployment was brought into sharp focus. If a high level of unemployment existed, it was because spending for business production was insufficient to cause businesses to operate at a full-employment level of production. Thus, insufficient spending was recognized as the cause of unemployment. To remedy high unemployment, spending had to be increased.

Economists refer to total planned spending for goods and services as aggregate demand. If full employment was accepted as a desirable economic and social goal, then Keynes argued that business should be induced to produce an output which would accomplish full employment. Since aggregate supply responds to aggregate demand, the government should assure that the level of aggregate demand would result in a full-employment level of aggregate supply. The difficulty lay in determining how aggregate demand could be manipulated by the government.

Keynes separated aggregate demand into its individual components. If aggregate demand is to be manipulated, then we should understand what we are trying to manipulate. We know that aggregate demand consists of spending from four different sectors of the economy as described in equation (9-1):

$$AD = C + I + G + (X - M), \qquad (9\text{-}1)$$

where AD = aggregate demand

$\quad C$ = planned spending by households for consumption purposes

$\quad I$ = planned spending by businesses for investment

$\quad G$ = spending by government for goods and services

$(X - M)$ = the net effect of spending resulting from foreign trade (exports-imports).

By examining equation (9-1), you can see that AD will increase if one or more of its components, $C, I, G,$ or $(X - M),$ increases.

It is obvious from equation (9-1) that a simple, direct way to increase AD is to increase G. Keynes recommended increases in government expenditures and this was done in several capitalistic economies. More importantly, Keynes developed a model of the economic system which demonstrated how the economy operated in the short run and how the government could act to promote full employment. This model is based on Keynes's theory of consumption spending; that is, his explanation of the cause of spending by individuals.

The Theory of Consumption Spending

Although Keynes acknowledged that there were several factors which influenced the level of consumption or consumer spending, he believed that, of these, income was most important. The Keynesian model is based on the idea that consumption spending is related to the amount of income available to the consumer. Keynes combined two old ideas (statements 1 and 2 below) with an idea of his own (statement 3 below) to develop his theory of consumption spending:

1. Consumption spending is directly related to disposable income. As disposable income increases, spending increases.

2. As disposable income increases, the portion of disposable income spent decreases.

3. For any change in disposable income, there is a corresponding, but smaller, change in spending that is stable and predictable.

consumption function   The relationship between the level of consumption demand and the economy's real disposable income.

In Chapter 10, we will develop an analytical framework for the economy based on this theory of consumer spending. Here, we want to develop a more intuitive understanding of Keynesian economics. The Keynesian *consumption function* is defined as the relationship between the current level of consumption spending *(C)* and the current level of disposable income *(Y_d)*. This consumption function is consistent with the above three statements regarding income and spending, and implies that a change in disposable income will result in a change in consumption spending.

Suppose that disposable income is at Y_{d1} and, therefore, consumer spending is C_1. Further, suppose that the economy is in a situation of high unemployment, and, to alleviate this, the government wants to increase aggregate demand without increasing its own expenditures. Consumer spending can be increased from C_1 to C_2 if disposable income is increased from Y_{d1} to Y_{d2}. But how can government accomplish this increase in disposable income? Since disposable income is essentially personal income less taxes, the government can change Y_d by changing the tax rate on personal income. Thus, Keynes argued that the government had indirect control over consumer spending through its ability to change disposable income by taxation. To increase consumer spending, income taxes should be lowered (disposable income increases), and to decrease consumer spending, income taxes should be raised (disposable income decreases).

Keynes and Investment Spending

Keynes recognized that business attitudes about the future had a significant influence on investment decisions. Attitudes about the future affected the calculations of expected sales revenue and expected profits. The decision to undertake an investment project requires that its expected rate of profit exceed the cost of financing. Keynes called attention to the fact that attitudes or expectations about the future are an important factor in the business investment decision.

One of the factors which has a strong influence on business expectations is the recent trend in sales. If consumption spending trends are up, then business expectations will be generally optimistic. This will have a positive influence on expected revenues and profits and will encourage business investment spending. If consumption spending trends are down, the process works in reverse and discourages business investment spending. Keynes believed that expectations sometimes would be more important than interest rates in determining business investment spending; that is, high interest rates may not necessarily discourage, nor low interest rates encourage, investment spending. During the 1930s, Keynes believed that the low (and declining) levels of investment were the result of bleak expectations concerning future business activity, despite extremely low interest rates.

THE KEYNESIAN EXPLANATION OF THE GREAT DEPRESSION

The Great Depression resulted from many complex forces and cannot be explained by a single cause or event. Keynesian economics offered the best explanation as to why aggregate demand fell so dramatically from 1929 to 1933. It also explained why the economy did not recover automatically as classical macroeconomics indicated it should.

Keynesian economics explained the decline in aggregate demand from 1929–1933 as follows: After several years of rising consumption and business investment spending brought on by the economic expansion of the 1920s, the rate of expansion began to slow. Business expectations did not become gloomy, but optimism about the future declined. Businesses responded by slowing the rate of investment spending which resulted in a decline in employment. When employment declined, income declined and consumption spending fell. This influenced investment spending decisions as falling consumption spending dampened expectations. As expectations became gloomier, business investment spending fell further, causing more declines in employment, income, and consumption spending. This spiral continued and aggregate demand plummeted.

The consumer sector decreased spending because there were fewer jobs and less income. Businesses reduced output because they couldn't sell their products. Businesses weren't spending for investment purposes because they had little confidence in the future. In fact, business decision makers had such a pessimistic attitude about the future that they weren't even replacing their machinery as it wore out. To many people, it seemed as though the whole system had become irrational. Nothing made sense. Table 9-1 shows how consumption and investment spending fluctuated during the Great Depression. Although these data do not prove that the Keynesian explanation was correct, they do show that the declines in C and I were correlated.

Keynesian economic theory suggested a solution to the Great Depression: The government should intervene in the capitalistic economy and use its power to tax and spend to increase aggregate demand. In particular, the government

**TABLE 9-1   CONSUMPTION AND INVESTMENT
EXPENDITURES DURING THE
DEPRESSION**
(billions of dollars)

Year	Consumption Expenditures	Investment Expenditures
1929	79.0	16.2
1930	71.0	10.3
1931	61.3	5.5
1932	49.3	.9
1933	46.4	1.4
1934	51.9	2.9
1935	56.3	6.3
1936	62.6	8.4
1937	67.3	11.7
1938	64.6	6.7
1939	67.6	9.3
1940	71.9	13.2
1941	81.9	18.1

Source: *Economic Report of the President,* various issues.

should spend more, or tax less, or both. This was difficult advice for government leaders to follow in an era of *laissez-faire* capitalism. With few exceptions, Keynes's prescriptions went unheeded until World War II. The process of rearming to fight the war forced the United States to increase aggregate demand through increased government spending without commensurate increases in taxation. By 1943, the unemployment rate in the United States had fallen to 1.9 percent. Keynesian economic policy had been used to end the Great Depression (not by choice) because war necessitated it.

THE POLITICS OF THE KEYNESIAN REVOLUTION

The Keynesian revolution was a huge political success, as well as an economic one. It is impossible to separate its success among economic thinkers from its success among politicians. It is easy to understand why Keynes's theories were so popular with politicians. The Depression brought a great deal of suffering. Classical economic theory offered no solution except to wait until prices fell, markets readjusted, and equilibrium was restored. In short, classical economic policy would suggest doing nothing until, in the long run, the economy returned to its full-employment equilibrium position. Keynes believed policy should be used to make things better now. Policy aimed at making things better is very attractive to politicians. Would you rather vote for a politician who said, "Do nothing—wait for things to get better," or for one who said, "We have a problem; here's how we can solve it"? Keynesian theory gave politicians a program designed to solve economic problems. They could be activists. You will see the political implications of Keynesian policy as we develop our analysis more fully in the next two chapters.

SUMMARY

1. This chapter focuses on three major points: the historical fluctuations in economic activity of the United States; Keynes's criticism of classical macroeconomic theory; and the Keynesian revolution which accompanied his alternative economic theories.

2. On the average, the United States has had a recession every four and one-half years since the Civil War. Before World War II, these recessions were accompanied by falling prices.

3. During the period 1950–1981, periods of recession were accompanied by inflation, giving rise to the term, stagflation. Simultaneous unemployment and inflation forces policymakers into a dilemma over which problem to deal with first.

4. The Great Depression began in August, 1929, when industrial production began to fall. This was two months before the stock market crash of October, 1929.

5. Between 1929 and 1933, the general level of prices and wages fell by about one third, as did real output. Unemployment rose from 3 percent to 25 percent of the labor force. One fifth of all banks failed, resulting in a loss of 10 percent of all bank deposits.

6. While the stock market crash didn't start the Depression, the crash, together with the bank failures, frightened investors badly. This drove down the prices of private sector securities (stocks and bonds) that were seen as risks.

7. The classical macroeconomic theory offered no practical explanation of the economic slump, nor any practical advice on how to get the economy going again. John Maynard Keynes found fault with this theory and pointed out its errors.

8. Keynes concluded that interest rates, prices, and wages were sticky downward and could not be counted on to prevent overproduction and unemployment. Keynes believed that, contrary to classical macroeconomic theory, the economy could go into a slump (recession) and stay there.

9. Focusing on insufficient aggregate demand as the cause of the high level of unemployment, Keynes urged governments to intervene to stimulate economic activity.

10. Keynes developed economic theories to explain the causes of consumer and business investment spending. He cited disposable income as the primary cause of consumer spending and identified the importance of expectations to business investment decisions.

11. Keynes explained the cause of the Great Depression by showing that consumer and business investment spending could interact to produce declines in economic activity. Most of the capitalistic economies were still mired in a state of economic depression as World War II began.

12. Keynesian analysis was popular with policymakers because it justified active intervention to improve economic conditions.

NEW TERMS

Great Depression
recession
bimetallism

stagflation
stock market crash
stabilization policy

countercyclical policy
speculative motive

sticky downward
consumption function

QUESTIONS FOR DISCUSSION

1. Explain the pressures for monetary reform during the late 1800s in the United States.

2. What is stagflation? In what sense is it a new phenomenon?

3. How has the pattern of inflation changed since the post-Civil War period?

4. What are some of the major facts that indicate the severity of the Great Depression?

5. Explain how the Keynesian revolution gained recognition and acceptance so easily.

SUGGESTIONS FOR FURTHER READING

Allen, Frederick Lewis. *Only Yesterday: An Informal History of the Nineteen Twenties.* New York: Harper and Row, Pubs., Inc., 1957.

Dauten, Carl A., and Lloyd M. Valentine. *Business Cycles and Forecasting,* 5h ed. Cincinnati: South-Western Publishing Co., 1978.

Friedman, Milton, and Anna Schwartz. *A Monetary History of the United States, 1867–1960.* Princeton, N.J.: Princeton University Press, 1963.

Galbraith, John Kenneth. *The Great Crash Nineteen Twenty Nine,* 3d ed. Boston: Houghton Mifflin Co., 1972.

Russell, Bertrand. *The Autobiography of Bertrand Russell, 1872–1914.* Winchester, MA: Allen & Unwin, Inc., 1967.

Schlesinger, Arthur. *The Age of Roosevelt.* Vol. I, *The Crisis of the Old Order, 1919–1933* (1957); Vol. II, *The Coming of the New Deal* (1959); Vol. III, *The Politics of Upheaval* (1960). Boston: Houghton Mifflin Co.

Shepherd, Jean. *In God We Trust: All Others Pay Cash.* New York: Doubleday and Co., Inc., 1966.

Terkel, Studs. *Hard Times: An Oral History of the Great Depression in America.* New York: Pantheon Books, 1970.

CHAPTER 10

The Keynesian Model

Learning Objectives

After studying the materials found in this chapter, you should be able to do the following:

1. Explain the major difference between Keynes and the classical economists regarding the equilibrium level of national income and output.

2. Define:
   (a) consumption function.
   (b) marginal propensity to consume.
   (c) marginal propensity to save.
   (d) expenditure multiplier.

3. Find the equilibrium level of national income by both tabular and graphical analyses using the following approaches:
   (a) aggregate supply equals aggregate demand.
   (b) leakages equal injections.

4. Explain how unintended business inventory changes act to bring aggregate supply into equality with aggregate demand.

5. Calculate the value of the multiplier, given either the MPC or the MPS.

6. Calculate the change in the equilibrium national income, given the initial change in aggregate demand and the value of the multiplier.

7. Explain the paradox of thrift.

In this chapter, the Keynesian model for the determination of national income and output will be developed. This theoretical view of the capitalistic economic system stands in sharp contrast to the classical macroeconomic theory. Based on a belief in Say's Law and self-regulating markets, classical economists concluded that the capitalistic economy would move automatically to an equilibrium level of national income and output which assured full employment of resources.

However, Keynes was highly critical of this view and the contention that a condition of full employment of resources was the only possible equilibrium for the economy. Keynes and others pointed out that the predictions of classical theory and the experience of the 1930s were inconsistent. To them, the Great

Depression demonstrated that the economy could become trapped at an equilibrium level of national income and output far below that required for full employment of resources. On one technical point Keynes and the classical economists were in total agreement; that is, Keynes agreed that the economy would move automatically to an equilibrium level of national income and output, where aggregate supply and aggregate demand were equal. However, Keynes contended that it was quite possible for the economy to reach this equilibrium with a high level of unemployment, and he developed a model of the economy which explained how this could happen.

Two of Keynes's insights, which we mentioned in Chapter 9, are essential to the development of the Keynesian model. First, Keynes argued that supply adjusts to demand; that is, businesses will adjust their level of output to meet the demand for output. For the macro economy, this means that aggregate supply is influenced by aggregate demand. But what determines the level of aggregate demand? Keynes believed that aggregate demand, particularly consumption expenditures, was strongly influenced by income. As we discussed, income (wages, salaries, rent, interest, and profit) is received by owners of factors of production which are used to produce society's output. Putting all this together, Keynes reasoned that aggregate demand determined aggregate supply and national income, but aggregate demand was itself influenced by national income. Thus, Keynes recognized that aggregate demand, aggregate supply, and national income were *interdependent;* that is, their values were jointly determined. The Keynesian model demonstrates that the equilibrium level of national income is determined through the interaction of aggregate demand and aggregate supply. It also shows that an equilibrium level of national income and output does not necessarily insure full employment.

This chapter focuses on the relationship between consumption expenditures and disposable income, a relationship known as the consumption function and the foundation upon which the Keynesian model is built. Following this, aggregate demand and aggregate supply are developed. We then demonstrate how the equilibrium level of national income and output is determined through the interaction of aggregate supply and aggregate demand. Next, the multiplier concept is introduced to show how changes in aggregate demand affect national income and output. Finally, the paradox of thrift is discussed, and the chapter concludes by showing how changes in export and import spending influence the domestic economy.

THE FOUNDATIONS OF THE KEYNESIAN MODEL

In Chapter 9, aggregate demand *(AD)* was defined as total planned spending for the economy's output. It was shown that aggregate demand was composed of spending from the consumer, business investment, government, and foreign sectors of the economy:

$$AD = C + I + G + (X - M). \tag{10-1}$$

The first step in constructing the Keynesian model is to develop the *aggregate demand schedule,* which shows the relationship between aggregate demand and national income at various levels of national income. We begin by explaining how consumption expenditures *(C)* are influenced by national income.

Consumption Expenditures (C)

Keynes argued that the amount consumers spend depends on their disposable income. Keynes called this relationship the consumption function and made it a key part of his theory. The consumption function is any equation, table, or graph which shows the relationship between income received by consumers (disposable income) and the amount they plan, or desire, to spend on currently produced final output. Assume that for a hypothetical economy, the consumption function is expressed by the equation

$$C = \$200 \text{ billion} + 0.8\ Y_d, \qquad (10\text{-}2)[1]$$

where C is consumption expenditures and Y_d is disposable income.

Notice that the Keynesian consumption function relates consumer spending to disposable income, not national income. In developing the Keynesian model, we want to relate aggregate demand to national income. From Chapter 7 we know that the relationship between national income and disposable income is:

$$Y_d = Y - T, \qquad (10\text{-}3)[2]$$

where Y is national income and T is personal taxes. By substituting equation (10-3) into (10-2), we can express consumption expenditures as a function of national income:

$$C = \$200 \text{ billion} + 0.8(Y - T). \qquad (10\text{-}4)$$

If we know the level of personal taxes *(T)*, the level of consumption expenditures can be determined for various levels of national income. In our hypothetical economy, we will assume that personal taxes are constant at $100 billion and, therefore, do not vary as national income changes.[3] Table 10-1 shows the consumption function in tabular form. It is derived by choosing various values for national income *(Y)* and then subtracting personal taxes *(T)* to determine disposable income *(Y_d)*. The values for planned consumption expenditures *(C)* are obtained by substituting the values of Y_d into equation (10-2) and solving for C. For example, if $Y_d = \$1,200$ billion, then $C = \$200$ billion $+ 0.8\,(\$1,200$ billion$)$

[1] This mathematical expression of the consumption function is consistent with Keynes's ideas regarding the relationship between consumer spending and disposable income discussed in the previous chapter. Virtually all presentations of the simple Keynesian model express the consumption function in this straight-line format.

[2] For simplification, we are ignoring the minor differences between personal income and national income, and we are assuming that the two income concepts are identical.

[3] In reality, personal taxes do vary as national income varies. While it would be more realistic to show that taxes are related proportionally or even progressively to income, this would complicate the analysis unnecessarily. In the computerized models of the economy used by consulting firms and the government, it is appropriate to use more realistic (and more complicated) relationships between variables. Through the assumptions we make in this and later chapters, the sophistication and complication of the economic models are reduced, while the essential features of their operation are maintained.

TABLE 10-1   PLANNED CONSUMPTION EXPENDITURES (C) AND PLANNED SAVING (S) AT VARIOUS LEVELS OF NATIONAL INCOME (Y) (billions)

National Income	Personal Taxes	Disposable Income	Change in Disposable Income	Planned Consumption Spending	Change in Consumption Spending	Planned Saving	Change in Saving
Y	T	Y_d	ΔY_d	C	ΔC	S	ΔS
(1)	(2)	(3)	(4)	(5)	(6)	(7)	(8)
$ 700	$ 100	$ 600	$ —	$ 680	$ —	$ −80	$—
900	100	800	200	840	160	−40	40
1,100	100	1,000	200	1,000	160	0	40
1,300	100	1,200	200	1,160	160	40	40
1,500	100	1,400	200	1,320	160	80	40
1,700	100	1,600	200	1,480	160	120	40
1,900	100	1,800	200	1,640	160	160	40
2,100	100	2,000	200	1,800	160	200	40

= $1,160 billion. Column 7 in Table 10-1 is Planned Saving. Where do those figures come from? Recall from Chapter 7 that saving (S) is that part of disposable income which is not spent. Therefore,

$$S = Y_d - C. \tag{10-5}$$

The MPC and MPS

Keynes believed that changes in disposable income caused consumer spending to change, but by a smaller amount. This idea was so important to his theories that Keynes gave it a name, the **marginal propensity to consume (MPC)**, which is defined as the ratio of the change in planned consumption spending (ΔC) to the change in disposable income (ΔY_d):

marginal propensity to consume (MPC) *The fraction of any change in income that is consumed; the MPS is greater than zero and less than one, and MPC + MPS = 1.*

$$\text{Marginal Propensity to Consume } (MPC) = \frac{\Delta C}{\Delta Y_d}. \tag{10-6}$$

A companion concept, the **marginal propensity to save (MPS)** is defined as the ratio of the change in planned saving to the change in disposable income:

marginal propensity to save (MPS) *The fraction of any change in income that is saved; the MPS is greater than zero and less than one, and MPC + MPS = 1.*

$$\text{Marginal Propensity to Save } (MPS) = \frac{\Delta S}{\Delta Y_d}. \tag{10-7}$$

Values of the MPC and MPS are not shown in Table 10-1, but can be easily obtained using the information in columns 4, 6 and 8. For instance, when Y_d increases from $1,000 to $1,200 billion, C increases from $1,000 to $1,160 billion and S increases from $0 to $40 billion. Thus, for ΔY_d = $200 billion, ΔC =

$160 billion and $\Delta S = \$40$ billion. To calculate the values of the MPC and MPS, we substitute this information into equations (10-6) and (10-7):

$$MPC = \frac{\Delta C}{\Delta Y_d} = \frac{\$160 \text{ billion}}{\$200 \text{ billion}} = 4/5 \text{ or } 0.8,$$

$$MPS = \frac{\Delta S}{\Delta Y_d} = \frac{\$40 \text{ billion}}{\$200 \text{ billion}} = 1/5 \text{ or } 0.2.$$

Note that the MPC is 4/5 and the MPS is 1/5 of the change in income, so the sum of the MPC and the MPS equals 1. That this will always be true, whatever the value of the MPC, follows from the fact that all consumer income not spent on final goods and services is saved. When income rises by $500 billion, the part spent is the MPC times $500 billion. The part *not* spent is $(1 - MPC)$ times $500 billion. The part not spent is the change in saving, the MPS times $500 billion. In other words:

$$MPS = 1 - MPC$$

$$MPC + MPS = 1.$$

If the MPC were .9, the MPS would have to be .1. If 9/10 of an increase in income is spent, only 1/10 is saved.

The consumption expenditure schedule shows consumption *demand,* or *planned* consumption, and the saving schedule shows *planned* saving. Of course, in reality, actual consumption expenditures and saving are not always equal to the planned values, but we can learn much from simple models. This basic Keynesian model assumes that households do consume and save the amounts they intend to.

Figure 10-1 graphically depicts the information in Table 10-1. The MPC shows up indirectly in Table 10-1, and is also implied by the consumption expenditures *(C)* line in Figure 10-1. The MPC is the slope of the consumption expenditure *(C)* line. You should recall (see the appendix of Chapter 2) that the slope of a line is the ratio of the change in the variable on the vertical axis to the change in the variable on the horizontal axis as you move along the line to the right. In this case, the slope is the ratio of the change in C to the change in Y. Symbolically, this is $\Delta C / \Delta Y$, which, by definition, is the MPC. In the same way, the slope of the saving function is the MPS ($\Delta S / \Delta Y$). Since the MPS equals 1 minus the MPC, the slope of the consumption function is greater than the slope of the saving function if the MPC is larger than 0.5. This explains why the two lines have different slopes in Figure 10-1.

Completing the Aggregate Demand Schedule

The relationship between consumption expenditures and national income shown in Table 10-1 is reproduced in columns 1 through 4 of Table 10-2. With this important foundation established, we can quickly complete the aggregate demand schedule by including expenditures from the other sectors of our hypothetical economy in Table 10-2.

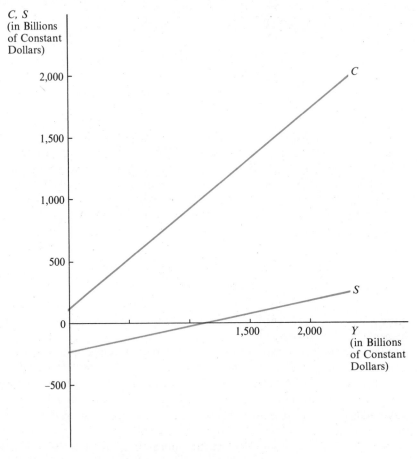

**FIGURE 10-1   PLANNED CONSUMPTION AND
PLANNED SAVING SCHEDULES**

The consumption function shows the relationship between planned consumption and
national income. Similarly, the saving function shows the relationship between
planned saving and national income.

In order to simplify our analysis we will assume that the levels of business
investment *(I)*, government *(G)*, and foreign sector spending *(X − M)* are
exogenously determined. This means that *I, G,* and *(X − M)* are determined by
economic or political forces which are resolved outside our simple Keynesian
model. These expenditures are independent of the level of national income. Later
we will consider the outside forces which influence *I, G,* and *(X − M)*.

Business Investment Expenditures (I)

Business investment expenditures *(I)* are assumed to be exogenously determined
and constant at $50 billion. This is shown in Table 10-2, column 6. Keynesian
economic theory holds that monetary policy influences *I* through changes in the
interest rate.

TABLE 10-2   THE AGGREGATE DEMAND *(AD)*
SCHEDULE (billions)

1 National Income (AS = Y)	2 Personal Taxes T	3 Disposable Income Y_d	4 Consumption Expenditures C	5 Business Investment Expenditures I	6 Government Expenditures G	7 Net Export Expenditures (X − M)	8 Aggregate Demand C + I + G + (X − M)
$ 1,100	$ 100	$ 1,000	$ 1,000	$ 50	$150	$100	$ 1,300
1,300	100	1,200	1,160	50	150	100	1,460
1,500	100	1,400	1,320	50	150	100	1,620
1,700	100	1,600	1,480	50	150	100	1,780
1,900	100	1,800	1,640	50	150	100	1,940
2,100	100	2,000	1,800	50	150	100	2,100
2,300	100	2,200	1,960	50	150	100	2,260
2,500	100	2,400	2,120	50	150	100	2,420
2,700	100	2,600	2,280	50	150	100	2,580

Government Expenditures (G)

Government expenditures are also assumed to be exogenously determined and constant at $150 billion. This is shown in Table 10-2, column 7. Later, we will see that by varying its expenditures, the government can significantly influence the equilibrium level of national income and output.

To complete the determination of the aggregate demand *(AD)* schedule we will assume that both export *(X)* and import *(M)* spending are exogenously determined and are constant at $200 billion and $100 billion, respectively. Thus, net exports *(X − M)* are constant and equal to $100 billion. Later in this chapter we will show how changes in the foreign sector influence the domestic economy according to the Keynesian model.

As we noted earlier, the aggregate demand schedule shows total planned spending in the economy at various levels of national income. Recall also that aggregate demand *(AD)* is calculated by summing up the spending from each sector of the economy:

$$AD = C + I + G + (X − M). \qquad (10\text{-}1)$$

Column 8 of Table 10-2 is the sum of $C + I + G + (X − M)$ and, therefore, shows the level of aggregate demand for each level of national income.

The information from Table 10-2 is shown graphically in the aggregate demand schedule in Figure 10-2. Because the graph conveys information more efficiently, we will utilize it extensively throughout the remainder of the text. Since an understanding of the *AD* schedule in its graphical form is important to the analysis which follows, let's look at how it is derived.

The aggregate demand *(AD)* schedule in Figure 10-2 is derived as follows: First, the consumption expenditure schedule is constructed by plotting the relationship between *C* and *Y* (columns 1 and 4 from Table 10-2). This gives us the *C* line. The *C + I* line is then constructed by vertically adding *I* (which is $50

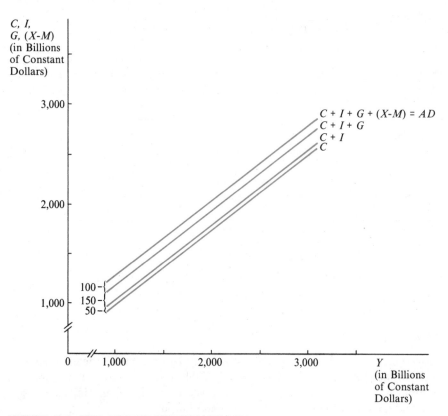

**FIGURE 10-2   THE AGGREGATE DEMAND (AD)
SCHEDULE**

Aggregate demand (AD) is equal to $C + I + G + (X - M)$. The AD schedule is constructed by first plotting the consumption expenditure schedule (C line); then, in sequence, by adding I, G, and $(X - M)$ values to obtain the $C + I$, $C + I + G$, and $C + I + G + (X - M)$ lines. By definition, the $C + I + G + (X - M)$ line is the aggregate demand (AD) schedule.

billion) to each amount of C. Similarly, the $C + I + G$ line is constructed by vertically adding G (which is \$150 billion) to each amount of $C + I$. Finally, the $C + I + G + (X - M)$ line is constructed by vertically adding $(X - M)$ (which is \$100 billion) to each amount of $C + I + G$. The $C + I + G + (X - M)$ line is, by definition, the aggregate demand line or schedule and shows total spending in the economy at each possible level of national income.

The Aggregate Supply Schedule

The aggregate supply schedule shows the relationship between aggregate supply (AS) and national income at various levels of national income. Conceptually, AS is identical to gross national product because both refer to the total value of output produced in the economy. Although GNP and national income are not identical concepts, the differences between them are minor and unimportant to the development of the Keynesian model. Thus, for purposes of simplification, the differences between GNP and Y will be ignored.

Since, within our model, AS and Y are both equal to GNP, they are equal to each other:

$$AS = Y. \qquad (10\text{-}8)$$

This is consistent with the idea that the total value of output and the total income generated from the production of output are equal. As equation (10-8) shows, aggregate supply and national income are the same for each level of national income.[4] The aggregate supply schedule described by equation (10-8) is shown in Figure 10-3. Various levels of AS are shown on the vertical axis and the corresponding, equal levels of Y are shown on the vertical axis. Since the scales on the two axes are identical, the aggregate supply schedule is a 45° line passing through the origin.

We can now combine the aggregate demand and aggregate supply schedules to determine the equilibrium level of national income and output.

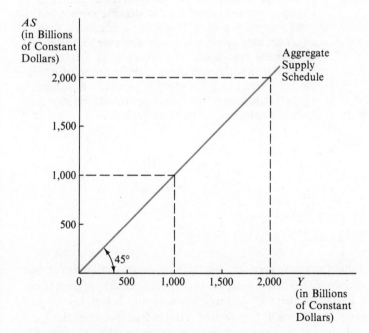

FIGURE 10-3   THE AGGREGATE SUPPLY SCHEDULE
          (45° line)

Given several simplifying assumptions made in this chapter, aggregate supply and national income are equal ($AS = Y$). The aggregate supply schedule is thus a 45° line passing through the origin. When $Y = $1,000$ billion, $AS = $1,000$ billion; when $Y = $2,000$ billion, $AS = $2,000$ billion; etc.

---

[4]This does not imply that Y causes AS. It is more correct to think in terms of aggregate supply determining income. As we noted earlier, the equilibrium level of AS, AD, and Y are jointly determined.

Tenn-Tom: Can Government Spending Projects Ever Be Stopped?

Keynesian economists suggest the institution of government spending and public works projects when the economy is at less than full employment. These public works projects, however, often take a great deal of time to finish. Their usefulness as a countercyclical tool is limited, because some of the spending may occur at the wrong part of the cycle. In addition, these projects are rarely stopped: once started, they seem to take on a life of their own.

The Tennessee-Tombigbee Waterway is a case study of such spending. The Tenn-Tom project is a channeling of the Tombigbee River between the Tennessee River and Demopolis, Alabama. The Tennessee River will then be opened to the Gulf of Mexico.

When the project began in 1971, the Corps of Engineers estimated its cost at $386 million. In 1981, with an estimated completion date of 1988, the estimated total cost was $1.8 billion. The General Accounting Office now warns that additional billions will be needed to open the river between Demopolis and Mobile. President Carter tried to stop the project, but ignited so much political heat that he dropped it. One argument that supporters made was that $1.1 billion had already been spent. The popularity of such arguments shows why public works projects are so hard to control. Once Congress starts a project, it is almost impossible to stop it. Even the Reagan administration's cutbacks have not yet touched Tenn-Tom.

EQUILIBRIUM IN THE MACRO ECONOMY—THE KEYNESIAN CROSS

Keynesian Cross   A graph that illustrates the intersection of the AD and AS lines. This intersection is the equilibrium level of national income.

Keynes concluded that the macro economy would move to an equilibrium at that level of national income *(Y)* where aggregate supply *(AS)* equals aggregate demand *(AD)*. The aggregate demand and aggregate supply schedules for our hypothetical economy are shown in Figure 10-4. Notice that the schedules have different slopes and, therefore, they intersect. A graph of the *AS* and *AD* schedules that shows this intersection is often referred to as the *Keynesian Cross,* because the point where the schedules cross defines the equilibrium level of national income. At $Y = \$2,100$ billion, the *AS* and *AD* schedules cross, and this, by definition, is the equilibrium level of *Y*.

In order to understand why the economy will move automatically to an equilibrium level of national income and output, we need to consider the crucial role that inventories and, particularly, unintended inventory changes play in business production decisions.

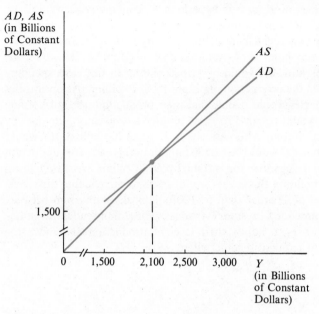

AD, AS
(in Billions
of Constant
Dollars)

FIGURE 10-4   THE KEYNESIAN CROSS

The equilibrium level of national income occurs where aggregate supply and aggregate demand are equal. Using graphical analysis, this equality of aggregate supply and demand occurs where the *AS* and *AD* schedules intersect. The term *Keynesian Cross* refers to the determination of equilibrium *Y* by the crossing of the *AS* and *AD* schedules. In this figure, equilibrium *Y* = $2,100 billion.

The Crucial Role of Unintended Business Inventory Changes

Inventories are the stock of goods which have been produced by businesses but have not yet been sold. Businesses maintain inventories because they do not want to risk losing sales to their competition when a desired item is out of stock.[5] Most businesses have determined the level of inventory that they wish to maintain and it is usually related in some way to sales. For instance, a firm may desire to maintain an inventory of goods equal to twice the amount usually sold during a month. In this sense, inventories act as a safety cushion or buffer between production and sales. When the actual level of inventory rises above or falls below the level desired by the firm, we say that **unintended business inventory changes** occur. Significant unintended changes in the level of inventories are a signal that the level of production is inconsistent with the trend in sales. Failure to respond to this situation could prove very costly. When sales exceed production, inventories decline and eventually put the business in a position of being unable to supply all its customers. When production exceeds sales, inventories increase, requiring the business to invest larger amounts of financial resources in inventories. Businesses, therefore, have very strong incentives to respond to unintended changes in the level of inventories.

inventories   The stock of goods that have been produced by businesses but have not yet been sold.

unintended business inventory changes   Changes that occur when the inventory level rises above or falls below that desired by the firm, because the production level is inconsistent with the trend in sales.

---

[5]Refer to your own experience. What did you do the last time you tried to purchase an item in a store and were told by the salesperson that the item was sold out? You probably went elsewhere to make your purchase. The store which was out of the item not only lost the sale, but created a poor image in your mind and allowed a competitor the opportunity to make you their customer.

The equilibrium level of Y for our hypothetical economy is $2,100 billion, because at other levels, unintended inventory changes occur. These unintended inventory changes bring aggregate supply into equality with aggregate demand.[6] Table 10-3 illustrates this point. For example, if $Y = \$1,500$ billion, then AS would be $1,500 billion and AD would be $1,620 billion. In this case, spending for output would exceed the production of output by $120 billion. As inventories begin to decline, businesses would realize that their production was not keeping pace with sales. They would respond to these unintended inventory changes by increasing their level of output. Alternatively, if $Y = \$2,700$ billion, AS would also be $2,700 billion, but AD would be $2,580 billion. In this case, the production of output would exceed spending for output by $120 billion, resulting in an unintended inventory buildup. Businesses would respond by reducing their level of output. At any level of Y other than $2,100 billion, disequilibrium between AS and AD causes unintended inventory changes. These unintended inventory changes prompt businesses to adjust their level of production and move the economy to the level of national income where $AS = AD$.

**TABLE 10-3   UNINTENDED INVENTORY CHANGES
AND THE EQUILIBRIUM LEVEL OF
NATIONAL INCOME (billions)**

National Income	Aggregate Supply	Aggregate Demand	Unintended Inventory Changes	Business Response	Effect on National Income
Y	AS	AD	$(AS-AD)$		
$1,500	$1,500	$1,620	$ −120	Increase AS	Increase
1,800	1,800	1,860	− 60	Increase AS	Increase
2,100	2,100	2,100	0	Maintain AS	No change
2,400	2,400	2,340	+ 60	Decrease AS	Decrease
2,700	2,700	2,580	+120	Decrease AS	Decrease

*Equilibrium in the Macro Economy—Leakages
Equal Injections*

An alternative method exists for determining the equilibrium level of Y. It involves finding the level of national income where leakages from and injections into spending are equal. Leakages include all national income which is not directly spent in the domestic economy: personal taxes (T), saving (S), and spending for imports (M). Injections include all spending in the domestic economy other than that derived directly from national income (i.e., consumption spending): investment (I), government expenditures (G), and spending for exports (X). Table 10-4 and Figure 10-5 demonstrate this method for determining equilibrium.

---

[6]In the simplest sense, the driving force of the Keynesian model is the self-interested behavior of business managers. Profit maximizing behavior requires that output be adjusted to the level of demand for the product.

TABLE 10-4   FINDING EQUILIBRIUM *Y* USING THE LEAKAGES EQUAL INJECTIONS APPROACH (billions)

National Income $AS=Y$	Personal Taxes T	Saving S	Import Expenditures M	Total Leakages $T+S+M$	Investment Expenditures I	Government Expenditures G	Export Expenditures X	Total Injections $I+G+X$
$1,100	$100	$ 0	$100	$200	$50	$150	$200	$400
1,300	100	40	100	240	50	150	200	400
1,500	100	80	100	280	50	150	200	400
1,700	100	120	100	320	50	150	200	400
1,900	100	160	100	360	50	150	200	400
2,100	100	200	100	400	50	150	200	400
2,300	100	240	100	440	50	150	200	400
2,500	100	280	100	480	50	150	200	400
2,700	100	320	100	520	50	150	200	400

Using the leakages equal injections approach, equilibrium *Y* occurs when

$$T + S + M = I + G + X. \qquad (10\text{-}9)$$

Determining equilibrium *Y* by use of Table 10-4 requires finding the value of leakages *(T + S + M)* and injections *(I + G + X)* at each level of *Y*, and then finding the level of *Y* where leakages equal injections. Using Figure 10-5, equilibrium *Y* occurs at the intersection of the leakages and injections lines. In either

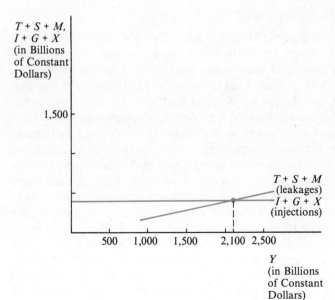

FIGURE 10-5   THE LEAKAGES EQUAL INJECTIONS APPROACH TO EQUILIBRIUM NATIONAL INCOME

In this figure, leakages and injections are shown as functions of national income. The intersection of the leakages and injections lines defines equilibrium national income. In this example, equilibrium *Y* = $2,100 billion.

case, equilibrium occurs when leakages and injections are $400 billion and $Y = $2,100 billion. Notice that this is the same value we obtained using the AD equals AS approach to equilibrium. Depending on the information available, you may use either the AS equals AD method or the leakages equal injections approach to find the equilibrium level of national income.

Changes in Aggregate Demand and the Keynesian Multiplier

Based on our hypothetical model of the economy, we have determined that the equilibrium level of Y is $2,100 billion. Now suppose that one of the elements of AD changes. What effect will this have on the equilibrium level of Y? As you may have already realized, a change in either C, I, G, or $(X - M)$ changes AD. When AD changes, equilibrium Y must also change. The change in Y depends on the magnitude and direction of the change in C, I, G, or $(X - M)$.

Suppose that the level of business investment expenditures increases by $100 billion to a new level of $150 billion at each level of national income. This causes the AD schedule to shift upward by $100 billion from AD_1 to AD_2, as shown in Figure 10-6. The original equilibrium at Y_1 ($2,100 billion) no longer holds, for at this level of national income, AD is $2,200 billion and exceeds AS by $100 billion. Unintended inventory declines occur and cause businesses to respond by increasing aggregate supply and national income. The new equilibrium point in Figure 10-6 occurs where AD_2 intersects the AS schedule. The new intersection is at a national income of $2,600 billion, $500 billion higher than the original equilibrium level. Thus, the $100 billion upward shift in AD results in a $500 billion increase in equilibrium Y. This is an example of the ***multiplier effect*** of a change in aggregate demand. The multiplier effect is that a given initial change in aggregate demand causes a final larger change in equilibrium national income. This is an important and powerful tool of Keynesian economic theory.

multiplier effect The ability of a given initial change in aggregate demand to cause a larger final change in equilibrium national income.

The Expenditure Multiplier Process

In our example the multiplier might work like this: Perhaps because of improved expectations about the future, say, businesses decide to increase or improve their capacity to produce goods and services. As a result, they increase investment expenditures by $100 billion. Since I has increased by $100 billion, AD increases by the same amount. But the process does not stop here. The additional investment spending is income to those who receive it. Expenditures and income received are two sides of any transaction. Remember Keynes's idea regarding the relationship between income and spending—when income changes, spending changes also, but by a smaller amount. The MPC tells us the relationship between changes in income and the *induced* changes in spending. Thus, the additional business investment of $100 billion caused incomes to increase by $100 billion. This is the "round 1" effect. As a result of receiving this income ($100 billion), the recipients will increase their spending by an amount dependent on the MPC. This "round 2" spending will increase AD further. If the MPC is 0.8, as in our example, the "round 2" increase in AD will be $80 billion ($100 billion × 0.8). But this spending becomes additional income to those who receive it, setting off a "round 3" increase in spending. This round-by-round process is shown in Figure 10-7. Each change in income causes a change in spending in the next

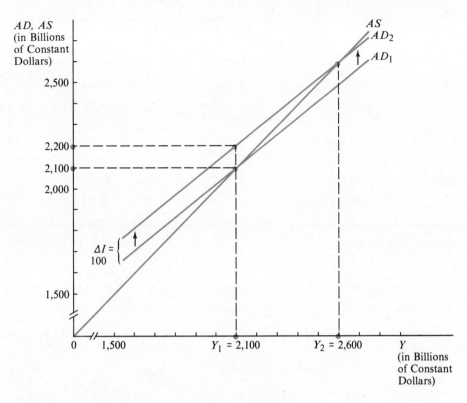

**FIGURE 10-6   CHANGE IN EQUILIBRIUM NATIONAL
INCOME**

With equilibrium national income at Y_1, business investment spending increases by $100
billion ($\Delta I = \$100$). This causes the aggregate demand schedule to shift up (from AD_1 to
AD_2) by $100 billion. Equilibrium national income increases (from Y_1 to Y_2) to $2,600 billion,
an increase of $500 billion.

round, which changes income, etc. How long does this income-spending process
go on? Figure 10-7 shows the process through the first five rounds and then
summarizes the remaining rounds. While the process theoretically goes on
forever, a mathematical tool is available to enable us to quickly determine the
cumulative change in Y. Notice that after "round 1," each column entry in Figure
10-7 is 80 percent of the entry above it. Thus, the spending and income columns
are declining at a uniform rate of 0.8 or 80 percent. It turns out that the cumulative effect of the round-by-round changes in national income is shown by,

$$\Delta Y_F = \Delta AD_1 \times \text{Expenditure Multiplier,}$$

where ΔY_F is the cumulative change in national income, ΔAD_1 is the initial
change in aggregate demand, and the *expenditure multiplier* is defined as

*expenditure multiplier   A
concept used to determine the
amount of the final change in
equilibrium national income
brought on by a change in
aggregate demand, defined as
$1/(1\text{-MPC})$.*

Round	Change in Aggregate Demand	Change in National Income
1	$100 billion (initial change)	$100 billion
2	80	80
3	64	64
4	51.20	51.20
5	40.96	40.96
All following rounds	163.84	163.84
Total	$500 billion	$500 billion

FIGURE 10-7 THE DYNAMICS OF THE MULTIPLIER PROCESS

$$\text{Expenditure Multiplier} = \frac{1}{1 - MPC} \qquad (10\text{-}11)$$

We can find the change in the equilibrium level of national income (ΔY_F) if the initial change in aggregate demand (ΔAD_1) and the MPC are known. First, equation (10-11) is solved by substituting for the actual value for the MPC:

$$\text{Expenditure Multiplier} = \left(\frac{1}{1-0.8}\right) = \left(\frac{1}{0.2}\right) = 5.$$

Second, we solve equation (10-10) for ΔY_F by substituting the known values for ΔAD_1 and the expenditure multiplier:

$$Y_F = \$100 \text{ billion} \times 5 = \$500 \text{ billion.}$$

This is the same change in Y we observed in Figure 10-6. It is also the value we would calculate by summing the effects of an infinite number of rounds in Figure 10-7. Figure 10-7 is obviously not practical for determining changes in equilibrium, but it is useful in showing the mechanics of the multiplier process. You should review both Figure 10-6 and equations (10-10) and (10-11) until you can find a change in the equilibrium level of national income using either approach.

The expenditure multiplier applies to a change in any of the components of aggregate demand, C, I, G, or (X − M). For instance, a $50 billion increase in net export spending is subject to the same expenditure multiplier (5) and would, therefore, cause a change of $250 billion in the equilibrium level of Y. The expenditure multiplier is the same no matter where the change in spending originates. A government dollar multiplies as well as a dollar from the foreign sector.

Alvin Hansen *(1887–1975)*

In the decades after the publication of Keynes's *General Theory* in 1936, *Alvin Hansen* gained a reputation as "the American Keynes." Many Keynesians argue that Hansen deserves major credit for the "fiscal revolution" in America and the redirection of U.S. macro policy in the three decades between 1938 and 1968.

Born in a small farming community in South Dakota, Hansen did his undergraduate work at Yankton College and his graduate work at the University of Wisconsin, where he received his Ph.D. in 1918. His dissertation was on *Cycles of Prosperity and Depression in the United States, Great Britain, and Germany,* so he was interested early in his career in the kinds of problems the world faced in the Depression of the 1930s. His interest in economic fluctuations continued, but he also did work on unemployment insurance, So-

cial Security, and United States foreign economic policy. By 1937, when he was invited to accept a newly created position at Harvard University, Hansen had established a solid and distinguished record in the economics profession.

However, it was his work in Keynesian economic theory and policy in the 20 years after he moved from the University of Minnesota to Harvard that truly established Hansen's reputation. Initially he was not particularly enthusiastic about the *General Theory* in 1936, but by the next year Hansen (at the age of 50) had started making important contributions to the new analysis. One vehicle he used was a Harvard seminar on fiscal policy, where he, some of his colleagues, and graduate students worked on analyzing important national problems and suggesting Keynesian policy prescriptions for them. Many of the most prominent Keynesians of the following 20 years participated in this seminar. They were influenced not only by Hansen's thought, but also by his desire to use theory to solve practical problems such as the unemployment of the 1930s, and his concern for the masses suffering from these problems. He participated vigorously in public debates in the years during and after World War II on the direction the economy should take and advocated Keynesian policies to get it there.

One problem that worried Hansen and many others in the 1930s was whether the United States and other countries were destined for stagnation; that is, very slow and sluggish growth in real income. When Hansen gave his presidental address to the American Economic Association in 1938, he stressed reasons for believing aggregate demand might be weak in the future, thus causing stagnation. He foresaw declining growth of population, the end of the western frontier, the depletion of natural resources, and the possibility that new inventions would not require the massive investment that went into railroads, new factories, etc., from the end of the Civil War through the 1920s. All these factors would tend to lower aggregate demand, but Hansen believed that this problem could be offset by using fiscal policy. In 1967, the American Economic Association awarded Hansen the Francis A. Walker medal, its highest honor.

Changes in Net Export Expenditures

Let's turn to a brief examination of how changes in net export expenditures $(X - M)$ influence the equilibrium level of national income. An increase in $(X - M)$ will shift the AD schedule up and cause an increase in equilibrium Y. A decrease in $(X - M)$ will have the opposite effect; the AD schedule will shift down and equilibrium Y will decrease. The change in Y will be equal to the change in $(X - M)$ times the expenditure multiplier.

What forces bring about changes in net export expenditures? Changes in relative prices and incomes between countries, tariffs, quotas, and embargos can all influence spending for imports and exports. Weather can also be a factor. For instance, if severe weather in the USSR ruined its wheat crop, the Soviets would turn to foreign suppliers for this essential grain. If the Soviets purchased American wheat, this would increase foreign spending for U.S. exports, and net export expenditures $(X - M)$ would increase. In Figure 10-8, this increase in $(X - M)$ would cause the aggregate demand schedule to shift upward from AD_1 to AD_2, and this would result in a higher equilibrium level of national income (Y_2).

Suppose that the price of an imported good suddenly rises, as was the case with OPEC oil in 1974. In the short run, expenditures on this good would increase. This would contribute to an increase in spending for imports and would cause net export expenditures $(X - M)$ to decrease. As shown in Figure 10-8,

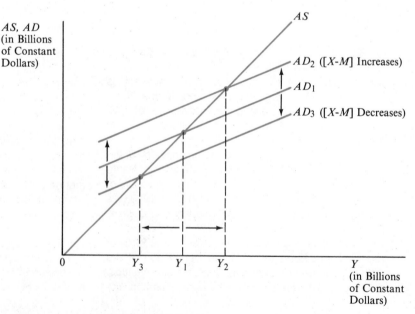

**FIGURE 10-8   CHANGES IN NET EXPORT
                          EXPENDITURES**

With aggregate demand and national income initially at AD_1 and Y_1: (1) Wheat sales to the USSR increase $(X - M)$. This causes aggregate demand to shift upward to AD_2. National income increases to Y_2; (2) OPEC raises the price of oil, causing $(X - M)$ to decrease. This causes aggregate demand to shift downward to AD_3. National income decreases to Y_3.

cause net export expenditures $(X - M)$ to decrease. As shown in Figure 10-8, the decrease in $(X - M)$ would cause the aggregate demand schedule to shift downward from AD_1 to AD_3, and would result in a lower equilibrium level of national income (Y_3).

The Paradox of Thrift

Many economists believe that a major contribution of Keynesian economics was its discussion of how an increase in planned saving may not be beneficial. Americans have traditionally believed that saving is a virtue. Benjamin Franklin said, "A penny saved is a penny earned." How can saving ever be bad?

When Keynesian economists criticize saving, they do so in the context of a nation which is operating with a deficiency of aggregate demand. In this case, equilibrium Y is less than the full-employment level of Y (the potential level of output of the economy). An increase in saving implies a decrease in consumption expenditures which causes aggregate demand to become more deficient. We can show what these economists have in mind by increasing planned saving in our previous example.

By an increase in planned saving, economists mean an upward shift in the saving schedule as plotted in Figure 10-1; equivalently, an upward shift in the $T + S + M$ line in Figure 10-5. If we focus on Figure 10-5, and assume that $T, M, I, G,$ and X remain constant, an increase in planned saving, S, causes an upward shift in the leakages line while the injections $(I + G + X)$ line remains unchanged. The increase in planned saving also means that consumers must spend less at each level of national income. This would be reflected by a downward shift of the consumption schedule in Figure 10-1 and a downward shift of the aggregate demand schedule in Figure 10-2. In Figure 10-9, we show both of these shifts; the upward shift in the leakages line from $T + S_1 + M$ to $T + S_2 + M$, and the downward shift in the aggregate demand line from AD_1 to AD_2, with each shifting by $100 billion.

In both cases, the new line is parallel to the original, because the MPC and the MPS stay the same and, therefore, the slopes do not change. Because consumption expenditures decrease by $100 billion when planned saving increases by $100 billion, the aggregate demand schedule shifts downward by exactly the amount that the leakage schedule shifts upward.

It is easy to see from Figure 10-9 that the equilibrium level of national income must fall. The downward shift in consumption expenditures means that the new aggregate demand schedule intersects the aggregate supply schedule at the lower level of Y. This is what Keynesians call the ***paradox of thrift***. As people become more thrifty, their thrift ultimately causes incomes to decline. Furthermore, the intention to increase saving does not result in any increase in actual saving. Notice that the new intersection of leakages and injections in Figure 10-9 occurs where injections equal $400 billion. But this is the same level as before the increase in planned saving. Thus, in equilibrium, $T + S_1 + M = \$400$ billion $= T + S_2 + M$. Since T and M have not changed, the equilibrium values of S_1 and S_2 must be the same. Thus, actual saving is unchanged.

As we have seen, the equilibrium level of national income occurs where aggregate supply and aggregate demand are equal. Equilibrium does not mean

paradox of thrift *The paradoxical result in the simple Keynesian model that when planned saving rises (the saving function shifts up), income falls and actual saving is no higher than before.*

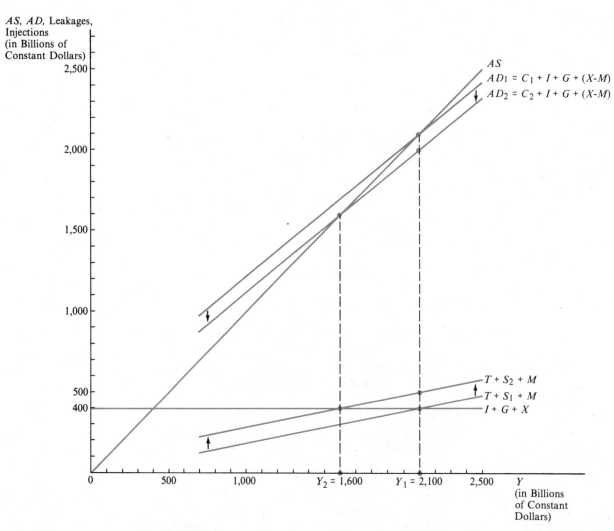

FIGURE 10-9   THE PARADOX OF THRIFT

An increase in planned saving implies a decrease in consumption expenditures. The $100 billion increase in planned saving shifts the leakage line upward from $T + S_1 + M$ to $T + S_2 + M$. Simultaneously, the $100 billion decrease in consumption expenditures shifts the aggregate demand schedule downward from AD_1 to AD_2. Equilibrium national income decreases from Y_1 to Y_2, a change of $500 billion. At the new equilibrium, (Y_2), $T + S_2 + M = $400 billion. But at Y_1, $T + S_1 + M$ was also equal to $400 billion, therefore, the equilibrium values of S_1 and S_2 are equal. An increase in planned saving caused Y to decrease while actual saving remained unchanged.

that the economy will operate at full employment with stable prices. If the economy does reach equilibrium with significant unemployed resources (as during the Great Depression), or with rampant inflation, what can be done to alleviate these conditions? In the following chapter, we will discuss the tools available to government to deal with undesirable equilibrium situations.

SUMMARY

1. In contrast to the classical theory of the macro economy, the Keynesian model shows that the economy can come to an equilibrium level of national income and output with a high level of unemployed resources.

2. The equilibrium level of national income occurs where aggregate supply equals aggregate demand. In the Keynesian model, the equilibrium levels of national income, aggregate supply, and aggregate demand are interdependent; that is, jointly determined.

3. The foundation of the aggregate demand schedule is the Keynesian consumption function. The consumption function shows how consumption expenditures (C) vary according to disposable income (Y_d).

4. The aggregate demand schedule is formulated by expressing each of the components of AD —C, I, G, and (X − M)—as a function of national income (Y).

5. By definition, aggregate supply is identical to national income. Plotting the aggregate supply schedule generates a 45° line which passes through the origin.

6. The intersection of the AS and AD schedules, referred to as the Keynesian Cross, defines the equilibrium level of Y. This level of Y does not assure full employment of resources.

7. At nonequilibrium levels of Y, differences between aggregate demand and aggregate supply result in unintended changes in business inventories. These unintended inventory changes act both as a signal and as an incentive, causing businesses to adjust their level of output to the level of spending for output (aggregate supply adjusts to aggregate demand).

8. Through the multiplier process, any initial change in aggregate demand will result in a larger change in the equilibrium level of national income.

9. Increases in foreign spending for U.S. exports increase AD and Y, while increases in U.S. spending for foreign imports reduce AD and Y.

10. An increase in planned saving may result in a decline in the equilibrium level of national income with no change in actual saving. This is referred to as the paradox of thrift.

NEW TERMS

marginal propensity to consume (MPC)
marginal propensity to save (MPS)
Keynesian Cross
inventories

unintended business inventory changes
multiplier effect
expenditure multiplier
paradox of thrift

QUESTIONS FOR DISCUSSION

1. Suppose the intercept of the consumption function is $300 billion and the MPC is 0.5. For all values of Y_d between $0 and $5,000 billion (by $500 billion intervals), develop a table relating C and S to Y_d, as in Table 10-1.

2. Construct a table similar to Table 10-2 based on the following information:

C is $200 billion when $Y_d = 0$
MPC = 0.75

$T =$ $500 billion
$I =$ $100 billion
$G =$ $400 billion
$X =$ $ 50 billion
$M =$ $150 billion.

3. Using the information from Question 2, construct a graph of the aggregate demand schedule similar to Figure 10-2.

4. Based on the information contained in Questions 2 and 3, what is the equilibrium level of Y?

5. Find the value of the multiplier given the following:

MPC = 0.4   MPS = 0.25

MPC = 0.67   MPS = 0.5
MPC = 0.9   MPS = 0.75

6. Assume the initial equilibrium level of national income is $4,800 billion and the MPC = 0.9. What will be the new equilibrium level of Y, if I decreases $100 billion from its initial level?

SUGGESTIONS FOR FURTHER READING

Dauten, Carl A., and Lloyd M. Valentine. *Business Cycles and Forecasting,* 5h ed. Cincinnati: South-Western Publishing Co., 1978, Chapter 7.

Samuelson, Paul A. "The Simple Mathematics of Income Determination," in *Income, Employment and Public Policy,* Lloyd A. Metzler, *et al.* New York: W. W. Norton & Co., Inc., 1964.

Fiscal Policy: Keynesian Policy Applied to the Economy

Learning Objectives

After studying the materials found in this chapter, you should be able to do the following:

1. Explain the Keynesian argument which states that active fiscal policy is necessary to assure a situation of full employment with price stability.

2. Distinguish between:
   (a) a deflationary gap and an inflationary gap.
   (b) a federal budget deficit and a federal budget surplus.

3. Define:
   (a) Keynesian fiscal policy.
   (b) Investment Tax Credit.
   (c) recognition, implementation, and impact lags.

4. Demonstrate how Keynesian fiscal policy can be used to offset the effects of changes in consumer, business, or foreign sector spending.

5. List the reasons that support the balanced budget multiplier effect.

6. Discuss the arguments for and against Keynesian fiscal policy.

7. Briefly describe the following U.S. experiences with Keynesian fiscal policy:
   (a) the Kennedy Tax Cut.
   (b) the Johnson Tax Surcharge.
   (c) the Ford Tax Rebate.

In this chapter we discuss the theory and practice of Keynesian fiscal policy. *Fiscal policy* refers to the government's policy regarding the level of its expenditures *(G)* and taxation *(T)*. **Keynesian fiscal policy** refers to the manipulation of *G* or *T* (or both) for the purpose of moving the economy toward a politically desirable level of income and output. First, we address the question of why Keynesian fiscal policy is necessary. We then show how Keynesian fiscal policy uses government expenditures and taxation to achieve certain economic goals. We consider the pros and cons of fiscal policy and discuss budget deficits, the national debt, and debt financing. In the final section of the chapter, we examine three episodes in recent American economic history when Keynesian fiscal policy was

fiscal policy *The use of government spending and taxation policies to influence the level of economic activity, inflation, and economic growth.*

Keynesian fiscal policy *Fiscal policy that manipulates government expenditures and taxation in order to move the economy toward a socially desirable level of income and output.*

practiced. Keep in mind that fiscal policy existed prior to Keynesian economic theory. Government expenditures and tax collections have always occurred daily. However, in response to particular economic problems, Keynesian fiscal policy endorses active government intervention in the capitalistic economy. Thus, it should not be confused with the continuous day-to-day activities of government spending and taxation.

WHY IS KEYNESIAN FISCAL POLICY NECESSARY?

In Chapter 10, we showed that according to the Keynesian view, the economy automatically moves to a level of national income where aggregate supply equals aggregate demand (or where leakages equal injections). We also pointed out the Keynesian contention that there is no assurance that this equilibrium level of Y will bring about full employment of resources at a stable price level.

In fact, Keynes believed that during the 1930s the world's capitalistic economies indeed reached equilibrium positions, but high levels of unemployment made these situations socially unacceptable. What should have been done and who should have been responsible for taking action? Keynes and his followers had answers to these questions.

Keynesian fiscal policy is based on the premise that aggregate demand should be manipulated to insure that the economy achieves an equilibrium level of Y which is socially desirable. For example, suppose the economy was in equilibrium but there was a high level of unemployment, as was the case in the 1930s. According to Keynesian economics, the problem could have been eliminated through an increase in aggregate demand *(AD)*. Aggregate demand can be increased if one or more of its components—C, I, G, or $(X - M)$—is increased. Although there are four possible sources for increased spending, Keynesians tend to eliminate the private and foreign sectors, leaving only government intervention as a reliable solution to the problem. Let's look at this argument.

An increase in spending from the foreign sector $(X - M)$ requires an increase in foreign spending for our exports or a decrease in domestic spending for imports, or both. Several methods exist that will accomplish an increase in $(X - M)$. First, a devaluation or depreciation of the domestic currency will make our products cheaper to foreigners and will increase our exports.[1] Second, imports of foreign goods and services can be restricted by tariffs and quotas, or even eliminated by an embargo.[2] These solutions come at the expense of our trading partners and are referred to as beggar-thy-neighbor policies.[3] Even if we were very callous

---

[1]Devaluation or depreciation reduces the price foreigners pay for United States currency and thus the price they pay for our products in terms of their currency. This is discussed in detail in the chapter on International Economics.

[2]A tariff is essentially a tax on foreign goods and services. Implementing a tariff (or raising an existing tariff) raises the price Americans must pay for foreign goods and services and reduces the quantity demanded. A quota restricts the amount of a foreign product which can be imported, while an embargo eliminates importing the product entirely. These ideas are discussed in detail in the chapter on International Economics.

[3]"Beggar-thy-neighbor" is the term given to any action of one country which improves its own condition but in the process hurts its trading partner's condition. For example, the United States could gain a trade advantage by devaluing the dollar in terms of the British pound. U.S. products would then be less expensive and the British would buy more of them. The United States economy would gain at the expense of the British economy.

and ignored the detrimental effects of such policies on our trading partners, their positive effect on our economy would be short-lived. Foreign countries could be expected to retaliate with similar policies of their own, thus eliminating our temporary advantage.[4] Consequently, manipulation of foreign sector spending is not a reliable source of increased spending.

What about consumption and business investment expenditures? Couldn't households and businesses be persuaded to voluntarily increase their expenditures in the social interest? Perhaps the president could appear on national TV and encourage people to spend more money. As we saw in Chapter 1, economists reason that both households and businesses are motivated more by self-interest than social interest. Neither of these groups could be expected to act in the interest of society if such action conflicted with the group's self-interest. For instance, acting in the social interest during the Depression would have required households to increase spending instead of saving, and businesses to increase investment expenditures in the face of stagnant demand for their products. However, the self-interest of these two groups dictated other behavior. During the Great Depression, households became more frugal and businesses reduced investment spending. Thus, Keynesians do not see voluntary changes in private sector spending as a solution to economic problems. They contend that self-interested behavior will cause private sector spending to move opposite to what is needed, decreasing during recessions and increasing during inflationary times.

Putting all this together, we can summarize the Keynesian argument for government fiscal policy intervention in the economy as follows:

1. Macroeconomic equilibrium does not assure that the economy will have full employment with price stability.

2. Instability in the private sector is a source of macroeconomic problems.

3. Only the government can be counted on to act in the social interest.

4. Keynesian economics provides the government with the tools necessary to correctly manipulate the economy.

Keynesians, therefore, conclude that it is the government's responsibility to insure that the economy achieves a level of national income consistent with full employment and price stability. In 1946 the Congress of the United States passed a landmark piece of legislation—the Full Employment Act (FEA). Political and business leaders feared that as the United States began the transition from wartime to peacetime production, the economy would plummet into another depression. The FEA made the U.S. government responsible for achieving and maintaining full employment through the use of fiscal and monetary policy. In 1978, Congress passed the controversial Full Employment and Balanced Growth Act, better known as the Humphrey-Hawkins Act, which defines targets and specifies the behavior required of the government. The Humphrey-Hawkins Act set goals of 4 percent unemployment rate and 3 percent inflation rate by 1983. The Act

[4]Refer to footnote 3. The British could eliminate the United States' advantage by devaluing the pound relative to the dollar. Activities such as these were common during the Great Depression, but no one really gained by them.

required that the government develop a five-year plan that would achieve these unemployment and inflation rate targets.

KEYNESIAN FISCAL POLICY

To set the stage for our discussion of fiscal policy, let's review the way in which the components of aggregate demand influence the equilibrium level of national income. The consumption schedule shifts for a number of reasons. In Chapter 10 we discussed the effects of an increased desire to save and the resulting downward shift in the consumption schedule. Conversely, economists believe that prolonged periods of inflation will cause the consumption schedule to shift up as people forego saving and increase spending to beat expected price increases. We have already discussed how investment expenditures shift in response to changing expectations about the future. We also learned in Chapter 10 how changes in prices, incomes, weather, and government policies influence exports and imports causing $(X - M)$ to shift up or down.

Because the forces which influence C, I, and $(X - M)$ are constantly changing, it is reasonable to expect that the expenditures from these sectors are seldom constant for long periods of time. As C, I, and $(X - M)$ fluctuate, aggregate demand changes and through the multiplier process, larger changes in income, output, and employment are induced.

Keynesian economists do not advocate government intervention to offset every shift in aggregate demand. They argue that Keynesian fiscal policy should be used to improve economic conditions which have significant, harmful effects. In practice, fiscal policy actions involving changes in government expenditures and taxation have occurred only on three occasions since World War II. We later discuss these occasions.

The Goal—Full Employment with Stable Prices

In order for the government to use Keynesian fiscal policy wisely, a target level of national income must be identified. If the equilibrium level differs significantly from the desired level, then the government can change taxes or spending to remedy the situation.

To be consistent with the Keynesian model, as well as with the FEA and the Humphrey-Hawkins Act, we will state the goal of the economy as the achievement of an equilibrium level of national income which generates full employment with price stability. As in earlier chapters, we will use Y^* to symbolize the full-employment level of national income. Through use of Keynesian fiscal policy, the government can manipulate AD so that the level of national income equals Y^*.

For simplicity and consistency, we will continue to use the Keynesian model developed in Chapter 10. As you recall, the aggregate demand schedule was derived by summing C, I, G, and $(X - M)$ at each level of national income. In our model, we assumed that consumption expenditures could be represented by the equation $C = \$200$ billion $+ 0.8 Y_d$. The MPC is 0.8 and, therefore, the value of the expenditure multiplier is 5.0. If we now make the assumption that the economy is at full employment with stable prices when national income is $2,100 billion, then we have numerically defined Y^* as $2,100 billion. As Figure 11-1 shows, Y^* occurs at the intersection of the AD_1 and the AS schedule. One way to understand the Keynesian viewpoint is that fiscal policy should be used to assure that the level of aggregate demand in the economy is AD_1 and not some lower or higher level such as AD_2 or AD_3. If aggregate demand is not at the desired level, a deflationary or inflationary gap will result.

Deflationary and Inflationary Gaps

A ***deflationary gap*** exists when the equilibrium level of Y is *less* than the desired level Y^*. In Figure 11-1, AD_2 results in a deflationary gap, because it generates an equilibrium Y of only $1,600 billion. The deflationary gap is measured at Y^* and is equal to the vertical distance between AD_1 and AD_2. The gap, shown by the distance DE, graphically depicts how much aggregate demand must be raised to bring national income up to the desired level. When a deflationary gap exists, demand is insufficient to purchase the output that can be supplied at full employ-

deflationary gap   If there is a deflationary gap, aggregate demand is less than the output that can be supplied at full employment, so output and prices fall.

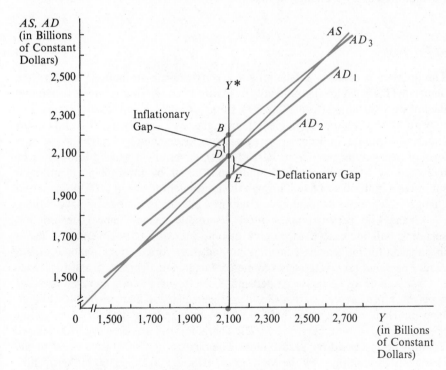

FIGURE 11-1   INFLATIONARY AND DEFLATIONARY GAPS

The full-employment level of national income is defined as Y^*. This target or goal is achieved when aggregate demand is AD_1. If aggregate demand is AD_2, then a deflationary gap equal to DE results. If aggregate demand is AD_3, then an inflationary gap equal to BD results.

ment. The resulting surplus causes businesses to respond by reducing output, or prices, or both. The reduction in output creates the unemployment we discussed previously.

An *inflationary gap* exists when the equilibrium level of Y is *greater* than Y^*. In Figure 11-1, AD_3 results in an inflationary gap because it generates an equilibrium Y of \$2,600 billion which is greater than our goal. The inflationary gap is also measured at Y^* and is equal to the vertical distance between AD_1 and AD_3. The gap, shown by the distance BD, depicts how much aggregate demand must be decreased to bring national income to the desired level. When an inflationary gap exists, aggregate demand exceeds full-employment output. Businesses operating at full capacity are unable to produce enough goods and services to meet the combined demands of households, other businesses, government, and the foreign sector. The resulting shortages cause inflation.

Now that we have defined national income ($Y^* = \$2,100$ billion) and have discussed possible problems, our next task is to show how Keynesian fiscal policy can eliminate a deflationary or inflationary gap and achieve the target national income. We will assume that initially the economy was at Y^*, but as a result of a downward shift of the consumption schedule, aggregate demand declined to AD_2. At the new equilibrium, Y is \$1,600 billion and a deflationary gap equal to DE exists. We will show how the gap can be closed by a change in government expenditures or by a change in taxes.

Changing National Income Using Keynesian Fiscal Policy

The problem is to close a deflationary gap by causing an increase in aggregate demand. This is depicted graphically in Figure 11-2. In order to increase national income by \$500 billion (from Y_2 to Y^*), the aggregate demand schedule must shift upward by the amount of the deflationary gap, DE. As Figure 11-2 shows, DE equals \$100 billion. In order to increase aggregate demand by \$100 billion at each level of national income (from AD_2 to AD_1), government expenditures must be increased by \$100 billion. Each additional dollar of government spending is subject to a multiplier of five. Through the multiplier process, a \$100 billion initial change in aggregate demand causes national income to change by \$500 billion.

Changes in personal taxes affect disposable income. Since consumption spending will increase if disposable income increases, the government has a mechanism for influencing consumption and, therefore, national income. It can reduce personal taxes if it wishes to increase aggregate demand, or increase taxes if it wants to decrease aggregate demand. To close deflationary gap DE, personal taxes must be decreased so that C and aggregate demand increase by \$100 billion. How much is enough? The MPC is 0.8, which tells us that for every dollar increase in Y_d, C will increase by \$.80. Therefore, to increase C by \$100 billion, Y_d must be increased by \$125 billion. The change in C is always equal to the change in Y_d multiplied by the MPC (\$125 billion $\times$ 0.8 = \$100 billion.) Thus, personal taxes must be reduced by \$125 billion at each level of national income. Again, the multiplier process will be at work as a \$125 billion decrease in personal taxes results in an initial increase in aggregate demand, which causes national income to increase by \$500 billion. It takes a \$125 billion decrease in taxes to accomplish the same change in Y as a \$100 billion increase in government

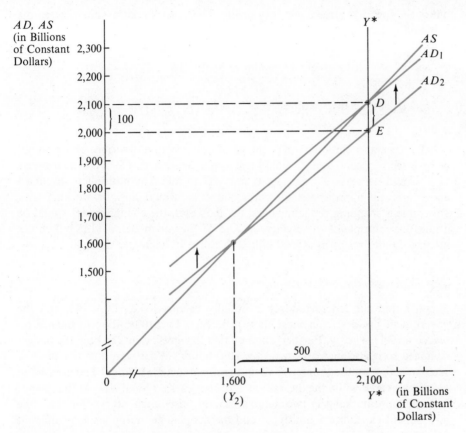

**FIGURE 11-2   CLOSING A DEFLATIONARY GAP WITH
FISCAL POLICY**

A deflationary gap is measured at Y^* and is the vertical distance between AD_2 and AD_1, which in this case is *DE*, or $100 billion. When aggregate demand is at AD_2, equilibrium Y is $1,600 billion, $500 billion less than Y^*. If aggregate demand is increased by the amount of the deflationary gap ($100 billion), national income will increase to the level of Y^* due to the multiplier effect.

spending. The multiplier associated with a tax change is less than the government multiplier. In our example, the tax change multiplier is 4 and the government expenditure multiplier is 5. This is because every dollar of additional government spending immediately contributes an additional dollar to aggregate demand, but every additional dollar reduction in personal tax is split between additional saving and spending. If, as in our example, the MPC is 0.8, then every dollar reduction in personal taxes contributes $.80 to aggregate demand (through an increase in C) and $.20 to increased saving. The tax change multiplier is less than the government expenditure multiplier, because a portion of the tax decrease leaks out of the spending stream and into saving. The general relationship between the two multipliers is:

$$\text{Government Expenditure Multiplier} = \frac{1}{MPS}$$

$$\text{Tax Change Multiplier} = -MPC\left(\frac{1}{MPS}\right) = -\frac{MPC}{MPS}$$

To close an inflationary gap, the fiscal policy action described above would be reversed. A decrease in G would result in a decrease in AD, while an increase in T would decrease Y_d, causing C and AD to fall. The multipliers discussed above are still appropriate. However, since we would now be working with government spending reductions and tax increases, the change in AD would be a negative multiple of the change in G or T. In our model, a $125 billion tax increase would result in a $500 billion decrease in aggregate demand.

The Balanced Budget Multiplier

Suppose that the federal budget is initially balanced (i.e., $G = T$), and the government decides to increase its expenditures by $100 billion to finance research on solar energy. Further, suppose that Congress wants to keep the budget balanced so it also increases taxes by $100 billion. What would be the effect of such an action on the economy? Would national income change? The increase in G increases AD, while the increase in T decreases Y_d, C, and AD. At first glance it might appear that the two actions exactly offset each other. But since the government expenditure multiplier and the tax change multiplier have different values, equal changes in government spending and taxes will change the level of national income. This effect is called the **balanced budget multiplier** and refers to the change in Y resulting from equal changes in G and T. To see how this works, consider the general effect on Y of changes in G and T:

balanced budget multiplier
Equal to unity; the balanced budget multiplier shows the change in national income when government expenditures and taxation receipts both increase by the same amount.

$$\Delta Y = \Delta G\left(\frac{1}{MPS}\right) + \Delta T\left(-\frac{MPC}{MPS}\right), \qquad (11\text{-}1)$$

where $\left(\frac{1}{MPS}\right)$ and $\left(-\frac{MPC}{MPS}\right)$ are the multipliers associated with changes in G and T respectively. If the changes in government spending and taxes are equal, then $\Delta G = \Delta T$ and equation (11-1) can be rewritten:

$$\Delta Y = \Delta G\left(\frac{1}{MPS}\right) + \Delta G\left(-\frac{MPC}{MPS}\right) \qquad (11\text{-}2)$$

$$\Delta Y = \Delta G\left(\frac{1 - MPC}{MPS}\right).$$

By definition, $1 - MPC = MPS$, so equation (11-2) can be rewritten:

$$\Delta Y = \Delta G\left(\frac{MPS}{MPS}\right) = \Delta G(1). \qquad (11\text{-}3)$$

Thus, equation (11-3) shows that equal changes in government spending and taxes result in a change in national income that is equal to the change in G times a multiplier of 1.0. This is always true because the value of the balanced budget multiplier equals $\left(\dfrac{MPS}{MPS}\right)$, which by definition is 1. As a result, the $100 billion increase in spending on solar research would increase national income by $100 billion.

KEYNESIAN FISCAL POLICY AND THE FEDERAL BUDGET

In the preceding analysis, we showed how Keynesian fiscal policy can eliminate a deflationary gap by increasing G or reducing T (or both). An inflationary gap can be eliminated by decreasing G or increasing T (or both). Keynesian fiscal policy works by changing the relationship between G and T, and, therefore, the balance of the federal budget, moving it towards deficit or surplus. To see why this is true, assume that initially the federal budget is balanced; that is, government expenditures are exactly offset by tax revenues, or $G = T$. If the government uses Keynesian fiscal policy to reduce or eliminate a deflationary gap, G is increased or T is decreased. No matter which action is taken, G will exceed T and there will be a *federal budget deficit (G > T)*. Alternatively, to eliminate an inflationary gap, G is decreased or T is increased, and a *federal budget surplus (T > G)* results. A federal budget deficit increases the national debt, while a surplus reduces it. Keynesian fiscal policy influences our national debt by creating deficits or surpluses.

federal budget deficit Federal government expenditures exceed taxation.

federal budget surplus Federal government tax receipts exceed expenditures.

Are we saying that Keynesian fiscal policy is responsible for the long series of federal budget deficits and the huge national debt? Absolutely not! The deficits and the debt are primarily the result of our congressional representatives voting to spend more than the government takes in. Only a small portion of our current national debt is the result of deficits incurred through the use of Keynesian fiscal policy. Most Keynesians argue strongly that the benefits of Keynesian fiscal policy (increased employment and economic growth) far offset the costs (budget deficits). The political difficulty is that many politicians have used Keynesian argument to avoid making hard decisions on the budget. In this sense, Keynesian theory created an intellectual escape for big spending members of Congress.

Federal Deficits and Surpluses

As we have seen, Keynesian fiscal policy works by moving the federal budget toward deficit or surplus. Let us examine the effects of the way the surplus is disposed of or the deficit is financed.

When individuals or businesses spend more than they receive as income, they must borrow to finance the deficit. Similarly, when G exceeds T, the government is forced to find a means to finance the deficit. The government has two alternatives for deficit financing: borrowing in the credit market or creating more money. The economic effects of the two alternatives are quite different.

Borrowing to Finance the Deficit—The Crowding-Out Effect

crowding-out effect   The increased demand for loanable funds by government causes the interest rate to rise; this reduces funds available for business investment, thus crowding out business investment.

If the government chooses to borrow, it must compete with individuals and businesses for funds in the credit market. The added demand resulting from government borrowing tends to drive up interest rates. As interest rates rise, some private sector borrowing is eliminated from the market. The elimination of this borrowing reduces private sector spending and investment and, therefore, reduces aggregate demand. Thus, borrowing by the government can result in a *crowding-out effect,* if the government's borrowing reduces (crowds out) private sector borrowing and spending. The crowding-out effect moderates the effectiveness of fiscal policy, because increased government spending comes at the expense of reduced private sector spending and investment. In terms of our model, the upward shift in G is partially offset by a downward shift of C and I. The crowding out of private investment also has long-run consequences. A reduction in investment spending means that the growth of our productive capacity is slowed. This will result in our economy's future output being less than it would have been if the government had not crowded out private investment spending.

Money Creation and Inflation

As an alternative, the deficit can be financed through money creation. The government could either instruct the U.S. Treasury to print enough new paper money to offset the deficit or have the Treasury borrow funds from the Federal Reserve Banking System. The Treasury pays bills by issuing checks (drawn on its account with the Fed) to the government's creditors. When these checks are deposited in the creditors' accounts, an expansion of the money supply results (as discussed in Chapter 5). The advantage of using money creation to finance a federal deficit is that it avoids the possibility of the crowding-out effect and does not reduce the effectiveness of increased government spending. The disadvantage of creating money is that it tends to have an inflationary impact if the economy is operating at, or near, full-employment capacity. In such cases, increased government spending is not offset by reduced spending in other sectors. As shown in Figure 11-1, with the economy at Y^*, G shifts upward causing the entire aggregate demand schedule to shift to AD_3. This produces an inflationary gap. From this simple analysis it is obvious that the government should not use money creation to finance a federal deficit if the economy is operating at or near Y^*.

Disposing of a Budget Surplus

On those rare occasions when tax revenues exceed expenditures, the government has had two options for disposal of the surplus: (1) retire (pay off) a portion of the national debt; or (2) impound the funds. Approximately 85 percent of our national debt is owned by (owed to) American citizens. If the government chose to use the budget surplus to retire part of the national debt, then the money would end up predominately in the domestic economy. If the recipients spent the money for consumption purposes, C would shift up. If, instead, the money was saved, it would be available for investment purposes and I would shift up. In either case, the intent of Keynesian fiscal policy would be partially offset. The contractionary effects of the budget surplus would contribute to increased spending in the private sector as the national debt was reduced. It is, therefore, apparent that the government's option to impound (or hold idle) the budget surplus is preferred, if Keynesian fiscal policy is not to be weakened.

KEYNESIAN FISCAL POLICY: PRO AND CON

Controversy over the use of Keynesian fiscal policy is quite pervasive in our society. The fundamental arguments are really quite simple. Its advocates claim that through the manipulation of government spending and taxes, we can reduce, if not eliminate, the social costs of unemployment and inflation. Furthermore, the increased government expenditures used to close a deflationary gap can be used to finance needed social goods (e.g., schools, parks, highways, etc.).

One of the arguments made by opponents of Keynesian fiscal policy is that it generates greater costs than benefits. They point out that it results in an increase in the size of the government sector (with an accompanying decrease in society's economic efficiency and productivity); that it results in the crowding-out effect previously discussed; and that it causes an undesirable change in the economy's mix of private and public goods. Others argue that Keynesian economic theory has been used to justify government intervention in the United States economy. Further, they claim that the Keynesian influence on fiscal policy is responsible for the deficits in the federal budget and increases in the national debt. These detractors might accept Keynesian policy if, over the long run, budget surpluses tended to offset deficits. However, they point out that since 1950, surplus budgets have totaled less than $20 billion, while deficit budgets have exceeded $500 billion. The tendency toward deficit budgets stems from two obstacles facing our representatives in Washington: first, it is very difficult to reduce or eliminate existing government programs in order to reduce G; second, voting for a tax increase makes a member of Congress unpopular and could even cause defeat in the next election. Many economists counter that these are weaknesses of the budgetary process, not Keynesian fiscal policy.

Not everyone agrees with the way government spends our dollars, regardless of whether the spending is associated with Keynesian fiscal policy. After all, some of the things government spending has given us since 1960 are: the Vietnam War; the damming of wild rivers; the destruction of associated ecologies; and investigations of people who disagreed with the government. When people look at the mistakes government has made, some say the best thing to do is keep government spending down to prevent future mistakes. Others say that there may have been problems in the past, but that good government in the future can prevent such problems as well as carry out effective social programs. It is important to note that Keynesian fiscal policy often means increased government spending.

Conflicts over social goals and values have a way of turning into a debate over whether to use government spending to stimulate the economy. Beginning in the 1930s, even before Keynes's *General Theory,* economists and politicians developed the idea of spending more on social projects when the economy had unemployment and cutting back on spending when there was full employment. For example, there might be cyclical shifts in the aggregate demand functions, making aggregate demand first too low and then too high, as with the AD_2 and AD_3 lines in Figure 11-2. If such a cycle were unacceptable, government spending could be used to keep national income close to full-employment national income, by increasing government spending when aggregate demand falls toward AD_2 and decreasing G when aggregate demand threatens to rise toward AD_3. For the people in favor of government programs, the main problem with this type of fiscal policy is the cutback in spending during the inflationary part of the cycle. It's unpleasant to be told your project is cancelled until the next recession. One can make a strong case that worthwhile projects shouldn't be cancelled. On the other hand, people who don't like social projects in the first place may argue that when inflationary pressures arise, the programs won't be cancelled. They fear that the programs instituted during a recession to stimulate the economy will go on forever. These people agree that an increase in G will make the whole pie larger when there is unemployment, but they also argue that the government's slice will remain large during good economic times and will be used for purposes they may not like.

It is interesting to note that, until the 1970s, Swedish stabilization policy was based on continuous shortages in the housing market. When unemployment threatened to rise, the government could have more housing built and thus keep employment fairly constant. When inflation was feared, housing projects were cut back. Housing was used as the sole tool of fiscal policy in this example.

PUTTING THEORY INTO PRACTICE—
THE U.S. EXPERIENCE

We will examine three episodes in recent American history when Keynesian fiscal policy was actually employed. Each of these episodes involved a macroeconomic problem that was dealt with by utilizing fiscal policy based on Keynesian theory.

The Kennedy Tax Cut

In 1960 John F. Kennedy ran against Richard M. Nixon for the presidency of the United States. Early in the campaign, many people thought Nixon would win. He had been vice-president for eight years, while Kennedy was a relative newcomer to the political arena, having served one term in the House of Representatives and one term in the Senate. Nixon wanted to make his experience and Kennedy's inexperience a major issue in the campaign. Kennedy countered, however, by arguing that Nixon had experience in how to run the country—but in how to run the country badly! Kennedy pointed out that during the Eisenhower-Nixon years, the U.S. economy had been generally stagnant and had suffered two major recessions. Kennedy further claimed that the Eisenhower-Nixon administration essentially did nothing to help the economy recover from high unemployment rates and sluggish, erratic economic growth. Annual rates of unemployment and economic growth are shown in Table 11-1.

Notice in Table 11-1 that real GNP decreased in 1958; the value of output was less in 1958 than it was in 1957. With negative economic growth, it is no wonder that unemployment averaged 6.8 percent in 1958. During this period, the

TABLE 11-1 UNITED STATES UNEMPLOYMENT AND ECONOMIC GROWTH RATES, 1958–1968

Year	Unemployment Rate (%)	Growth Rate of Real GNP (%)
1958	6.8	−0.3
1959	5.5	6.0
1960	5.5	2.1
1961	6.7	2.6
1962	5.5	5.7
1963	5.7	4.1
1964	5.2	4.3
1965	4.5	6.0
1966	3.8	6.1
1967	3.8	2.7
1968	3.6	4.6

Compiled from U.S. Department of Commerce, *Business Conditions Digest* (Washington: U.S. Government Printing Office, January 1959–January 1969.)

growth rate of the Russian economy averaged 6 percent per year. Kennedy promised that he had a plan to get the economy going again. After taking office, he worked with his Council of Economic Advisers, which included Keynesian economists Walter Heller and James Tobin, to formulate a program that would both reduce the unemployment rate and increase economic growth.

In terms of the simple, theoretical Keynesian model, we could say that the U.S. economy was experiencing a deflationary gap. The economy was in equilibrium, but national income and output were below full employment. As we have shown, a deflationary gap can be eliminated by an increase in aggregate demand. The increase in aggregate demand can be accomplished through fiscal policy, either by an increase in G, a decrease in T, or both.

In 1962, Kennedy proposed a fiscal policy action based on traditional Keynesian economics. His proposal called for a decrease in personal and corporate taxes together with an increase in government spending. The proposal was designed to cause an increase in C, I, and G. Through the multiplier process, the increase in aggregate demand would increase Y and eliminate the deflationary gap. In addition, the **Kennedy Tax Cut**, as it was called, contained an innovative idea designed specifically to encourage business investment spending, the **Investment Tax Credit (ITC)**. As its name implies, the ITC is a tax write-off, or credit, given to business for undertaking investment spending. In effect, the ITC was a government subsidy to the business sector which allowed individual firms to deduct a certain percentage of investment spending from taxes owed.[5] The subsidy was justified

Kennedy Tax Cut A fiscal policy designed by the Kennedy administration to close the deflationary gap through a decrease in personal and corporate taxes and an increase in government spending.

Investment Tax Credit (ITC) A tax write-off or credit given to business for undertaking investment spending.

---

[5]The original level of the ITC was 7 percent. If a firm spent $1 million on an investment project, it could deduct $70,000 from the taxes it owed to the government. In effect, the ITC increases the expected rate of profit of all investment projects. Given that the interest rate remains stable, the ITC will cause an increase in investment spending.

Walter W. Heller *(1915–   )*

Arthur M. Okun *(1928–1981)*

The high point of fiscal activism, fine-tuning, and Keynesian aggregate demand management took place during the Kennedy-Johnson administration from 1961 to 1969. The early years provided some of the greatest successes for this policy, but by the last years of the Johnson administration, evidence was accumulating that controlling the economy was not as easy as some had thought.

The chairperson of John F. Kennedy's Council of Economic Advisers was *Walter W. Heller* of the University of Minnesota, who continued to serve under Lyndon B. Johnson until the 1964 election. *Arthur M. Okun* served on the three-member Council from late 1964 until the end of the Johnson administration and, in early 1968, was named chairperson of the Council.

In his book, *New Dimensions of Political Economy,* Heller said, "Today's (1967) talk of a 'new economics' arises not out of startling discoveries of new economic truths but out of the swift and progressive weaving of modern economics into the fabric of national thinking and policy." When he talks of "modern economics," Heller means Keynesian economics, with an emphasis on fiscal policy. From his viewpoint, what seemed to be the "new economics" to the noneconomist of the early and mid-1960s was simply the economic truths that had been around since the Keynesian revolution of the 1930s and 1940s. These truths had finally come into their own in influencing the thinking of the high level policymakers about the macro economy. In the preface to his book, Heller cited challenges to the "new eco-nomics," and even a few partial failures, but exuded confidence that the new outlook would solve pressing macro problems.

In his 1970 book, *The Political Economy of Prosperity,* Arthur M. Okun was noticeably less optimistic. By this time the inflation that was to plague the 1970s had already been at work for more than two years. Furthermore, it had become clear that macro policies often could benefit one group in the economy only by hurting another group. It began to seem that macro policies designed to stimulate the economy could often have the side effect of causing higher inflation and injuring those groups particularly hurt by inflation, such as those on fixed incomes. Still, Okun remained convinced in his book that with care and good Keynesian economic policymaking, the performance of the economy could be improved. However, over the next decade, the outlook for using fiscal and monetary policies to improve economic performance became much more gloomy; one example of this is the changing view toward the nature of the trade-off between inflation and unemployment, as we shall discuss in Chapter 15.

Heller remains a prominent figure in current macro policy debates and very often is on the activist end of the spectrum. Nevertheless, it is clear that policymaking is a much more difficult and imprecise activity than it seemed in the early 1960s and that the economy is far more obstinate and contrary than was at one time believed.

on the basis that, in the short run, investment spending would aid the economy by creating jobs, income, and spending. In the long run, investment spending would increase productive capacity and contribute to economic growth.

Kennedy was unsuccessful in obtaining congressional approval for his proposal. Congress was hesitant about the Kennedy Tax Cut. It was the first attempt to use Keynesian economic theory as a justification for the government to directly intervene in the economy. Many resisted the proposal because it would result in an increased federal deficit (tax revenues would fall while government expenditures would be increased). With the proposal stalled in Congress, Lyndon Johnson became president following Kennedy's assassination. In early 1964, Johnson was finally successful in getting congressional approval for the Kennedy Tax Cut. Did the policy work? Refer again to Table 11-1. Beginning in 1965, the unemployment rate declined and the economic growth rate increased, a trend that was to continue for the next several years. While these statistics do not prove conclusively that Keynesian fiscal policy was responsible for the rapid expansion of the U.S. economy from 1964 until 1969, Keynesian economists feel that they make a strong case in its behalf. Generally, economists agreed that Keynesian fiscal policy had worked as theory indicated it would. Some Keynesian economists went so far as to claim that the business cycle had been eliminated. These economists claimed that with the proper use of the tools of Keynesian economics, we need never fear another Great Depression.

The Ford Tax Rebate

A second example of closing a deflationary gap through the use of Keynesian fiscal policy occurred during the administration of Gerald Ford. Upon taking office during the summer of 1974, Gerald Ford declared inflation "public enemy number one," and formulated a fiscal policy action designed to reduce aggregate demand. To increase public awareness of inflation and to gain support for his program, Ford encouraged people to wear WIN (Whip Inflation Now) buttons.[6] As Ford prepared to have his WIN policies brought before Congress, many economists were concerned that restrictive fiscal policy would be harmful to the economy. They argued that inflation had peaked and the economy was about to slip into a recession. A tax increase would make the situation worse, not better. Ford was advised to drop his WIN campaign and begin work on an expansionary fiscal policy to deal with rising unemployment. Although Ford and the Democratic Congress finally agreed that a tax cut was needed, they disagreed on its size and distribution. The Democrats proposed a $23 billion tax rebate to be spread over a wide segment of the population, with individuals receiving a maximum of $200. Ford believed the Democrats' proposal would be dangerously inflationary. In terms of Figure 11-2, he believed the proposal would overshoot the target level of national income and produce another inflationary gap (from AD_2 to AD_3). He countered with a $16.7 billion tax rebate to be distributed in larger amounts to

---

[6]At the time, many Democrats who disagreed with Ford's actions wore the buttons upside down so that they read NIM. This, they said, represented their belief that there would be *No Immediate Miracles*.

Ford Tax Rebate *A fiscal policy designed by the Ford administration that featured tax cuts in the form of a rebate to individual taxpayers and tax incentives for buying a new house.*

a smaller segment of the population.[7] The Democrats prevailed and Ford signed the $23 billion tax rebate into law in the spring of 1975. The **Ford Tax Rebate** also included an innovative tax incentive designed to help the ailing housing industry. A housing purchase tax credit was available on any unsold, new home which had been started on or before April 15, 1975. The buyer was allowed to deduct 5 percent of the purchase price of the new home from the federal tax return. The goal was to create a tax incentive to help remove the large inventory of newly built, unsold homes on the market. As the Ford Tax Rebate took effect, aggregate demand increased and the unemployment rate fell. By election year, 1976, unemployment had fallen to below 8 percent from a high of over 9 percent in 1975. The inflation rate was around 6 percent, half what it had been in 1974 when inflation reached its peak. In both 1964 and 1975, fiscal policy based on Keynesian economic theory produced the intended results.

The Johnson Tax Surcharge

Following the Kennedy Tax Cut in 1964, the U.S. economy experienced a period of sustained economic growth. During this time, President Johnson initiated his program to produce the "Great Society." Johnson declared a "war on poverty" and introduced legislation designed to raise the living standard of low-income families. Beginning in the second half of the 1960s, American involvement in Southeast Asia, especially in South Vietnam, increased significantly. With the economy operating at a full-employment level of output (Y^*), Johnson added another burden, the war in South Vietnam. To fight both wars, the government needed a larger share of the economy's output. Johnson did not want to reduce spending on the domestic war on poverty nor did he want to increase taxes to provide revenues to fight in Vietnam. Johnson, therefore, chose to increase G without an increase in T, while the economy was at Y^*. This resulted in a deficit in the federal budget which was largely financed through money creation. The result of the increase in G while the economy was operating at Y^* was to generate an inflationary gap similar to that shown in Figure 11-1. As noted earlier, an inflationary gap gets its name from the economic problem it creates—inflation. Annual rates of unemployment and inflation for 1961–1971 are shown in Table 11-2. As you can see, the unemployment rate was below 4 percent (the full-employment target level at the time) from 1966 through 1969. Notice that the inflation rate rose, while the unemployment rate declined. We will have more to say about this inverse relationship in Chapter 14.

By 1967, Johnson was convinced that inflation was becoming a problem. With the aid of his economic advisers, he designed a Keynesian fiscal policy program designed to close the inflationary gap. Aggregate demand was to be reduced causing Y to decline to Y^*. The decline in income and output was intended to reduce inflationary pressures. It was understood that a necessary

---

[7]Ford believed that the tax rebate should be structured to encourage spending for automobiles and large appliances, since unemployment was most severe in these industries and the steel industry. He argued that the tax rebates should be given to a small portion of taxpayers in amounts sufficient to stimulate sales in the most depressed industries. The Democrats wanted the tax rebate to partially compensate low income groups for the effects of the recent inflation. This could be accomplished, they argued, by keeping the individual rebates smaller, but making them available to more people.

TABLE 11-2   UNITED STATES UNEMPLOYMENT AND
INFLATION RATES, 1961–1971

Year	Unemployment Rate (%)	Inflation Rate (%)
1961	6.7	1.0
1962	5.5	1.1
1963	5.7	1.2
1964	5.2	1.3
1965	4.5	1.7
1966	3.8	2.9
1967	3.8	2.9
1968	3.6	4.2
1969	3.5	5.4
1970	4.9	5.9
1971	6.0	5.0

Source: Compiled from U.S. Department of Commerce, *Business Conditions Digest* (Washington: U.S. Government Printing Office, January 1962–January 1972.)

consequence of the program to reduce inflation was an increase in the unemployment rate.

The program proposed by Johnson was standard Keynesian medicine for closing an inflationary gap. Aggregate demand was to be reduced by a tax increase, a temporary 10 percent surcharge on individual income and corporate profit.[8] The surcharge was to be effective for one year with the presidential option to extend it for a second year.[9] The program also called for the elimination of the investment tax credit and promised to slow the rate of increase of government spending. Similar to the earlier Kennedy Tax Cut, the **Johnson Tax Surcharge** did not receive speedy congressional approval. Although Johnson had great influence with Congress, the idea of voting for a tax increase did not appeal to many members of Congress. However, in 1968, after a delay of more than a year, the surcharge was passed, and President Nixon extended the tax surcharge program.

This first test of restrictive fiscal policy failed. Look at the data in Table 11-2. Unemployment rose as expected, but the intended decline in the inflation rate failed to materialize. In fact, by 1970, the inflation rate was up to 5.9 percent from a level of 4.2 percent in 1968.

As a result of these three episodes, many people believed that fiscal policy could be used successfully to close a deflationary gap, but that it was not capable of closing an inflationary gap.

Johnson Tax Surcharge   A fiscal policy designed by the Johnson administration to reduce inflation. The program included a 10 percent tax surcharge on individual and corporate income effective for one year, with a presidential option to extend it for another year. It also included the elimination of the investment tax credit and a decrease in the rate of government spending.

[8]For instance, an individual tax payer would calculate his or her tax liability as that person had in the previous year. Then he or she would add 10 percent to that amount and pay the total to the government. Corporations would do the same.

[9]Many economists believe the nonpermanent feature of the tax surcharge diminished its chance for success. They argued that people would not reduce consumption expenditures in response to a temporary reduction in disposable income.

Hey Man, Do You Want to Buy a Tax Credit?

Pity the corporation that is spending great amounts of money on retooling in order to compete more effectively with modern firms! It is allowed huge tax credits by President Reagan's 1981 tax package, but it doesn't have enough income to offset these credits. To solve the dilemma, it can sell these tax credits to a firm that has income to offset, but doesn't need to retool.

Tax credits are "sold" through a leasing arrangement. The firm that can't use its tax credits sells its equipment to a firm that can use the credits. The firm buying the equipment then leases it back to the original firm. When the lease expires, the first firm buys the equipment back for one dollar.

Many firms are jumping on this bandwagon. It is estimated that IBM bought $200 million in tax benefits from Ford Motor Company in late 1981. Proponents of this activity see it as a salvation to ailing firms. It encourages firms to retool and compete against foreign industries.

The cost is high. Tax experts estimate that the loss of tax revenues could be as high as $3 billion. This means that profitable firms and individuals pay more taxes in order to give ailing firms an incentive to retool. Many argue that it is a subsidy to make some sick firms profitable—a subsidy paid by taxpayers.

THE PROBLEM OF LAGS

recognition lag   Time lapse associated with the time it takes to recognize an economic problem.

As a result of our experiences over the past 25 years, economists have identified several lags associated with economic policymaking. The *recognition lag* occurs because it takes time to become aware of, or recognize, an economic problem. Our statistical measures (unemployment rate, consumer price index, and GNP) take from one to three or more months to compile. At best, when these statistics become available, they tell us about economic conditions during the previous months or quarter. Once a problem is recognized, additional time passes as the president and Congress formulate a fiscal policy solution. More time passes as the bill moves through Congress. Even after Congress has finished its debate and passed the legislation, more time may lapse before the president signs the bill into law. This lag is called the *implementation lag,* because it is associated with the delay in formulating and researching agreement on an appropriate fiscal policy response. President Kennedy's Council of Economic Advisers recommended a tax cut in 1961. He, in turn, made the proposal to Congress in late 1962, and it wasn't until February 1964 that the Kennedy Tax Cut was signed into law. Johnson's Tax Surcharge was held up in Congress for nearly a year before being enacted in 1968. As a result of these congressional delays, many economists thought that limited discretionary power to change tax rates should be accorded

implementation lag   Once an economic problem is identified, there is a lapse of time that passes while appropriate action is formulated and moved through legislative channels.

the president. It would save valuable time, they argued, if the president could either raise or lower taxes within a narrow, well-defined range, without requiring prior approval by Congress. However, many of these same advocates changed their minds about granting discretionary power to the president as a result of the experience with *impounded funds* during the Nixon administration. After Congress had approved expenditures for a project, the funds were impounded and not spent. In this way, Nixon was able to circumvent Congress and use restrictive fiscal policy without the approval of Congress. After a fiscal policy action has been signed into law, additional time passes before we see an improvement in the economy. Thus the *impact lag,* which is a time lapse between the implementation of a policy and the time when the policy begins to influence economic activity, results.

In the next two chapters, we will see that monetary policy is susceptible to the same lags. Most economists agree that the implementation lag is longer for fiscal policy than monetary policy, and that the impact lag is longer for monetary policy than for fiscal policy. Taken together, recognition, implementation, and impact lags may involve a considerable amount of time. It is quite possible that combined lags can take up so much time that a tax cut or an increase in government spending will not have full effect until after the economy begins to move out of recession by itself. The expansionary fiscal policy may then simply help start inflation. Similarly, anti-inflationary tax increases or expenditure cutbacks may not begin to work until after the economy has turned into a recession.

impounded funds   After Congress has approved expenditures for a project, the funds are not spent. In this way, the president can circumvent Congress and use restrictive fiscal policy without the approval of Congress.

impact lag   The time lapse between the implementation of a fiscal policy and the time when it begins to influence economic activity.

SUMMARY

1. Keynesian fiscal policy is based on the following beliefs: (1) an equilibrium may result in high rates of unemployment or inflation; (2) changes in private or foreign sector spending may cause macroeconomic problems; and (3) only the government can be counted on to act in the social interest.

2. The Full Employment Act of 1946 makes the government responsible for achieving and maintaining full employment through the use of fiscal and monetary policy.

3. Changes in private and foreign sector expenditures can cause deflationary or inflationary gaps. A deflationary gap occurs when aggregate demand is insufficient to purchase society's full-employment output, while an inflationary gap occurs when aggregate demand exceeds society's full-employment output.

4. Keynesian fiscal policy can be used to close either a deflationary or an inflationary gap. Closing a deflationary gap requires increasing

G, reducing T, or both. Closing an inflationary gap requires reducing G, increasing T, or both.

5. Through the balanced-budget multiplier effect, equal, offsetting changes in G and T will cause Y to change by the same amount as G.

6. Advocates of Keynesian fiscal policy claim it allows us to reduce, if not totally avoid, the social costs of unemployment and inflation. Opponents claim that fiscal policy (1) causes inefficiency through large government, (2) crowds out private sector spending, (3) is inflationary, and (4) increases the national debt.

7. The U.S. experience with Keynesian fiscal policy has produced mixed results. Tax cuts by Kennedy and Johnson in 1964 and Ford in 1975 reduced deflationary gaps while a tax increase by Johnson (and Nixon) failed to reduce an inflationary gap in 1968 to 1970.

8. Keynesian fiscal policy is hindered by lags in recognition, implementation, and impact.

NEW TERMS

fiscal policy
Keynesian fiscal policy
deflationary gap
inflationary gap
balanced budget multiplier
federal budget deficit
federal budget surplus
crowding-out effect

Kennedy Tax Cut
Investment Tax Credit
Ford Tax Rebate
Johnson Tax Surcharge
recognition lag
implementation lag
impounded funds
impact lag

QUESTIONS FOR DISCUSSION

1. Do you think economists who subscribe to classical macroeconomic theory would advocate the use of fiscal policy to eliminate a deflationary or an inflationary gap? Why or why not?

2. Suppose the MPC is 0.9, the consumption function intercept is $300 billion, and I, G, $(X - M)$, and T are each equal to $100 billion. What are the equilibrium levels of Y, C, and S?

3. In Question 2, if G rises to $200 billion, *ceteris paribus*, by how much do the equilibrium levels

of Y, C, and S change? What would be the equilibrium levels of Y, C, and S, if T was reduced by $200 billion, *ceteris paribus*?

4. Using the information in Question 2, suppose Y^* is $5,600 billion. How much would G have to change to bring the economy to full employment? How much would T have to change?

5. Why are economists concerned about the lags associated with fiscal policy actions? What solutions can you offer?

SUGGESTIONS FOR FURTHER READING

Blinder, Alan. *Economic Policy and the Great Stagflation.* New York: Academic Press, Inc., 1981.
Dauten, Carl A., and Lloyd M. Valentine. *Business Cycles and Forecasting,* 5h ed. Cincinnati: South-Western Publishing Co., 1978.
Friedman, Milton, and Walter Heller. *Monetary Versus Fiscal Policy.* New York: W. W. Norton and Co., Inc., 1969.
Heller, Walter. *New Dimensions of Political Economy.* New York: W. W. Norton and Co., Inc., 1967.
Okun, Arthur. *The Political Economy of Prosperity.* New York: W. W. Norton and Co., Inc., 1970.

APPENDIX: A GENERAL ALGEBRAIC SOLUTION OF THE MODEL

In analyzing fiscal policy, it is often useful to work with algebraic formulas rather than numerical ones. For example, instead of using the specific consumption function,

$$C = \$200 \text{ billion} + 0.8(Y - T),$$

we might use the more general consumption function,

$$C = a + b(Y - T), \tag{11-4}$$

where $a > 0$ and where $0 < b < 1$; b is the MPC.

These general formulas offer additional insights into how the models work and offer shortcuts in solving them. Suppose we set

$$I = I_0$$
$$G = G_0$$
$$(X-M) = (X-M)_0$$

and

$$T = T_0,$$

where I_0, G_0, $(X-M)_0$, and T_0 are some fixed but unspecified numbers. We can then write the Keynesian model in general terms as

$$Y = C + I + G + (X-M) \tag{11-5}$$

$$C = a + b(Y-T) \tag{11-6}$$

$$I = I_0 \tag{11-7}$$

$$G = G_0 \tag{11-8}$$

$$(X-M) = (X-M)_0 \tag{11-9}$$

$$T = T_0. \tag{11-10}$$

We have a, b, I_0, G_0, $(X-M)_0$, and T_0 as givens. This leaves six variables—Y, C, I, G, $(X-M)$, and T—in the six equations (11-5)—(11-10). We can substitute the consumption function (11-6) into the equilibrium condition (11-5) to give

$$Y = a + b(Y-T) + I + G + (X-M). \tag{11-11}$$

Then, we can substitute for I, G, and $(X-M)$ from equations (11-7), (11-8), and (11-9) to find

$$Y = a + b(Y-T) + I_0 + G_0 + (X-M)_0. \tag{11-12}$$

Then using equation (11-10), we substitute for T in (11-12) to obtain

$$Y = a + b(Y-T_0) + I_0 + G_0 + (X-M)_0. \tag{11-13}$$

Since Keynesian fiscal policy does not involve changes in investment or foreign spending, we can simplify (11-13) slightly by defining

$$Z_0 = I_0 + (X-M)_0.$$

Then (11-13) becomes

$$Y = a + b(Y-T_0) + G_0 + Z_0. \tag{11-14}$$

We can rearrange (11-14) to find

$$Y = a + bY - bT_0 + G_0 + Z_0$$
$$Y - bY = a - bT_0 + G_0 + Z_0$$
$$(1 - b)Y = a - bT_0 + G_0 + Z_0$$
$$Y = (\frac{1}{1-b})(a - bT_0 + G_0 + Z_0). \qquad (11\text{-}15)$$

From equation (11-15), we can see that the equilibrium value of Y is equal to the aggregate demand function intercept $(a - bT_0 + G_0 + Z_0)$ times the multiplier $\frac{1}{1-b}$.

Now, let us hold a, b, T_0, and Z_0 constant and solve for the value Y_0 associated with the level of government spending G_0. We have

$$Y_0 = (\frac{1}{1-b}) (a - bT_0 + G_0 + Z_0).$$

Similarly, if G increases to a higher level, G_1, then Y will change to a higher level also, as in

$$Y_1 = (\frac{1}{1-b}) (a - bT_0 + G_1 + Z_0).$$

If we define the change in Y as $\Delta Y = Y_1 - Y_0$ and the change in G as $\Delta G = G_1 - G_0$, then

$$\Delta Y = Y_1 - Y_0 = (\frac{1}{1-b}) (a - bT_0 + G_1 + Z_0) - (\frac{1}{1-b})(a - bT_0 + G_0 + Z_0)$$

$$= (\frac{1}{1-b}) (a - bT_0 + G_1 + Z_0 - a + bT_0 - G_0 - Z_0)$$

$$= (\frac{1}{1-b}) (G_1 - G_0)$$

$$= (\frac{1}{1-b}) \Delta G.$$

Thus, if government spending changes by ΔG, the resulting change in Y is given by the multiplier times ΔG.

Let's try a similar experiment by raising taxes from T_0 to T_1. Then,

$$Y_0 = (\frac{1}{1-b}) (a - bT_0 + G_0 + Z_0)$$

and

$$Y_1 = (\frac{1}{1-b}) (a - bT_1 + G_0 + Z_0).$$

Thus,

$$\Delta Y = Y_1 - Y_0 = (\frac{1}{1-b})(a - bT_1 + G_0 + Z_0) - (\frac{1}{1-b})(a - bT_0 + G_0 + Z_0)$$

$$= (\frac{1}{1-b})(a - bT_1 + G_0 + Z_0 - a + bT_0 - G_0 - Z_0)$$

$$= (\frac{1}{1-b})(-bT_1 + bT_0)$$

$$= (\frac{1}{1-b})(-b \Delta T)$$

$$\Delta Y = (\frac{-b}{1-b}) \Delta T$$

So, the change in Y is equal to the taxation multiplier $\frac{-b}{1-b}$ times the change in taxes. Recall that the tax change multiplier is just $-(MPC/MPS)$.

The Algebra of the Balanced Budget Multiplier

Recall that the budget deficit is defined as $(G-T)$. If $G=T$, the budget is balanced. Let's suppose that we raise both G and T by the same amount. The budget remains balanced, but we can show that Y will rise. To see this, write the initial Y as

$$Y_0 = (\frac{1}{1-b})(a - bT_0 + G_0 + Z_0)$$

and then let both T and G rise, so

$$Y_1 = (\frac{1}{1-b})(a - bT_1 + G_1 + Z_0).$$

The change in Y is

$$\Delta Y = Y_1 - Y_0 = (\frac{1}{1-b})(a - bT_1 + G_1 + Z_0) - (\frac{1}{1-b})(a - bT_0 + G_0 + Z_0)$$

$$= (\frac{1}{1-b})(a - bT_1 + G_1 + Z_0 - a + bT_0 - G_0 - Z_0)$$

$$= (\frac{1}{1-b})(-bT_1 + bT_0 + G_1 - G_0)$$

$$= (\frac{1}{1-b})(-b \Delta T + \Delta G)$$

$$\Delta Y = (\frac{-b}{1-b}) \Delta T + (\frac{1}{1-b}) \Delta G.$$

If T and G rise by the same amount, $\Delta T = \Delta G$, so

$$\Delta Y = \left(\frac{-b}{1-b}\right)\Delta G + \left(\frac{1}{1-b}\right)\Delta G$$

$$\Delta Y = \left(\frac{1-b}{1-b}\right)\Delta G = \Delta G. \tag{11-16}$$

The multiplier $\left(\frac{1-b}{1-b}\right)=1$ is known as the *balanced budget multiplier*. The result that equal increases in G and T cause Y to rise by the same amount is called the *balanced budget multiplier theorem*. Note, however, that equation (11-16) holds for equal changes in G and T, whether the budget was initially balanced or not. Thus, the theorem really says that increases in G and T that don't change the budget deficit nevertheless have real effects.

It is important to realize that the balanced budget multiplier theorem only makes sense if there are unemployed resources in the economy so Y can, in fact, rise when G goes up. If Y can't rise, the increase in G means that either C, I, or $(X-M)$ must fall.

The Modern Quantity Theory of Money

Learning Objectives

After studying the materials found in this chapter, you should be able to do the following:

1. Describe the two major challenges faced by the economists who developed the modern quantity theory (MQT) of money.

2. Discuss the revision in the demand for money concept which allowed the MQT economists to explain short-run variations in the velocity of money.

3. Explain why a decrease in the expected yield and/or an increase in the risk of holding bonds would cause an increase in the demand for money.

4. Describe and explain the importance of the Friedman-Meiselman tests and the St. Louis Fed model to the Keynesian-MQT debate.

5. Explain how the formation of expectations by the public is important to:
   (a) the effect on prices and output given a change in the money stock or a change in fiscal policy.
   (b) the time lag between a change in the money supply and the observed change in prices and output.

6. Briefly discuss the following statement: "The question of whether the Keynesian or modern quantity theory is better must be resolved on empirical grounds."

After the Keynesian Revolution of the 1930s and 1940s, the Keynesian model, which was presented in Chapters 10 and 11, became the most important view of the macro economy. However, the influence of the quantity theory of money, which was discussed in Chapter 8, led some economists to disagree with the Keynesian view and to construct a modern quantity theory of money as an alternative to the Keynesian model. This chapter discusses the *modern quantity theory (MQT)*, how it differs from the Keynesian model, and how it challenges the Keynesian revolution. We will discuss how the MQT evolved from the older quantity theory and show some of its main propositions.

Two main challenges faced those economists who wanted to build a modern quantity theory. First, the modern quantity theory would have to develop a theory of the demand for money that would allow for, and help explain, variations

modern quantity theory   A modern reformulation of the quantity theory of money intended to remove the older theory's shortcomings. It tries to explain shorter run changes in the price level and real output and income, as well as the determination of the long-run price level.

in velocity such as those that occurred during the Great Depression. You will remember that the quantity theory could not satisfactorily explain these changes in velocity. Second, the modern quantity theory would have to show how changes in the money stock affect output and prices in the short run.

ORIGINS OF THE KEYNESIAN REVOLUTION AND THE MODERN QUANTITY THEORY

We learned in Chapter 9 that the Keynesian model filled the need for an explanation of what was going on in the Great Depression of the 1930s; that is, what caused the fall in real output from 1929 to 1933 and the high levels of unemployment. (The unemployment rate was almost 25 percent in 1933 and close to 10 percent even in 1941.) Further, Keynesian theory proposed a solution to the high unemployment problems of the 1930s; according to the theory, expansionary fiscal policy could be used to eliminate unemployment. The earlier economic explanations of the Depression, such as those based on the classical quantity theory and the many business cycle theories, did not seem to explain these times nearly as well as Keynesian theory, nor did these other explanations offer much in the way of solutions for the terrible problems of the 1930s. The Keynesian model seemed to be the best way to look at the economy and its problems, and it offered the best alternative for solving these problems.

For these reasons, the Keynesian revolution swept through American and British economic thought. We must emphasize that there was very little statistical evidence either *for* or *against* the Keynesian theory; there was little factual evidence that compared the Keynesian theory to other explanations.

econometrics The use of mathematics, statistics, economic models, and data to test economic theory and forecast developments in the economy.

Econometrics is that branch of economics that combines economic theory with mathematical and statistical methods to forecast economic events, to explain various economic occurrences (such as the Depression, the inflation of the late 1960s and 1970s, the recession of 1974, and so on), and to compare how well different theories explain how the economy behaves. In the 1930s and 1940s, econometrics was in its infancy. Even in the early 1960s, many economic researchers had only limited access to the computers that are necessary to carry out extensive econometric research on how the economy behaves. In the 1960s, when computers became accessible to economists and the level of econometric skill had improved greatly from the 1930s and 1940s, Keynesian theory was the dominant theory. Our point is that it had become dominant without a large amount of supporting econometric research.[1]

The lack of econometric support does not mean Keynesian theory was wrong. Rather, it means that those who opposed Keynesian economics could now try to attack it on the basis of empirical, or econometric, research; that is, they

---

[1]Some truly fine econometricians were at work in the 1930s and 1940s; for example, Jan Tinbergen of the Netherlands, who shared the first Nobel Prize in Economics in 1969. But most economists of that period were not this sophisticated and interested in empirical questions in economics. Indeed, there often was a bias against empirical work. Even in the 1970s, economists were able to earn Ph.D.'s with only very basic skills in statistics and econometrics. This merely means that economics has only begun to seriously face empirical issues in the past few decades, not that such nonempirical economists are bad economists.

could compare the theory with the facts. This is precisely what happened with the evolution of the MQT. The monetarists who developed and support the MQT present two main attacks on the Keynesian theory. First, they offer a rival theory, the revised MQT, that attempts to remedy the major flaws in the older quantity theory. Second, they argue that the MQT does a better job of explaining the world and forecasting the future than does the Keynesian theory. They argue that the empirical evidence is on their side. By the mid-1970s, the debate had reached the point where it was in large part an empirical one. Each side acknowledged that the other side was not making some basic mistake in logic and agreed that the issue of *which theory is better* must be resolved on empirical grounds.[2]

THE KEYNESIAN THEORY DIDN'T PREVAIL EVERYWHERE

The Keynesian revolution swept up some of the very best minds in economics. For example, Paul A. Samuelson of MIT, the Nobel prizewinner in economics in 1970, wrote:

> I have always considered it a priceless advantage to have been born as an economist prior to 1936 and to have received a thorough grounding in classical economics. It is quite impossible for modern students to realize the full effect of what has been advisably called "The Keynesian Revolution" upon those of us brought up in the orthodox tradition. What beginners today often regard as trite and obvious was to us puzzling, novel, and heretical.
>
> To have been born as an economist before 1936 was a boon—yes. But not to have been born too long before!
>
> > Bliss was it in that dawn to be alive,
> > But to be young was very heaven!
>
> The *General Theory* caught most economists under the age of thirty-five with the unexpected virulence of a disease first attacking and decimating an isolated tribe of south sea islanders. Economists beyond fifty turned out to be quite immune to the ailment. With time, most economists in-between began to run the fever, often without knowing or admitting their condition.[3]

However, it was to be expected that not everyone would convert to the new views. First, economic theory is quite hard to master, and, once understood and accepted, its logical strength is so convincing that it is not easily discarded. Thus, many economists who had mastered and adopted the quantity theory continued to hold to it and teach it.[4] Second, no theory is without flaws (or at least shortcomings), and those who see the flaws are tempted to find another theory that does

---

[2]Representatives from both sides did make logical mistakes and continue to do so. However, both sides acknowledge that a valid case can be made for the other side's view. Each side may believe the other side is fundamentally mistaken and will be proved wrong in the long run, but the evidence that refutes the other side must be mainly empirical evidence.

[3]See Paul A. Samuelson, "The General Theory," *Econometrica,* Vol. 14 (July, 1946). Samuelson was not the only distinguished economist greatly influenced by the Keynesian revolution. Joan Robinson of Cambridge University was a student and colleague of Keynes who did a great deal to extend aspects of the theory. J. R. Hicks of Oxford was substantially influenced, while at the same time making significant contributions to Keynesian theory.

[4]Keynes wrote of how hard it was for him to throw off the grounding he received in the quantity theory from Alfred Marshall (see Chapter 8 for Marshall's place in the history of the quantity theory).

a better job. Thus, some economists turned to the modern quantity theory as an alternative to the Keynesian theory. For example, the Keynesian model of Chapters 10 and 11 did not mention the money supply at all. Even in the 1960s, one could find Keynesian models, designed to guide the entire economy, that did not even mention the money stock. Such neglect turned some people toward the MQT because their views held that money did play a significant role in the economy.[5]

The quantity theory approach lived on at a number of universities but with particular strength at the University of Chicago. Beginning in the early 1950s, published work from Chicago, as well as from other universities, attempted to rebuild the quantity theory and also to mount an empirical attack on Keynesian theory. Major contributors to the evolution of the MQT were Milton Friedman, long at the University of Chicago (and now retired but still active at the National Bureau of Economic Research), Karl Brunner (University of Rochester), and Allan Meltzer (Carnegie-Mellon University).

FROM THE QUANTITY THEORY TO THE MODERN QUANTITY THEORY

Let's consider the evolution from the quantity theory to the modern quantity theory. One major step was the development of a more sophisticated theory of the demand for money than the theory used by the older quantity theorists. As we saw in Chapter 8, the quantity theory focused on the long-run questions concerning the price level, adopting the very simple hypothesis that the demand for money was related to the level of GNP by a constant. For example, in Alfred Marshall's discussion, the quantity of money that people demanded to hold (M^d) was equal to a constant—the Cambridge k—times GNP, or

$$M^d = k \cdot GNP. \qquad (12\text{-}1)$$

Marshall and his followers interpreted k as simply that fraction of a year's income that people desired to hold in the form of money. It is very reasonable to suppose that the quantity of money that people want to hold will depend on GNP. A major reason for holding money is to use it for transactions involving the goods and services that make up the gross national product.

If we suppose, as the older quantity theorists did, that real output is constant in the long run, then the only long-run changes in GNP are due to price changes. We may let $Y = Y^*$ (the long-run full-employment output), as we did in Chapter 8. We know from our discussion of national income accounting that GNP in current dollars is the price level times real output, or $GNP = P \cdot Y$. Thus, in the long run, when $Y = Y^*$, we will have

$$GNP = P \cdot Y^*,$$

where P is the price level. Let us further assume the money supply is a constant

---

[5]That is, for some people Keynesian theory went too far in its neglect of money. These economists would not focus on the money supply as exclusively as did the older quantity theorists, but they thought money mattered very much to the overall state of the economy.

M^s. (Once the principles involved are understood, it is not too difficult to generalize to the case where M^s and Y^* can grow over time.) Finally, let us state the equilibrium condition that money demand equals money supply, or

$$M^d = M^s.$$

Then, from equation (12-1) we have

$$M^s = k \cdot P \cdot Y^*. \qquad (12\text{-}2)$$

It can be seen that doubling both M^s and P will satisfy equation (12-2). As Chapter 8 explained, quantity theorists viewed this relationship as meaning that, in the long run, when Y returns to Y^* and money demand and supply are equal, a doubling of M^s causes P to double; or, more generally, a change in the money supply causes the general level of prices to change in the same proportion as the change in M^s.

The key assumption here is that k is constant. As Chapter 8 discussed, Irving Fisher argued that in the long run a change in the money supply causes a proportionate change in the price level. Fisher started with the equation of exchange,

$$M^s V = P \cdot Y, \qquad (12\text{-}3)$$

which always has to be true since income velocity *(V)* is defined as

$$V = \frac{P \cdot Y}{M^s} = \frac{GNP}{M^s}. \qquad (12\text{-}4)$$

He reasoned that V was constant in the long run (or at least V didn't depend on P or M). When Y settled down to Y^* in the long run, equation (12-3) would become

$$M^s V = P \cdot Y^* \qquad (12\text{-}5)$$

and the price level, P, would have to be proportionate to the money stock, M^s. Thus, in either the Cambridge or Fisher versions of the quantity theory, a key assumption was that k or V was constant. As can be seen by comparing equations (12-2) and (12-5), in the long run k has to be the same as $\frac{1}{V}$, or V has to equal $\frac{1}{k}$. Clearly the two theories are very closely related.

The quantity theorists knew that neither k nor V was constant over the short run; they knew that Y did not always equal Y^*; and they knew that P was not always at its long-run value. In fact, it was precisely the inability of the older quantity theory to explain movements in k, V, P, and Y that made the Keynesian theory appear to be better. A natural line of development of the MQT was to try to remedy these gaps and to explain variations in k and V, as well as changes in Y and P. In the following section, we will discuss the MQT developments regarding k and V, and, later in this chapter, we will discuss MQT views on how P and Y change in reaction to changes in the money supply.

Karl Brunner *(1916–)*   Allan H. Meltzer *(1928–)*

Among the most influential and active of modern quantity theory economists are *Karl Brunner* of the University of Rochester and *Allan Meltzer* of Carnegie-Mellon University. The resurgence of the quantity theory and its substantial reformulation as the modern quantity theory of money is sometimes viewed as a result of the work at the University of Chicago by Milton Friedman and his colleagues and students. Brunner and Meltzer are the developers of a separate and very active strand of the modern quantity theory, and, with their students scattered across many countries, they provide a distinctive outlook on U.S. and international economic developments.

Born in Switzerland, Brunner received his doctorate in 1943 at the University of Zurich. He taught at UCLA from 1951 to 1966. In 1966 he moved to Ohio State University, where he was the founding editor of the *Journal of Money, Credit, and Banking,* which he edited from 1969 to 1974. Since 1971 he has been at the University of Rochester, and in 1975 he became the founding editor of the *Journal of Monetary Economics,* an important journal in the areas of monetary theory and policy.

Born in Boston, Meltzer received his Ph.D. at UCLA in 1958, writing his dissertation under Brunner. He is the Maurice Falk Professor of Economics and Social Sciences in the Graduate School of Industrial Administration at Carnegie-Mellon University and has served on the editorial boards of a number of distinguished journals.

Beginning in the early 1960s, Brunner and Meltzer produced a series of articles dealing with the process by which money is supplied to the U.S. economy; emphasis on money-supply theory is one of their contributions to the modern quantity theory. Individually and together, they made contributions in the area of monetary theory, the theoretical and policy implications of predicting velocity, and the micro foundations for the use of money. Separately (and jointly), both authors have made numerous contributions to monetary policy analysis.

Brunner and Meltzer founded the Shadow Open Market Committee to provide an alternative analysis of the questions faced by the Federal Open Market Committee of the Federal Reserve System. The Shadow Open Market Committee has generally emphasized control of the money supply and the desirability of moving gradually and in preannounced stages to a steady rate of monetary growth. Brunner and Meltzer have also been instrumental in another "shadow" group monitoring the monetary policies of European countries.

THE DEMAND FOR MONEY AND THE BEHAVIOR OF k AND V

During the Great Depression, there was a significant decline in velocity. This is shown in Figure 12-1. One way of explaining the sharp decline in V is to explain why k increased. For instance, if people increase the amount of money they wish to hold relative to GNP, then k will increase. In response to this increase in M^d, we would expect $\frac{GNP}{M^s}$ to decline and therefore V would fall. When people attempt to increase their money holdings, they engage in fewer transactions and, on average, hold each dollar longer. This causes GNP to decline and therefore $\frac{GNP}{M^s}$ (and V) to decline. Thus, for the monetarists who wished to reconstruct and modernize the quantity theory of money, the first step was to explain why the demand for money varied in the short run.

The MQT is based on the idea that the demand for money can be explained within the same framework used to explain the demand for goods and services. According to this view, people hold cash balances (demand money) for the utility or satisfaction it affords them. In Chapter 3, we saw that the demand for a good or service will vary in predictable ways as such important factors as income and

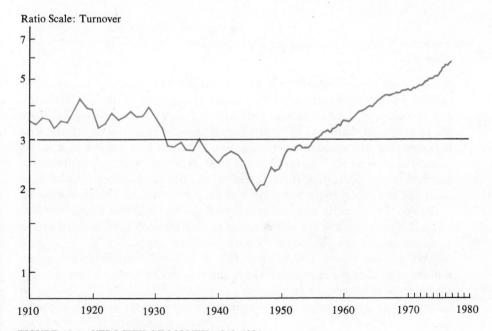

FIGURE 12-1   VELOCITY OF MONEY, 1910–1981

Velocity is equal to GNP by the money supply—in this case the M_1 money supply. There was a sharp fall in velocity in the early years of the Depression and also in the World War II years. However, in the post-World War II period, velocity has grown, though with ups and downs around the upward trend. (Source: *Historical Chart Book,* Board of Governors of the Federal Reserve System.)

price expectations change. The MQT identifies the important factors affecting people's decisions to hold money and shows how changes in these factors result in predictable changes in the demand for money.[6] In the following sections, we will consider why people hold money and how changes in expected yields, risk, and the price level influence the demand for money.

Motives for Holding Money

Today, most economists agree that the decision to hold money depends upon a comparison of the satisfaction obtained from holding money with the satisfaction obtained from holding alternative assets. Money is very useful. It allows us to make purchases and provides us with some degree of security against unexpected events which might require an outlay of cash. There are many transactions where only cash will do. For example, you cannot use a parking meter without cash. If you use a credit card for most of your transactions, you still need to pay the credit card bill with money. Thus, we can identify strong *transaction* and *precautionary motives* for holding money.

Since we derive a great deal of satisfaction from holding money, why don't we keep all of our income or wealth in cash or checking accounts? Monetarists point out that there are costs associated with holding money. First, there is an opportunity cost: when we hold money we forego the possible gains from holding alternative assets. Second, money's value or purchasing power fluctuates with changes in the price level. Holding money will be costly during periods of rising prices.

precautionary motive Holding money as a precaution against unexpected requirements for using it.

Expected Yields, Risk, and the Demand for Money

What do you expect to get from holding assets other than money? For example, suppose you reduce your money holdings to buy one share of stock in IBM. You will probably get some dividends, although you can't be sure how much. Also, the value of your share may go up although there is no guarantee that it will. You may come out $10 ahead in a particular year for every $100 you invest, a return or *yield* of 10 percent.[7] This is the actual yield. However, when you compare the desirability of holding your funds in cash or in IBM stock, you want to look at what you can expect to get out of both of these investments. This is an *expected yield*. You are uncertain what the actual yield will be for almost all assets. Thus, you will want to look at the *risk* attached to each asset. We can think of risk as some measure of the possibilities of both gains and losses.

We can use Figure 12-2 to show how k and the demand for money are influenced by changes in expected yields and risk. As we proceed, keep in mind that a decision to decrease holdings of securities (stocks and bonds) implies an increase in money holdings. Since we are interested in how changes in expected

yield The rate of return on funds invested in an asset.

expected yield The expected rate of return on an asset.

risk The idea that the actual outcome may be better or worse than expected.

---

[6]See Milton Friedman, "The Demand for Money," in Milton Friedman (ed.), *Studies in the Quantity Theory of Money* (Chicago: University of Chicago Press, 1956).

[7]For example, if you buy one share for $100 and a year later you receive a dividend of $4, while the price of the share has risen to $106, you could sell the share and be $10 ahead, $4 from the dividend and $6 from the increase in the price of one share. You made $10 on your investment of $100, or the investment yielded a 10 percent annual rate of return.

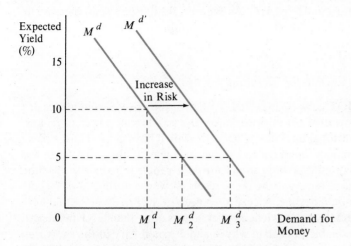

FIGURE 12-2 CHANGES IN EXPECTED YIELD AND RISK INFLUENCE THE DEMAND FOR MONEY

The demand for money line (M_d) shows that at lower expected yields on assets such as stocks and bonds, people will act to increase their cash balances. For example, if expected yield decreases from 10 percent to 5 percent, the quantity of money demanded would increase from M_1^d to M_2^d.

An increase in the risk associated with holding alternative assets would result in an increased desire to hold cash balances at any expected yield. This is shown by the shift of the demand for money line from M^d to $M^{d'}$. If the expected yield was 5 percent, an increase in risk would lead to an increase in the demand for money. This is shown by the increase from M_2^d to M_3^d.

yields and risk influence the decision to hold money, we will assume that the level of GNP is constant throughout our analysis. First, let's also hold risk constant and see how M^d responds to a change in the expected yields of securities from 10 percent to 5 percent. We would expect that a decline in expected yields would cause people to reduce their holdings of securities, and, therefore, increase their holdings of money. Why? Think of the expected yield on securities as the opportunity cost for holding money. When we hold money, we forgo the expected yield of our alternative, securities. When the expected yield declines, the opportunity cost of holding money also declines, so we would adjust to the change by holding less securities and more money. The M^d line in Figure 12-2 shows this relationship. As the expected yield decreases from 10 percent to 5 percent, the quantity of money demanded increases. Since GNP is assumed constant, an increase in M^d will increase k $(k = \frac{M^d}{GNP})$. More money is demanded in response to the decrease in the expected yield on securities, and this implies an increase in k. Now let's look at the effect of a change in risk with both GNP and expected yield held constant. Again, refer to Figure 12-2. With an expected yield of 5 percent, an increase in the risk associated with holding securities will result in a decrease in demand for securities and an increase in money holdings. An increase in the demand for money given a constant expected yield is shown by a shift of the demand function from M^d to $M^{d'}$. As Figure 12-2 illustrates, an increase in risk with expected yield constant at 5 percent results in an increase in money holdings from M_2^d to M_3^d.

Price Level Changes and the Demand for Money

According to the MQT, how do expected changes in the price level influence M^d and k? Consider how changes in prices affect the purchasing power of money. When prices rise, the dollar buys less; when prices fall, it buys more. Thus, a rising price level causes money holdings to decline in value. If the price level was expected to rise, this would provide an incentive for people to reduce the portion of their wealth held in money form. As a result, k would decline and, for any level of GNP, M^d would decline. An expected drop in the price level would have just the opposite effect. By acknowledging that factors other than GNP influenced M^d, monetarists were able to explain why k and V could vary in the short run.

Let's turn to the record of the 1930s. With the stock market crash of 1929 and the many bankruptcies of the early 1930s, it was no wonder that many people wanted to hold their assets in the form of money. The expected return on holding stock and bonds looked small and quite risky. Government bonds appeared safe but only gave relatively small yields. Thus, we would expect an increase in k and a decline in V and that is, in fact, what happened. It is not surprising that both the price level and real output fell during the Depression in response to this fall in velocity. Output fell by 25 percent and prices by more than 30 percent. The price level decline added further to people's desire to hold money and contributed to the decline in V.

By investigating the short-run demand for money, MQT economists found a way to account for variations in k and V. This also helped to account for historical episodes such as the Great Depression where the Keynesian theory seemed superior.[8] In later sections of this chapter, we talk about the MQT explanation of the split between price and output changes. For the moment, however, we will continue to examine velocity and GNP without asking how changes in GNP are split between price and output changes.

Changes in Velocity and the Stability of Velocity

MQT proponents didn't want to go too far with the idea of velocity being variable. Look at it this way. From Chapter 8, we know that the equation of exchange tells us that

$$M^s V = PY$$

is always true, where V is velocity, P is the price level, and Y is real income. Suppose that every time M^s increases, V changes in the opposite direction and in an exactly offsetting way. If M^s is doubled, for example, V falls to one half its previous value. This would mean that changes in M^s would have no effect at

[8]For such a discussion, see Milton Friedman and Anna Schwartz, *A Monetary History of the United States, 1867–1960* (Princeton, N.J.:Princeton University Press, 1963).

all on PY; that is, on GNP. Or, consider another example: Suppose V took on absolutely unpredictable values between 1 and 1,000. Then there would be absolutely no way to change M^s to keep GNP constant or even to help control GNP. However, if V changed very steadily and gradually from 5 to 4 or from 2 to 3, the Fed could gradually and steadily change M^s to exactly offset these changes in V.

Many Keynesian economists would agree that the demand for money does depend on expected yields and on risk, just as monetarists believe. However, Keynesians often argue that velocity is not very stable or predictable. For example, Keynesian economists often believe that velocity is unstable in the sense that it changes widely in response to changes in the money supply. Most Keynesian econometric models forecast that almost nothing happens to price in response to growth in the money supply. Further, such models forecast that almost nothing happens to output. Clearly these model builders believe that velocity falls to offset the growth in the money supply. From their point of view, then, money supply growth is not very important for either prices or real output. Those who believe in the MQT argue that changes in the money supply *are* important for both prices and output in the short run, and particularly for prices in the long run, just as the older quantity theory argued. Thus, for the MQT to make sense, V must be relatively *stable*. Velocity may change, but not by enormous amounts and not in an entirely random or erratic way.

Notice that the question of how velocity changes is an empirical one. Monetarists have put forward arguments that V changes in relatively small amounts and in ways that can be explained by changes in the expected yields and risks of other assets, such as stocks and bonds. Keynesians have put forward reasons why changes in V are likely to be large and very erratic, so that variations in the money stock are not at all likely to have a predictable effect on GNP, and why V can change to offset the impact of changes in M^s. Conflicting arguments that do not have logical mistakes must be settled by appeals to fact. This is one of the main roles of empirical work in economics.

THE FRIEDMAN-MEISELMAN TESTS

Econometric tests are rarely convincing to everyone; economists on opposite sides of the argument are seldom swayed to the other side. This is because no test can ever prove that a theory is right or wrong; it can only make your opinion more or less strong. Your pet theory may do badly in a given test because of chance or because the test wasn't appropriate or well designed. If you flip a quarter ten times, you may get ten heads, just by chance. Still, your best guess for the next ten flips is five heads and five tails. Put another way, every theory in the natural sciences, as well as in the social sciences, will be wrong at some time or other and in some degree or other.

An important test was carried out in the early 1960s by Milton Friedman, who has been the main force behind MQT at the University of Chicago, and by David Meiselman, who was Friedman's student and is now a professor at Virginia Polytechnic Institute.[9] Friedman and Meiselman adopted the view that if the

---

[9]Milton Friedman and David Meiselman, "The Relative Stability of Monetary Velocity and the Investment Multiplier in the United States, 1897–1958," *Stabilization Policies* (Englewood Cliffs, N.J.: Prentice-Hall, Inc., 1963), pp. 165–268.

MQT was to be very useful, then V must be stable. But how stable must V be? We know that V does vary and should vary in the view of the MQT. Friedman and Meiselman chose to compare the predictive power of M^s to the sort of simple Keynesian theory developed in Chapters 10 and 11. They asked, How well do changes in GNP correlate to changes in M^s? They compared their results with the answer to the question, How well do changes in GNP correlate to changes in autonomous expenditures? By autonomous expenditures, they meant investment demand in the Keynesian model, plus the government deficit. Recall that in Chapters 10 and 11, changes in investment demand, government spending, and taxation had major roles in explaining changes in real income through the multiplier process. If this theory is to be useful, the multiplier must be stable in the same way that velocity must be stable if the MQT is to be useful. Friedman and Meiselman asked whether changes in M^s did a better job of explaining changes in GNP as compared to the explanation that was provided by changes in autonomous expenditures. In their view, the results of this test seemed to indicate that velocity was more stable than was the Keynesian multiplier.

Notice that Friedman and Meiselman actually compared two different theories to see how well each could explain the same data. Many empirical projects in economics do not compare theories; for example, you might conduct experiments to see whether GNP and investment spending were related or whether GNP and the money supply were related. It turned out that both relations seemed to hold. Friedman and Meiselman went one important step further and asked which was the better relationship. They found that changes in M^s did a better job of explaining changes in GNP. Of course, most monetarists welcomed the results of the *Friedman-Meiselman tests,* and most Keynesians refused to change their opinions on the basis of these tests. However, the important point is that, based on these tests and other work with economic data by monetarists, empirical tests became an important part of the debate. Keynesians proposed other tests in which their theories looked superior to monetarist theories and offered explanations of why the monetarists' results should not be accepted. Monetarists, of course, responded to these attacks in kind.

Keynesians objected to the Friedman-Meiselman tests by identifying what they considered to be weaknesses in the statistical methods used. In particular, they questioned the direction of causation between the money supply and GNP. According to the MQT, changes in M^s cause changes in GNP. The Keynesians argued that the reverse was also possible. For instance, an increase in GNP would increase the amount of money necessary for transactions purposes, prompting the Fed to increase the money supply. The way the Keynesians saw it, changes in GNP could be responsible for changes in the money supply. In short, the direction of causation was uncertain. This debate proved quite productive as it prompted further theoretical and empirical efforts on both sides.

Friedman-Meiselman tests
Tests carried out by Milton Friedman and David Meiselman, from which they concluded that the MQT outperformed the simple Keynesian model.

THE ST. LOUIS FED MODEL

In the late 1960s, a group of economists at the Federal Reserve Bank of St. Louis developed a more sophisticated model of the U.S. economy, building on the earlier work of Friedman and Meiselman.[10] The *St. Louis Fed model* took into account some of the earlier Keynesian criticisms of the Friedman-Meiselman tests. The first tests of the model, based on U.S. data from the period 1953–1968, were particularly damaging to Keynesian economics. First, the model did a better job of explaining and predicting than did the existing Keynesian models; but more important, it showed that monetary policy worked better, faster, and more predictably than fiscal policy. In addition, the first tests showed that the value of the Keynesian multiplier was practically zero. Think what this would mean. If the multiplier is close to zero, then fiscal policy is practically useless. Again, the Keynesians objected to the MQT arguments on the basis of statistical techniques, especially the direction of causation between the money supply and GNP.

If the initial tests of the St. Louis Fed model were a victory for the MQT, the later tests must be considered a partial victory for the Keynesians. The later tests utilized U.S. data over a longer period, 1953–1973, and were not nearly so one-sided in their results. In particular, these tests, and others which followed, showed that the value of the multiplier was not zero, but closer to 1.5 over the period.[11] It appeared that fiscal policy had been buried prematurely by the MQT economists.

So what has all this model building and testing accomplished? While the MQT economists were unable to present final, conclusive evidence that monetary policy worked and fiscal policy didn't, they managed to destroy any lingering doubts about whether money mattered or not. In the 1950s and even as late as the mid-1960s, many Keynesian economists believed that the money supply did not have much influence on the U.S. economy. Now, virtually all economists agree that the money supply does matter; the arguments are now concerned with how much, when, and in what way it influences the economy.

St. Louis Fed model A model of the U.S. economy that took into account some of the earlier Keynesian criticisms of the Friedman-Meiselman tests.

CHANGES IN THE MONEY STOCK, OUTPUT, AND THE PRICE LEVEL

Both the older quantity theory and the MQT would agree that if the money supply suddenly doubles, the long-run effect is simply a doubling of the price level (if the long-run level of equilibrium output is not growing). As we saw in Chapters 8 and 9, a major defect of the quantity theory was its inability to show how the price level and output reacted on the way to the new long-run equilibrium. This defect was particularly telling when the quantity theory could not effectively explain the Great Depression's severe fall in output from 1929 to 1933. The money stock fell by more than one third from August, 1929, to March, 1933. An important task of the modern quantity theorists was to explain how this fall in the money stock influenced prices and particularly output. In this section we want

---

[10]See Leonall C. Andersen and Jerry L. Jordan, "Monetary and Fiscal Actions: A Test of Their Relative Importance in Economic Stabilization," *Review of the Federal Reserve Bank of St. Louis,* Vol. 50 (November, 1968), pp. 11–23.

[11]See Benjamin M. Friedman, "Even the St. Louis Model Now Believes in Fiscal Policy," *Journal of Money, Credit and Banking* (May, 1979), pp. 365–367 and Leonall C. Andersen and Keith M. Carlson, "The St. Louis Model Revisted," *International Economic Review,* Vol. 15, No. 2 (June, 1974), pp. 305–327.

Paul A. Volcker *(1927–)*

Paul A. Volcker was appointed chairman of the Federal Reserve Board of Governors in August, 1979, by President Carter. He continues in this role under President Reagan because the Fed chairmanship is independent of political change in the White House. When President Carter appointed Volcker, he introduced him as a Democrat, but Volcker later indicated that he was no longer a party member. Many Republicans are happy that Volcker remains on the job. The monetarists in the Reagan administration appreciate Volcker's toughness in setting monetary policy.

Volcker did his undergraduate work at Princeton University, graduating *summa cum laude*. He received a master's degree in government and economics from Harvard University and then enrolled in the London School of Economics. Volcker never completed his work there because he thought writing a thesis was a waste of time.

Volcker was named chairman of the Federal Reserve Board of Governors after four years as president of the Federal Reserve Bank of New York. Volcker had to take a salary cut to become chairman of the board. As president of the Federal Reserve Bank of New York, he was paid $116,000 annually, but as chairman of the board that oversees the entire Fed system, he is paid only $57,500.

to examine what the MQT has to say about changes in output and prices in the short run, on the way to long-run equilibrium.

The MQT faces the same problems that the quantity theory did when asking the question, What happens to velocity, prices, and output between two long-run equilibria? We have already seen that the MQT has a better answer than the quantity theory as to what happens to velocity. The MQT can explain some of the variations in velocity in terms of changes in expected yields of assets such as stocks and bonds and also in terms of changes in the risk of such assets. We now want to show how the MQT approaches changes in prices and changes in real output.

Suppose there is no growth in full-employment real output (Y^*) in the long run.[12] Up to time t_1, the economy has been in equilibrium with the money stock M_1, real output equal to its long-run value Y^*, and the price level P_1 determined by

$$P_1 = \frac{M_1 \cdot V}{Y^*}.$$

---

[12]It is only for convenience that we assume that there is no growth of output. Our main points can easily be made (though with a little more complicated arithmetic) in a world where output and the money stock are allowed to grow over time.

At time t_1, the money supply suddenly increases to M_2. By time t_2 we assume that Y is back to the long-run equilibrium value Y^*, and P has adjusted to its new higher long-run value (P_2) given by

$$P_2 = \frac{M_2 \cdot V}{Y^*}.$$

Also, V has returned to its constant long-run level. A very important set of questions, however, is how Y, P, and V move to their equilibrium values; that is, what happens in the short run? The MQT focuses on expectations to explain these questions.

Correct Expectations

Let's look at two extreme examples. First, suppose every business sets its price on the first day of the month and that time t_1 corresponds to that first day. At one extreme, the president of the United States, the Speaker of the House, the chairperson of the Board of Governors of the Federal Reserve System, and other dignitaries announce a jump of 10 percent in the money supply and assure everyone that the money supply will be kept at this new, higher level forever. They could explain that this means prices will eventually have to increase in proportion to the increase in the money supply and that output will have to settle down at Y^* over the long run. They could even assure everyone that if every business now raises prices—and wages—in proportion to the increase in the money supply, and output and production are kept the same, the economy will remain in equilibrium. Suppose the populace fully believes the government and the assorted dignitaries when they say that the money stock will remain at the new, higher level and that a price increase in proportion to the increase in the money stock and no output change will continue to result in equilibrium. Then we might well find all businesses raising prices (and wages) in proportion to the increase in the money stock, not changing the rate of output, and the economy settling right into equilibrium at the new, higher price level with the same initial output of Y^*. The key point in this case is that everyone has been told what to expect about the money supply, the changes in prices and wages, and output, and everyone thoroughly believes what has been said.

Mistaken Expectations

In the other extreme case, the money supply is increased as before, but a wide variety of different announcements is made. Some distinguished leaders say the increase is temporary and will have no effect. Others say that it is temporary and will have good effects. They are contradicted by others who claim that the effects will be bad. Still others claim that the effects are good and that there should be further increases in the stock of money. Indeed, until the past 15 years, nobody would have known of the increase until after a quarter of a year had passed, because money supply statistics were only published quarterly. Before the Great Depression, it might have taken more than a year to receive an estimate of money supply growth. Today, money supply growth statistics are reported weekly and have become one of the most closely watched economic indicators in our society.

Businesses must decide how to react to these changes and to various people's views of what the changes mean. In this case, it is quite hard to form accurate expectations. Business does, however, learn by experience. The increase in the money supply means that people have more money to spend, and banks and other financial institutions will probably make more loans to allow firms and individuals to buy more. This causes the demand for output of all kinds to increase, as is shown by the demand curve shifting to the right, from D_1D_1 to D_2D_2, in Figure 12-3. Now, if business has simply ignored the increase in the money supply, it might keep its prices at OP_1 and produce OQ_1 units of output. However, at OP_1, people will now demand the quantity OQ_2, though business would like to supply only OQ_1. Many businesses, however, will go ahead and sell the OQ_2 units by selling units from their inventories. Selling these units results in inventory disinvestment, a negative addition to inventories. Output has not yet changed, but sales have risen, so inventories fall. Further, if business was satisfied with its level of inventories, this fall in inventories is *unintended inventory disinvestment,* and business won't be pleased by this. Why not? Many businesses are in the position of having an informal promise to sell as many units as are demanded at the price the business has set. For example, if you go to a hardware store for a doorknob, you expect to find doorknobs there and at the price marked. You would not be happy to be told that there will be a new shipment in next week, nor would you like to be told that the price is twice as high this week as last week (or as it will be next week) because many more people want the doorknobs this week. You would likely go to another store that kept inventories of doorknobs and didn't change doorknob prices, up or down, too frequently. The first store runs a good chance of losing a customer, perhaps permanently.

Many businesses, then, will see their inventories falling because of the demand increase depicted in Figure 12-3. They will order new inventories from their suppliers (or begin to produce more themselves if they don't rely on suppliers),

FIGURE 12-3   AN INCREASE IN DEMAND FOR OUTPUT DUE TO AN INCREASE IN THE MONEY SUPPLY

When the money supply increases, demand for the output of the typical good or service will rise. If sellers keep price constant, they will reduce their inventories by selling OQ_2 units while only OQ_1 units are being produced. This will put upward pressure on prices.

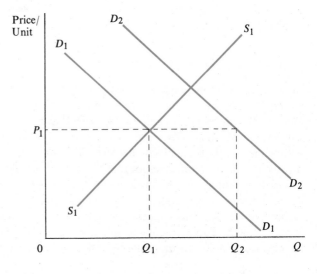

and output will start to rise. Prices will also start to rise. Any business that holds price at OP_1 will find inventory falling period after period. The important point is that businesses will be forced to change their expectations about demand, and the change in expectations will cause them to set higher prices. In addition, the increased demand by businesses to rebuild their inventories will cause suppliers to charge higher prices to other businesses once the suppliers' expectations change to cause them to expect higher demand, so the supply curve in Figure 12-3 will start to shift left, as Figure 12-4 shows. Figure 12-4 shows a higher equilibrium price, but the price is not high enough to keep output at OQ_1, although we will ultimately end up back at OQ_1. Price is lower and output is higher in Figure 12-4 than they ultimately will be because the supply curve has not shifted left as much as it eventually will. This is because expectations have not yet completely adjusted. Suppliers have not made their full adjustments yet, and workers are not yet making the full wage demands that they will make when they completely understand the new, higher price level.

Figure 12-5 shows how the economy will ultimately reach the new equilibrium. The demand curve has fully adjusted to the new, higher money supply and so has the supply curve. The market has settled back to the initial output OQ_1, but at the new, higher price level OP_3 which is required by the higher money supply.

It might well be that output first expands, as in Figure 12-3, without price changing, because people's expectations of inflation have not yet changed. Over the next several periods, demand may still be larger than expected, even though prices have started to rise, as in Figure 12-4. Output finally fully adjusts, as in Figure 12-5, when everyone has come to expect the new, higher demand and price levels.

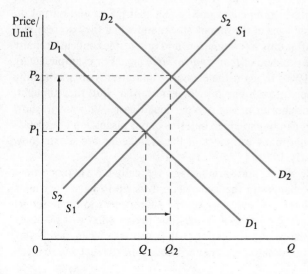

FIGURE 12-4   THE DEMAND AND SUPPLY CURVES SHIFT DUE TO INFLATION

Sellers raise price from its initial level to prevent any further declines in their inventories and because, as prices rise throughout the economy, sellers find their costs rising. That is, price rises to OP_2 because demand increased and supply has fallen (the supply curve has shifted left).

FIGURE 12-5   DEMAND AND SUPPLY ADJUST FULLY TO THE INCREASE IN THE MONEY SUPPLY

In the new long-run equilibrium, price has increased but quantity is at its initial level of OQ_1. The supply curve has shifted left by as much as the demand curve shifted right, and reflects the general increase in costs in the economy.

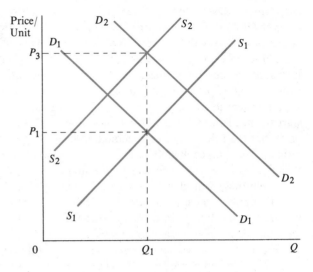

The Crucial Role of Expectations

It might seem that the *MQT* is no more precise than was the quantity theory. After all, the two extreme cases we talked about were far apart in their results concerning the movements from one long-run equilibrium to the other, and the possibilities for the time path of the economy in the second case seem very large. But the important point to notice is that what happens depends on expectations. If you can say what businesses expect, the MQT can predict what will happen to the paths of price, output, and velocity.

LONG AND VARIABLE LAGS

long and variable lags   The time span between a change in monetary policy and a resulting change in income and prices.

Many MQT economists have commented on the fact that prices and output do not respond instantly to changes in the money stock, and when they do respond, they sometimes respond after only a few quarters and other times only after many more quarters. This is the problem of *long and variable lags.* For example, many MQT economists in the 1960s thought the economy in a given year was mainly influenced by money supply growth one to two years earlier. But, they thought, this lag might be longer or shorter in any one particular case. We want to show that long and variable lags can be explained in terms of our discussion of expectations, and we also note that many estimates of the average lag are shorter now than in the 1960s and early 1970s.

In discussing the issue of long and variable lags, we really have two questions to answer. First, why do changes in the money supply seem to have their main effects one to two years later? Second, why do the effects seem to come sooner in some cases than in others? As for the first question, review what we said above about the two extreme cases of expectations. In any case, when people are surprised by a change in the money stock, they will take time to react and to revise their expectations. We are not surprised, then, to find that the economy shows a lag in reacting to changes in the money supply.

Further, business and labor cannot react instantly to changes in the money supply. Wage contracts are often signed for two to three years in advance. Sears, Roebuck catalogs are good for six months at a time. Restaurants don't change their prices every few days, and grocers don't change their prices of canned goods every day. All this results in *sluggish or sticky price and wage behavior.* Business and labor would find it difficult and costly to negotiate new wage contracts every week. If there were frequent renegotiations, business could not count on a given wage rate when pricing its products. You probably wouldn't want to place a Sears order today if you didn't know what the price would be when the goods were delivered, and you also probably would like to have a few days to think over purchases even at a given price. Restaurants must pay to have new menus printed with different prices, and customers are reluctant to go to restaurants where prices are changing all the time. How do you know you'll have enough money? And, even if you can pay, will you feel you got your money's worth?

sluggish or sticky price and wage behavior   Prices and wages may respond slowly to some economic changes.

Let us suppose that in one case where the money supply increases, it takes the average firm one year to catch on to this change and to understand what it means for prices; that is, in this case there is a year lag before expectations change. Further, suppose that some firms change their prices every day, some firms only once a year, and the average firm once every six months. Thus, about six months after firms have caught on to the change in the money supply (that is, a year after it happens in this case), firms will be changing prices, resulting in an overall lag of one year and six months. And, by the time most firms have altered prices to account for the higher money supply, two years have gone by.

The above example was fictitious, but we can look at the early and mid-1960s for a real example. Inflation was low and relatively constant. When the monetary growth of the late 1960s hit the economy, it was only natural that it took the economy substantial time to react. Business and labor had become used to low inflation, and there was a lag in their reactions. But by the mid-1970s, the lags seemed much shorter. Both business and labor had been hurt by the inflation of the past ten years and were on the lookout for signs of more of it.

Comparing the 1960s with the 1970s and early 1980s, the lags between changes in monetary growth rates and reactions to their changes seem to many people to be shorter now. We can explain this by arguing that people now react faster and adjust their expectations more quickly since they have had more experience with changing monetary and fiscal policies, and they have caught on to how changes in these policies can lead to inflation.

SUMMARY

1. Following the Great Depression and the publication of the *General Theory,* Keynesian economics became the dominant macroeconomic view among American economists. This theory did not become dominant because of empirical evidence, but because it offered a more acceptable explanation of the short-run ups and downs of the economy.

2. Keynesian theory proposed practical ways out of the unemployment problems of the Great Depression through the use of fiscal policy. Classical macroeconomics could offer no active solutions to the economy's problems.

3. Two problems faced those economists who wished to rebuild the quantity theory of money.

First, they had to explain why and how velocity varied in the short run. Second, they had to explain the short-run movements in price and output due to a change in the money supply.

4. By including expected yields and risk on non-money assets as factors influencing the demand for money, the MQT economists were able to explain short-run variations in velocity.

5. The speed and correctness with which people change their expectations regarding a change in the money supply determines the extent to which output changes in the short run and how quickly prices adjust.

6. Empirical work by Friedman and Meiselman and by economists at the Federal Reserve Bank of St. Louis led them to conclude that the MQT was better than Keynesian economics at explaining variations in GNP. These early econometric tests were important because they established that money did matter and initiated further empirical work by both MQT and Keynesian economists.

7. During the last 20 years, the lag between money supply changes and price level changes has shortened. Most economists believe this is because people now understand the effects of monetary policy and can more quickly form correct expectations about changes in the money supply.

NEW TERMS

modern quantity theory (MQT)
econometrics
precautionary motive
yield
expected yield

risk
Friedman-Meiselman tests
St. Louis Fed model
long and variable lags
sluggish or sticky price and wage behavior

QUESTIONS FOR DISCUSSION

1. Why would an MQT economist want to explain why velocity can change? After all, don't these economists believe V is constant in the long run (or at least independent of M^s and P)?

2. Suppose you are holding bonds issued by a city. Suddenly you become convinced there is a good chance the city might go bankrupt and not pay off its bonds. Might you switch out of these bonds and hold more money? If you thought all bonds had become riskier, would you want to hold more money?

3. Why were the Friedman-Meiselman tests important?

4. The text discussed an increase in the money supply. Look at Figures 12-3, 12-4, and 12-5 and explain how they would appear if instead we considered a *decrease* in the money supply growth rate.

5. If the average firm sets prices once a year, do you suppose monetary policy will usually take longer to have an effect than if the average firm sets prices once a month? Explain why or why not.

SUGGESTIONS FOR FURTHER READING

Friedman, Milton. "The Demand for Money," in Milton Friedman (ed.), *Studies in the Quantity Theory of Money*. Chicago: University of Chicago Press, 1956.

Friedman, Milton, and David Meiselman. "The Relative Stability of Monetary Velocity and the Investment Multiplier in the United States, 1897–1958." *Stabilization Policies*. Englewood Cliffs, N.J.: Prentice-Hall, Inc., 1963.

Friedman, Milton, and Anna Schwartz. *A Monetary History of the United States, 1867–1960.* Princeton, N.J.: Princeton University Press, 1963.

Laidler, David E. W. *The Demand for Money.* New York: Dun-Donnelley Publishing Co., 1977.

Samuelson, Paul. "The General Theory." *Econometrica,* Vol. 14 (June, 1946). Reprinted in Robert Lechachman (ed.). *The General Theory: Reports of Three Decades.* New York: Macmillan Co., 1964.

Wonnacott, Paul. *Macroeconomics.* Homewood, Ill.: Richard D. Irwin, Inc., 1978.

Monetary Policy and Economic Performance

Learning Objectives

After studying the materials found in this chapter, you should be able to do the following:

1. Explain how the yield on a bond is inversely related to its price.

2. Describe how an open market action by the Fed which raises the price of government bonds will reduce the yield on corporate bonds.

3. Describe how monetary policy works according to Keynesian economic theory.

4. List some of the advantages and disadvantages of using monetary policy instead of fiscal policy to bring about a change in the economy.

5. Explain the proposition that an increase in the expected rate of inflation will result in an increase in the interest rate.

6. Define and contrast:
   (a) the investment demand schedule and the marginal efficiency of investment schedule.
   (b) nominal and real interest rates.
   (c) the money multiplier and the monetary base.

7. Discuss the reasons why Keynesians believe monetary policy should be used to stabilize interest rates.

8. Explain the MQT argument that when the Fed misses its money supply target, inflation may result.

9. Contrast Fed monetary policy before and after October, 1979.

10. Describe the argument by Milton Friedman that the Fed should be required to achieve a constant money supply growth rate.

In this chapter we will discuss monetary policy which is activity by the Federal Reserve System (Fed) to influence money supply growth, credit conditions, and the level of interest rates. We will examine the differences between Keynesian and MQT economists regarding monetary policy. First, we will discuss the Keynesian view that monetary policy should be aimed at stabilizing the level of interest rates. Then we will present the monetarist view that the Fed should conduct monetary policy to insure that the money supply grows at an appropriate rate. As we present these contrasting positions, we will review the criticisms that have been made about each. We will discuss the relationship between inflationary expectations and the level of nominal interest rates, and the proposition that the higher the expected rate of inflation, the higher interest rates will be. The chapter concludes with a discussion of the controversy over whether the Fed should be governed by rules or discretion.

KEYNESIAN VIEWS ON THE INFLUENCE OF MONETARY POLICY

Keynesian economists think of monetary policy as interest-rate policy. They feel the Federal Reserve System can control interest rates to influence investment decisions. Investment changes cause changes in output and income through the multiplier process. Thus, monetary policy works by influencing interest rates, which influence investment, which then affects output and income. Figure 13-1 shows this relationship. Let's examine each step of the Keynesian conception of monetary policy shown in Figure 13-1 to better understand how it works.

Bond Prices and Bond Yields

In order to understand how monetary policy influences interest rates, we must examine the relationship between the price of a bond and its yield. A *bond* is an interest-bearing certificate of public or private indebtedness. Federal, state, and local governments, as well as private corporations, sell bonds to raise revenues. Bonds are attractive investments for several reasons: First, many are traded in

bond Interest-earning certificate issued by governments or corporations as a way of borrowing money.

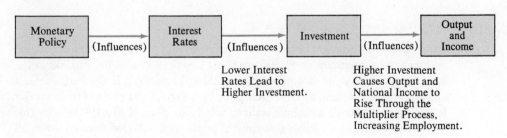

FIGURE 13-1 THE EFFECTS OF MONETARY POLICY IN THE KEYNESIAN ANALYSIS

In the typical Keynesian analysis, monetary policy affects output and income through the interest rate. For example, the Fed can use an open market operation to buy bonds, thus driving down interest rates. At lower interest rates, a greater level of investment is forthcoming, driving up aggregate demand. The higher aggregate demand causes output and income to rise through the multiplier process, as discussed in Chapters 10 and 11.

maturity date *The point at which a bond matures and is paid off.*

face value *The amount printed on a bond's face that the issuer promises to pay when the bond matures.*

active markets and, therefore, may be sold quickly if the need arises. Second, they pay an annual premium or interest to the holder. Third, in many cases the bond may be resold for a profit. There are several different types of bonds, but the kind that is relevant to our discussion has three important characteristics: (1) a *maturity date* which indicates when it will be paid off (e.g., ten years from today); (2) a *face value* which indicates how much the bond will pay at maturity; and (3) an annual premium or interest payment to the bondholder which is some fixed percentage of the face value.

Suppose that you have just received a large sum of money from the estate of a relative. You want to invest part of the money in an interest-bearing security and are considering the purchase of a government bond with a face value of $10,000. It pays an annual interest premium of $1,500 and matures in ten years. In order to make a decision regarding the purchase of the bond, you need to compare it with alternative investment possibilities. The yield of the bond should be compared with, say, the yield of a saving certificate at your local bank. But what is the yield of the bond described above? You are probably tempted to say that the bond's yield is 15 percent, because it pays $1,500 each year and has a face value of $10,000. But notice that so far we've said nothing about the price of the bond. The bond's face value, maturity date, and annual interest premium are fixed. The price of the bond is variable and its yield depends on the price you pay. If you pay $10,000 for the bond, you will earn $1,500 annually on an investment of $10,000. After ten years you will also get your original investment back (remember the bond pays its face value at maturity). Your annual yield in this case would be 15 percent. But suppose you only have to pay $8,000 for the bond. Now you will earn $1,500 annually on an $8,000 investment and get $10,000 back in ten years. That is an annual yield of more than 18 percent.[1] Alternatively, if you pay $12,000 for the bond, you will earn $1,500 annually on a $12,000 investment, and at maturity, you will receive only $10,000. In this case the annual yield is about 12.5 percent. Not only does the price of the bond determine its yield, but there is a systematic relationship between bond prices and bond yields. The higher the bond's price, the lower its yield; the lower its price, the higher its yield. Using more technical language, we can say that bond prices and bond yields are inversely related. This statement is true of all bonds, government or corporate, as long as they have the three characteristics mentioned above.

Monetary Policy and Bond Yields

Suppose that government bonds maturing in ten years with a face value of $10,000 and an annual premium of $1,500 are being bought and sold for $10,000 in the open market today. At this price, their yield is 15 percent. If the Fed wants, it can buy enough of them to raise their price by $100. All the Fed has to do is offer to buy as many bonds as people want to sell at the price of $10,100 apiece. This will lower the yield on these government bonds and will also tend to lower all bond yields in the economy, including the interest rates faced by business.

---

[1]When a bond carries a stream of interest payments, as well as being paid off at face value on its maturity date, it is rather complicated to find the exact yield (though there are books of tables that you can use for this purpose). Our point is that if the price of the bond is less than its face value, the yield is greater than the stated interest rate on its face (15 percent in our example); if the price of the bond is greater than its face value, the yield is less than the stated interest rate.

To see this more clearly, imagine that both government and corporate bonds are priced at $10,000 with identical yields. Under these circumstances, you would not prefer one to the other. But if government bond prices rise to $10,100, their yield will fall. Thus, corporate bonds become more attractive because, so far, their yields have not fallen. However, if people begin to demand more corporate bonds, prices will be driven up and yields will fall. So, the open market operation reduces the yields of government and corporate bonds alike.

These open market operations affect the interest rates that business faces in another way—through the banking system. The Fed's open market purchases of bonds will lead to an increase in the reserves banks hold, as discussed in Chapter 5. In turn, banks will be more likely to lend to business and on better terms (lower interest rates).

Investment Spending and the Rate of Interest

In Chapters 9 and 10, we discussed the Keynesian theory of investment spending. We said that the fate of any proposed business investment would depend on the expected rate of profit relative to the interest rate; that is, its earnings compared to its costs to the firm. The same reasoning applies on a macroeconomic basis; the aggregate amount of business investment spending will be determined by comparing the interest rate to the expected rate of profit on all possible investments. To see this more clearly, let's start with a hypothetical firm.

The Investment Demand Schedule

Assume that a manufacturing firm is considering three investment projects for the coming year: (1) an automated welding machine which costs $20,000; (2) a computerized bookkeeping system which costs $60,000; and (3) a forklift which costs $30,000. The firm has calculated the expected revenues and costs of operation for each alternative over its useful life to the firm. It has also taken into account the initial cost and salvage value of each investment. With this information the firm has calculated that the annual expected rate of profit is 14 percent for the welding machine, 22 percent for the bookkeeping system, and 8 percent for the forklift.

Based upon this information, an investment demand schedule can be constructed. An **investment demand schedule** shows a ranking of all possible investment projects in declining order of their expected rates of profit. The investment demand schedule for our hypothetical firm is shown in Figure 13-2.

The schedule looks like a series of steps rather than a smooth line. This is because we have only three projects to consider and each requires a lump-sum expenditure. If we were to total the schedules of every firm in the economy, we would generate a smoother line, as in Figure 13-3. The economy's investment demand schedule in Figure 13-3 is also known as the **marginal efficiency of investment (MEI) schedule,** because it ranks all of society's investment possibilities according to their expected rate of profit or, as Keynes put it, their marginal efficiency.

Given that we know the investment demand schedule for the economy, we need only know the interest rate in order to determine the amount of investment spending. Every investment with an expected rate of profit exceeding the interest rate will be undertaken.

investment demand schedule A ranking of all possible investment projects in declining order of their expected rates of profit.

marginal efficiency of investment schedule A ranking of all of society's investment possibilities according to their expected rate of profit or their marginal efficiency.

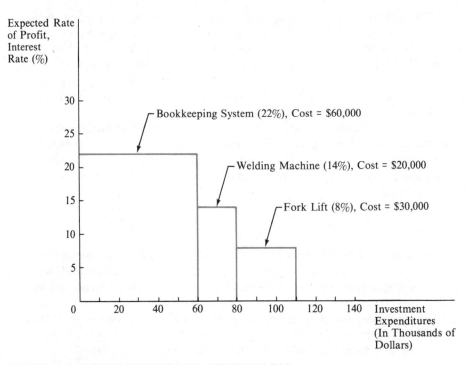

**FIGURE 13-2   INVESTMENT DEMAND SCHEDULE FOR
A FIRM**

The three possible investment alternatives for a firm are ranked according to their expected
rate of profit. The decision about which investment to undertake will depend on a comparison
of the alternative expected rates of profit and the interest rate.

For instance, if the interest rate were 20 percent, the level of investment
expenditures in the entire economy would be $50 billion, as shown in Figure 13-3;
that is, there are $50 billion worth of investment projects with an expected rate
of profit exceeding 20 percent. Our firm would invest in the computerized accounting system because its expected rate of profit (22 percent) exceeds the
interest rate. Neither the welding machine nor the forklift would be purchased.
If the interest rate were 12 percent, then the firm would invest in the automatic
welding machine as well as the accounting system. For the economy, a 12 percent
interest rate would result in $100 billion of investment expenditures. Investment
demand and the interest rate are inversely related; that is, when interest rates rise,
investment spending *(I)* declines, and when interest rates decline, investment
rises.

Investment Spending, Output, and Income

As discussed in Chapters 9 and 10, a change in any of the components of
aggregate demand causes a shift of the *AD* schedule and a change in the equilibrium level of national income. Thus, a decline in the interest rate which causes

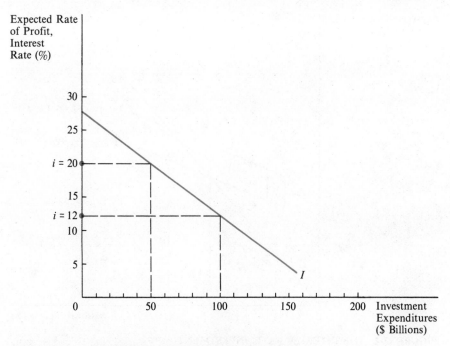

**FIGURE 13-3   INVESTMENT DEMAND SCHEDULE FOR
                THE ENTIRE ECONOMY**

Given a hypothetical investment demand schedule for the macro economy, the amount of
investment expenditures will depend on the interest rate *(i)*. If *i* = 20 percent, then
investment expenditures will be $50 billion; if *i* declines to 12 percent, investment
expenditures will increase to $100 billion. In general, investment demand is inversely related
to the interest rate.

---

an increase in I will shift the AD schedule upward. This effect is shown in Figure
13-4. The increase in aggregate demand from AD_1 to AD_2 causes the equilibrium
level of national income to increase from Y_1 to Y_2. An increase in the interest rate
has the opposite effect; investment declines, aggregate demand shifts downward,
and national income and output decline.

Problems Keynesians See with Monetary Policy

In the Keynesian view, monetary policy works as follows: The Fed buys government bonds in an open market operation, and this increase in the demand for
bonds drives up their prices and reduces their yields. This action also affects
corporate bonds, driving up their prices and reducing their yields. In addition,
the open market operation creates additional reserves that banks want to lend at
lower interest rates. At these lower interest rates, business wants to invest more,
and this increase in investment causes real income and output to rise through the
multiplier process.

   In the Keynesian view there are a great many steps in moving from monetary
policy to a change in real output, and many things can go wrong along the way.

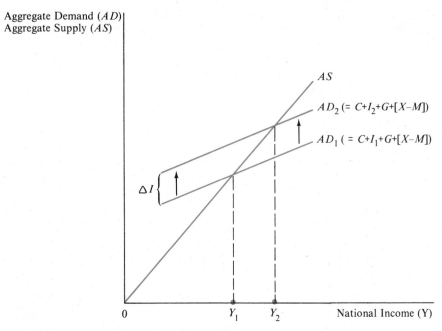

**FIGURE 13-4   THE INTEREST RATE, INVESTMENT
                EXPENDITURES, AND INCOME AND
                OUTPUT**

A decrease in the interest rate causes the amount of investment expenditures to rise from I_1 to I_2. This change in investment expenditures ($I_2 - I_1 = \Delta I$) causes aggregate demand to shift upward from AD_1 to AD_2. The increase in aggregate demand causes income and output to rise from Y_1 to Y_2.

We saw from our previous example that if the Fed decides to buy as many bonds as the market wants to sell, it can move bonds prices up from $10,000 to $10,100. However, it is difficult to know how great an effect a given change in bond prices or yields will have. Suppose the Fed purchases bonds and succeeds in reducing yields on corporate bonds from 16 percent to 15 percent. This may have very different effects, depending on whether the investment demand curve is $I_1 I_1$ or $I_2 I_2$ in Figure 13-5. Investment is initially OI_1 at an interest rate of 16 percent. With $I_1 I_1$, the fall in i to 15 percent causes a large increase in I to OI_3, but with $I_2 I_2$ the increase in I is much smaller, moving to OI_2. The point is, the Fed cannot be sure what effect such changes will have on I unless it is sure of the slope of the investment demand schedule that it faces. Even worse, suppose the investment demand schedule shifts a good deal; at one time it might be $I_1 I_1$ in Figure 13-6, and at other times it might be $I_2 I_2$ or $I_3 I_3$. Government economists might decide that investment demand of OI_1 is needed to move the economy to full employment. If the Fed cannot guess which investment demand schedule it will face, it cannot very easily choose the proper interest rate to set. For example, if it picks i_1, the desired OI_1 results *if* the investment demand schedule is $I_1 I_1$. But with either $I_2 I_2$ or $I_3 I_3$, the ratio i_1 gives the wrong quantity of investment goods demanded. With $I_2 I_2$, I would be too large; and with $I_3 I_3$, I would be too

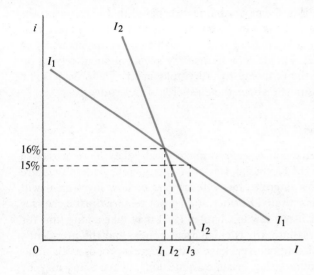

FIGURE 13-5 THE EFFECT ON INVESTMENT DEMAND OF A FALL IN CORPORATE BOND YIELDS

A given fall in the interest rate from, say, 16 percent to 15 percent, will cause a larger increase in investment if investment demand is very responsive (as with curve I_1I_1) than if investment demand is not as responsive (as with curve I_2I_2). If policymakers are mistaken in their beliefs about the responsiveness of investment demand, they may incorrectly change the interest rate.

small. In fact, many Keynesian economists believe investment demand *is* fairly unstable and shifts a good deal as expectations change.

Furthermore, suppose the investment demand schedule is very *inelastic;* that is, a large change in the interest rate produces a very small change in investment. Suppose i falls by 1 percent. Investment demand might rise by only, say, ¼ percent. Thus, a relatively large change in i may produce a relatively small change in I. If full-employment real income requires a large change in I, it would then require a very large change in i.

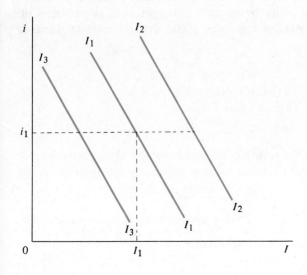

FIGURE 13-6 INTEREST-RATE POLICY WHEN THE INVESTMENT SCHEDULE CAN SHIFT POSITION

If the investment demand schedule shifts a good deal, policymakers cannot be sure they will achieve the appropriate level of investment for a particular interest rate. For example, suppose investment of OI_1 is desired. If the investment demand curve is I_1I_1, an interest rate of i_1 will give OI_1. But if i_1 is set, I will be too large if the actual investment demand curve turns out to be I_2I_2 and will be too small if investment demand turns out to be I_3I_3.

Until the mid- or late 1960s, many economists believed that investment was quite inelastic with respect to changes in the interest rate; so inelastic, in fact, that no positive rate of interest could make I large enough to move the economy to full-employment output. This made economists very skeptical about relying on monetary policy to move the economy to full employment. These days, some economists are not so pessimistic about the elasticity of investment.

Monetary Policy Vs. Fiscal Policy

The problems with monetary policy seem to make fiscal policy more attractive than monetary policy from the Keynesian viewpoint. Fiscal policy doesn't require the authorities to guess how interest rates will respond or how investment will react to changes in the interest rate.[2] Further, it does not require drastic changes in interest rates. Of course, as we saw in Chapter 11, it may take a long time for a president to talk Congress into a particular fiscal policy, and the president's advisers may not like the fiscal policy package that Congress proposes. In situations where the implementation lag becomes quite long, Keynesians may be forced to turn to monetary policy. They may try to influence the Fed to take monetary policy actions which would move the economy in the same direction as would the fiscal policy action.

The Appropriate Role of Monetary Policy in the Keynesian View

According to Keynesians, the proper role of monetary policy is to supplement fiscal policy. For example, suppose the economy is at less than the full-employment level of real income. An increase in G or a cut in T will drive income up. If the Fed forces or allows interest rates to rise at this time, then investment will fall, partially offsetting the expansionary effect of the rise in G or cut in T. From this viewpoint, it is important that monetary policy be used in conjunction with fiscal policy.

Keynesians believe that, in this situation, monetary policy should insure that interest rates remain stable or, better yet, decline. Thus, the Fed could accommodate the expansionary fiscal policy by increasing its open market purchases of securities. The resulting lower interest rates would keep investment demand strong.

MODERN QUANTITY THEORY VIEWS ON INFLATION AND THE INTEREST RATE

Monetarists tend to focus on the growth of the money supply. Monetarists revived the quantity theory's view that the money supply plays a key role in determining

---

[2]Of course, there is much guesswork involved in judging how households will react to a tax cut. Will most of it be spent or saved, and how long will it take households to spend the fraction that isn't saved? Further, government spending may crowd out investment spending, as discussed in Chapter 11.

James Tobin *(1918–)*

Born in Champaign, Illinois, *James Tobin* did his undergraduate work at Harvard University and also received his Ph.D. from Harvard in 1947. He has been at Yale University since the beginning of his academic career and is currently Sterling Professor of Economics at Yale. His list of publications is long, distinguished, and wide ranging. Among numerous honors, he has served as president of the American Economic Association. He is a central figure in the criticism of the tide of monetarism that has been rising for the past two decades.

In 1981 Tobin was awarded the Nobel Prize in Economics for his work on portfolio analysis. After win-

ning the prize, Tobin commented that his portfolio selection theory was, ". . . just the theory of not putting all your eggs in one basket."

Tobin has long had faith in the possibilities of using active government policies for good purposes, both at the micro level on such issues as poverty and on the macro level to stabilize the economy and promote economic growth. Indeed, Tobin served on John F. Kennedy's Council of Economic Advisers from January, 1961, until July, 1962, and was one of the originators of macroeconomic policy of the Kennedy-Johnson years.

Among Tobin's major contributions are his articles on money from the 1950s. He introduced a risk-return framework for analyzing the choice of combinations of assets, including money, to hold in a portfolio. This "portfolio balance" approach has been very fruitful and is widely used in analyzing domestic monetary questions, as well as international financial problems. One of the basic insights of this portfolio analysis is that the overall risk of a portfolio of assets depends on how much the yields on individual assets tend to move together. Suppose asset *A* sometimes has very good years, but sometimes very bad years; some years it yields a 15 percent return, others a −5 percent return. This asset then offers a good deal of risk concerning its return. Suppose asset *B* also is very risky. However, it may be that holding both assets *A* and *B* is *not* very risky. Suppose when asset *A* has a bad year, asset *B* usually has a good year; and when asset *A* has a good year, asset *B* usually has a not-so-good year. Then, holding both of them offers a moderate overall yield each year with much less risk than holding either alone. This is the idea of selecting assets whose yields show a great deal of negative correlation.

the price level and that changes in the money supply play a major role in determining changes in the price level. They believe that monetary policy should be used to control the money supply in order to control price changes over time. This point of view depends upon the belief that real output tends to return to its long-run full-employment level on its own and that the money supply has no *long-run* effect on *Y*. They believe that in the *short run,* the split of the effects between *P* and *Y* depends on people's expectations.

This does not mean that monetarists think the interest rate is irrelevant or unimportant. Indeed, monetarists have spent a great deal of time developing an explanation of the interest rate in which *expected rates of inflation* play a major role.

Suppose we use the GNP deflator as our measure of the price level. Also, suppose the GNP deflator in one year is 100 and in the next year is 110. The percentage change in the price level is the *actual* inflation rate—it's the percentage change in the price level that actually took place. To explain the interest rate, monetarists look at what people expect the inflation rate to be, or the *expected* rate of inflation. To see how this works, look at the demand and supply of loanable funds in Figure 13-7. The interest rate, *i,* influences the amount of funds people want to borrow. At a 10 percent rate of interest, if you borrow $100 for a year, you have to pay back $110 at the end of the year. If the interest rate is 5 percent, then you have to pay back only $105; it is obviously cheaper to borrow at lower interest rates. We expect, then, that people will want to borrow more funds at lower rates. The demand curve slopes down, just as would a demand curve for any good or service. For people who lend money, the higher the interest rate, the larger the return they make from each $100 they lend. We expect them to lend more at higher rates of interest. The supply curve slopes upward. Equilibrium occurs at the interest rate i_1, where the quantity of funds people want to borrow is OF_1; this just equals the quantity of funds lenders want to lend. An important question is, How does the *expected* rate of inflation influence the equilibrium rate of interest?

Expected Inflation and the Demand and Supply of Loanable Funds

Changes in expected inflation rates cause shifts in both the demand and supply of loanable funds and thus lead to a new equilibrium value of *i.* Suppose people come to expect a higher rate of inflation. In Figure 13-8, we see that the demand

FIGURE 13-7   THE DEMAND AND SUPPLY OF LOANABLE FUNDS

The demand curve slopes downward, showing that at lower interest rates borrowers want to borrow a larger amount. The upward sloping supply curve shows that at higher interest rates, lenders are willing to lend larger amounts. At the interest rate i_1, the amount borrowers want to borrow equals the amount lenders want to lend, and there is equilibrium.

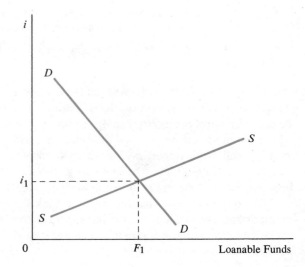

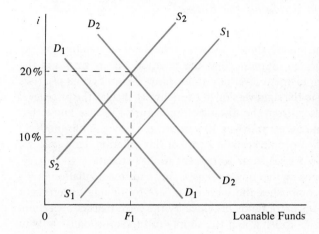

FIGURE 13-8 INCREASE IN THE EQUILIBRIUM INTEREST RATE DUE TO A RISE IN THE EXPECTED RATE OF INFLATION

If there is an increase in the expected rate of inflation, the demand for borrowing rises from D_1D_1 to D_2D_2 because it is now easier to pay back loans. However, lending looks less attractive, so the supply of loanable funds falls; that is, the supply curve shifts left. The demand and supply curves shift the same distance, intersecting at an interest rate that is higher by the amount of the increase in expected inflation. This new interest rate leaves the real equilibrium, after taking inflation into account, the same as before.

curve shifts to the right, from D_1D_1 to D_2D_2. People will borrow more now if they think the inflation rate is going to be higher. The reason for this is that the higher the inflation rate, the less valuable are the dollars you must repay. This makes you want to borrow more; or, looking at it a different way, you would be willing to pay a higher interest rate to borrow any given amount. In either case, the demand curve shifts to the right. Exactly the same sort of reasoning applies to business demand for borrowing. Business is much more willing to borrow at any given interest rate when it expects rising prices for the goods it produces.

We also expect the supply curve to shift left if there is an increase in expected inflation. Note that this shift is actually a fall or decrease in the supply of funds. This is because the people who lend the funds are thinking in terms of what they can buy when they get their funds *plus interest* back from the borrower. For example, if they lend $100 at 10 percent interest for one year, they will get back $110 at the end of that year. If the price level is the same as it was at the start of the year, they can buy 10 percent more real goods by having made the loan. But suppose the price level also rises by 10 percent. Then the $110 they get back will buy only the same amount of goods the $100 would have bought at the start of the year. If lenders demand 10 percent extra in real goods, they won't lend at 10 percent interest if they expect 10 percent inflation. In fact, to get a 10 percent return in terms of real goods, they will demand an interest rate of 20 percent. The supply curve will shift by the amount of the change in the expected rate of inflation.

Thus, both the demand and supply curves shift as in Figure 13-8, and when the expected rate of inflation rises, so does the equilibrium interest rate. In fact, monetarists expect the interest rate to rise by about the same amount as the expected rate of inflation rises.

Changes in the Inflation Rate and the Rate of Interest

Let's see how changes in money supply growth influence i, depending on the inflation rate that is expected. Suppose that the inflation rate is zero and the economy is at the full-employment level of output. Now the money supply rises by 10 percent. According to the rigid version of the quantity theory, the price level will rise by 10 percent also. From the discussion of Figure 13-8, we know that if the original equilibrium interest rate was 10 percent, the new equilibrium level of i will be 20 percent when people become aware of this inflation. However, we are now interested in how i rises from 10 percent to 20 percent.

We will begin by supposing that no one *expects* any additional inflation. Let's assume that the Fed accomplishes the increase in M^s by buying government bonds from banks. With the extra funds provided by the open market operation, banks now have more funds to lend, and the supply of funds for loans shifts in Figure 13-9 from $S_1 S_1$ to $S_2 S_2$. The demand curve doesn't shift yet because no one expects any higher inflation than before. Hence, the new rate of interest is the lower rate i_2. The quantity of loans rises from OF_1 to OF_2. Notice that up to this point the results are the same as in the Keynesian view: The Fed's open market operations reduce the interest rate.

Business and consumers use the borrowed amount $F_1 F_2$ to make additional purchases. Eventually this increase in demand for goods drives up prices; people see this increase in prices and begin to expect inflation. As people begin to realize that inflation will be 10 percent now instead of zero, the demand and supply curves in Figure 13-9 will both begin to shift until they reach positions similar to those in Figure 13-8. In this case, the Fed's attempt to reduce interest rates by increasing the money supply ultimately leads to higher interest rates.

FIGURE 13-9   THE EFFECT ON THE INTEREST RATE OF AN INCREASE IN THE MONEY SUPPLY GROWTH RATE WITH NO ADDITIONAL INFLATION EXPECTED

If the Fed buys bonds in an open market operation, the money supply is increased and banks have extra reserves to lend. By itself, this increases the supply of funds to lend (from $S_1 S_1$ to $S_2 S_2$) and drives down the interest rate. Notice, however, that we have assumed that people have not become aware of the extra inflation that can be expected from this increase in the money supply. When they do, the demand and supply curves will shift as in Figure 13-8, and i will rise instead of fall as it did here.

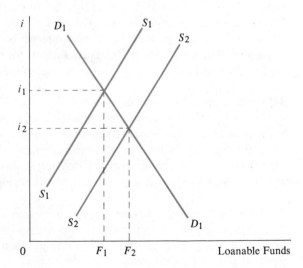

Real Interest Rates Vs. Nominal Interest Rates

Suppose the interest rate at which you can borrow is 10 percent. This is called the *nominal (market) interest rate.* Monetarists emphasize the *real rate of interest,* which is defined as the nominal interest rate minus the expected inflation rate. In our example, before the money supply and prices start to increase, the interest rate is 10 percent and the inflation rate is zero, so the real rate of interest is 10 percent. In the long-run equilibrium, the interest rate is 20 percent and inflation is 10 percent, so the real rate of interest is again 10 percent (= 20 percent − 10 percent). As long as people underestimate inflation, they must be expecting a real rate of interest that is larger than the real rate actually turns out to be. For example, if people expect 5 percent inflation and the interest rate is 15 percent, then they expect a real rate of interest of 10 percent (= 15 percent − 5 percent).

nominal (market) interest rate The rate of interest established in the market but not adjusted for inflation as the real rate of interest is.

real rate of interest The nominal (or market) rate of interest minus the expected inflation rate.

When Is an Interest Rate Too High?

If you review the section of this chapter dealing with Keynesian monetary policy, you can see why many Keynesians would be alarmed at seeing the interest rate rise from 10 percent to 15 percent. This would seem likely to curtail investment, reduce aggregate demand, and start a recession. Hence, these Keynesians might well argue for an increase in the money supply in order to bring the interest rate back down to 10 percent. MQT economists, however, would argue that the interest rate should be allowed to rise, even to 20 percent, to take into account the higher expected and actual long-run inflation rate (10 percent in the example we have been using).

Monetarists have emphasized that what matters to people is real rates of interest, not just the *nominal* (or stated) interest rate. It is not clear whether a nominal interest rate of 15 percent is so high that it will lead to a recession or so low that it will lead to a great expansion of output. To judge this, the expected rate of inflation and the long-run equilibrium real rate of interest must also be known. For example, if inflation is 10 percent and the equilibrium real rate of interest is 5 percent, then the 15 percent nominal interest rate is neither expansionary nor recessionary. But if the inflation rate is 5 percent and the equilibrium real rate of interest is 5 percent, then the nominal interest rate of 15 percent gives a real rate of 10 percent, which would discourage investment.

Many Keynesians now agree with the main elements of this discussion on the importance of looking at the real rate of interest rather than just the nominal rate of interest. Nevertheless, Keynesians and monetarists often disagree about whether the interest rate is too high or too low. One reason for this is that you know the nominal interest rate for money borrowed for one year, but you have to guess what inflation will be for the next year in order to guess at the real rate of interest you will receive or pay. Keynesian and MQT economists often disagree on their inflation guesses. If the interest rate is 15 percent and MQT economists think inflation will be 15 percent, then i looks too low if the equilibrium real rate of interest is, say, 5 percent. If Keynesians believe inflation will be zero, that same i of 15 percent can look far too high. In fact, many monetarists believe it is precisely this sort of miscalculation that has led the Fed into making serious mistakes in monetary policy. To avoid these mistakes, they would like the Fed to pay much more attention to money supply growth and less attention to the level of interest rates. The next section discusses this line of reasoning.

CONTROLLING THE MONEY SUPPLY

The Fed can direct its attention either to controlling money supply growth or to controlling the level of interest rates. Monetarists usually favor policy which focuses on controlling money supply growth and which permits interest rates to rise and fall according to market conditions. Keynesians historically have favored using monetary policy primarily to manipulate the interest rate and only second-arily to control money supply growth. This is because they believe that stable interest rates are an important, positive influence on business activity. In addition, they would argue that it is quite difficult, if not impossible, for the Fed to control money supply growth within narrow limits.

money multiplier (m) Equals the money stock divided by the monetary base.

This argument is based on the fact that the Fed does not exercise direct control over the money supply. The Fed can influence bank lending by influencing reserves, but it cannot directly control lending and the money supply. One device for looking at this problem is the ***money multiplier*** (not to be confused with the multipliers of Keynesian theory that we saw in Chapters 10 and 11). The money multiplier relates to the money supply and the ***monetary base***. The monetary base is equal to the sum of cash in the hands of the public plus bank reserves. Thus, the monetary base can be used either as cash holdings—cash in your pocket— or as reserves to support bank deposits. The money supply can be defined by the relationship

monetary base (B) Equals currency in the hands of the public plus reserves held by banks; the funds available to support the money supply.

$$M^s = m \times B, \qquad (13\text{-}1)$$

where M^s is the money supply, B is the monetary base, and the money multiplier, m, is defined as

$$m = \frac{M^s}{B}. \qquad (13\text{-}2)$$

Thus, m is just a number that relates B to M^s.[3] It is useful to look at m because the Fed can control the monetary base, and we can see from equation (13-1) that changes in M^s are caused by changes in the monetary base, by changes in the money multiplier, or both.

If the Fed wants to increase B, it can simply use an open market operation to buy government securities, and B rises by the amount of this purchase. If the Fed buys from a bank, the purchase price is automatically added to the bank's reserves. If it buys from a private citizen, the citizen will ultimately deposit the

---

[3]Thus, we will get a different money multiplier corresponding to the different money supply concepts. For example, suppose $M_1 = \$400$ billion, $M_2 = \$1,000$ billion, and $B = \$200$ billion. Then the M_1 money multiplier is

$$m_1 = \frac{M_1}{B} = \frac{\$400}{\$200} = 2,$$

and the M_2 money multiplier is

$$m_2 = \frac{M_2}{B} = \frac{\$1,000}{\$200} = 5.$$

The Attraction of Gold

Requests for a return to a gold standard appear with predictable frequency. However, in recent years these requests have become stronger and the government is actively studying proposals for a gold standard. Supply-side economists are leaders in this appeal to the virtues of the gold standard. Such economists as Robert Mundell of Columbia University and Arthur Laffer of the University of Southern California are outspoken proponents of a gold standard. They argue that monetary discipline is altogether absent in domestic monetary policy. They believe that a gold standard (Mundell proposes a band of $400–$450/ounce of gold) with both citizens and governments being able to exchange dollars for gold would force monetary discipline. Thus, as people feared governmental policy that would be inflationary, they would exchange dollars for gold. The key idea is that the unit of account will never change.

Most economists scoff at these ideas, and sharp divisions exist between supply-siders and monetarists. Monetarists, such as Allan Meltzer of Carnegie-Mellon University, argue that the gold standard advocates are to be commended for their concern over the lack of monetary discipline, but a gold standard is not the solution. Meltzer points out that gold is a commodity such as oil, wheat, or silver, and that the dollar price of gold should change when the supply and demand conditions in the gold market change. Meltzer notes that the last experiment in the United States with a gold standard (1882–1913) is often misinterpreted. Proponents of the gold standard point to the price stability over these three decades, as prices were almost the same in 1913 as they were in 1882. But closer examination shows that the prices of goods and services fell 47 percent from 1882–1896 and then rose 41 percent from 1896 to 1913, hardly a period of price stability.

Monetarists such as Professor Meltzer advocate a monetary rule rather than a gold standard as a way to create discipline in monetary policy.

Fed's check in a bank. In either case, B rises by the amount of the open market purchase. If m is constant, M^s increases by m times the change in B. For example, a $1 billion increase in B would cause M^s to rise by $2 billion if m is 2, by $3 billion if m is 3, and so on. The money multiplier, however, is not constant, and changes in the money multiplier affect M^s. Suppose B is $200 billion and m is initially 2.5; then M^s equals $500 billion ($200 billion $\times$ 2.5). A fall in m by only .1, to 2.4, means M^s becomes $480 billion (2.4 $\times$ $200 billion), or M^s falls by $20 billion. Thus, a very small change in m has a large effect on M^s.

The Fed controls B and thus controls one source of the change in M^s. The other source of change, variations in m, are not entirely under the Fed's control. An increase in B would go partially to extra currency holdings, so there is less than a 100 percent increase in reserves. In this case, the public's decisions on the holding of currency and coin versus deposits would keep M^s from rising as much as it otherwise would. Or, if the increase in B goes entirely to reserves, banks could decide not to lend all these reserves. In either case, this means that an attempt to make M^s rise by, say, \$2 billion by increasing B could be frustrated in part by an offsetting fall in m. Many monetarists argue that over periods of a few quarters, the money multiplier is fairly stable, and that most changes in the money supply are therefore due to changes in the monetary base. Thus, to the monetarists, controlling the money supply is very important, and control of the monetary base can allow the Fed to control the money supply fairly well.

CONTROLLING INTEREST RATES

Until very recently, the Fed paid more attention to interest rates than to the money supply. One reason for this was the idea, resulting from Keynesian theory, that interest rates are important in stimulating adequate investment, as we discussed. Letting interest rates rise too far could curtail investment and cause a recession.

The Fed had another reason for focusing on interest rates; it wanted to stabilize interest rates. If you look at a newspaper's financial page, you will see that interest rates change daily. In fact, they change frequently during any day that the bond markets are open. Interest rates appear to rise and fall in irregular patterns that often seem, to the Fed, to make no sense. Instead of letting interest rates rise and fall and rise again, why not stabilize them around some average value? This idea was based on the assumption that financial markets are often mistaken about equilibrium rates and that well-timed open market operations can improve their performance by smoothing out unnecessary fluctuations. It was also greatly reinforced by the fact that the Treasury has to borrow by selling United States government securities to the public. The government finances the government budget deficit through these sales, and the Treasury prefers low, stable rates to high, unstable rates. Thus, the Fed had three reasons for attempting to stabilize interest rates. First, Keynesian theory indicates this stability is important; letting interest rates rise can retard a recovery or contribute to a recession. Second, the Fed thought that actors in financial markets often make mistakes and that their performance can be improved by actions to stabilize interest rates. Third, the Fed wanted to stabilize markets to assist the Treasury in selling bonds to finance the government budget deficit.

Many economists believe that the Fed's purchases and sales of securities do not help the market. Interest rates change frequently because people are often receiving news that makes them change their minds about what the equilibrium rate is. Unless the Fed has better information concerning the equilibrium rate, intervention by the Fed is as likely to move the market away from equilibrium as to move it toward equilibrium. But even if the Fed has better information, why not make this information available to everyone and allow the market to digest it and move the interest rate toward the level the market thinks best? Furthermore, many economists of both the Keynesian and monetarist schools are suspicious of Fed efforts to help the Treasury sell securities to the public. Between the outbreak of World War II and 1951, the Fed bought Treasury securities to keep the interest rate on them very low, generally below 2 percent.

Beginning in the 1970s, more attention has been focused on the money supply and its growth. The Fed now sets targets for the growth of the money supply. A major issue which divides Keynesian and MQT economists is whether the Fed should use interest rate targets in its attempt to achieve its money supply targets.

October, 1979, was a watershed date for the Fed's approach to monetary policy. Prior to that date, the Fed placed significant focus on *interest rate targets.* Since then, the Fed has been almost totally concerned with money supply growth targets, virtually ignoring interest rates. Let's look at these contrasting Fed policies.

interest rate targets Targets where authorities would like interest rates to be; sometimes targets are designed to control money supply growth.

Controlling the Money Supply Through Interest Rate Targets

Many economists believe that instead of looking at the monetary base, a better way for the Fed to control the money supply (M^s) is by using interest rate targets. They argue that there is some interest rate which, if maintained by the Fed, will cause M^s to grow by just the desired amount. The Fed will sometimes be off in its guesses about what will happen to M^s, but it will do a better job of controlling M^s by using interest rate targets than by using money supply targets.[4]

Actually, the monetarists won quite a victory in convincing the Fed to pay attention to M^s at all. Through the 1950s and 1960s, the Fed was concerned more about interest rates than about the growth of the money supply, and it was primarily developments in the MQT that forced the Fed's attention toward M^s. First, monetarists developed evidence of the importance of the money supply— for example, the Freidman-Meiselman tests and the St. Louis Fed model discussed in Chapter 12. Second, these economists kept up a steady barrage of information on the MQT and gradually convinced more people that there was an alternative to Keynesian theory.

The Fed's approach to controlling M^s by using interest rate targets works in the following way. The Fed tries to keep the *federal funds rate* within a certain target zone. The federal funds rate is the rate banks pay when they borrow reserves from each other. If, for example, bank A needs \$1 million in reserves to meet the reserve requirement, it can borrow them from bank B, and pay interest at the federal funds rate to bank B. Bank B notifies the Fed to transfer \$1 million from its reserve account to bank A. It's as simple as that.

federal funds rate The rate of interest that banks pay when they borrow reserves from each other.

The Fed will set a target zone of, say, 10 to 10.25 percent for the federal funds rate. If the demand for federal funds rises, this tends to drive the rate above 10.25 percent. The Fed then injects new reserves into the system to prevent the rate from rising above 10.25 percent by buying government securities. Figure 13-10 shows the demand and supply of federal funds. If demand is D_1D_1, the rate is in the target zone of 10-10.25 percent. If demand temporarily goes up from D_1D_1 to D_2D_2, the equilibrium rate would rise above 10.25 percent; put another way, at a rate of 10.25 percent the market would demand more than is supplied by the amount AB. If the Fed buys securities worth AB, it injects reserves of AB into the market, and the federal funds rate stabilizes at 10.25 percent.

---

[4]This approach to money supply targets is discussed by Benjamin Friedman, "Public Disclosure and Domestic Monetary Policy," in Richard D. Erb (ed.), *Federal Reserve Policies and Public Disclosure* (Washington: American Enterprise Institute for Public Policy Research, 1978).

FIGURE 13-10   CHANGES IN RESERVES TO STABILIZE THE FEDERAL FUNDS RATE

Suppose the Fed has set a target rate zone of 10 to 10.25 percent for the federal funds rate. It will use open market operations to supply reserves if the rate threatens to move above 10.25 percent and will remove reserves if the rate threatens to move below 10 percent. If supply is SS and demand is D_1D_1, the Fed doesn't have to add or subtract reserves. When demand rises to D_2D_2, the Fed must supply an extra amount of reserves equal to AB to keep the rate from rising above 10.25 percent. When demand falls to D_3D_3, the Fed must drain reserves equal to CE to keep the rate from falling below 10 percent. On balance, using this target zone leads the Fed to add reserves equal to $AB - CE$ (where $AB - CE$ could be negative or positive, depending on how D_2D_2 and D_3D_3 bracket the target zone).

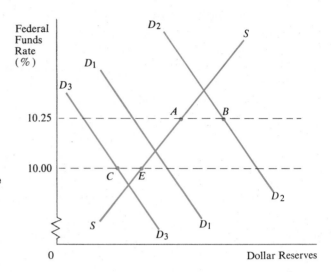

If, on the other hand, demand for borrowing reserves falls in the federal funds market and the rate seems likely to fall below 10 percent, the Fed would sell securities, reducing banks' reserves and putting upward pressure on the rate. In Figure 13-10 suppose demand falls to D_3D_3. The Fed must drain an amount of reserves equal to CE to keep the federal funds rate from falling below 10 percent. It thus sells Treasury securities in the amount of CE.

Using this strategy, the Fed tries to control the money supply by estimating how much M^s would grow at each federal funds rate and then stabilizing the rate at the level that gives the desired money supply growth. The Fed also picks a **money supply target zone** and attempts to keep the actual growth of the money supply in the target zone by keeping the federal funds rate in its target zone. Figure 13-10 illustrates how this works. Sometimes demand for federal funds is high, as with D_2D_2, and the Fed injects reserves (AB in Figure 13-10). At other times, demand is low, as with D_3D_3, and the Fed drains reserves (CE in Figure 13-10). On balance, though, reserves rise by the amount $AB - CE$. Banks then lend some of this net increase in reserves, and the money supply grows, as discussed in Chapter 5. If the Fed has guessed correctly, $AB - CE$ is just the right increase in reserves to cause M^s to grow by the desired amount.

money supply target zone   The band in which monetary authorities want money supply growth rates to be.

Money Supply Targets Often Were Missed by the Fed

From all indications, this approach to control the money supply did not work very well. Evidence indicates that during the 1970s, the Fed achieved most of its interest rate targets and missed many of its money supply targets. Proponents argue that other methods of controlling the money supply—for example, by controlling the monetary base—would not have done any better.

Missed Targets as One Cause of Inflation

Many monetarists believe that these money supply "misses" contributed to inflation. We can look at their argument in terms of Figure 13-10. Suppose that, on average, demand is really D_2D_2 rather than the D_1D_1 that the Fed expects. In this case, the Fed must continue to add reserves in the amount AB to the system in order to stabilize the federal funds rate at 10.25 percent. Since the Fed must, on balance, add reserves in the amount AB rather than the smaller amount $AB - CE$, this will lead to larger than planned increases in the monetary base, B. Through the money multiplier, this rise in B will cause the money supply to rise by a multiple of the rise in B. In Figure 13-10, reserves and the monetary base rise by AB, and with a multiplier of 2.5, the money supply rises by 2.5 times AB. This rise in M^s leads to higher prices, according to the MQT, and people begin to expect higher inflation. We have seen before, in Figure 13-8, how expected inflation causes the demand and supply for funds to rise, driving up interest rates. Over time, then, we expect to see the curves for the demand and supply of federal funds shifting up in a way similar to the curves in Figure 13-8. This means that the Fed must inject even more reserves into the system than before to keep the federal funds rate at 10.25 percent. In Figure 13-11, the Fed first has to inject AB reserves to keep the rate at 10.25 percent. As inflation rises and people come to expect this higher inflation, the demand curve shifts to D_2D_2 and the supply of funds falls, or the supply curve shifts from S_1S_1 to S_2S_2. Now the Fed must

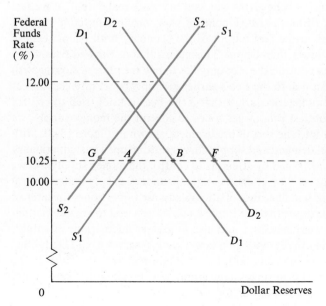

FIGURE 13-11 INFLATION AND THE DEMAND AND SUPPLY OF FEDERAL FUNDS— RESERVES CONTINUE TO RISE

The Fed attempts to keep the federal funds rate at 10.25 percent when the equilibrium rate (at the $D_1D_1 - S_1S_1$ intersection) is above this rate. It thus supplies more reserves (AB) and thereby generates more inflation by increasing the money supply. As people come to expect inflation, both the demand and supply curve shift to D_2D_2 and S_2S_2, respectively. To keep the rate at 10.25 percent, even more reserves (GF) must be injected, which would lead to higher inflation, further upward shifts in D and S, and even larger reserve injections. In the monetarist view, the only way out of this spiral is to let the rate rise to the point where the quantities demanded and supplied are equal (in this case, 12 percent); no additional inflationary reserve injections would then be required. In this view, the attempt to control the federal funds rate has added to inflation.

inject the larger amount of *GF* reserves to stabilize the rate at 10.25 percent. As time goes on, the demand and supply curves continue to shift, and injected reserves grow at an even faster rate. Inflation continues to rise. Eventually the Fed must set a higher interest rate target or the reserves will rise explosively. Many monetarists argue that when the Fed raises its target, it will not raise it by enough. We'll end up with D_2D_2 and *SS* in Figure 13-10, with the demand-supply intersection above the high end of the target zone (which is now, of course, above 10.25 percent). This leads to further increases in reserves, the monetary base, and the money supply, as well as to more inflation.

HOW TO STOP INFLATION: A MONETARIST APPROACH

Monetarists thought that the only way to break out of this spiral was to slow the growth of the monetary base without regard to what happened to interest rates. They said that money supply growth targets should be the only concern of the Fed. In October, 1979, Paul Volcker, chairman of the Federal Reserve Board of Governors, announced that the Fed would drop the interest rate target and concentrate only on maintaining the growth of the money supply within a target band. For instance, in 1982, the target band for M_1 was set between 2.5 and 5.5 percent. Thus, the Fed would attempt to increase the monetary base at a rate which would allow M_1 to grow at a rate between 2.5 and 5.5 percent during 1982. Let's see how the Fed would act using this strategy.

In Figure 13-11, if the Fed does not inject additional reserves when the demand and supply curves rise to D_2D_2 and S_2S_2, then the federal funds rate rises to 12 percent, but reserves don't grow. The sharp rise in interest rates is the price that has to be paid to reduce the growth of reserves and the money supply. Of course, most other interest rates will rise when the federal funds rate does. Most Keynesians and monetarists believe this will tend to reduce real output, as we saw earlier in this chapter. From the MQT point of view, declines in money supply growth lead to declines in the real output of the economy until people believe inflation is going to be lower than before. This means that as the Fed tries to get the money supply under control, the economy has to pay the price of slow growth and high unemployment due to the Fed's earlier attempts to set interest rates at too low a level. Many monetarists argue that if the Fed had not tried to control interest rates, or use interest rate target zones to control the money supply, we would not have gotten into the sort of predicament shown in Figure 13-11, with bank reserves rising and demand and supply curves shifting up. Thus, inflationary episodes would not be worsened by attempts to control the money supply. As we saw, output will be depressed by attempts to get the money supply under control once it has gotten out of hand because of attempts to use target zones for interest rates. Thus, monetarists argue that the interest rate targets lead to greater fluctuations in inflation than were necessary and also to greater fluctuations in output. Note that if the Fed tried to set too high a target zone, reserves would be drained from the banking system, reducing both inflation and real growth. Thus, in the view of many monetarists, mistakes concerning the target zone were costly whether the zone was set too high or too low.

RULES VS. DISCRETION

Prior to October, 1979, the Fed frequently used discretion in order to modify policies to meet changing conditions and circumstances. Those monetarists who believed that attempting to achieve interest rate targets contributed to inflation argued against any discretionary action by the Fed. Instead, they favored a set of rules that would strictly control what the Fed can do in conducting monetary policy. This monetary issue, *rules versus discretion,* divides Keynesian and MQT economists, and even divides MQT economists among themselves. Many observers of Fed policy believe that its recent actions are designed to eliminate discretionary activity and represent a first step toward a rule to govern monetary policy.

rules vs. discretion   The argument over whether monetary policy should be dictated by a set of simple rules or should be left to the discretion of the monetary authority.

The most famous and influential suggestion regarding this issue was made by Milton Friedman. He argued that the Fed should set a target of a constant money supply growth rate. One possibility was a money supply growth rate equal to the long-run growth rate of real output. Thus, if output and the money supply grow at, say, 3.5 percent per year, the price level will be constant as long as velocity does not change.[5]

Even without interest rate targets, there are reasons why the discretionary monetary actions of the Fed might do more damage than good. These reasons all involve lags. One such lag occurs between the time things go wrong with the economy and the time the Fed recognizes that things have gone wrong. Because it takes time to formulate a new policy even after the need is seen for some policy change, another lag occurs. There is a third lag because it takes time to put the policy into operation. (This is less time than it takes to get fiscal policy into action in most cases, as we saw in Chapter 11, but it can take several months for the Board of Governors and the Federal Open Market Committee to agree on a new policy.) And fourth, there is a lag between the time action is taken and the time it affects the economy (see the discussion in Chapter 12 of long and variable lags). The problem is that by the time the policy takes effect, it may do more harm than good. For example, the Fed might adopt an expansionary policy because the economy is in a recession, with rising unemployment and falling output. Suppose output growth has already started to turn up and is nearly back to normal by the time the effects of the expansionary monetary policy reach the economy. Then, the expansionary policy will only make output grow even faster than normal and will eventually lead to more inflation.

The basic argument in favor of an inflexible rule is that it ties the Fed's hands. The public would have no uncertainty about what the Fed would do if it really had to follow the rule; private decision makers wouldn't have to guess about future changes in Fed policy. Further, the Fed couldn't take actions that would make things worse than they would be if it followed the rule. The argument against a strict rule is that it would not allow the Fed to take actions that could make things better than they would be under the rule. Monetarists argue that the

---

[5]In the United States the M_1 velocity, $\dfrac{GNP}{M_1}$, has risen at an average annual rate of somewhat over 3 percent for the past few decades. Thus, price level stability would require that M_1 rise at a rate somewhat less than the growth in Y, because increases in velocity tend to raise prices. M_2 velocity, $\dfrac{GNP}{M_2}$, has been more nearly constant.

historical record of the Fed's use of its current discretionary powers proves that we would be better off with a strict rule.

Some economists associated with the Minneapolis branch of the Fed have recently argued that even the best discretionary policy can't do better than a strict monetary rule. This idea is based on the theory of rational expectations which we will discuss in detail in a later chapter. The argument is that the public will, after a while, begin to anticipate Fed policy moves and change prices to offset these moves; so why not follow a rule and avoid the guessing and price changes? Others dispute this view, arguing that discretionary policy can help when prices and wages cannot change very quickly. We do not want to advocate one argument over another, but rather point out that the usefulness of discretionary monetary policy is open to serious question. The next time you read pronouncements by the chairman of the Fed, you should ask yourself if what is being proposed will really make things better than they would be if we just followed a rule similar to that suggested by Friedman.

SUMMARY

1. In the Keynesian view, monetary policy is thought of as interest-rate policy. Interest rates affect investment demand which affects income, output, and employment through the multiplier process.

2. Monetary policy can influence interest rates by changing the yields on government and corporate bonds. The Fed, by selling or buying bonds, can lower or raise bond prices. Bond prices and bond yields are inversely related.

3. Investment demand is inversely related to the interest rate. As interest rates decline, a larger number of potential investment projects have expected rates of profit which exceed the interest rate.

4. Changes in investment spending change aggregate demand and, therefore, change the equilibrium level of national income, output, and employment.

5. Many Keynesian economists believe that investment demand is very unresponsive (inelastic) to changes in the interest rate. They argue that investment demand is unstable and shifts a great deal as expectations change. Because of this, they argue for strong fiscal policy, with monetary policy used only as a supplement.

6. According to monetarists, the money supply determines prices and the inflation rate in the long run, but it does not affect real output. In the short run, changes in monetary policy affect both price and output.

7. In the MQT view, expected inflation affects the interest rate, with higher expected inflation increasing the demand for funds and reducing the supply. If monetary policy changes so that the long-run inflation rate rises, the interest rate will rise by approximately the same amount.

8. In the short run, before the economy understands that the money supply is growing faster, the interest rate may fall. Eventually, expectations are revised and the interest rate rises to incorporate the new, higher rate of inflation.

9. Many monetarists argue that the use of interest rate target zones led the Fed to create too much money in inflationary times and too little during recessions, thus magnifying the fluctuations within the economy. Economists like Milton Friedman argue that the economy would be better off if the Fed had no discretion over monetary policy but had to follow a money supply growth rate rule; that is, make the money supply grow at some fixed rate every year.

10. Prior to October, 1979, Fed monetary policy was essentially Keynesian; that is, interest rate targets held a high priority. Since that time, the Fed has concentrated on achieving money supply growth targets, a monetarist view of monetary policy.

NEW TERMS

bond
maturity date
face value
investment demand schedule
marginal efficiency of investment schedule
nominal (market) interest rate
real rate of interest

money multiplier *(m)*
monetary base *(B)*
interest rate targets
federal funds rate
money supply target zone
rules vs. discretion

QUESTIONS FOR DISCUSSION

1. Using the investment demand schedule shown in Figure 13-3, suppose that i declined from 20 percent to 15 percent. What change in I would occur?

2. If the $MPC = 0.75$, what change in Y would occur if i decreased from 20 percent to 15 percent? Use Figure 13-3 to determine your answer.

3. Suppose that $i = 15$ percent and the $MPC = 0.9$. Further, suppose the economy is in equilibrium and $Y = \$2,000$ billion. If $Y^* = 2,200$, what change in i would be necessary to bring the economy to the full-employment level of national income? Use the information in Figure 13-3 to determine your answer.

4. Suppose a one-year bond will pay $1,000 at maturity. Give the yield on this bond for prices of $999, $975, $950, $925, $900, $850, and $800.

5. Suppose the equilibrium real rate of interest is 3 percent and that in every period people try to earn this real rate. If they believe inflation will be 5 percent, what i is set? What if they believe inflation will be 12 percent? Suppose they believe inflation will be 12 percent, but it actually is 15 percent. What is the actual real rate of interest that people receive? (Hint: In this case, where people set i to try to earn the equilibrium real rate in every period, the difference between the expected real rate of interest and the actual real rate is just the expected inflation rate minus the actual inflation rate.)

6. Suppose the monetary base is $200 billion. If m is 3 and then rises to 3.2, what is the change in M^s? What is the dollar change in M^s if B rises from $200 billion to $225 billion and m is constant at 3?

7. According to the Keynesian view, what are some of the problems that might arise in using the interest rate to help control the economy?

8. Discuss the monetarist argument that interest rate targets contribute to fluctuations within the economy.

9. What is the case against *discretion?* What is the case for it?

SUGGESTIONS FOR FURTHER READING

Friedman, Milton. *A Program for Monetary Stability.* New York: Fordham University Press, 1975.

Friedman, Milton, and Walter Heller. *Monetary Versus Fiscal Policy.* New York: W. W. Norton and Co., Inc., 1969.

Poole, William. *Money and the Economy: A Monetarist View.* Reading, MA: Addison-Wesley Publishing Co., Inc., 1978.

Policy Alternatives to Affect Unemployment and Inflation

Learning Objectives

After studying the materials found in this chapter, you should be able to do the following:

1. Define:
   - (a) the Phillips curve.
   - (b) the natural rate of unemployment.
   - (c) frictional unemployment.
   - (d) structural unemployment.

2. Explain the implications for economic policy of the Phillips curve trade-off between inflation and unemployment.

3. Explain Friedman's argument that the long-run Phillips curve is vertical.

4. List and discuss three reasons why there is a positive rate of unemployment even when the economy is performing satisfactorily.

5. Present arguments pro and con for the following statements:
   - (a) Labor unions are the cause of inflation.
   - (b) Businesses are the cause of inflation.
   - (c) Excessive monetary growth is the only possible cause of inflation.

Phillips curve   A curve which seems to illustrate a short-run trade-off between the level of unemployment and the rate of inflation.

This chapter focuses on two of the most pressing problems facing the U.S. economy: inflation and unemployment. It begins with an explanation of inflation and unemployment according to the simple Keynesian model. Since actual data on inflation and unemployment rates did not conform very closely to the theory's predictions, a modification in the Keynesian theory was called for. This came in 1958 with the idea that a systematic trade-off existed between inflation and unemployment. This trade-off was called the *Phillips curve*. Using Phillips curve analysis, U.S. policymakers attempted to manipulate this trade-off. Later, when the performance of the economy significantly departed from the Phillips curve predictions, the idea of a shifting Phillips curve was developed. MQT economists developed their own ideas regarding the inflation-unemployment relationship. The monetarist view denied any permanent trade-off between inflation and unemployment and stated that neither expansionary fiscal nor monetary policy could permanently reduce the unemployment rate. The chapter examines four possible causes of price increases: government spending, unions, big business, and money supply growth.

INFLATION AND UNEMPLOYMENT IN
THE SIMPLE KEYNESIAN MODEL

Up to this point we have discussed inflation and unemployment as if they were separate economic problems. According to the simple Keynesian model, inflation occurs when the economy's level of aggregate demand exceeds the full-employment level of output, and unemployment results when aggregate demand is insufficient to purchase the full-employment level of output. Given these assumptions, the simple Keynesian model predicts that inflation and unemployment will not occur simultaneously.

This Keynesian relationship between inflation and unemployment is shown in Figure 14-1. Inflation rates are shown on the vertical axis, and unemployment rates are shown on the horizontal axis. Point A shows a situation of full employment with stable prices. The inflation-unemployment combinations form an L-shaped line because of the following assumption of the simple Keynesian model: If the economy is operating at less than the full-employment level of output and

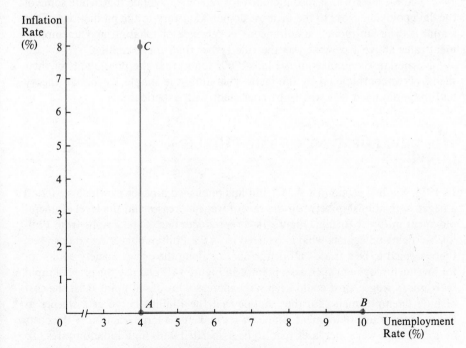

**FIGURE 14-1   INFLATION AND UNEMPLOYMENT IN
                THE SIMPLE KEYNESIAN MODEL**

The L-shaped figure above shows various possible combinations of inflation and unemployment in the economy according to the simple Keynesian model. If the economy was experiencing a deflationary gap (e.g., point B), an increase in aggregate demand would move the economy toward Y^* (point A). As increased aggregate demand moved the economy from B to A, unemployment rates would decline. If aggregate demand were increased after the economy reached Y^*, then prices would be pulled up. The inflation rate would increase with no further decreases in the unemployment rate. This is shown by the movement from A to C.

a deflationary gap exists, increases in aggregate demand cause increased output with no increase in prices. Once the economy reaches the full-employment level of output, further increases in aggregate demand cause increased prices without an accompanying increase in output (an inflationary gap exists).[1] Thus, with the economy at point B, an increase in aggregate demand would result in increased output and employment without any increase in the price level. The unemployment rate would decline with no increase in inflation as the deflationary gap was closed. This is shown by the horizontal segment of Figure 14-1. With the economy experiencing full employment and stable prices, further increases in aggregate demand would result in price increases without an increase in output or employment. The unemployment rate would remain unchanged and the inflation rate would increase as an inflationary gap was opened.[2] This is illustrated by the vertical segment of Figure 14-1.

In Figure 14-1, we have chosen an unemployment rate of 4 percent as the full-employment level of national income and output. This was the generally accepted definition of full employment during the 1950s and 1960s, and it determines the position of the vertical segment of the L-shaped curve. Notice that according to Figure 14-1, simultaneous inflation and unemployment are not possible.

The unemployment and inflation rates for 1957–1969 are shown in Figure 14-2. The Keynesian L is also included for reference. Notice that while some of the data points lie close to the L, most do not. Contrary to the predictions of the simple Keynesian model, simultaneous occurrence of inflation and unemployment rates above 4 percent was the rule rather than the exception.

Keynesian economists of the late 1960s found that the predictions of their theory were contradicted by the facts. Therefore, the simple Keynesian theory had to be modified if it was to be consistent with experience.

THE DEVELOPMENT OF THE PHILLIPS CURVE

In 1958, English economist A. W. Phillips published a paper in which he found a negative relationship between the rate of wage increases and the level of unemployment in Great Britain. Figure 14-3 reproduces one of the graphs from Phillips's article and depicts what is referred to as the Phillips curve. As you can see, there seemed to be a trade-off open to society along the curve. Society could opt for low unemployment such as at point A in Figure 14-3 and pay the price of rapid increases in wages, or it could keep wage increases low, as at point B, at the cost of high unemployment. Further, notice that the Phillips curve gets steeper at lower levels of unemployment. Since wages make up a large fraction of the costs of goods, high wage increases tend to be associated with high inflation rates,[3] so

---

[1] This is equivalent to the assumption that as aggregate demand is increased and the deflationary gap is closed, all businesses reach full-employment capacity output simultaneously.

[2] Inflation which occurs when the economy is at the full-employment level of output is called "demand-pull inflation." Since the economy cannot respond to increased spending by increasing output, demand pulls up prices and causes inflation.

[3] For example, labor's share of income in the United States tends to be around 75 percent of gross national product.

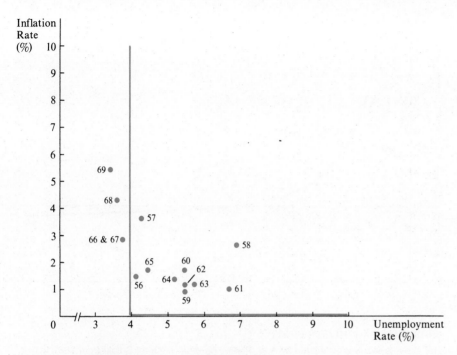

**FIGURE 14-2 INFLATION AND UNEMPLOYMENT,
                1957–1969**

Actual inflation and unemployment rates for the U.S. economy are shown above. The
L-shaped relationship between inflation and unemployment rates is reproduced from Figure
14-1 for reference. Notice that most of the data points are not very close to the *L*. (Source:
Economic Report of the President, 1982.)

the Phillips curve is usually thought of as relating price inflation to unemployment.

    While Phillips presented evidence which suggested that a trade-off existed between inflation and unemployment, he offered no justification for the trade-off. For this reason, the Phillips curve was at first described as an empirical finding in search of a theory. Early explanations for the Phillips curve focused on how changing conditions in the labor market influenced prices; when aggregate demand is increasing, businesses expand output and increase employment. As the unemployment rate falls, the labor market becomes tighter and it grows increasingly difficult to hire workers at prevailing wage rates. Businesses must therefore offer higher wage rates to attract additional workers. With aggregate demand increasing, the demand for individual products is strong and the rising wages can be passed along to consumers in the form of higher prices. Thus, falling unemployment rates are associated with increases in the inflation rate.

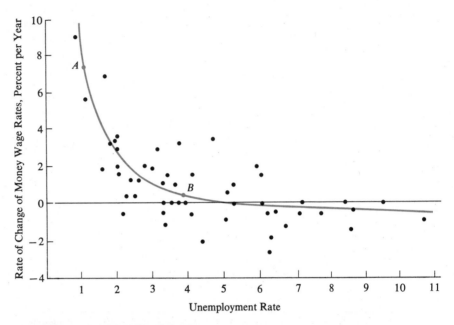

FIGURE 14-3   A PHILLIPS CURVE

The above curve was estimated by A.W. Phillips on data for Great Britain from 1861 to 1913. In addition to the negative relationship between the rate of change of money wages and the unemployment rate, note that the curve is not very steep at high rates of unemployment (say, 10 percent) but is quite steep at low rates of unemployment (say, 1 percent). Thus, reducing unemployment from 10 percent to 9 percent would not cost much in extra wage inflation, but reducing unemployment from 2 percent to 1 percent would result in substantial extra wage inflation. (Source: A.W. Phillips, "The Relation Between Unemployment and the Rate of Change of Money Wage Rates in the United Kingdom, 1861–1957," *Economica*, Vol. XXV [1958], pp. 283–300.)

The Phillips Curve—A Menu of Choice?

Early proponents of the Phillips curve argued that the unemployment-inflation trade-off did exist, that it was stable, and, therefore, that it represented a menu of choice for economic policymakers. Let's use Phillips curve analysis to examine the U.S. experience from 1961–1967. In Figure 14-4, a Phillips curve for the U.S. economy has been constructed using unemployment and inflation data from that period. Recall that in 1964 the Kennedy Tax Cut was introduced. The tax cut was intended to reduce the unemployment rate and it was successful in doing so. As Figure 14-4 shows, from 1965 through 1969, lower unemployment rates were traded for higher inflation rates. In 1969, the Johnson Tax Surcharge was enacted to close an inflationary gap. This restrictive policy was supposed to move the U.S. economy back down the Phillips curve to a more favorable position; that is, to a position with less inflation and a little more unemployment. Figure 14-5 illustrates the intention and results of the Johnson Tax Surcharge. In 1969, with the economy operating at point *A,* taxes were increased. According to the revised Keynesian theory, the resulting decline in aggregate demand should have moved the economy downward and to the right along the Phillips curve to point *B.*

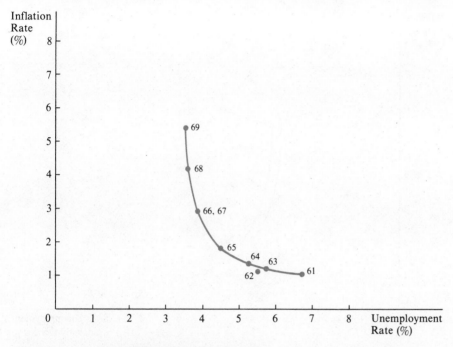

**FIGURE 14-4   A PHILLIPS CURVE FOR THE U.S.
ECONOMY, 1961–1969**

In the above figure, a smooth curve has been constructed using actual inflation and
unemployment data for the period 1961–1969. The data seem to verify the
inflation-unemployment trade-off implied by the Phillips curve.

Instead, in 1970, the economy moved to a point like *C* with a higher level of
unemployment (as expected) but also with a higher rate of inflation. One explanation for the movement from point *A* to point *C* was that something had caused
the trade-off between unemployment and inflation to worsen; that is, the Phillips
curve had shifted to the right.

The Shifting Phillips Curve

Keynesian economists were left with the problem of explaining forces which
could have caused the Phillips curve to shift as shown in Figure 14-6. Early
explanations for the shifting Phillips curve focused on random economic shocks
and changes in the labor force composition.

Random Economic Shocks

Several random shocks occurred to the U.S. economy in the early 1970s and these
had the effect of increasing the price level without lowering the unemployment
rate. These shocks included the devaluation of the dollar vis-à-vis other currencies

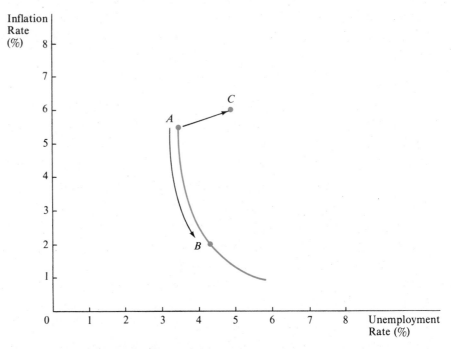

**FIGURE 14-5   THE 1969 JOHNSON TAX SURCHARGE—
INTENTION AND RESULT**

In 1969, the inflation and unemployment rate for the U.S. economy was at point *A* on the Phillips curve shown above. The Johnson Tax Surcharge was enacted with the intention of reducing the inflation rate. A small increase in the unemployment rate was the expected cost of the trade-off. This is shown by a movement down along the Phillips curve from *A* to *B*. Instead, both the unemployment and inflation rates increased in 1970—the economy moved from *A* to *C*.

from 1971–1973 and the dramatic increase in the price of OPEC oil beginning in 1973.[4]

Devaluation meant that the dollar bought fewer units of foreign currency. As a result, the dollar price of foreign products (imports) increased.[5] The rising cost of imports contributed to general price increases in the economy without reductions in the unemployment rate.

The rise in oil prices had an even more pervasive effect on the U.S. economy causing gasoline prices to quadruple between 1973 and 1980. Oil and its derivatives have many other uses in addition to fueling motor vehicles. Fuel oil is important for heating homes, schools, hospitals, and offices. Petroleum and its

---

[4]Another shock was the failure of Soviet agriculture in 1973–1974. The Russians were forced to import massive quantities of grains, particularly wheat. As a result, U.S. supplies of wheat were diminished, resulting in subsequent price increases for wheat and flour.

[5]For example, suppose that a West German exporter sold VW vans for 16,000 marks. At an exchange rate of $1 = 4 marks, an American importer could have purchased a van for resale in the United States for $4,000. After the devaluation, if $1 bought only 3 marks, the U.S. importer would have to pay $5,333 for the same van.

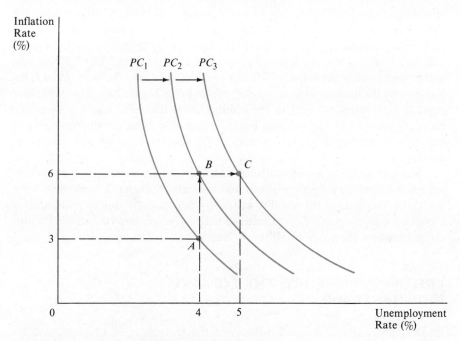

**FIGURE 14-6 EXPLANATION FOR THE SHIFTING
PHILLIPS CURVE**

Random economic shocks (e.g., the devaluation of the dollar and rapid increase of OPEC oil prices) during the early 1970s caused the inflation rate to increase with no improvement in unemployment. This is shown by the movement from A to B and the shift in the Phillips curve from PC_1 to PC_2. Changes in the composition of the labor force (i.e., the influx of women and teenagers) caused the unemployment rate to rise without an accompanying decline in the inflation rate. This is shown by the movement from B to C above, and the shift in the Phillips curve from PC_2 to PC_3.

derivatives are also used as raw materials for many industries. Thus, rapidly rising prices for imported oil set off price increases throughout the economy.

The increased cost of imported oil caused total spending for imports to increase and resulted in a downward shift in net export spending $(X-M)$. According to the Keynesian model, this would result in a decrease in national income and output and an increase in unemployment.

The price increases resulting from the random shocks would cause the inflation rate associated with any given unemployment rate to be higher than before the shocks. This is depicted in Figure 14-6, where point A represents an inflation-unemployment rate combination prior to the random shocks and point B the combination after the shocks. The movement from A to B implies a shift in the Phillips curve from PC_1 to PC_2. Thus, random economic shocks provided one plausible explanation for why the Phillips curve shifted.

Changing Labor Force Composition

Another argument to explain the shifting Phillips curve focuses on the changing composition of the U.S. labor force. During the last 20 years, the proportion of women and teenagers in the labor force has risen significantly. Historically, the unemployment rate of these two groups has been above that of adult men. As these groups become a larger portion of the labor force, the overall unemployment will tend to rise. Thus, the unemployment rate associated with any inflation rate will be higher after the influx of women and teenagers into the labor force. This is shown by the movement from point B to point C in Figure 14-6. The movement from B to C implies a shift in the Phillips curve from PC_2 to PC_3. Thus, the changing labor force composition has the effect of shifting the Phillips curve to the right, indicating a less favorable trade-off between inflation and unemployment.

Many economists were dissatisfied with these explanations for the deteriorating trade-off between unemployment and inflation. Monetarist economists were especially skeptical of the stability of trade-offs brought about by fiscal and/or monetary manipulation. They countered with an alternative view of the Phillips curve based on the work of Milton Friedman.

FRIEDMAN'S THEORY: THE LONG-RUN PHILLIPS CURVE

In December, 1967, Milton Friedman of the University of Chicago gave his presidential address to the American Economics Association.[6] In this address he was very critical of the Keynesian view that the Phillips curve represented a menu of permanent combinations of inflation and unemployment. In his words, "There is always a temporary trade-off between inflation and unemployment; there is no permanent trade-off."[7] To develop this argument, Friedman made an important distinction between what he called the long-run Phillips curve and the short-run Phillips curve we have been discussing. Friedman stated that the short-run trade-off between inflation and unemployment was temporary and that in the long run, the Phillips curve was vertical at the **natural rate of unemployment.** The natural rate of unemployment is defined as the unemployment rate which results when the labor market is in long-run equilibrium. Long-run equilibrium prevails when the inflation rate expected by workers and the economy's actual inflation rate are equal.

natural rate of unemployment The idea that there is some level of unemployment to which the economy naturally tends to move and which is not affected in the long run by the inflation rate or by government monetary and fiscal policies.

Friedman showed why the Phillips curve was vertical in the long run but had a negative slope in the short run, as well as why the short-run curve tended to shift over time. His explanation was based on the premise that decisions in the labor market which determine the level of employment and wage rates are influenced by workers' expectations of inflation. Friedman argued that the short-run trade-off between inflation and unemployment was possible only if the actual inflation rate turned out to be different than what workers expected it to be.

Friedman and Edmund Phelps, of the University of Pennsylvania, developed what is referred to as the **accelerationist theory** of the trade-off between inflation and unemployment. According to Friedman and Phelps, the government can maintain unemployment below the natural rate only at the cost of ever-increasing rates of inflation.

accelerationist theory Theory that states that the government can maintain unemployment below the natural rate only at the cost of ever-increasing rates of inflation.

---

[6]Milton Friedman, "The Role of Monetary Policy," *American Economic Review* (May, 1968), pp. 1–15.
[7]*Ibid.*, p. 11.

We can examine both the accelerationist theory and Friedman's idea of the vertical long-run Phillips curve with the following hypothetical example: assume that the economy initially is in a position of long-run equilibrium as shown by point A in Figure 14-7. This means that the labor market is in equilibrium at the natural rate of unemployment, which we are assuming is 6 percent. We further assume that there has been no recent inflation in the economy and, therefore, none is expected. Thus, actual inflation and inflation expectations are the same— 0 percent. The level of aggregate demand is just sufficient to purchase business output under these conditions without generating any change in employment or prices.

Now suppose government policymakers decide that the existing unemployment rate of 6 percent is socially undesirable and take action to reduce the unemployment rate to 4 percent. The government abruptly and unexpectedly increases the level of aggregate demand through fiscal or monetary policy (the

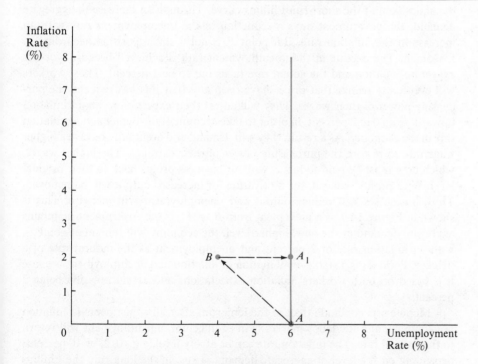

**FIGURE 14-7 THE VERTICAL LONG-RUN PHILLIPS
CURVE**

According to Friedman, the inflation-unemployment trade-off implied by the traditional Phillips curve is temporary and unstable. An increase in aggregate demand which produces an unexpected increase in the inflation rate can cause a temporary reduction in the unemployment rate. This is shown above as a movement from A to B. After workers have had time to adjust their expectations of inflation to a higher actual rate, the temporary reduction in unemployment will disappear. This is shown above as movement from B to A_1. After workers adjust their expectations to actual inflation, unemployment always returns to the natural rate, assumed here to be 6 percent. Thus, according to Friedman, in the long run, after workers adjust their expectations there is no trade-off between inflation and unemployment, and the Phillips curve is vertical.

unexpectedness of this action is important, as we shall explain shortly). The increased aggregate demand causes temporary shortages at prevailing prices and begins to pull prices upward. Rising prices result in rising profits for business. Businesses respond to this signal from the market by increasing output. In order to produce more output, businesses must employ more workers. Job vacancies increase and many unemployed workers find jobs. As the expansionary process begins, newly employed workers take jobs at the prevailing wage rate. Even though prices are beginning to rise, wage rates do not quickly respond to the changed conditions, because the price increases which are occurring are small and not immediately recognized. Even after the price increases are recognized, wages are slow to adjust, because many wage rates are tied to contracts which are negotiated only once every two or three years. As a result, there is a considerable lag between rising prices and the upward adjustment of wage rates, and this creates increased profits for businesses.

As a consequence of the sudden and unexpected increase in aggregate demand, the economy moves from point A to point B in Figure 14-7, with unemployment declining to 4 percent and inflation rising to 2 percent.[8] These are the dynamics behind the short-run Phillips curve. Through an increase in aggregate demand, the government buys a reduction in the unemployment rate with an increase in the inflation rate. But point B is not a stable position according to Friedman. The decline in the unemployment rate is achieved because workers expect no inflation and the actual rate turns out to be 2 percent. Thus, workers will eventually realize that prices have risen and that this has reduced the purchasing power of their wages. They will adjust their expectations about inflation upward, from 0 to 2 percent, in order to take account of the higher actual inflation rate in the economy. As a result, they will demand and eventually receive a higher wage rate to restore the purchasing power of their earnings. The higher wages, which now must be paid to labor, will cut business profits back to their original level. With profits reduced, the motivation for increased output will be removed. Thus, businesses will reduce output and unemployment will increase. This is shown in Figure 14-7 as a movement from B to A_1. If the government maintains aggregate demand at the new, higher level, the economy will remain at point A_1 with an inflation rate of 2 percent and unemployment at the natural rate of 6 percent. Point A_1 is a stable combination of inflation and unemployment because it is based on both workers' inflation expectations and actual inflation being 2 percent.

Monetarists conclude that, in the long run, after all adjustments to inflation are complete and the labor market is in equilibrium, unemployment will return to the natural rate. The inflation rate can be at any level (e.g., 0, 2, or 10 percent) depending on the level of aggregate demand. Thus, in the long run, the Phillips curve is vertical at the natural rate of unemployment as shown in Figure 14-7.

Now let's return to our example and illustrate the argument made by Friedman and Phelps that unemployment below the natural rate can be maintained only at the cost of increasing rates of inflation.

---

[8]The inflation rates used in these examples are hypothetical and are chosen to simplify the presentation.

THE ACCELERATIONIST THEORY

Let's pick up our example with the economy at point A_1 in Figure 14-8. Having been thwarted in the first attempt to maintain the unemployment rate at 4 percent, government policymakers again attempt to reduce unemployment with fiscal or monetary policy. Aggregate demand is increased to an even higher level. As before, prices and profits are driven up and firms increase output. This increases the demand for labor; employment rises and the unemployment rate declines to 4 percent. Rising output prices cause the inflation rate to rise above 2 percent to, say, 4 percent, and the economy moves off the long-run Phillips curve from point A_1 to point B_1. Point B_1 is unstable for the same reason that point B was unstable. It is achieved because the actual rate of inflation (now 4 percent) is greater than expectations (2 percent). As people become aware of the

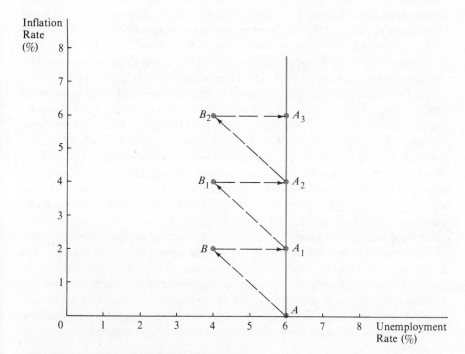

FIGURE 14-8   THE ACCELERATIONIST VIEW

According to the accelerationist view, unemployment rates below the natural rate (assumed to be above 6 percent) can be achieved only if government policies generate accelerating rates of inflation. With the economy at point A, a government-induced increase in aggregate demand causes a temporary decline in the unemployment rate and unexpected inflation from A to B. After workers adjust their expectations to the higher actual inflation rate, the temporary reduction in unemployment disappears (B to A_1). To reduce unemployment below the natural rate, government policy must become more expansionary. This causes a further increase in the inflation rate and a temporary decline in unemployment from A_1 to B. After workers adjust their expectations to the higher inflation rate, unemployment returns to the natural rate (B_1 to A_2). In order to keep the unemployment rate below the natural rate (points B, B_1, B_2, etc.), the government must follow a policy which generates accelerating rates of inflation (2 percent, then 4 percent, then 6 percent, etc.).

difference, they revise their expectations of inflation upward to 4 percent. Wage rates eventually rise, profits decline, production falls, and unemployment increases. The economy moves back to the long-run Phillips curve at point A_2, but with a higher level of aggregate demand and an inflation rate of 4 percent. As the government persists in its attempts to reduce unemployment below the natural rate, the process described above is repeated. The economy moves to point B_2, and after workers adjust their expectations of inflation, it moves back to the long-run Phillips curve at point A_3. The cost of persistent attempts to reduce the unemployment rate below the natural rate is not 2 percent inflation, but a continually increasing rate of inflation; first 2 percent, then 4 percent, then 6 percent inflation, and so on.

According to the accelerationist theory, the unemployment rate can be maintained below the natural rate for an extended period of time provided that expectations are never allowed to completely adjust to actual inflation. What is required is that actual inflation rates continually accelerate ahead of inflation expectations. For example, with the economy at point B in Figure 14-8, the reduction in unemployment will be eliminated as workers revise their inflation expectations upward from 0 to 2 percent. By increasing aggregate demand while the economy is at point B, the government can generate a 4 percent inflation rate while expectations are being revised upward from 0 to 2 percent. Thus, the movement back to the long-run Phillips curve (B to A_1) is thwarted, and instead, the movement is from B to B_1. Later, when workers adjust their expectations to the higher actual inflation rate of 4 percent, aggregate demand is again increased and a 6 percent inflation rate is generated. Rather than moving from B_1 to A_2, the economy moves to B_2. According to the accelerationist theory, the economy can trace out a short-run Phillips curve by joining points A, B, B_1, B_2 etc., if government policy is used to generate inflation rates which continue to rise faster than expectations can adjust. Many economists believe that the inflation-unemployment combinations of the 1960s were the result of conditions similar to those we have just described. Government policy from 1964 until 1969 produced actual inflation rates which accelerated ahead of expectations. Thus, unemployment rates were maintained below the natural rate because workers systematically underestimated actual inflation rates for several years. When the Johnson Tax Surcharge took effect in 1969–1970, the stimulus to aggregate demand was reduced. The accelerationist theory would predict a rise in the unemployment rate without any decrease in the inflation rate as the economy moved back toward the long-run Phillips curve. Today, most economists, including many Keynesians, accept the accelerationist view of the unemployment-inflation rate movements since 1964.

More recently, a group of economists headed by Robert Lucas of the University of Chicago and Thomas Sargent of the University of Minnesota have formulated an even more discouraging scenario for government policy and the inflation-unemployment trade-off. According to their theory, monetary and fiscal policy may generate increased rates of inflation, but cannot lower unemployment below the natural rate. This idea, known as rational expectations, is controversial.[9] It is reviewed in the appendix to this chapter.

---

[9] A well-written summary of the rational expectations theory is presented in Mark H. Willes, "Rational Expectations—Fresh Ideas That Challenge Some Established Views of Policymaking," *Federal Reserve Bank of Minneapolis Annual Report* (1977), pp. 1–13.

John Muth *(1930–)*

Robert E. Lucas, Jr. *(1938–)*

By the mid-1970s, a radical new idea was sweeping economics concerning the way expectations are formed. The basic idea, "rational expectations," is credited to *John F. Muth,* and its most influential exponent in macroeconomics has been *Robert E. Lucas, Jr.*

It is clear that people's expectations about future developments are important for their actions today. But how are expectations determined? This question has long puzzled economists. In 1961, Muth proposed a simple, radical solution. He hypothesized that people in the economy base their expectations on the best economic theory available as they understand the basic relationships involved. For example, if the price of wheat depends on the wheat harvest, and the harvest depends on the weather, people will base their expectations of wheat prices on what they see happening to the weather. Furthermore, said Muth, people will *on average* be right about the relationship between the weather and the price of wheat; in any particular year, their guesses will be somewhat off, but their mistakes will be random, and an economist couldn't do a better job.

Lucas applied this idea to macroeconomics. Suppose that the price level ultimately depends on the money supply. Then, according to the rational expectations hypothesis, people will catch on to this relationship. If the money supply is expanding, people will un-

derstand that this means higher prices and wages and will thus raise prices and wages now. Furthermore, many economists in this camp believe that it is only mistaken expectations that affect real variables such as real income. This is a very monetarist view. Thus, they think that monetary policy that is anticipated by the economy will not affect real output, and the monetary authorities can thus affect national income only by "fooling" the citizenry. In their view, changes in monetary policy thus merely cause consumers and producers to make mistakes, thereby ultimately hurting the economy. Their recommendation is to leave the economy alone and simply adopt an "*x* percent annual growth rate" of the money supply, since monetary policy can't make things better and may make things worse. This view that even the best monetary policy doesn't do any good and can do much harm is rather radical.

John F. Muth earned his Ph.D. at Carnegie-Mellon University in 1962 and has taught at Carnegie-Mellon and Michigan State. He is now at Indiana University's Graduate School of Business Administration. Robert E. Lucas, Jr., was awarded his Ph.D. from the University of Chicago in 1964 and is currently a professor of economics at the University of Chicago. He has also taught at Carnegie-Mellon.

THE FULL-EMPLOYMENT RATE OF UNEMPLOYMENT

Even when demand and supply are roughly balanced in the labor market, we expect to have reported unemployment of, say, 6 percent. It is important to see why this is true so we can interpret the unemployment statistics we read in the newspaper. In addition, this discussion is closely related to the idea of the natural rate of unemployment.

It is useful to gain some historical perspective. When the United States entered World War II, the unemployment rate was still almost 10 percent. The country had not yet recovered from the Great Depression that began in August, 1929. However, the lowest unemployment rate during World War II was about 1.2 percent, in spite of the fact that almost 11.5 million Americans were in the armed forces and patriotic appeals were made for the elderly to come out of retirement and for women to take jobs outside their homes in order to further the war effort. Unemployment averaged about 4.5 percent in the 1950s, 4.8 percent in the 1960s, and 6.3 percent for most of the 1970s. Thus, the level of unemployment in the United States has varied greatly but has always been positive. We want to examine why, even in labor markets with the strongest demand, we have to expect unemployment as measured by the Bureau of Labor Statistics (BLS).

The definition of unemployment used by the BLS insures that we will always have a positive unemployment rate. The BLS takes a survey each month to determine the unemployment rate. They ask a sample of 60,000 people if (1) they had jobs in the preceding month, and (2) if not, whether they were actually looking for work. These questions don't take into account certain conditions that guarantee the answers will always show a positive rate of unemployment. First, they don't ask what kind of job the individual is looking for or would accept. If you would like to be the manager of the New York Yankees, the president of an automobile company, or a professor of English literature at Harvard, you may have to wait a very long time before you get a job offer that you will accept. Put another way, there are newspaper ads for dishwashers in even the most severe recessions, and almost anyone who is willing to accept such a job can get one.

Second, the questions don't take into account the individual's incentives to accept a job. In the early 1930s, those out of work could not count on welfare or unemployment payments, and their labor unions couldn't offer much in the way of unemployment benefits. In the 1980s, there are welfare and unemployment insurance benefits, and often unions have negotiated rather good payments that have to be made by companies to workers who are laid off. For example, some auto workers who are laid off can count on several months of pay from their companies at up to 90 percent of the salary they would be making if they were back on the job. We aren't saying that this is wrong; but we have to recognize that these workers won't accept jobs that pay very much less than their old ones, and will thus be counted as unemployed.

Third, if you are unemployed, you probably won't take the first job that comes along but will continue to search for a job that looks good compared to what you think you can expect to find. The longer you search, the better an idea you have of what you can expect. After a time, you will decide that it doesn't seem worthwhile to go on looking—the prospects of finding a better job do not look that attractive—and so you will take a job. Until you do, you are one of the unemployed. Some people are out of work *and* looking for work because they have just entered the labor force (students graduating, homemakers returning to the labor force, and so on); others have been laid off; some have been fired; and others have simply quit. Whatever the reason, a certain percentage of the work force is always between jobs. For these three reasons, we always expect to see a positive rate of unemployment, as we did even in World War II.

Many economists distinguish between *frictional* and **structural unemployment.** When a worker at an aircraft plant in Los Angeles is laid off, that worker has many alternative opportunities available, and the unemployment until a new job is found is called *frictional* unemployment; it is due to the frictions of moving from one job to another. However, a coal miner in West Virginia, laid off by the closing of the only mine in an area with no other employment, cannot very well look forward to finding another job without moving to another geographical area. This is referred to as *structural* unemployment because it is due to a change in the structure of the economy and because elimination of this unemployment requires a shift in people's locations or changes in their job skills. Another cause of structural unemployment would be a change in technology that makes a whole class of jobs obsolete, such as when hand looms were replaced by mechanical looms. One person operated each hand loom and it was a skilled job, while one person with little skill could tend several mechanical looms.

Thus, there will always be people who have just entered the labor force, who have quit, or who have lost jobs, and there will always be people who are temporarily laid off or who are out of work in jobs that depend on such factors as the weather. The rate of unemployment that we expect to find when demand and supply are in balance is what we mean by the natural rate of unemployment. According to some economists, such as Milton Friedman, the natural rate of unemployment is a number given by the vertical Phillips curve, say, 6 percent. For many Keynesian economists, the natural rate of unemployment depends on where the economy is on the long-run Phillips curve that is *not* vertical; that is, according to these economists, society has some control over the rate of unemployment.

A very important issue is when and why the natural rate changes. From the above discussion, we can see that the natural rate will increase when people become more particular about the jobs they will take and when their incentives for accepting jobs decrease due to, say, an increase in unemployment benefits. The natural rate will also increase when people begin to quit jobs more frequently or get fired more frequently. Further, the natural rate will rise when more people who tend to have a difficult time getting jobs enter the labor force. For example, we can easily imagine that a college graduate with a general liberal arts degree will have more trouble getting a job in business than would a graduate with an emphasis in business or economics. Similarly, a high school graduate will often have more trouble than a college graduate, and a high school dropout can be in a very bad position. If the composition of the labor force shifts to more of these relatively difficult-to-place groups, then the natural rate of unemployment will rise.

In the United States economy, the groups with the highest unemployment rates are women, young people, and minorities. This is partly due to discrimination and partly due to these groups *as a whole* having less training and less salable job skills. For both reasons, these groups tend to have high unemployment rates.

frictional unemployment
Unemployment due to frictions in the economy, such as the time it takes to move from one job to the next, to select a job out of the number of offers available, and so on.

structural unemployment
Unemployment due to structural shifts in the economy; for example, skills not matching job openings, workers being located in one area and jobs in another area, and so on.

We are not blaming these groups for having higher than average unemployment rates or for raising the overall natural rate of unemployment. These groups very often have no control over this situation. The point is this: Whether you think the long-run Phillips curve is vertical or has a negative slope, the composition of the labor force will shift the position of the long-run Phillips curve. Thus, whether an economist is in the Keynesian or MQT camp—or somewhere between the two—the changes in labor force composition lead to the belief that the long-run Phillips curve has shifted. It isn't true that conservatives think the curve has shifted while liberals do not, or that Keynesians and MQT economists disagree that these changes in labor force composition cause shifts in the long-run Phillips curve. The main difference among economists on this score is whether they believe there is any long-run inflation-unemployment trade-off at all.

DO UNIONS CAUSE INFLATION?

Many business people are quite sure that unions cause inflation, and many union people firmly believe that it is all they can do to keep up with the price increases caused by the policies of business. This section explains how both groups can reasonably hold these positions and why neither view is really correct.

Look back at Figure 14-7 or 14-8, and recall that we started the process shown there by expanding aggregate demand with monetary and/or fiscal policy. When demand rises because of expansionary fiscal and/or monetary policy, business feels justified in raising prices. From a worker's viewpoint, higher wages are needed just to keep up with the cost of living. It is easy to see how people can become convinced that there is a wage-price spiral, with wage increases leading to price increases, which in turn lead to more wage increases, and so on.

In the above analysis, however, the real cause of both the price and wage increases was the expansionary fiscal or monetary policy. Once this policy was introduced, both prices and wages had to rise in order to return the system to equilibrium. In fact, the argument about whether business or labor causes inflation is an example of how people involved in a process often see very clearly the small picture of what is happening to them but miss the big picture of what is going on within the whole economy.

If government applies further expansionary policies every period, prices can be expected to rise every period. These ongoing price increases are what we mean by continuing inflation. However, this does not mean that government policies alone explain rises in the general level of prices. Earlier in this chapter we presented the argument that the sharp rise in OPEC oil prices in 1973–1974 resulted in random shocks throughout the economy. This sort of occurrence can cause prices to rise for a year or two but cannot cause them to continue rising year after year, as happens in continuing inflation. For inflation to continue, new disturbances must occur year after year.

The same thing is true of the labor market and inflation; continuing inflation requires continuing disturbances. In Figure 14-9, we show a case where unions raise wages from the equilibrium level OW_1 to the higher rate OW_2. This causes unemployment of $ON_3 - ON_2$. In response to this higher level of labor costs, we would expect business to raise prices. But if unions do not raise wages again, there is no ongoing inflation. Of course, we could imagine that unions will raise wages

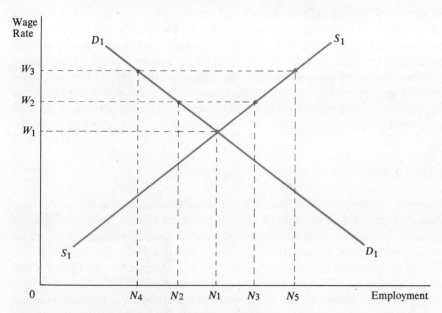

**FIGURE 14-9   UNIONS, WAGE INCREASES, AND
UNEMPLOYMENT**

If unions can exert some monopoly power, they can raise wages from OW_1 to, say, OW_2.
This will cause an increase in unemployment. Further, business will raise the price level
and pass along some of the increased wage costs. But unless unions once again raise
wages, we won't have ongoing price increases; that is, we won't have inflation. However,
if government reacts to the unemployment $ON_3 - ON_2$ by starting expansionary
monetary and fiscal policies, we can expect inflation. Thus, unions can't cause inflation
by themselves, but they might be able to start the process that government then
continues, or *ratifies*. (The same analysis applies if business uses its monopoly power to
shift the Phillips curve.)

again in response to any price increase, but as they do, unemployment rises, as
we see in comparing OW_3 with OW_2. At some point, this increasing unemployment will halt further wage and price increases. Any wage-price spiral has to stop
unless it is fed by further disturbances, particularly by expansionary monetary
and fiscal policy.

If the unemployment at wage rates OW_2 and OW_3 in Figure 14-9 is politically
unacceptable, the government can attempt to reduce it by using expansionary
monetary and fiscal policy. In effect, the unions' actions have shifted the long-run
Phillips curve to the right. Consequently, as we have seen, the success of the
government policy will depend on whether the long-run curve has a negative slope
or is vertical. In the latter case, of course, expansionary policy will only succeed
in increasing the rate of inflation at the now higher natural rate of unemployment.

A large majority of economists in the United States now agree that unions
can cause inflation in the longer run only if the government *ratifies* their attempts
to raise wages by running expansionary monetary and fiscal policies. We still have
to answer the question of whether unions can in fact kick off the inflationary
process. Here opinion is much more divided. Union members constitute less than

*ratifying price increases   The
idea that if either businesses or
unions manage to raise prices
government will use
expansionary policy so that the
price increases won't reduce
aggregate demand, output, and
employment.*

20 percent of the United States work force. Further, the 20 percent figure of union membership can substantially overstate union power. The unions that have been most successful in raising their members' wages—such as those representing construction workers and airline pilots—make up a small fraction of total union membership. Many economists view the suggestion that this 20 percent causes inflation as arguing that the tail wags the dog. Other economists hold that this 20 percent is quite large enough to set off the wage-price spiral when coupled with government expansionary policy. This question, then, must be left unanswered.

DOES BUSINESS CAUSE INFLATION?

It should be fairly obvious from the preceding discussion that we don't think business causes much inflation in the United States either. Any price increases initiated by business must be ratified by fiscal or monetary policy to set off an ongoing inflationary process. Business may be able to adopt policies that shift the Phillips curve, but an increase in ongoing inflation can develop only if government adopts a more expansionary policy in reaction to these shifts.

There is no doubt that the 500 largest United States firms have some degree of monopoly control over the prices of the goods they sell, and these firms also have a good deal of interest in making large profits. It is important to note here that once these firms have exercised their monopoly power, they have no incentives to change price unless something else also changes. In other words, if you initially set price to maximize profits, you have no incentive to change price unless demand or cost conditions change. However, government policy that ratifies price increases is precisely the ingredient that will cause demand conditions to change, as well as change cost conditions as workers try to keep up with price increases.

Most economists would now agree that business actions can cause ongoing inflation only if ratified by government macro policy. It remains an open question as to whether business plays a significant role in setting off the inflationary process.

INFLATION AND THE GOVERNMENT BUDGET DEFICIT

Do deficits in the government budget cause inflation? Keynesians and monetarists respond with different answers. Keynesians believe that if the economy is far from the full-employment output, increases in government spending or tax cuts (both of which raise the deficit) will increase output without increasing inflation (or without increasing inflation very much). This argument can be thought of in terms of the inflationary gap analysis. Alternatively, in terms of the short-run Phillips curve analysis, when unemployment is quite high, a decrease in unemployment will add very little to inflation. However, when the economy is close to full employment, an increase in the deficit through active fiscal policy will cause inflation, in the view of many Keynesians.

Many monetarists believe that the deficit contributes to inflation primarily by leading to increases in the money supply. When the government deficit increases, it must somehow be financed. The government is literally paying out more than it is taking in, and it must get those extra dollars somewhere. One way is to borrow by selling new government bonds to the public. As more bonds are put on the market, their prices fall; this means that their yields rise, or the general level of interest rates goes up. This is unattractive to policymakers. Hence, they often urge the Fed to buy some of these bonds to keep the bond prices higher and the yields lower than they otherwise would be. But as we saw in Chapter 13, these purchases by the Fed result in the monetary base being expanded, so the money supply rises. In other words, the Fed buys these bonds by creating new money. In the monetarist view, this leads to inflation and, after a while, to higher interest rates. In this way, deficits cause inflation only to the extent that they are partly financed by money supply creation.

MONEY AND ONGOING INFLATION

In the first two or three decades after the *General Theory,* many Keynesians were sure that monetary policy didn't matter. Rather remarkably, by the late 1960s and into the 1970s, the large majority of economists in the United States agreed that excessive money supply growth was a necessary ingredient of substantial, long-term inflation. Most economists would agree that inflation of more than a few

Inflation and OPEC

When we think of inflation we think of a rise in the price of an item that we consume or purchase. This is because we are constantly reminded of the effects of inflation when we purchase specific goods or services. However, we must be careful. Inflation is not the increasing price of a certain product, such as oil. Instead, it is an increase in the price level, which is measured by the amount of spending on a bundle of goods.

Products can increase in price, but this does not mean we have inflation. Many politicians, including Presidents Nixon, Ford, and Carter, said that OPEC was causing our inflation. Many reporters seemed to agree. However, they all failed to distinguish between changes in relative prices and inflation. If OPEC increases the price of oil, it must cut production to cause the price to rise. If we maintain the same money stock and the supply of goods available remains unchanged, the price level will rise. This is a once-and-for-all change in the price level. We are worse off and the members of OPEC are better off. But inflation is a steady, ongoing increase in the price level from period to period.

It is interesting to understand why the president, Congress, and even the Fed might blame OPEC. It doesn't need American votes and doesn't respond to accusations. However, it is difficult to understand why reporters allow politicians and political institutions to get away with this finger pointing.

percentage points above average that went on for, say, three years would have to be accompanied by above normal money supply growth. In other words, ongoing inflation is not possible without ongoing excessive money supply growth.

As we saw earlier in this chapter, expansionary government policy which is initiated with the economy at Y^* will drive up the price level. Alternatively, increases in C or I will also bring about price increases. These will result in a temporary, one-time increase in the price level and, therefore, in a temporary increase in the inflation rate. If the price increases are to continue, we would need further increases in government spending, or upward shifts in the consumption or investment functions. Put another way, ongoing inflation can't be explained by a one-time increase in government spending from 20 percent to, say, 22 percent of GNP. This generates price increases that die out, resulting in a new, higher price level but not in continuing inflation. Ongoing inflation caused by government spending would require G to rise to 22 percent of GNP, then 24 percent, 26 percent, and so on. Or, we could have ongoing inflation if G and the consumption and investment functions took turns rising. However, the problem with this explanation is that we have had a fair amount of historical experience with inflation where G, C, and I all seem to be either increasing very moderately or have even been somewhat depressed. For example, the inflation of the 1970s was *not* accompanied by either consumption or investment booms, and government's share of GNP was not growing steadily or significantly.

This recognition left the Keynesian picture as follows. Fluctuations in government spending or the consumption (or investment) functions could set off multiplier-type changes in real output and income and could also cause bursts of price changes that lasted for a rather long period. Something else, however, was needed to explain why the average inflation rate of the 1960s was about 2.3 percent, while that of the 1970s was about 7.0 percent. By this time it was accepted that money mattered, as we discussed above, so many Keynesians could now agree with the MQT view that, over the longer run, the average rate of money supply growth has a substantial influence on the average rate of price inflation. In this view, one-time changes in the consumption or investment functions could cause a change in the price level, but further price changes would require accommodating money supply growth.

SUMMARY

1. Because of its analytical framework, the simple Keynesian model developed in previous chapters predicts that inflation and unemployment will not occur simultaneously.

2. The simple Keynesian theory was modified to include the idea that a systematic and exploitable relationship existed between inflation and unemployment. The Phillips curve implied that the economy could choose from a variety of possible inflation-unemployment combinations.

3. When the trade-off between inflation and unemployment appeared to worsen, economists tried to explain the shifts in the Phillips curve. Causes included random shocks to the economy and the changing composition of the labor force.

4. Milton Friedman countered these Keynesian views with the idea that any inflation-unemployment trade-off was temporary and that the long-run Phillips curve was vertical at the natural rate of unemployment.

5. The accelerationist theory predicts that the unemployment rate can be maintained below the natural rate if people form expectations adaptively and are continually fooled by expansionary government policy.

6. We expect to observe positive rates of unemployment even when society experiences full employment; that is, when labor markets are in long-run equilibrium.

7. The possibility that unions or big businesses cause inflation is questioned. Unions and big business can contribute to a wage-price spiral by demanding higher wages and prices; but without ratification by government, these inflationary demands cannot be maintained.

NEW TERMS

Phillips curve
natural rate of unemployment
accelerationist theory

frictional unemployment
structural unemployment
ratifying price increases

QUESTIONS FOR DISCUSSION

1. Why are simultaneous inflation and unemployment impossible according to the simple Keynesian model?

2. The simple Keynesian model was modified to include the Phillips curve relationship. Why did this occur? What is the relationship between inflation and unemployment according to the Phillips curve?

3. Why did economists search for ideas to explain shifting Phillips curves?

4. What is Friedman's argument about the Phillips curve being vertical in the long run? How do expectations of inflation affect it? Why do we see a short-run Phillips curve?

5. According to the accelerationist theory, the government must generate increasing rates of inflation in order to maintain unemployment below the natural rate. Explain this conclusion.

6. Why do we expect to see positive measured rates of unemployment?

7. What is meant by the natural rate of unemployment? Why isn't it zero?

8. Can either business or unions cause *ongoing* inflation? What is meant by the government ratifying inflation?

SUGGESTIONS FOR FURTHER READING

Friedman, Milton. "The Role of Monetary Policy." *American Economic Review* (May, 1968), pp. 1–15.

Kareken, John H. "Inflation: An Extreme View." *Federal Reserve Bank of Minneapolis Quarterly Review* (Winter, 1978), pp. 7–13.

Phelps, Edmund S. "Money Wage Dynamics and Labor Market Equilibrium," *Microeconomic Foundations of Employment and Inflation Theory.* New York: W.W. Norton & Co., Inc., 1970, pp. 124–166.

Phillips, A.W. "The Relation Between Unemployment and the Rate of Change of Money Wage Rates in the United Kingdom, 1861–1954." *Economica,* Vol. XXV (1958), pp. 283–300.

Willes, Mark H. "Rational Expectations—Fresh Ideas That Challenge Some Established Views of Policymaking." *Federal Reserve Bank of Minneapolis Annual Report* (1977), pp. 1–13.

Wonnacott, Paul. *Macroeconomics,* rev. ed. Homewood, Ill: Richard D. Irwin, Inc., 1978, Chapter 13.

APPENDIX: THE RATIONAL EXPECTATIONS THEORY

Rational expectations theorists agree with Milton Friedman's proposition that expansionary policy can reduce the level of unemployment by causing price increases which surprise the labor force. But they contend that people cannot be continually surprised by expansionary policy. When the government or the Fed is no longer able to surprise people, expansionary policy will produce only higher rates of inflation without even a temporary reduction in unemployment. The views of Lucas and Sargent and other rational expectations theorists are based on a unique idea regarding the way people form their expectations about the future.

In the accelerationist model, unemployment rates below the natural rate could be achieved if workers' inflationary expectations were less than actual inflation. As soon as workers realized their error, the employment gains would disappear unless the actual inflation rate (driven by expansionary fiscal or monetary policy) continued to accelerate ahead of workers' rising expectations. As long as expectations are slow to adapt to abrupt changes in the actual inflation rate, accelerated rates of inflation can keep unemployment below the natural rate.

Lucas and Sargent believe that this view of how expectations are formed is out of touch with basic economic behavior. They contend that it is more correct to assume that expectations are formed rationally, not adaptively. The idea of *rational* expectations is based on the following assumptions about people's behavior:

1. People make economic decisions using all available information which bears significantly on the future consequences of their decisions. This includes knowledge of government policy actions already taken as well as knowledge of strategies or approaches that government policymakers regularly take when economic conditions (unemployment and inflation) begin to change.

2. People tend to avoid repeating previous errors. Because they must make their plans in an environment of considerable uncertainty, people are likely to make occasional mistakes. But, because the economic environment rewards those who make good forecasts and penalizes those who don't, people will learn to avoid repeatedly misusing information that affects their future.[10]

Those who subscribe to the rational expectations theory conclude that if people behave in this way, the government will be unable to bring about lower levels of unemployment with policies which generate higher (even accelerating) rates of inflation.

If we accept the Friedman premise that the unemployment-inflation trade-off exists only when workers are surprised by unexpected inflation, then the above conclusion is not difficult to follow. Let's examine the rational expectations theory within the context of the short-run/long-run Phillips curve analysis.

---

[10]Mark H. Willes, "Rational Expectations—Fresh Ideas That Challenge Some Established Views of Policymaking," *Federal Reserve Bank of Minneapolis Annual Report* (1977), pp. 1–2.

Again, we will assume that the economy is initially at point A on the long-run Phillips curve shown in Figure 14A-1. The actual and expected inflation rates are assumed to be 0 percent. The government attempts to reduce the unemployment rate below the natural rate with expansionary fiscal or monetary policy. Because people are surprised about the inflationary consequences of the government's policy, unemployment decreases to 4 percent and the economy moves to point B on the short-run Phillips curve. After workers adjust their expectations to the new, higher inflation rate, the economy moves back to the natural rate of unemployment with a higher level of aggregate demand and a higher inflation rate. Up to this point, the accelerationist and rational expectations views are identical. As before, let's suppose that the government is persistent in its attempts to reduce the unemployment rate. But now, let's assume that expectations are formed

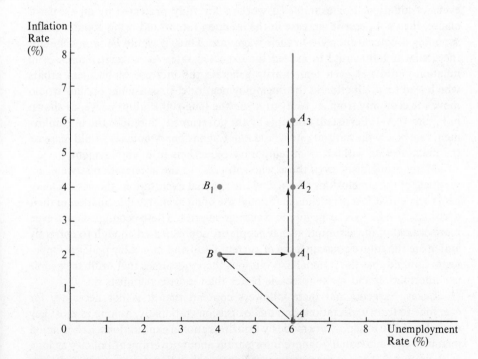

FIGURE 14A-1   THE RATIONAL EXPECTATIONS VIEW

According to the rational expectations view, people will eventually catch on to the inflationary consequences of expansionary government policy. If expectations are then formed rationally, the government will be unable to achieve reductions in the unemployment rates even with accelerating rates of inflation. Expansionary policy initially fools people, producing unexpected inflation. The unemployment rate declines and the economy moves from A to B. The temporary reduction in unemployment disappears as workers adjust their expectations of inflation from B to A_1. When the government tries again to reduce the unemployment rate through expansionary policy, people anticipate the inflationary consequences and adjust their expectations rationally. Instead of gaining a reduction in the unemployment rate (A_1 to B_1), the expansionary policies result in an increase in the inflation rate without even a temporary reduction in unemployment. If people form their expectations rationally, further expansionary policy by government will generate only increases in the inflation rate as the economy moves along the long-run Phillips curve from A_1 to A_2, to A_3, etc.

rationally instead of adaptively. When the government initially increased the level of aggregate demand, people were surprised (fooled) and suffered the consequences. Their error was that they failed to see that the government policy which was causing production to expand was also causing inflation. The inflation cut into the purchasing power of their wages, leaving most of them worse off than before. Now, as the government increases aggregate demand to an even higher level in an attempt to reduce the unemployment rate (from A_1 to B_1 in Figure 14A-1), people refuse to be surprised again and form their expectations rationally rather than adaptively. Having been through the process once and having paid a price (declining purchasing power of their wages), they anticipate that expansionary government policies will generate inflation. Knowing that inflation is inevitable, workers bargain for wage agreements which will protect them from its consequences. They demand contracts which keep up with inflation and protect the purchasing power of their income.

The most common form of protection for the purchasing power of wages are escalator clauses in labor contracts which call for automatic wage increases in the event of inflation. For example, if workers are fully protected by an escalator clause, then a 4 percent increase in the inflation rate would bring about a corresponding 4 percent increase in their wage rate. Thus, it would be impossible for the actual inflation rate to exceed the expected rate. As a result, increases in inflation could not even temporarily generate the increase in business profits which lead to a reduction of the unemployment rate. Expansionary policy would move the economy from A_1 to A_2 to A_3 on the long-run Phillips curve, as shown in Figure 14A-1. Persistent attempts by the government to reduce the unemployment rate below the natural rate would fail. Expansionary policies would increase the inflation rate without even temporary reductions in unemployment.

Many economists, even those who subscribe to the accelerationist view, are skeptical of the conclusions reached by the rational expectations theorists. Opponents argue that few people make rational use of all available information in their decisions to take jobs or negotiate wages or salaries. These economists are even more critical of the assumption that people are sophisticated enough to correctly anticipate the future consequences of current fiscal and monetary policies. Opponents contend that the rational expectations theory assumes that ordinary people use information and make forecasts better than most economists do.

Lucas, Sargent, and their followers contend that it is not necessary for everyone to form expectations and make decisions rationally, as long as most key decisions in the economy are made by utilizing rational expectations. Labor union members can individually ignore information about government policies as long as their contract negotiators act according to the rational expectations theory. Lucas and Sargent believe that many key decision makers in society (union negotiators, financial analysts, business and economic forecasters) have learned from costly mistakes of the past, and now realize that they must anticipate the inflationary consequence of current or proposed government policies. As more and more key decision makers catch on to the consequences of fiscal and monetary policy, they will act rationally and this will reduce the effectiveness of government's policies.

Macroeconomic Policy and Economic Performance

Learning Objectives

After studying the materials found in this chapter, you should be able to do the following:

1. Contrast the ideas of Keynesian and MQT economists on the following issues:
   (a) the stability of the private sector of the economy.
   (b) the use of government macroeconomic policy to improve the performance of the economy.
   (c) the use of rules vs. discretionary fiscal and monetary policy.

2. Summarize the arguments for and against the use of fiscal, as opposed to monetary, policy.

3. Explain how, according to MQT economists, a reduction in the money supply growth rate will lead to a decrease in the inflation rate.

4. Discuss arguments for and against using wage and price controls as a tool to fight inflation.

In this chapter we will see how Keynesian and MQT economists agree and disagree on the timing, extent, and usefulness of fiscal and monetary policy. The chapter examines the basic views of these two schools of economists on how the macro economy works, and it tries to relate these views to policy prescriptions.

A substantial part of the disagreement between Keynesian and MQT economists is not whether to use monetary or fiscal policy but whether to make *active* use of either sort of macro policy. A key issue here is whether the economy would be better off if policymakers followed strict rules rather than using their discretion to set policies. There are, however, some important differences in how Keynesians and monetarists view the usefulness of fiscal or monetary policy. The first part of this chapter discusses the differences in the ways Keynesians and monetarists would use macro policy in general, and the second part of the chapter examines the pros and cons of fiscal vs. monetary policy. Following this, the chapter discusses two alternatives for dealing with stagflation. Next, the MQT proposal for controlled money supply growth is examined, followed by a discussion of wage-price controls as a tool to reduce high inflation rates.

THE STATUS OF THE DEBATE ON MONETARY POLICY

By the late 1960s and early 1970s, the debate on monetary policy was far from where it had been in the 1930s and 1940s. We want to summarize these changes to show where the debate stands at the beginning of the 1980s.

In the 1930s and 1940s, the quantity theory and monetary policy were widely discredited. Economists looked more and more to Keynesian theory to explain the macroeconomic world and looked to the use of fiscal policy to stabilize the economy. The quantity theory was discredited in large part because it appeared that it could neither explain the Depression nor offer solutions for it. Monetary policy was discredited because it didn't seem to be important in the Keynesian theory, nor did it seem to have worked at all in the 1930s, particularly in the period between 1929 and 1933.

By the early 1960s, the monetarists had a theory to counter Keynesian theory. The modern quantity theory provided an explanation of the Depression. It showed how velocity could change, as it did in the 1930s. Furthermore, Milton Friedman and Anna Schwartz argued that, with the fall in the money supply by one third from 1929 to 1933, the Depression was to be expected.[1] The Depression could have been avoided, they suggested, if the Fed had not allowed this decline in the money supply. Had monetary policy been formulated correctly, there would have been a fairly bad recession, but it would have been nothing like the Depression.

But the MQT didn't immediately convert economists or gain immediate acceptance. Instead, acceptance was achieved in small stages. As Chapter 12 emphasized, empirical work by monetarists challenged Keynesian conclusions. While such challenges did not quickly convince many people to change their views, they did make the MQT case more respectable, one that could not be simply dismissed.

By the mid-1970s, most economists had come to agree with one or more of the following propositions regarding the role of money and monetary policy:

1. Monetary policy has a significant influence on the overall behavior of the economy.

2. In the long run, monetary policy does not affect real output, employment, or unemployment, but determines almost exclusively the rate of inflation.

3. Monetary policy should focus on the quantity of money in the economy, not the level of interest rates.

4. The best rule governing the conduct of monetary policy is to stabilize the rate of growth of the money supply.

These four propositions are listed in descending order of agreement among economists; that is, the fourth would arouse more controversy than the first. But

[1]Milton Friedman and Anna Schwartz, *A Monetary History of the United States, 1867–1960* (Princeton, N.J.: Princeton University Press, 1963).

even the third and fourth propositions are generally more accepted now than ten years ago.[2]

There is no longer any argument that fiscal policy works and monetary policy does not. Instead, the arguments of the 1980s turn on the certainty of results of using monetary or fiscal policy and on the sort of goals macro policy should try to achieve.

With the credibility of the MQT established both in theory and in practice, we turn now to a discussion of Keynesian vs. MQT views of the world. We will tie together many of the ideas studied in previous chapters and attempt to show their relevance in economic policymaking.

KEYNESIAN VS. MQT VIEWS OF THE WORLD

The following sections are designed to orient you to the Keynesian vs. MQT debate rather than to tell you exactly what Keynesians think as opposed to exactly what monetarists think. Economics is not a road with armed camps at either end, one Keynesian, the other monetarist. Instead, there is a continuum of views in macroeconomics, and many economists hold views that fall somewhere between the strict Keynesian view and the strict monetarist view. There are, however, certain ideas that seem to distinguish Keynesians from monetarists and that help explain some of their positions on policy issues. Within either school, too, there are differences in the degree to which people hold these views and in how important they think these views are. The following pages outline some major differences between the two broad groups.

Is the Private Sector Unstable?

One important question which divides the Keynesian and MQT camps is that of whether the private sector is inherently unstable. Keynesians tend to believe that it is and point to the statistical evidence on consumption and investment spending as illustrated in Figures 15-1 and 15-2. According to the multiplier framework, Keynesians believe that these fluctuations in spending are translated into fluctuations in real national income and output. Consequently, the Keynesian prescription for the economy's ills is the use of government expenditure and taxation policies to offset private sector instability. Monetary policy could be used to change interest rates in order to guide investment toward a full-employment level of real output and income.

Monetarists tend to doubt that the private sector is unstable. Few MQT economists would claim that the private sector never has fluctuations or that consumption and investment functions never shift. But they do believe that many of the major economic problems of the twentieth century (and certainly of the years since 1945) have resulted from unfortunate changes in government fiscal and monetary policy rather than from disturbances originating in the private sector.

---

[2]For a discussion of the differing attitudes economists hold regarding the role of money and monetary policy, see Herbert Stein, "Monetarism Under Fire," *The American Enterprise Economist* (September, 1981).

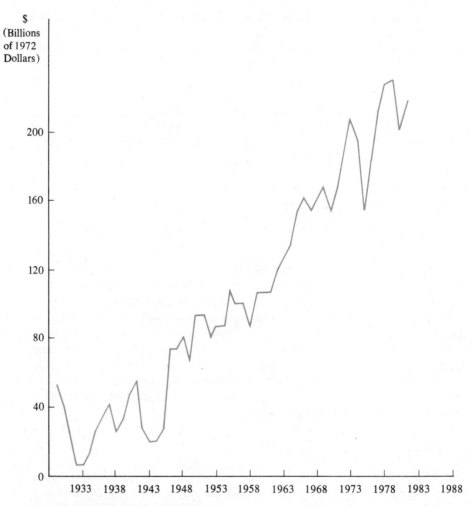

**FIGURE 15-1   GROSS PRIVATE DOMESTIC
INVESTMENT, 1929–1981**

This figure shows that there has been an upward trend in the level of real investment. However, there have been many severe fluctuations associated with this trend. One Keynesian view is that fiscal and monetary policy could be used to offset these fluctuations. (Source: *Survey of Current Business*.)

Does Government Macroeconomic Policy Make Things Worse?

A second difference between monetarists and Keynesians is that the MQT camp is not nearly as favorably disposed to the use of government policy to improve the macro economy as are the Keynesians. In many instances, monetarists believe government policy has only made things worse. An example of bad policy they frequently mention is the way the Federal Reserve System allowed the money stock to fall by almost one third at the start of the Great Depression and watched one fifth of the banks in the country close their doors due to financial difficulties.

Keynesians often deny charges about specific historical instances in which monetarists allege that government macro policy has been misused. However, a

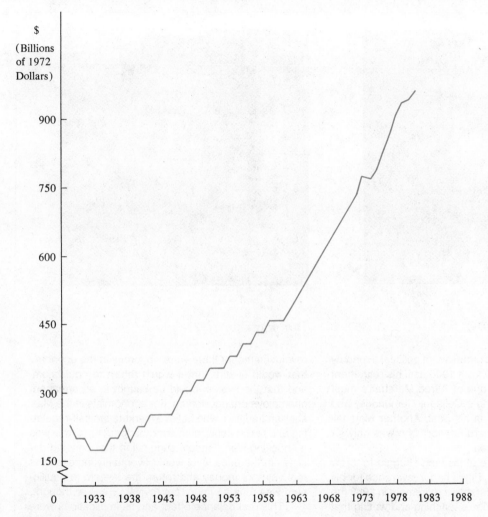

FIGURE 15-2 PERSONAL CONSUMPTION EXPENDITURES, 1929–1981

As with investment, the level of real consumption has shown an upward trend. There have been many fluctuations above and below the upward trend, though the fluctuations have not been as sharp as those in real investment. (Source: *Survey of Current Business.*)

large majority of economists would agree that the record of macroeconomic policymaking is spotted by a rather large number of bad decisions. Monetarists think of this record as an indication that macro policy will always be biased toward mistakes and toward making things worse rather than better. Hence, monetarists favor rules for monetary (and fiscal) policy over the discretion of the policymakers. An example of such a rule is, "Allow the money supply to grow by only 3 percent per year." If policy is determined by rules, there may be no way to change policy to improve a situation, but at least there is no danger that discretionary policy will be used in such a way as to make the macro situation worse.

A.C. Pigou *(1877–1959)*

Arthur C. Pigou was professor of political economy at Cambridge University from 1908 until his retirement in 1943. He had been one of Alfred Marshall's most brilliant students at King's College, Cambridge, and succeeded his teacher in his post. Another Marshall student was John Maynard Keynes, who was only six years younger than Pigou.

While Keynes wrote of his long struggle to throw off Marshall's influence, Pigou had a reverence for his teacher. Indeed, after Marshall's retirement in 1908 (he died in 1924), it was Pigou's teaching and writing that firmly implanted Marshall's approach to demand and supply and partial equilibrium analysis in the minds of students for decades to come. For Pigou, it was "all in Marshall." Pigou did, however, make substantial contributions in his own right, particularly in welfare economics, where he looked at conditions for maximizing society's welfare, how those conditions may be violated, and what government policies might be used to improve the situation.

In his *General Theory,* Keynes highlighted his differences with his predecessors, including particularly stinging remarks about the inadequacies of the work by Marshall and Pigou. Apparently Pigou found the criticism of Marshall more difficult to accept than that of himself, and he gave the *General Theory* a bad review. Later, however, the two men were reconciled.

In the early years after the publication of the *General Theory,* many economists thought the Keynesian

Don Patinkin *(1922–)*

revolution meant there were no forces in the economy that would ensure that it would return to equilibrium, and that the system could be caught in a permanent unemployment equilibrium. For economists in the Marshallian tradition, who believe markets are self-regulating and reach equilibrium over the longer run, this was a shocking idea. Pigou's suggestion that ongoing declines in the price level would eventually increase the real value of money and return the system to equilibrium was thus an important revival of earlier thought.

This real balance effect and its implications were extensively analyzed by *Don Patinkin* in a series of articles beginning in the late 1940s (where he initially referred to the real balance effect as the Pigou effect) and in his book *Money, Interest, and Prices* (1956). By the mid- to late 1960s, the logic of the real balance effect was generally acknowledged. It was, however, asserted that the real balance effect was small, that prices and wages didn't fall very quickly, and that it could take the economy a long time to return to equilibrium. What was gone, however, was the belief that the macro system could be trapped into a permanent unemployment equilibrium.

Don Patinkin was awarded his B.A., M.A., and Ph.D. degrees from the University of Chicago. He is currently professor of economics at the Hebrew University of Jerusalem. He has made numerous contributions to monetary economics, the history of economic thought, and the study of the economy of Israel.

Keynesians respond strongly to this argument on a number of grounds. First, they believe there have been clear successes in policy. They offer the following defense of the cases of failure cited by MQT critics: While policy did not completely solve the problems in these instances, policy did prevent the situations from being as bad as they would have been had monetarists' advice been taken. Thus, the evidence presented by monetarists is rejected or downplayed by Keynesians. Second, even in the cases where clear mistakes were made, Keynesians can argue that it is better to use good, sound policy than to pursue no policy at all. Third, Keynesians argue that some past mistakes were based on a lack of knowledge of how the economy works, and, with more and better knowledge currently available, these kinds of mistakes can be avoided.

In response, monetarists often adopt what may seem to be a cynical viewpoint. They point out the delays involved in fiscal and monetary policymaking, and they also point to the political pressures on politicians to adopt policies that are designed to win elections rather than help the overall performance of the economy. If these practical considerations operate on policy, perhaps it is better to give policymakers no freedom at all in order to prevent what will probably be mistakes. As we saw earlier, many Keynesian economists have become somewhat discouraged about getting Congress and the presidential administration to agree and act on policy at the time the economists think is right. This, combined with wide-spread acceptance that the long-run Phillips curve is steeper than was believed in the early 1960s (perhaps even vertical), has made many Keynesians more cautious about actively using fiscal and monetary policy to improve the economy's performance. To them, government policy is like a medicine that won't cure everything, a medicine you have to be careful with; but this doesn't mean the medicine is of no use at all.

How Fast Does the Economy Adjust?

Another MQT viewpoint is that even the *best* policy is likely to do as much damage as good. Not all monetarists share this view by any means, and it is a relatively new one. It is part of the broader question of how fast the economy adjusts to a new equilibrium if there is a disturbance and, in fact, whether the economy tends to adjust at all.

Most economists now would agree that the United States economy does adjust to disturbances and will eventually return by itself to equilibrium. This idea is a noticeable change from the theories of the 1930s, 1940s, 1950s, and even 1960s, when many economists believed that underemployment equilibrium was a permanent, rather than a temporary, situation. However, many Keynesian economists argue that the economy will take far too long a time to return to equilibrium if left to its own natural equilibrium forces. Instead, they argue, society as a whole will be better off if government uses macro policy to (1) keep the economy from getting too far from full-employment equilibrium, and (2) hasten any necessary adjustment back to full-employment equilibrium.

Figure 15-3 shows some of the considerations involved in this argument. Suppose people lose interest in Rubik's cube puzzles and the demand for them falls from D_1D_1 to D_2D_2. This will drive down prices as well as the quantity produced and sold. Ultimately, price must fall to OP_2 and the quantity produced and sold to OQ_2. At some later period, demand may rise again to D_1D_1, driving price and quantity back to OP_1 and OQ_1. Both of these shifts in demand require

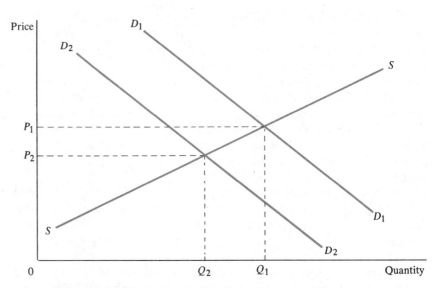

FIGURE 15-3 THE NEED FOR ADJUSTMENT TO CHANGE IN A SINGLE MARKET

If demand falls from D_1D_1 to D_2D_2, output must adjust from OQ_1 to OQ_2 and price must fall to OP_2 in order for the market to return to equilibrium. This adjustment will take time, and very likely businesses in this market will make mistakes in the adjustment process.

adjustment of price and quantity, and, of course, these quantity changes require adjustments in the number of workers employed, the machines bought, the number and length of work shifts, the number of firms in the industry, and so on.

Every time such adjustments are necessary, the firms are quite likely to make many mistakes. After almost any period of adjustment, you can ask firm managers, "Is there anything you would have done differently if you had known then what you know now?" If you get an honest answer, it will almost always be yes.

Such mistakes cannot be totally avoided. Managers don't have convenient diagrams such as Figure 15-3 to guide them. Once they realize that demand has fallen, they might guess that price and quantity will settle at OP_2 and OQ_2, but they can't be sure, and often their guesses will be wrong. Clearly, adjustments take time, and moving too fast or too slow can be very costly. Managers, then, have incentives to adjust at the right pace. Very often they misjudge the pace, whether of expansion or contraction, but we don't suppose they do this purposely or even in a *consistent* way. That is, we don't suppose managers always react too slowly (or always too quickly), for otherwise they or their bosses would begin to notice these consistent mistakes and take steps to eliminate them.

Many economists and many people in the general public would agree that government intervention in the adjustment process of one industry would not lead to improvement, on average, and would indeed probably be costly and inefficient. Some monetarists would further argue that when we are talking about the adjustment of the economy as a whole, the behavior of private markets can be relied upon to produce adjustment at just about the right speed, *on average*. Many Keynesian economists regard this as quite untrue for the economy as a whole, even though many of them would agree that a single, isolated industry should probably be left to adjust by itself. Many monetarists would also agree that the economy as a whole probably doesn't adjust at the right speed, on average, and, in fact, generally adjusts too slowly.[3] However, they would argue that, in practice, government policy is so poorly used that active fiscal and monetary policy shouldn't be employed, even if these policies are good in theory.

The Keynesian view, then, is that the private economy will adjust too slowly if left to itself. Some monetarists would agree, but they would argue that (1) the economy adjusts more quickly than most Keynesians believe, and (2) government policy attempts to increase the speed of adjustment are more likely to hurt than to help because of poor design, timing, and execution of policy. Other monetarists would be inclined to deny that the economy adjusts too slowly if left to itself. They believe that even the best designed and executed policy would not help the economy, but would simply make it adjust too fast. Notice that the issue here is not whether the economy does or should adjust instantly; no one argues that. The issue is whether the economy adjusts as quickly as is desirable and, if not, whether it can be helped to adjust.

The Costs of Adjusting Too Fast

Monetarists often argue that the use of expansionary fiscal and monetary policy to speed adjustment will lead to high costs for the whole economy. It isn't just that business loses profits when it adjusts too fast; this may be unimportant compared to putting the unemployed back to work more quickly. But monetarists argue that reducing unemployment in this way will only lead to higher unemployment later and that the trade-off isn't worthwhile. In this view, expansionary policy goes too far and causes inflation to rise. When restrictive policy is used to fight inflation, unemployment rises to higher levels than before. This argument is based on the MQT outlook that policy, as it is actually used, only seems to worsen the economic situation. The inflation and unemployment experience of the late 1960s through the early 1980s seems to be consistent with this idea.

A Keynesian response would stress three points. First, the record isn't as bad as monetarists claim. Second, the best Keynesian advice was sometimes *not* followed by policymakers, so the poor results shouldn't be blamed solely on Keynesian policy. Third, though Keynesian advice sometimes proved wrong, Keynesians will offer better advice in the future as they learn more about the economy.

THE SPEED OF ADJUSTMENT, THE MULTIPLIER, AND THE PERMANENT INCOME HYPOTHESIS

The Keynesian idea that the economy seems to adjust too slowly if left to itself goes back to the Great Depression and the multiplier reasoning. During the

---

[3]Some monetarists—and many Keynesians—believe prices take a very long time to adjust to, say, a change in monetary policy (in fact, too long to adjust in comparison to the ideal speed). Other monetarists think that prices adjust much more quickly than the first group believes. Both groups have some empirical evidence to support their beliefs. This remains an area of dispute, but much work is going on in this area and progress in resolving the issue can be expected.

Depression there were many workers who couldn't get jobs to earn income; if they could have found jobs and earned income, they would have demanded output. But since output wasn't demanded, business laid off more workers and income fell even more, resulting in further reductions in demand for consumption goods, and the Depression became worse and worse through the multiplier process.

The MQT finds fault with this theory on the grounds that the multiplier is usually quite insignificant, so we don't ordinarily need to worry about the multiplier process. This argument relies mainly on the ***permanent income hypothesis*** developed by Milton Friedman.[4] Its essential point is simple and quite attractive. If you get paid once a month, you don't base your daily consumption on your daily income. Instead, you base consumption on some idea of what can be covered by the income stream you expect over time. Similarly, anyone with widely varying annual incomes would not change consumption very much from year to year. This idea has widespread applications. Have you ever known people in school who consume at high levels even though they don't have a very large income at the time? They are basing their consumption on some notion of what their income will be on a permanent basis, rather than basing their consumption on transitory ups and downs of income as it actually comes to them. Similarly, construction workers in unfavorable climates can only work, say, eight months of the year. They plan for this, and, rather than drastically reducing their consumption during the winter, they maintain consumption, and some of them even go on vacation. Workers in industries subject to strikes can often maintain their consumption level when strikes eliminate income because they've built this possibility into their plans. The same thing is true of workers who are subject to periodic layoffs; often they can withstand the loss of income with little effect on consumption for quite a long period of time.

In all these cases, the loss of income has to cut into consumption if it continues long enough. The family that planned on a two-week strike is in bad shape if the strike is still going on after three months. Laid-off workers who counted on being out of work for a month will probably have to cut back on consumption if they are out of work six months. The construction worker who waits through a longer than usual winter that is followed by such a wet spring that there is no work finds it hard to keep up consumption. Maintaining a given consumption level is, in part, determined by an individual household's ***liquid assets***; that is, the assets that can quickly be turned into cash without a significant loss in value, such as checking and savings accounts, savings bonds, and assets such as corporate stocks and bonds. When a household has sold off such assets, it is left with such things as its car and house, which are not very liquid. In any case, conditions have become very grim when a household must consider selling such assets, and by this time, it will have cut back on consumption, perhaps substantially.

The important point is this: As long as people don't base their consumption on transitory ups and downs in income, the multiplier is equal to one. If investment spending falls by $100 billion, causing income to fall by $100 billion, people will maintain their consumption expenditures. In the permanent income view, they expect such ups and downs and have built them into their average consump-

permanent income hypothesis *The hypothesis that people don't base their consumption decisions on their current income but on some longer run average of the level of income they can expect.*

liquid assets *Assets that can be quickly converted into cash with little or no loss in value.*

---

[4]Milton Friedman, *A Theory of the Consumption Function* (Princeton, N.J.: Princeton University Press, 1957).

tion level; this doesn't mean that they expected the downturn exactly when it occurred, but they knew there would be one someday. While the economy is adjusting and returning to full-employment equilibrium, they continue to consume as before. Thus, the initial $100 billion decrease in income isn't multiplied to a larger decrease in income. This result depends on (1) people actually reacting according to the permanent income hypothesis, and (2) the downturn not being more severe or long-lasting than people had planned on.

Some economists argue that the Great Depression was the single major instance where economic conditions got so bad that the multiplier process took over from the permanent income hypothesis. The argument is simply that the Depression was so severe and so long-lasting that people couldn't maintain consumption at its usual level. Further, many households exhausted their liquid assets long before the economy was back to anything approaching normal. However, the Depression was quite unusual compared to average recessions.

THE ADJUSTMENT OF INVESTMENT

Several other reasons have been suggested as to why the macro adjustment process might be too time-consuming, even if the process for a particular industry is not. One major reason depends on the behavior of investment.

Suppose households decide to consume $10 billion less and save $10 billion more. When monetarists claim the private sector is stable, they don't deny that such shifts in the consumption function can happen. They do argue that large and frequent shifts in the consumption function—say, plus or minus 10 percent in a quarter—will not happen. Further, they argue that if one component of private sector demand falls—in this case, household demand for consumption goods— another component will rise to return aggregate demand to the full-employment level. This means monetarists believe that, in this case, investment demand would rise by $10 billion. Of course, no one would expect expenditures on investment to rise by $10 billion at the exact time that consumption expenditures fall by $10 billion.[5] On the demand side, business must evaluate investment opportunities, decide it wants $10 billion more in investment, raise the funds to pay for the investment, place orders for the goods, start the process to have a trained and ready work force in place for the new plants and equipment, and so on. On the supply side, firms producing new plant and equipment must evaluate demand, expand their activities by hiring the people laid off by the consumer goods' industries because of the decrease in consumption demand, improve their own plants and equipment, and so forth. The point is, the shift in demand and reallocation of factors of production takes some time, perhaps a fair amount of time, especially if the resource shifts are large and involve considerable retraining and relocation of people. Many monetarists would argue that usually the process

---

[5]This might happen. Farm households might cut back on consumption to finance more investment by the family business. More generally, the decrease in consumption demand and increase in planned saving would be used to finance increased household demands for money, bonds, and other securities. In this case, adjustments of prices and interest rates would encourage business to invest more. Even after business decides to invest more, there is still a period of adjustment required, as the text explains.

would be half finished in a year to a year and a half and completed or almost completed within three years.

Keynesian economists believe that investment does not respond at all like the way we just described it. This is for two reasons. First, the increase in saving—because of the decline in the consumption function—will make more funds available for investors to borrow and this will drive down interest rates. Keynesians used to say frequently that business does not respond very strongly to the fact that funds are cheaper to borrow. However, the great majority of economists now agree that investment is sensitive enough to the interest rate that there will be some positive rate of interest low enough to cause investment, and thus aggregate demand, to rise to the full-employment level. Admittedly, it will take some time for resources to shift fully, but the real question here is whether such shifts will take too much time; the insensitivity of investment to the interest rate doesn't have much to do with how long the adjustment will take.

The second adjustment problem often raised goes right to the heart of this matter by talking about *business confidence.* One way to think of this is to consider how confident business is that it can sell the extra goods it will be able to produce if it invests more now. Business managers in many industries would say that the outlook for future sales is considerably more important than the interest rate in their investment decisions. If business people become less confident at the same time consumption falls by $10 billion, we can't expect them to expand investment very quickly.

The real problem with lack of business confidence is that it can be self-fulfilling for quite a period of time. If you believe the economy will eventually return to full-employment equilibrium, you know that investment will have to rise in the long run by the extra $10 billion. However, if in the first year every business has very little confidence and no one invests, then sales that year will be less than the full-employment level because no one invested the extra amount to get the economy to the full-employment level of income and output. The lack of confidence thus appears justified; that is, it is self-fulfilling and can go on for quite some time. In such a situation, why shouldn't the government use policy to increase aggregate demand and thus increase business confidence by increasing the economy's sales and income?

Many monetarists insist that the primary reason for any lack of business confidence is that business worries about unsound government policies. Consequently, government ought to adopt sound policies and stick to them. When business is convinced that sound policies have been adopted and will be carried out in the future, confidence will be restored and investment demand will rise to move the economy toward full-employment equilibrium.

GOVERNMENT POLICY AND BUSINESS CONFIDENCE

There are, of course, other policies that government could adopt that would hurt business, such as higher inflation and higher taxes on business. If business basically distrusts the government in power, it will take much longer to muster the confidence to invest the extra $10 billion per period required in our previous example to move the economy to full-employment equilibrium.

On the conservative end of the economic spectrum, many economists believe that the best strategy for government in such a case is to prove it won't harm business, and when business believes this, investment and the economy will recover. At the more liberal end of the spectrum, many Keynesians believe that the business sector should not be indulged in this fashion.[6] If business can't get the economy moving in a short time, government should do it. Many of these economists agree that, *ceteris paribus,* they would rather have business do the job because business is more efficient in producing output than government; but they feel this efficiency isn't worth the delay in returning to full-employment output. Further, some economists are willing to say that society needs many goods and services that business does not provide but which government will, so there really is little or no loss in relying on government spending to stabilize the economy.[7] Examples of such spending might include hiring poor, unemployed minority youth to work on projects to rehabilitate central cities, cleaning up the environment, and providing more health and social services to urban and rural poor.

Most conservative economists are in favor of providing tax breaks for business and for investors in the household sector in order to stimulate investment, both by making such investment more profitable and by showing that the government isn't against these groups. This was an argument made in support of the 1981 Reagan tax cuts. Many liberal economists ridicule this as *trickle-down theory;* that is, tax breaks are given to business and the rich in the hope that some of the benefits may trickle down to the unemployed and the poor. It is argued that this will not necessarily happen; that the breaks given to the rich and privileged are very large in relationship to the benefits the underprivileged and unemployed might receive from them; and that it would be better, fairer, and quicker to rely on government expenditures to stimulate and stabilize the economy.

Notice that there is an argument over a question of *fact.* For example, Will benefits trickle down? In contrast, questions of *values* include, What is fair or just? Is it right to give tax breaks to business when a large number of people are unemployed? Is it good to neglect the cities in favor of private sector consumption and investment? Factual questions are ones that we can hope, as economists, to answer (though the answers aren't clear-cut or easy to find). The questions about what is fair, good, or just are ones that economists have no particular expertise in answering. These questions were with us long before the first recorded philosopher and will continue to haunt politicians.

POLICIES TO DEAL WITH STAGFLATION

Now that we have summarized the general differences between the Keynesian and MQT views regarding the economy and economic policy, we can turn to the

---

[6]Economic conservatives need not be monetarists, and they certainly need not be political conservatives in the sense of supporting politicians who are considered conservatives. By the same token, economists who would call themselves economic liberals need not accept the label Keynesian, nor need they be political liberals as the term is used currently in American politics.

[7]John Kenneth Galbraith would take the view that there is no loss but rather a positive gain. He continues to argue, as he did in his book, *The Affluent Society* (Boston: Houghton Mifflin Co., 1958), that public sector spending is too small compared to private sector spending.

important macroeconomic question of the 1980s—how should we deal with stagflation, the problem of simultaneous high levels of inflation and unemployment?

Stagflation presents a difficult dilemma for economic policymakers. First, there appears to be no combination of fiscal and monetary policies which will simultaneously reduce inflation and unemployment. Second, fiscal and monetary policies designed to reduce the level of unemployment tend to increase the rate of inflation, while policies designed to reduce the rate of inflation tend to increase the level of unemployment. Given this dilemma, it is not surprising to find economists strongly divided on the question of how best to deal with stagflation. Most monetarists favor a policy calling for restrictive economic policy with primary emphasis on strict control of the growth of the money supply. Many Keynesians favor the implementation of wage-price controls. Supply-side economics advocates policies designed to increase saving, investment, labor productivity, and economic growth. In the remainder of this chapter we will discuss the first two of these proposals: controlled money supply growth and wage-price controls. In the next chapter we will examine supply-side economics in detail.

Stagflation—The MQT View

Most economists who subscribe to the MQT begin by asserting that society must accept the unemployment rate given by long-run equilibrium conditions in the labor market. Thus, dealing with stagflation amounts to first eliminating inflation and then letting the labor market return to the natural rate of unemployment at whatever inflation rate may be deemed acceptable. According to monetarists, eliminating inflation requires that the growth of the money supply be reduced to whatever rate is consistent with the acceptable rate of inflation.

How quickly the money supply growth rate is reduced will determine the magnitude and duration of unemployment. The process for eliminating inflation, according to the MQT view, requires government to pursue a restrictive economic policy and to defeat inflationary expectations, as explained in Chapter 14.

Assume that for several periods the money supply has been growing at a rate of 6 percent annually and the economy has reached equilibrium with an unemployment rate of 6 percent and an inflation rate of 6 percent. This situation, depicted by point A_3 in Figure 15-4, might be the result of previous persistent attempts by the government to maintain the unemployment rate below the natural rate (6 percent), a situation discussed in detail in Chapter 14. Now, convinced that its expansionary policies produce only accelerating rates of inflation, the government decides to bring the economy back to a position of 0 percent inflation at the natural rate of unemployment (point A in Figure 15-4). This is to be accomplished using the MQT prescription of slowing the growth of the money supply gradually from 6 percent to 0 percent annually.[8]

Thus, with the economy at point A_3, and the actual and expected rates of inflation equal at 6 percent, the government reduces the money supply growth rate from 6 percent to 4 percent. However, wage contracts for the coming period

---

[8]To keep the examples as simple as possible, we are assuming that the economy is not experiencing any growth of real output. Under this condition, the noninflationary growth rate of the money supply would be 0 percent per year; that is, the money supply would remain constant.

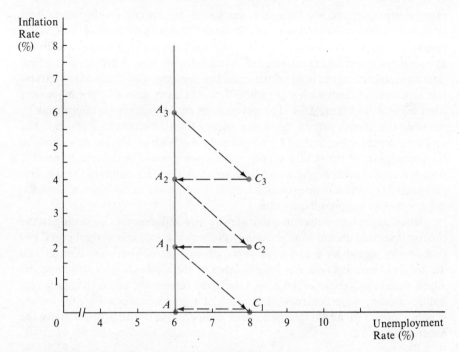

**FIGURE 15-4   DEALING WITH STAGFLATION—THE
                MQT VIEW**

With the economy experiencing a high inflation rate and unemployment at the natural rate, such as point A_3, restrictive monetary policy is initiated to reduce inflation. The reduction in aggregate demand causes a decline in the rate of price increases, a decline in sales and output, and an increase in the unemployment rate. This is shown by the movement from A_3 to C_3 as unemployment increases to 8 percent and inflation falls to 4 percent. When workers adjust their inflation expectations downward to 4 percent, labor is no longer overpriced, and output and employment increase. Unemployment declines to the natural rate (6 percent) as shown by the movement from C_3 to A_2. With successive gradual reductions in the money supply growth rate, followed by downward adjustments in inflation expectations by workers, the economy will follow the path from A_2 to C_2, C_2 to A_1, A_1 to C_1, and C_1 to A. At point A, the economy is at the natural rate of unemployment with no inflation.

have been based on people's expectations of 6 percent inflation. The higher wage rates are reflected in higher product prices as businesses attempt to maintain output and profit levels. But, with the money supply now growing at a slower rate, the rate of growth of aggregate demand is also slowed. As a result, aggregate demand is insufficient to purchase all output at the higher prices. Throughout the economy, demand schedules in individual markets shift left. Unintended inventory increases occur and profit levels decline, prompting businesses to reduce output and employment. The unemployment rate increases to 8 percent as the economy moves from A_3 to C_3 in Figure 15-4. The short-run trade-off indicated by this movement occurs because the actual and expected rates of inflation are not equal. Expected inflation exceeds actual inflation, causing labor to be temporarily overpriced, and resulting in a decrease in output and employment.[9] This is shown by a movement along the short-run Phillips curve from A_3 to C_3. But point C_3 is unstable for reasons we have previously discussed. It has been achieved as a result of incorrect expectations of inflation by workers. After workers adjust their expectations to the lower actual rate, the economy will return to the natural rate of unemployment with 4 percent inflation. This is shown by the movement from C_3 to A_2 in Figure 15-4. The government could then repeat the process by reducing the growth rate of the money supply from 4 percent to 2 percent. The economy would move first to C_2 and then to A_1. With successive reductions in the growth rate of the money supply, the economy could be brought to point A with 6 percent unemployment and 0 percent inflation. To maintain these unemployment and inflation rates would require government to maintain a noninflationary money supply growth rate.

How long might it take to eliminate the high inflation rate according to the process described above? Most economists believe it would take several years, and that society would have to accept unemployment rates above the natural rate during this time. It takes this long because of the slowness with which people adjust their expectations of inflation. One of the reasons for this is the multi-year nature of many wage contracts. The result of a gradual reduction of the money supply growth rate would thus be an extended period of unemployment above the natural rate.

Speeding Up the Adjustment Process

Many people say that a long period of high unemployment is not a politically feasible solution to our inflation problems. Could the adjustment process be speeded up? Some economists say it could, but only if society were to accept a *very* high unemployment rate as the cost. Let's look at this argument. First, with the economy initially at point A_3 in Figure 15-5, suppose that the money supply growth rate is reduced abruptly from 6 percent to 0 percent. Wage rates and, therefore, product prices would be severely out of line with the reduced level of aggregate demand. Business sales and profits would plummet, production would be reduced, and unemployment would rise significantly. This is shown by the movement from A_3 to C_3'. The inflation rate would decline rapidly to 0 percent, but unemployment would increase drastically to, say, 14 percent or higher. After expectations adjusted to actual conditions, the economy would move from C_3' to A. No one is suggesting such a severe policy to deal with high inflation rates. Monetarists simply point out that while such a policy would be unpopular, it is a possible way to reduce inflation very quickly.

WAGE AND PRICE CONTROLS

Given the potentially high social costs of the MQT solution, some economists call for the implementation of wage and price controls as a way of dealing with

---

[9]Labor is overpriced in the sense that given the increased wage rate and the level of aggregate demand, businesses cannot profitably maintain employment at the present level. The wage increases negotiated by workers cannot be fully passed on to the final consumer without (1) some output remaining unsold causing unintended inventory increases or (2) a decline in the profit level. In either case, businesses will reduce output and employment.

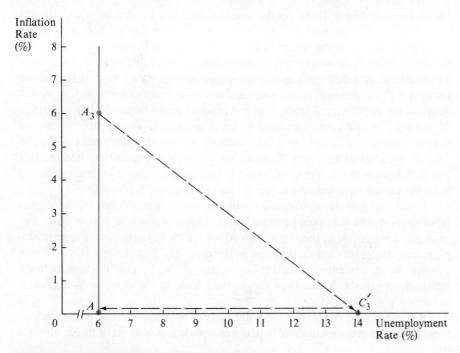

**FIGURE 15-5   SPEEDING UP THE ADJUSTMENT
PROCESS**

According to monetarists, a very large decrease in the money supply growth rate would
produce a dramatic decrease in aggregate demand. The inflation rate would decline quickly,
but the unemployment rate would rise to a very high level. This is shown by the movement
from A_3 to C_3'. As inflation expectations are adjusted downward, the economy moves from
C_3' back to the natural rate of unemployment at A.

stagflation. Their analysis rests on the concept of the short-run Phillips curve. At
any given expected rate of inflation, there is a given temporary trade-off between
unemployment and inflation. An increase in aggregate demand drives up prices
and reduces unemployment. Thus, declining unemployment rates are associated
with rising inflation rates, and rising unemployment rates are associated with
falling inflation.

Most economists believe that people form their expectations about the future
adaptively. This means that last period's actual rate of inflation has a very strong
influence on the rate that people expect in this period. A change in the actual
inflation rate will result in a corresponding, but lagged, change in the inflation
rate people expect. In addition, the expected inflation rate influences the actual
inflation rate through wage contracts and pricing decisions by business. The rate
which will actually prevail in the economy is determined by the interaction of
labor market forces and inflation expectations.

For instance, suppose the economy has experienced a 10 percent inflation rate
with unemployment at the natural rate for several periods. A firm making its
pricing decisions for the coming period would likely expect its labor and materials
costs to increase by 10 percent and also expect its competitors to raise their prices

by 10 percent. Given these conditions, the firm has good reason to expect a continuation of 10 percent inflation and would presumably raise its own prices by 10 percent. In the absence of any changes in the labor market (i.e., increases or decreases in the unemployment rate or wage rates), labor costs would rise by 10 percent, as expected. As a result, the actual inflation rate would be 10 percent. However, if the unemployment rate declined as a result of increased aggregate demand, we would expect labor costs and product prices to increase by more than 10 percent. In this case, aggregate demand conditions would push the actual inflation rate to, say, 12 percent. Alternatively, if the unemployment rate rose as a result of decreased aggregate demand, we would expect labor costs and product prices to increase by less than 10 percent. In this case, aggregate demand would keep the actual inflation rate below 10 percent at, say, 8 percent.

Fiscal and monetary policies influence inflation through their impact on the labor market and the unemployment rate. This is shown in Figure 15-6. For example, a reduction in the rate of growth of the money supply will raise unemployment and reduce actual inflation as the economy moves along the short-run Phillips curve. This lower, actual inflation rate will lead people to expect a lower inflation rate in the future than they would have in the absence of restrictive monetary policy.

Keynesians argue that the main difficulty with using restrictive monetary or fiscal policy to reduce inflation is that unemployment may have to remain at a

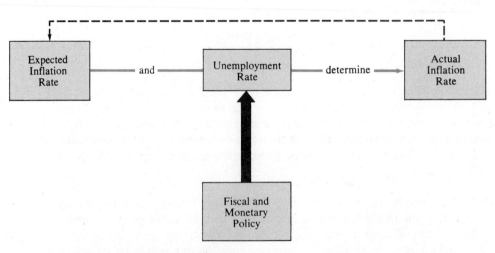

**FIGURE 15-6 INFLATION, EXPECTATIONS,
UNEMPLOYMENT, AND POLICY**

This illustration shows a view of the inflation process that is similar to the way many economists believe the expected inflation rate helps determine the actual inflation rate. Restrictive monetary and fiscal policy will raise the unemployment rate, and this increase in unemployment will reduce the actual inflation rate (through the Phillips curve) in this view. A reduction in the actual inflation rate will reduce the expected inflation rate. However, this approach to reducing inflation may require high unemployment for a long time, especially if business is slow to adjust to the rate of inflation it expects.

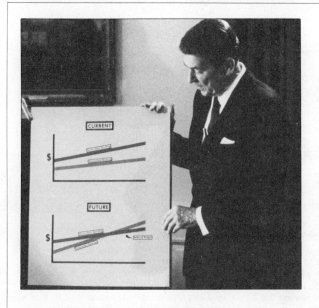

Key Indicators-Leading Indicators: What to Watch

Economists and other forecasters are often asked for predictions on future economic activity. There are, of course, many sophisticated models that forecasters use to predict future economic conditions. As an alternative to these sophisticated models, there are a series of indicators that business people and amateur forecasters can use in order to make educated guesses and to get a feel for future economic conditions. Often these educated guesses turn out to be as accurate as the forecasts that are based on sophisticated models.

One of the most frequently reported indicators of the U.S. economy is the Commerce Department's monthly index of leading indicators. This index includes such things as new orders, layoffs, prices of raw materials, and the money supply. It is generally believed that if this index moves in the same direction for a few consecutive months, the GNP will follow.

Other key indicators to assess economic performance are reported weekly or monthly in the financial press. Such economic statistics as gross national product, industrial product, personal income, retail sales, consumer prices, producer prices, employment, and housing starts are indicators of activity in various sectors of the economy. If you want to track the performance of the economy, you will want to keep abreast of these key indicators of economic performance.

high level for quite a long time before inflation expectations decline to whatever level gives an acceptable rate of actual inflation. This is because unemployment must remain high to drag down actual inflation, with expected inflation then falling (with a lag) in response to decreases in actual inflation. If people adjust their expectations quite slowly, this may be a very long process.

Many economists believe that expectations are slow to adjust. That is, if expected inflation is 10 percent, it takes many periods of 8 percent actual inflation before people come to expect 8 percent inflation.

Instead of inducing a recession with restrictive economic policy in order to reduce inflation, some economists offer an alternative solution: use wage and price controls to reduce actual inflation. They believe this is the preferred solution because it does not require any increase in the unemployment rate. This is shown in Figure 15-7. Because of government-imposed controls, prices and wages are simply not allowed to rise as fast as before. As a result, the actual inflation rate declines and this causes a downward adjustment in the expected inflation rate. As long as the controls are maintained, the expected inflation rate will continue to decline. Once the expected inflation rate has been reduced to an acceptable level, the wage and price controls can be lifted without inflation rising again. Thus, proponents argue that controls can eventually break the wage-price inflationary spiral without forcing society to endure sustained periods of high unemployment.

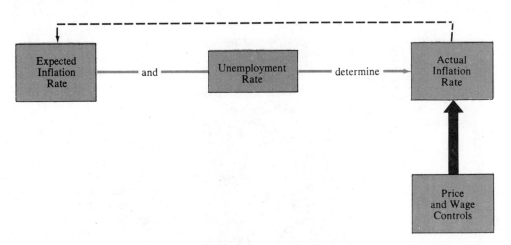

FIGURE 15-7   CONTROLS AND INFLATION
An alternative to the policy approach discussed in Figure 15-8 is to use wage and price controls. This
is supposed to allow the government to bring down the actual inflation rate without increasing
unemployment. Controls work, in this view, by reducing the actual inflation rate. In turn, this decline in
the actual inflation rate is supposed to lead business to expect a smaller inflation rate than before.
Thus, several periods of controls that reduce the actual inflation rate are supposed to lead to a
reduction in the expected inflation rate, so that when controls are lifted, the expected inflation rate is
lower than before, which makes the actual inflation rate lower than before.

This was the strategy of the Nixon administration's wage-price freeze in
August, 1971. In a televised speech to the American people, President Nixon
stated that he hoped the controls he was implementing would produce a six to
twelve month period when no prices would rise while some prices would fall. In
effect, he was trying to reduce inflationary expectations with controls.

Opponents argue that controls don't work, and even if they did, they would
require that the market not be allowed to perform its functions freely, which
would be extremely costly to society. Those who favor controls acknowledge that
society must temporarily function without the full benefit of the free market.
However, this cost must be balanced against the benefit that unemployment
doesn't have to rise to bring down the actual inflation rate.

Economists who favor controls believe they could be made to work better if
a stronger incentive system existed. A suggestion for holding down wage and
price increases which has received considerable publicity is the ***tax-based incomes
policy (TIP)***. Under this incentive system, a firm which granted any wage increase
in excess of that allowed by the wage-price controls would be penalized by an
increase in the corporate income tax it pays. For example, if the controls allowed
a 3 percent wage increase and a firm granted its workers a 6 percent increase, then
the corporate income tax paid by the firm would be increased by some multiple
of the excessive 3 percent. If the government set the penalty multiple at 3, then
the corporate income tax would be increased by 9 percent (3 percent × 3). This
would raise the violating firm's tax rate from 46 percent to 55 percent. The TIP
plan would thus create a strong incentive for management to resist the wage
demands of unions which exceeded the limits of the wage-price controls.

tax-based incomes policy (TIP)
*An incentive system under which
a firm that granted any wage
increase in excess of that allowed
under wage-price controls would
be penalized by the corporate
income tax it pays.*

Supporters of TIP claim that it would also work to limit price increases. They argue that most firms set prices by marking up production costs. Further, they argue that the largest component of product costs is labor's wages. By controlling wage rates, TIP limits cost increases and, therefore, price increases.

An Explanation of Why Wage and Price Controls Don't Work

In practice, wage and price controls haven't worked the way we outlined above, which is why most economists are usually not in favor of them. We need to look at how firms set prices to see why wage and price controls haven't worked well. Some markets in the United States economy are competitive, with suppliers having little or no pricing power, and we can use demand and supply analysis to analyze them. For example, each firm in agriculture thinks of itself as having no pricing power; firms in the retail clothing outlet business have some pricing power; and firms in the steel industry have substantial pricing power. The general forces of inflation work in much the same way in all these markets. We will start by discussing industries where firms have pricing power.

When firms try to decide what price to set, they consider their costs and the demand they think they will face. After all, they are interested in profits, and profits depend both on how much they can sell at different prices and on how much it costs to produce the goods they sell. In inflationary times, firms see that period after period, the price they can charge without a decrease in sales is rising; that is, their demand curves are shifting, as we show in Figure 15-8 where the

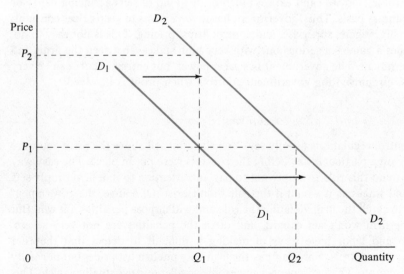

FIGURE 15-8 SHIFTING DEMAND CURVES IN THE INFLATIONARY PROCESS

Inflation means that the demand curves facing an industry or firm are shifting to the right over time. This is why the average business could sell the same amount in each period, OQ_1, but charge a higher price as time goes on (price can increase from OP_1 to OP_2).

quantity OQ_1 can now be sold at OP_2 instead of OP_1. They also find their costs are rising because labor is demanding more in order to keep up with or stay ahead of inflation, and prices are also rising for the inputs they must buy from other firms. Thus, regardless of whether an individual firm has pricing power, we would expect to see prices rise as demand and costs rise.

The effect of wage and price controls is to keep costs from rising; if wages and input prices can't rise, costs can't rise either. However, the other part of the push for higher prices is rising demand, and wage and price controls cannot affect this, at least for a considerable period of time (if ever), meaning that pressures remain for prices to rise. Demand will continue to rise for one or both of two reasons. First, demand will continue to rise because of expansionary monetary and fiscal policy. In this case, demand will not stop rising until these policies are reversed. Second, many economists would argue that increases in demand have a built-in momentum. Once you become accustomed to paying 10 percent more each period, it takes some time for your expectations to adjust to lower rates of price increases. This is the sort of argument we used above to discuss how some economists justify wage and price controls in the first place.

With demand rising but costs constant, firms could undertake a combination of raising prices and increasing output. For example, a firm could hold output at OQ_1 in Figure 15-8 and raise price to OP_2 or keep price at OP_1 and expand output to OQ_2. Naturally, you can imagine that firms will want to raise prices in the face of rising demand. Government, however, doesn't want prices to rise —that's the whole point of wage and price control! Further, if most prices rise, costs begin to rise and the program has to break down as prices and costs resume their upward spiral. Consequently, government fights these price rises, but it's a tough battle for the following reasons.

Asking firms not to raise prices when demand is rising is asking them to forego profits, and we can't expect much of this kind of self-sacrificing behavior on a voluntary basis. Thus, government has to *force* firms to keep prices constant; it has to investigate, supervise, and control firms' pricing. This is not easy to do. It becomes a game—a serious one with very high stakes—between the firms and the government. The government has great power, but entrepreneurs can be very clever in circumventing government controls when profit is involved.

How Business and Labor Circumvent Controls

Price control regulations usually say, You shall not sell above the price you were charging on a particular day before the controls were put in place. The easy way to get around this rule is simply not to pay any attention to it; a firm simply sets prices and wages as it would if the rule didn't exist. Of course, the government will try to catch the firm violating the rule and will impose penalties if it can. But often the firm won't get caught, and often the penalties are not very severe. Business and labor have ways of making it difficult to detect that they are violating the controls. For example, the firm may publish list prices but normally sell at discounts. These discounts can become smaller and eventually vanish. This is an example of the general problem of knowing what the price was when the controls were put in place and what it is now. The list price stays the same but the transaction price rises. This means that price indexes (based on list prices) may show no increase when the prices being paid are in fact rising. Further, firms that now get smaller discounts find their costs rising, putting upward pressure on their prices.

Business has other ways of getting around controls. A firm can, for example, claim that each project is custom tailored, so that a project that cost $1,000 before controls, now costs $1,250 but is defined as a different project, even though the two projects are very similar. Business can also change the size or quality of the product and leave the price unchanged. Producing smaller candy bars at the same price is an example of this. Government agencies know these tricks, of course. The problem is having enough enforcement personnel to deal with them.

Wages are also raised in defiance of controls. Typically, controls allow firms some room to promote people. Further, new employees can usually be brought in at higher job classifications and salary levels than they had elsewhere. Thus, controls tend to result in an above-average number of promotions where people get new titles and higher pay but do the same job as before. Also, people will change jobs more often to get higher pay.

Unions may be able to get benefits for their entire membership during times of controls. Controls generally provide for increases in wages if they are justified by productivity increases. Unions can sometimes get management and government to agree to recognize productivity increases larger than those that actually occurred. At other times, unions have simply demanded and received wage hikes larger than allowed (as in Great Britain, for example), and the government couldn't, or didn't dare, oppose them.

In some cases, special exceptions to the wage controls are granted certain employees. If members of the fire department make less than police officers, they may be allowed raises to remove this difference; it's then up to the police to find a special reason why they need a raise. Eventually the public realizes that the controls are being evaded by some, but not all, groups. This seems unfair and undermines support for the control program.

Consequences of Wage and Price Controls

It might seem that business, labor, and government are playing a game that can harm the economy. Individual firms and workers may gain, but the overall economy loses because of the continuing inflation. These price and wage increases do, however, serve two legitimate economic goals. First, when demand rises, a price increase is often called for. In Figure 15-9, we show an increase in demand in a competitive industry. The upward-sloping supply curve, SS, means that per-unit costs are rising as the output of the industry increases. The rise in price from OP_1 to OP_2 shows that, with the increase in demand, price would rise if the market were left to itself. If price is held at OP_1 when demand shifts to D_2D_2, producers would want to supply OQ_1 but buyers would demand the quantity OQ_3, so there is a shortage equal to $OQ_3 - OQ_1$. In other words, if price isn't allowed to rise, the result is a shortage. One way to handle such a shortage is to resort to non-price *rationing*; that is, limiting the number of units that people are allowed to buy at price OP_1. This can be done by requiring that people have both money and rationing tickets or coupons to buy the good. This technique was used by most of the countries fighting in World Wars I and II. Other ways to handle such a shortage are to allow long lines (queues) to form, to use favoritism, or to

rationing Limiting the amounts of various goods that people are allowed to buy.

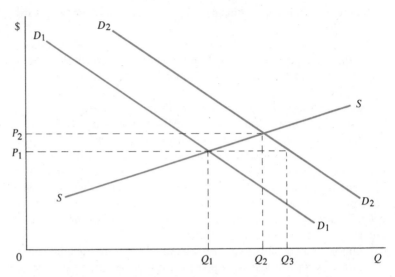

FIGURE 15-9   PRICE CONTROLS AND SHORTAGES

Inflation means that demand curves are shifting to the right over time, as was shown in Figure 15-8. If there are no controls, prices will rise with an increase in demand, as from OP_1 to OP_2. If controls keep the price at OP_1, then there will be a shortage of $OQ_3 - OQ_1$ equal to the quantity demanded (OQ_3) minus the smaller quantity supplied (OQ_1).

black markets   *Markets in which goods are illegally sold at prices above government regulated levels.*

allow **black markets** to form (where price is above the official controlled price); all these are used to some degree whenever prices are not freely adjustable.

Another difficulty with price controls, which is unrelated to general upward shifts of all demand curves, comes about when a particular industry's demand curve moves more than the average. For example, if people lose interest in *Star Wars* memorabilia and turn to Pacman games, we would expect to see Pacman sales and production rise (because of a more than average upward shift in demand) and *Star Wars* memorabilia sales and production to fall (because of a downward shift in demand or a less than average increase in demand). At the same time, we should expect the price of Pacman games to rise compared to the price of *Star Wars* memorabilia. If price controls don't allow the price of the Pacman games to rise, we will see a shortage of Pacman games. This problem is due to shifts in *relative* demand. The longer price and wage controls are in effect, the more likely it is that *relative demands* will tend to get away from their initial pattern, and the worse will be the shortages.

Shortages arise from (1) overall demand increases for the entire economy, and (2) relative demand shifts. The shortages have to be dealt with somehow. If government does nothing, business will simply raise prices, and the control program won't work. Thus, government has to enforce the program. In the early stages of a control program, the shortages are not too bad; but, as time goes on, overall demand increases make shortages worse, as do relative demand shifts. Governments must almost always have some way of allowing some prices to rise so that particular shortages don't become too severe. For example, Americans don't like giving up beef, as was shown by severe reactions to beef shortages after World War II and in the early 1970s. Thus, a bureaucracy is required to give permission for some price increases. The people who work in this bureaucracy have to be paid fairly well. Further, dealing with the bureaucracy takes time, involves filling out forms and so forth, and is quite expensive for business, as well as causes a great deal of uncertainty as to what the final bureaucratic decision will be.

Why Controls Are Removed

Let us sum up the forces that work against the success of a program of wage and price controls. First, every business and worker will have a large incentive to try to circumvent the controls, even if controls seem like a good idea for the other sectors of the economy. Second, controls lead to shortages, and these shortages get worse over time. This means the incentives to try to get around the controls increase. Third, a bureaucracy is required to enforce the controls and also to grant exceptions to them. This bureaucracy is costly to support, but, more important, it requires the people it regulates to fill out many forms and thus causes great hostility. Fourth, the controls appear not to work, both because some prices go on rising and because shortages develop. This interacts with the cost and interference of the bureaucracy to cause the entire program to look unattractive, and thus the program loses some of its public support. As time goes on, all these factors become worse, and eventually the program has to be abandoned. Most control programs in the western world are ultimately abandoned as failures. Governments don't like to admit failure, so sometimes they abandon the program after declaring it a success. In a few cases, governments adopt anti-inflationary macro policies at the same time as controls, and when the anti-inflationary policies work, they mistakenly think the controls are a success.

Why Are Controls Ever Put in Place?

Why, then, do the general public and economists sometimes favor wage and price controls? Often this occurs when other policies, such as monetary and fiscal policy, have been tried and don't seem to work, or they create high levels of unemployment. In this case, the general public and economists feel they have no alternative but to try controls. Additionally, some economists, like John Kenneth Galbraith, disagree with our analysis of inflationary pressures in terms of rising costs and demand. In their view, there is a wide range of prices that, say, the 500 largest firms in the United States economy could set without causing shortages. They believe government should control the prices set by these firms to minimize inflation. This group of economists is a minority in the profession, but often the general public agrees with them.

SUMMARY

1. Economists agree that monetary policy has a significant influence on the overall behavior of the economy. In the long run, monetary policy does not influence real output or employment, but determines only the rate of inflation.

2. Keynesians tend to believe that a large portion of the disturbances to the economy originate in the private sector. Monetarists do not agree and argue that, to a substantial degree, the cyclical nature of the economy is caused by government policy.

3. Keynesians believe that if left alone, the economy will adjust very slowly to eliminate high unemployment. They recommend expansionary fiscal and monetary policies to speed up the adjustment process. Monetarists believe the economy adjusts well enough if left alone. They argue that government policy is likely to do more harm than good.

4. Keynesian policy prescriptions rely heavily on the belief that the expenditure multiplier gives government a powerful tool to use for improving economic conditions. Based on the permanent income hypothesis, monetarists argue that the expenditure multiplier is insignificant.

5. Keynesians argue that monetarists rely too heavily on investment adjustments to offset changes in the consumption function. They believe that a lack of business confidence can prevent the increase in investment demand; therefore, they think that government policy should be used to increase aggregate demand.

6. Monetarists respond that the lack of business confidence is based on fears about government policy. For example, monetarists argue that increased government spending frequently crowds out private investment spending by driving up interest rates.

7. Monetarists favor very simple rules for monetary and fiscal policy that give very little discretion to policymakers. Keynesians argue that good discretionary policy will yield better results than rules.

8. Keynesians favor government expenditures as having more certain effects on aggregate demand than monetary policy or tax cuts.

9. To deal with stagflation, monetarists favor using restrictive monetary policy to reduce aggregate demand. According to this view, rising unemployment rates are a necessary ingredient to the process which forces down inflation expectations. Successive and gradual reductions in the money supply growth rate will eventually reduce inflation to the desired level. Following this, unemployment will return to the natural rate.

10. Given that restrictive monetary policy generates high unemployment rates, Keynesians favor wage and price controls to reduce inflation. According to this view, controls directly reduce actual inflation without requiring increased unemployment.

11. Opponents of wage and price controls argue that they don't work as supporters claim. Both businesses and labor have strong incentives to raise prices and wages and have found many ways to do so. To the extent that controls can be enforced and made to work, market forces are subverted and shortages occur. In the past, the public has come to see controls as ineffective and eventually they have been removed.

NEW TERMS

permanent income hypothesis
liquid assets
tax-based incomes policy (TIP)

rationing
black markets

QUESTIONS FOR DISCUSSION

1. Explain what is meant by the view that the private sector is unstable.

2. What are the pros and cons of the argument that active government policy makes the economy worse off?

3. Distinguish between the view that the economy adjusts at about the right speed and the view that it adjusts too slowly, but that active policy to increase the speed is not wise.

4. What is the permanent income hypothesis? What is the multiplier in this case? Why?

5. Explain how a lack of confidence on the part of the business sector can make adjustment too slow. What are the pros and cons of using government policy in this case to speed up adjustment?

6. Explain the MQT solution for bringing inflation under control. Why do many Keynesians oppose this solution?

7. Explain the argument that wage and price controls can break the vicious cycle between expected inflation and actual inflation.

8. Explain how shortages tend to arise under a controls program. Distinguish between shortages in most industries and those due to relative demand shifts.

9. How do business and labor try to circumvent controls? Why do they do this?

10. In a nutshell, what is the argument for rules vs. discretion? for discretion vs. rules?

SUGGESTIONS FOR FURTHER READING

Friedman, Milton. "Why Economists Disagree." *Dollars and Deficits: Inflation, Monetary Policy and the Balance of Payments.* Englewood Cliffs, N.J.: Prentice-Hall, Inc., 1978.

_____. *An Economist's Protest,* 2d ed. Glen Ridge, N.J.: Thomas Horton and Daughters, 1975.

Gordon, Robert J. *Macroeconomics,* 2d ed. Boston: Little, Brown & Co., 1981, Chapter 12.

Stein, Herbert. "Monetarism Under Fire." *The American Enterprise Economist* (September, 1981).

Willes, Mark H. "Eliminating Policy Surprises: An Inexpensive Way to Beat Inflation." *Annual Report, Federal Reserve Bank of Minneapolis,* 1978.

Supply-Side Economics: Theory and Policy for the Eighties

After studying the materials found in this chapter, you should be able to do the following:

1. Explain how Say's Law is part of the theoretical underpinning of supply-side economics.

2. Show how growth in productivity has slowed in the United States.

3. Discuss supply-side economics in terms of:
   (a) self-interested behavior.
   (b) the tax wedge.
   (c) taxes and productivity.

4. Show how marginal tax rates have an impact on:
   (a) work effort.
   (b) savings.
   (c) risk taking.
   (d) the allocation of investment.
   (e) tax avoidance.

5. Define supply-side economics.

6. Discuss the Laffer curve and its implications for tax cuts.

7. Distinguish between supply-side economics and Reaganomics.

8. Explain how tax changes have an impact on the economy as seen by a supply-sider and a Keynesian.

Supply-side economics is the term that has been given to the macro theory and policy proposals which have been championed by President Reagan. To most people, supply-side economics and "Reaganomics" are synonymous. While many of Reagan's key policy advisers advocate supply-side economics, some made a reluctant conversion. For example, during the presidential primaries of 1980, Vice-President George Bush, then an opponent of Reagan, characterized supply-side economics as "voodoo economics"; now he is an advocate.

This chapter places supply-side policies in historical perspective. It reviews some tenets of supply-side economics and discusses the policy propositions that have emerged from the political debate. We will return to the distinctions between supply-side economics and Reaganomics at the end of this chapter.

HISTORICAL PERSPECTIVE

We have seen in previous chapters that classical macroeconomics, which was based on the quantity theory of money, gave way to the Keynesian revolution. During the 1960s and 1970s, the Keynesian revolution was challenged by the modern quantity theorists, and the two groups stood far apart regarding macro policy. Starting in the mid-1970s, and with significantly increased activity in the 1980s, supply-side advocates entered the debate, giving a third alternative for macro policy. These supply-siders drew heavily on the work of classical economists for their theory.

Say's Law—The Beginning of Supply-Side Economics

As we saw in Chapter 8, Say's Law was a basic tenet of classical macroeconomics. Say's Law said, supply creates its own demand. It concentrated on supply as the driving mechanism of the macro system, and it brought into focus the idea that people worked and produced in order to consume.

A basic premise of Say's Law was that the economy, if left alone, would correct itself. There was little, if any, need for government intervention. Production would always generate sufficient income to purchase the goods produced. This was because the entrepreneurs and the owners of land, labor, and capital always received in income the exact value of what was produced. These individual factor owners would then purchase the goods that would be produced. Gluts of certain goods could appear, but they would be short-lived, because suppliers of these unwanted goods would be punished by falling prices for their goods.

With the onset of the Keynesian revolution, concern about supply-side factors faded. Remember that Keynesian economics assumes that aggregate supply responds passively to aggregate demand. Also recall that Keynesian economics developed in response to the Great Depression—a period of high unemployment and excess productive capacity. Given the high level of idle resources, it seemed apparent that aggregate supply simply responded to government-induced increases in aggregate demand. Most economists still believe Keynes was correct in focusing attention primarily on aggregate demand manipulation in order to solve a deflationary gap such as the Great Depression. Today, however, many economists believe that Keynesian economics is not a general theory of macroeconomics, but a special theory that explains the causes and solutions for economic depressions. Supply-siders argue that since the Great Depression, Keynesian economics has diverted attention away from other important factors such as work effort, labor productivity, and incentives to save and invest.

Moreover, some economists point out that Keynes's theory and Keynesian economics, as applied in a democratic setting, are quite different. Keynes viewed macro policy as being set by an elite group of advisers. These advisers use budget deficits and surpluses to adjust aggregate demand. In the United States, we almost always run deficits.[1]

Productivity Growth—The Concern of Supply-Side Economics

Concern about the slow growth of productivity in the United States caused many economists to reemphasize the supply side. Figure 16-1 illustrates that growth in productivity of the American economy has declined significantly since 1950. However, there have been periods of trend reversal; in particular, the period from 1962 to 1968, which was accompanied by investment tax credits, liberalized

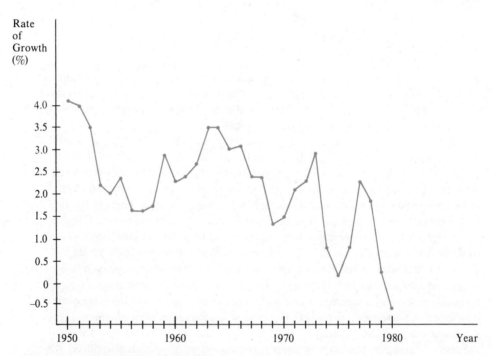

**FIGURE 16-1   LONG-TERM TRENDS IN
PRODUCTIVITY GROWTH, 1950–1980**

This figure shows the average annual growth rate in productivity in the private nonfarm sector. Productivity growth in the United States has declined significantly since 1950. However, the period from 1962 to 1968, which was characterized by investment incentives and reduced corporate taxes, saw a temporary reversal of the downward trend. Three-year averages have been used to smooth out cyclical fluctuations around the trend. (Source: Michael Evans, "An Econometric Model Incorporating the Supply-Side Effects of Economic Policy," *The Supply-Side Effects of Economic Policy*, Federal Reserve Bank of St. Louis [May, 1981], p. 45.)

---

[1]See James Buchanan and Richard Wagner, *Democracy in Deficit: The Political Legacy of Lord Keynes* (New York: The Academic Press, 1977).

depreciation, and reduced corporate taxes. This sort of argument has drawn attention to the supply side and has caused policymakers to examine exactly what affects productivity trends.

SOME BASIC TENETS

Supply-side economics has not yet developed a tight theoretical model that can be clearly laid out. This makes it different from the Keynesian theory or the modern quantity theory. A Keynesian or a monetarist can also be an advocate of supply-side policy. In fact, some monetarists are also active supply-siders. While we cannot yet propose a theoretical model for supply-side economics, we can describe some of the basic tenets which underlie it.

Self-Interested Behavior

The supply-siders rely on many of the basic concepts of economics that were developed in the beginning of this book. They remind policymakers that economic incentives are important and that the driving force in economic theory is the self-interested behavior of individuals. Individuals, in their roles as workers, managers, investors, and savers, respond in predictable ways to changes in the reward structure of their environment. Supply-siders point out that the government has a great deal of influence on this reward structure. It isn't that monetarists and Keynesian economists don't understand or appreciate the concept of self-interested behavior, it's just that supply-siders believe that Keynesian policy, with its demand-side emphasis, has interfered with this important aspect of economics.

The Growth of Government and the Tax Wedge

Supply-siders think that Keynesian intrusions into the market are partly responsible for the dramatic growth of the public sector. We discussed this phenomenon in Chapter 6. This growth has drained resources from the private sector. As taxes rise, costs of production rise to pay for increased governmental activity. Supply-siders contend that taxes are ultimately treated by businesses as costs of production, which they pass on to consumers in the form of higher prices. Thus, taxes to support government activity are seen as a **tax wedge** between the cost of production and the retail price of the product. The growth of government has necessitated large tax revenues and has, therefore, increased the tax wedge. In this way, growth of government has contributed to rising costs and is inflationary. In terms of the Phillips curve, which was discussed in previous chapters, the growth of government can be seen as a cause of the deteriorating inflation-unemployment trade-off; that is, a shift of the Phillips curve.

tax wedge   Taxes are treated by businesses as costs of production, which are then passed on to consumers in the form of higher prices.

The Tax-Transfer System and Productivity

As we have seen, supply-side economics concentrates on the declining growth of productivity in the United States. Supply-siders point out that the growth of the tax-transfer system has reduced incentives and has thus reduced the productivity of the economy. The basis of this argument is that marginal tax rates influence an individual's decision to work, innovate, invest, and save, and they encourage tax avoidance. The progressive tax system has generated behavior patterns which lead to lower productivity and inefficient utilization of scarce resources.

While more labor effort usually results in a higher wage rate, increases in income drive workers into higher marginal tax brackets. As a result, a significant portion of the return to increased effort and productivity is taxed away. Consequently, workers opt for more leisure (e.g., longer vacations, increased absenteeism, less moonlighting, and earlier retirement).

The same proposition holds for saving. An individual's reward for saving depends upon both the interest rate and the marginal tax rate on income. Given the interest rate, the higher the marginal tax rate, the less incentive there is for saving. Consequently, less credit is available to borrowers. Thus, our progressive tax structure retards saving. The same holds for risk taking. When considering options to expand productive facilities or to implement new and more efficient technologies, managers must weigh the risks that are involved against the expected profits *after taxes*. The higher the marginal tax rate, the less the expected profit, and the less eager investors will be to assume risks. As a result, less new technology is adopted, and both output and productivity are negatively influenced.

Supply-siders also point out that our progressive tax structure causes resources to be allocated inefficiently. They refer to situations where resources flow to certain sectors of the economy because of special tax advantages. This is presently the case with real estate investment. Because all depreciation, taxes, and interest expenses are deductible, individuals in high marginal tax brackets find their after-tax yields higher in real estate investment than in other types of securities. Thus, supply-siders argue that too many financial resources flow into the real estate market and are, therefore, unavailable for more productive uses.

Finally, supply-siders stress that the high marginal tax rates cause too many of our scarce resources to be utilized in avoidance of taxes. Significant time is spent looking for tax loopholes by individuals and their hired attorneys and accountants.

In summary, supply-siders see the progressive tax structure with its high marginal tax rates as generating disincentives to work, save, innovate, and invest, and as generating incentives for tax avoidance. These disincentives lead to declining productivity, inflation, and economic stagnation. Critics of supply-side economics point out that econometric studies indicate that marginal tax rates have only a slight impact on work effort. However, supply-siders believe that marginal tax has an impact on saving, investment, and risk taking. Michael Boskin of Stanford University has demonstrated that a 10 percent increase in the rate of return on saving will generate a 4 percent rise in the saving rate.

A DEFINITION OF SUPPLY-SIDE ECONOMICS

Supply-side economics has not yet developed a theoretical model that can be clearly defined. This makes it different from Keynesian theory or monetarism. Supply-side economics consists of a set of propositions, rather than a theory. One set of supply-side propositions has been offered by Herbert Stein, who is a professor of economics at the University of Virginia and who also served as President Nixon's chairman of the Council of Economic Advisers. Stein lists 11 propositions and classifies them according to how they relate to supply-side economics.[2] He begins with eight propositions that have been a part of economic theory for decades. You will recognize them from the material you have already studied.

1. Supply is an important element of economic analysis.

2. Increasing the supply of total output is important for individual welfare and national strength.

3. The supply of output depends on the supply of resources or inputs.

4. The supply of resources and, therefore, total output are affected by public policy.

5. The supply of resources will be influenced by the tax system.

6. A tax reduction will make the national income higher than it would otherwise have been and the revenue loss from the tax reduction will, therefore, be less than if the national income had not been induced to rise.

7. A tax reduction will raise the national income by more than the amount of the tax reduction.

8. A tax reduction will increase the total tax revenue.

Stein lists three more propositions from supply-side economics that he believes contribute to policy analysis.

9. A tax reduction not accompanied by a reduction of government spending will raise total revenue, and will do so by operating on the supply-side of the economy.

Stein accepts the proposition as true, but thinks the debate should be over the size of changes in governmental revenues rather than their existence. The difference in this supply-side proposition and Keynesian analysis is that supply-siders attribute the increase in tax revenue to the production stimulated, while Keynesians first see an increase in demand, which causes business to increase production.

10. Less political and ambitious supply-siders might be willing to settle for the proposition that a tax-rate cut not accompanied by an expenditure cut will nonetheless increase real output, even if it also reduces total revenue.

As with Proposition 9, Stein points out that the size of the production increase is the important thing. Most economists would not dispute the proposition that production will increase. The important question is, how much?

---

[2]Herbert Stein, "Some Supply-Side Propositions," *The AEI Economist,* April 1980. A good discussion of Stein's article appears in Thomas J. Hailstones, *A Guide to Supply-Side Economics* (Richmond, Va.: Robert F. Dame, Inc., 1982).

The Disincentive Effects of Taxation

"All Work, Small Pay Makes Little Red Hen Rue the Day."[1]

Once upon a time, there was a little red hen who scratched about and uncovered some grains of wheat.

---

[1]Author unknown.

She called her barnyard neighbors and said, "If we work together and plant this wheat, we will have some fine bread to eat. Who will help me plant the wheat?"

"Not I," said the cow.

"Not I," said the duck.

"Not I," said the goose.

"Then I will," said the little red hen, and she did. The wheat grew tall and ripened into golden grain.

"Who will help me reap my wheat?" asked the little red hen.

"Not I," said the duck.

"Out of my classification," said the pig.

"I'd lose my seniority," said the cow.

"I'd lose my unemployment," said the goose.

Then it came time to bake the bread.

"That's overtime for me," said the cow.

"I'd lose my welfare benefits," said the pig.

"If I'm the only one helping, that's discrimination," said the goose.

"Then I will," said the little red hen, and she did. She baked five loaves of fine bread and held them all up for the neighbors to see. They all wanted some and demanded a share. But the red hen said, "Now I can rest for awhile and eat the five loaves myself."

"Excess profits," cried the cow.

"Capitalistic leach," screamed the duck.

"Company fink," grunted the pig.

"Equal rights," yelled the goose. And they hurriedly painted picket signs and marched around the little red hen. "Look at the oppressed cow. Look at the disadvantaged duck. Look at the underprivileged pig. Look at the less fortunate goose. You are guilty of making second-class citizens of them." They formed a government and taxed the hen four loaves.

"But . . . but," said the little red hen. "I earned the bread."

"Exactly," said the wise farmer. "That is the wonderful free enterprise system. Anybody in the barnyard can earn as much as he wants. You should be happy to have this freedom. In other barnyards, you would have to give all five loaves," said the farmer. "Here you give four loaves to your suffering neighbors."

And they lived happily ever after, including the little red hen, who clucked and smiled: "I am grateful."

But her neighbors wondered why she never baked any more bread.

11. The way to tackle the inflation problem is from the supply-side, especially by cutting taxes.

Stein points out that Proposition 11 is the most visible policy prescription of supply-side economics. Stein argues that inflation has been averaging about 10 percent and output has been growing by about 2 percent. This means that an 8 percent increase in output would be needed for a supply-side solution to inflation. Stein thinks this unlikely, regardless of the size of any tax cuts.

We saw earlier that supply-siders view the decline in productivity as, in large part, a result of U. S. tax policy. But how do supply-side tax reductions improve productivity, reduce inflation, and promote economic growth? An excellent definition of how the tax cuts work has been developed by Michael K. Evans. Evans, an economic consultant, is best known for his work at the Wharton Business School and at Chase Econometrics, where he helped develop sophisticated forecasting models of the U. S. economy.

Evans points to the simplicity of supply-side economics. He says that all that supply-siders advocate is that policymakers take into account the economy's ability to produce when setting economic policy. He believes that the rise of Keynesian economics is responsible for the fact that this simple proposition was ignored in the 1960s and 1970s.

Evans' list of ten supply-side propositions is as follows:[3]

1. A reduction in tax rates increases the incentive of individuals to save by raising the rate of return on assets held by individuals. This higher savings leads to lower interest rates and higher investment.

2. Corporate tax-rate cuts or similar measures, such as increasing the investment tax credit or liberalizing depreciation allowances, improve investment directly by increasing the average after-tax rate of return.

3. Higher investment leads to an increase in productivity, which means that more goods and services can be produced per unit of input.

4. The transfer of resources from the public to the private sector increases the overall growth rate in productivity, since productivity gains in the public sector are small or nonexistent.

5. The faster growth in productivity provides the needed capacity to produce additional goods and services demanded because of the tax cut, thus leading to balanced growth without bottlenecks or shortages.

6. Lower tax rates result in more modest demands for wage increases, since real income has risen by virtue of the tax cut and workers do not suffer a loss of real income by moving into higher tax brackets.

---

[3]Michael Evans, "The Bankruptcy of Keynesian Econometric Models," *Challenge* (January-February, 1980).

7. Lower inflation leads to an increase in real disposable income, and hence, a rise in consumption, output, and employment.

8. Lower tax rates improve work effort, resulting in an increase in the quality and quantity of work. This, in turn, raises productive capacity still further, thereby contributing to the slowdown in the rate of inflation.

9. The lower rate of inflation causes an increase in net exports, which strengthens the value of the dollar. This leads to further reductions in the rate of inflation, because imported goods decline rather than advance in price.

10. The increase in capacity also permits the production of more goods for export as well as domestic consumption, thereby providing additional strength for the dollar and less imported inflation.

Studying the definitions of Stein and Evans makes it clear that supply-side economics is primarily a set of propositions or beliefs about the value of tax cuts. Figure 16-2 schematically shows how supply-siders believe tax cuts will ultimately lead to reduced inflation and increased productivity, output, income, and tax revenues.

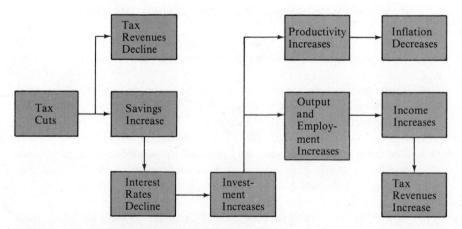

**FIGURE 16-2 HOW TAX CUTS WORK IN THE
SUPPLY-SIDE ANALYSIS**

Supply-siders believe that tax cuts will work to reduce inflation as well as to reduce unemployment through their effect on labor productivity and output. In addition, although tax cuts initially mean declining tax revenues, later, as a result of increased output, employment and income tax revenues will be larger.

THE LAFFER CURVE

To some, the *Laffer curve,* developed by Arthur Laffer, has become the center-piece of supply-side economics. The idea of the Laffer curve is presented in Figure 16-3. At zero tax rates, the government generates zero tax revenue. At 100 percent tax rates, the government also receives zero revenue, because incentives to work and invest disappear. Laffer contends that as tax rates rise, as from 0 to t_2 in Figure 16-3, the revenue generated increases, but after that point, tax revenue declines as disincentives to work and invest become more significant. Laffer did not offer any statement as to where the U.S. economy was on the Laffer curve, but since he advocated huge tax cuts and didn't fear loss of revenue, one must hypothesize that Laffer believed that the U.S. tax rates were above t_2 in Figure 16-3.

> *Laffer curve* Curve illustrating the fact that as taxes rise, the revenue generated increases up to a certain point when revenues start to decline. This is because as taxes increase, disincentives to work and invest become more significant.

Although the popular press views the Laffer curve as a supply-side proposition, many supply-siders disclaim association with it. They argue that the Laffer curve draws too much attention to the association between tax rates and tax revenue, and that it suggests that one should set tax rates to maximize tax revenue. They would instead wish to set tax rates so as to maximize supply, or aggregate output. A curve such as the one drawn in Figure 16-4 suggests that certain public expenditures enhance productivity and there is a level of govern-

Arthur Laffer

Arthur Laffer, who developed the Laffer curve, is one of the best known representatives of supply-side

economics. It is reported that he first drew the Laffer curve on a napkin in a restaurant in 1974 to demonstrate to a colleague how a tax cut could increase government revenue. This is really not a new idea, but an idea that Laffer popularized.

Laffer believes that David Stockman, director of the Office of Management and Budget (OMB), has done much to undo the Reagan experiment with supply-side economics. Laffer recently called the 1981–1982 recession "the Stockman recession and the Stockman deficit."[1] Laffer believes that Stockman's concern over deficits caused the tax cut to be watered down and delayed. As a result, the supply-side experiment was not given a chance to work.

Laffer, a Reagan adviser in the 1980 campaign, is now a member of Reagan's Economic Policy Board, but he removed himself from consideration for governmental jobs. *Newsweek* quotes Laffer as saying, "The silliest thing you can do is have an economist run your country. The second silliest thing you can do is not listen to him."[2]

Laffer is a professor of business economics at the University of Southern California.

[1] *U.S. News & World Report,* January 18, 1982.
[2] *Newsweek* (June 29, 1981), p. 13.

FIGURE 16-3   THE LAFFER CURVE

The Laffer curve purports to show that a decrease in tax rates from t_1 to t_2 will cause tax revenues to increase from TR_1 to TR_2.

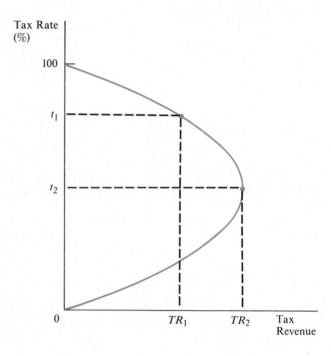

FIGURE 16-4   OUTPUT AND TAX RATES

This curve, which shows the effect of tax rates on supply, suggests there may be a tax rate, t^*, that maximizes aggregate output, A.

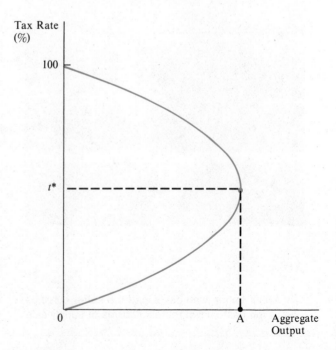

ment and its underlying tax rate that would produce a maximum level of aggregate output. Supply-siders would be in agreement that the tax rate in the U. S. economy is presently much higher than t^* in Figure 16-4 and that a decrease in taxes will cause aggregate output to increase.

REAGANOMICS AND SUPPLY-SIDE ECONOMICS

President Reagan is an eager proponent of supply-side economics. In his first State of the Union Address, he laid out a program heavily influenced by supply-side thinking. His program outline, as we saw in Chapter 6, was highlighted by a large tax cut. It included:[4]

1. A reduction of $5.5 billion in the current 1981 budget.

2. A $49.9 billion cut in federal expenditures for fiscal 1982, a $79.7 billion cut for 1983, and a $126.8 billion cut for 1986.

3. An across-the-board (Kemp-Roth style) 10 percent annual personal income tax reduction for three years beginning in July, 1981.

4. A reduction over a three-year period in the maximum marginal tax rate on investment income (unearned income) from 70 percent to 50 percent to make it equal to the maximum rate on wage and salary income. (See Chapter 6 for recent changes in personal income taxation.)

5. An increase in the income level at which the maximum tax rates take effect.

6. Accelerated depreciation via a version of the Capital Cost Recovery Act (10-5-3 Bill).

7. A continuation and increase in the use of tax credits for new investment.

In January, 1982, Reagan's second State of the Union Address contained a similar theme. Despite a great deal of criticism in his first year as president and despite advice to increase taxes in the face of rising budget deficits, President Reagan remained firm in his advocacy of supply-side tax cuts.

Some supply-siders are upset with President Reagan's advisers. They believe that Reagan has not really attempted a supply-side experiment à la Evans's list of propositions. Instead, they believe the tax cut only moderated and set back increases that had occurred in the late 1970s.

Stephen A. Meyer and Robert J. Rossona of the Federal Reserve Bank of Philadelphia have examined tax data. They have concluded that by 1983 most people will be in higher tax brackets.[5] Meyer and Rossona calculated marginal tax rates for a cross-section of households. Assuming inflation rates of 8 percent, they found that households with an adjusted gross income of $13,000 to $40,000 in 1980 (in 1978 dollars) would face rising marginal tax rates until 1983. For

[4]Summary Fact Sheet, *A Program for Economic Recovery,* February 18, 1981.
[5]*Business Week,* December 28, 1981, p. 15.

example, families earning $22,500 in 1980 (again 1978 dollars) would face a 50 percent higher marginal rate in 1983 than they did in 1980.

This example explains the unhappiness of true believer supply-siders. They feel that we haven't had a supply-side experiment, but that the public views **Reaganomics** and supply-side economics as one and the same. As a result, a failure of Reaganomics could well be viewed by the public and by politicians as a failure of supply-side policy. Supply-siders argue that this should not be the conclusion, as Reagan has not yet developed a supply-side policy proposal.

Reaganomics Economic policy as advocated by President Reagan. It emphasizes deregulation and tax cuts to spur investment and production.

Deregulation and Supply-Side Economics

Deregulation is an important aspect of President Reagan's economic policy. As we saw in Chapter 6, deregulatory matters are high on the agenda in Washington. Murray Weidenbaum, chairman of President Reagan's Council of Economic Advisers, is a leader in the policy initiatives to decrease the governmental regulatory thrust.

While most supply-siders are avid and committed to deregulation, this is not a unique proposition of supply-side economics. Most monetarists, particularly those who advocate a monetary rule, are also proponents of deregulation. This deregulatory activity is associated with supply-side economics, with monetarism, and most certainly with Reaganomics. Keynesians, on the other hand, are less likely to condemn government regulatory behavior. This does not come from any aspect in Keynesian analysis, but rather from the tendency of Keynesian economists to be allied with active governmental policy.

Competing Policy Advice and Policy Tools

The policymaker-politician is confronted with competing economic advice on questions of macro policy. When analyzing inflation, the Keynesian would recommend increasing taxes or reducing governmental spending. The major Keynesian tool is fiscal policy. The monetarist would recommend contractionary monetary policy. The major monetarist tool is a reduction of the money supply. The supply-sider would recommend an increase in supply as a way to ease inflationary pressures. Massive tax cuts that increase incentives and spur investment would be the tool of the supply-sider. These tax cuts would be aimed at marginal tax rates.

We are now in a position to make an important distinction between Keynesian views and supply-side views. Both groups advocate tax cuts to stimulate a stagnant economy. Beyond this point of agreement, however, lie two important differences. First, Keynesians believe that the absolute size of the tax cut is the important consideration. The impact on the economy depends on the size of the tax cut and the tax reduction multiplier. However, supply-siders would argue that it is not the absolute amount of the tax reduction which is important, but rather the effect on marginal tax rates; that is, how individual incentives are influenced. Second, Keynesians believe that tax changes influence the economy by changing the level of aggregate demand; that is, through their impact on consumption spending. Supply-siders emphasize that changes in marginal tax rates have their primary impact on the economy by influencing saving, investment, innovation, and productivity. The increase in aggregate demand is believed to be a secondary impact.

SUMMARY

1. Say's Law, a basic tenet of classical macroeconomics, is a theoretical underpinning of supply-side economics.

2. Concerns about declines in productivity in the United States have, in part, been responsible for the renewed interest in supply-side economics.

3. Supply-side economics draws increased attention to the macroeconomic impact of macroeconomic policy. Market behavior of self-interested individuals is stressed.

4. Supply-side economics examines the tax wedge caused by government in private markets. Taxes are costs of production and cause prices to rise.

5. Taxes, particularly high marginal tax rates associated with progressive taxes, adversely affect incentives.

6. High marginal tax rates cause people to work less, consume more leisure, save less, take fewer risks, invest in areas with tax advantages, and spend money seeking to avoid taxes.

7. Supply-side economics does not have a theoretical base; it is instead a set of policy propositions related to tax policy.

8. The Laffer curve shows that, as taxes rise, the government generates more revenue to a point, but after that point higher taxes produce less governmental revenue. This falling revenue is caused by the disincentives of higher tax rates.

9. President Reagan's economic policy is influenced by supply-side propositions, but Reaganomics is not synonymous with supply-side economics.

10. Some supply-siders argue that President Reagan has not attempted a supply-side policy experiment.

11. Deregulation is advocated by supply-side proponents but also by economists of other policy camps.

12. Keynesians measure the significance of a tax cut by its absolute size in dollars.

13. Supply-siders measure the significance of a tax cut by its impact on marginal tax rates.

NEW TERMS

tax wedge
Laffer curve

Reaganomics

QUESTIONS FOR DISCUSSION

1. A reporter returning from London writes that economists who claim the British economy is sick are surely wrong because he saw many Rolls Royce cars and other displays of wealth in London. Do you agree? How would a supply-sider use this example as a symptom that something was wrong with the economy?

2. How do marginal tax rates affect saving decisions, investment decisions, and work decisions?

3. Explain the impact of a tax cut as viewed by supply-siders and Keynesians.

4. How does a supply-sider think a tax cut will reduce inflation?

SUGGESTIONS FOR FURTHER READING

Hailstones, Thomas J. *A Guide to Supply-Side Economics.* Richmond, Va.: Robert F. Dame, Inc., 1982.
Kaufman, Henry. "Reganomics: Why Isn't Wall Street Concerned?" *Challenge* (September/October, 1981).
Meyer, Laurence (ed.). *The Supply-Side Effects of Economic Policy.* St. Louis: Federal Reserve Bank of St. Louis, 1981.

PART 4

The Basics of Microeconomics

Elasticity: Measure of Responsiveness

Learning Objectives

After studying the materials found in this chapter, you should be able to do the following:

1. Define elasticity.

2. Calculate the coefficients of elasticity for the following measures:
   (a) price elasticity of demand.
   (b) income elasticity of demand.
   (c) cross elasticity of demand.
   (d) price elasticity of supply.

3. List and define the values for the coefficient of price elasticity of demand when the demand is:
   (a) elastic.
   (b) inelastic.
   (c) unit elastic.

4. List and define the values for the coefficient of the income elasticity of demand when the good is:
   (a) inferior.
   (b) normal.

5. List and define the values of the coefficients of cross elasticity of demand when two goods are:
   (a) substitutes.
   (b) complements.
   (c) independent.

elasticity *A measure of the sensitivity or responsiveness of quantity demanded or quantity supplied to changes in price (and other factors).*

In Chapter 3 we developed the tools of supply and demand. In this chapter we expand on these concepts and develop another tool of the microeconomist, the elasticity measurement. *Elasticity* is the measure of the *sensitivity* or *responsiveness* of quantity demanded or quantity supplied to changes in price (or other factors). We will develop several elasticity measures and then demonstrate their usefulness in discussions of public policy.

SUPPLY AND DEMAND, AGAIN

Supply and demand are so basic to our analysis in economics that it is worth reviewing them before we begin expanding our kit of economic tools.

When we examine demand, we look at shifts in demand curves and movement along demand curves. Any movement along a demand curve is in response to a change in price and is referred to as a *change in quantity demanded.* Any shift of the demand curve is called a *change in demand.* These changes in demand are in response to changes in one or more of the other *ceteris paribus* conditions that underlie the demand curve—the tastes of the group demanding the good, the size of the group, the income and wealth of the group, the prices of other goods and services, or expectations concerning all these *ceteris paribus* conditions.

In a similar fashion, we can talk about changes in supply and changes in quantity supplied. The term *quantity supplied* indicates to the economist that the change which occurred was in response to a change in price. When we use the phrase *change in supply* we know that the change occurred not because of a change in price, but because of a change in one or more of the other *ceteris paribus* conditions affecting supply—the prices of the factors of production, the number of sellers, the level of technology used to produce the good, or expectations about these conditions.

In Chapter 3 we learned that demand curves always have a negative slope, and that supply curves usually have a positive slope. We also learned about changes in supply and demand and changes in quantity demanded and quantity supplied, using these terms to describe price formation in markets.

These economic principles and the use of this new terminology are useful in explaining economic happenings. Figure 17-1 is a diagram of the market supply and demand for automobiles. Given *ceteris paribus* conditions such as quality,

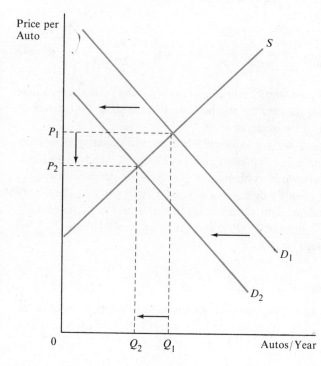

FIGURE 17-1   THE MARKET FOR AUTOMOBILES

If the price of gasoline, a complementary product to automobiles, rises, there will be a decrease in the demand for automobiles. The price will fall from OP_1 to OP_2 and the equilibrium quantity will decrease from OQ_1 to OQ_2. We say there has been a decrease in the quantity supplied.

size, and mileage, we determine an equilibrium price of OP_1 and quantity sold of OQ_1. Now suppose the price of gasoline increases. Gasoline and automobiles are complements, so you know that the increase in the price of gasoline is going to cause the demand for automobiles to decrease from D_1 to D_2 in Figure 17-1. This decrease in demand causes the price to fall to OP_2, and the quantity supplied to decrease to OQ_2.

The important point about supply and demand analysis is that it allows you to think logically about what is happening in markets. If you can draw a demand and supply curve for a product, you can analyze what effect changes in price or in any *ceteris paribus* condition can have. Understanding supply and demand is the bedrock of microeconomic analysis. If you do not understand how to use this tool, go back to Chapter 3 and review it thoroughly.

ELASTICITY AS A GENERAL CONCEPT

dependent variable The variable that changes in response to the independent variables in an equation.

independent variable The variable or variables in an equation which are determined outside the equation.

Elasticity measures the way one variable changes in response to changes in other variables. The *dependent variable* is the variable that changes in response to some other variable, called the *independent variable.* In formula form we express the dependent variable *(x)* as a function of an independent variable *(y)*, as in equation (17-1).

$$x = f(y_1, y_2, y_3, \ldots y_n).$$ (17-1)

Elasticity measures how the x variable responds to changes in any one of the different y variables. The formula to determine this responsiveness can be expressed as in equation (17-2):

$$E_1 = \frac{\% \Delta x}{\% \Delta y_1}, E_2 = \frac{\% \Delta x}{\% \Delta y_2}, \ldots, E_n = \frac{\% \Delta x}{\% \Delta y_n}.$$ (17-2)

E denotes elasticity, and the formula says that elasticity is the percentage change in the dependent variable divided by the percentage change in the particular independent variable we are looking at.

In examining demand, we are interested in how the quantity demanded responds to changes in price (we represent changes by the Δ symbol) and how the quantity demanded responds to changes in the other *ceteris paribus* factors that affect demand. The quantity demanded of good x (QD_x) is thus the dependent variable, and the independent variables are the price of x (P_x), income (I), tastes (T), the price of complements (P_c), and the price of substitutes (P_s). We can thus rewrite equation (17-1) as

$$QD_x = f(P_x, I, T, P_c, P_s).$$

We can now determine how QD_x responds to any of the factors by holding all but one of them constant and calculating the elasticity coefficient using equation

(17-2). For example, to see how quantity demanded responds to price, we would calculate

$$E_d = \frac{\% \, \Delta \, QD_x}{\% \, \Delta \, P_x},$$

where E_d is defined as the coefficient of price elasticity of demand. This formula gives us the ***price elasticity of demand.***

price elasticity of demand   A measure of the responsiveness of the quantity demanded to changes in price.

PRICE ELASTICITY OF DEMAND

The famous English economist, Alfred Marshall, writing in the late 1800s, developed the concept of elasticity to compare demands for various products. When comparisons are made, it is necessary to concentrate on the *relative* responsiveness of the quantity demanded to price rather than concentrating on the absolute responsiveness. We are interested in relative comparisons because we want to be able to measure and then label the sensitivity of the demand relationship. To understand this concept, examine Figure 17-2. Two demand curves are drawn— one is the demand curve for coffee, the other is the demand curve for orange juice. As the price increases by the same amount for each curve, we see different changes in the quantity demanded. The two goods have different sensitivities to the price change; that is, they have different elasticities.

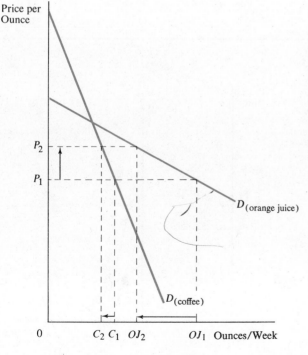

FIGURE 17-2   DEMAND CURVES WITH DIFFERENT ELASTICITIES

Demand curves may have different elasticities or exhibit different responses to changes in price. The same price change can be seen to have quite a different impact on the quantity demanded of coffee and orange juice. The price change has a much greater impact on the quantity of orange juice demanded, so we say the demand for orange juice is more elastic than the demand for coffee.

The *coefficient of price elasticity of demand* (E_d) is defined as the percentage change in quantity demanded divided by the percentage change in price. The equation for the price elasticity of demand is, as we have seen,

$$E_d = \frac{\% \, \Delta \, QD_x}{\% \, \Delta \, P_x}.$$

Since what we mean by the relative change (or percentage change) is the change in the variable divided by the base amount of the variable, this reduces to

$$E_d = \frac{\dfrac{\Delta \, QD_x}{QD_x}}{\dfrac{\Delta \, P_x}{P_x}}. \tag{17-3}$$

With most demand curves, the elasticity coefficient varies along the curve; however, some demand curves have a *constant* price elasticity of demand. This is not normal, but we shall first examine these cases.

Figure 17-3 depicts a vertical demand curve, showing that quantity demanded is totally unresponsive to changes in price. As price changes from OP_1 to OP_2, there is no change in the quantity demanded. If we calculated the elasticity coefficient, we would find:

$$E_d = \frac{\dfrac{OQ_1 - OQ_1}{OQ_1}}{\dfrac{OP_1 - OP_2}{OP_1}} = \frac{0}{\dfrac{OP_1 - OP_2}{OP_1}} = 0.$$

**FIGURE 17-3   PERFECTLY INELASTIC DEMAND
             CURVE**

On a perfectly inelastic demand curve, the quantity demanded has no responsiveness to changes in price. A relatively inelastic demand curve is a demand curve which is not very responsive to changes in price.

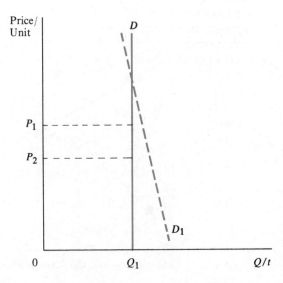

This is a limiting case which violates the law of demand and is not known to exist in the real world. This curve is called a ***perfectly inelastic*** demand curve. Although it doesn't exist in the real world, there may be demand curves that are very close to it, such as curve D_1, represented by the dashed line in Figure 17-3. We would refer to this curve as a *relatively* inelastic demand curve. A highly inelastic demand exists for goods such as heroin for an addict or heart medicine for someone with a heart condition. These individuals probably do not respond very much to changes in price, particularly if they are wealthy.

In Figure 17-4, which depicts a horizontal demand curve, we have another limiting case. At OP_1 or at any price below OP_1 an infinite quantity of the good would be demanded; if price rises above OP_1, the quantity of the good that would be demanded is zero. If we calculate the coefficient for a price change from OP_1 to OP_2, we get:

$$E_d = \frac{\dfrac{\infty}{OQ_1}}{\dfrac{OP_1 - OP_2}{OP_1}} = \infty.$$

perfectly inelastic   A price elasticity of demand coefficient of zero. There is no response in quantity demanded to changes in price. The demand curve is vertical.

We refer to such a curve as a ***perfectly elastic*** demand curve because the response to changes in price is infinite or perfect. We would refer to a curve such as D_1, the dashed demand curve in Figure 17-4, as a *relatively* elastic demand curve. A highly elastic demand exists for the wheat production of an individual farmer in the United States. The price of a bushel of wheat is determined by the market. At that price (or any lower price), all the farmer's wheat that is available will be demanded. But if a farmer raises the price even slightly, demand for that farmer's wheat will go to zero.

A third kind of elasticity curve is drawn in Figure 17-5. It is represented by a rectangular hyperbola. Any percentage decrease or increase in price is met by

perfectly elastic   A price elasticity of demand coefficient of infinity. The quantity demanded responds in an infinite way to a change in price. The demand curve is a horizontal line.

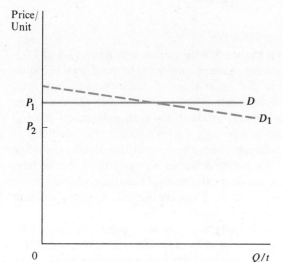

FIGURE 17-4   PERFECTLY ELASTIC DEMAND CURVE
On a perfectly elastic demand curve, the quantity demanded has an infinite response to changes in price. A relatively elastic demand curve is a demand curve which is very responsive to changes in price.

FIGURE 17-5   UNITARY ELASTIC DEMAND CURVE

A unitary elastic demand curve is a rectangular hyperbola. A change in price brings about an equal relative change in quantity demanded.

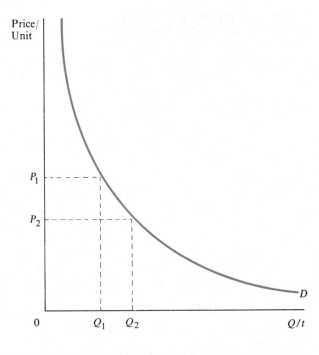

an exactly equal percentage increase or decrease in the quantity demanded. This means that the elasticity coefficient at any point along the demand curve is equal to one. For example, if we calculated the elasticity coefficient for a price change from OP_1 to OP_2, we would find that:

$$E_d = \frac{\dfrac{OQ_1 - OQ_2}{OQ_1}}{\dfrac{OP_1 - OP_2}{OP_1}} = 1.$$

unit elastic   A price elasticity of demand coefficient of one. The change in quantity demanded responds at the same rate as any change in price. The demand curve is a rectangular hyperbola.

We refer to such a curve as **unit elastic.**

Most demand curves are not shaped like the curves in Figures 17-4 or 17-5. Most straight line demand curves have a shape similar to the one drawn in Figure 17-6. Demand curve D in Figure 17-6 has a *range* of elasticity coefficients from infinitely elastic (at the y-axis intercept) to infinitely inelastic (at the x-axis intercept). Table 17-1 presents a handy guide to the nomenclature of demand elasticities. When the coefficient is *less* than one, we refer to the elasticity as *inelastic.* This is because the percentage change in quantity demanded is less than the percentage change in price. When the coefficient is *greater* than one, we refer to the elasticity as *elastic* because the quantity demanded changes relatively more than price. Of course, there are degrees of responsiveness. As the coefficient becomes larger, the responsiveness or elasticity increases.

The best way to understand elasticity is to calculate some elasticity coefficients. Using Figure 17-6, which is produced from the demand schedule in Table 17-2, we can calculate elasticity coefficients for the demand curve in Figure 17-6.

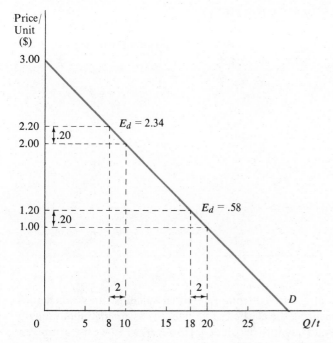

FIGURE 17-6 STRAIGHT LINE DEMAND CURVE WITH CHANGING ELASTICITY

A straight line demand curve has changing elasticity coefficients from the *y*-axis intercept to the *x*-axis intercept.

First, however, we need to understand some technicalities. The first problem is whether we are calculating the elasticity at a single point or between two points. If we are examining the elasticity between points, we are actually calculating the *average* elasticity over the space between the points. This is called **arc elasticity.** Most economists use a different, but related, concept called **point elasticity.** This refers to the responsiveness of quantity demanded to price at a particular point

arc elasticity   Average elasticity over the space between two points.

point elasticity   The responsiveness of quantity demanded to price at a particular point on a curve.

TABLE 17-1 A GUIDE TO ELASTICITY COEFFICIENTS

Numerical Coefficients	Responsiveness of Quantity Demanded to a Change in Price	Terminology
$E_d = 0$	NONE	perfectly inelastic
$0 < E_d < 1$	Quantity changes by a smaller percentage than the percentage change in price	inelastic
$E_d = 1$	Quantity changes by an equal percentage as the percentage change in price	unit elastic
$1 < E_d < \infty$	Quantity changes by a larger percentage than the percentage change in price	elastic
$E_d = \infty$	Quantity goes to zero or to all that is available	perfectly elastic

TABLE 17-2   DEMAND SCHEDULE FOR FIGURE 17-6

Price	Quantity Demanded
$ .50	25
1.00	20
1.20	18
1.40	16
1.60	14
1.80	12
2.00	10
2.20	8
2.40	6
2.60	4
2.80	2
3.00	0

on a curve. The concept is derived from differential calculus.[1] In mathematics, we are technically measuring the elasticity at a point by assuming infinitesimally small changes in price and quantity demanded. However, when we use arithmetic to calculate particular coefficients, we are working with a sizable, discrete change. This is the concept of arc elasticity. A second technicality is that the formula will always produce a negative number because demand curves are negatively sloped. This means there is an inverse relationship between the variables.[2] In practice, we ignore the sign and consider an E_d of -5 larger than an E_d of -4. It will be important later, when considering other elasticity measures, to keep track of the sign, but when considering price elasticity of demand, we ignore it.

We can now calculate some price elasticity of demand coefficients using the demand schedule of Table 17-2. The formula again is

$$E_d = \frac{\text{percentage change in quantity demanded}}{\text{percentage change in price}}.$$

For analytical purposes, this reduces to

$$E_d = \frac{\dfrac{\Delta Q}{(Q_1 + Q_2)/2}}{\dfrac{\Delta P}{(P_1 + P_2)/2}}.$$

It is necessary to divide the sum of the beginning price and ending price by two, and to divide the sum of the beginning and ending quantity by two. This is a technicality based on the fact that we are calculating arc elasticity and we need

---

[1]Elasticity at a particular point can be measured by the formula:

$$E_d = \frac{dQ}{dP} \cdot \frac{P}{Q}$$

[2]See the appendix to Chapter 2.

averages. If we didn't find an average quantity and price, the coefficient would be different depending on whether we calculated it as a price increase or price decrease.

We will now compute the elasticity coefficients for two different changes on the demand curve in Figure 17-6. First, the elasticity coefficient for the increase in price from $1.00 to $1.20:

$$E_d = \frac{\dfrac{20 - 18}{(20 + 18)/2}}{\dfrac{1.00 - 1.20}{(1.00 + 1.20)/2}}$$

$$E_d = \frac{\dfrac{2}{19}}{\dfrac{.20}{1.10}}$$

$$E_d = \frac{.1053}{.1818}$$

$$E_d = .58.$$

Now for the elasticity coefficient for the increase in price from $2.00 to $2.20:

$$E_d = \frac{\dfrac{10 - 8}{(10 + 8)/2}}{\dfrac{2.00 - 2.20}{(2.00 + 2.20)/2}}$$

$$E_d = \frac{\dfrac{2}{9}}{\dfrac{.20}{2.10}}$$

$$E_d = \frac{.2222}{.095}$$

$$E_d = 2.34.$$

You can see that the elasticity is different at different points along this constant slope demand curve. In fact, all constant slope or linear demand curves except those that are perfectly vertical or horizontal have points that range from elastic to unit elastic to inelastic. On a demand curve such as D in Figure 17-7, all points above price OP_1 have an elasticity coefficient greater than one and are elastic; at price OP_1 the elasticity is equal to one (unit elasticity); and all points below OP_1 have an elasticity coefficient less than one and are inelastic.

To prove how important it is to average the quantity and price when making actual calculations, calculate the effect of an increase in price from $1.00 to $1.20 and then of a decrease in price from $1.20 to $1.00 using equation (17-3), which does not average. If you do this, you will get different elasticity coefficients. Often when we examine a demand curve or schedule, we don't know if the price is decreasing or increasing. We want to know the average or arc elasticity between the points and we find this by employing the averaging technique.

FIGURE 17-7   VARYING ELASTICITY DEMAND CURVE

A straight line demand curve has changing elasticity coefficients from the *y*-axis intercept to the *x*-axis intercept. At all prices above the unit elastic price (OP_1), demand is elastic. At all prices below the unit elastic price, demand is inelastic.

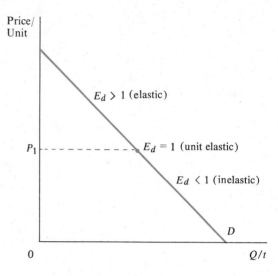

This example also clearly demonstrates that elasticity is an entirely different concept than the geometric concept of slope. The demand curve in Figure 17-6 has a constant slope, but the elasticity coefficients you calculated varied along the curve.

Elasticity and Substitutability

Price elasticity of demand depends, in large part, on the number of substitutes a product has. If a product, such as table salt, has relatively few substitutes, it will have a relatively inelastic demand. This is just another way of saying that the quantity demanded of a good like table salt isn't very responsive to changes in price over a wide range of prices. Because of this, the elasticity coefficients for general groups of commodities will be lower than for specific commodities. For example, the elasticity of salt in general will be lower than the elasticity of Morton salt.

A related point is that the longer the period of time consumers have to adjust, the more elastic the coefficient of price elasticity becomes. This is because there are more opportunities to modify behavior and substitute different products over a longer time period. A good example would be the price elasticity of demand for natural gas. In the short run it is likely very inelastic; but over time, as industry and homes convert to other sources of energy, the price elasticity will increase. To become familiar with the price elasticity of demand for a range of commodities, see Table 17-3, which lists some estimated elasticity coefficients.

TABLE 17-3 SELECTED ESTIMATED ELASTICITIES

	E_d
Fresh Tomatoes	4.60
Medical Care	3.60
Canned Tomatoes	2.50
Airline Travel	2.40
Radios and TV Receivers	1.25
Automobiles	0.80

Source: David R. Kamerschen and Lloyd M. Valentine, *Intermediate Microeconomic Theory* (2d ed.; Cincinnati: South-Western Publishing Co., 1981), Chapter 3, p. 58.

Price Elasticity of Demand and Total Revenue

When we are dealing with demand curves, we are dealing with price and quantity relationships. Quantity, or the number of items sold, multiplied by price, equals the *total revenue* generated. We can now use the principle of elasticity to establish a pricing technique and can examine the relationship of total revenue to price elasticity of demand. In order to grasp the relationship, consider a famous illustration in economics. The famous French mathematician and economist, Augustin Cournot, wondered what the owner of a mineral spring should charge for the spring's water, which was wanted for its healing powers. Cournot assumed that the spring cost nothing to operate, it produced an unlimited quantity of output, and the owner wanted to be as wealthy as possible under the principle of self-interest.

total revenue The quantity of a good or service that a firm sells multiplied by the price of a good or service.

To determine the correct price, we must first recognize that a price change has two (opposite) effects on total revenue. The first effect is that a price decrease will decrease total revenue. The other is that with a price decrease, quantity demanded increases, thus increasing total revenue. The net effect on total revenue depends on whether the relative price decrease exceeds the relative quantity demanded increase or vice versa. This is exactly what the price elasticity of demand coefficient tells us. Consider, for example, a situation where total revenue is given by

$$TR = OP_1 \times OQ_1.$$

In Figure 17-8, a decrease in price from OP_1 to OP_2 will decrease total revenue if the price elasticity of demand coefficient is inelastic. This results because the percentage increase in quantity demanded would be less than the percentage decrease in price.

To see the same principle in numerical form, consider Figure 17-6 and Table 17-2 once more. At a price of $2.00, the total revenue *(TR)* is $20.00. An increase in price from $2.00 to $2.20 causes *TR* to fall from $20.00 to $17.60. This is because the 10 percent increase in price caused an even greater percentage decrease in quantity demanded. The elasticity was greater than one. Conversely, if price rises from $1.00 to $1.20, *TR* increases from $20.00 to $21.60 because the

FIGURE 17-8 TOTAL REVENUE AND ELASTICITY

A price decrease in the elastic portion of a demand curve will increase total revenue. A price decrease in the inelastic portion of a demand curve will decrease total revenue.

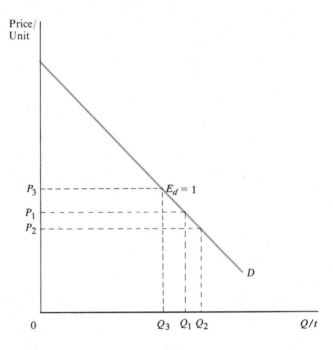

percentage increase in price is greater than the percentage decrease in quantity demanded. The elasticity is less than one.

To see the principle in a more general way, consider Figure 17-9. On both demand curves the price falls from OP_1 to OP_2 and output increases from OQ_1 to OQ_2. This change causes the total revenue to change. Some revenue is lost and some revenue is gained due to the price change. In Figure 17-9, the crosshatched area represents revenue that has been lost and the shaded area represents revenue that has been added. In the case of the relatively elastic curve, panel (b) of Figure 17-9, the decrease in price has brought about an increase in total revenue; in panel (a), the decrease in price has brought about a decrease in total revenue.

In other words, we can determine what will happen to total revenue when we change price if we know the elasticity coefficient. A reduction in price will always cause an increase in quantity demanded, but total revenue will decrease with inelastic demand and increase with elastic demand. Likewise, a rise in price will cause total revenue to fall with elastic demand and to rise with inelastic demand. These relationships are summarized in Table 17-4.

A good example of this principle occurred in the U.S. airline industry in the late 1970s. The airline industry, believing that the demand for air travel was inelastic, had historically been against lower fares and the deregulation of the industry that would produce lower fares. When deregulation was forced in the late 1970s, the revenues of the airline companies increased dramatically in the face of lower fares. The experience indicates that the demand for air travel is relatively elastic or at least much more elastic than the airlines had thought.

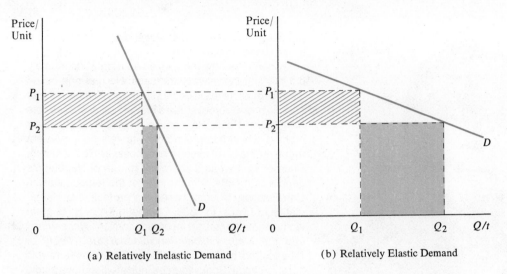

FIGURE 17-9   CHANGES IN TOTAL REVENUE
Equal price changes bring about different changes in total revenue, depending on the relative elasticities of the demand curves. If the curve is relatively inelastic, a decrease in price will bring about a decrease in total revenue; and if the curve is relatively elastic, this same decrease in price will bring about an increase in total revenue.

We can now answer Cournot's question. The owner of the mineral spring should not try to charge the highest possible price or sell the largest possible amount. The owner should set price where the elasticity coefficient is *unitary*. To see why, set price where the elasticity is, say, .5, or inelastic. If the owner raises price, quantity demanded will decrease, but by only one half the rate of the price increase, so *TR* will rise. On the other hand, if the $E_d = 2$, or is elastic, the owner should decrease price. If the price is lowered, the quantity demanded increases

TABLE 17-4   ELASTICITY AND TOTAL REVENUE

Price Change	Quantity Demanded Change	Elasticity	Total Revenue
Rise	Decrease	$E_d > 1$	Decrease
Rise	Decrease	$E_d = 1$	Unchanged
Rise	Decrease	$E_d < 1$	Increase
Fall	Increase	$E_d > 1$	Increase
Fall	Increase	$E_d = 1$	Unchanged
Fall	Increase	$E_d < 1$	Decrease

Antoine Augustin Cournot *(1801–1877)*

Antoine Augustin Cournot was one of the first economists to view economic theory as a set of tools that could be used to analyze economic and social problems. Cournot was one of the first to show that both supply and demand determine price, and that, in time, price influences both supply and demand. Cour-

not used simple two-dimensional diagrams to demonstrate these relationships.

Cournot is now recognized as a great economist, but this was not always the case. He had one of the great original minds in economic theory, but his life was a tragic one. Cournot studied mathematics at the École Normale in Paris. He had an insatiable appetite for reading, which he pursued despite very poor eyesight that eventually resulted in blindness. While a student, Cournot worked as a secretary to one of Napoleon's generals. In 1834, with the help of the famous statistician Poisson, Cournot became a professor of mathematics at Lyons. In 1838, Cournot published his great work in mathematical microeconomics, *Researches into the Mathematical Principles of the Theory of Wealth*. This book did not have much impact and was hardly noticed. Some sources indicate that not a single copy was sold! In later years, as his sight was failing, Cournot published less mathematical versions of his previous work, which were more widely read. When Cournot died in 1877, his highly original and innovative work in economic theory was largely unnoticed.

The irony of Cournot's life is that, although he was not well known during his own lifetime, his vision of economics as a set of highly mathematical tools that could be used to examine a large number of social problems is very close to the thinking of most present day economists. If Cournot were to return today, he would surely be surprised to see how his vision has come to be the practiced role of the economist.

---

at twice the rate of the price decline. The owner will maximize total revenue when $E_d = 1$, or is unitary elastic. So the mineral spring owner would set a price of OP_3 in Figure 17-8. At price OP_3, the area $OP_3 \times OQ_3$ represents maximum total revenue.

Price Elasticity of Demand and Public Policy

Using a hypothetical example based on some "reasonable" estimates of consumption, price, and price elasticities, we can see how useful a tool price elasticity of demand is to the economist who is a policy adviser. Suppose you are picked by the president to be an adviser to his "energy czar." On your first day on the job, the czar, after meeting with the president, tells you that as part of a new "Project Independence" gasoline consumption must be decreased by 3 billion gallons per year. You discuss the matter and decide against lowering the speed limit, patriotic appeals, or legislated rationing. You decide that the market should ration the quantity available and that the best solution is to raise price by putting an additional excise tax on gasoline. Your job then becomes one of determining what the appropriate tax should be.

You return to your office and check the latest figures on gasoline consumption, which you find to be 30.5 billion gallons per year. Next it is necessary to determine the price elasticity of demand for gasoline. Research into statistical work by economists tells you that the best estimates are that the long-run price elasticity of demand for gasoline in the United States is .45, with estimates for individual states ranging between .4 and .5. The short-run elasticity, in sharp contrast, is approximately .09, with estimates ranging between .07 and .11.[3] Remember that as the time under consideration is lengthened, elasticity increases. In this case the long-run elasticity is five times that of the short-run elasticity. Over a period of time people will buy more fuel-efficient cars, but they won't do it overnight. It will happen in the normal course of car replacement. Of course, a huge increase in price might speed up the replacement process.

It is now a simple matter to compute the tax necessary to have the desired effect on consumption. For simplicity, assume the current price is $1.00 per gallon. If the $E_d = .45$ and you wish to decrease consumption by 3 billion gallons in the long run, *ceteris paribus,* you need only to substitute into the formula to determine the tax.

$$E_d = \frac{\% \Delta QD}{\% \Delta P} = \frac{\dfrac{3 \text{ billion}}{30.5 \text{ billion}}}{\% \Delta P}$$

$$E_d = \frac{.098}{\% \Delta P}$$

$$.45 = \frac{.098}{\% \Delta P}$$

$$\% \Delta P = .218$$

Thus, in order to have the 9.8 percent decrease in quantity demanded, it is necessary to have a 21.8 percent increase in price. The required additional excise tax would, therefore, be 21.8 cents per gallon of gasoline ($1.00 $\times$ 21.8%), making the price of gasoline $1.22 per gallon.

In this hypothetical case, you have used a simple economic tool in the same way that economists giving policy advice would use it. Although it was hypothetical, the estimates were real and the exercise is similar to exercises performed many times by government economists during recent energy crises.

PRICE ELASTICITY OF SUPPLY

The equation for the *price elasticity of supply* is

$$E_s = \frac{\text{percentage change in quantity supplied}}{\text{percentage change in price}},$$

price elasticity of supply **A** *measure of the responsiveness of the quantity supplied to changes in price.*

---

[3]Data Resources, Inc. *A Study of the Quarterly Demand for Gasoline and Imports of Alternative Gasoline Taxes* (Lexington, Massachusetts; December, 1973).

which again reduces into the more workable formula of

$$E_s = \frac{\dfrac{\Delta QS}{QS}}{\dfrac{\Delta P}{P}} \,.$$

As with E_d, if $E_s = 1$, it is unit elastic. If $E_s > 1$, it is elastic; and if $E_s < 1$, it is inelastic. The analogy to price elasticity of demand stops there. A major difference is that the ***coefficient of the price elasticity of supply (E_s)*** is usually positive because we normally have positively sloped supply curves. Since the curves are positively sloped, the relationship between elasticity and total revenue that we established for price elasticity of demand doesn't hold; higher prices result in higher total revenue, regardless of whether supply is elastic or inelastic.

We can classify supply curves as perfectly inelastic, unit elastic, or perfectly elastic. The designations again measure the responsiveness of changes in quantity to changes in price.

Consider Figure 17-10. The quantity supplied is totally unresponsive to changes in price. It is perfectly inelastic. Examples of perfectly inelastic supply curves are infrequent, but in the very short run it is often impossible to produce more of a good regardless of what happens to price. This inability to produce more will, of course, affect the supply curve, which depicts the amount people are willing to supply at various prices. Consider the supply of Rembrandts, for example, or the supply of Rose Bowl tickets. A rise in the price of Rembrandts (even in the long run) or Rose Bowl tickets (in the short run) does not cause the supply of these items to increase. We usually represent these supply curves as being perfectly inelastic.

Figures 17-11 and 17-12 depict a perfectly elastic and unit elastic supply curve, respectively. Any straight line supply curve that is drawn through the

coefficient of the price elasticity of supply (E_s) The numerical measure of price elasticity of supply. The percentage change in quantity supplied divided by the percentage change in price.

FIGURE 17-10 PERFECTLY INELASTIC SUPPLY CURVE

A perfectly inelastic supply curve is a vertical line. It would exist if suppliers dumped a certain stock of a commodity on a market in such a way that changes in price would not affect the quantity supplied.

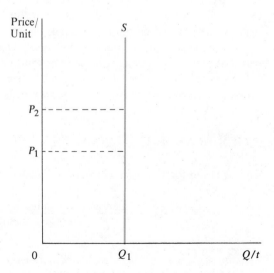

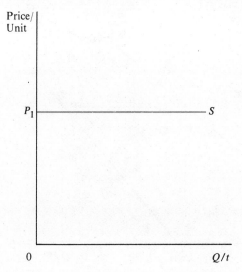

FIGURE 17-11   PERFECTLY ELASTIC SUPPLY CURVE

A perfectly elastic curve is a horizontal line. A change in price produces an infinite response in the quantity supplied.

origin, as in Figure 17-12, is unit elastic over its entire range. This is because the percentage changes of the two variables are always equal to each other. Throughout their range, other linear, or straight line, supply curves are elastic if they intersect the price axis and inelastic if they intersect the quantity axis, though elasticity changes along both curves. Two such curves are drawn in Figure 17-13.

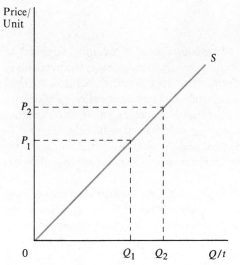

FIGURE 17-12   UNIT ELASTIC SUPPLY CURVE

A straight line supply curve drawn through the origin has a unitary coefficient of elasticity along the entire curve.

FIGURE 17-13 INELASTIC AND ELASTIC SUPPLY CURVES

A straight line supply curve that intersects the *y*-price axis will be elastic over its entire length, and a straight line supply curve that intersects the *x*-quantity axis will be inelastic over its entire length.

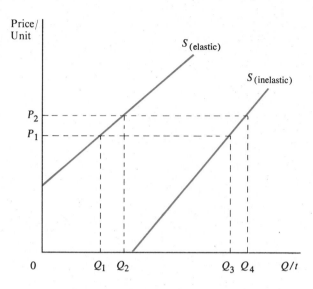

Price Elasticity of Supply and Cost

The elasticity of supply depends to a large degree on how the cost structure in the market for the good under consideration responds to changes in output. If costs rise rapidly as output is expanded, the quantity supplied will not be very responsive to changes in price; the curve will be inelastic. Alternatively, if costs don't increase very much as output is increased, the rise in price will increase the profits of supplying firms and the output response could be significant. This would be the case for an elastic curve. We will discuss this subject in detail.

Price Elasticity of Supply and Time

Elasticity of supply is the measure of responsiveness of quantity supplied to changes in price. The major factor affecting this responsiveness is the availability of inputs that can be attracted away from other uses. Another factor is the time period under consideration. As the time period increases, the possibility of obtaining new and different inputs to increase the supply increases. In our two examples of stock supply, Rembrandts and Rose Bowl tickets, you will recognize that in the long run the stadium could be expanded and the quantity of tickets increased; Rembrandts, however, have a perfectly inelastic supply because additional inputs don't exist.

These two factors—availability of inputs and time—affect elasticity of supply. We can predict that the elasticity of supply coefficient becomes larger as the time frame increases, and is larger for products that use relatively unspecialized or abundant inputs.

Price Elasticity of Supply and Public Policy

If we examine another hypothetical policy question, we can see how important and useful the elasticity of supply coefficient is. Suppose that you are hired as an adviser to the secretary of defense and you are instructed to determine how to make the volunteer army work better. You are told that the army is presently enlisting 57,500 volunteers per month, but 30 percent more are needed to keep the ranks at full strength. If you could calculate the elasticity of supply, it would be a simple matter to determine the pay increase necessary to reach full strength. Note that you don't even need to know what the present level of pay happens to be if you can calculate the elasticity.

During the early 1970s the military commissioned many elasticity studies. These studies agree on an $E_s = 1.25.$[4] Thus, working from $1.25 = \frac{.30}{\% \Delta P}$, you can now report to your boss that the army can meet its personnel requirements by raising pay levels by 24 percent $\left(24\% = \frac{.30}{1.25} \times 100 \right)$. But before you turn this figure into your boss you have some second thoughts. You know that elasticity of supply depends on the availability of inputs. In this case we are looking at the elasticity of supply of a factor and it depends on the availability of that factor. Not all potential volunteers are equally available; the more intelligent have more options in civilian jobs and colleges, and would probably be less responsive to the pay increase. This leads you to forecast that a simple pay increase for all potential enlistees might change the mental mix of enlistees and attract fewer intelligent ones. You gather more data and find that at present the army breaks its personnel into three groups—Mental Categories I and II, Mental Category III, and Mental Category IV, based on how high they score on the AFQT (Armed Forces Qualifying Test). The test is similar to an IQ test, with Categories I and II being the smartest. Assuming the present army has one third of its strength from each group, and speculating that the elasticity coefficients for the three groups are 0.5, 1.25, and 2.0, you now have some important policy information to report. If the pay raise of 24 percent that you calculated was to go into effect, the number of Mental Category IV enlistments —which have the highest elasticity because the volunteers have fewer options— would increase by 48 percent, while the number of Categories I and II enlistments would increase by only 12 percent. This would mean the ability (as measured by mental category) of the army would decrease substantially. To counteract this problem, you could suggest a differential pay increase. Assuming you want to keep enlistments by mental category at the present share, you could now calculate the needed increases. Mental Categories I and II would have to go up by 60 percent $\left(.5 = \frac{.30}{\% \Delta P} \right)$, Mental Category III pay would have to go up by 24 percent $\left(1.25 = \frac{.30}{\% \Delta P} \right)$, and Mental Category IV pay would only need to go up by 15 percent $\left(2 = \frac{.30}{\% \Delta P} \right)$. As you can see, imaginative application of this simple tool can have important implications for policy. This example,

---

[4]For one such study, see *Innovations for Achieving an All Volunteer Army.* General Electric TEMPO (January 3, 1972).

though hypothetical, is very similar to exercises that were actually performed in the early years of the volunteer army.

OTHER ELASTICITIES

As we saw at the beginning of this chapter, we could calculate the elasticity of almost anything because what an elasticity coefficient measures is the responsiveness of one measurable quantity to another. There are, however, two other elasticity coefficients which are quite common in economics.

income elasticity of demand A measure of the way in which quantity demanded responds to changes in income.

The first is the *income elasticity of demand.* This measures the responsiveness of changes in quantity demanded to changes in income, assuming all other things, including price, are held constant. The formula is expressed as

$$E_I = \frac{\text{percentage change in quantity demanded}}{\text{percentage change in income}}.$$

The sign of the coefficient is important when we calculate income elasticity. If the sign is negative, indicating an inverse relationship between income and demand, the good is an inferior good. If the sign is positive, the good is a normal good.

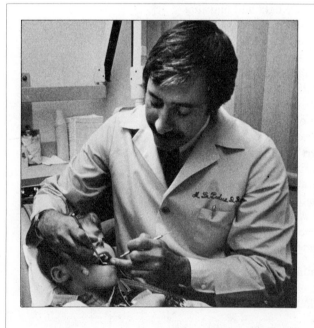

Income and the Price of a Straight Smile

Have you ever seen so many braces in your life? Depending on where you live, it may seem as if every other kid has braces. On top of it all, middle-aged men and women are wearing braces with increasing frequency. Can we explain this phenomenon in economic terms, or is it that we see more braces because society has finally realized the inherent worth of straight teeth?

Let's think back to our simple supply and demand models and the *ceteris paribus* factors that affect demand and supply. We saw earlier that tastes are important. Thus, tastes can be a partial explanation. What else? How about income? If a good is a normal good, demand for it will increase as income increases. If it is income elastic, changes in income will have a significant impact on demand.

Let's use some casual empiricism. Who gets braces? Middle and upper-middle income kids (and their parents). We now have an explanation; we may even call it a simple predictive model. We see more braces these days because the demand for straight teeth is very income elastic and incomes have increased significantly in the last decade.

Some testable hypotheses now emerge from our model. We would expect to find that the higher the income level, the higher the incidence of braces. What do you think would happen to an orthodontist's income during a recession? Would it be more variable than, say, a general practitioner's income?

For normal goods we use the same designations for the elasticity coefficient that we used before. If the coefficient is greater than one, $E_I > 1$, we say the good is income elastic. If $E_I < 1$, we say the good is income inelastic. Goods that have high and positive income elasticities are usually thought to be luxury goods. Indeed, you might use the concept of income elasticity of demand as a definition of what a luxury good is. Necessities, such as salt, would have an inelastic income elasticity coefficient. Luxuries, such as diamonds, would have an elastic income elasticity coefficient.

The other elasticity concept we make use of is *cross elasticity of demand*. It measures the responsiveness of changes in quantity demanded for one product to changes in the price of another product. It assumes the goods are related; they are either complements or substitutes. Two goods that are completely unrelated (independent of one another) would have a zero cross elasticity of demand. The formula can be stated as

cross elasticity of demand   A measure of the responsiveness of changes in the quantity demanded of one product to changes in the price of another product.

$$E_{x,y} = \frac{\text{percentage change in quantity demanded of good } x}{\text{percentage change in price of good } y}.$$

If the sign of $E_{x,y}$ is negative, we know the relationship is an inverse one and that an increase in the price of good y will bring about a decrease in the quantity demanded of good x. A negative cross elasticity coefficient would thus indicate that good x and good y are complements. A positive coefficient would indicate a substitute relationship between good x and good y, because an increase in the price of good y will lead to an increase in the quantity demanded of good x. The size of the coefficient tells us how strong the complementary or substitute relationship is between the two goods.

SUMMARY

1. Elasticity is the measure of the sensitivity or responsiveness of quantity demanded or quantity supplied to changes in price (and to changes in the other *ceteris paribus* factors).

2. Linear demand curves, except for those that are perfectly vertical or horizontal, have points on them that range from elastic to inelastic and one point that is unit elastic.

3. Price elasticity of demand is a measure of substitutability. The more substitutes an item has, the more elastic demand will be. This simply means that consumers have more options and, as a result, respond more readily to changes in price.

4. As time increases, elasticity of demand increases because individuals have more opportunity to substitute other goods.

5. Total revenue is dependent on elasticity because a demand curve is a price-quantity line. When price changes, the quantity demanded changes and this changes total revenue. The amount of the change in total revenue will depend on the responsiveness of consumers to changes in price, and this is precisely what elasticity measures.

6. Price elasticity of supply is a measure of the responsiveness of changes in quantity supplied to changes in price.

7. As time increases, the elasticity of supply increases, because the longer the time period, the more chance there is for adjustments to take place.

8. Income elasticity measures the responsiveness of changes in quantity demanded to changes in income.

9. Cross elasticity of demand measures the responsiveness of changes in the quantity demanded of one good to changes in the price of other goods.

NEW TERMS

elasticity
dependent variable
independent variable
price elasticity of demand
coefficient of price elasticity of demand (E_d)
perfectly inelastic
perfectly elastic
unit elastic

arc elasticity
point elasticity
total revenue
price elasticity of supply
coefficient of price elasticity of supply (E_s)
income elasticity of demand
cross elasticity of demand

QUESTIONS FOR DISCUSSION

1. If the government wants to place a tax on a certain commodity for the purpose of generating revenue, should it look for goods that have relatively inelastic or relatively elastic demand curves?

2. Suppose that in your city the manager of the transit authority increases the bus fares and subsequently finds that revenues decline. The bus line is losing money and the manager calls for still higher fares to break even. Can you suggest any other solution?

3. To demonstrate the importance of calculating average price changes and quantity changes when determining elasticity, use the correct formula for calculating a change in price from $2.20 to $2.40 in Table 17-2, then calculate it again as a price increase from $2.20 and as a price decrease from $2.40, without using the averaging formula. Explain the difference in your answers.

4. Would the elasticity of demand for Miller High Life be higher or lower than the elasticity of demand for beer? Why?

5. Why is public policy that is aimed at decreasing the importation of oil frustrated by the fact that demand for gasoline is income elastic and price inelastic?

SUGGESTIONS FOR FURTHER READING

Ferguson, C. E., and S. Charles Maurice. *Economic Analysis.* Homewood, Ill.: Richard D. Irwin, Inc., 1978, Chapter 2.
Kamerschen, David R. and Lloyd M. Valentine. *Intermediate Microeconomic Theory,* 2d ed. Cincinnati: South-Western Publishing Co., 1981, Chapter 3.

CHAPTER 18

The Basic Micro Tools: Some Applications

Learning Objectives

After studying the materials found in this chapter, you should be able to do the following:

1. Calculate the expected cost of a crime given:
   (a) probability of arrest and conviction.
   (b) penalty.

2. Diagram the economic effects of an excise tax to determine the incidence of the tax.

3. Define:
   (a) price ceiling.
   (b) price floor.
   (c) shortage.
   (d) surplus.
   (e) black market.

4. Diagram the economic effects of:
   (a) rent control.
   (b) minimum wages.
   (c) target prices in agriculture.
   (d) natural gas price regulation.

5. List the economic aspects of the health care crisis.

In this chapter we make use of the basic microeconomic models and theories that we developed in previous chapters. These simple tools of economics can yield profound insights into diverse social issues. You will see in this chapter that you are now equipped with tools of analysis that can help you understand diverse issues such as crime, taxation, rent control, minimum wages, the energy crisis, and the farm problem.

THE ECONOMICS OF CRIME: USE OF THE SELF-INTEREST HYPOTHESIS

We can use one of our assumptions, the self-interest hypothesis, to analyze crime problems and prevention. Let's assume that the criminal is a rational person who commits a crime when it is in the criminal's self-interest to do so. A criminal calculates the costs and benefits of each crime and commits those crimes where the benefits exceed the costs. In other words, crime is an economic activity.

We have generated the simple hypothesis that a criminal calculates costs *(C)* and benefits *(B)* of criminal activities and commits those crimes where $B > C$. Crime is an economic activity and the criminal behaves like any other entrepreneur.

If we go deeper into the cost and benefit calculation, we can analyze the situation in more detail. The benefits are what the criminal hopes to realize by the activity. We want to place a value on this. In crimes involving the theft of property, this is relatively easy. The anticipated benefit is the anticipated market value of the take. For other crimes such as murder, illegal parking, or littering, we have to impute some value to the activity.

The cost is the penalty *(P)* adjusted for the probability (π) that the criminal will be caught and the penalty will be imposed. So we need to compare B to $P \cdot \pi$. In other words, if the fine for littering is $500, but on the average one will be caught and fined for littering only once every 500 times, the expected cost of littering is $1 (=$500 \times 1/500$). The economic model we have just developed thus tells us that if some people get more than $1 worth of benefit from littering, they will litter.

The Economics of Robbery

Our model can now be applied to crimes more serious than littering. If we want to do something about the amount of armed robbery that is taking place in our society, we can analyze this crime and its prevention in terms of our model. There are three elements to our model. It says that crime depends on the benefits from the activity so, *ceteris paribus,* as the take goes up, so will the amount of robbery. Second, it says that as the penalty goes down (with no change in the probability of being caught), criminal activity will go up. Third, it says that if the probability of being caught goes down, *ceteris paribus,* the amount of robbery will go up.

We can now advise policymakers. If we want to decrease the amount of armed robbery, we can do any or some combination of all three things. We could decrease the potential take, or profit. This is difficult to do, but you probably have noticed that most late-night gas stations advertise that they don't keep much cash on hand. We could also increase the penalty. We could say that if a person is caught robbing a gas station and using a gun during the robbery, the criminal will have the hand that is holding the gun cut off. Now increasing the penalty is sometimes difficult because society deems some penalties too severe. In some countries, the hands of robbers are cut off, but in the United States penalties for robbery usually are limited to prison sentences. Recently, in one suburb outside Washington, D.C., the local police chief announced that squad cars would be equipped with rifles with exploding shells (outlawed by the United Nations as being too inhumane for warfare), and that officers had been instructed to shoot first and ask questions later when investigating robberies. Almost immediately the robbery rate fell in this jurisdiction and increased in adjacent jurisdictions. The reason is predicted by our model which says as the potential penalty rises, criminal activity will fall. Of course, we might object to this policy even if it does reduce crime. But economic models are positive, telling us only what the consequences of such a policy will be. They don't say if it's good or bad in a moral sense. The third option which could reduce the robbery rate would be to increase the probability of arrest and conviction of would-be robbers. This might be accomplished by more police, speedier justice, television cameras in banks, or other similar measures.

The Economics of the Death Penalty

The preceding analysis has probably led you to the conclusion that economists would argue that the death penalty deters crime. Indeed, a University of Buffalo economist, Isaac Ehrlich, has statistically argued that the death penalty does act to reduce the amount of murder.[1] If you are a doubter, answer this question: Would you ever litter if the probability of getting caught was one in five hundred and the penalty was death? You would have to place a high value on being able to litter, or a low value on your own life, if you answered in the affirmative. However, some people argue that murderers have such a distorted view of reality that they underestimate the probability of being caught, convicted, and sentenced to death. These people argue that the death penalty provides little deterrence. More importantly, just because positive economic theory says the death penalty provides deterrence does not mean that you, or anyone else, has to accept it on moral, or normative, grounds.

The Economics of Illegal Parking

There probably are some of you who are still skeptical about our simple model of crime, so let's analyze a criminal activity that you have probably committed or at least contemplated committing—illegal parking on campus. On almost all college campuses, parking is in short supply and as a result there are benefits to parking in an illegal parking space. Let's suppose that the fine for illegal parking is $2.00, and you find from experience that you get a ticket one out of every four times you park illegally. The expected cost of the crime is thus $.50 ($2.00 × .25). Now it would be almost impossible to estimate the benefits that accrue to those who illegally park, but since there are many violators, we know that benefits are substantial. Assume you are appointed to a committee formed by the university's president to solve the parking problem. You have three options: You could lower the benefits by buying shuttlebuses to transport students from their parking areas to the classroom buildings; you could increase the likelihood of being caught by hiring more police and increasing the number of times they check the parking areas; or you could raise the cost of the crime. A common way to do this is to tow away illegally parked cars. This raises the cost of the crime significantly, because violators now have to pay towing fees in addition to the basic fine. This includes a great deal of time and trouble.

If you still don't believe the model, here is an empirical test you can carry out. Observe the amount of illegal parking on a nice sunny day. Then, the next time it rains, observe the criminal activity again. What does the model predict? On rainy days the benefits of the crime go up, *ceteris paribus*, because the benefit is the proximity to class plus arriving in class dry. The probability of being caught

[1]Again, this does not mean that you should necessarily support the death penalty. You can still be opposed to the death penalty on humanitarian grounds even though you accept the implications of the model. For the study, see I. Ehrlich, "The Deterrent Effect of Capital Punishment: A Question of Life and Death," *American Economic Review* (June, 1975).

also goes down, *ceteris paribus,* because campus police don't like to get wet either. Our model thus predicts that there will be more illegal parking on rainy days. Check it out—test the model!

WHO PAYS WHAT TAX: AN EXERCISE IN SUPPLY AND DEMAND

excise tax   A tax that is placed on the sale of a particular item, such as liquor, cigarettes, or electricity.

An *excise tax* is a tax that is placed on the consumption of a particular item, such as liquor, cigarettes, or electricity. Excise taxes can be specific, being placed on one particular item, such as cigarettes, or they can be general, being placed on a broad class of goods, such as food. It is even possible to view the income tax as an excise tax on labor. We can look at excise taxes, then, as we try to understand who actually pays an imposed tax.

If you listen to the rhetoric of the debates over taxation, you know it is quite confusing. Consumers often are convinced that they ultimately pay all taxes, yet business often fights hard to prevent tax increases on their products. If consumers pay all taxes, why should business care if it is taxed or not? The answer is not simple. The correct answer to the question of who ultimately pays what tax is, it depends. It depends on the supply and demand conditions in the relevant markets.

Let's examine a case in which we have normally sloped supply and demand curves, as in Figure 18-1, which illustrates the market for beer. Assume we have a market and the market settles at a price of $1.50 per six-pack, with X_e six-packs per week representing the equilibrium quantity. Now suppose the government places a tax of $.50 per six-pack on beer and collects this tax from producers. This means that the supply curve will shift up by the amount of the tax. The costs of production for the beer producer have been increased $.50 per six-pack. One way to view the tax is that the producer must pay $.50 per six-pack for the permission to produce beer. In terms of Figure 18-1, the supply curve shifts up at all points by $.50. The post-tax supply curve is S_t. Price will rise to $1.75 per six-pack and the new equilibrium quantity is X_t. But note that this new price is less than the old price plus the tax. If the entire tax had been shifted forward to consumers, the consumer would now pay the old price of $1.50 plus the tax of $.50, or $2.00 per six-pack. It is also clear that the amount of money the producer actually keeps has fallen. Before the tax, the producer kept $1.50 per six-pack, but now the producer keeps $1.25 per six-pack [$1.75 (price) minus the $.50 tax]. The tax caused prices to rise, which meant the quantity demanded fell. The beer producers must sell the lower quantity at a lower received price than before. In this example, then, part of the tax was paid by consumers and part was paid by producers. Each paid half of the excise tax.

The amount of the tax that each pays depends on the supply and demand elasticities for the goods being taxed. To see this more clearly, examine the four panels in Figure 18-2. Using Figure 18-2, we can easily see how the elasticity of supply and the elasticity of demand affect the *tax incidence.* Tax incidence is the economist's phrase for who really pays the tax.

tax incidence   The place where the burden of any tax actually rests; those who pay the tax after all shifting has occurred.

In panel (a) of Figure 18-2, we have a normally sloped supply curve and a perfectly inelastic demand curve. When the excise tax is placed on the good, the supply curve shifts to S_t. The result is that price rises from OP_e to OP_t. Price

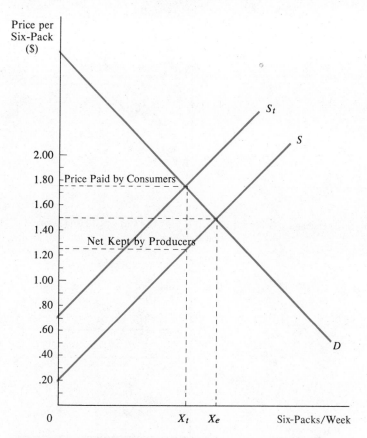

FIGURE 18-1 AN EXCISE TAX ON BEER

A per unit tax on a commodity causes the supply curve to shift up by
the amount of the tax. Less of the commodity is purchased at a higher
price. Part of the tax is borne by consumers and part of the tax is borne
by producers.

has risen by the full amount of the tax and the equilibrium quantity is unchanged.
In this case, the incidence of the excise tax falls fully on the consumers of this
good. The tax has been shifted forward to consumers by the full amount of the
tax.

In panel (b) of Figure 18-2, we have a normally sloped supply curve and a
perfectly elastic demand curve. The post-tax supply curve is S_t. After the tax is
imposed, price is unchanged at OP_e and equilibrium quantity falls to OQ_t. Since
the price to consumers is unchanged, the producer is paying the entire tax. The
incidence of the tax falls fully on the suppliers of this good.

The principle involved in panel (a) and panel (b) is clear: The more inelastic
the demand for a good, the more any excise tax placed on the good will fall on
consumers of that good. Secondly, the more elastic the demand curve, the more
any excise tax placed on the good will fall on the producers of that good.

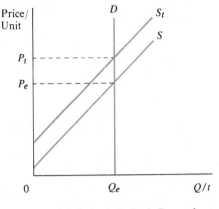

(a) Perfectly Inelastic Demand

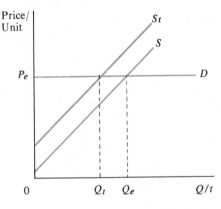

(b) Perfectly Elastic Demand

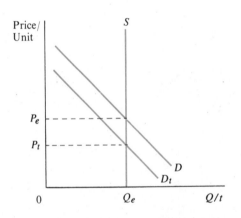

(c) Perfectly Inelastic Supply

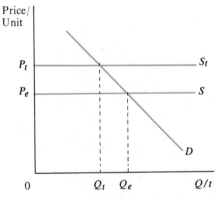

(d) Perfectly Elastic Supply

FIGURE 18-2   ELASTICITY AND TAX INCIDENCE
Tax incidence, or who pays the tax, can be easily determined in the case of perfectly elastic or perfectly inelastic demand and supply curves. With perfectly inelastic demand [panel (a)], the consumer pays the entire tax. With perfectly elastic demand [panel (b)], the producer pays the entire tax. With perfectly inelastic supply [panel (c)], the supplier pays the entire tax. With perfectly elastic supply [panel (d)], the consumer pays the entire tax.

Now examine the supply curves in panels (c) and (d) of Figure 18-2. In panel (c) we have a perfectly inelastic supply curve. Consequently, it is necessary to alter the geometric presentation slightly. The usual way to represent a tax increase on a graph is by a parallel increase in the supply schedule. We can also represent a tax increase by a parallel decrease in the demand schedule. In the case of perfectly inelastic supply, we must use the alternative of shifting the demand schedule, because it is impossible to shift the supply schedule.

In this case the tax cannot affect that given quantity. We view the demand curve as the curve the industry faces with the amount of the tax netted out. The equilibrium quantity is unchanged after the shift and the price the firm receives falls from OP_e to OP_t. In other words, the entire amount of the tax has been paid by the suppliers of the good. In panel (d) we have a perfectly elastic supply curve. An excise tax shifts the supply curve to account for the higher price at each output. After the shift, the price of the item has increased from OP_e to OP_t, the exact amount of the tax. In this case, consumers are paying the entire tax. Of course, less is being sold so some producers may be worse off, but consumers are paying more for OQ_t, and this increased amount is exactly equal to the amount of the tax.

This exercise in shifting supply and demand curves demonstrates some general principles of excise tax incidence:

1. The more inelastic the demand, the more price rises, meaning that the tax falls more heavily on consumers.

2. The more elastic the demand, the less price rises, indicating that the tax falls more heavily on producers.

3. The more inelastic the supply, the more the tax is paid by producers.

4. The more elastic the supply, the more price rises, and more of the tax is paid by consumers.

The answer to the question of who pays the excise tax should now be clear. The answer again is, it depends. It depends on the relative elasticities of supply and demand for the good on which the tax is placed.

INTERVENTION IN MARKETS

In Chapter 3, we saw how free markets reach equilibrium. It is possible for this market process to be interfered with, and this interference is sometimes the result of governmental action. *Price ceilings* result when the government establishes a price as a limit and will not allow the market price to rise above the limit. *Price floors* are prices below which the authority will not permit the market price to fall. Price ceilings and price floors cause disruptions in the market clearing process, and our economic tools allow us to see the effects of these disruptions.

price ceilings Prices imposed by a governmental unit that are set as a limit. The ceiling is a price that cannot be exceeded.

price floors Prices established as minimum prices. A governmental unit sets a price which cannot be undercut.

Price Ceilings

A price ceiling that is set below the equilibrium price prohibits the market from clearing. The amount that consumers wish to purchase at the imposed ceiling is greater than the amount suppliers are willing to supply at this price. Figure 18-3 demonstrates this. In Figure 18-3, the equilibrium price is OP_e and the equilibrium quantity is OQ_e. The government imposes a price ceiling of OP_c. The amount that consumers wish to consume at price OP_c is OQ_d, and the amount the suppliers are willing to supply at the ceiling is OQ_s. The result is a *shortage*. It is important to realize that the shortage is created by the ceiling. Without the ceiling, price would rise, the quantity demanded would decrease, and the quantity supplied would increase until price reached OP_e and the market cleared. If the ceiling is to be maintained, government must replace the market with some other way to allocate the goods. Consumers are frustrated as they try to obtain the good

shortage The amount that consumers wish to purchase at some price exceeds the amount suppliers wish to supply. A shortage can only occur on a lasting basis when a price ceiling is in effect.

FIGURE 18-3   PRICE CEILING

A price ceiling that is set below the market clearing price
creates a shortage. At the price imposed by the government,
potential purchasers demand a larger quantity of the good than
suppliers are willing to sell.

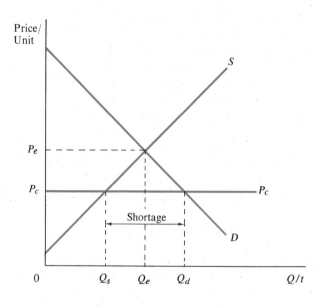

or service at the lower price, and some institution other than the market must
be imposed to determine who will get the good or service.

In almost all cases where price ceilings are imposed, ***black markets*** spring up.
Black markets are markets in which people buy and sell the goods or services that
are controlled by price ceilings at prices above the imposed price ceiling.[2] We'll
have more to say about black markets a little later.

*black markets   Markets in
which people buy and sell goods
or services at prices above
imposed price ceilings.*

Rent Control.   Price ceilings are used by various levels of government. Later in
this chapter we will discuss how price ceilings have created the natural gas crisis
which we have today. Consider now the effect of price ceilings on apartment
rentals.

Many cities, including New York City and Washington, D.C., have imposed
price ceilings on apartment rents. This usually is referred to as ***rent control.*** At
first glance, the goals of rent control are admirable; i.e., to keep rents low so that
everyone, including the poor, can find a place to live at a reasonable price. For
the effect of rent control, refer again to Figure 18-3. At a price less than the
market clearing price, there will be a shortage of rental units. More people will
be looking for rental units than the number available. Something other than the
market mechanism will now allocate the rental units. The landlord can now
impose criteria on who the tenants will be because for any vacancy, the landlord
has a number of people waiting in line to rent the apartment. The landlord can
now inexpensively discriminate in a choice of tenant because it is now costless
to discriminate. Without rent control, the landlord is more likely to rent to any
prospective tenant rather than leave the apartment vacant because the market is
clearing. With rent control the landlord can choose from the backlog of prospec-

*rent control   Price ceilings that
are imposed by governmental
units on apartment rentals.*

[2]You should be able to show why a price ceiling that is imposed *above* the equilibrium price has no
effect on the market.

Price Ceilings and Queues

Markets ration goods and services. To intervene in markets with ceilings or floors, the government must ration the goods in shortage or purchase the goods in excess.

Nowhere is this more visibly demonstrated than in planned economies. The pictures coming out of Poland before and immediately after the imposition of martial law graphically illustrate the effect of market intervention.

Newspapers reported that the lines to get meat in August, 1981, were as long as 8 hours' waiting time. This effectively excludes those who work as they cannot stand in line that long.

Prices are set by the state and markets are not allowed to clear. As a result, black markets spring up and barter takes place. Cigarettes become a surrogate currency. People get their ration of cigarettes so if they don't smoke, they can trade the cigarettes for something they do want. The *Wall Street Journal* (October 23, 1981, p.1) reports a conversation with Miss Dzoitek, a hospital switchboard operator who does not smoke or drink. She does get a quota of cigarettes and points out, "Tobacco and alcohol are the best currencies nowadays. Money no longer matters."

tive tenants. The landlord can exclude those who are young (or old), or those who have children (or dogs). The point is that the interference in the market has replaced the nondiscrimination of the market mechanism.

Black Markets. As mentioned earlier, black markets tend to develop when price ceilings are imposed. Let's say the market in Figure 18-4 represents the market for tickets to one of the biggest college football games of the year, the Rose Bowl. The stock of tickets is perfectly inelastic in the short run at the 70,000 seating capacity of the stadium. The university is selling the tickets at a price ceiling of $15 per ticket. For this game, the market clearing price would be $30, so the $15 imposed price has created a shortage of 30,000 tickets. This means that there is going to be a larger quantity of tickets demanded than there are tickets. The university has to allocate these tickets by some other means than the market, so it discriminates; it sells tickets to those fans who are willing to wait in line the longest or those who donate to the booster club. The shortage of tickets will produce a black market. Some of those who are able to get the tickets for $15 will be willing to sell them. These people will engage in black market activity by selling them to those who are willing to pay more. In the black market for tickets to such events, these black marketeers are referred to as scalpers. Scalping generally has a bad connotation. But consider: the scalper is performing the service of

FIGURE 18-4   THE ROSE BOWL

A price ceiling is often imposed by universities in selling tickets to popular events. Such a price ceiling, if it is below the market clearing price, creates a black market for the underpriced tickets.

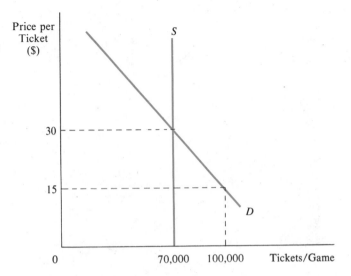

transferring tickets from people who value other goods more highly than they value the tickets to individuals who value the tickets more highly than other goods. Thus, the scalper is being paid for performing this service.

Why Ceilings? If price ceilings are so disruptive, why do we have them? One answer is that not all people are hurt by ceilings. Those who are able to purchase the good or service at the artificially low price are better off and they, as a result, approve of the ceiling. In the apartment example, if you already have an apartment and you don't want to move, you would be better off with rent control. You would probably vote for rent control because it would make you better off. In the ticket example, if you don't mind waiting in line, or if you will get a ticket because you are a booster, you would like low ticket prices. It is important to realize, though, that price ceilings do not, as is often claimed, generally help the poor. If there is one ticket left at $15 for the big game, who do you think will get it? A poor fan who likes football more than anything else that the $15 would buy, or the governor who thinks it would be good politics to be seen at the game? When the market is replaced, another mechanism must be substituted to allocate goods. This mechanism usually depends heavily on power and influence, and thus the poor, who lack power and influence, are not generally helped by the ceiling.

Price Floors

A price floor that is set above the equilibrium price prohibits the market from clearing. The amount that suppliers offer for sale at the imposed floor is greater than the amount consumers wish to purchase at this price. Figure 18-5 demonstrates this case. In Figure 18-5 the equilibrium price is OP_e and the equilibrium

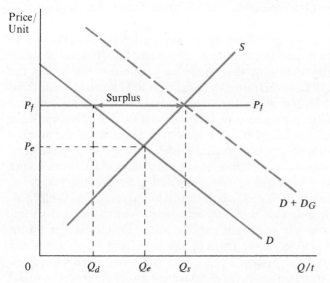

FIGURE 18-5   PRICE FLOOR
If the government imposes a price above the market clearing price, a surplus will be created. At the higher than equilibrium price, suppliers will desire to sell more units than consumers will be willing to purchase.

quantity is OQ_e. The government imposes a price floor of OP_f, with the result that the quantity supplied at price OP_f is OQ_s, and the quantity consumers demand is OQ_d. The result is a **surplus** equal to $OQ_s - OQ_d$. This surplus is created by the price floor. If the floor didn't exist, price would fall and the quantity demanded would increase while the quantity supplied would decrease until the market cleared.

It can be difficult for the governmental unit that imposes a price floor to maintain the floor. Some suppliers will attempt to cut prices in order to sell the desired quantity. The most effective way for the government to prevent this price cutting is to purchase the unwanted quantity supplied. By purchasing the surplus, the government in effect is shifting the demand curve outward to create a new equilibrium at the desired price. In Figure 18-5, the dashed demand curve represents the previous demand curve plus the added governmental demand. Such a shift would allow the price to remain at OP_f. The best example of price floors that worked in this way were the price supports for grain during the 1960s. The government wanted to maintain a price that was above the market clearing price. To maintain this price floor, it was necessary for the Department of Agriculture to purchase the grain; the effect of this was to shift the demand curve to the right so the higher price could be maintained.

surplus   The amount that suppliers wish to supply at some price exceeds the amount that consumers wish to purchase. A surplus can only occur on a lasting basis when a price floor is in effect.

The Minimum Wage

The **minimum wage** is a price floor in the labor market. In terms of Figure 18-5, a minimum wage of OP_f that is set above the market wage (OP_e) causes a surplus of labor ($OQ_s - OQ_d$). In terms of our analysis, if the minimum wage is set above the market clearing wage rate, the amount of labor that laborers will supply at

minimum wage   A price floor imposed by a governmental unit in labor markets.

that wage will be greater than the amount of labor that firms will wish to employ, resulting in unemployment.

Economists generally agree that minimum wage legislation causes unemployment to be higher than it would be otherwise. This is particularly true for young people, where the market clearing wage might be significantly lower than the minimum wage. In 1978 Congress raised the wage floor to $2.65 an hour, up from the $2.30 an hour which was set in 1974. In addition, a formula was adopted which insured automatic increases up to $3.35 an hour in 1981. This was done despite the fact that teenage unemployment was almost 18 percent at the time the bill was passed and despite strong statistical evidence from a large number of economists that the increase would raise youth unemployment to even higher levels. Professor Robert Goldfarb of George Washington University and Dr. Edward Gramlich, then of the Brookings Institution, reviewed, in two independent publications, eight empirical studies by economists. The studies overwhelmingly agreed that increases in minimum wages would cause increases in unemployment. The studies differed, however, as to how significant the impact would be. They predicted that the 15 percent increase in the minimum wage, which took place in 1978, would increase teenage unemployment anywhere from 3.4 to 5.3 percentage points.[3]

If there is so much agreement among economists about the deleterious effects of minimum wages, why are they enacted? The reason is very similar to the one for enacting price ceilings. Not all people are hurt by the wage floor. Some workers receive pay increases when the legislation is enacted. Those who are laid off or are unable to find employment at the new minimum wage usually don't understand why they can't find employment. The result is that it is politically popular among some groups, particularly organized labor, to support minimum wage legislation. Remember, economics only tells us that minimum wage legislation causes decreased employment. It does not tell us that minimum wage legislation is a good or bad thing. We may decide that it is better to have fewer people employed at a higher wage rate than to have everyone who wants to work employed at a lower, market clearing wage rate.

THE CONTINUING SAGA OF NATURAL GAS REGULATION

In 1978 President Carter held a fireside chat to talk to the American public about the energy crisis. He declared that the energy crisis was the moral equivalent of war. President Carter ultimately ordered a deregulation of natural gas coupled with a windfall gains tax on large oil companies. President Reagan continued the phased deregulation and eliminated the windfall gains tax in his 1981 tax reform. We can, using the tools developed in previous chapters, analyze many aspects of the energy crisis. As an example, we will examine the natural gas shortage.

---

[3]See Edward M. Gramlich, "Impact of Minimum Wages on Other Wages, Employment and Family Incomes," *Brookings Papers on Economic Activity,* No. 2 (1976), pp. 409–451; and Robert Goldfarb, "The Policy Content of Quantitative Minimum Wage Research," Industrial Relations Research Association Proceedings, December, 1974, pp. 261–268.

The Creation of a Crisis: Regulation of Natural Gas

In 1938 Congress passed the Natural Gas Act, and in 1954 the Supreme Court placed all firms selling interstate natural gas under the regulation of the *Federal Power Commission (FPC)*.[4] The law was intended to keep prices "just and reasonable" for consumers by allowing suppliers only a "fair" rate of return. After the 1954 Supreme Court ruling, the FPC attempted to regulate the price received by each individual producer engaged in the interstate sale of natural gas. The system broke down in 1960 when a giant backlog of hearings developed in response to the attempted regulation of more than 4,000 firms. A former Harvard Law School dean has called this "the outstanding example in the federal government of the breakdown of the administrative process."[5] In response to this administrative breakdown, the FPC ruled in 1965 (affirmed by the Supreme Court in 1968) that it would set prices separately for each geographical area and each individual petroleum commodity. This decision took eight years to be enacted, and during this entire period prices were kept at 1960 levels. This individual commodity approach to pricing is next to impossible to implement because natural gas is jointly produced with crude oil. The FPC method requires that certain costs be allocated to the production of natural gas even though it is produced in a joint process. Recognizing the administrative history and difficulty of these controls, let us determine what the effects of regulation were.

Paul W. MacAvoy, a professor of economics at M.I.T. and a member of President Ford's Council of Economic Advisers, has extensively examined the natural gas industry. In a series of books and articles in professional journals, he has simulated the market for natural gas to determine the effects of regulation. He has concluded that regulation has held prices below free-market levels. Between 1964 and 1967, prices would have been about twice as high without regulation. The result of these artificially depressed prices is that 40 percent fewer new reserves were added to production than would have been added in the free-market context. The result of these lower reserves is painfully obvious. In the absence of the price-rationing function of the market system, there is a shortage. Existing supplies must then be rationed and consumers (including industry) must substitute more expensive alternative fuels for the cheaper natural gas that is not available. The curious result is that the government, in order to keep the price of natural gas low, produced a shortage that required consumers to buy even more expensive gasified coal, imported liquid natural gas, or some other alternative fuel.

We can see this graphically in Figure 18-6. Assume the price originally set by the FPC was near or at equilibrium. This produced a price represented by P_{1960} and an equilibrium quantity of Q_{1960}. The 1960 decision to set prices on a geographical area basis resulted in a price ceiling that was not changed for eight

Federal Power Commission (FPC)   An independent agency that controls hydroelectric projects and regulates the interstate sale of electricity and natural gas.

---

[4]The brief discussion that follows does not do justice to the complexity of natural gas regulation. The interested reader should see Edward J. Mitchell, *U.S. Energy Policy: A Primer* (Washington: American Enterprise Institute for Public Policy Research, June, 1974). Mitchell's study cites much of the relevant literature on natural gas regulation. See Mitchell for references to the data and the other studies mentioned.

[5]Quoted in Edward J. Mitchell, *U.S. Energy Policy: A Primer* (Washington: American Enterprise Institute for Public Policy Research, June, 1974), p. 7.

FIGURE 18-6   THE MARKET FOR NATURAL GAS

In 1960, the price, P_{1960}, was an equilibrium price. The amount consumers *wished* to purchase was exactly equal to the amount suppliers *wished* to sell. A shortage is created if the price is frozen at P_{1960} and demand increases to D_{1968} or D_{1981}. Allowing the price to rise reduces the shortage, but some shortage remains as long as the price is controlled at a level below equilibrium.

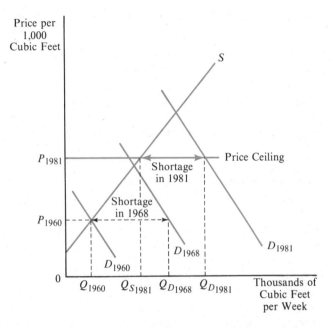

years while the case was in litigation. During this period there were tremendous changes in the *ceteris paribus* demand conditions. For one, income increased substantially during this period. The demand for natural gas is very income elastic. Thus, by 1968 the demand curve had shifted to the curve represented by D_{1968}. We now have a shortage. At P_{1960} the quantity supplied is Q_{1960} and the quantity demanded is Q_{D1968}. We had 40 percent less production than we would have had in a free market. In 1981 the problem was still present. Demand had increased to D_{1981}. To be sure, the FPC allowed the price to rise to P_{1981}, but the price rise lagged behind the demand increase. So in 1981 we still had a government-created shortage, because at P_{1981} the quantity supplied is Q_{S1981} and the quantity demanded is Q_{D1981}.

It is important to realize that the shortage was caused by the price ceiling. Natural gas is scarce, but scarcity and shortage are different concepts. Scarcity simply means that the item is not as plentiful as we would like; with scarcity, rising prices insure equilibrium. Shortage means that at the prevailing price, the quantity demanded exceeds the quantity supplied. This distinction is important because much of the talk about an energy crisis confuses these two concepts.

Predictions of doom for the users of energy are not new. As early as the beginning of the nineteenth century some commentators were predicting our first energy crisis. In the early 1800s houses were lit by oil-burning lamps. Demand for these lamps was increasing rapidly because of income and population growth. The lamps were fueled by oil from sperm whales. Many people predicted that the whale population would soon be depleted and, therefore, houses would be dark. In other words, they were predicting greater scarcity of this particular product. What happened? Prices rose rapidly, from about 40 cents per gallon to about $2.50 per gallon in 30 years. These higher prices caused the quantity demanded to decrease, as substitutes for the whale oil were sought. The important point is that a shortage did not occur because prices rose in the face of greater scarcity. Shortages can only occur with artificially imposed low prices. It is particularly disturbing that the shortages of natural gas occurred in a market where there was a potentially large and relatively elastic supply.

The Dilemma of Earlier Regulation

Perhaps even more disturbing is that, even after it is generally recognized that government regulation is creating havoc in important markets, it is politically very difficult to remove the controls. This is understandable if we examine the behavior the controls bring about. Those individuals who are lucky enough, or have enough political power, purchase the natural gas at below market prices. When Congress becomes convinced that the crisis may be the result of regulation, it is politically very unpopular to change the law. This is easy to understand. In 1977 the regulated price of natural gas was $1.34 per thousand cubic feet. At that time it was estimated that markets would have cleared at $3.00 per thousand cubic feet. But markets change, demand has continued to grow, and energy supplies have been disrupted. A recent report by the Energy Action Educational Foundation calculates that price will average $7.25 per thousand cubic feet in 1984. The dilemma is clear: being an advocate of deregulation makes it appear to consumers as if the deregulator, not market forces, produced the sharp rise in fuel bills, and voters might turn against a member of Congress who votes to deregulate. It is important to realize that if Congress had not interfered with the market mechanism in the first place, voters would probably not hold Congress responsible for subsequent higher gas prices after deregulation.

It was a major goal of the Carter administration to lift the price ceiling in 1978–1979, and the necessary legislation was approved by Congress in the fall of 1978. The Carter deregulation, which was a hard fought legislative battle, immediately raised prices 25 percent and allowed for a 10 percent increase per year until 1985, when all ceilings on newly found natural gas would be removed. There is, however, disagreement over what impact the bill will have on natural gas consumption. The White House hailed the bill as a major energy victory. Critics disagree, saying that the bill is vague and complex and that it will be too hard to administer. Reagan, who has been an advocate of deregulation, does not plan to interfere with the scheduled deregulation.

This brief review of natural gas regulation was not meant as a lesson of one industry, but as an illustration of the effect that regulation and political interference can have on market forces. Similar regulation can be found throughout the U.S. economy. One need only scan the headlines for this month's crisis; be it the meat shortage, the cement shortage, or the capital shortage. The distortion is very likely caused by well-intentioned interference with market forces.

THE HEALTH CARE INDUSTRY

The rapidly rising price of health care is receiving considerable attention from journalists and politicians these days. In large part, this increased interest is a natural outgrowth of the fact that health care has become one of the fastest growing industries in the United States. Between 1950 and 1980, total expenditures on health care increased from $11 billion annually to more than $200 billion annually, and they are expected to more than double again between 1980 and 1985. In 1950 these expenditures represented 4.5 percent of total national income. They are expected to represent more than 10 percent of national income by 1984. Let's look at the potential problems of the health care industry using the basic economic tools we have developed.

We can see what is happening in the health care industry by examining Figure 18-7. The market in 1950 is represented by supply curve S_{1950} and demand curve D_{1950}. Equilibrium is OP_1 and OQ_1. Between 1950 and 1980 there were substantial changes in the *ceteris paribus* conditions in the health care market. On the supply side, hospitals and doctors have greatly increased the sophistication of the care they supply. There has been a virtual explosion in the industries that make diagnostic, surgical, and therapeutic equipment. This equipment is very expensive and increases the cost of supplying health care (even if it does mean improved health care). The effect of all this improved, expensive care has been to shift the supply curve from S_{1950} to S_{1980} in Figure 18-7.

On the demand side, the changes have been equally significant. First and foremost, the income of U.S. citizens has risen significantly over this period. Assuming health care is a normal good and that the demand for it is income elastic, increased income will increase the demand for health care, and the more income elastic this demand, the more significant will be the increase in demand. Second, the very success of medical health care delivery creates more demand for health care in the future. This is because older people demand more health care than younger people. As the health care of the population improves, the population lives longer. More health care is then demanded because the population is now older. For example, one of the reasons we have more people demanding

FIGURE 18-7   THE MARKET FOR HEALTH CARE

The health care market can be characterized by decreasing supply due to increasing costs and increasing demand due to rising incomes and the continued aging of our society. As a result, the equilibrium price of health care has been rising rapidly.

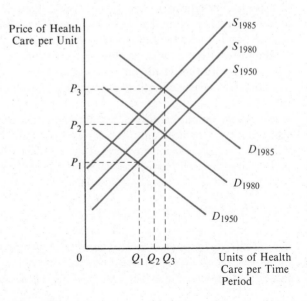

health care related to the heart is because we have an older population. Twenty years ago many of these people would have died of measles, polio, or tuberculosis before they would have been old enough to develop heart problems. In any event, the demand for health care has increased significantly. This increase is represented by the shift from D_{1950} to D_{1980} in Figure 18-7. The result of these changes in supply and demand has been for price to rise to OP_2 and a new level of consumption to be established at OQ_2.

The Coming Crisis in Health Care

What about the future? Let's speculate as to what might happen, using our basic tools. It is likely that the supply curve will continue to shift leftward, representing an increase in the price of the factors of production used to produce health care. It is also likely that demand will continue to increase as incomes rise and the population ages. We would predict, then, that in response to a shift in demand from D_{1980} to D_{1985}, and a shift in supply from S_{1980} to S_{1985}, there will be an increase in price to OP_2 and an increase in the equilibrium quantity to OQ_2. But this supposes that the government does not intervene in this market. A quick review of congressional interest in the health care industry would be enough to convince you that this is not a realistic assumption. As it stands now, the most likely governmental solution to the rapidly rising prices is twofold. Currently, the most popular solution is some form of national health insurance. Senator Edward Kennedy has made national health insurance a major political issue. The economic effects of such a program are easy to predict. Since national health insurance would lower the effective price of health care and make health care affordable to more citizens, it would increase the demand curve even beyond the one represented by D_{1985}. This would put even greater upward pressure on prices. While a national health insurance program is seen as an antidote to rising costs, there is also increasing pressure to intervene in the market with price controls. Congress is beginning to talk about the "immorality" of the high price of health care. Wage and price controls have been suggested as a solution. The effect can be predicted by examining Figure 18-7. At a ceiling price of OP_2, demand, coupled with rising costs, causes supply to decrease even more. The effect would be a shortage. The severity of the shortage would depend upon the magnitude of the increase in demand and decrease in supply. We would have the same type of crisis we discussed earlier when examining the natural gas market. An interesting point is that just at the time Congress has demonstrated that it is beginning to understand how controls implemented in the 1950s helped create the energy crisis, it is flirting with similar controls for the health care industry.

A Liberal's Dilemma?

Does this discussion and an understanding of these basic economic tools mean that we can't support a national health program that would insure health care to all citizens? Not at all! All that economics tells us is that such a program would increase demand and put upward pressure on prices of health care. We may well decide that this upward pressure on prices is worthwhile and that we want such a program. The point of economics is to tell us that these pressures are there, that we can't ignore them, and that to resort to controls will probably create a crisis.

THE FARM PROBLEM

We hear and often read in the news about the demise of the family farm and the crisis in agricultural markets. In some areas of the country, traditionally conservative farmers have even borrowed the tactics of the protest movements in efforts to draw political attention to their economic problems. The farm problem and agricultural economics present some very complicated problems, but our basic tools can provide many insights into what the situation is and how the problem came about.

In the short run the problem is simple enough to understand. First, agricultural production takes place in a very competitive market which closely resembles the basic supply and demand model we developed in Chapter 3. Second, the demand for the products produced in this market tends to be price inelastic. Third, weather plays a significant role in determining the size of any particular crop. These things taken together mean that the revenue a farmer receives in any one year can be highly variable. The irony for farmers is that in good harvest years they may be in worse shape than in poor harvest years. This can be seen by examining Figure 18-8. Let's say that in the previous year farm output sold at a price of OP_1, so OQ_1 units were sold with farmers receiving a total revenue of $OP_1 \cdot OQ_1$. The next year is very good and the crop is bountiful, so the supply curve shifts to S_2. Price falls to OP_2 and consumers purchase OQ_2 units. Since demand is so inelastic, farmers are now making less revenue than they did the year before ($OP_1 \cdot OQ_1 > OP_2 \cdot OQ_2$); the large fall in price brought only a small increase in sales. An individual farmer can do nothing about the fact that the bountiful harvest caused prices to fall.

Good Weather and Bumper Crops Mean Higher Taxes

It doesn't seem to make much sense, but good weather and big crops do not necessarily mean that farmers are better off. Since the demand for food is relatively price inelastic, a bumper crop means significantly lower prices and lower incomes for some farmers. The government then gets into the act with support prices and parity payments.

We have been hearing a great deal about trimming the budget. However, in 1982 Congress wasn't too hard on farmers. The dairy lobby was beaten back a little: support prices were pegged at 70 percent of parity, down from 80 percent. Thus, in 1983 farmers will only get $1 billion from taxpayers instead of $2 billion. Restrictions on peanut growing were also abolished, but the price supports were raised.

Good weather may mean good crops and lower prices for consumers. But if you're a taxpayer that isn't necessarily good. The 1983 farm subsidy bill comes in at about $2 billion . It doesn't seem to make sense, unless you're a senator from a farm state.

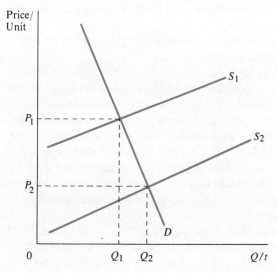

FIGURE 18-8 THE MARKET FOR FARM OUTPUT

The market for farm output is characterized by erratic supply and inelastic demand. This means that the total revenue a farmer receives in any one year can be highly variable.

The Long-Run Problem

The long-run problem for the farmer is caused by the fact that there have been huge increases in farm productivity in the United States in the last century. It takes fewer and fewer farmers to supply the food we need. In the early 1800s, more than half the U.S. labor force was engaged in farming, but now less than 5 percent of the work force is engaged in agriculture. A surplus of farmers manifests itself in insufficient income to service the huge capital investment it takes to run a farm. As a result, we witness the curious phenomenon that while farmers don't have adequate income, they are quite wealthy because the value of their land and buildings is very high. Farmers who enjoy their life-style are, of course, against future reductions in the agricultural labor force. Many of the political arguments to save the family farm are arguments to stop this trend toward fewer and fewer agricultural workers. If farmers have political power, and some would argue that they have disproportionate political power because reapportionment of political districts lags population shifts, we would expect a governmental response to their calls for action. One such governmental response has been the agricultural support program.

The Political Response

Prior to 1973, the **agricultural support program** consisted of attempts to decrease supply or increase demand. Price floors were enacted to create parity. *Parity* prices are an attempt to define fair prices; that is, prices that are necessary to establish the purchasing power of the farmer at some past level which is selected as the proper level. Farmers like to view 1910–1914 as a "golden age" and often think parity should be established with this period. The idea is to link farm prices

agricultural support program The political response to the pressure to increase farm incomes. Most programs in agricultural support are aimed at decreasing supply or increasing demand for raw agricultural production.

parity   Parity prices are an attempt to define fair prices—those which establish agricultural purchasing power at some past level. The period of 1910–1914 is usually viewed as the golden age of agriculture and parity is often linked to this period.

to an index of the purchasing power of farmers as it was in the period selected as the appropriate one, such as 1910–1914. Parity is an argument for higher relative prices in the agricultural sector. In practice, parity creates price floors, which are prices above equilibrium levels.

We saw the effect of price floors in Figure 18-5. The quantity supplied exceeds the quantity demanded at the imposed price and a surplus develops. If the government is to maintain this price floor, it must act as the buyer of last resort. The government must purchase the surplus. After the government purchases the surplus, it has a dilemma. It can't sell the product on domestic markets or the price will fall back to the equilibrium price. In the 1950s and early 1960s, the government reacted to this dilemma by building storage bins and storing the farm product. At the high point of this storage activity, which occurred in 1961, the government had 1.3 billion bushels of wheat and 1.7 billion bushels of corn in storage.

There are some other things that could be done. The government could destroy the surplus grain, but this will upset those who consider it wasteful.[6] The government could give the produce away, perhaps to poor countries, but this might upset other countries who are trying to sell to these poor countries. The government could sell the grain to other countries if customers could be found. Still another alternative would be to hold on to the surplus for future emergency needs. It is, however, absolutely necessary for the government to buy the surplus it has created.

Managing Production

As early as the mid-1950s, the U.S. government decided that the purchase and storage of the surplus was too costly and that managing production was a better alternative. The idea is that the government can maintain the price floor by keeping the quantity supplied at lower levels than would exist without government intervention. In this case, the government is trying to shift the supply curve to maintain the higher price.

soil bank program   A program which attempts to raise farm income by paying farmers who allow their land to lay idle.

acreage allotment   A farm program that sets a limit on the total number of acres that can be placed in production.

marketing quota system   A farm program which specifies how much output a farmer can bring to market.

The first such attempt to manage production was known as the *soil bank program.* In the soil bank program, which was started by President Eisenhower, farmers were paid to let their land lay idle. This would thus reduce the supply.[7] A second attempt was an *acreage allotment.* An acreage allotment sets a limit on the number of acres that can be put into production. The government then must determine who gets what acreage allotment. In producing tobacco, for example, the decision is based on historical levels of production. If your parents were tobacco producers and you bought or inherited their farm, you would get an allotment equal to their share of past production. Still another way to decrease supply is a *marketing quota system.* A marketing quota system simply specifies how much a farmer can bring to market.

---

[6]The Canadian government once destroyed 28 million eggs. See Patrick Howe, "Unscrambling the Egg Market: A Lesson in Economics," *Common Sense Economics,* Vol. 2, No. 2 (Spring, 1977), pp. 42–47.
[7]Predictably, farmers took their least productive land out of production and the supply didn't change very much.

All these attempts to manage farm production have had profound effects on farmers. In the case of the soil bank, the farmer was paid out of general tax revenues not to produce on the least productive land. In the acreage allotment method, farmers have had an incentive to cultivate the allowed acres very intensively in an effort to produce larger crops on fewer acres. In the marketing quota system, the farmer cannot benefit by increasing productivity and output since the allowed output is specified by the government.

The Political Response Since 1973

Since 1973 and the period when Earl Butz was President Nixon's secretary of agriculture, the system of agricultural support has changed. We no longer have price floors or *support prices,* which had been the term for floors in the pre-1973 period. Instead, we now have *target prices.* Target prices are prices the government considers to be fair for farmers. The market is allowed to clear and the equilibrium price is compared to the target price. The government then pays each farmer the difference between the target price and the market clearing price. In the Carter administration, this governmental transfer grew to a large amount of money. For example, the 1978 price of winter wheat in the Texas panhandle was as low as $1.92 per bushel. This was compared to a 1977 average price of $3.00 per bushel and an average of $5.00 to $6.00 per bushel in 1971–1972. The target price in May, 1978, was raised to $3.40 per bushel. It was estimated by the government that the differential between the market clearing price of $1.92 per bushel and the target price of $3.40 per bushel cost taxpayers $4.4 billion in 1978. The Reagan administration made an attempt to curtail these programs. The first attempt in early 1981 was successful and kept a scheduled rise in milk price supports from going into effect. It did not do away with supports, but did prevent an increase at that time. Other congressional battles loom on the horizon. Senator Jesse Helms of North Carolina has been a leader in dismantling welfare programs such as food stamps. As a result, many northern members of Congress want to retaliate by evaluating price supports and acreage allotments in tobacco.

Currently, the Reagan administration has yet to turn its attention to the myriad of transfer programs that are available to farmers. These programs range from federal money for building farm ponds to state subsidized soil testing and extension services. If a reduction in governmental regulation starts to affect agriculture, the results will be interesting.

support prices Price floors in agriculture that were used before 1973.

target prices Prices that the government determines are fair to farmers. After the market clearing price is determined, the government pays each farmer the difference between the target price and the market price.

Solutions?

Like the other social problems discussed in this chapter, the tools of economics cannot solve the farm problem, but can point out some fundamental truths. The fundamental truths are that there are too many resources in the agricultural industry and these resources are kept there by transfers from general tax revenues. Taxpayers' income is being redistributed to farmers and this keeps resources in the farm industry that would otherwise be attracted to other industries. The basic tools of economics cannot tell us if this is good or bad, nor can they predict if anything will be done to change the situation. The answer to the first question is a value judgment concerning whether you think it is good or bad to maintain the present level of resources in agriculture. The answer to the second question will in part depend on the political strength of farmers and the farm constituency.

SUMMARY

1. This chapter used the basic tools developed in the previous chapters to demonstrate how useful economics is in analyzing a wide range of social policy questions.

2. Crime is an economic activity and can be analyzed as a rational decision of the criminal. To decrease criminal activity, one need only decrease the benefits the criminal receives or increase the costs the criminal must pay. This holds for the entire range of crime, from illegal parking to armed robbery or murder.

3. The concepts of supply, demand, and elasticity can be used to determine tax incidence. The more inelastic the demand for a product and the more elastic the supply, the greater the amount of the tax paid by the consumer. Conversely, the greater the elasticity of demand for a product and the more inelastic the supply, the more the tax is paid by producers. In other words, relative elasticities determine tax incidence.

4. Price ceilings are attempts to keep prices from rising to their equilibrium level. Price ceilings cause shortages, and black markets often de- velop in response to the shortage. Rent con- trol is an example of a price ceiling.

5. Price floors are attempts to keep market prices from declining below a certain level. Price floors cause surpluses that must be absorbed to prevent the price from falling. Agricultural support prices and minimum wages are exam- ples of price floors.

6. The energy crisis as it pertains to natural gas is a good example of how price ceilings disrupt markets. The lesson is that price ceilings are very difficult to remove even after the damage they cause is well understood. This type of intervention seems likely in the health care in- dustry.

7. The farm problem has in part been caused by the supply and demand characteristics of the industry and in part by the rapid productivity gains in agricultural production. The govern- ment has been active in agricultural markets for a long time and the effects of this activity can be examined by using the concepts of sup- ply and demand.

NEW TERMS

excise tax
tax incidence
price ceilings
price floors
shortage
black markets
rent control
surplus
minimum wage

Federal Power Commission (FPC)
agricultural support program
parity
soil bank program
acreage allotment
marketing quota system
support prices
target prices

QUESTIONS FOR DISCUSSION

1. Why does a price ceiling that is set above the equilibrium price have no effect on the market?

2. Can you think of other areas where models like the simple economic model of crime might be formulated? What about the economics of the deci- sion to have children? the economics of marriage and/or divorce?

3. How is the minimum wage maintained at higher than market clearing rates? Why don't the

unemployed workers agree to work for lower wages and thereby circumvent the imposed price floor?

4. If you were the taxing authority, would you place an excise tax on items with elastic or inelastic demand? Why?

5. Should the government stay out of the farm sector? What would be the consequences for farmers of no government intervention? for consumers?

6. Do you favor price controls on rentals (rent control)? Explain your position.

SUGGESTIONS FOR FURTHER READING

Fellner, William, (ed.). *Contemporary Economic Problems: 1978.* Washington: American Enterprise Institute for Public Policy Research, 1978.

Hailstones, Thomas J., and Frank V. Mastrianna. *Contemporary Economic Problems and Issues,* 6h ed. Cincinnati: South-Western Publishing Co., 1982.

LaForce, J. Clayburn. *The Energy Crises: The Moral Equivalent of Bamboozle.* Los Angeles: International Institute for Economic Research, 1978.

Leftwich, Richard H., and Ansel M. Sharp. *Economics of Social Issues,* 3d ed. Dallas: Business Publications, Inc., 1978, Chapter 2.

McKenzie, Richard B., and Gordon Tullock. *The New World of Economics,* revised ed. Homewood, Ill.: Richard D. Irwin, 1978.

North, Douglass C., and Roger LeRoy Miller. *The Economics of Public Issues,* 4h ed. New York: Harper & Row, Publishers, Inc., 1978.

CHAPTER 19

The Utility Approach to Consumer Behavior

Learning Objectives

After studying the materials found in this chapter, you should be able to do the following:

1. Define utility.

2. Given marginal utility, calculate total utility and derive a marginal utility curve from a total utility curve.

3. Use the equation for maximizing total utility to determine an individual's consumption pattern.

4. Derive an individual demand curve for a good based on:
   (a) the equation for maximizing total utility.
   (b) the principle of diminishing marginal utility.

5. Solve the diamond-water paradox based on:
   (a) marginal utility and total utility.
   (b) value in exchange and value in use.

6. Discuss the theory of progressive income taxation based on:
   (a) the marginal utility of income.
   (b) interpersonal utility comparisons.

We have spent a considerable amount of time using demand curves to develop predictions concerning the outcome of market processes. Most of our analysis makes use of market demand curves, which we derive by aggregating individual demand curves. Since these individual demand curves form the bedrock of the analysis, we need to consider the factors that underlie the individual consumer's demand curve.

The first approach economists took to examine consumer demand—the classical approach—involved the concept of measurable utility. We will use this approach to examine some problems and suggest some applications. The second approach to consumer demand—indifference curve analysis—will be discussed in the next chapter.

DEMAND AND UTILITY

It is important that economists be able to derive an individual's demand curve for a commodity. The demand curves of all individuals can then be aggregated to form the market demand curve for the commodity.

Why does a person demand a certain good or service? An obvious answer is that the good or service is expected to satisfy some need or desire of the consumer. Economists are content with this superficial answer. Psychologists, however, want to probe much more deeply into the question. They want to distinguish between wants and needs. Psychologists are also interested in the qualities or intensities of the needs being satisfied.

There may be moral, or ethical, dimensions to the desires people have. Why do people want to buy guns? pornography? narcotics? sports cars? liquor? cigarettes? These are questions to which psychologists, moralists, and many others devote a great deal of attention. But economists generally are not interested in why desires exist or why people should buy some goods and not others. It is not because they think such questions are unimportant. Indeed, such questions may be more important than the questions economists try to answer, such as, What would happen to the sales of Porsches if their price increased by $1,000? or, What would happen to the sales of potatoes if the price of wheat went up $1 per bushel? Economists accept the fact that people have a certain psychological or ethical makeup and, without approving or disapproving of it, the analysis starts from there.

UTILITY

In the early development of the discipline of economics, the major issue was determining the value of goods and services. Some believed that value depended on the scarcity of the commodity or the difficulty of producing it. Others looked for some intrinsic or inherent value attached to the consumption of the commodity. It wasn't until the beginning of this century that the great British economist, Alfred Marshall, spelled out the importance of both ideas. One point of view involved supply; the other, demand. In a famous analogy, Marshall said that you could no more say whether supply or demand determined value than you could say which blade of a pair of scissors did the cutting. Thus, value, or price, is determined by the interaction of supply and demand.

Let's consider the influence of demand on value first, and leave supply for later chapters. Demand theorists used the notion of *utility.* The ordinary meaning and dictionary definitions of utility always include something about usefulness, but this meaning is much more restricted than the one used in economics. In economics, if an individual wants a commodity, then that commodity has utility. The good or service has whatever qualities are inherent to it, and, given those qualities, the individual decides how much utility it has. Thus, the same commodity may have a great deal of utility for one person, and none or very little for some other person. Like beauty, utility is in the eye (or mind) of the beholder.

utility   The satisfaction that an individual receives from consuming a good or service.

Utility is strictly an *ex ante* concept; that is, utility measures the way an individual feels about a commodity *before* the individual buys or consumes it. You may see a cake in a bakery window and have great desire for it—that's utility. If you buy and eat the cake, you may get sick and receive no satisfaction from its consumption—that's irrelevant economically. Utility is the satisfaction you *expect* to get, not what you actually get. The reason for this distinction is that we use utility in the development of the demand curve, and the demand curve shows the amounts that people will buy based on anticipated satisfaction, not the amounts that they would have bought after having made the purchase.

ex ante   A Latin phrase meaning "before the event."

util An arbitrary unit used to measure utility.

utility function A preference function ordering a consumer's desire to consume differing amounts of goods.

A good unit for the measurement of utility, like pounds or gallons or miles, does not exist, but since utility is unique to the individual, an arbitrary unit called the *util* can be employed. As long as no attempt is made to compare the number of utils of different people, this is a satisfactory measuring device. For example, suppose you try to construct your *utility function* for some commodity, say, a particular brand of beer. First, choose a convenient time period, say, a day for this example. Then, for one unit (one can) of beer per day assign a number of utils, say, 20. (You can choose any number at all: 1; 1,000; 1/10; 47½.) Ask yourself, if I get 20 utils from one can, how many would I get if I consumed two cans of beer per day rather than just one? Suppose, after much reflection, you say, 38. Ask yourself the same question about three cans of beer per day, four, five, six, and so on.

An economist would expect you to establish a schedule something like that shown in Table 19-1. The important characteristic of the schedule is that, while the total utility becomes larger the more you consume per day (up to a point), the additions to total utility from each additional unit consumed become smaller. This feature—the fact that additional, or marginal, utility declines as consumption increases—is called *diminishing marginal utility*.

diminishing marginal utility The fact that marginal utility declines as consumption increases. Less satisfaction is obtained per additional unit as more units are consumed.

Marginal utility is the amount of utility that an additional unit of consumption adds to total utility. The formula for determining marginal utility *(MU)* is

$$MU = \frac{\text{change in total utility}}{\text{change in quantity consumed}}.$$

marginal utility The amount of utility added by an additional unit of consumption.

Marginal utility is thus the change (increase or decrease) in total utility that is brought about by consuming one more unit or one less unit of the good. In Table 19-1, the marginal utility is determined by calculating how much each additional can of beer adds to total utility. For example, the first can of beer adds 20 utils to total utility. The fourth can of beer adds 13 utils to total utility. This is found by subtracting the total utility of consuming three beers from the total utility of consuming four beers (67 − 54 = 13).

TABLE 19-1   UTILITY SCHEDULE FOR BEER

Cans of Beer per Day	Total Utility	Marginal Utility
0	0	
1	20	20
2	38	18
3	54	16
4	67	13
5	77	10
6	84	7
7	88	4
8	89	1
9	87	−2
10	82	−5

Principle of Diminishing Marginal Utility

The principle of diminishing marginal utility holds that for a given time period, the greater the level of consumption of a particular commodity, the lower the marginal utility. In other words, as you consume more units of a commodity, the additional units yield less of an addition to total utility than the preceding units did. For instance, the seventh beer is expected to provide less additional pleasure than the sixth beer. This principle is reflected in Table 19-1 and Figure 19-1. In

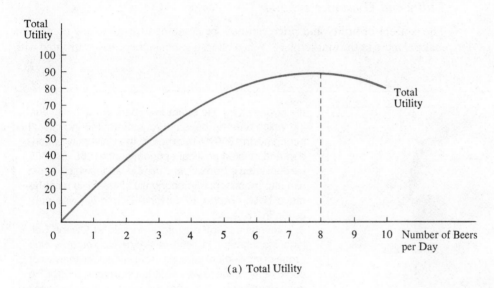

(a) Total Utility

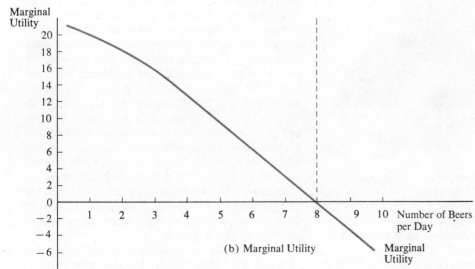

(b) Marginal Utility

FIGURE 19-1 TOTAL AND MARGINAL UTILITY

Total utility increases as consumption increases to a certain level, in this case 8 beers per day, and then it declines. When total utility is increasing, marginal utility is declining, illustrating the principle of diminishing marginal utility. At the point that total utility begins to decline, marginal utility becomes negative.

Table 19-1, marginal utility falls from 20 utils for the first beer to 18 utils for the second beer. The seventh beer only adds four utils to total utility.

Figure 19-1, panel (b), shows the marginal utility curve that corresponds to the total utility curve in panel (a). Note that when the total utility curve reaches its maximum, marginal utility is zero. This makes sense because if total utility is to decline, marginal utility must become negative. In Table 19-1, total utility reaches a maximum at eight, because the ninth beer has a negative marginal utility. And, the only way a total can decline is for additions to that total to be negative.

Utility and Consumer Behavior

The concept of utility and price can now be combined to show how consumers make choices in the marketplace. When choosing, consumers are confronted with

William Stanley Jevons *(1835–1882)*

William Stanley Jevons had one of the great original minds in the history of economic thought. Jevons combined utility theory with marginal analysis and applied it to consumer choice. He thus constructed the theory that underlies the theory of demand, much as we have done in this chapter.

Jevons led a strange life. He was both an esoteric intellectual and a practical economist. He was born in Liverpool and studied chemistry and mathematics at University College, London. Financial problems caused him to move to Australia to accept a job with the Sydney Mint. He spent five years in Australia, during which time he became very interested in political economy. In 1859 he returned to the University of London and studied political economy until 1865. In 1865 he published a book, *The Coal Question,* which thrust him into prominence in economic circles. His most famous book, *Theory of Political Economy,* was published in 1871.

Jevons accepted a professorship at Owens College, Manchester, in 1866, where he worked on a wide range of intellectual pursuits, from statistical analysis of commodity prices to very abstract economic theory. He even developed a sun spot theory to explain business cycles. His work generated a great deal of interest in political circles, but Jevons himself had little impact on economic policy or economic thought. This was largely because of his personal habits. He was, perhaps, the original "strange professor." He once wrote to his sister that he had never attended a party "without impressing upon all friends the fact that it is no use inviting me." He didn't regret this solitude; in fact, he argued that reserve and loneliness are necessary to develop ideas. He felt that social intercourse insured that thoughts would "never rise above the ordinary level of the others." A colleague of Jevons wrote: "There never was a worse lecturer, the men would not go to his classes, he worked in flashes and could not finish anything thoroughly, the only point about Jevons was that he was a genius."

Unfortunately for economics, Jevons died at the early age of 47. He drowned while at a health resort in the south of England. At the time of his death, Jevons was working on a massive book entitled *Principles of Economics.* The book, of course, was never completed.

a range of items and also a range of prices. You may not choose the item which has the greatest utility, because price and your income are also important factors. In other words, consumers don't always buy their first choice. Such behavior is commonplace. You may prefer a Porsche to a Chevette, but you may purchase the Chevette. This is rational behavior, and we can see why by looking at price and utility.

Suppose, for example, you are considering purchasing a six-pack of beer. You are presented with three possibilities listed in Table 19-2. Heineken is your first

TABLE 19-2   UTILITY PER DOLLAR COMPARISONS

	Marginal Utility (Utils)	Price	MU per Dollar
Heineken	30.0	$3.00	10
Miller	27.0	2.25	12
Pabst	20.0	2.00	10

choice because it yields the most utility. But the relevant question is not which beer has the most utility, but which has the most utility *per dollar*. Therefore, you choose to buy a six-pack of Miller. This choice implies that the extra satisfaction of Heineken over Miller is not worth $.75, but the extra satisfaction of Miller over Pabst is worth the extra $.25 it costs. Thus, in deciding how to spend your money, you look at marginal utility per dollar rather than marginal utility alone. You do this because money is the common denominator. Dollars can be used to buy any available good. So for the last dollar you spend, you want to choose the item with the highest utility per dollar; and in so doing, you economize by getting the most satisfaction per dollar. There are other things you can do with your money, and you are saying in this example that $.75 spent on something other than Heineken will yield more utils than the Heineken will, but that $.25 spent on other goods will not yield more utils than spending it on Miller.

Maximizing Total Utility

The self-interest hypothesis lets us assume that individuals will act to maximize their total utility. To see how marginal utility and price influence how a consumer maximizes total utility, let's look at a market with only two goods, Coke and pizza, where a unit of Coke costs $.50 and a unit of pizza costs $1. The utility schedules for the two goods are presented in Table 19-3. The consumer has a given amount of income, called a *budget constraint*. For this example, let's endow our consumer with $13 worth of purchasing power, and see how that income will be allocated between the two goods, so as to achieve maximum utility.

The first purchase will be pizza, because pizza yields 32 utils of satisfaction compared with 29 utils for a dollar's worth of Coke. The next purchase also will be pizza, because it yields 31 utils, which is still greater than Coke, the alternative purchase. In other words, the consumer buys two pizzas before buying any Coke. The third purchase is Coke, because the 29 utils of satisfaction gained from purchasing two Cokes are greater than the 28 utils that are yielded by a third

budget constraint   A given level of income that limits the amount of goods that may be purchased by an individual.

TABLE 19-3   UTILITY SCHEDULE

Coke				Pizza			
Quantity per Week (Cans)	MU (Utils)	MU/P (P = $.50)	TU (Utils)	Quantity per Week (Small Pizzas)	MU (Utils)	MU/P (P = $1.00)	TU (Utils)
1	15	30	15	1	32	32	32
2	14	28	29	2	31	31	63
3	13	26	42	3	28	28	91
4	12	24	54	4	24¾	24¾	115¾
5	11	22	65	5	20¼	20¼	136
6	10¾	21½	75¾	6	18	18	154
7	10¼	20½	86	7	17	17	171
8	10	20	96	8	16	16	187
9	9	18	105	9	14	14	201
10	8	16	113	10	12	12	213
11	7	14	120	11	11	11	224
12	6½	13	126½	12	9	9	233

pizza. The process continues until the income of $13 is spent. In maximizing total utility, the consumer will spend $5 on ten cans of Coke and $8 on eight pizzas. This allocation produces 300 utils of satisfaction—the maximum total utility that can be purchased with $13 of income. You cannot find an expenditure pattern which will produce more satisfaction (try reducing Coke consumption by two cans and increasing pizza consumption by one pizza, or vice versa).

What we have done is to follow a maximization rule which says that an individual maximizes total utility when the last dollar spent on A yields the same utility as the last dollar spent on B. In algebraic form, total utility is maximized where,

$$\frac{MU_A}{P_A} = \frac{MU_B}{P_B}.$$

Thus, the marginal utility of a can of Coke, when ten cans per week were consumed, was 8 utils, and the price of Coke was $.50, so

$$\frac{MU_{Coke}}{P_{Coke}} = \frac{8}{\$.50},$$

or 16 utils per dollar. For pizza, at the optimum consumption rate the MU was 16 and the price was $1, so

$$\frac{MU_{pizza}}{P_{pizza}} = \frac{16}{\$1},$$

or 16 utils per dollar.

This can be generalized to include all goods by saying an individual maximizes utility where

$$\frac{MU_x}{P_x} = \frac{MU_y}{P_y} = \ldots = \frac{MU_n}{P_n}.$$

Of course, individuals don't spend all their income on goods. Sometimes, individuals hold money (let's use $ as the symbol) as they do any other commodity. We now write our equation for maximization as

$$\frac{MU_A}{P_A} = \frac{MU_B}{P_B} = \frac{MU_\$}{P_\$}.$$

Now the price of one dollar is one dollar, so

$$\frac{MU_\$}{P_\$}$$

can be simply written as,

$$MU_\$.$$

We thus have total utility being maximized where,

$$\frac{MU_x}{P_x} = \frac{MU_y}{P_y} = \ldots = \frac{MU_n}{P_n} = MU_\$.$$

This is a very complete expression for **utility maximization.** It has been extended to include all commodities, including money, and says that in order to maximize total utility, the marginal utilities per dollar of expenditures have to be equal and also have to equal the marginal utility of money. If this is not the case, a change in consumption patterns, for a given budget constraint, can produce more satisfaction. This is just a formal way of saying that people allocate their income so as to yield the most satisfaction possible. When utility is being maximized, the additional satisfaction from any use of $1 will equal the additional satisfaction from any other use of $1. When this is not the case, the individual will, by reallocating personal income, consume more of the good that yields more additional satisfaction per dollar.

To see how a given consumption pattern can be adjusted to achieve maximum utility, return to Table 19-3. Let's give the individual a $9 income and say that $3 worth of Coke and $6 worth of pizza are being consumed. Obviously the expression

$$\frac{MU_{Coke}}{P_{Coke}} = \frac{MU_{pizza}}{P_{pizza}}$$

doesn't hold, because

$$\frac{10\frac{3}{4}}{.50} > \frac{18}{1}.$$

utility maximization The way a consumer adjusts consumption, given a budget constraint and a set of prices, in order to maximize the total amount of satisfaction.

The individual isn't maximizing because the last dollar spent on Coke yields more utils than the last dollar spent on pizza. The individual should reallocate consumption outlays. By giving up one dollar's worth of pizza, the consumer would lose 18 utils but would gain 20¼ utils by spending one more dollar on Coke. Total utility would thus rise by 2¼ utils. Now substituting back into the equation, we get,

$$\frac{10}{.50} = \frac{20}{1}$$

(20¼ rounded off); the consumer is maximizing.

Marginal Utility and the Law of Demand

With the tools we've developed, we can now derive an individual's demand curve for a good. Suppose that there are only two goods, x and y. Remember, we draw demand curves in a *ceteris paribus* experiment so income, tastes, and the prices of all other goods (good y) are held constant. We start with our consumer in equilibrium, maximizing utility when

$$\frac{MU_x}{P_x} = \frac{MU_y}{P_y}.$$

At this equilibrium, MU_{x_1} corresponds to the consumption of x_1 units of x in Figure 19-2. P_{x_1}, the price of x_1, is represented by OP_{x_1} in Figure 19-2. So our equation should now be written

$$\frac{MU_{x_1}}{P_{x_1}} = \frac{MU_y}{P_y}.$$

FIGURE 19-2   DEMAND CURVE FOR GOOD x

When price falls from OP_{x1} to OP_{x2}, consumer maximization is thrown out of equilibrium. Equilibrium will be restored if the consumer increases consumption to Ox_2.

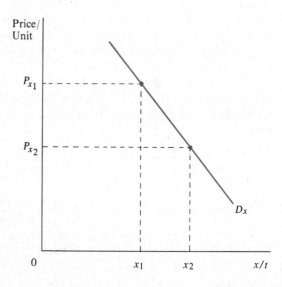

Now lower the price of x to OP_{x2}. This throws the expression out of equilibrium because the denominator on the left side is now smaller, making the left side of the expression larger:

$$\frac{MU_{x1}}{P_{x2}} > \frac{MU_y}{P_y}.$$

In order to get the expression back into equality, the individual has to lower the value of the left side of the expression and/or raise the right side. How can this be done? If the individual consumes more of x, MU_x will decline because of the principle of diminishing marginal utility. As consumption moves to Ox_2 on Figure 19-2,

$$MU_{x2} < MU_{x1}.$$

When this happens, the expression will move toward

$$\frac{MU_x}{P_x} = \frac{MU_y}{P_y}.$$

But as more x is purchased, less y is bought, so the MU of y increases, as the MU of x declines.

Consumer maximization behavior requires that when the price of a commodity falls (as from OP_{x1} to OP_{x2} in Figure 19-2), the consumer will increase the consumption of x. Since this is necessary for utility maximization, it proves that the demand curves of individuals must have a negative slope; that is, the lower the price, the greater the quantity demanded.

SOME APPLICATIONS OF UTILITY THEORY

You have practiced and observed utility maximization even though you may not have thought of it in the formal terminology of economics. Suppose, for a moment, you are organizing the beer concession for a club fund-raising event. There are two ways to finance the concession: you can charge an admission fee to the event and then allow free consumption, or you can charge a set price for each beer, say, $.50 per glass. Our theory predicts different levels of consumption and hence different requirements for planning the supply. In the first case beer drinkers will consume beer until the marginal utility per glass is zero, because the price per additional glass is zero. In the second case beer drinkers will consume beer until the marginal utility per glass equals the marginal utility of $.50. You can predict, then, that there will be more drunken, rowdy behavior if the party is financed by an admission charge. If you don't agree with this analysis, reflect back on group parties you have attended. Were the most rowdy ones the pay-as-you-go type or the admission type?

This may seem like an insignificant example because the consumption of beer isn't a very earth-shaking issue. So let's change the good from beer to medical services. If we consider a *free* national health service, what do you predict will happen to the consumption of these services?[1] Of course, people will consume them until the marginal utility is zero! This is exactly what happens in a socialized medicine program. If you have ever participated in such a program in the army, at a university, or under one of the new health maintenance plans, you probably have consumed more of these services than before. Since the services are free, more are consumed. You also may have noticed that with the free system the waiting time is usually longer, the waiting rooms are less comfortable, and the workers are less congenial than with a paid system. The effect of all this is to reduce the marginal utility and, therefore, decrease the demand for service. Lowering the quality of a good or a service is equivalent in many ways to increasing the price.

The Diamond-Water Paradox

Classical economists argued that utility (and thus demand) could not be a determinant of price because diamonds, while less useful than water, were more expensive than water. These classical economists spent a great deal of time discussing this problem, which became known as the *diamond-water paradox.* It should be clear that the paradox is caused by the failure to separate total utility and marginal utility. The total utility of water is high, but since there is a great deal in existence and large quantities are consumed, its marginal utility is low. The total utility of diamonds, on the other hand, is relatively low, but since diamonds are rare, their marginal utility is high. Price, then, is determined by marginal utility, not total utility. We say that marginal utility determines *value in exchange* (price) and that total utility determines *value in use.* Scarcity, then, is related to value through utility. If something is scarce and has a low marginal utility, it will have a low price; but if something is scarce and has a high marginal utility, it will be valuable and hence be expensive.

The Uneasy Case for the Progressive Income Tax[2]

One of the main arguments (but not the only one) for a *progressive income tax* is based on the principle of diminishing marginal utility. This argument assumes that we can measure utility (which we have seen is impossible), and further, that we can make *interpersonal utility comparisons* or say that individuals all have the same utility schedule for equal increments of income. With these two assumptions, proponents of the progressive income tax argue that we can maximize utility within society by taking income away from the high income individuals who have lower marginal utilities of income and transferring it to the low income individuals who have higher marginal utilities of income.

Proponents of a progressive income tax who apply principles of individual utility maximization to the society as a whole are on very shaky ground, however. First of all, economists are in agreement that interpersonal utility comparisons are meaningless. People are different. There really is no accounting for taste.

diamond-water paradox *The problem that classical economists faced when they argued that value in use could not determine price (demand), because diamonds, while less useful than water, were more expensive than water.*

value in exchange *Price, or value in exchange, is determined by marginal utility. Scarcity is related to value through utility.*

value in use *Usefulness, or value in use, is often thought of as the total utility an item supplies. Water is thus very valuable in use, but not very valuable in exchange (price), because it has a low marginal utility.*

progressive income tax *An income tax which applies a higher tax rate to taxpayers with higher levels of income. The tax rate and income level are positively correlated.*

interpersonal utility comparisons *Attempts to compare levels or amounts of utility between consumers. This is impossible because utility is subjectively determined.*

[1] By *free,* we mean there is no monetary cost to the patient; i.e., price is zero.
[2] For a comprehensive treatment of this subject, see Walter J. Blum and Harry Kalven, Jr., *The Uneasy Case for Progressive Taxation* (Chicago: University of Chicago Press, 1970).

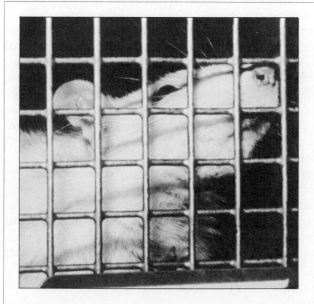

Experimental Economics: Economics According to Rats

Economics is beginning to borrow from experimental psychology. Economists at the University of Arizona and Texas A&M University, among others, are carrying out work in a lab setting to test some fundamental propositions in economoics.

At the University of Arizona, Vernon Smith has conducted research on market behavior using human subjects, usually students. At Texas A&M , economists Ray Battalio and John Kagel have experimented with human and animal subjects. In male and female mental wards, the economists did experiments with token economies. Patients were paid tokens for tasks and were free to spend these tokens on personal items. Some of the results of these investigations were fascinating. They found that the distribution of income earned was closely parallel to that in the U.S. economy. Perhaps even more startling was the fact that earning differences between male and female patients were similar to those in the macro economy.

This led the two economists to experiment with rats. They found that rats trained to do work for pay (i.e., hit a bar for food) reduced their work effort after some point, choosing more leisure over additional income. They also found that among low-income rats (those that had to work hard for a little food), work reduction was more common.

There is no way you can prove that an additional $100 of income gives less satisfaction to Elizabeth Taylor than to an unemployed auto worker. In fact, Liz may get more satisfaction because she is such an expert consumer. It is impossible to prove that one individual gets more or less satisfaction from an increment to income than does any other individual.

A second and more fundamental problem with this analysis is that it assumes a diminishing marginal utility for income (money). This proposition cannot be verified. The principle of diminishing marginal utility, you will remember, states that the marginal utility of a *particular commodity* declines as consumption is increased. Increased income, however, represents an increase in the consumption of all goods. If wants are insatiable, as we determined in Chapter 1, there is no reason to believe that the principle of diminishing marginal utility holds for money. Even so, it is probably the case that most people think that money has diminishing marginal utility. What about you? Do you think a $100 bill will give your "rich" economics instructor more or less satisfaction than it will give you?

PROBLEMS WITH UTILITY THEORY

There are two major difficulties with a demand theory based on utility. They center on the indivisibility and immeasurability of utility. In working through the theory, we have traced what happens to the consumer's satisfaction when we vary units of consumption during a given period in which tastes are held constant, and we have seen that adjustments in consumption can be made in order to maximize utility. The theory works well enough when we consider the consumption of certain kinds of goods, such as ice cream cones or beer or shirts. When we consider the purchase of an automobile or a home, however, we see that it is difficult to talk about additional units because the purchase is what economists call *lumpy*. It is difficult to consume a part of a house or a part of a car, while it is possible to consume part of a case of beer. The theory is somewhat weakened, then, by the fact that the consumer can't make continuous decisions about successive amounts of consumption.[3]

A greater problem is the inability to measure utility. We have proceeded as if there was a way we could strap a meter to a consumer and with exactness measure the utility expected from consuming one more beer. This is, of course, not possible. Psychology has not yet developed to such a technological level. But before you reject utility theory as useless, remember that we are developing a theoretical tool, much as is done in a physics class. It really isn't that important for our theory that we be able to measure utility. Our purpose is to develop propositions about how quantity demanded will change when prices change, not about how utility changes.

lumpy *Indivisibilities in consumption. Consumption of houses is lumpy, for example, because 10 percent of a house cannot be easily purchased and consumed.*

SUMMARY

1. Total utility is the total amount of satisfaction expected from consuming an item or group of items.

2. Marginal utility is the addition to total utility from consuming one more unit of a good.

3. Consumers, in deciding among items, choose those items with the highest marginal utility per dollar.

4. An individual maximizes total utility by consuming all items so that the marginal utilities per dollar spent are equal.

5. Utility theory has been criticized on the grounds that utility is not measurable and that items consumed are not perfectly divisible as the theory of utility maximization requires. Despite these criticisms, utility theory is a useful tool for analyzing consumer behavior.

NEW TERMS

utility
ex ante
util
utility function
diminishing marginal utility

marginal utility
budget constraint
utility maximization
diamond-water paradox
value in exchange

---

[3]This is really not such a debilitating flaw. Consumers can still make adjustments even with most lumpy purchases. Consider a house as an example. Suppose the individual decides after the purchase that the house is too large and that other purchases would yield more marginal utility. Over time, the house can be depreciated by a lessening of routine maintenance so that more can be spent on the other goods which yield a higher marginal utility. Buying a smaller house, or one at a less desirable location, or renting are also available alternatives.

value in use
progressive income tax

interpersonal utility comparisons
lumpy

QUESTIONS FOR DISCUSSION

1. Does something have to be useful to have utility? What does it mean for a good or service to be useful?

2. What is happening if the price of a good, such as a petroleum product, is increasing without a decrease in consumption?

3. Does the fact that water is inexpensive and diamonds are expensive conflict with the theory developed in this chapter? Explain.

4. If the marginal utility of one good is 4 and the price is $2, and the marginal utility of another good is 5 and its price is $1, is the individual consumer maximizing total utility? If not, how could more utility be obtained?

5. Does advertising increase or decrease the utility you get from consuming certain goods? Is this good or bad?

6. A survey shows that a group of consumers prefers light beer to regular beer. What does this mean in terms of the utility analysis we have presented in this chapter?

7. What would you expect to happen to a normal consumer's total utility curve for bacon, if the surgeon general established a link between bacon and cancer? How would this announcement affect the demand curve for bacon?

SUGGESTIONS FOR FURTHER READING

Easterlin, Richard A. "Does Money Buy Happiness?" *Public Interest* (Winter, 1973), pp. 3–10.
Kamerschen, David R. and Lloyd M. Valentine. *Intermediate Microeconomic Theory,* 2d ed. Cincinnati: South-Western Publishing Co., 1981, Chapter 4.

CHAPTER 20

An Alternative Approach to Consumer Behavior: Indifference Analysis

Learning Objectives

After studying the materials found in this chapter, you should be able to do the following:

1. Define indifference curve analysis.

2. List and define the following elements of indifference curve analysis:
   (a) indifference curve.
   (b) budget line.
   (c) the equilibrium point in terms of the slope of the budget line and the marginal rate of substitution.

3. Derive the following, using indifference curve analysis:
   (a) an income-consumption curve.
   (b) a price-consumption curve.
   (c) the income effect and the substitution effect.
   (d) a demand curve.

indifference curve analysis   *A technique of analyzing consumer behavior that does not require the concept of measurable utility.*

The primary shortcoming of marginal utility theory is the immeasurability of utility. This shortcoming does not mean that the theory has no value. The value, however, is to be found in the theoretical insights that it offers rather than in any precise applications. Marginal utility theory was first explained in the 1870s. Then, in the late 1800s, Italian economist Vilfredo Pareto and British economist F.Y. Edgeworth, working separately, developed another consumer behavior theory—*indifference curve analysis.* It wasn't until 1939, when Nobel prizewinning British economist Sir John Hicks published his classic book *Value and Capital,* that this analysis became popular with economic theorists and teachers. The theory swept the economics profession, and for a while marginal utility analysis fell into disrepute.

Pareto, Edgeworth, Hicks, and others were not trying to dispute utility analysis, but rather were proposing an alternative way of viewing consumer behavior. Its major improvement is that it does not require the ability to measure utility. All that is necessary is that consumers are able to rank bundles of goods in the order, from low to high, in which they prefer them.

INDIFFERENCES

The concepts of indifference and preference seem to fit more closely the way consumers actually make decisions than does the concept of utility. Individuals

Sir John R. Hicks *(1904–)*

Sir John R. Hicks is one of the most significant contributors to modern microeconomic theory. In his book *Value and Capital* (1939), he reconstructed demand theory using indifference curves. Hicks developed the theories discussed in this chapter. In 1972

Hicks was awarded the Nobel Prize in Economics (along with Kenneth Arrow) for ". . . pioneering contributions to general economic equilibrium theory and welfare theory."

Hicks was born in Leamington Spa, England, and attended Balliol College, Oxford. His first teaching post was at the London School of Economics, where he taught from 1926–1935. He later taught at Cambridge and the University of Manchester. In 1946 he moved to Nuffield College at Oxford and remained there until his retirement.

Hicks's main contributions to economic literature center on the theory of demand. Hicks showed that if a consumer maximizes something (we call it utility) and if the consumer's choices can be ranked, it is possible to deduce the consumer's reaction to price changes as well as to substitute and complementary goods. Hicks then went on to establish clearly the difference between income and substitution effects by developing the idea of the *compensated demand curve,* which is the demand curve along which an individual consumer's real income is unchanged.

Sir John Hicks made contributions to a host of theoretical economic areas, including international trade, public finance, macroeconomics, and monetary theory. Most of his theoretical work was done in the 1930s and 1940s. He clearly ranks as a major figure in the history of economic theory.

make choices between bundles of goods. For example, you might choose between four tickets to a football game and two tickets to a concert. In indifference analysis, we view the consumer as making choices between collections of goods and services. We assume only that the individual is able to state preferences for different bundles of commodities or to profess indifference among some of them. Suppose we offer an individual different combinations of Coke and Miller beer, as indicated in Table 20-1. Carton *A* contains 16 Cokes and 6 beers. When we

TABLE 20-1 AN INDIFFERENCE SET

Cartons	Good x (Coke)	Good y (Miller)
A	16	6
B	12	8
C	10	10
D	8	14
E	6	18

offer the individual carton B, which contains 12 Cokes and 8 beers, the individual states that neither one is preferred over the other; they are equal in the amount of satisfaction the individual expects to derive and, therefore, the individual is indifferent between the two cartons. Offering the individual the choice among cartons C, D, and E yields the same response, or indifference. The individual has indicated that all five cartons of beer and Coke yield the same amount of satisfaction. We have created an ***indifference set*** for our consumer. We can geometrically represent this indifference set by drawing an ***indifference curve.*** An indifference curve corresponding to the indifference set in Table 20-1 is drawn in Figure 20-1. An indifference curve shows all combinations of the two commodities among which a consumer is indifferent. It is the geometric representation of an indifference set.

indifference set   Bundles of goods among which a consumer is indifferent. The bundles yield equal satisfaction.

indifference curve   A graphing of an indifference set. An indifference curve shows all combinations of two commodities among which the consumer is indifferent.

Indifference curves are negatively sloped because there is an inverse relationship between the quantities of the two goods available in each combination. In other words, each combination represents a trade-off. In our example, if carton B is to have more beer than carton A, it must have less Coke, since the bundles are to yield the same level of satisfaction. If one carton had more beer and more Coke than any other, or if it had more of one good without having less of the other, it would be preferred and the consumer would no longer be indifferent.

The indifference set represented by a higher indifference curve is preferred to that represented by a lower indifference curve. As we move from I_1 to I_2 to I_3 to I_4 in Figure 20-2, the individual receives more satisfaction. Such a series of indifference curves is called an ***indifference map.*** Every individual consumer has such a map, and movement to higher curves on the map represents a gain in utility.

indifference map   A series of indifference curves representing different levels of satisfaction for the consumer.

Extreme Indifference Curves

The shape of the indifference curves in Figure 20-2 is considered to be typical for most goods. To understand why this shape is typical, let's look at two extreme shapes first. One extreme is shown in Figure 20-3, where each indifference curve

---

FIGURE 20-1   INDIFFERENCE CURVE

Indifference curves geometrically represent combinations of two goods among which the consumer is indifferent. All combinations represent the same level of satisfaction.

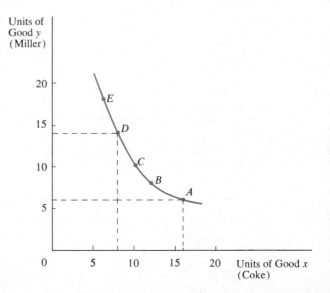

Units of Good y (Miller)

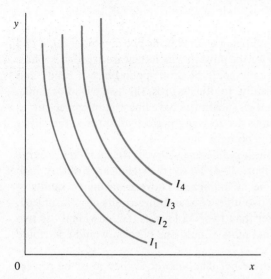

FIGURE 20-2   INDIFFERENCE MAP

An indifference map is a series of indifference curves. Higher curves on the map represent higher levels of satisfaction.

is a straight line (linear curve). On indifference curve I_3, the individual is indifferent among all combinations between 40 units of y and no x, and 20 units of x and no y. For instance, this person is indifferent between a bundle made up of $20y$ and $10x$ and a bundle made up of $10y$ and $15x$. We can generalize and say that the consumer is indifferent between all combinations offering two units of

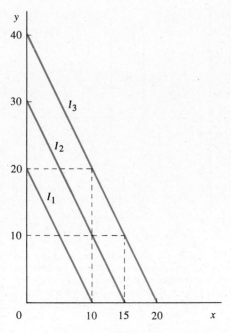

FIGURE 20-3   LINEAR INDIFFERENCE CURVES

On a linear indifference curve the consumer always has the same trade-off between the two goods, regardless of the amount of either good the consumer may have. The two goods are perfect substitutes.

y in compensation for the loss of one unit of *x*. The trade-off is always two *(y)* to one *(x)*.[1]

Indifference curves like this could happen only if the two commodities, *x* and *y*, are the same commodity except for the units in which they are expressed. Thus, *y* could be nickels and *x*, dimes; or *y* could be a one-pound bag of candy and *x*, a two-pound bag of the same candy. In other words, this is a trivial example, except that it demonstrates that perfect substitutes have linear indifference curves and that the closer two commodities are to being perfect substitutes, the closer the indifference curves are to being straight lines.

The extreme opposite of the linear indifference curve is the indifference curve with a right angle, as shown in Figure 20-4. To see the significance of this, look at I_1. I_1 indicates that the consumer is indifferent between having two units of *x* and two units of *y*, and having two units of *x* and three units of *y*, or indeed, two *x* and any number of *y* greater than two. As long as the individual has two units of each commodity, additional units of only one of them would contribute nothing to utility.

What kind of goods might these be? The answer is they must be perfect *complements,* and the examples usually given are: *y* = left shoes and *x* = right shoes, or *x* = coats and *y* = linings. Again, this is a trivial case since perfect complements are usually combined and sold as one good. We can observe from this, however, that goods that are complements to each other will have indifference curves which approach the right-angled ones, being very concave or bowed toward the origin and almost parallel to the axes.

**FIGURE 20-4   RIGHT-ANGLED INDIFFERENCE
                        CURVES**

An indifference curve with a right angle indicates that more of good *y*, once an equal amount of good *x* has been purchased, adds nothing to satisfaction. The goods are perfect complements.

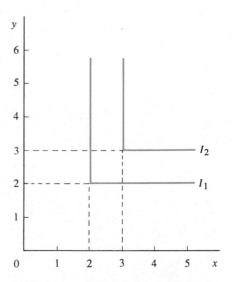

---

[1]The equation for I_3 is $y = 40 - 2x$. In this case the slope is -2, meaning that two units of *y* will compensate the consumer for the loss of one unit of *x*. Remember that since this is an indifference curve, any point on the curve has the same utility as any other point on the curve. The equation for I_2 is $y = 30 - 2x$, and for $I_1, y = 20 - 2x$. Obviously I_3 is preferred to I_2, which is preferred to I_1.

Typical Indifference Curves

The typical indifference curve for two goods will lie between the extremes of perfect substitutes and perfect complements; that is, it will have some curvature and some degree of concavity. It will have a negative slope, which means that for the individual to be indifferent between two bundles of commodities some extra amount of one good is necessary to compensate for the loss of some amount of the other. Saying the same thing in another way, every combination of two goods represented on the same indifference curve will have more of one of the goods but less of the other than any other combination on that indifference curve.

The concavity feature means that as a consumer attains more units of one good and fewer units of the other good, it takes more and more units of the more abundant good to compensate for the loss of one unit of the good that is becoming more scarce. See Figure 20-5 for a depiction of this.

At point A the individual is consuming relatively large amounts of y and small amounts of x. In order to compensate for a reduction in consumption of 1 unit of y, the person would only require 2 units of x in order to be satisfied with such a trade; but at point B, since less of y and more of x are being consumed compared to point A, it will take a larger quantity of x (5 units) to compensate for the loss of 1 unit of y. At point C, the individual now consumes a large amount of x and very little y, so to give up 1 unit of y, 20 units of x would be needed to retain the same utility as before.

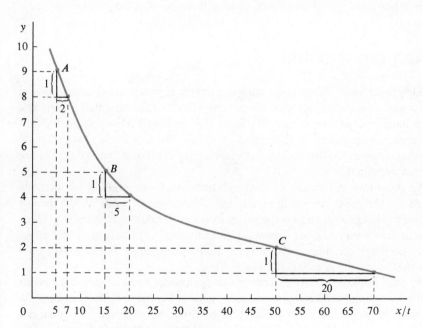

FIGURE 20-5 CONCAVITY FEATURE OF INDIFFERENCE CURVES

A typical indifference curve is concave. This concavity means that it takes increasingly larger amounts of the abundant good to compensate for losses of the good that is becoming more scarce.

There is no law that says such preference relations must hold, but it is usually the case. First, upon introspection most of us would say that this is the way we would behave in this trade-off situation. Second, the opposite proposition seems highly unlikely. It would say that the less you had of a good, the less you would want of it relative to other goods, and the more you had of a good, the more valuable additional units of it would become. If this were the case, you would eventually only consume one good!

DIMINISHING MARGINAL RATES OF SUBSTITUTION

marginal rate of substitution The consumer's trade-off between two goods represented on an indifference curve. The slope of the indifference curve represents this trade-off.

The trade-off ratio we have been discussing represents the **marginal rate of substitution**. The marginal rate of substitution of x for y, MRS_{xy}, shows the number of units of good x that must be gained to compensate along an indifference curve for a one-unit decrease in good y; that is,

$$MRS_{xy} = \frac{\text{number of units of } y \text{ given up}}{\text{number of units of } x \text{ gained}}.$$

In Figure 20-5, the MRS_{xy} at point A is ½; that is, one unit of y must be sacrificed to gain two units of x. At point B, the MRS_{xy} is 1/5 and at point C, it is 1/20. The declining value of MRS_{xy} is a reflection of the **principle of diminishing marginal rates of substitution**, showing that as more of one good *(x)* is substituted for the other good *(y)*, the value of good x in terms of good y declines.

principle of diminishing marginal rates of substitution As a consumer receives more and more of a particular good, its value in terms of other goods declines. This is represented by the changing slope of the indifference curve.

BUDGET CONSTRAINTS

An indifference map allows us to compare points representing combinations of goods x and y in such a way that we can say whether the individual prefers one or feels indifferent among several. We know that all points on any single indifference curve are equivalent to each other in utility. We also know that points on indifference curves located to the right and above other indifference curves are preferred combinations.

We must now determine which combinations of commodities are actually possible for the consumer we are studying. The answer depends on the income available to that person and on the prices of the commodities in question. These two factors, income and price, constrain the individual from buying all that might be desired. Together, the factors form a **budget constraint**. When shown on a graph the constraint is called the **budget line**.

We shall limit our analysis to two goods (you could think of one of the goods as "all other goods"). To remain consistent with our earlier example, assume the individual can consume either Miller beer or Coke. Suppose the individual has a disposable income *(DI)* of $10.00 and now Miller and Coke each sell for $.50 per unit. The construction of the budget line is illustrated in Figure 20-6. If the

budget constraint A given level of income that limits the amount of goods that may be purchased by an individual.

budget line The graphing of the budget constraint, indicating achievable levels of consumption given the prices of goods and the consumer's income.

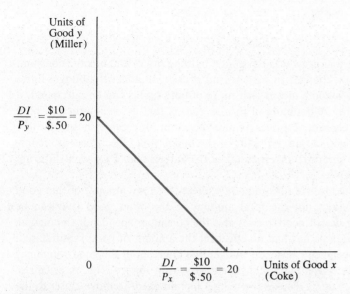

FIGURE 20-6   BUDGET LINE
A budget line graphically depicts the consumption combinations that
are attainable with a given level of income. Any combination outside
(to the northeast of) the line is unattainable.

individual spends the entire income *(DI)* on Miller, 20 units of beer can be
purchased. This is determined by dividing income by the price of the good

$$\left(\frac{DI}{P_y}\right).$$

In this case,

$$\frac{\$10.00}{\$.50} = 20 \text{ units of beer.}$$

Thus, 20 is the *y* intercept. The *x* intercept is calculated in the same manner:

$$\frac{DI}{P_x} = \frac{\$10.00}{\$.50} = 20 \text{ units of Coke.}$$

With a straight line, we connect the two points that represent buying all of
good *y* (Miller) or all of good *x* (Coke), and we thus express all possible combinations that can be purchased with a given income level. It is a budget line because
any combination outside (to the northeast of) the line is unattainable at that
income level; it is outside the budget constraint. In other words, the budget line
is the dividing line between those combinations that are attainable and those that
are unattainable, at a given level of prices and a given level of income.

CHANGES IN INCOME AND CHANGES IN PRICES

The budget line we just drew was developed holding prices and income constant. We need to see how changes in income and prices will affect the budget line.

An increase in income means that more of both goods can be purchased, if prices stay the same. A doubling of income means that twice as much of both goods can be purchased, if prices remain constant. Increases in income are represented by a parallel outward shift of the budget line. Decreases in income are represented by a parallel inward shift of the budget line. Two such shifts are shown in Figure 20-7.

A change in the price of one good only affects the total amount of that good that can be purchased, not the total amount of the other good that can be purchased. If the price of good x rises and the consumer spends all the income on good y, the price rise has had no effect on the amount of good y purchased. A price rise, then, will only affect the budget line intercept of the good which has experienced the price rise. Such a change is shown in Figure 20-8. A price rise for good x from P_{x_1} to P_{x_2} causes the budget line intercept to move closer to the origin, reflecting the fact that less x can now be purchased with the constant income. A decrease in the price of good x to P_{x_3} would mean more x could be purchased and the intercept would move away from the origin, reflecting increases in the potential consumption of good x.

Price changes cause the slope of the budget line to change. The slope of the budget line is, of course, $\Delta y / \Delta x$. Notice that we can compute the slope by

FIGURE 20-7   THE EFFECT OF INCOME CHANGES ON BUDGET LINES

An increase in income is represented by a parallel outward shift of the budget line. A decrease in income is represented by an inward parallel shift of the budget line.

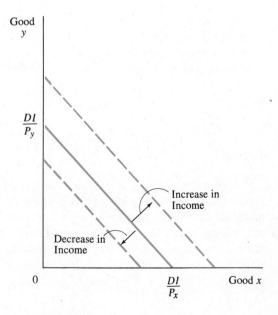

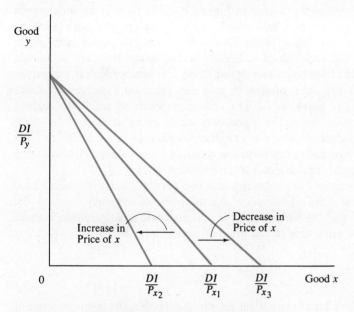

**FIGURE 20-8   THE EFFECT OF PRICE CHANGES ON
BUDGET LINES**

An increase in the price of one good changes the slope of the
budget line. An increase in price means that if all disposable income
is spent on the item, less of it can be purchased. As a result, the
intercept of the budget line will shift closer to the origin. The
opposite holds for a decrease in price.

---

taking the negative of the ratio of the vertical intercept to the horizontal intercept.
The ratio of the intercepts is   .

$$-\left(\frac{DI}{P_y} \Big/ \frac{DI}{P_x} \right),$$

which is equal to

$$-(P_x/P_y).$$

So, we can say that the slope of the budget line changes when the ratio of prices
changes. A change in income, on the other hand, represents no change in relative
prices, so the slope of the budget line remains the same, as reflected by the *parallel*
shifting of the budget line described above.

MAXIMIZATION OF SATISFACTION

We can now demonstrate maximization of consumer satisfaction. If we combine
a set of indifference curves with the budget line, we can see where an individual

consumer maximizes satisfaction, as in Figure 20-9. At point A on indifference curve I_2, the budget line and indifference curve I_2 are tangent. Any point on I_3, such as point B, is of course preferred to point A, because higher indifference curves represent higher levels of utility. However, point B is not attainable because it is outside the budget line. Point C on I_1 is attainable, but a point on indifference curve I_2 is also attainable, and any point on I_2 represents more satisfaction than any point on I_1. The consumer wants to reach the highest attainable indifference curve. The highest attainable curve would be one which is tangent to the budget line because no higher indifference curve can be reached with the given income and prices. So in this example, our consumer is maximizing utility, or is in equilibrium at point A on indifference curve I_2.

You may remember from geometry that two curves which are tangent have equal slopes at the point of tangency. At the point of tangency between the indifference curve and the budget line, the marginal rate of substitution is equal to the ratio of the price of x to the price of y; that is,[2]

$$MRS_{xy} = P_x/P_y.$$

This may seem like a lot of theoretical mumbo jumbo, but the common sense of it is that the marginal rate of substitution expresses the willingness of the consumer to trade a certain amount of x for a certain amount of y and the slope of the budget line reflects the market's willingness to trade a certain amount of x for a certain amount of y. The impersonal forces of the market impose the relative

---

FIGURE 20-9   CONSUMER MAXIMIZATION

An individual maximizes consumer satisfaction where the budget line is tangent to the highest attainable indifference curve.

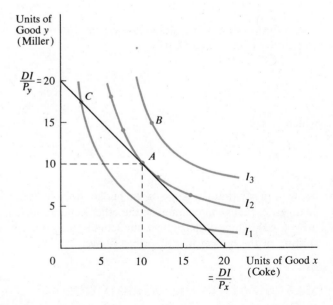

---

[2]Technically, MRS_{xy} is equal to the negative of the slope of the indifference curve. The price ratio, as we have seen, is the negative of the slope of the budget line. Therefore, at the (equilibrium) point of tangency between the indifference curve and the budget line, $MRS_{xy} = P_x/P_y$.

price on the consumer, so the consumer adjusts consumption amounts in such a way that his or her trade-off is the same as that of the market.

Look at Figure 20-10. Suppose you are consuming 15 units of y and 5 units of x (you are at point A). According to your indifference curve (I_1), you would be willing to give up 5 units of y if you were compensated by 2 units of x; but the market is willing to give you 5 units of x in exchange for 5 units of y (note point B). We should then expect to see you consuming less y and more x. In fact, until your indifference curve says you are willing to give up exactly 1 unit of x in exchange for 1 unit of y when the prices of the two commodities are the same, as in this example, you will be able to increase your utility by moving in the direction of the tangency of some indifference curve and the budget line.

Household Reaction to Income Changes

We can now trace through the adjustment process that takes place when a household experiences a change in income. In Figure 20-11, if the consumer's income is DI_1, and x and y sell for P_x and P_y respectively, the optimum utility is at point A. A decrease in income is represented by DI_0, and two increases in income are represented by DI_2 and DI_3. The respective optimum positions representing tangencies of a budget line and an indifference curve are points B, C, and D. If we connect these points, we get what is called an ***income-consumption curve.*** This curve shows how consumption of the two goods changes as income changes. Now recall our discussion of the income elasticity of demand. The income elasticities of both good x and good y in Figure 20-11 are positive because consumption of both goods increases as income increases. Remember that a positive income elasticity indicates that a good is a normal good. An inferior good would have

income-consumption curve A curve that shows how the consumption of two goods changes as income changes.

FIGURE 20-10   TANGENCY SOLUTION ONCE AGAIN
Lower indifference curves that are within the budget constraint represent lower levels of utility than the highest, but still attainable, indifference curve.

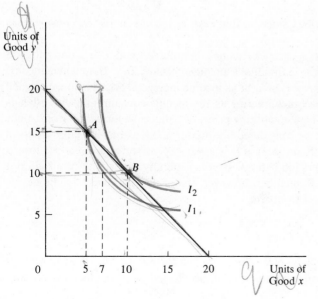

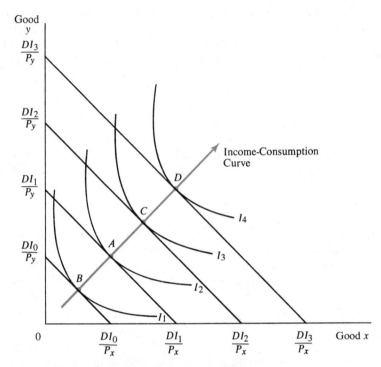

**FIGURE 20-11   INCOME CHANGES AND THE
INCOME-CONSUMPTION CURVE**

An income-consumption curve traces the response of consumption patterns
to changes in income.

a negative income elasticity since, in that case, as income increases, consumption of the good decreases.

Figure 20-12 shows a case where one commodity, good x, is a normal good for this person until the individual's income reaches DI_3. But, when income increases above DI_3, less x is bought as income increases. So x is a normal good up to point A, then becomes inferior as the income-consumption curve bends backward. There is, of course, nothing pejorative about the term "inferior." Your daily newspaper might be considered an inferior good; as income falls, a person buys the paper more often, because it is a less expensive form of entertainment and also because it offers job listings. Beer is generally thought to be an inferior good, as are potatoes. Remember, however, that a normal good to some people may be an inferior good to others.

Household Reaction to Price Changes

We saw in Figure 20-8 how price changes affect the budget line. We can now see how the optimum consumption point will be affected by price changes. Initially,

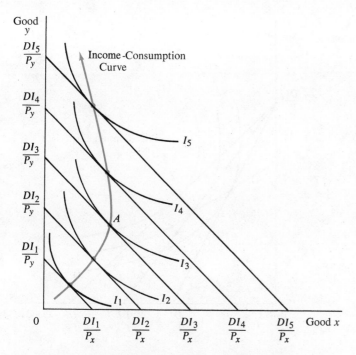

**FIGURE 20-12   INCOME-CONSUMPTION CURVE FOR
AN INFERIOR GOOD**

The income-consumption curve for an inferior good bends backward,
indicating that less of the good is consumed as income increases
beyond a certain level.

the consumer is at the point of maximum utility (point *A* in Figure 20-13). As
the price of *x* falls from P_{x_1} to P_{x_2}, the budget line rotates out to intersect the
x-axis at $\dfrac{DI}{P_{x2}}$, and the consumer now has a new optimum at point *B* on
indifference curve I_2. Another decrease in price to P_{x_3} allows the consumer to
reach a still higher indifference curve, I_3, and a new optimum at point *C*. Connecting the points produces a ***price-consumption curve,*** which shows how consumption changes when relative prices change.

We will not spell out the theoretical mechanics here, but it is worth noting
that when the price of a commodity falls, there are two forces at work to cause
the consumer to increase purchases of that commodity. First, when the price of
a good falls, the market trade-off, or the *substitution,* rate changes. This is referred
to as the ***substitution effect.*** Second, the individual has a larger *real income,*
meaning that with the same money income, more of both (or all) commodities
can be purchased (and will be as long as the good is not an inferior good). We
refer to this as the ***income effect.***

*price-consumption curve   A
curve that shows how the
consumption of two goods
changes as the price of one of
the goods changes.*

*substitution effect   When the
price of a good falls, it becomes
less expensive relative to all other
goods and more of it is
consumed, substituting for other
goods.*

*income effect   As the price of a
good falls (rises), the consumer's
real income rises (falls), and the
consumer buys more (less) of all
normal goods.*

FIGURE 20-13   PRICE-CONSUMPTION CURVE

A price-consumption curve graphically depicts how consumption changes when relative prices change.

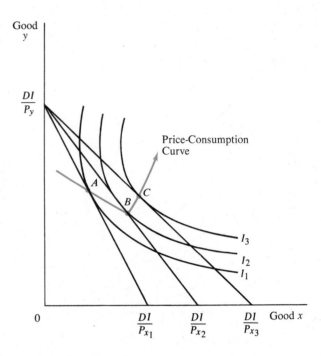

INDIFFERENCE ANALYSIS AND THE LAW OF DEMAND

We can now derive an individual's demand curve and demonstrate the law of demand. This is a *ceteris paribus* experiment in which we will change the price of one commodity and observe what happens to the quantity demanded. In Figure 20-14, we have an indifference map and a budget line for goods x and y. Let x be the particular good in which we are interested and let y represent all other goods. The consumer is at an optimum at point A. At point A the individual consumes O_{x_1} of x at a price of P_{x_1}. Price and quantity are plotted on Figure 20-15. Now let the price of x fall to P_{x_2}. As before, this decline in price causes the budget line to rotate outward. A new optimum is reached at point B, where the new budget line is tangent to indifference curve I_3. The change in price has caused consumption to increase from O_{x_1} to O_{x_2}. This increase in consumption is also plotted on Figure 20-15. If a line is drawn through the two price-quantity points, we have two points on a demand curve which has the negative slope we expect of demand curves.

INDIFFERENCE CURVE ANALYSIS: APPLICATION

Although indifference curve analysis is not one of the basic tools you need for rudimentary economic analysis, virtually every advanced economics course makes extensive use of indifference curves. To demonstrate how useful such analysis is, we can analyze the effect of a proportional income tax on the work-leisure choice.

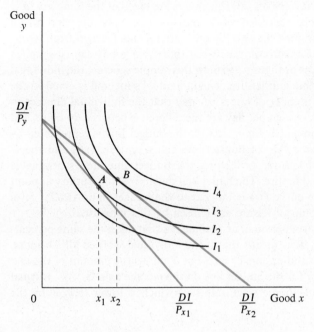

FIGURE 20-14 INDIFFERENCE MAP AND BUDGET LINES FOR THE DERIVATION OF A DEMAND CURVE

When the price of one good decreases, the consumer reaches a higher indifference curve. On this higher indifference curve, the consumption of the good that experienced the decrease in price will have increased.

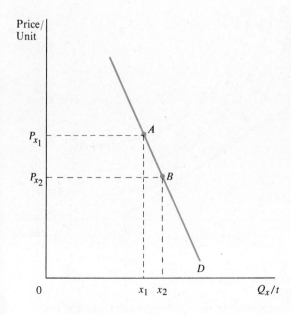

FIGURE 20-15 DERIVING A DEMAND CURVE

When the price of good x decreases, the consumer can reach a higher indifference curve. This increased consumption of good x at a lower price means that the demand curve must have a negative slope.

proportional income tax *An income tax which applies the same tax rate to all taxpayers regardless of their level of income.*

With a ***proportional income tax,*** all consumers are taxed at the same *tax rate.* An individual's preferences between work and leisure can be depicted on an indifference curve. We assume the two "goods" are income (earned from work) and leisure. The trade-off relationship between these two goods can be graphed as an indifference curve, as in Figure 20-16. In this simple scheme, the individual can choose between income and leisure. The individual's income is equal to the wage rate (w) times the number of hours per day that the individual chooses to work. The hours of work chosen per day are the difference between 24 hours and the amount of leisure chosen. In Figure 20-16, the budget line is represented by the line *SL.* The S intercept is 24 hours times the wage rate (w), and the L intercept is 24 hours of leisure. As before, the budget line shows attainable combinations of work and leisure. The individual maximizes total utility at point *A,* where an indifference curve (I_2) is tangent to the budget line. An OS_1 level of income and OL_1 amount of leisure are chosen by this individual.

Now consider the introduction of an income tax that takes the same percentage of everyone's salary. This means that if the individual worked all 24 hours, the amount of income would no longer be S but S minus the amount of the tax. So we get a new intercept for the budget line on the income axis, S^*. S^* is equal to 24 hours times the take-home wage rate (w_1) which is lower than w by the

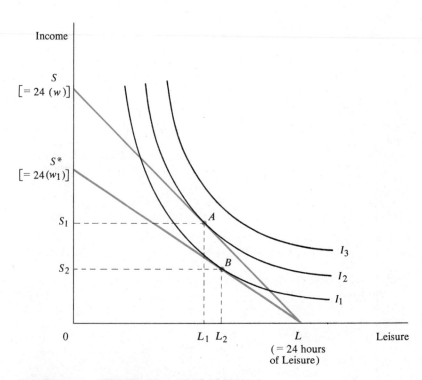

FIGURE 20-16   EFFECTS OF A PROPORTIONAL INCOME TAX

A proportional income tax increases the "price" of income and results in the individual opting for less income and more leisure.

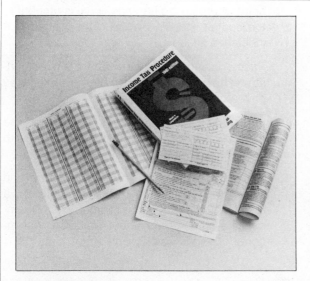

Taxes and Leisure

Do taxes affect work incentives? It's a hard question to answer. Many economic studies lead to the conclusion that they do, but that the amount of work effort affected is not too large. Think about it. Most of us want to be paid for our work because it is work. If it weren't work, it would be entertainment, play, leisure, or just plain fun.

In short, most people would rather do something else (at least most of the time) than work. In terms of demand theory, we want to know what the price of doing something else happens to be. In opportunity cost terms, the price of sitting under a shade tree is the income we give up. If we could earn $10 an hour, the price of shade-tree sitting would be $10 an hour. If the government takes 70 percent of the $10, the price of sitting under the tree is $3 an hour. It now comes down to a simple question: Do you think there will be more shade-tree sitting at a price of $3 an hour than at a price of $10 an hour?

Taxes lower the price of leisure; and leisure, like any other good, has a negatively sloped demand curve. In this chapter, there is a more precise demonstration of this fact.

percent of the tax. The individual now maximizes total utility at point B, which represents a tangency with the highest attainable indifference curve, I_1. In effect, the prices of all the goods the individual buys have increased relative to the price of leisure (the price of leisure is the income foregone per hour of not working).

Imposition of the tax has had three effects on the individual. First, the individual is on a lower indifference curve and is, therefore, at a lower level of satisfaction or well-being. This ignores what the government did with the tax receipts and implicitly assumes the government spent them in a way different than our hypothetical individual would have spent them. This is not an outlandish assumption because if the individual would have spent the money in the same way the government would, there would have been no need for the tax. A second effect is that the individual's spendable income fell from OS_1 to OS_2. The third effect is that the individual increased the amount of leisure taken from OL_1 to OL_2. The income tax has definitely had an effect on the work-leisure trade-off.

What you have just worked through is the standard explanation of how income taxes change the relative price of leisure and thereby create incentives to take more leisure and work less. Income taxes can thus be shown to have a disincentive effect on work and the supply of labor.

SUMMARY

1. Indifference sets and indifference curves show combinations of goods that yield equal amounts of satisfaction.

2. The slope of an indifference curve shows the marginal rate of substitution between the goods.

3. Diminishing marginal rates of substitution mean that as more of one good is substituted, its value in terms of the other good declines.

4. A budget constraint is represented by a budget line which shows the combinations of consumption baskets that are attainable at a given level of income and a given set of prices.

5. Changes in income and prices can be represented by changing the budget line. A change in income is represented by a parallel shift of the budget line. A price change is represented by moving the intercept of the good whose price has changed; this changes the slope of the budget line.

6. A consumer maximizes satisfaction at the point where an indifference curve is tangent to the budget line. This is the highest attainable indifference curve.

7. Price-consumption curves graphically demonstrate how consumption patterns change as prices change.

8. Income-consumption curves show how the consumption of each good changes with changes in income.

9. When price changes, there are income and substitution effects. The substitution effect is a result of the change in relative prices. The income effect comes about because real income changes as prices change.

NEW TERMS

indifference curve analysis
indifference set
indifference curve
indifference map
marginal rate of substitution
principle of diminishing marginal rates of substitution
budget constraint

budget line
income-consumption curve
price-consumption curve
substitution effect
income effect
proportional income tax

QUESTIONS FOR DISCUSSION

1. What does it mean to say that you are "indifferent" between two choices?

2. If the tuition at your college or university were doubled, what income and substitution effects would you experience?

3. Show the effects of a 20 percent increase in the price of all goods (x and y). Then show the effect of a 20 percent decrease in income. Is there any difference? Can inflation be viewed as a tax on income?

4. Why does it take more and more of an abundant good to compensate for the loss of one unit of a good that is becoming scarcer?

5. Would you expect brain surgeons to take more vacations than college professors? Why or why not?

SUGGESTIONS FOR FURTHER READING

Ferguson, C. E., and S. Charles Maurice. *Economic Analysis.* Homewood, Ill.: Richard D. Irwin, Inc., 1978, Chapters 3 and 4.

Kamerschen, David R. and Lloyd M. Valentine. *Intermediate Microeconomic Theory,* 2d ed. Cincinnati: South-Western Publishing Co., 1981, Chapters 5 and 6.

PART 5

The Organization of Product Markets

Production
and Cost

Learning Objectives

After studying the materials found in this chapter, you should be able to do the following:

1. List the advantages and disadvantages of the various forms of business organization.

2. Calculate the least-cost method of production to determine economic efficiency.

3. Define:
   (a) explicit and implicit cost.
   (b) normal and economic profit.

4. Use a production function to:
   (a) define increasing and diminishing returns.
   (b) define economies and diseconomies of scale.
   (c) calculate cost when given the prices of the inputs.

5. Diagram *TPP, APP,* and *MPP.*

6. Define the stages of production in terms of *APP* and *MPP.*

7. Use the definition of $TC = TFC + TVC$ to calculate:
   (a) *ATC.*
   (b) *AFC.*
   (c) *AVC.*
   (d) *MC.*

8. Diagram *TC, TVC, TFC, ATC, AVC, AFC, LRATC,* and *MC.*

9. List the sources of economies of scale and diseconomies of scale.

10. Determine the profit-maximizing level of production using:
    (a) total revenue and total cost.
    (b) marginal revenue and marginal cost.

11. Calculate the present value of a stream of income using a present value table.

This chapter sets the stage for examining the behavior of firms. Before we can analyze firms as sellers of products in different types of markets, it is necessary to understand firms as purchasers of factors of production and to analyze their activities as producers of commodities. The firm buys factors of production (the terms "factors of production" and "inputs" are used as synonyms) and attempts to transform them into marketable outputs. This chapter examines that transformation, which we shall call *production.* It is especially important that this chapter be understood clearly because it provides the foundation for the next four chapters.

production   The transformation of inputs into marketable outputs.

THE FIRM

The *business firm* is organized by an entrepreneur or group of entrepreneurs to combine inputs of raw materials, capital, labor services, and organizational technology to produce outputs of goods and services. Firms are parts of industries. There are many ways to define an *industry,* but, in general, what economists mean by an industry is a group of firms producing similar or related products. For example, when we refer to the automobile industry, we might include just the big four—General Motors, Ford, Chrysler, and American Motors. Or, we might extend the coverage to include all foreign makers and all small domestic producers. We might also include firms which supply parts, materials, and services to automobile producers or to automobile consumers. There are no absolute rules on how to define a particular industry. The definition usually depends on our purpose or the particular problem or issue we wish to study.

business firm   An organization formed by an entrepreneur to transform inputs into marketable outputs.

industry   A group of firms producing similar or related products.

In the United States, firms are organized primarily in one of three ways. These are legal, not economic, categories, and they differ mainly as to the legal liability of the owners. There are some interesting economic questions which arise because of the differences in treatment under the law, but these need not concern us at this point.

Sole Proprietorships

In the *sole proprietorship* form of enterprise, no legal distinction is made between the owner and the firm. The financial resources of the firm are limited to those of the individual owner and what can be borrowed from friends or financial institutions. Thus, the profits and losses accrue solely to that individual. Success of the firm is success of the owner; bankruptcy of the firm is bankruptcy of the owner. This intimate relationship usually means a constant involvement of the owner with the affairs of the firm; and obviously, there are great incentives for hard work and diligence.

sole proprietorship   The form of business enterprise where no legal distinction is made between its owner and the firm.

Compared to other forms of business enterprise, a proprietorship can go in or out of business very easily. In certain lines of business, government approval is required, as licenses or permits may be needed, but typically the single proprietor starts and ends a business by simply doing so. More than 75 percent of the business firms in the United States are sole proprietorships. Most farmers, many professionals such as doctors, lawyers, and consultants, and many small firms, especially in retailing, are sole proprietorships. Although dominant in numbers, sole proprietorships account for only 10 percent of annual business sales.

Partnerships

partnership *The form of business enterprise where there is more than one owner, and these owners and the firm have no legal distinction.*

Partnerships are similar to sole proprietorships except they have more than one owner. There are more personal and financial resources available to a partnership than if only one person formed the firm. Each partner brings to the relationship special skills, knowledge, energy, and decision-making powers. Offsetting these advantages are the inevitable frictions that arise in operating the firm. Partners have to agree on the proportions of ownership owned by each partner, which may be dictated by the amounts of funds contributed, the amounts of work, or the amounts of other kinds of value contributed (such as ideas or patents). Joint rights and responsibilities have to be agreed upon. The partners share in any profits but are also legally liable for any debts incurred by the enterprise.

The disadvantages of the partnership arrangement apparently outweigh the advantages since less than 10 percent of the business organizations and only 5 percent of annual business sales in the United States are accounted for by this form of business. As with sole proprietorships, firms organized as partnerships tend to be quite small and are typically found in professional services—medicine, law, consulting, and some financial services.

Corporations

corporation *The form of business enterprise where stockholders are the legal owners of the firm. Their legal liability is limited.*

The dominant form of business organization in the United States, measured in any way except by absolute number, is the *corporate* form. *Corporations* account for slightly less than 15 percent of business firms but about 85 percent of annual business sales.

stockholders *The owners of a corporation.*

A corporation is a more formal and complex organization than the others. Owners are *stockholders.* Their numbers may run into the hundreds of thousands, although some corporations have only a few stockholders. The stockholders vote, according to the number of shares held, for a *board of directors,* who in turn appoint officers of the corporation to manage the corporation along the guidelines set by the charter of incorporation and the directors.

board of directors *The individuals elected by the stockholders of a corporation to select the managers and oversee the management of the corporation.*

One of the strengths of the corporate form of business organization is the relative ease of acquiring capital, either by issuing additional shares of *stock,* which are certificates demonstrating ownership in the corporation, by borrowing through the issuance of *bonds,* which are interest-earning certificates issued by the corporation, or by borrowing directly by loans from banks or other financial agencies.

stocks *Certificates of ownership in a corporation.*

bonds *Interest-earning certificates issued by governments or corporations as a way of borrowing money.*

The attractiveness of the corporation as a form of organization stems from the fact that the stockholders of the corporation are the legal owners and have rights to the profits, but their legal liability is very limited. This *limited liability* aspect is the critical advantage of the corporate form of business. In fact, in many countries corporations are referred to as limited liability companies and often have the letters *Ltd.* after the name of the firm to stress this feature to anyone who might deal with the enterprise. The letters *Inc.* after the name of a firm in the United States denote the same thing. A stockholder cannot be sued for failure of the corporation to pay its debts; only the corporation can be sued. Thus, the corporation, defined in law as a legal person in its own right, can go bankrupt without the owners going bankrupt. Of course, if individuals have most of their wealth in the stock of one corporation, they might go bankrupt because the stock would no longer have any value. A second and very important attraction of

limited liability *The fact that the stockholders of a corporation cannot be sued for failure of the corporation to pay its debts; only the corporation itself can be sued.*

corporate organization is the ease of transferring ownership. Ownership rights can be transferred through the sale of stocks, and markets (stock exchanges) have evolved to facilitate the transfer. The costs of transfer of ownership are for this reason significantly lower for corporations than for partnerships or single proprietorships.

Different types of ownership cause managers of firms to behave in different ways. For instance, an owner-manager of a single proprietorship may make decisions that are different from those of the hired manager of a large corporation. For now, we will ignore these differences and assume that firms, however they are organized, exist for only one purpose: to increase the wealth of owners. To do this, firms try to maximize their profits. This assumption of profit maximization allows us to develop a powerful predictive theory about the economic effects of different market structures.

ECONOMIC EFFICIENCY

The entrepreneur must combine the factors of production efficiently if the firm is to maximize profits. To do this, entrepreneurs must decide among competing ways of producing a given output. Suppose, for example, South-Western Publishing Company, in deciding how to produce this book, was faced with the alternatives listed in Table 21-1. The production engineer has told the production chief that 100,000 copies of this book could be produced in any of four ways. The engineer has determined the alternative ways to produce the book; it is now up to the entrepreneur to decide how to actually produce the books. The entrepre-

TABLE 21-1 ALTERNATIVE WAYS TO PRODUCE 100,000 COPIES OF THIS BOOK

	Capital (Machines)	Labor (Worker/Years)	Land (Acres)	Output
Method A	5	5	1	100,000
Method B	4	10	1	100,000
Method C	3	15	1	100,000
Method D	2	25	1	100,000

Price of:

Capital Services	$30,000 per Machine
Labor Services	$ 4,000 per Worker/Year
Land Services	$10,000 per Acre

Cost of:

Method A = $150,000 + 20,000 + 10,000 = $180,000
B = $120,000 + 40,000 + 10,000 = $170,000
C = $ 90,000 + 60,000 + 10,000 = $160,000
D = $ 60,000 + 100,000 + 10,000 = $170,000

neur must have a decision rule in order to select a production alternative. This is where profit maximization comes into play. Without profit maximization as a goal, the entrepreneur would have to choose on some other basis—perhaps on a physical-units basis. The method that would minimize the inputs in a physical sense would be method *A,* which uses the fewest inputs. This method of choosing is based on **technical efficiency.** A drawback of this method is that it compares physical units of machines, acres of land, and worker/years of labor. To make sense of such a rule, there needs to be some further rule. For example, the entrepreneur might want to conserve on machines this year. The entrepreneur would then choose method *D* of production.

technical efficiency   A method of production which minimizes physical usage of inputs according to some rule.

Such rules might be needed in a command economy, such as the Soviet Union. A market system, however, puts the inputs into dollar terms and lets the entrepreneur choose the least-cost method of producing. The least-cost method is based on **economic efficiency.** The least-cost method, or the economically efficient method, would always be chosen by the entrepreneur because of the assumption of attempted profit maximization. In Table 21-1, the entrepreneur would choose method *C* to produce the books. Regardless of the price of the books, method *C* maximizes profits (or minimizes losses) because costs are minimized.

economic efficiency   The least-cost method of production.

OPPORTUNITY COST ONCE AGAIN

We just saw how the entrepreneur attempts to minimize costs to achieve economic efficiency. But we need to be careful how we define cost. Costs of the inputs are expressed in terms of their *opportunity cost.* You have been introduced to the concept of opportunity cost, and now you need to apply it with a vengeance. This can be a problem if you are not used to thinking in terms of opportunity cost and are more used to thinking in terms of *explicit cost.* Explicit costs are bookeeping costs or money outlays. We will not ignore explicit costs, but we want to include *implicit costs.* Implicit costs are those costs implied by the alternatives given up. In sum, when we talk of costs, we include all the opportunity costs, not just the part that is explicit.

explicit cost   Bookkeeping cost or money outlay.

implicit cost   The cost implied by the alternatives given up. The opportunity cost of production.

Some examples can make this clearer. Suppose you have the option of working two hours overtime at $10 an hour or going to a concert that costs $5. The *cost* of attending the concert is the $5 ticket plus the $20 you could have earned working overtime. Attending the concert will cost you $25.

Let's return to the example of Suzy Sizzle's lemonade stand. In Chapter 3, we developed supply curves for Suzy's lemonade stand. Table 21-2 presents the financial picture of Suzy's lemonade stand as a bookkeeper would prepare it. Only the explicit costs of doing business are considered. Suzy pays $2,800 for materials, $3,000 to her father for rent, and $4,000 to her only employee, herself. Considering explicit costs only, she shows a profit of $5,200.

Now let's consider the problem the way an economist would. Suppose that Suzy could have re-rented the land, for which she paid her father $3,000, to her Uncle Billy for $5,000. In addition, she could have served beer in her uncle's bar for $7,200 rather than the $4,000 she paid herself for serving lemonade. Since the opportunity cost of the land is $5,000 and the opportunity cost of her labor is $7,200, these are the amounts that should be used in the calculation of her

**TABLE 21-2 SUZY SIZZLE'S PROFIT AND LOSS
STATEMENT: EXPLICIT COSTS ONLY**

Total Revenue from Sales:	$15,000
Less Cost of:	
Cups	500
Sugar	1,000
Lemons	1,100
Water	200
Land	3,000
Suzy's Salary	4,000
	9,800
Bookkeeping Profit	$ 5,200

financial statement. Table 21-3, column *A*, shows these costs, and we see that Suzy has made zero economic profit. This is not necessarily bad. By earning zero profits, Suzy has at least earned her opportunity cost, which means that her resources could not have been better used elsewhere and so are optimally employed. By saying that these resources are optimally employed, we mean Suzy could not do anything else with these inputs that would earn a greater rate of return.

Now let's change the example slightly. Instead of working for her uncle and earning $7,200, let's assume she can earn $15,000 as a model for a major magazine. The opportunity cost for Suzy's labor is now $15,000. As we see in Table 21-3, column *B*, the lemonade firm now shows a profit of −$7,800; that is, a loss of $7,800. In this case, Suzy is not meeting her opportunity cost and should thus leave the lemonade business, rent her land to Uncle Billy, and work for the magazine. Very different results are obtained from those in Table 21-2. The bookkeeper's assessment, which only considers explicit costs, has Suzy making

**TABLE 21-3 SUZY SIZZLE'S PROFIT AND LOSS
STATEMENT: EXPLICIT AND IMPLICIT
COSTS**

	A	*B*	*C*
Total Revenue from Sales:	$15,000	$15,000	$15,000
Less Cost of:			
Cups	500	500	500
Sugar	1,000	1,000	1,000
Lemons	1,100	1,100	1,100
Water	200	200	200
Land	5,000	5,000	5,000
Suzy's Salary	7,200	15,000	5,000
Economic Profit	$ 0	$ − 7,800	$ 2,200

Opportunity Cost

Opportunity cost pervades all economic calculations. Every activity has an opportunity cost, because the decision to undertake one activity precludes the undertaking of another.

Professor Charles A. Lave of the University of California, Irvine, applied this basic economic concept in a study of the 55 MPH speed limit.[1] Lave examined statistics that showed that the cost of wasted travel time

---

[1]Charles A. Lave, "The Costs of Going 55," *Newsweek* (October 23, 1978).

is enormous per life saved or energy saved by driving at 55 MPH rather than at 65 MPH. Let's examine the opportunity cost of driving at 55 MPH and compare it to the benefits. Studies show that commuters value their travel time at 42 percent of their hourly wage. If we calculate the time it takes to drive the same distance at 55 MPH instead of 65 MPH, and value the increased travel time at 42 percent of commuters' hourly wages, we find that a 55 MPH speed limit costs about $6 billion in travel time per year. The government tells us that a 55 MPH speed limit saves 4,500 lives per year. Therefore, it costs about $1.3 million per life saved. In addition, we save roughly 1 to 2 percent of our gasoline. This is a trivial amount of savings and one which could be duplicated or exceeded by proper maintenance of air in tires. So the primary benefit is in lives saved.

In his article, Lave reports on some other costs of saving lives. He reports that putting a smoke detector in every home would cost about $5,000 per life saved, kidney dialysis machines save lives for about $30,000 per life, mobile cardiac care units cost about $2,000 per life saved, and highway improvements cost between $20,000 and $100,000 per life saved. The conclusion is pretty obvious: Driving 55 MPH is a very costly way of saving lives. No wonder it is so unpopular! It is a good example of the government forcing people to purchase a commodity, in this case safety, which the public views as too costly.

If you don't think that a 55 MPH speed limit is too costly, what about a 45 MPH speed limit, or a 35 MPH speed limit? A 5 MPH speed limit would virtually insure no deaths from automobile accidents. Do you think a 5 MPH speed limit is a reasonable opportunity cost to insure no highway deaths? Probably not. So you see, it's a decision at the margin concerning what you think the proper trade-off between costs and benefits for safety happens to be. As Lave points out, the cost of saving one life by moving from 65 MPH to 55 MPH is 102 person-years of extra travel time per year.

a "profit" of $5,200. The economist's assessment, which considers opportunity costs, shows a loss of $7,800 and has Suzy closing her business to work for a magazine.

Let's change the example once more. Suppose Suzy's best alternative is to pick lettuce for her brother Jack and earn $5,000. As Table 21-3, column *C*, shows, the lemonade stand now earns an economic profit of $2,200. This ***economic profit*** is a return above explicit and implicit costs. It is extra; that is, it is not needed to keep resources in this industry. Of course, Suzy likes making this economic profit—in fact, other entrepreneurs would also like to earn more than

economic profit   *Return to the firm in excess of the explicit and implicit costs of production.*

their opportunity cost. It is inevitable, then, that additional resources in the form of more lemonade stands will move into this industry in an attempt to earn some of these economic profits. Those who enter the market will be those whose opportunity costs are lowest.

ECONOMIC COST AND NORMAL PROFIT

The concepts of cost and profit which we have just introduced are important and will be used throughout this book. The opportunity cost of capital and entrepreneurship is referred to as *normal profit*. A normal profit represents the rate of return that is necessary to keep capital in an industry. Say, for example, a normal rate of return is 12 percent. We would say that a firm earning a 12 percent rate of return is earning zero profits because its capital could earn 12 percent elsewhere. The concept of normal profit is relevant in utility pricing. If an electric utility is not granted a price increase and the rate of return on capital falls below the normal rate of return, capital will leave the industry because it can earn its opportunity cost elsewhere.

normal profit   The opportunity cost of capital and entrepreneurship. This is the level of profit that is necessary for a firm to remain in a competitive industry.

Our definition of costs is important because we predict behavior from it. When economic profits are positive, we predict that firms will enter an industry; when negative, that firms will leave; and when zero, that firms will remain. Profits signal movements into or out of an industry. If a firm isn't earning normal, or average, profits in the industry in which it presently produces, the resources of this firm will flow to an industry where average, or normal, returns can be earned. If more than average, or normal, returns are earned in an industry, resources will be attracted to it.

We now turn to three production relationships. First, we will discuss the relationship between inputs and outputs, or the production function. Next, we will show how output changes when inputs are varied. Finally, we will discuss how costs of production are related to levels of output.

PRODUCTION FUNCTIONS IN THE SHORT AND LONG RUN

A *production function* is a description of the amounts of output expected from various combinations of input usage. It is usually expressed in tabular or graphic form, but it can also be shown by a mathematical formula. The production function describes a technical or technological relationship. The input combinations and their corresponding output quantities, which make up the production function, are determined by engineers, agronomists, chemists, and other technical experts. Only the best input combinations are included. For example, it might be that an output of 100 units of a commodity could be produced by 5 units of capital, 20 units of labor, and 2 units of land, or by 6 units of capital, 30 units of labor, and 3 units of land. Since the second combination is obviously inferior to the first, that method of production would be ignored. The production function is a reflection of the best technology available for a given level of output in the production process.

production function   A description of the technical relationships that transform inputs into outputs. Production functions can generally be described by mathematical relationships.

fixed factors　The factors of production that cannot be varied in the short run, such as the size of the plant.

variable factors　The factors of production that can be varied in the short run.

short run　The period of time too short to vary all the factors of production. Short-run decisions are those concerned with using the existing plant more or less intensively.

long run　A period of time in which all inputs, including plant and equipment, can be varied.

Usually we are interested in only a portion of the production function. For instance, it is often convenient to ask what would happen to total production if all inputs were at a given, fixed level and only one was allowed to change in amount. Then we can speak of *fixed factors* and *variable factors*. Which factors are fixed and which are variable usually depends on the problem we are studying, although in many cases it is natural to think of the land and the buildings of a firm as the fixed factors and labor as the variable factor. When we distinguish between fixed and variable factors, we are considering what is called the *short run*. In the *long run,* all factors are variable. *Short-run* decisions are those concerning the profit-maximizing use of the existing plant and equipment. The plant is used more intensively as the amount of variable factors, such as labor or additional machines, is increased. *Long-run* decisions are those concerning the selection of a plant size that will maximize profits.

These different time horizons may not correspond to time in the calendar sense. Some industries may be able to increase in size very rapidly. In addition, contractions in size may take longer than expansions since the only way to decrease the amount of fixed factors may be to use them until they wear out. In some cases contractions can occur more quickly, depending on whether the plant and equipment are adaptable for use in other industries. It is primarily for convenience of analysis that we treat decisions as being either short-run or long-run decisions. You should keep in mind that these decisions are inherently related. Once a long-run decision to build a plant of a certain size is made, a whole series of short-run decisions are influenced because they must deal with this certain-size plant.

Increasing and Diminishing Returns

As we add more and more units of a particular variable factor to a given set of fixed factors, we may at first obtain larger increments in output, but we eventually obtain smaller increments in output. This economic phenomenon is referred to as the *principle of diminishing returns*. It is plausible that returns are diminishing because, otherwise, all the wheat needed to feed the world could be produced on one acre of land by just adding more seed, more fertilizer, more water, and more labor to that acre of land.

principle of diminishing returns　As more and more units of a variable factor are added to a set of fixed factors, the resulting increments of output will eventually become increasingly smaller.

The principle of diminishing returns is a fascinating and pervasive phenomenon. Nobody knows why, but we never find the principle contradicted in real-world observations. Why is it that a tree grows more slowly as it grows larger? Why do little pigs put on more weight from a given amount of corn than do big ones? Why is it more costly to add a floor to a twenty-story building than to a ten-story building? Why is it that adding water to parched soil yields remarkable results whereas adding the same amount of water to already moist soil may add very little to the crop? Why is it that if a firm adds a worker when the labor force is already large, the increase in output is less than if one is added at a time when the labor force is small? These are only a few examples of the principle of diminishing returns.

Note that diminishing returns is a short-run phenomenon and says nothing about the long-run production function. It only says that if you add more and more variable input to a fixed factor, after a while the return will decline. Think of your own experience in studying for exams. The output is your score on a test and the variable factor is the time you spend studying. Assume you could get 55 percent without studying. One hour of studying boosts your score to 66 percent; two hours, to 75 percent; three hours, to 80 percent; four hours, to 84 percent; five hours, to 86 percent, and so on. You see that each additional variable input (hour spent studying) produces a smaller increment in output than the previous input. In this example, the first hour produced an improvement of 11 percent; the second hour, 9 percent; the third, 5 percent, and so on. We see a diminishing return to studying. It is up to you to decide when the return for an additional hour of studying is not worth the opportunity cost of that hour in terms of the other things you could be doing. So you see, even deciding how much to study is an exercise in rational economic calculation.

Marginal and Average Physical Product

In order to describe more precisely the changing relationship between inputs and outputs, economists use the concept of the **marginal physical product** (*MPP*) of the factors of production. The marginal physical product of labor, say, is the change in total output per unit change in the use of labor service. Formally,

$$MPP_L = \frac{\Delta \, TPP}{\Delta \, L},$$

where MPP_L is the marginal physical product of labor, $\Delta \, TPP$ is the change in the total physical product, and $\Delta \, L$ is the change in the number of units of labor employed. The **average physical product (APP)** of a factor of production is simply the **total physical product (TPP)** divided by the number of units of the factor employed. For example, the average physical product of capital is

$$APP_K = \frac{TPP}{K},$$

where APP_K is the average physical product of capital and where K is the number of units of capital used.

We can see these relationships arithmetically by examining Table 21-4, which represents a short-run production function. All factors of production are fixed factors except labor. Labor, the variable input, can vary between 1 and 10 units. You can see, by examining Table 21-4, that as more variable input is added to the fixed inputs, output goes through three distinct stages. When the first three units of labor are added, output increases at an increasing rate. Adding the fourth unit of labor causes output to increase, but by a smaller amount than the third unit of labor produced. The eighth unit of labor produces no increase in output and the ninth unit of labor causes output to decline. We sometimes refer to these phases as **stages of production.** Stage I is where we experience increasing returns to the variable factor; stage II is the area of diminishing returns; and stage III is the area of negative returns. Table 21-4 shows these stages. This same relationship is represented graphically in Figure 21-1. Total product increases at an increasing rate in stage I reflecting increasing returns. It increases at a decreasing rate in stage II reflecting diminishing returns, and declines in stage III reflecting negative returns.

The average product curve and marginal product curve in panel (b) of Figure 21-1 reflect the phenomena in another way. When increasing returns are being

marginal physical product   The change in physical output that is produced by a unit change in a factor of production.

average physical product   The total physical product (output) divided by the number of units of a factor used.

total physical product   The amount that a firm produces in physical units.

stages of production   Stage I is where we experience increasing returns to the variable factor. Stage II is the area of diminishing returns. Stage III is the area of negative returns.

TABLE 21-4 STAGES OF PRODUCTION

Variable Input	Total Output	Marginal Product	Average Product	Stage of Production
(Units of Labor)	(Units of Product)			
1	6	6	6	
2	14	8	7	Stage I
3	24	10	8	
4	32	8	8	
5	38	6	7.6	Stage II
6	42	4	7	
7	44	2	6.3	
8	44	0	5.5	
9	42	−2	4.7	Stage III
10	36	−6	3.6	

experienced in stage I, marginal physical product is rising. In stage II, diminishing returns is equivalent to declining marginal physical product. Similarly, declining total product means negative marginal physical product.

A very important relationship between average values and marginal values can be developed. Think of your grade point average. If your grade in this course (the marginal grade) is below your grade point average for all courses taken, your average will fall. If your grade in this course is above your grade point average, your average will rise. The same holds for every marginal-average relationship. If a basketball player's lifetime shooting percentage (average) is higher this week than last week, you know that in the intervening (marginal) games, the player has shot a higher-than-average percentage. If the average is rising, the marginal must be above average, or putting it the other way around, if the marginal is above average, it will pull the average up. If the average is falling, the marginal must be below the average.

COST IN THE SHORT RUN

The production function relates inputs to outputs. These inputs have prices and represent costs to the firm. These prices are determined in factor markets and may or may not be affected by the firm itself. Given the prices of inputs and the production function, we can derive cost data for the firm. Although the derivation can be done formally, we will derive the costs in a simpler fashion and leave the formal derivation to more advanced texts and courses.

Costs Defined

total cost The sum of all the costs of production.

Total Cost (TC) is simply the total cost of producing different levels of output. A total cost profile for a hypothetical firm is given in column 4 of Table 21-5.

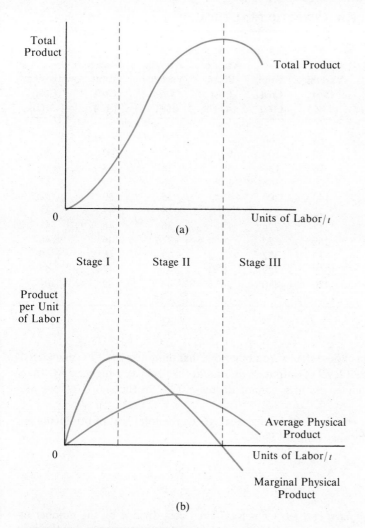

FIGURE 21-1 PRODUCT CURVES

Total product increases at an increasing rate in stage I, reflecting increasing returns. In stage II, diminishing returns set in. Diminishing returns mean that marginal physical product is declining. Stage III is characterized by negative returns.

Total cost is made up of two components: *total fixed cost (TFC)* and *total variable cost (TVC)*. Total fixed cost is the cost of the fixed factors and, therefore, does not vary in the short run. These total fixed costs will be the same regardless of how many units of output the firm produces. Total variable costs vary directly with output, increasing as more output is produced. This happens because more variable factors have to be purchased if more output is to be produced. Total fixed costs and total variable costs are represented by columns 2 and 3 in Table 21-5. Note that we have said that $TFC + TVC = TC$. We assume that for every level

total fixed cost   The cost of the fixed factors of production. Total fixed cost does not vary in the short run.

total variable cost   The total of costs that vary directly with output, increasing as more output is produced.

TABLE 21-5   COST FOR A HYPOTHETICAL FIRM

1 Output per Week (Q)	2 Total Fixed Cost (TFC)	3 Total Variable Cost (TVC)	4 Total Cost (TC)	5 Average Fixed Cost (AFC)	6 Average Variable Cost (AVC)	7 Average Total Cost (AC)	8 Marginal Cost (MC)
0	60	0	60		0		0
1	60	40	100	60	40	100	40
2	60	76	136	30	38	68	36
3	60	108	168	20	36	56	32
4	60	140	200	15	35	50	32
5	60	175	235	12	35	47	35
6	60	216	276	10	36	46	41
7	60	262	322	$8^{4/7}$	$37^{3/7}$	46	46
8	60	312	372	$7^{1/2}$	39	$46^{1/2}$	50
9	60	369	429	$6^{2/3}$	41	$47^{2/3}$	57
10	60	430	490	6	43	49	61

of output, the firm chooses factor combinations that minimize the *TVC* associated with producing that level of output. Why should the firm pay a higher *TVC* than it has to? (Of course, the firm cannot decrease *TFC* in the short run we are considering.)

average total cost   *Total costs of production divided by the number of units of output.*

Average total cost, hereafter designated *AC*, is the total cost of producing an output, divided by that output. Thus,

$$AC = \frac{TC}{Q}.$$

average fixed cost   *Total fixed costs of production divided by output. Average fixed costs decline as production is increased.*

Likewise, *average fixed cost (AFC)* is total fixed cost divided by the number of units of output, and *average variable cost (AVC)* is the total variable cost divided by the number of units of output. *AFC, AVC,* and *AC* appear in columns 5, 6, and 7 of Table 21-5, respectively.

average variable cost   *Total variable costs divided by the number of units of output.*

Marginal cost is the addition to (change in) total cost of producing one more (or one less) unit of output. Therefore,

marginal cost   *The change in total cost of producing one more (or one less) unit of output.*

$$MC = \frac{\Delta TC}{\Delta Q} = \frac{\Delta TVC}{\Delta Q}.$$

This means that marginal costs are really marginal *variable* costs, because there are no marginal fixed costs.

These cost measures are all mathematically interrelated, and you can make calculations to move from one to the other. As practice, be sure to work the problem in the study guide which gives you a table like Table 21-5 with blank cells. If you can fill in the blanks, you understand the relationship between the different measures of cost. All these relationships are summarized in Table 21-6.

TABLE 21-6 COST MEASURES SUMMARIZED

Total Cost = TC
Total Fixed Cost = TFC
Total Variable Cost = TVC
Average Total Cost = AC
Average Fixed Cost = AFC
Average Variable Cost = AVC
Marginal Cost = MC

$$TC = TFC + TVC$$

$$AC = \frac{TC}{Q}$$

$$AC = AFC + AVC$$

$$AFC = \frac{TFC}{Q}$$

$$AVC = \frac{TVC}{Q}$$

$$MC = \frac{\Delta TC}{\Delta Q} = \frac{\Delta TVC}{\Delta Q}$$

Cost Curves

We can draw a series of cost curves for the production function described by the numerical data given in Table 21-5. The curves are drawn smoothly to better emphasize the relationship between the curves.[1]

The total fixed cost, total variable cost, and total cost curves are drawn in Figure 21-2. If you are confused as to how the curves are related, review Tables 21-5 and 21-6. The shapes of the total cost curve and the total variable cost curve determine the shape of the production function. When the variable factor is increased, output increases and costs increase. If output increases more rapidly than factor cost, total cost (as well as total variable cost) increases at a decreasing rate, and returns are increasing. In Figure 21-2, this is what happens as output increases from zero to OQ_1. From OQ_1 to higher levels of output, output increases less rapidly than the factor cost increases, so total cost (along with total variable cost) increases at an increasing rate. The principle of diminishing returns is operating.

If this is not clear, consider this simple example. Suppose that a firm hires one more worker and output increases by ten units. The variable cost increases by the wage of that worker (for a given time period). Now, if it takes two workers to increase output by ten more units, total variable cost would increase by the wage rate times two. Clearly the cost has increased at an increasing rate.

Now, let's look at average costs within a production function. Figure 21-3 shows the *AFC, AVC, AC,* and *MC* curves of a hypothetical firm. The *AFC* curve declines continuously, getting closer and closer to the *x*-axis of the graph. This

---

[1]By drawing the curves smoothly, we are assuming that the gaps between the discrete points in Table 21-5 can be filled in with a continuous curve.

FIGURE 21-2 TOTAL COST CURVES

The shape of the total cost curve and total variable cost curve is a reflection of the shape of the production function. From zero output until an output of OQ_1, total cost and total variable cost increase at a decreasing rate. After output OQ_1, diminishing returns set in and these costs increase at an increasing rate.

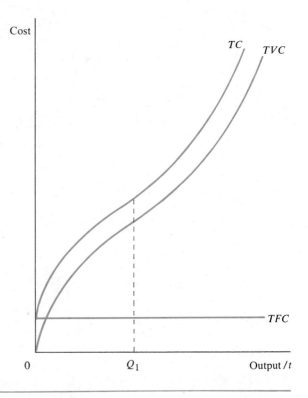

**FIGURE 21-3   MARGINAL AND AVERAGE COST
           CURVES**

Average fixed cost declines continuously. Average variable cost declines, reaches a minimum, and then increases, as does average cost, resulting in a *U*-shaped cost curve. The marginal cost curve intersects the average variable cost and average cost curves at their minimum points.

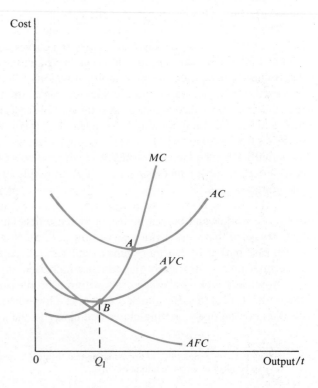

is because fixed costs are constant and average fixed cost is derived by dividing a constant cost amount by an ever-increasing quantity. The AFC thus becomes smaller and smaller as output increases.

AVC declines and then increases, as does AC. This U-shape represents at first increasing returns and then diminishing returns, as we discussed earlier. At first, returns to the fixed-size plant (we are looking at the short run) increase. This is represented by the output up to OQ_1 in Figure 21-3. OQ_1 in Figures 21-2 and 21-3 are the same. After OQ_1, returns to the variable factors decline. We have reached diminishing returns. In other words, increasing returns mean decreasing average costs and diminishing returns mean increasing average costs. The AVC and AC curves are U-shaped because of decreasing costs (increasing returns) for small levels of output and increasing costs (diminishing returns) at eventual higher levels of output.

The minimum point on the AC curve is referred to as the **least-cost combination.** The least-cost combination is the lowest attainable per-unit cost for a given plant size. The least-cost combination in Figure 21-3 is point A. For a fixed plant size, it is impossible to produce at a lower per-unit cost than that represented by the least-cost combination.

It is very important to note that the MC curve intersects the AC and AVC curves at their lowest points, points A and B in Figure 21-3. This relates to our earlier discussion of the average-marginal relationship. For the average curves to be declining, the marginal must be below the average, and in order for the average to be rising, the marginal must be above the average. This requires that the marginal and average be equal when the average curve is at its minimum point. If you don't see why this has to be the case, think back to the example of how your grade point average goes up or down depending on the grade in an added (marginal) course. Also, notice that when the marginal cost curve starts to rise, it is still below the average variable cost curve; thus, average variable cost is still falling. An average value falls as long as the marginal value is below it, regardless of whether the marginal value is falling or rising.

least-cost combination The lowest attainable per-unit cost for a given plant size. It is represented by the minimum point on the average cost curve.

COST IN THE LONG RUN

In the long run, there are no fixed factors of production. As a result, there are no fixed costs; all costs are variable. In fact, we define the long run as that period long enough to vary all inputs.

In essence, the long-run decision focuses on a determination of which size plant to build. Each plant size is represented by a short-run AC curve, so the long-run decision is the selection of the desired short-run cost curve. The decision will be based on the output the firm expects to produce. Figure 21-4 graphically illustrates this decision. Suppose that the technological factors (given by the production function) are such that only three plant sizes are feasible. These plants are represented by AC_1, AC_2, and AC_3 in Figure 21-4. The long-run decision of which short-run curve to be on would depend on the planned output of the firm. If output is to be less than OQ_1, then the plant represented by AC_1 should be built because it represents the plant size that will produce an output level between O and OQ_1 at the lowest attainable per-unit cost. Likewise, if outputs between OQ_1 and OQ_2 are planned, the plant represented by AC_2 should be built. If

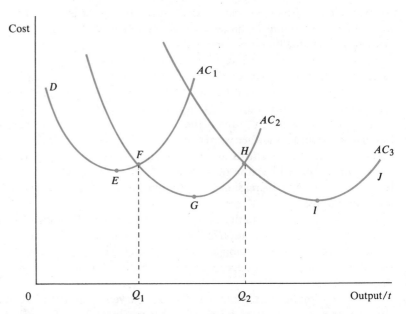

FIGURE 21-4   ALTERNATIVE PLANT SIZES
The long-run decision of the firm is the determination of which size plant to build.
This decision is the selection of the desired short-run cost curve.

outputs greater than OQ_2 are planned, plant AC_3 should be built. In the long run, the average cost curve facing this firm is *DEFGHIJ*.

It is likely that more than three alternative plant sizes are available, and in the planning stage they would all be examined. Assume the firm faces all the alternative short-run curves as depicted in Figure 21-5. All the possible short-run curves are tangent to a curve that is sometimes referred to as a *planning curve*. It is called a planning curve because in the planning stage any point on the curve could be chosen by building a certain-size plant. Such a planning curve, more commonly called the *long-run average cost curve (LRAC)*, is shown in Figure 21-5. The long-run average cost curve then represents the lowest attainable average cost of producing any given output. For example, if you knew you were going to produce exactly OQ output, plant size AC_4 would have the lowest average cost of doing so.

Only at point A on Figure 21-5, which represents an output of OQ_1 units, is there a tangency between the minimum point on the short-run average cost curve (the least-cost combination) and the minimum point on the *LRAC* curve. This point is referred to as the *optimal-size plant*. This is the optimal-size plant because it represents the short-run AC curve with the lowest attainable per-unit costs.

Economies and Diseconomies of Scale

The *LRAC* curve drawn in Figure 21-5 is *U*-shaped. This *U*-shape means that, at first, as plant size and firm output increase, average costs fall. Increasing

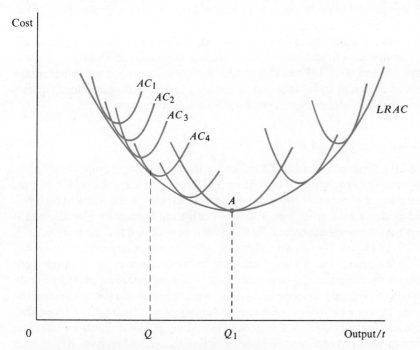

FIGURE 21-5 LONG-RUN AVERAGE COST CURVE
All the possible short-run cost curves are tangent to a curve called a planning curve.
This planning curve is the long-run average cost curve and represents the lowest
attainable average cost of producing any level of output. The optimal plant size
would be found at point *A*, where the minimum point on a short-run average cost
curve is tangent to the long-run average cost curve at its minimum point.

returns result from the firm becoming larger. After a certain point (point *A* on
Figure 21-5), however, bigness starts becoming costly. As the plant continues to
increase in size, average cost begins to rise. Economists refer to these returns and
costs to increased plant size as *economies and diseconomies of scale;* that is, as
scale (plant size) increases, economies (savings) result. After a while, further
growth results in diseconomies (costs).

It is easy to see how economies of scale result from a growth in plant size.
As a firm increases its scale of operations, it can usually employ more specialized
machinery and jobs can be more specialized. Equipment can be used more efficiently. By-products of the operation which might be uneconomical to recover,
or exploit, in a small-scale plant may become significant for a large operation. A
large firm is often able to obtain quantity discounts and to purchase more precise
amounts of intermediate products from other firms. Even political influence of
economic value is more likely to accrue to a large, rather than a small, firm. These
are just a few of the factors that account for the negative slope of the *LRAC* curve
as the scale of plant increases.

*economies of scale   Declines in
average cost that are due to
increased plant size. Declining
long-run average costs.*

*diseconomies of scale   Increases
in average cost that are due to
increased plant size. Increasing
long-run average costs.*

Diseconomies of scale are perhaps harder to grasp, although anyone who has dealt with giant bureaucracies, public or private, will have seen evidence of them. Diseconomies result primarily from the fact that as an organization becomes very large, communication and coordination become more difficult and time-consuming, and control from the top diminishes. So when a firm has taken advantage of most of the gains to be achieved by growing larger, managerial inefficiencies set in and the *LRAC* curve turns upward with further growth.

Optimal-Size Plants in the Real World

Figure 21-5 depicted a smooth *LRAC* curve that had a single optimal-size plant corresponding to an output of OQ_1. If we look around in the real world, however, we see many different-size firms operating side by side in the same industry.

Economists have spent much time investigating economies of scale, and it appears that the range of actual *LRAC* curves is represented in Figures 21-6, 21-7, and 21-8. In Figure 21-6 we see economies of scale over a large range of output. This situation occurs in the steel and auto industries, where we see a few very large firms that seem to get larger and larger. The optimal-size plant in Figure 21-6 would be OQ_1, which conceivably might represent all the normal sales of the industry. In some industries a ***natural monopoly*** occurs because the economies of scale justify the existence of only one firm. Many public utilities, for instance, in order to become large enough to be of optimal size, need to have all the sales in a market.

In Figure 21-7 we see that a large number of different-size plants can be optimal. Distinctly different-size firms can all produce efficiently in the same industry at the same per-unit (or average) cost. In Figure 21-7 any firm producing

natural monopoly   A monopoly that emerges because of economies of scale. The size of the market is such that there is room for only one optimally sized firm.

FIGURE 21-6   ECONOMIES OF SCALE AND A FEW VERY LARGE PLANTS

When economies of scale exist over large ranges of output, one large plant or a few large plants are most efficient.

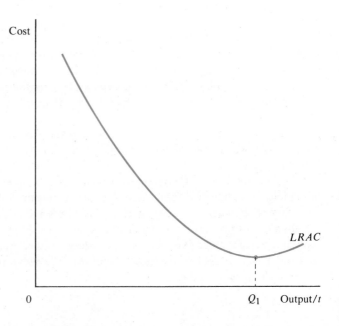

Cost

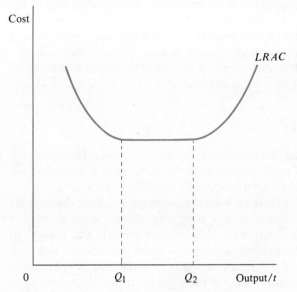

LRAC

0   Q_1 Q_2 Output/t

**FIGURE 21-7   MANY OPTIMAL-SIZE PLANTS OF
DIFFERENT SIZES**

A range in the output of the optimal-size plant can exist. When
this situation exists, plants of distinctly different sizes can all
produce efficiently in the same industry.

an output between OQ_1 and OQ_2 would be efficient, and if the demand for the
product was large enough to support many firms of this size, a very competitive
situation would exist. This situation prevails in many industries.

In Figure 21-8 we see rapidly achievable economies of scale and then rapid
diseconomies of scale. This would be the case when all the firms in an industry
(where sales are large relative to OQ_1) are of a very similar size. The optimal-size
plant in Figure 21-8 is, of course, OQ_1.

Cost

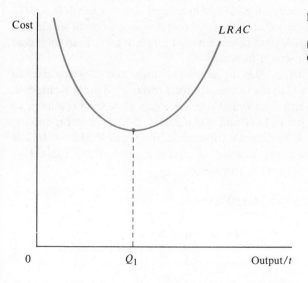

LRAC

0   Q_1 Output/t

**FIGURE 21-8   MANY OPTIMAL-SIZE PLANTS OF
SIMILAR SIZES**

If there is a unique minimum point on the long-run average cost
curve, all the plants will be of a very similar size.

The concept of economies of scale is important. We observed that if the bigness of a firm is due to economies of scale, it is efficient to have production carried out by large firms. This is very important for antitrust policy because these large-scale firms may exert monopoly pricing powers. We will return to this problem in some detail when we examine some actual studies of economies of scale and monopoly power in selected industries.

PROFIT MAXIMIZATION

Soon we will examine production and sales under different market structures, but now we must cover a few more preliminaries. First, we need to discuss profit maximization, and second, we need to examine choice over time.

We will assume that the firms we will examine in the next four chapters are all profit-maximizing firms. But what does profit maximization mean in terms of production decisions? It means that in the short run, the firm will attempt to choose the output that maximizes the difference between total revenue and total cost. *Total revenue (TR)* is the price an item sells for multiplied by the number of units sold. *Marginal revenue (MR)* is the addition to (or change in) total revenue from selling one more unit. Our operational rule for profit maximization, then, is to produce that output at which marginal revenue equals marginal cost *(MR = MC)*. Notice that the directive to produce where $MR = MC$ is just another way of saying, Produce where total profit is at its maximum, or alternatively, Produce where total revenue exceeds total cost by the largest amount. These are simply different ways of saying the same thing. Generally, the $MR = MC$ rule is the most convenient one with which to work.

First, let us convince you that profit is maximized where $MR = MC$. Since MR is the change in total revenue per unit change in quantity sold, if you add up all the marginal revenues from zero to the current quantity (say OQ_1), you will get the total revenue at OQ_1. Likewise, if you add up all the marginal costs from zero output to the current output, you will get the total variable cost of the current output. Anytime MR is greater than MC, total revenue is increasing faster than total cost when output and sales are increased. This means that profit is increasing (or losses are decreasing). If you decreased output when $MR > MC$, total revenue would decline by more than total cost declines, so profit would fall. But if output were increased, total revenue would increase more than total cost would increase, and profit would increase.

On the other hand, if $MC > MR$, an increase in output and sales would cause total cost to increase more than the increase in total revenue, so profit would fall. But a decrease in output and sales would decrease costs more than revenues, so profit would increase. So far we have said that if $MR > MC$, expand production and sales, and if $MC > MR$, decrease production and sales. If $MR = MC$, it would be unprofitable to either increase or decrease production. Table 21-7 summarizes these rules for profit maximization.

total revenue The quantity of a good or service that a firm sells multiplied by the price of the good or service.

marginal revenue The change in total revenue from selling one more (or one less) unit.

TABLE 21-7   RULES FOR PROFIT MAXIMIZATION

$MR > MC$	Expand Output
$MR = MC$	Profits Maximized, Output Unchanged
$MR < MC$	Reduce Output

It's easy to see this same relationship on a graph. In Figure 21-9, the firm is a *price taker,* which means that the price is fixed as far as this firm is concerned. Thus, the total revenue curve in Figure 21-9, panel (a), is a straight line from the origin, and the *MR* curve in panel (b) is a horizontal line and is equal to the price of the product. The total cost curve is consistent with the law of diminishing

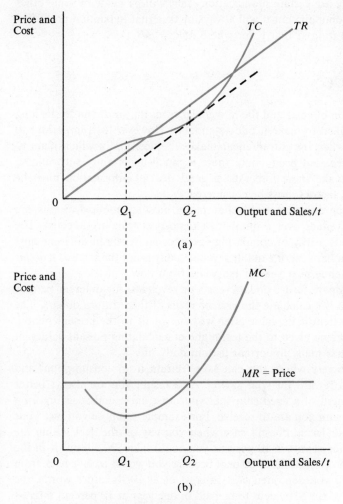

(a)

(b)

**FIGURE 21-9 PROFIT MAXIMIZATION UNDER
CONDITIONS OF PURE COMPETITION**

Profit maximization occurs where marginal cost is equal to marginal revenue. The vertical distance between total revenue and total cost is greatest [panel (a)] at the same level of output where marginal cost equals marginal revenue [panel (b)].

returns after output OQ_2. (From zero output to OQ_2, the cost curve represents increasing returns and decreasing average costs.)

The vertical distance between TR and TC is greatest at output OQ_2, and at that point the slopes of TR and TC are equal. The slope of TR is MR and the slope of TC is MC, so it is clear that $MR = MC$ at output OQ_2. This can be seen clearly in Figure 21-9, panel (b). Note that if output were decreased from OQ_2, MC would fall below MR and TR would fall by more than TC, so profit would fall. If output increased from OQ_2, TC would increase more than TR and MC would be greater than MR, so again profit would fall. Profit is at a maximum at OQ_2.

This decision rule, to produce that output where marginal revenue equals marginal cost, will come up again and again, so it is important to make sure you understand it. There are certain modifications that will be made in some other contexts, such as monopoly, but it will always be true that maximum profit will be obtained by operating at that point where $MR = MC$.

PRESENT VALUE

So far, our discussion of costs and the movement from the short run to the long run has been simplified to make it understandable. However, it is important to keep in mind that when the entrepreneur makes the decision of which plant to build, based on forecasted production, there is much uncertainty surrounding that decision. To make these forecasts, a great deal of information must be gathered and many factors must be considered.

When production decisions, or for that matter most economic decisions, are made, costs and revenues over a number of periods of time are affected. The decision maker needs a way of comparing revenues and costs in different time periods, because a dollar cost or a dollar revenue today is not the same as a dollar cost or a dollar revenue next year or ten years from now.

present value The capitalized value of an item to be paid for or sold in the future. A future value discounted to the present.

In order to compare future dollars (costs or revenues) for different periods with present dollars, we calculate the *present value* of these future dollars. The present value of an item is its value after we *discount* it to the present period. *Discounting* is the name given to the technique of calculating present values. It works simply and has many important uses in daily life.

discounting The term given to the technique of calculating present values.

We live in a society where you can save (refrain from consumption) and receive interest as a reward for your saving. As a result, you are always better off delaying a payment of a fixed sum that you must make and speeding up a payment of a fixed sum you are to receive. For example, suppose you owe your friend $100 and your friend doesn't care when you pay off the debt within the next year. If the interest rate is 10 percent you could take $90.90, put it in the bank, and in one year pay off the $100 debt because you would receive back from the bank the $90.90 you deposited *plus* interest of $9.10. In other words, the present value *(PV)* of the $100 debt to be paid in one year at 10 percent interest is only $90.90. Another way of saying this is that the $90.90 you put in the bank today will be equivalent to the $100 you pay to your friend a year from now. Conversely, if you were owed $100, you would want the money now so you could put $100 in the bank and have $110 at the end of a year. Two principles emerge from this example of discounting. The first is: the higher the interest rate, the lower the present value. The second is: the longer the time period, the lower the present value.

The formula for calculating present value is

$$\frac{V_t}{(1+r)^t},$$

where V_t is the value in year t, r is the interest rate, and t is the number of years. The formula is rarely used in calculations, however, since present value tables, like Table 21-8, are readily available. This table shows the present value of one dollar received in any future year (up to 50 years) at different interest rates. You can easily read the table to see, as in our previous example, that the present value of $100 for one year at a 10 percent interest rate is $90.90 (.909 × $100).

APPLICATIONS OF PRESENT VALUE

Applications of present value calculation surround you in your day-to-day life. Let's look at an example.

Suppose that on your first job as an executive you are given the task of planning a new phase of operations. The engineer tells you the operation can be

TABLE 21-8 PRESENT VALUE OF $1.00

Year	3%	4%	5%	6%	7%	8%	10%	12%	15%	20%	Year
1	.971	.962	.952	.943	.935	.926	.909	.893	.870	.833	1
2	.943	.925	.907	.890	.873	.857	.826	.797	.756	.694	2
3	.915	.890	.864	.839	.816	.794	.751	.711	.658	.578	3
4	.889	.855	.823	.792	.763	.735	.683	.636	.572	.482	4
5	.863	.823	.784	.747	.713	.681	.620	.567	.497	.402	5
6	.838	.790	.746	.705	.666	.630	.564	.507	.432	.335	6
7	.813	.760	.711	.665	.623	.583	.513	.452	.376	.279	7
8	.789	.731	.677	.627	.582	.540	.466	.404	.326	.233	8
9	.766	.703	.645	.591	.544	.500	.424	.360	.284	.194	9
10	.744	.676	.614	.558	.508	.463	.385	.322	.247	.162	10
11	.722	.650	.585	.526	.475	.429	.350	.287	.215	.134	11
12	.701	.625	.557	.497	.444	.397	.318	.257	.187	.112	12
13	.681	.601	.530	.468	.415	.368	.289	.229	.162	.0935	13
14	.661	.577	.505	.442	.388	.340	.263	.204	.141	.0779	14
15	.642	.555	.481	.417	.362	.315	.239	.183	.122	.0649	15
16	.623	.534	.458	.393	.339	.292	.217	.163	.107	.0541	16
17	.605	.513	.436	.371	.317	.270	.197	.146	.093	.0451	17
18	.587	.494	.416	.350	.296	.250	.179	.130	.0808	.0376	18
19	.570	.475	.396	.330	.277	.232	.163	.116	.0703	.0313	19
20	.554	.456	.377	.311	.258	.215	.148	.104	.0611	.0261	20
25	.478	.375	.295	.232	.184	.146	.0923	.0588	.0304	.0105	25
30	.412	.308	.231	.174	.131	.0994	.0573	.0334	.0151	.00421	30
40	.307	.208	.142	.0972	.067	.0460	.0221	.0107	.00373	.000680	40
50	.228	.141	.087	.0543	.034	.0213	.00852	.00346	.000922	.000109	50

lion ten-year salary. Winfield was a good enough bargainer that he received a 10 percent cost of living adjustment. Neither the Yankees nor Winfield would disclose details of the offer, but the papers reported the details as leaked by executives of other teams.

It was reported that Winfield's salary for 1981 would be $1.5 million and would increase 10 percent per year for ten years, making his salary $3,536,921 in the tenth year. The news wires reported the ten-year worth of this contract at $23,906,134.

Let's calculate the present value of Winfield's contract using a 12 percent interest rate, which was a modest rate at the time of the contract, and assuming (for simplicity) that his annual salary is paid in a lump sum on December 31 each year. The calculations show that the reported $23.9 million contract was really worth $11.8 million. This still may be the most lucrative contract in sports history, but it is far less than the headlines indicated.

WINFIELD'S SALARY

Year	Salary in Millions of Dollars	Present Value in Millions of Dollars (12% discount rate)
1	1.5	1.3
2	1.7	1.4
3	1.8	1.3
4	2.0	1.3
5	2.2	1.2
6	2.4	1.2
7	2.7	1.2
8	2.9	1.2
9	3.2	1.2
10	3.5	1.1
Total	$23.9	$11.8

Present Value and the Headlines

In 1980, Dave Winfield entered the free agent baseball players' market. He eventually signed with the Yankees for what the papers reported was a $24 mil-

built in any of three ways and over a period of three years, but the firm's cash outlay will be spread out differently over the years. The alternatives are listed in Table 21-9. All alternatives are equal in the sense that they do not affect the operation of the project and have the same date of completion, and all payments are made at the end of the year. Which should you choose? Each plan costs $600. The only way to determine which alternative will maximize profit is to use present value analysis and discount the future dollar amounts. Using Table 21-8, we can calculate the present value of each amount in Table 21-9. The present values, using a 10 percent interest rate, are in parentheses in Table 21-9. We can then

TABLE 21-9 **PRESENT VALUE EXAMPLE** (10 percent
interest rate)

Alternative	Cost in Year 1	Cost in Year 2	Cost in Year 3	Total Cost
A	$200 (181.80)	$200 (165.20)	$200 (150.20)	$600 ($PV = 497.20$)
B	$400 (363.60)	$100 (82.60)	$100 (75.10)	$600 ($PV = 521.30$)
C	$100 (90.90)	$100 (82.60)	$400 (300.40)	$600 ($PV = 473.90$)

total the present value amounts to find the least-cost method of production, which
turns out to be alternative *C*. Alternative *C* turns out to be 5 percent cheaper than
alternative *A* and 9 percent cheaper than alternative *B,* meaning a substantial
savings for the firm.

SUMMARY

1. Firms are organized by entrepreneurs to produce outputs by combining inputs. The entrepreneur does this in such a way as to maximize
profits.

2. While single proprietorships are the dominant
form of business organization by number, corporations account for about 85 percent of annual business sales in the United States.

3. Economic efficiency means selecting that
combination of resources that minimizes the
cost of producing a certain output.

4. Economists calculate both implicit and explicit
costs of production. Implicit costs are those
costs implied by alternatives given up, and explicit costs are expenditure, or bookkeeping,
costs.

5. When total costs (both implicit and explicit) are
equal to total revenues, economists say there
is zero economic profit. This means the firm is
covering all opportunity costs, including a normal return on profit. When costs exceed reve-

nues, firms and resources will leave an industry in order to earn the opportunity cost
associated with those resources.

6. A production function is the technical relationship between factors of production and outputs.

7. In the short run, some factors are fixed.

8. In the long run, all factors are variable.

9. In the short run, as variable factors are added
to the fixed factor, the firm may experience
increasing returns at low levels of output but
eventually will incur diminishing returns at
some higher levels of output.

10. Increasing and diminishing returns account for
the *U*-shape of the short-run average cost
curve.

11. The *U*-shape of the long-run average cost
curve is due to economies and diseconomies
of large-scale production.

12. Profit maximization means that an entrepreneur will produce that level of output that equates marginal cost and marginal revenue, thus insuring that total revenue exceeds total cost by the largest possible amount.

13. Present value calculations are techniques for making dollar amounts to be received or paid in the future comparable with dollar amounts in the present.

NEW TERMS

production
business firm
industry
sole proprietorship
partnership
corporation
stockholders
board of directors
stocks
bonds
limited liability
technical efficiency
economic efficiency
explicit cost
implicit cost
economic profit
normal profit
production function
fixed factors
variable factors
short run
long run
principle of diminishing returns

marginal physical product
average physical product
total physical product
stages of production
total cost
total fixed cost
total variable cost
average total cost
average fixed cost
average variable cost
marginal cost
least-cost combination
planning curve
long-run average cost curve
optimal-size plant
economies of scale
diseconomies of scale
natural monopoly
total revenue
marginal revenue
present value
discounting

QUESTIONS FOR DISCUSSION

1. Why are cost curves normally *U*-shaped both in the long and in the short run?

2. What is a normal profit? Why is it necessary for a firm to earn a normal profit?

3. The famous epigram of the Chicago School of Economics is: There is no such thing as a free lunch. What does this mean?

4. How does the short run differ from the long run? What would be the short run in farming? in the lemonade-stand business? in electricity generation?

5. Is there a parallel between diminishing utility in consumption and diminishing returns in production? Describe any similarities you see.

6. List as many things as you can think of that cause diseconomies of scale.

7. At what size do universities start experiencing diseconomies of scale? What does the existence of many different sizes of universities indicate about the optimal-size university?

8. Does a university have to reach a certain size to have an efficient (winning) sports program? How would you gather empirical evidence on this?

9. What is the difference between diminishing returns and diseconomies of scale?

10. If we were to change the assumption of profit maximization, how would we predict what output the firm would decide to produce? Do certain organizations that you have dealt with operate by motivations other than profit maximization? Name some.

SUGGESTIONS FOR FURTHER READING

Dean, Joel. "Opportunity Versus Outlay Costs." Reprinted in *Readings in Introductory Economics,* by John R. McKean and Ronald A. Wykstra. New York: Harper & Row, Publishers, Inc., 1971.

Kamerschen, David R., and Lloyd M. Valentine. *Intermediate Microeconomic Theory,* 2d ed. Cincinnati: South-Western Publishing Co., 1981, Chapters 8 and 10.

North, Douglass C., and Roger Leroy Miller. *The Economics of Public Issues,* 4h ed. New York: Harper & Row, Publishers, Inc., 1978.

CHAPTER 22

The Model of Pure Competition

Learning Objectives

After studying the materials found in this chapter, you should be able to do the following:

1. List the assumptions of pure competition.

2. Diagram the interaction of a representative firm and the total market.

3. Calculate profits, given information on *TC* and *TR*.

4. Calculate profits, given information on *Q, MR, MC, AC,* and price.

5. Define the shutdown point in terms of:
   (a) price and *AVC.*
   (b) *TFC* and losses.

6. List the characteristics of a:
   (a) constant cost industry.
   (b) increasing cost industry.
   (c) decreasing cost industry.

7. List the rules for the firm-industry equilibrium system based on *MC* and *MR*.

We have developed the principles of production and the general cost relationships that are derived from the production process. Any firm making production decisions will relate potential or forecasted revenues to these costs in determining output levels. However, the forecasted revenues will depend on the market conditions faced by the firm.

In the next four chapters we will look at four different models, and we will refer to them as *market structures.* The first model we will discuss is the model of ***pure (or perfect) competition.*** It is important to keep in mind that this is a theoretical model. It does not describe reality but rather allows the development of tools that indicate what would be produced if conditions were close to pure competition. In other words, the purely competitive model is the abstract ideal to which we will compare other market structures. This purely competitive model underlies the basic supply and demand model we developed earlier.

pure competition The market structure in which there are many sellers and buyers. The firms produce a homogeneous product and there is free entry and exit of these firms to and from the industry.

CHARACTERISTICS OF PURE COMPETITION

We require five basic assumptions for the model of pure competition. In developing the theory, we assume these five characteristics exist in the market in which the firm is selling its product.

First, we assume that there are large numbers of sellers in the industry. We don't specify any particular number as being large, but instead say that a large number means there are so many sellers of the product that no single seller's production can affect price. A wheat farmer would be an example of this. No single wheat farmer can influence the price of wheat. The farmer could sell the entire crop, or none of the crop, and as far as the farmer could tell, it wouldn't affect the price one bit. This is because the market is large relative to any single producer.

Second, we assume that there are large numbers of buyers. Again, large numbers mean that no one buyer can affect the price in any perceptible way. In other words, no single purchaser has any *market power*.

Our third assumption is that purely competitive firms produce a homogeneous product. The product of one firm is no different from the products of other firms in the industry. Since this is the case, purchasers have no preference for one producer over another. If you are a miller and want to purchase wheat, you don't care if Farmer Jones or Farmer Smith produced the wheat—a bushel of number 1 winter wheat is a bushel of number 1 winter wheat!

Fourth, and very important, we assume that there is free entry into, and free exit out of, the industry. This means that if one firm wishes to go into business or if another firm wishes to cease production, they do so without governmental or any other kind of constraint. Keep this assumption in mind because it is crucial in distinguishing pure competition from monopoly, which we will examine in the next chapter.

Last, we assume there is perfect knowledge and perfect mobility of resources. This assumption, even more unrealistic than the others, means that when economic profits exist, firms will find out about these profits and enter the industry. Resources are costly to move and information is costly to acquire. Still, the assumptions are valuable because the abstraction allows us to see the adjustments which take place in an ideal setting.

market power The ability of firms or buyers to affect price. Large numbers of buyers and sellers insure that no one buyer or seller affects price.

COMPETITIVE ADJUSTMENT IN THE SHORT RUN

Recall that a profit-maximizing firm always produces where marginal cost is equal to marginal revenue. Now that we know what costs look like, we need to determine what the firm's marginal revenue looks like. Since the firm is small relative to the market, and its product is indistinguishable from the product of other firms, the purely competitive firm views itself as having no influence on market price. If the purely competitive firm wants to sell any of its output, it must sell at the market price. For this reason the purely competitive firm is referred to as a *price taker*. The firm takes the market price as its selling price. If it sets a higher price, none of its output will be sold because buyers can purchase an

price taker A firm in pure competition is a price taker because the firm views itself as having no influence on price. It can sell any amount at the market clearing price.

identical product for the market price elsewhere. By the same token, it makes no sense to sell below market price because the firm can sell all it wants to sell at the established market price.

The market demand and supply curves and the firm's resultant demand curve are drawn in Figure 22-1. Market demand *(D)* and supply *(S)* curves are such that the market equilibrium price is OP_1. If the market is in equilibrium, the purely competitive firm can sell as much of the product as it wishes at price OP_1. From the firm's viewpoint, it faces a perfectly elastic demand curve at price OP_1.

The total revenue of a firm is the price times the quantity sold ($TR = P \times Q$). ***Average revenue (AR)*** would then be $\frac{TR}{Q}$, which is also the price-quantity relationship we depict in a demand curve. Demand curves are thus average revenue *(AR)* curves. The firm's perfectly elastic demand curve in Figure 22-1 is, as a result, also a perfectly elastic *AR* curve. Average revenue is the revenue per unit sold, which in this case is the price of the product. Marginal revenue is the change in total revenue of selling one more or one fewer unit ($MR_n = TR_n - TR_{n-1}$). In Figure 22-1, the change in total revenue, if sales increase from x_1 to x_2 to x_3, etc., is $OP_1 (Ox_2 - Ox_1)$, $OP_1 (Ox_3 - Ox_2)$, etc., where each change in x is one unit of x. In other words, in the case of a perfectly elastic demand curve, such as the firm's demand curve in Figure 22-1, $D = P = AR = MR$. The marginal revenue curve of a perfectly elastic demand curve is the same as the demand curve.

Using marginal cost and marginal revenue, we can now determine how the firm will adjust its output in the short run. The market and ***representative firm*** are depicted in Figure 22-2. A *representative firm* is an average firm—one of the many firms in this market. In Figure 22-2, the firm's marginal cost curve is also

average revenue   Total revenue divided by the quantity sold. A demand curve is an average revenue curve.

representative firm   A firm used to represent the firms of an industry; an average firm.

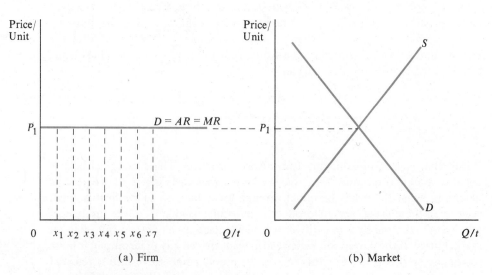

FIGURE 22-1   ELASTIC DEMAND AT MARKET EQUILIBRIUM

A firm's demand curve in pure competition is perfectly elastic at the market equilibrium price.

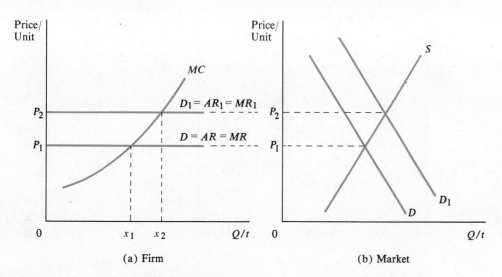

FIGURE 22-2   PROFIT MAXIMIZATION

An increase in demand in the market causes equilibrium price to rise. The demand curve the firm
faces adjusts by the amount of the increase in equilibrium price. The firm increases its output to
equate marginal cost and marginal revenue. The adjustment process is such that the firm's marginal
cost curve is its short-run supply curve.

drawn in. We see that the firm maximizes profits by producing Ox_1 when the price
per unit is OP_1, because at Ox_1, $MR = MC$. Now assume the market demand
increases to D_1. This causes the price to rise to OP_2 and the firm's demand curve,
average revenue curve, and marginal revenue curve to change to D_1, AR_1, and
MR_1, respectively. The firm responds by increasing its output to Ox_2, where MR_1
$= MC$. What we have seen in Figure 22-2 is that the firm's short-run marginal
cost curve is the same as its ***short-run supply curve***. As demand increased, the firm
moved up along its MC curve. Another increase in market demand would cause
the firm to move further up its MC curve. The higher price would lead it to supply
more output.

*short-run supply curve   The
supply curve in the short
run--the period in which the size
of the plant cannot be varied. In
pure competition, the short-run
marginal cost curve is the
short-run supply curve.*

Profits, Losses, and Shutting Down

We have just seen how the firm adjusts in the short run to changes in market
demand, but we don't yet know if the firm is making a profit or a loss and how
large this profit or loss is. To find out, we need to add the average cost curve to
the graph. Also, in order to decide if the firm should continue to produce if losses
are encountered, we need to add the average variable cost curve.

In Figure 22-3 the firm is maximizing profit by producing Ox_1 at price OP_1
where $P = MR = MC$. The average cost of producing Ox_1 can be seen to be
x_1C on Figure 22-3. The total cost of producing Ox_1 is represented by the area
of the rectangle OP_1Cx_1. The total revenue is also OP_1Cx_1, so $TR = TC$. The
firm is thus making zero economic profits, although it is meeting its opportunity

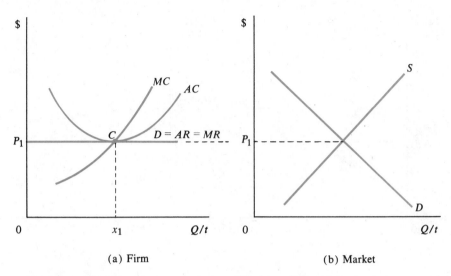

(a) Firm   (b) Market

**FIGURE 22-3   FIRM EARNING ZERO ECONOMIC
PROFIT**

The average cost curve can be used to determine if the firm is making an economic profit.
If price (average revenue) is equal to average cost, the firm is making zero economic
profit.

costs. Remember that this includes *normal profit,* which is the return on capital
necessary to keep firms in the industry.

If the firm's average cost curve is as drawn in Figure 22-4, the average cost
of producing Ox_1 would be x_1A. Total revenue is still OP_1 times Ox_1, or the area

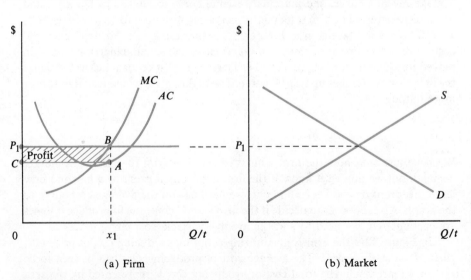

(a) Firm   (b) Market

FIGURE 22-4   FIRM EARNING AN ECONOMIC PROFIT

If the firm's average revenue is greater than its average cost at the level of output being
produced, the firm is making an economic profit.

OP_1Bx_1. Total cost is now $OCAx_1$. $TR > TC$, so there is an economic profit equal to CP_1BA in Figure 22-4. Alternatively, if the average cost curve is represented by the one drawn in Figure 22-5, the average cost of producing Ox_1 would be x_1A. Total revenue is OP_1Bx_1 and total cost is $OCAx_1$. In this case $TC > TR$, so losses are being incurred. The loss is equal to P_1CAB in Figure 22-5.

Now an important question is whether the firm in Figure 22-5 should continue to produce, and if so, for how long. After all, it is suffering a loss, which means the factors could earn more in some other use. Opportunity costs are not being met. But keep in mind that this is the short run, which means that some factors are fixed. These fixed factors represent the fixed costs and thus cannot be removed. Fixed costs must be paid in the short run even if production ceases. We need, then, to include the AVC curve to determine the conditions under which the firm should cease production. A firm is depicted in Figure 22-6 with several equilibrium points represented. At a price of OP_1, which represents a marginal revenue of MR_1, the firm maximizes profits by producing Ox_1. At OP_1 the firm is thus making an economic profit because total revenue (OP_1 times Ox_1) is greater than total cost (x_1D times Ox_1). At price $OP_2 = MR_2$, the firm would produce Ox_2 and make zero economic profit because TR ($= OP_2Bx_2$) is equal to TC ($= OP_2Bx_2$). Examine carefully what happens when price falls to OP_3 and marginal revenue to MR_3. The profit-maximizing or loss-minimizing output is now Ox_3. At output Ox_3, losses are incurred because total revenue is now OP_3Sx_3 and total cost is $OCEx_3$. Losses are thus represented by the rectangle P_3CES. The question we need to answer is, Should the firm produce and incur this loss or should it cease production? Remember, if production is halted, fixed costs must still be paid. In Figure 22-6, if price is OP_3, the firm is earning a total

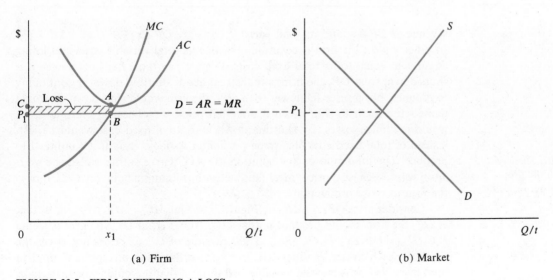

(a) Firm   (b) Market

FIGURE 22-5   FIRM SUFFERING A LOSS

If the firm's average cost is greater than its average revenue at the level of output being produced, the firm is incurring a loss.

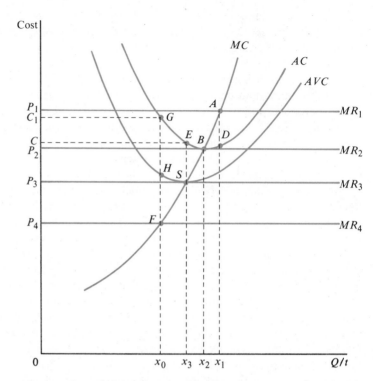

FIGURE 22-6   THE SHUTDOWN POINT

If average revenue is greater than average variable cost, the firm will be able to cover total variable costs and make a payment toward total fixed costs. If price falls below average variable costs, the firm will lose less money if it shuts down than if it continues to produce.

revenue of OP_3Sx_3 and its total variable costs are OP_3Sx_3 ($TVC = AVC \cdot Q$). In other words, the firm is covering (exactly) its total variable costs and losing an amount equal to its total fixed costs. It must pay these fixed costs even if it shuts down, so at OP_3 the firm is indifferent about shutting down or continuing to produce, but if price fell lower than OP_3, the firm would shut down. It would make sense for it to shut down if price fell below OP_3 because shutting down would minimize losses. By shutting down, only total fixed cost would be lost, instead of total fixed cost plus some portion of variable costs if it continued to produce. The minimum or low point on the AVC curve is thus called the **shutdown point**, because if price *(MR)* falls below the minimum point on AVC, it pays the firm to cease production.

shutdown point   The level of output at which the firm minimizes its losses by ceasing operation.

Consider price $OP_4 = MR_4$ on Figure 22-6. Our $MC = MR$ rule tells us that at OP_4 the firm should produce output Ox_0. However, at Ox_0 the firm is losing P_4C_1GF ($=OP_4Fx_0 - OC_1Gx_0$). Total revenue of OP_4Fx_0 does not cover the TVC of x_0, which is x_0H times Ox_0. In other words, the firm is losing more than total fixed cost. It is making variable cost outlays that it wouldn't have to make if it stopped production entirely. The firm would be better off to shut down and only incur its fixed costs. (We give a numerical example on page 453.) Consider now our earlier statement that the firm's marginal cost curve represents its short-run supply curve; we see that this statement is not exactly correct. A firm's short-run supply curve is represented by its marginal cost curve *above* point *S*, the shutdown point. Below point *S*, the firm would produce no output, so we consider the marginal cost curve starting at the minimum point on the *AVC* curve to be the firm's supply curve.

To review, we should note that the minimum point on the *AC* curve is the least-cost combination, and the minimum point on the *AVC* curve is the shutdown point. The *MC* curve above the *AVC* is the purely competitive firm's supply curve. Also keep in mind that these are all short-run phenomena. We will trace the long-run adjustment later.

A Numerical Example

We can see the same short-run adjustments just discussed using a numerical example. Table 22-1 reproduces some of the production data which we used in the last chapter. We can assume that different market prices are the result of different market equilibrium situations, and we can then calculate the response

TABLE 22-1 PRODUCTION DATA

Output	AVC	AC	MC	TC
1	$40	$100	$40	$100
2	38	68	36	136
3	36	56	32	168
4	35	50	32	200
5	35	47	35	235
6	36	46	41	276
7	$37^{3/7}$	46	46	322
8	39	$46^{1/2}$	50	372
9	41	$47^{2/3}$	57	429
10	43	49	61	490

the firm would make to these changes. In Table 22-2, six different market prices corresponding to different market conditions are assumed. When the market price is $61, we know that the demand and marginal revenue curves the firm faces are

TABLE 22-2 PRICING PROBLEM

Market Price (MR)	Firm's Output (equate MR with MC)	TR	TC	Firm's Profit
$61	10	$610	$490	$120
50	8	400	372	28
46	7	322	322	0
41	6	246	276	−30
35	5	175	235	−60
32	4	128	200	−72

perfectly elastic at $61. The firm would then produce 10 units ($MR = MC = 61) and earn an economic profit of $120. This numerical example corresponds to the geometric example in Figure 22-4. At a market price of $46, the firm maximizes profit where $MR = MC = 46, which is at an output of 7 units. Since $TR = TC$ at 7 units, there is zero economic profit. This corresponds to Figure 22-3. When market price falls to $41, the firm reacts by decreasing its output to 6 units ($MR = MC = 41), and at 6 units it incurs a loss of $30. This corresponds to Figure 22-5. The firm will continue to produce in the short run until price falls below $35 because the minimum point on the AVC curve is at $35. To see why, examine the adjustment when market price falls to $32. At $32 the firm would produce 4 units, but if it does, it loses $72. ($TR = 4 \times $32 = 128; $TC = 4 \times $50 = 200; and $128 - $200 = -$72$.) If it shuts down, the firm loses only $60 in total fixed cost, as the total variable cost *(TVC)* would have been $140 if production had taken place. ($TVC = 4 \times $35 = 140; $TFC = $200 - $140 = 60.) So it loses less if it ceases production. At any price less than $35, the firm will shut down.

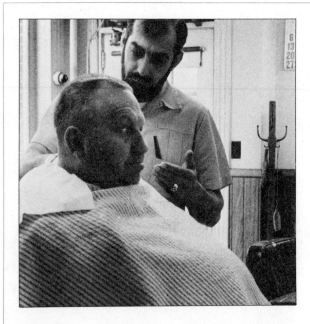

Government and the Price of a Haircut

Wouldn't you think that the production of haircuts would fit the competitive model developed in this chapter? Entry should be easy and relatively inexpensive. Required equipment amounts to scissors, a chair, perhaps a hair dryer, and a mirror. But barbers and beauticians are one group that has been able to interfere with the free flow of resources. They have been successful in getting most states to regulate entry in the guise of protecting the consumer from bad products and services. The state legislature does this by setting up a board of licensure which is usually controlled by the people being licensed. The board restricts entry into the profession with the result that prices charged for haircuts are higher than they would otherwise be.

In the state of Arizona, for example, the requirements to be licensed have grown to ridiculous, but predictable, proportions. More hours of instruction are required to give haircuts than are required to complete a law degree in one of Arizona's state law schools.

From what are they protecting you? A bad haircut! What would happen if you were given a bad haircut? Well, it would be embarrassing for a week or two. But the market would punish the haircutter pretty quickly. People wouldn't return for another poor job. So why in the world do we license barbers? To keep out new entrants.

You probably know someone that chisels on the licensing board and gives black market haircuts below the price of the licensed shops. Wouldn't it be nice if this same system was available everywhere?

Haircuts may seem to be a trivial example, but such interference with free entry, which is a necessary part of the competitive model, is rampant. There are more than 850 occupations and businesses that are licensed by various states.

The Market Supply Curve

We can now look at the interaction between supply and demand in the market in terms of the relationship between the firm's marginal cost curve and the market supply curve. We saw that the firm's marginal cost curve represents its output response to increased market prices. If we were to add all the individual supply curves, we would construct the market or industry short-run supply curve. The market supply curve is simply the aggregate of all the firms' supply curves. The short-run market supply curve, then, is the aggregate of all the firms' marginal cost curves that lie above their average variable cost curves. In the long run, more firms can enter an industry as a response to economic profits. The market supply curve will shift to the right because it is now made up of more individual firm supply curves. Conversely, as firms leave an industry due to losses, the market, or industry, supply curve will shift to the left, representing a decrease in supply. This time the decrease is due to the fact that there are fewer individual firm supply curves to be summed.

COMPETITIVE ADJUSTMENT IN THE LONG RUN

To trace the adjustment process when firms have time to adjust the fixed factors, thus allowing new firms to enter the industry, consider the example in Figure 22-7. The solid D_1 and S_1 lines in Figure 22-7, panel (b), show the industry in equilibrium. The industry is in equilibrium when there are no economic forces working that would cause it to expand or contract. In Figure 22-7, panel (a), equilibrium prevails because the representative, or average, firm is making zero economic profit at price OP_1 and output Ox_1. Let's assume this representative firm is one of 1,000 identical firms, so the market supply curve (S_1) in Figure 22-7, panel (b), is the summation of 1,000 MC curves (above the AVC curve). Since these firms are making zero economic profits at price OP_1, the industry is in equilibrium with an industry output of OQ_1 and each firm producing Ox_1, where $1,000 \cdot (Ox_1) = OQ_1$. Now suppose there is an increase in market demand to D_2. Let's say this increase is brought about by an increase in real income and the good under consideration is a normal good. When market demand shifts to D_2, market price rises to OP_2 and the demand curve facing the firm rises to be perfectly elastic at price OP_2. The firm's new demand curve is represented by D_2, AR_2, MR_2. These changes are all represented by dashed lines. The firm's initial (short-run) response is to increase its output to Ox_2 because $MR_2 = MC$ at output Ox_2. Thus, the initial increase in market demand (from OQ_1 to OQ_2) is met by each of the 1,000 firms increasing their output from Ox_1 to Ox_2. Note, however, that each firm is now making an economic profit equal to the shaded area in Figure 22-7, panel (a). Profit, you recall, means that factors are earning more than their opportunity cost. This profit means the industry is out of equilibrium. Other firms are going to attempt to grab some of this profit. The existence of profit, then, is the signal for new firms to enter this industry.

Since we initially assumed that free entry and perfect knowledge are characteristics of pure competition, entrepreneurs will be aware of this profit and will enter the industry. As firms enter the industry, the market supply curve will shift,

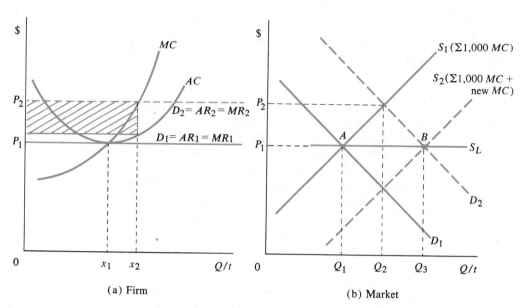

**FIGURE 22-7   ADJUSTMENT TO AN INCREASE IN
                DEMAND**

An increase in market demand will cause price to rise and the demand curve the representative firm faces
to shift upward. Profits will result and new firms will enter in response to this profit. As new firms enter the
industry, the market supply curve shifts to the right, causing price to fall to the point at which the
representative firm is again earning zero economic profit.

because it now is the summation of the 1,000 original MC curves plus the MC
curves of the new entrant firms. In fact, firms will keep entering the industry until
equilibrium (zero profit) is restored. This is illustrated in Figure 22-7. If all firms
have the same costs (that is, all firms are exactly like this representative firm) and
if nothing happens to change these costs (in Figure 22-7 we assume that this is
the case), equilibrium will be restored when the price has been reduced to OP_1,
the original equilibrium price. If the new equilibrium price is OP_1, and industry
output is OQ_3, each firm is producing Ox_1, and the summation of the firm's output
$(1,000 +$ the new number of firms times Ox_1) is equal to the industry output,
which is OQ_3. If we connect the market equilibrium points, points A and B in
Figure 22-7, we get the industry's long-run supply curve (S_L). This represents
what occurs after all adjustments have had time to take place.

You can check your understanding of this adjustment process by going
through the adjustments for a decrease in demand. Figure 22-8 illustrates this.
The industry is initially in equilibrium at price OP_1 and output OQ_1. Firms are
making zero profits and producing Ox_1 units of output. Something or someone,
perhaps the government, says the product is dangerous to your health and this
causes demand to decrease to D_2, represented by the dashed line in Figure 22-8,
panel (b). Market price falls to OP_2 and industry output falls to OQ_2. Firms adjust
their output to Ox_2, where $MC = MR_2$. At Ox_2, however, firms are incurring
losses represented by the crosshatched area. (We are assuming OP_2 is above AVC,
so the firm continues production.) The industry is now out of equilibrium. Just

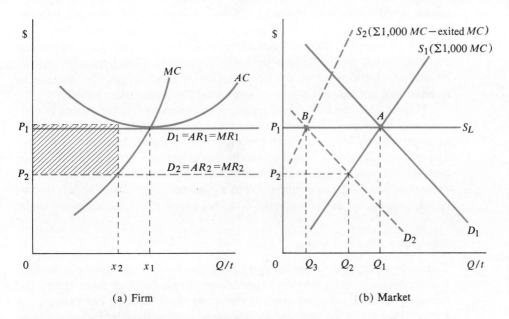

**FIGURE 22-8   ADJUSTMENT TO A DECREASE IN
                DEMAND**

A decrease in market demand will cause price to fall and the demand curve the representative firm
faces to shift downward. Losses will be incurred and some firms will leave the industry. As some firms
leave the industry, the market supply curve shifts to the left, causing price to rise until a remaining
representative firm is earning zero economic profit.

as profits were the signal for firms to enter, losses are the signal for firms to exit
the industry. Entrepreneurs move their factors to the production of other commodities, seeking to earn their opportunity cost elsewhere. We assumed perfect
knowledge, so the entrepreneurs will know where they can earn their opportunity
cost. As firms leave the industry, the short-run market supply curve will shift,
because it is now derived by adding up fewer firms' MC curves. Firms will leave
the industry until those remaining firms have zero economic profits. This equilibrium is restored when the market supply curve shifts so as to restore a price of
OP_1. Industry output is now OQ_3 with each of the 1,000 minus the exited firms
producing Ox_1 units of output. As before, the long-run supply curve (S_L) can be
found by connecting the industry's equilibrium points, which are represented by
points A and B in Figure 22-8, panel (b).

The adjustment we traced in Figures 22-7 and 22-8 assumed that factor prices
and thus costs were unaffected by the quantity of output the industry produced.
This meant that as firms entered the industry (Figure 22-7) or exited the industry
(Figure 22-8), the prices of the factors of production did not change and, as a
result, the cost curves didn't change. When this is so, the industry is referred to
as a *constant cost industry.* In a constant cost industry, as more steel, labor,
electricity, or whatever is purchased to increase output, the cost of those inputs
does not increase. This would probably be the case where the industry's purchase
of inputs is small relative to the market supply of these inputs. If the industry's
use of inputs is small relative to the market supply, the increased demand for

*constant cost industry   An
industry in which expansion of
output does not cause average
costs to rise. The long-run supply
curve is perfectly elastic.*

inputs would not increase the price of these same inputs. For example, take the citizens' band radio industry. If profits exist and firms enter, these firms will demand more inputs. They will demand more steel, more labor, more transistors, etc. If all the CB-producing firms have similar production functions and comprise an insignificant amount of the consumption of these inputs, the increase in demand will not cause the price of steel, labor, and transistors to rise.

Figures 22-7 and 22-8, then, represent contractions and expansions in constant cost industries. The short-run response to a contraction in demand was a decrease in price. An expansion in demand produced a short-run increase in price. The market adjustment, however, returned price to its original level with fewer firms in the case of the contraction and additional firms in the case of the expansion. The long-run supply curve in a constant cost industry is thus seen to be perfectly elastic, even though the short-run supply curve has a positive slope.

Increasing Cost Industries

increasing cost industry An industry in which expansion of output causes average costs to rise in the long run. The long-run supply curve has a positive slope.

Sometimes an expansion in industry output will cause costs to increase in the long run. In this case, as an industry expands output and demands more inputs, the increased demand will cause prices to rise in the input markets. For example, an increase in demand for wine causes new firms to enter the wine industry and to demand more grapes, grape pickers, land, and wine makers. If the increased demand causes the price of grapes, grape pickers, land, or wine makers to rise, the average production costs of the firm will increase as a result of the increased demand for wine. Also, less efficient factors and firms will be drawn into the industry. This is the case in an *increasing cost industry.*

Figure 22-9 illustrates the long-run adjustment process in an increasing cost industry. The industry is originally in equilibrium at price OP_1 and output OQ_1. Each firm is producing Ox_1. Market demand increases to D_2 and, as a result, market price rises to OP_2. The firm now faces a demand which is perfectly elastic at OP_2. The firm's demand is now represented by $D_2 = AR_2 = MR_2$. The firm's short-run response is to increase output to Ox_2, where $MC_1 = MR_2$. Industry's output is now OQ_2. At this increased output, two things will happen. First, new firms will enter the industry because of the economic profits that now exist. Second, costs are rising as a result of the increased demand for inputs. This rise in cost is represented by the upward shift to MC_2 and AC_2 in Figure 22-9, panel (a). This upward shift of MC and AC assumes all costs are increased proportionately. In most cases this would not be exactly true, as some inputs (the scarcer ones) would rise faster in price, but the illustration is clearer if we assume all factor prices rise proportionately, and this assumption does not seriously affect the analysis. Firms, as consumers of inputs, are likely to be a significant influence in some input markets and insignificant in others. In our previous example, as the demand for wine increased and firms entered the industry, there may have been no effect on the price of land but a significant effect on the salaries of wine makers. It is also possible that firms less able to produce the good in question will be attracted to the industry. In this case, a representative firm would have higher costs, indicating less efficient production.

The net result of the increased number of firms and increasing costs is a rightward shift in the short-run market supply curve. The supply curve shifts to the right because there are more firms' MC curves to add up, but it will not shift

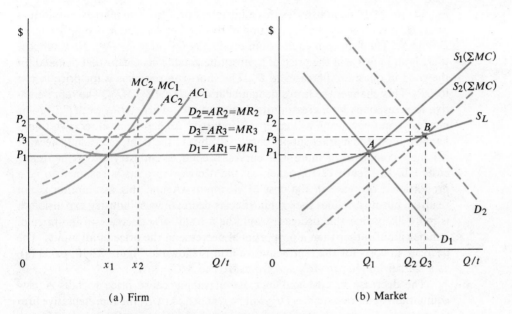

(a) Firm　　　　　　　(b) Market

**FIGURE 22-9　ADJUSTMENT IN AN INCREASING COST
INDUSTRY**

When demand increases in an increasing cost industry, the firms that enter the industry bid up the
prices of the factors of production for all firms in the industry. As a result, price does not return to the
previous equilibrium. Instead, a new equilibrium with the representative firm earning zero economic
profit is established at a price above the old equilibrium price but below the initial increase in price.

---

as far as before because costs have risen for every firm. A new short-run market
supply curve will be created when equilibrium is reached at price OP_3 where firms
are no longer making profits. Industry output is now OQ_3 and each firm is
producing Ox_1 where $MR_3 = MC_2$.

As before, we can find the long-run supply curve by connecting the industry's
equilibrium points. Connecting points A and B in Figure 22-9, panel (b), produces
a long-run supply curve (S_L) with a positive slope, indicating an increasing cost
industry. We will leave it to you to diagram the adjustment process reflecting a
decrease in demand for an increasing cost industry.

Decreasing Cost Industries

To complete the analysis, we must examine a ***decreasing cost industry.*** In a
decreasing cost industry, expansion in industry output causes input prices to fall,
and, as a result, costs decrease. A real-world example is hard to come up with.
In a decreasing cost industry, as more firms enter the industry, causing the
demand for inputs to increase, input prices fall. This implies that there are
economies of scale in an industry that is supplying an input to the industry under
examination. For example, as more electricity is demanded, more efficient generators are built and the price of this input falls.

*decreasing cost industry　An
industry in which an expansion
of output causes average costs to
fall in the long run. The
long-run supply curve has a
negative slope.*

Figure 22-10 demonstrates this adjustment process. The market equilibrium price, OP_1, is given by the intersection of the market demand and supply curves, D_1 and S_1. The firm is in equilibrium producing Ox_1 at price OP_1. Now suppose there is an increase in the price of a substitute good. This means that demand for the good in question increases to D_2. The short-run response is for price to rise to OP_2. This changes the firm's demand curve to D_2, AR_2, MR_2. The representative firm responds by increasing its output to Ox_2, where $MR_2 = MC_1$. Profits now exist and new firms will enter this industry. As new firms enter, two things happen. First, the market supply curve will shift to the right, increasing, because it is now composed of more MC curves. Second, as industry output increases, costs fall. In Figure 22-10, panel (a), the decrease in costs is assumed to be a proportional decrease in the cost of all inputs. Again, this assumption is not realistic, but it simplifies the graph. If costs decrease with industry expansion, it is more likely that this decrease would be a result of a decrease in the price of a major input rather than a proportional decrease in the price of all inputs. The decrease in costs for the representative firm is shown in Figure 22-10, panel (a), as a shift from AC_1 to AC_2 and from MC_1 to MC_2.

The decrease in cost and increase in supply cause price to fall. A new equilibrium at a price such as OP_3 will be reached. At OP_3 the representative firm faces demand curve D_3. Equilibrium is reached at output Ox_1 where $MC_2 = MR_3$. No economic profits exist.

As before, we can now connect the equilibrium points in the market. These points are represented by points A and B. The long-run industry supply curve

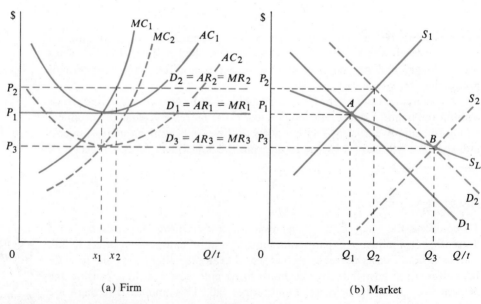

(a) Firm   (b) Market

FIGURE 22-10   ADJUSTMENT IN A DECREASING COST INDUSTRY

When demand increases in a decreasing cost industry, the firms that enter the industry cause the prices of the factors of production for all firms in this industry to fall. As a result, a new equilibrium price is established that is below the initial equilibrium price.

is represented by the S_L curve in Figure 22-10, panel (b). The curve has a negative slope. This would mean that an increase in market demand would eventually lead to a new equilibrium at lower product prices. Decreasing cost industries thus have negatively sloped long-run supply curves. (The short-run supply curves are still positively sloped since they are the aggregate of firms' MC curves.) Industries with decreasing costs are very unlikely but theoretically conceivable. We leave diagramming the effects of a decrease in demand to your understanding of the adjustment process in decreasing cost industries.

EQUILIBRIUM: SO WHAT?

The model of pure competition is such that the firm and industry are driven to equilibrium at zero economic profit. Herein lies the appeal of pure competition as a standard against which to judge other market structures. Economists view this equilibrium as an ideal, a social optimum. In equilibrium, resources are optimally allocated among competing uses. Figure 22-11 shows a firm in equilibrium. At equilibrium, price (P) is equal to average cost (AC) and also is equal to marginal cost (MC).

First, consider $P = MC$. This means that *allocative efficiency* is being met, or that the resources of the firm are being allocated exactly as consumers wish. It means that firms are expanding production exactly to the level desired by consumers. If $P > MC$, it would mean that the firm was not putting enough resources into the production of the good in question. Consumers would be willing to pay more than it costs to produce another unit of the good. If $P < MC$, too many resources are being devoted to the production of the good. Consumers would not be willing to pay as much as it costs to produce another

allocative efficiency When price is equal to marginal cost, firms expand production to the exact level that consumers desire, as measured by the market price.

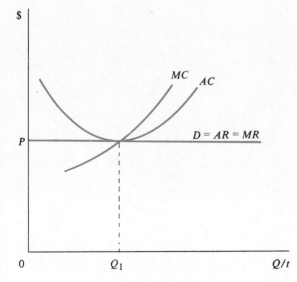

FIGURE 22-11 EQUILIBRIUM CONDITION
In short-run equilibrium, allocative efficiency is being met. This means that the resources of the firm are being allocated as consumers wish.

unit of the good. In other words, where $P = MC$, the correct amount of resources is being devoted to producing the good.

Second, consider $P = AC$. This means that firms are only earning normal profits. There is no incentive for firms to enter or leave the industry.

Third, consider $MC = AC$. This means that AC is at a minimum, and, therefore, the firm is at the least-cost combination. This means that the variable resources are being combined as efficiently as possible.

In the long run, the short-run average cost curve (AC) will also be tangent to the long-run average cost curve at its minimum point, $AC = LRAC$, as in Figure 22-12. This means that all firms are at the efficient size and are also combining variable resources efficiently. The firms are at the least-cost combination and at the optimal plant size. All firms must be efficient or they will be driven from the market by incurred losses. If any one firm is more efficient than normal, or more efficient than the representative firm, it will be able to make an economic profit even though the other firms don't.

At long-run equilibrium, then, we have $P = AC = MC = LRAC = LRMC$. The purely competitive model is thus the ideal of efficiency to which we will compare other market structures.

PROFITS: THE DRIVING FORCE

It is important to note the role of profits in the purely competitive model. Profits serve as the signal for firms to move in and out of an industry. When profits exist, entrepreneurs rush in to attempt to capture them and the industry is forced to equilibrium. Likewise, when losses are present, firms leave to earn higher returns elsewhere. Equilibrium is forced by the profit-seeking nature of firms. In equilibrium, we have efficiency. It is not because of some altruistic behavior on the part

FIGURE 22-12   LONG-RUN EQUILIBRIUM
In long-run equilibrium, average cost is equal to long-run average cost. This means that all firms are at the technically efficient size and are also combining variable resources efficiently.

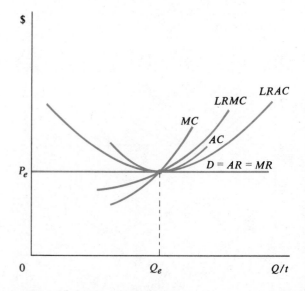

of the entrepreneur that the firm is efficient; rather, the entrepreneur is assumed to be a profit maximizer interested solely in individual self-interest, and this brings about efficiency. In the competitive model, self-interest and the quest for profits produce the efficiency that benefits consumers. The firm is not striving for efficiency but for profits.

EXAMPLES OF PURE COMPETITION

Perhaps the closest we can come to the model of pure competition in the U.S. economy are the markets for various agricultural products. In these markets there are large numbers of buyers and sellers and there is a homogeneous product. This

Our Shrinking Farmlands?

Farming comes very close to the model of competition. There are large numbers of producers, and entry into production is relatively easy. Almost everyone with a small plot of land is a potential producer. Casual empiricism, therefore, leads us to conclude that as the price of food rises, many of these small part-time farmers will produce for home use. At the margin, this can have a powerful impact as home producers drop out of the market as demanders of the products they produce.

Despite ease of entry and exit from farm produc-

tion, we often read that the shrinkage of our farmland is, or should be, an area of national concern. Prime acreage disappears each year as new homes, shopping centers, and industrial plants are built. In some cities, such as Phoenix and Los Angeles, the speed of this transition is visually demonstrated as new developments race away from the central city, thereby devouring farmland.

Economic principles tell us that the fear that this is a national problem is unjustified. The market is a very effective allocator of land. As scarce farmland becomes more valuable in agricultural uses, the conversion to other uses will cease.

Moreover, it is not factually correct that farmland has disappeared in the United States. Clifton Luttrell of the Federal Reserve Bank of St. Louis has looked at the facts. Between 1910 and 1979, there were ups and downs in the amount of cultivatable land. Our model of pure competition would predict this, as farm products rose and fell in price and profitability. In 1969, the number of acres under cultivation was at an all-time low. Since 1969, there has been a significant increase; in 1979, the amount of land under cultivation was at an all-time high for the past 40 years.

In addition, one needs to examine output per acre. An acre under cultivation in the 1980s is not the same as an acre under cultivation in the 1880s.

The concern raised over shrinking acreage and land use is more serious than a simple misunderstanding of the facts. One wonders what alternative would be proposed in order to let the market allocate the use between agriculture, homes, shopping centers, and factories. One suspects use of a government agency. Most economists would prefer the workings of the market as opposed to the "wisdom" of any farmland czar.

homogeneity is reflected in the fact that there are no brand names associated with most farm products. In addition, there is relatively free entry into and exit out of the industry. Anyone with capital, or the ability to borrow capital, can enter the agriculture industry. There are very few, if any, educational requirements, in the sense of having a degree or passing a test, and little in the way of licenses, inspection codes, or officials who must be bribed. So, if you don't like thinking in abstract terms all the time, you can use agriculture as an industry and a wheat farm as a firm to illustrate our theory of pure competition. Of course, the example is not perfect because resources tend to be immobile in agriculture and our model assumes relatively mobile resources. Agriculture is, however, a very useful example of pure competition.

The model of pure competition is not meant to be a perfect description of reality. Nor in every case is it the ideal state that we should be striving to reach. In certain industries it may be too costly to bring about the necessary conditions to make that industry purely competitive, in which case we would accept less than the ideal. The model of pure competition is a tool for the economist. The economist can compare the real-world situation to the hypothetical world of pure competition to determine what would be the case if pure competition existed. In this sense, pure competition is a benchmark, or yardstick, by which analysts can measure the costs of other market structures.

SUMMARY

1. Pure competition is characterized by large numbers of buyers and sellers, homogeneous products, ease of entry into and exit from the industry, and perfect knowledge and mobility of resources.

2. The firm in a purely competitive market faces a perfectly elastic demand curve at the price determined by equilibrium in the market.

3. The firm's short-run supply curve is its short-run marginal cost curve above the minimum point on the average variable cost curve, otherwise known as the shutdown point.

4. Long-run adjustments to changes in market demand are dependent on the cost characteristics of the industry under consideration. Since entry is easy, firms will enter as long as

profits are present. As a result, economic profits brought about by an increase in demand will bring about new entry.

5. An industry is characterized by constant, increasing or decreasing costs. The slope of the long-run supply curve will depend on these different cost situations.

6. In equilibrium, $P=AC=MC=LRAC=LRMC$. This is the efficiency ideal to which we hold other market structures up for comparison.

7. Profits are the force that drives the model to efficiency. The firm is not seeking efficiency but profits. This search for profits produces the efficiency which characterizes the model of pure competition.

NEW TERMS

pure competition
market power
price taker
average revenue

representative firm
short-run supply curve
shutdown point
constant cost industry

increasing cost industry
decreasing cost industry

allocative efficiency

QUESTIONS FOR DISCUSSION

1. Show how the long-run market supply curve will be brought about by short-run supply adjustments in an increasing cost industry.

2. Diagram a situation showing a market in equilibrium and a representative firm. Then show a decrease in market demand. Trace through the short-run and long-run adjustment, assuming this is a decreasing cost industry.

3. "If the price of wheat doesn't rise, farmers will lose money and the long-run price will be even higher." Discuss this often-heard argument.

4. Why does profit maximization bring about efficiency?

5. What situations cause long-run supply curves to be positively sloped?

6. Explain in your own words why you might keep producing in the short run even if you were incurring a loss.

7. What does it mean to say that in pure competition long-run equilibrium means that $P = AC = MC = LRAC = LRMC$?

SUGGESTIONS FOR FURTHER READING

Kamerschen, David R., and Lloyd M. Valentine. *Microeconomic Theory,* 2d ed. Cincinnati: South-Western Publishing Co., 1981, Chapters 11 and 12.

Leftwich, Richard H. *The Price System and Resource Allocation,* 6h ed. Hinsdale, Ill.: Dryden Press, 1979, Chapter 9.

Stigler, George J. *The Theory of Price,* 3d ed. New York: Macmillan, Inc., 1966, Chapter 10.

The Model of Monopoly

Learning Objectives

After studying the materials found in this chapter, you should be able to do the following:

1. Define pure monopoly.

2. Calculate and diagram average revenue and marginal revenue, given data on price and output.

3. Label sections of a downward-sloping demand curve according to elasticity, given information on *MR*.

4. Diagram a monopolistic firm (in terms of *AR, MR, MC,* and *AC*) making:
   (a) an economic profit.
   (b) a loss.
   (c) an economic profit of zero.

5. List natural and artificial barriers to entry into an industry.

6. Define the misallocation of resource by a monopolist in terms of *P, AC,* and *MC*.

7. Show that a monopolist does not have a supply curve.

8. Define two types of price discrimination.

9. Define and illustrate consumer surplus.

10. Discuss the alternative theories to profit maximization.

11. Define:
    (a) dumping.
    (b) local monopoly.
    (c) natural monopoly.

monopoly   The market structure in which there is a single seller of a product that has no close substitutes.

Pure monopoly is at the other end of the market continuum from pure competition. The word ***monopoly*** is derived from the Greek words *mono* for "one" and *polein* for "seller." Monopoly is the market structure in which the firm is a single seller of a product that has no close substitutes. It is necessary that there be no close substitutes to insure that there is only one firm in the industry. If a close substitute product exists, the firm is not a single seller.

It is important to keep in mind that pure monopoly is a theoretical model and as with pure competition, real-world examples are almost nonexistent. The theory is still useful, however, as a tool to examine real-world situations. The definition of a pure monopoly as a single seller of a product with no close substitutes makes finding examples quite difficult, but there are many firms that have some of the same economic effects as pure monopoly. We say these firms have **monopoly power.** (Technically these firms are called *oligopolies,* and we will examine oligopoly in detail later.)

Perhaps the best example of monopoly in U.S. history is the Aluminum Company of America which, prior to World War II, was the only aluminum producer in the United States. But even this example contradicts our model to some extent because aluminum does have some close substitutes. For example, beer can be put into bottles, steel cans, or even wooden kegs; golf clubs can be made with steel or even wooden shafts; and not long ago tennis players got along with wooden racquets. So, before we worry too much about finding a *real* monopoly, let's analyze adjustment under monopoly and then compare the allocation of resources under pure monopoly to those under pure competition.

monopoly power   The ability to exercise some of the economic effects as predicted in the model of pure monopoly.

DEMAND AND MARGINAL REVENUE

In the last chapter we saw that the purely competitive firm faced a perfectly elastic demand curve and, as a result, price and marginal revenue were equal. However, a monopolistic firm faces the *market* demand curve because the firm is the single seller and is, therefore, the industry. This is a very important distinction because market demand curves have negative slopes. Since the demand curve has a negative slope, the marginal revenue curve is going to lie below the demand curve, which is, as we saw before, the average revenue curve. The commonsense reason for the relationship of the demand and marginal revenue curves or the fact that the marginal revenue curve lies below the average revenue curve is that the monopolist must lower price in order to sell more units of output. Price reductions apply to *all* units of output that the monopolist sells. Each additional unit sold thus adds to total revenue by the amount it sells for—its price—but takes away from total revenue by the reduction in price times the previous units sold, so this change in total revenue (which is equal to marginal revenue) must be less than price.

An arithmetic example is presented in Table 23-1. When three units are being sold, the total revenue is $186 (=3 × $62). In order to sell four units, the monopolist must reduce the price from $62 to $60. Total revenue will then increase by $60 because an additional unit is being sold for $60, but it will also decrease by $6 because the first three units now sell for $2 less each, or for $60 each rather than for $62. The net result is that the monopolist has added $54 (=$60 − $6) to total revenue by reducing the price from $62 to $60. Notice that *MR* is $54 and price (average revenue) is $60 for four units. *MR* has to lie below *AR* whenever there are previous units that suffer a price reduction.

This relationship can be seen graphically in Figure 23-1. You may remember our discussion about the relationship between elasticity and total revenue. We can now relate that discussion to marginal revenue and the monopolist. When demand is inelastic, price decreases cause total revenue to decline. If total revenue is declining, it must mean that the additions to total revenue are negative, or that the *MR* is negative. This is graphically demonstrated in Figure 23-1. Price

TABLE 23-1   DEMAND AND MARGINAL REVENUE
RELATIONSHIPS

Units Sold	Price (Average Revenue)	Total Revenue	Marginal Revenue
1	$64	$ 64	$ 64
2	63	126	62
3	62	186	60
4	60	240	54
5	58	290	50
6	56½	339	49
7	55	385	46
8	52	416	31
9	47	423	7
10	40	400	−23

reductions below OP_1 will decrease total revenue because marginal revenue is negative. This corresponds to the inelastic portion of the curve. Conversely, a reduction in price from OP_2 to OP_1 would increase total revenue because the demand curve is elastic in this range.

Think back to our discussion of elasticity and the problem of the mineral spring. In that problem we determined that the monopoly owner of a mineral spring with no production costs would set price at the point where the price elasticity of demand was unitary. We can now see this same principle using our

FIGURE 23-1   DEMAND AND MARGINAL REVENUE

The marginal revenue curve lies below the average revenue curve in the case of a negatively sloped demand curve. In drawing the relationship between average and marginal revenue, the marginal revenue curve will intersect the x-axis exactly halfway between the origin and the point where the average revenue curve intersects the x-axis.

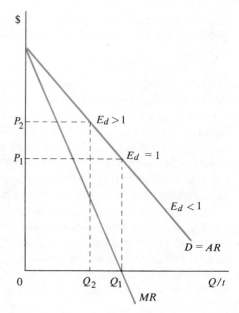

profit maximization rule of $MR = MC$. If costs are zero, the MC curve would be superimposed on the quantity or x-axis. In Figure 23-1, the monopolist would maximize by producing OQ_1 at price OP_1, where $MC = MR = 0$. What is happening is that the mineral spring monopolist will increase sales of the product as long as marginal revenue is positive since it costs nothing more to produce another unit. You should note that this does not mean the mineral spring monopolist sells as much as possible, but rather sells the quantity which maximizes total revenue, which in this case happens to be the same as the quantity where profit is maximized, since costs are zero.

PRICE AND OUTPUT DECISIONS

The monopolist searches out the profit-maximizing price and output by equating marginal cost and marginal revenue. Whereas the purely competitive firm is a price taker, we say that the monopoly firm is a *price searcher.* A monopolist sets the profit-maximizing price, not the highest price. We can see this process graphically by looking at cost relationships under monopoly.

In Figure 23-2 we see a monopolist producing good x. The market demand is D_1, from which MR_1 is derived. The monopolist's AC curve and MC curve are also drawn in. The monopolist will maximize profit by producing Ox_1 units of x because at Ox_1, $MR = MC$. If $MR > MC$ (that is, if output is less than Ox_1), the monopolist can increase profits by expanding output because additions to output add more to total revenue than to total cost. On the other hand, if $MR < MC$ (that is, if output is greater than Ox_1), the monopolist would contract output because additions to output add more to total cost than to total revenue.

price searcher   A firm that sets price in order to maximize profits. A price-searching firm has monopoly power.

FIGURE 23-2   THE PROFIT-MAXIMIZING POSITION OF A PURE MONOPOLIST

The profit-maximizing monopolist will produce output Ox_1, where $MR = MC$. Since average cost is less than average revenue (price) for output Ox_1, the monopolist is making an economic profit.

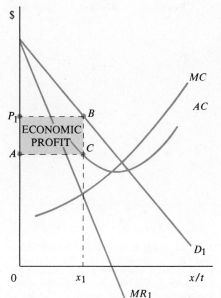

After output Ox_1 is produced, the monopolist will search for the highest price it can charge and still sell all its output. In Figure 23-2, this price is OP_1. The monopolist can sell output Ox_1 at price OP_1 because the demand curve in Figure 23-2 shows that OP_1 is the maximum that consumers will pay for output Ox_1.

At OP_1 and Ox_1, the monopolist is making an economic profit. The average revenue (price) is OP_1. OA is the average cost, so $OP_1 > OA$ and thus the monopolist is making a profit of $OP_1 - OA$ per unit, or a total profit of $(OP_1 - OA) \cdot Ox_1$. In Figure 23-2, total cost is represented by rectangle $OACx_1$ and total revenue is represented by rectangle OP_1Bx_1. TR minus TC equals profit, or rectangle AP_1BC. Since the costs depicted in the cost curves include both explicit and implicit costs, this profit means that the monopoly firm is making more than its opportunity cost, that is, the firm is making more than is necessary to keep its resources employed in this industry.

We can also determine price and output numerically. Table 23-2 combines the revenue data of Table 23-1 and the cost data of our chapter on production. We see that the monopolist would maximize profits at 7 units, where $MC = MR = \$46$. Price would be $52 because the demand curve (AR) tells us that 7 units will sell for $52 each. At a price of $52, total revenue is $364 ($=7 \times \$52$) and total cost is $322 ($=\$46 \times 7$), which means that the monopolist is making a profit of $42 ($=\$364 - \$322$). If you don't believe this is maximum profit, construct an eighth column for Table 23-2 and call it profit. Calculate the profit at each level of output from 1–10 units and you will see it is maximized at 7 units, because at 7 units, $MR = MC$.[1]

TABLE 23-2   MONOPOLIST'S COST AND REVENUE DATA

Output and Sales	Total Cost	Average Cost	Marginal Cost	Average Revenue	Total Revenue	Marginal Revenue
0	60	—	—	—	0	—
1	100	100	40	58	58	58
2	136	68	36	57	114	56
3	168	56	32	56	168	54
4	200	50	32	55	220	52
5	235	47	35	54	270	50
6	276	46	41	53	318	48
7	322	46	46	52	364	46
8	372	46½	50	51	408	44
9	429	47⅔	57	50	450	42
10	490	49	61	49	490	40

[1]If you undertake such a calculation, you will find that profit is $42 at an output of 6 units and at an output of 7 units. This result obtains from the fact that in numerical examples we use discrete data. The principle is that profit maximization implies producing where $MC = MR$, but a unique point only exists when dealing with functions and using calculus. In this example the actual profit-maximizing output would be somewhere between 6 and 7 units of output.

Profits and New Entry

Other entrepreneurs will want some of the profits the monopolist is receiving. As a result, there will be pressure from new firms entering the industry in order to cash in on some of these profits. But wait! A monopoly is a single seller producing a product for which there are no close substitutes, so if there is new entry, we no longer have monopoly. If a monopoly is to exist, there must be some forces at work to keep new firms from entering. Economists say there must be **barriers to entry.** Barriers to entry are natural or artificial obstacles that keep new firms from entering an industry.

barriers to entry Natural or artificial obstacles that keep new firms from entering an industry.

A *natural* barrier to entry is economies of scale. If the long-run cost curves are such that an optimal-size plant occurs only when the firm is very large relative to the size of the market, it could be that there is room for only one cost-efficient firm in the industry. If there are significant economies of scale, one firm which gets bigger than any of the others will be able to undersell them. In such a case the bigger firm will cut price below its rivals and eventually become the only firm in the industry. When just one firm emerges in this way—and this happens in very few industries—the firm is called a **natural monopoly.** Public utilities fit this category. The government recognizes that these are natural monopolies and therefore regulates them. Difficulties in such regulation will be discussed in the chapter titled "Theory in the Real World: The Structure of American Industry." As you might guess, the incidence of natural monopoly is very low. Some would argue that even public utilities are not natural monopolies. If the frequency of natural monopoly is low, then any monopoly power that exists in our economy must be due to artificial barriers.

natural monopoly A monopoly that emerges because of economies of scale. The size of the market is such that there is room for only one optimally sized firm.

An *artificial* barrier to entry is one which is contrived by the firm (or someone else) to keep others out. It doesn't take much imagination to come up with a list of such barriers. The least sophisticated, but perhaps the most effective, would be the use of violence. Say you have a monopoly on the illegal numbers racket in south Chicago. If a new entrepreneur ("family") moves in to reap some of these profits, you simply blow them away—very effective! This sort of tactic may sound preposterous, but business history contains many examples of such activity. The early history of oil exploration and drilling is one example where violence was sometimes used and private armies were often a must.

On a more civilized level, you may be able to erect artificial barriers that are legal, or at least quasi-legal. If you could capture ownership of all the raw materials in an industry, you could then control entry by not selling to potential new entrants. The classic example of this behavior is the Aluminum Company of America which, before World War II, controlled almost all the known free-world sources of bauxite, the essential ore for the production of aluminum.

Another technique would be to get a patent on a process or machine that is vital in production. Patent rights give sole authority to use the process or machine to the holder of the patent. The problem with a patent is twofold. First, it expires after 17 years in the United States, and then everyone is entitled to use the idea. Second, to get a patent you must provide detailed plans on how the item is produced, and these plans are available to potential competitors at the Library of Congress. So it appears a patent is not a very effective entry barrier to anyone who is willing to risk a lawsuit brought by the offended patent holder (and patent holders don't always win their cases). You may have already thought of a good alternative to patents—secrecy. If you can keep your vital process secret, you can keep new firms out of your industry. So now you know why there is barbed wire around research and development offices, why you aren't told the formula for Pepsi Cola, and why corporate spying is big business.

The Government and Barriers to Entry

In the final analysis, it is very difficult to be a monopolist because it is very hard to keep new entrants out of your industry—unless you can get the government to help you. Consider the industries you regard as monopolies or near monopolies. Let's look briefly at two industries with significant market power, the steel industry and the taxicab industry.

Suppose that firms in the steel industry are earning economic profits. Firms that are producing steel in Europe see these profits being earned and gear up to export steel to the United States in order to earn some of these profits. In effect, these foreign steel firms are entering the U.S. industry. The domestic firms then appeal to Congress or the president to keep these firms out, to block their entry, and tariffs or quotas are then put into effect. These tariffs or quotas serve as artificial barriers to entry by raising the price of foreign goods or prohibiting their sale.

Next, consider the taxicab industry. You decide to start a cab business. You already own a car, so the entry costs are relatively small. All you need to do is to mark your vehicle so that it can be recognized as a cab, and perhaps install a meter. However, you will need a permit, which in some cities will be very difficult and expensive to obtain. If you operate as a "jitney," an underground cab that avoids city regulations, you will make the existing monopoly cab owners very unhappy.

In these examples government supplied the artificial barrier to entry. Federal, state, and local governments all restrict entry and thereby insure protected market positions. It should not be too surprising that many of the graft cases in government have centered on the granting of monopoly privileges. A government official or agency protects a monopoly by keeping competitors out, and the monopolist is often willing to pay for this with campaign contributions, favors, or outright bribes such as direct cash payments, free vacations, or jobs for relatives.

When you examine industries that possess monopoly power, keep in mind that governments help monopolies exist by erecting barriers to entry. If the monopoly power persists for a long period of time, there is very likely some explicit or implicit government support of that monopoly. This is because monopoly profits are a very powerful and attractive force, and new entry is very difficult for the firm alone to block. As a result, monopolies usually try to enlist governmental support of one kind or another.

RESOURCE ALLOCATION WITH MONOPOLY

No entrepreneur likes to sell in a purely competitive industry. A firm that can create a successful monopoly is rewarded with profits. (This ability to use power in markets is stressed in marketing and management courses—hence, there are no marketing courses for wheat farmers!) Obviously monopoly is good for the monopolist. But as we are about to see, monopoly can be bad for society.

To see what's so bad about monopoly, let's examine Figure 23-3. First, suppose that Figure 23-3 represents a purely competitive market. The market demand curve is that faced by the numerous sellers and the MC curve is the summation of all the individual firm marginal cost curves. The competitive price and output would be OP_c and OQ_c. Now, suppose that the industry is monopolized by one firm that has bought up all the individual competitive firms and that this doesn't change any of the cost curves. The monopoly firm, then, would face the same cost conditions that the aggregate competitive firms faced. The *market* supply curve would represent the monopolist's marginal cost curve, because it would be the summation of the purchased firms' marginal cost curves. Likewise, the monopoly firm faces the *market* demand curve and its corresponding marginal revenue curve. The monopoly firm will produce OQ_m at price OP_m. It is thus a very simple matter to contrast pure monopoly to pure competition. The monopolist produces a smaller output ($OQ_m < OQ_c$) and charges a higher price ($OP_m > OP_c$) than does the purely competitive firm. This is possible because the monopolist excludes entry into the industry. Since the monopolist excludes entry, consumers are not getting the correct amounts of those goods that are produced by monopolized industries. Monopoly restricts output. This is the classical argument against monopoly.

The monopolistic output and price, then, represent monopoly misallocation, with monopoly having the same cost conditions as the aggregate of the competitive firms. You should note that the misallocation of monopoly might even be worse if, in buying up the individual firms, the monopoly introduced diseconomies of organization. This would be represented by an upward shifting of the cost curves in Figure 23-3.

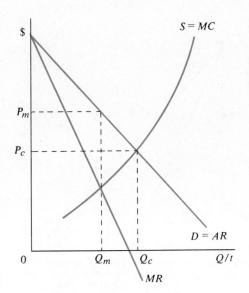

FIGURE 23-3   PRICE OUTPUT DETERMINATION UNDER PURE MONOPOLY AND PURE COMPETITION

The monopolist, equating marginal cost and marginal revenue, produces output OQ_m at price OP_m. If this same industry were competitive, the price would be OP_c and output would be OQ_c.

We can learn more about this misallocation of resources by examining Figure 23-4. The monopoly is in equilibrium producing OQ_1 at a price of OP_1. Monopoly profits are represented by rectangle CP_1AB. Let's examine closely what is going on at this equilibrium. First, price OP_1 is not equal to AC (average cost), which is OC per unit; that is, $P > AC$. This means that economic profits are being earned. Second, $P > MC$, which means the value consumers place on the item (P_1) exceeds the opportunity cost of producing more units (MC). This means, from a welfare point of view, that more should be produced, but the monopolist prohibits that from happening by restricting entry. Third, average cost at output OQ_1 is not equal to marginal cost at OQ_1, as $AC > MC$. This means that OQ_1 is not being produced at the least-cost combination of factors. That could happen only at output OQ_2. The monopolist is not forced to be fully efficient, although the firm does produce its actual output for the lowest cost possible. You can easily see, then, what we mean when we say that monopoly misallocates resources.

THE MONOPOLIST'S SUPPLY CURVE?

A monopoly firm does not have a supply curve in the same sense that a purely competitive firm's marginal cost curve can be viewed as its supply curve. A supply curve shows how much output will be supplied at any price, but a monopolist sets the price, so it doesn't make sense to ask how much will be supplied at various prices. For a monopoly, the profit-maximizing output where MC is equal to MR will depend on how the demand curve shifts. In order to determine a supply curve, it is necessary to show that at a given and unique price, a firm will supply a given and unique output. Examine Figures 23-5 and 23-6. In Figure 23-5 we

FIGURE 23-4   MONOPOLY MISALLOCATION OF RESOURCES

A monopoly misallocates resources because price is greater than marginal cost. This means the value consumers place on the item exceeds the opportunity cost of producing more units.

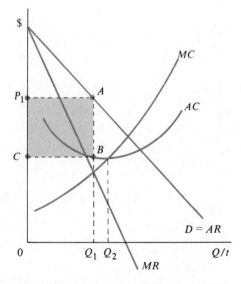

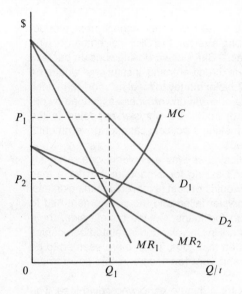

FIGURE 23-5 ONE OUTPUT—TWO PRICES
We can graph a supply curve if we can show a unique price, given a certain output. There are at least two prices, OP_1 and OP_2, consistent with output OQ_1, so we cannot draw the monopolist's supply curve.

see that two prices, OP_1 and OP_2, are consistent with output OQ_1. The demand curves D_1 and D_2 have marginal revenue curves with the property that they intersect the monopolist's marginal cost at the same level of output. In Figure 23-6, two different output levels, OQ_1 and OQ_2, are produced at OP_1.

The analysis of Figures 23-5 and 23-6 shows that it is impossible to sketch a supply curve for a monopolist. There is no way we can predict what the

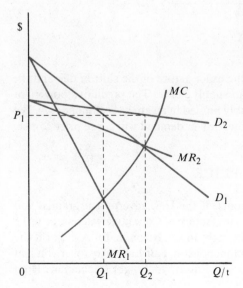

FIGURE 23-6 ONE PRICE—TWO OUTPUTS
We can graph a supply curve if we can show a unique output for a given price. There are at least two outputs, OQ_1 and OQ_2, consistent with price OP_1, so we cannot draw the monopolist's supply curve.

The New Chrysler Corporation

Economists often draw attention to entry conditions when looking at monopoly and monopoly behavior. It is, however, important that firms also be allowed to exit from industries in which losses are being incurred. Chrysler Corporation was the latest firm to seek government aid in order to stay in business. The case made for Chrysler was a classic example of government intervention and interference in the economic give-and-take of markets.

For whatever reason—poor management, production of the wrong-size car, the OPEC oil embargo, high labor costs, etc.—Chrysler was losing huge amounts of money. Private credit-granting institutions would no longer loan Chrysler money to meet its short-term cash crisis because of credit unworthiness as judged by private loaners of funds. So Chrysler appealed to the government, making a political case for governmental loan guarantees.

The political case was a powerful one. After all, Chrysler wasn't asking for a handout, but for a loan guarantee. It would not cost taxpayers anything unless, of course, Chrysler failed and the government had to make good on the loans. On the benefit side, thousands of workers in Chrysler and in related companies would be spared their jobs. Thus, there seemed to be only gainers and very few losers in this government guarantee.

But think for a minute as to who could lose. The supply of loanable funds is not perfectly elastic; the government alters the flow of funds in capital markets. Thus, many new entrepreneurs could not get funds; many productive enterprises could not expand; inefficiency was rewarded with a flow of capital; and a firm that should have been punished by the market wasn't.

Nonetheless, the political arguments won, and Chrysler received its guarantee. What was correct? You decide. Do you think Conestoga wagons would still be running between St. Louis and California if the wagon train suppliers had developed a politically important lobby?

monopolist will do without knowing the exact nature of the shift in demand. In this sense, then, the monopolist has no supply curve. The predictive powers of the economist are, therefore, considerably limited in an analysis of monopoly. We can no longer say, *ceteris paribus,* an increase in demand will cause price to rise.

MONOPOLY, PROFITS, AND PRICE

Monopoly is not a license to make profits. If the U.S. government granted you an absolute monopoly in the sale and manufacture of Conestoga wagons, or if the Israeli government granted you the sole right to sell bacon in Tel Aviv, or if the Mormon church made you the coffee monopolist in Salt Lake City, or if you had a monopoly in the sale and manufacture of Edsels, you might lose money. High costs and/or insufficient demand may cause the monopolist to lose money. Still, there is a common misconception that a monopoly situation guarantees profits.

Figure 23-7 graphs a monopoly suffering a loss. The monopoly is producing OQ_1 and charging the profit-maximizing price, OP_1. Average costs of producing OQ_1 are OC per unit. As a result, the monopolist is incurring losses equal to rectangle P_1CAB. Since the demand curve is below the average cost curve, there is no way to avoid losses. The next question is, Will the monopolist continue to produce? If price is above AVC, as is the case in Figure 23-7, the monopolist will be better off in the short run to continue rather than stop production. In the long run, if demand does not increase, the monopoly will go out of business. This is because the presence of losses indicates that the factors are not earning their opportunity cost. The factors will move or be moved to more productive uses.

Consider the case of the Penn Central Railroad. It clearly had monopoly power because it had sole authority (granted by the government) to provide rail transportation between different east coast cities. However, costs rose (as the price of capital and labor increased); at the same time demand declined because of competing modes of transportation. Eventually, losses were incurred. The market was signaling that the factors of production were more valuable elsewhere. In this case, the government granted subsidies to make up the losses. This raises an interesting question: Should government subsidize (certain) monopolies that are incurring losses? If so, how do you decide which to subsidize? Should we subsidize the steel companies by helping them keep out less expensive foreign steel? The government granted a direct subsidy to Penn Central, but refused to give one to Lockheed.

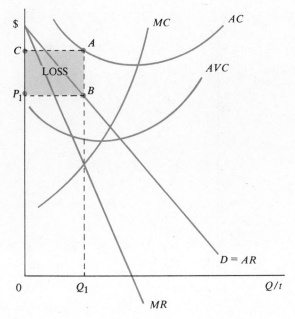

FIGURE 23-7 A MONOPOLY SUFFERING LOSSES
The monopolist might suffer losses in the short run. If average cost exceeds average revenue, the monopolist is suffering a loss.

Just as monopolists can suffer losses, it is also possible that a monopoly might earn only normal profits. Figure 23-8 illustrates. The monopoly is producing OQ_1 and charges OP_1. TR is equal to TC, rectangle OP_1AQ_1. In this instance, the monopoly is earning its opportunity cost and there will be no incentive for other firms to enter this industry or for this firm to leave the industry. $P = AC$, which means that producers are not earning economic profits. It still is the case, however, that $P > MC$, indicating that more units should be produced.

So we see, then, monopolies don't always make profits. In fact, they can often incur losses and go out of business. Also, monopolists do not charge the highest price possible. Remember the mineral spring example? Monopolists charge the *profit-maximizing* price, and this price will depend on the demand conditions, and costs, in that industry.

MONOPOLY IN THE LONG RUN

The monopolist, unlike the purely competitive firm, can continue to earn economic profits in the long run. As long as the entry barriers remain, economic profits can be maintained. Long-run maintenance of entry barriers is very difficult, however, because the economic profits will bring about new firms and processes to compete for any economic profits that exist. In principle, then, even with government help, the power of any single monopoly is likely to decline in the very long run. In the railroad example, entrepreneurs will be attracted by the profits existing in other industries, and trucks, buses, private cars, barges, and planes will decrease the demand for rail transportation.

**FIGURE 23-8   A MONOPOLY EARNING NORMAL
                   PROFITS**

It is possible that a monopoly might only earn normal profits. In this instance, there is no incentive for other firms to enter the industry, and there is no need for barriers to entry.

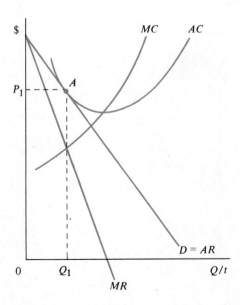

PRICE DISCRIMINATION

In analyzing monopoly behavior, we have assumed that the monopolist charges the same price to all consumers and the same price for all units sold to a particular consumer. If, on the other hand, the monopolist is able to charge different consumers different prices, or charge a particular consumer different prices depending on the quantity purchased, we say the monopolist is able to practice *price discrimination*. First, we will examine a monopolist practicing price discrimination with one consumer, and then we will examine a case where price discrimination means different prices for different consumers.

Consider the demand curve for a single consumer or group of homogeneous consumers in Figure 23-9. At price OP_1, the individual will consume OQ_1 units of the good. You will remember from our discussion of utility-maximizing behavior, that the marginal utility of the last unit purchased is equal to the price of the unit. This means that the marginal utility of each previous unit purchased was greater than price OP_1. The consumer would have been willing to pay higher prices for these previous units, so at the market price of OP_1, the consumer receives a bonus in terms of utility. The total purchase is worth more to the consumer than the total amount (price times quantity) that is paid. This extra utility gained is called *consumer surplus* and is represented by the shaded area in Figure 23-9.

A monopoly producer might be able to deal separately with the consumer for each unit purchased. In terms of Figure 23-10, the monopolist could say, "You may buy OQ_1 units for OP_1, $OQ_2 - OQ_1$ units for OP_2, $OQ_3 - OQ_2$ units for OP_3, and $OQ_4 - OQ_3$ units for OP_4." By doing this, the monopolist has extracted most of the consumer surplus and converted it into revenue for the firm. Compare the shaded areas in Figure 23-10 to the shaded area in Figure 23-9. Both represent consumer surplus. In Figure 23-10, by charging different prices for

price discrimination   The practice of charging different consumers different prices or a particular consumer different prices for different quantities purchased.

consumer surplus   The extra utility gained from the fact that some consumers pay less for an item than they would be willing to pay.

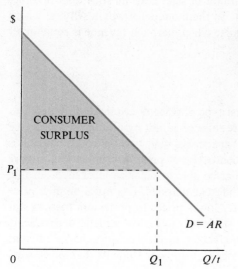

FIGURE 23-9   CONSUMER SURPLUS
Consumer surplus is the difference between the total utility received from the purchase of a product and the total revenue generated by the product. It exists because the marginal utility of each previous unit purchased was greater than price OP_1.

FIGURE 23-10   A DISCRIMINATING MONOPOLIST

A discriminating monopolist can expropriate most of the consumer surplus by charging different prices for different amounts of consumption.

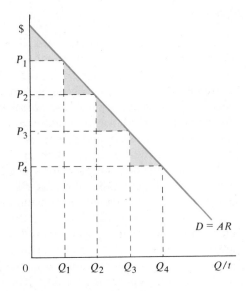

different amounts of consumption, the monopolist has expropriated much of the consumer surplus. It is theoretically possible for the monopolist to get all of this consumer surplus by perfectly discriminating in differential prices for each unit.

A second type of price discrimination which isn't as advantageous to the monopoly, but which is more feasible, occurs when a monopolist can separate markets and charge different prices to different consumers or groups of consumers. If the monopoly can separate the markets and prevent resale, it can price discriminate by adjusting for the different demand elasticities in the two markets. The monopolist does this by equating marginal revenue in each submarket. If marginal revenue is not equal in each submarket, a switching of sales between markets would increase total revenue. This makes sense if you have a good grasp of marginal analysis. Given any level of sales, it makes for profit maximization to sell in any submarket where a given unit of sales adds most to total revenue; i.e., where marginal revenue is highest. So the monopolist would sell first where marginal revenue is highest and maximize when marginal revenue is equal in all markets.

Price Discrimination in Practice

In practice, we very seldom see the first type of price discrimination. It requires the seller to have the power to separate sales on a unit-by-unit basis. We do see some crude approximations, such as "artichokes 40¢, two for 65¢," but this is hardly close to Figure 23-10. The second type of price discrimination is more common. It only requires that the seller be able to separate markets according to the elasticity of demand in these different markets. Examples of such price discrimination abound. Bookstores offer lower prices to professors than to students; airlines charge lower fares for students; university athletic departments offer lower priced tickets to students and faculty; medical doctors charge different patients different fees for the same service (less to poor students than professors, but more to rich students). Consider plane fares. If you fly to Europe and can stay for 14–21 days, the fare is cheaper than if you stay for less than 14 days. If you stay for 21–48 days, flights are even cheaper. Why? Which class of consumers of air transportation have the most inelastic demand? Business people, of course, who tend to travel on tight schedules and have bosses who don't want them playing in France for 14 days!

It should be clear that two conditions are necessary in order to practice price discrimination. First, you must be able to separate consumers into groups that have different demand elasticities. These groups need to be economically identifiable (if it costs too much to identify the groups, discrimination might not pay). So when economists talk about price discrimination, they're not talking about creed, color, or sex, unless certain creeds, colors, or sexes have different demand elasticities for certain products. In our example of air fares, you can separate the classes of consumers by length of stay. Business people seldom travel to a destination for more than a few days; rarely do they travel for more than 14 days.

The second major requirement for price discrimination is that the monopolist *must* prevent the resale of goods or the movement of customers between markets. Consider the case of charging different prices to different classes of consumers for a football game. It only works if you prohibit the lower priced customers from reselling. If you don't, you are no longer a monopolist in the sale to the higher priced market. Is it any wonder that the athletic department requires you to show your picture I.D. card *and* your ticket at the gate? The higher priced ticket holders are only required to present their tickets. You might have guessed that price discrimination works well where resale is very difficult. Medical doctors are very successful in practicing price discrimination because they have easily recognizable submarkets with different elasticities (by income category) *and* because resale is almost always ruled out. Little wonder that Dr. David Reuben, the doctor who told you all you ever wanted to know about sexual problems, when asked to explain his pricing policy, replied, "I have an infinitely sliding scale. Everyone should pay, but nobody can pay more than he can afford. So I charge some patients five dollars an hour and others one hundred."[2]

Is Price Discrimination Bad?

Price discrimination does have a positive side effect in that it will usually cause output under monopoly to increase. We saw earlier in this chapter that monopoly is undesirable because it restricts output. If a monopoly can, however, sell output one unit at a time, output will be pushed to the point where $P = MC$. This is just common sense, because the single monopolist restricts output in order to keep price from falling. If price will only fall on the increments in output (not other units), production will be pushed to the point where $P = MC$. This is the same solution as obtained in pure competition. The difference, of course, is that the profits accrue to the monopolist. Price discrimination turns consumer surplus into monopoly profits. This means monopolists are wealthier and consumers are worse off. It is important to note that this is a transfer of wealth and doesn't change any of the other good or bad effects of the monopolist.

---

[2]Reported in the *Chicago Sun-Times*, June 23, 1974, and cited in James V. Koch, *Microeconomic Theory and Applications* (Boston: Little, Brown & Company, 1976), p. 233.

On another level, many people believe price discrimination is unfair or immoral because it means different people pay different amounts for the very same product. Why should an airplane ticket be cheaper because someone is a tourist rather than a business traveler? Why should professors get their books and pens for lower prices than students? Why should students pay less for a football ticket than nonstudents?

Interestingly, it is sometimes the group that benefits from price discrimination that complains. Price discrimination is common in international trade because the separation of national markets is often easy to maintain. Tariffs and transportation costs can help prevent resale. When firms in a country sell in a foreign market at a lower price than they do at home, they are engaging in price discrimination. Demand in the foreign country is more elastic than domestic demand, so the foreign monopolist sells to foreigners at a lower price than at home. The U.S. Treasury calls this practice *dumping.* Dumping occurs, for example, when the Japanese sell televisions in the United States at a lower price than they sell the same sets at home. The odd thing is that dumping has an unfavorable connotation. When the Japanese dump televisions in the United States, the U.S. government takes action against Japan. This is curious because Japanese firms are giving U.S. consumers a better deal than Japanese consumers. Complaining about the lower price is a little like writing to the school paper to say that you, as a student, don't like the fact that you can get tickets to the big game for one third the regular price. Seen from another angle, however, dumping is an objectionable practice: You can understand why domestic manufacturers don't particularly approve of the lower priced products offered by foreign competitors.[3]

dumping   The practice of selling in foreign markets at lower prices than in domestic markets. This is a form of price discrimination.

SOME OTHER COSTS OF MONOPOLY

There are other costs associated with monopoly that are often ignored. These are the inconveniences and rudeness often associated with monopolies, particularly the regulated monopolies. Consider the telephone company. Students at some colleges are required to place a $100 deposit plus wait three weeks at the beginning of the year before telephone service begins. Can you imagine such treatment from a firm where there are close substitutes? The reason the telephone company is able to get away with this is that most of us don't consider the mail, or cans connected with waxed string, a good substitute for telephone service.

WHO RUNS THE FIRM? ALTERNATIVES TO PROFIT MAXIMIZATION

We have consistently assumed in this chapter and the previous chapter that firms are profit maximizers. This assumption allowed us to predict how the firm would

---

[3]There may be some other objections to dumping. The government may fear that the Japanese are selling below cost to drive U.S. firms out of business in an attempt to corner the market on televisions. Or the Treasury may fear Japan is transmitting macroeconomic disturbances to the U.S. by weakening the U.S. television industry. But the bottom line is that we are objecting to someone selling us goods too cheaply.

adjust in the two distinct market structures of pure competition and pure monopoly.

The profit-maximizing assumption might have seemed reasonable for firms such as wheat farms when we were concerned with competitive firms, but what happens when we move into the realm of monopoly power and giant firms run by professional managers? We saw earlier that corporations account for about 85 percent of the annual business sales in the United States. Yet corporations are run by hired managers, not owners. Managers might operate by some principle other than profit maximization. This proposition is sometimes referred to as the hypothesis of the *separation of ownership and control* and simply means that managers who control corporations may behave differently than would owner-managers. This different behavior would result only if the managers have different goals *and* owners can't control managers.

The hypothesis that behavior deviates from the profit-maximization assumption of economic theory is based on organizational theory which you have probably studied if you have taken a course in social psychology or management. The hypothesis assumes that management will follow standard procedures even if these procedures result in lower profits. Managers of big business are seen as bureaucrats who react conservatively to avoid mistakes and to cover their liability, much as managers in the military, the federal bureaucracy, or any large organization do. Those who argue that a firm does not maximize profits offer several competing hypotheses to the standard profit-maximization hypothesis. Let's look briefly at some of these.

The *satisficing* hypothesis argues that the management of a firm does not seek maximum profits but rather certain target levels of output and profits that are satisfactory to the ownership interests. Unfortunately, in order to perform empirical tests of this hypothesis to determine its validity, it would be necessary to specify what a firm's target happens to be; otherwise any result that is found would be consistent with satisficing behavior. The proponents of the satisficing hypothesis have not as yet accomplished this specification. As a result, the predictive value of the hypothesis is very low.

Another alternative hypothesis has been suggested by Professor William Baumol of Princeton University. Baumol argues that given some numerical level of profits, the managers' primary goal is to increase the *sales* of the firm. In essence, Baumol is saying that managers are rewarded by stockholders, according to the relative size of their firm in the market, for any increase in their percentage share of the market, say, from 15 to 20 percent. This is called the *constrained sales maximization* hypothesis. The implication of this hypothesis is that monopoly might not be as bad as we concluded earlier. If sales, rather than profits, are the primary goal of a monopoly, the firm will lower prices and increase output. The lower prices and increased output will insure that the misallocation of resources will not be as bad as we had predicted with profit maximization.

A rejoinder to these competing hypotheses is the *long-run profit maximization* hypothesis. Following this hypothesis, if the firm maximizes sales, it is doing so because this will lead to higher profits in the long run. Likewise, if the firm is concerned with social responsibility and philanthropic or altruistic projects, the long-run profits of the firm may be maximized by consolidating its goodwill. The problem with this hypothesis is that unless we specify a distinct time period, almost any behavior would be consistent with long-run profit maximization. The

separation of ownership and control Corporations are run by hired managers, not owners. These managers might operate by some principle other than profit maximization. This behavior results if managers have goals different than the owners' and if the owners cannot control the managers.

satisficing Management does not seek to maximize profits, but rather seeks target levels of output and profits that are satisfactory to the interests of ownership.

constrained sales maximization Occurs when a manager's primary goal is to increase the sales of the firm because managers are rewarded by stockholders for increasing the firm's relative share of the market.

long-run profit maximization The argument that even if managers follow satisficing behavior or constrained sales maximization, they do so only because this leads to higher profits in the long run.

Herbert Simon *(1916–)*

Herbert Simon was born in Milwaukee, Wisconsin, and educated at the University of Chicago. Professor Simon has held teaching positions at the University of California, the Illinois Institute of Technology, and the University of Pittsburgh. He is presently at Carnegie-Mellon University.

Simon has never held a teaching post as an economist. Instead, he has held professorships in political science, administration, psychology, and information sciences. He is thus an economist in the broadest sense of the word, like the early classical economists.

In awarding the 1978 Nobel Prize in Economics to Simon, the Royal Swedish Academy paid particular attention to his work which was concerned with the development of alternatives to profit maximization. The committee made the following statement in its official announcement:

In his epoch-making book, *Administrative Behavior* (1947), and in a number of subsequent works, he described the company as an adaptive system of physical, personal, and social components that are held together by a network of intercommunications and by the willingness of its members to cooperate and to strive towards a common goal. What is new in Simon's ideas is, most of all, that he rejects the assumption made in classic theory of the firm as an omnisciently rational, profit-maximizing entrepreneur.[1]

Professor Simon has had an important impact on more academic disciplines than any of the other Nobel prizewinners in economics. His work in management science and public administration is credited with bringing scientific approaches to the "art" of management. Professor Simon is perhaps the best example of an economic theorist who has made a major impact on business and public administration.

---

[1]"The Nobel Memorial Prize in Economics," *The Scandinavian Journal of Economics,* Vol. 81, No. 1 (1979), pp. 72–73.

theory then becomes a cataloging exercise; there is no way to refute such a theory because it is consistent with everything and, therefore, can predict or explain nothing.

If monopoly firms substitute other goals for profit maximization, one goal that might be substituted is religious or racial discrimination. In other words, they may sacrifice some profits in order to sell to or hire the type of people with whom they identify. A very interesting test of this hypothesis was conducted several years ago by Professor Armen Alchian of UCLA and the late Professor Rubin Kessel of the University of Chicago. They examined the employment of Jewish and non-Jewish graduates of the Harvard Business School according to the market structures in which they were employed. In the years examined, 36 percent of the graduates were Jewish. Comparing the employment of these Harvard MBAs in monopolized and relatively competitive industries, they discovered that the monopolized category was 18 percent Jewish and the competitive category was 41 percent Jewish.[4] This evidence is consistent with the hypothesis that monopoly power makes discrimination against minorities easier (less costly) and points to yet another cost of monopoly power.

Recently Professor Thomas DiLorenzo of George Mason University has argued that rational utility maximizing behavior of managers of private monopolies will not be more lax than their counterparts in competitive firms. This is the case because monopoly managers are claimants to monopoly wealth through salary increases and increased expenditures on managerial perquisites.[5]

Before we go too far afield developing a list of behavioral hypotheses about firm behavior, we need to think back to our discussion of what theory is and what it does. Theory abstracts from the real world by concentrating on the important aspects or effects of a phenomenon. If profit maximization is a valid assumption, it will yield reasonably accurate predictions about firm behavior. The profit-maximization assumption is a cornerstone of many hypotheses that have been empirically tested and found to be valid. Alternative assumptions have yet to be as rigorously tested.

EXAMPLES OF MONOPOLY

We have pointed out that there are no examples of pure monopoly in the real world. Our theoretical definition prohibits this. There are, however, firms with monopoly power, and we can use the monopoly model to explain the behavior of, and to predict economic outcomes for, these firms. Public utilities, for example, are considered natural monopolies (and are regulated as a result). State trading monopolies that are set up by some nations to engage in international trade are also monopolistic. They have been demonstrated to practice price discrimination by selling to different countries at different prices. *Local monopolies* are another form of real-world monopoly. If you grew up in a small, remote town, there may have been only one movie theater or perhaps only one grocery store. A firm in such a situation is a local monopoly because the close substitutes are costly in that you must travel to reach them. In all these real-world examples of monopoly, we can use the model of pure monopoly to examine the effects of monopoly power.

local monopoly A firm which has monopoly power in a geographic region. Even though close substitutes exist, the distance between sources of supply creates monopolies.

SUMMARY

1. Pure monopoly is a market situation in which there is a single seller of a product with no close substitutes.

2. The monopoly firm faces a negatively sloped demand curve and a marginal revenue curve that lies below that demand curve.

3. The monopolist maximizes profits by producing the output at which $MC = MR$ and sets the price at which exactly that output can be sold. Since price is often greater than average cost in the monopoly case, economic profits often exist.

---

[4]A.A. Alchian and R.A. Kessel, "Competition, Monopoly, and the Pursuit of Money," in H.G. Lewis, et al., *Aspects of Labor Economics* (Princeton, N.J.: Princeton University Press, 1962).
[5]Thomas J. DiLorenzo, "Corporate Management, Property Rights, and the X-istence of X-efficiency," *Southern Economic Journal* (July, 1981), pp. 116–124.

4. The monopolist is sometimes able to erect barriers to entry which allow profits to exist in the long run. These barriers are very difficult to maintain and, as a result, monopolists often appeal to the government for help in maintaining entry barriers.

5. Monopolies produce a lower output at a higher price than do competitive firms. At equilibrium, the monopoly firm is producing at a level of output where $P \neq AC \neq MC$.

6. Monopoly power is not a guarantee of profits. Some monopolies go out of business because of persistent losses; others make only normal profits.

7. A monopoly can increase its revenues if it practices price discrimination. For price discrimination to be successful, the monopolist must have customers with different demand elasticities and they must be separated and prohibited from reselling the product.

8. The satisficing hypothesis and the sales maximization hypothesis are both derived from the idea of the separation of ownership and control. They argue that hired managers, as opposed to owner-managers, attempt to maximize sales or meet *satisfactory* profit targets rather than maximize profits.

9. Although no examples of *pure* monopoly exist, the model of pure monopoly is useful in analyzing monopoly power.

NEW TERMS

monopoly
monopoly power
price searcher
barriers to entry
natural monopoly
price discrimination
consumer surplus

dumping
separation of ownership and control
satisficing
constrained sales maximization
long-run profit maximization
local monopoly

QUESTIONS FOR DISCUSSION

1. Explain in your own words why marginal revenue is less than average revenue under conditions of monopoly.

2. Should business firms be socially responsible? Respond to the argument that they should maximize profits and leave social responsibility to elected and appointed officials.

3. List as many barriers to entry as you can. Which are the most effective?

4. Why will a monopolist never attempt to produce in the inelastic portion of the demand curve?

5. Do electric utilities practice price discrimination? If so, why do demand elasticities differ? How can the utility separate markets?

6. Should government subsidize monopolies that are losing money in order to keep them in business?

SUGGESTIONS FOR FURTHER READING

Baumol, William J. *Business Behavior, Value and Growth,* rev. ed. New York: Harcourt, Brace & World, 1967.

Mansfield, Edwin (ed.). *Monopoly Power and Economic Performance,* rev. ed. New York: W. W. Norton & Co., 1968.

Mason, Edward S. "Corporation," *International Encyclopedia of the Social Sciences,* edited by David L. Sills, Vol. 3. New York: Macmillan Publishing Co., 1968.

Sherman, Roger. *The Economics of Industry.* Boston: Little, Brown & Company, 1973, Chapter 9.

CHAPTER 24

The Model of Monopolistic Competition

Learning Objectives

After studying the materials found in this chapter, you should be able to do the following:

1. Define monopolistic competition.

2. List the characteristics of the model of monopolistic competition.

3. List the parts of the market structures continuum.

4. Diagram a representative firm in monopolistic competition making:
   (a) an economic profit.
   (b) a loss.
   (c) an economic profit of zero.

5. Diagram the long-run equilibrium in monopolistic competition compared to such an equilibrium in pure competition.

6. Define:
   (a) excess capacity.
   (b) product differentiation.

7. Define the relationships between:
   (a) excess capacity and product differentiation.
   (b) product differentiation and elasticity of demand.

In the last two chapters we have developed the two poles of a theoretical spectrum of market structures. At one extreme, we have pure monopoly and at the other we have pure competition. Figure 24-1 illustrates these polar cases. There are no perfect, theoretically correct real-world examples of either polar case, but for many years all real-world industry structures were analyzed by appealing to these two. In the 1930s all this changed and theories were developed that filled in the continuum in Figure 24-1. We call the space between these two poles *imperfect competition.* We can further divide imperfect competition into *monopolistic competition,* which we will analyze in this chapter, and *oligopoly,* which we leave to the next chapter.

The development of monopolistic competition is usually associated with Edward Chamberlin and Joan Robinson. Chamberlin, who died in 1967, was a Harvard professor and published a book in 1933 entitled *The Theory of Monopolistic Competition.* Joan Robinson published *The Economics of Imperfect Compe-*

imperfect competition The market structures of oligopoly and monopolistic competition.

monopolistic competition The market structure in which a large number of firms produce a differentiated product. Entry into the industry is relatively easy.

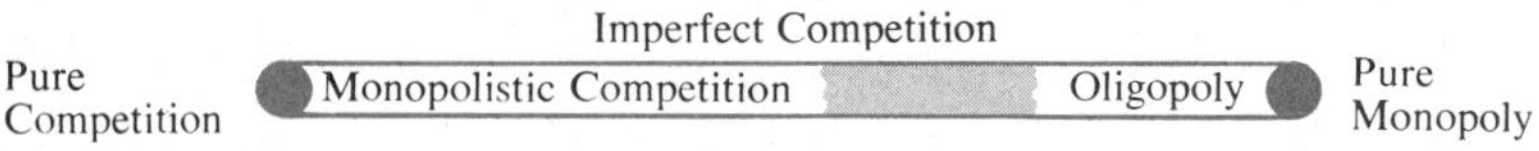

FIGURE 24-1 MARKET STRUCTURES CONTINUUM
The two poles of the theoretical spectrum are pure competition and pure monopoly. The real-world space between the two poles is called imperfect competition. Imperfect competition consists of monopolistic competition and oligopoly. There is a shaded area between monopolistic competition and oligopoly because it is not always clear where one ends and the other begins.

tition, also in 1933. Robinson was only 30 years old when this classic was published and she is still a professor at Cambridge University in England. These two books presented the basics of monopolistic competition.

CHARACTERISTICS OF MONOPOLISTIC COMPETITION

In developing the model of monopolistic competition, we assume that the industry is composed of a large number of sellers. Each of these sellers produces a product that is ***differentiated,*** which means that the products of these firms have either real or imagined identifiable characteristics that are different from each other. All that this means is that there is a difference in the product of one firm when compared to others. This differentiation can take many forms. It might be that the salespeople are nicer, that the packaging is prettier, that the credit terms are better, or that the service is faster. It could even be that a famous person is associated with the product, such as Joe DiMaggio endorsing a coffee maker, or Reggie Jackson promoting a brand of video-cassette recorders. It is important to note that a product is differentiated if consumers view it as different. Chemists tell us that aspirin is aspirin, that there is no difference among the brands. Yet if consumers view the brands as different, we have product differentiation.

differentiated product A good that has real or imagined identifiable characteristics that are different from other goods.

In monopolistic competition, we have an industry characterized by a large number of firms, each producing a differentiated product. A third and very important assumption we make is that entry into this industry is relatively easy. New firms can enter the industry and start producing products that are similar to those already being produced. In his original description of monopolistic competition, Chamberlin called the market for a good that was differentiated but had a large number of close substitutes a ***product group.*** Chamberlin characterized monopolistic competition as the large group case where there was rivalry between many firms in a product class.

product group A market for a good that is differentiated but has a large number of close substitutes.

You will probably recognize monopolistic competition as the market structure of most firms that you are familiar with since retail firms often fit this description. Monopolistic competition is generally what most people think of when they think of competition. Pure competition, with its required product homogeneity, simply does not fit commercial reality, where people are madly trying to make their products different.

Joan Robinson *(1903–   )*

Edward Chamberlin *(1899–1967)*

Joan Robinson and *Edward Chamberlin* are given joint credit for developing the theory of monopolistic competition. Chamberlin published his *Theory of Monopolistic Competition* (1933) six months before Robinson published *The Economics of Imperfect Competition* (1933). Chamberlin, in later years, was preoccupied with trying to differentiate his ideas from Robinson's. Robinson is reported to have commented on Chamberlin's anguish over her receiving joint credit by saying at one point, "I'm sorry I ruined his life."

Chamberlin was born in the state of Washington, but attended high school in Iowa, where he was an all-around student and a successful athlete. He later attended the University of Iowa, then went to the University of Michigan to study, and ultimately received his Ph.D. at Harvard. He taught at Harvard until his death.

Joan Robinson developed her ideas quite independently of Chamberlin (they did not know each other) while a junior faculty member at Cambridge University. After the appearance of her path-breaking book, Robinson expanded her interests and research over a wide range of economic policy issues. Still a very

active economist and social critic, Robinson is an outspoken foe of the market system. Her more recent antimarket publications include *An Essay on Marxian Economics* (1956), *Economic Philosophy* (1962), and *Freedom and Necessity* (1970). Both Professor Robinson and Professor Chamberlin have had a significant impact on economics, but their careers were strikingly different. Chamberlin's career was characterized by a single pursuit: the development of the theory of monopolistic competition. Few economists have applied themselves to so singular a purpose and yet achieved fame. Perhaps this singleness of purpose in part explains Chamberlin's pain at having to share his fame with Robinson. Unlike Chamberlin, Robinson's interests have been wide ranging. After contributing to micro theory, she worked with Keynes and helped to develop macroeconomics. Subsequently, she became a fiery social critic with varied interests. It is likely that she views her work on monopolistic competition as important, but in no way the dominant part of her contribution to economic analysis.

SHORT-RUN ADJUSTMENT

Analysis of the short-run position of the monopolistically competitive firm is remarkably similar to the analysis of the purely competitive firm. In Figure 24-2 we have a firm's demand curve. We start the analysis by depicting a representative firm rather than the market and then deriving the demand curve faced by a representative firm as we did with pure competition. This is necessary because, with product differentiation, each firm faces its own demand curve. The firm's demand curve in Figure 24-2 is negatively sloped, unlike the perfectly elastic demand curve of the purely competitive firm. This slope is caused by the differentiated nature of the product the firm is producing. If the product's price is raised, the firm will not lose all its customers because some will prefer this product to those of competing firms. Likewise, if price is lowered, the firm will gain customers, but some customers will be loyal to the products produced by other firms. It's easy to see that the elasticity of the demand curve is a measure of the degree of differentiation within the industry. If the goods are only slightly differentiated, they are then close substitutes and each firm's demand curve will be very elastic. If the differentiation is significant, the curve will be relatively inelastic, indicating that the firm could more easily raise price without losing many customers. Its customers are more loyal. Think of the aspirin example. If some people are willing to pay more for Bayer than for Brand X aspirin because they think it is different, the makers of Bayer will be able to raise price without losing a large number of customers. The more people are convinced that the products are different, the greater the degree of price autonomy. Thus, the Bayer people will be limited in their price autonomy by the amount of differentiation they are able to create. At some price, too few people will be willing to pay for the differentiation. In other words, some people may be willing to pay 10¢ more for Bayer, but as price is raised higher, more and more people will shift to other brands.

**FIGURE 24-2   SHORT-RUN PROFITS IN
                  MONOPOLISTIC COMPETITION**

In the short run, economic profits can exist in monopolistic competition. These profits will cause new firms to enter the industry.

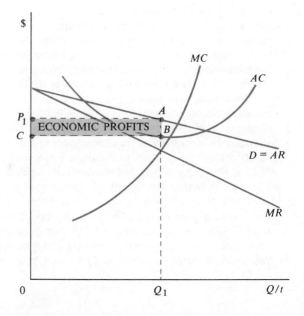

The demand curve in Figure 24-2 has a negative slope, indicating product differentiation, but the curve is very elastic, indicating that there are many good substitutes. Since the curve is negatively sloped, the marginal revenue curve will lie below the demand (average revenue) curve for the same reasons it did in the case of pure monopoly. The firm will, of course, maximize profits at price OP_1 and output OQ_1, where marginal revenue is equal to marginal cost. The representative firm in Figure 24-2 is earning economic profits because average revenue, OP_1, exceeds average cost, OC. Total revenue is represented by rectangle OP_1AQ_1 and total cost is represented by rectangle $OCBQ_1$. Total profits are thus shown by the shaded rectangle CP_1AB.

LONG-RUN ADJUSTMENT

What about long-run equilibrium in monopolistically competitive industries? In Figure 24-2, we saw a short-run equilibrium with economic profits. This signals profit-seeking entrepreneurs to enter this industry. Since we assumed that entry into monopolistically competitive industries is relatively easy, new firms will enter the industry. As firms enter the industry, the demand curve that any single representative firm faces will shift to the left because the new firms will be attracting customers away from firms already in the industry. This is what happens in an area when a new retail grocery store opens. It draws customers away from the existing firms. The demand curve will continue to shift to the left as new firms enter, and new firms will enter as long as economic profits are to be made. Long-run equilibrium thus must occur at the zero economic profit (or normal profit) number of firms. Such an equilibrium is depicted in Figure 24-3. Price is OP_1 and output is OQ_1. Total revenue and total cost are represented by

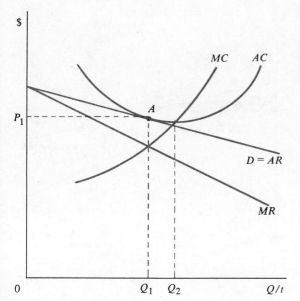

FIGURE 24-3 LONG-RUN EQUILIBRIUM IN MONOPOLISTIC COMPETITION

Since entry into monopolistically competitive industries is relatively easy, there can be no long-run profits. Firms will enter until the existing firms are earning only normal profits.

rectangle OP_1AQ_1. There are no economic profits being earned and no additional new firms will attempt to enter this industry.

Of course, too many firms might enter the industry in the mistaken anticipation of economic profits. If this happened, losses would be realized and firms would leave the industry as the long-run adjustment proceeded. In Figure 24-4, a monopolistically competitive firm making losses of P_1CBA is shown. Firms would respond by leaving the industry, which would cause the demand curves faced by the remaining firms to increase (shift to the right) until the equilibrium shown in Figure 24-3 is restored. The long-run adjustment process thus produces a situation in which zero economic profits exist.

EXCESS CAPACITY

excess capacity   Under-utilization of existing plant size. In monopolistic competition, the firm produces less than the efficient capacity of the plant.

The adjustment process we have just examined causes the firm to choose an output which produces an underutilization of existing plant size. This underutilization is called *excess capacity* and is depicted in Figure 24-3. The profit-maximizing output was seen to be OQ_1, where $MR = MC$. This is not, however, the output that would have resulted under pure competition because under pure competition the firm is producing at the least-cost combination. The least-cost combination is where average cost is at a minimum and is the socially optimal output because it represents maximum attainable efficiency. This efficient output is represented by OQ_2 in Figure 24-3. In other words, in long-run equilibrium, the monopolistically competitive firm produces less than the efficient capacity of the firm. Economists call this excess capacity.

Is this excess capacity a bad thing? To answer this, it is necessary to understand what causes it. The firm is producing less than the socially ideal output

---

FIGURE 24-4   SHORT-RUN LOSSES IN MONOPOLISTIC COMPETITION

Short-run losses will cause some firms to exit the industry. Firms will exit until the existing firms are earning normal profits, as in Figure 24-3.

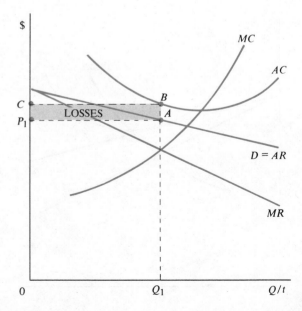

because it maximizes profits by producing the lower output. This comes about because the demand curve is downward sloping. We can see this by examining Figure 24-5. Begin with demand curve D_1. The monopolistically competitive firm would produce OQ_1 at price OP_1. Now make the demand curve more elastic by rotating it, as in Figure 24-5. As the demand curve becomes more and more elastic and finally perfectly elastic, like D_2, the output would increase to the socially efficient output OQ_2 and price would fall to OP_2. The excess capacity is thus easily seen to be a result of the negative slope in the demand curve. This negative slope, you recall, is a result of the product differentiation. The excess capacity, therefore, results from product differentiation.

It might be argued that this excess capacity is a good thing because consumers willingly accept the extra cost it implies in return for the differentiation that results.[1] It would indeed be a very boring world without product differentiation. We might all be wearing khaki-colored shirts, for example. How should we evaluate this argument? The major problem lies in separating desired from undesired product differentiation. If a consumer is faced with considerable product differentiation, but little price competition, the consumer is not able to choose whether or not to pay extra to get the differentiated product. This doesn't seem to be too important a problem when there are many firms, however, as in monopolistic competition. Consider aspirin. If the only products in the industry were produced by Bayer, Anacin, Tylenol, and Bufferin, the consumer really would not have a low-price choice, since these firms compete almost exclusively by advertising rather than by lowering prices. But the consumer does have a choice of lower priced aspirin brands. So in choosing Bayer over Brand X, we can say that the

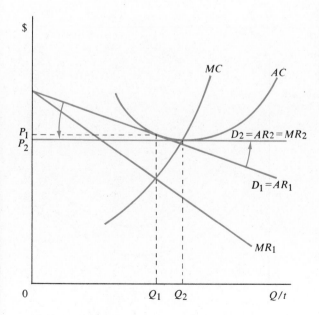

FIGURE 24-5 EXCESS CAPACITY
Excess capacity results from the negative slope of the demand curve. As the demand curve becomes more elastic, the excess capacity diminishes and disappears when the curve becomes perfectly elastic. The slope and, therefore, the excess capacity are a result of product differentiation.

---

[1] In fact, Professor Chamberlin argued this himself.

consumer voluntarily chooses the product differentiation. In this case, product differentiation seems to be a good thing because the consumer is maximizing individual utility by choosing. If, on the other hand, there are no options for lower priced products and the consumer must choose among those products that compete only through advertising, then the consumer may not have a choice about bearing the cost of the differentiation except, of course, by doing without the good altogether.

PRODUCT DIFFERENTIATION AND ADVERTISING

The firm in monopolistic competition will try to differentiate its product because this shifts its demand curve to the right *and* makes it more inelastic by developing consumer loyalty. This means that it will advertise as well as make changes in color, style, quality, and so on. This advertising can inform consumers of higher quality or it can develop brand loyalty, either of which creates differentiation. Competing with rivals through advertising, style changes, color changes, and the like is referred to as *non-price competition.*

non-price competition
Competing with rivals through advertising, style changes, color changes, and techniques other than lowering price.

Advertising does not necessarily cause an increase in price. Even though costs rise with advertising, it is possible that the increased output that advertising generates could result in lower prices because of economies of scale. You can see this by examining Figure 24-6. In Figure 24-6, AC_1 represents a firm's long-run average costs before advertising. With sales of OQ_1, the price consumers pay is OP_1. Advertising raises costs, as represented by AC_2, but if output increases because the firm gains sales by advertising, price can fall to OP_2 because of

FIGURE 24-6   ADVERTISING AND A POSSIBLE DECLINE IN PRICE

AC_1 represents long-run average costs without advertising. AC_2 represents costs made higher by advertising. If the firm increases output from OQ_1 to OQ_2 because of advertising, it is possible for price to the consumer to fall from OP_1 to OP_2. If sales do not increase, price will rise to OP_3.

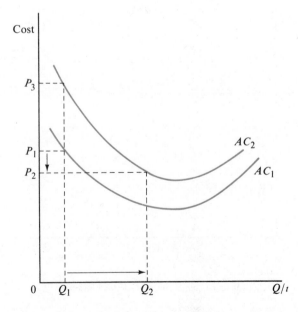

economies of scale. On the other hand, if sales stay at OQ_1, average cost will rise to OP_3.

If a firm, by effective use of non-price competition, can successfully differentiate its product so that other firms' products do not seem to compete, the firm can earn economic profits in the long run. Such a firm has in essence turned its share of the monopolistically competitive market into a mini-monopoly.

Consider McDonald's as an example. Fast food preparation is a monopolistically competitive industry. There are large numbers of firms and entry is relatively easy. If a firm is able to successfully differentiate its product so that consumers don't consider the products of other firms as close substitutes, the firm is then able to earn long-run profits because it can keep would-be competitors out of its segment of the industry. For example, McDonald's can't keep firms out of the hamburger market, but it can keep firms out of the McDonald's hamburger market—if everyone believes there's nothing like a Big Mac!

It is easy to determine how successful a firm is at this type of differentiation by examining its prices relative to its competitors' prices. You may go to McDonald's if a Big Mac is $.15 more than the competition, but would you if it was $.55 more or $1.15 more? There is some price at which the other products will become

Where Have All the Breweries Gone?

In 1933, the United States repealed Prohibition; breweries opened their doors (legally). At this time there were more than 750 breweries in the United States. Some states with high proportions of German immigrants, such as Wisconsin and Pennsylvania, had a brewery in almost every medium-sized town.

In the 1960s and 1970s, there was a major consolidation in the beer industry. The leaders, Anheuser-Busch, Schlitz, Pabst, Miller, and Coors, have significantly increased their share of the U.S. market. In some markets such as in the West, a few breweries (such as Coors) dominate sales. This consolidation or increase in concentration is the result of several factors. Good transportation facilitated marketability and, thus, larger economies of scale. Advertising created national markets for beer and altered allegiance to local brands. Some breweries suffered from poor management and poor products. Some local breweries claim that the major producers practiced predatory pricing to drive them out of business.

In any event, the facts are clear. The beer industry, which would have been characterized earlier in U.S. history as being monopolistically competitive, no longer is characterized as such. The industry structure you studied in this chapter has been replaced by oligopoly in the beer industry, a subject that you will study in the next chapter.

Some beer afficionados are bothered by this change in industry structure. Some economists believe that this change in structure is bad for consumers, and that government should take action to prevent it. Others believe it is a natural phenomenon and consumers are better off because of increased efficiencies.

In any event, beer making is big business, and it is getting bigger. When you tip your next glass of suds, consider if industry structure is affecting the price and quality of your favorite drink.

good substitutes. That price is a measure of the effectiveness of the product differentiation. It may be that a Big Mac is worth more to you because it has a higher quality or it may be that it is worth more only because McDonald's has a very successful advertising and public relations program. The point is that it doesn't matter what causes the differentiation; the economic impact is that McDonald's can earn an economic profit in the long run.

RESOURCE ALLOCATION IN MONOPOLISTIC COMPETITION

Our theory of monopolistic competition has several implications for the allocation of resources that are different from the social ideal developed in pure competition. First, at the zero economic profit, long-run equilibrium, there will be excess capacity. This means that price will be greater than marginal cost. So, consumers are paying only the average costs of production, but these costs are higher than the most efficient level of production would produce.

Second, if costs are the same under pure competition and monopolistic competition, prices will be higher in monopolistic competition. Third, firms in monopolistic competition will provide a wider variety of styles, colors, qualities, and brands. This, of course, is related to the differentiation and excess capacity which caused average costs to be higher.

Fourth, there will be advertising and other forms of non-price competition. This is not necessarily bad; to the extent that it adds to satisfaction and as long as the product is voluntarily purchased, it can be viewed as a good thing. Some social critics view any advertising that does more than convey information as a bad thing. As economists, we would argue that it is a bad thing only if people don't have options to consume alternative goods.

MONOPOLISTIC COMPETITION: HAVE WE LEARNED ANYTHING NEW?

The theory that we have presented in this chapter has been the focus of much debate by economists. This debate has sometimes been referred to as "Chamberlin vs. the Chicago School."[2] Economists at Chicago, notably Professor George Stigler, argue that the theory of monopolistic competition doesn't offer any additional insights or predictions that the model of pure competition hasn't already offered. This goes back to our earlier discussion of the role of theory. Stigler admits that monopolistic competition is more descriptive of the real world than pure competition, but he contends that this does not make it more useful. Stigler argues that usefulness as a description of the real world is not important. The crucial question is whether or not the model of monopolistic competition offers different insights or more correct predictions than the model of pure competition. Professor Stigler argues that it does not offer either.

---

[2]See G. Chris Archibald, "Chamberlin Versus Chicago," *Review of Economic Studies* (October, 1961), pp. 1–28.

It would be a mistake for us to make too much of this controversy. It may be acceptable for academic economists to argue over such matters; after all, academic careers have been based on such arguments. For the purposes of this course, the model of monopolistic competition is useful, and most economists view it as useful. The general usefulness of the model lies in its attempt to fill in the gap between pure competition and monopoly. The way we view non-price competition, the way we analyze advertising, and the way we view the costs of product differentiation owe much to the development of the model of monopolistic competition. So, even if we could get by with only the tool of pure competition, the model of monopolistic competition enriches the analysis.

SUMMARY

1. Monopolistic competition is a market situation characterized by many producers of a heterogeneous product.

2. Key assumptions in the model of monopolistic competition are: large numbers of producers; product differentiation; and relative ease of entry. This means that economic profits can exist in the short run, but entry of new firms will insure a long-run equilibrium with zero economic profit.

3. Because of product differentiation, a firm at equilibrium produces less than the socially optimal output. This underproduction is referred to as excess capacity.

4. Monopolistically competitive firms produce a smaller output at a higher price than firms (with the same costs) engaged in pure competition.

5. Marginal cost is not equal to average, long-run equilibrium cost in monopolistic competition.

6. Some economists argue that no insights can be derived from the monopolistic competition model that cannot be derived from the pure competition model. In general, however, most economists feel that the model of monopolistic competition adds richness to the theory of the firm.

NEW TERMS

imperfect competition
monopolistic competition
differentiated product

product group
excess capacity
non-price competition

QUESTIONS FOR DISCUSSION

1. Is advertising wasteful?
2. Firms in monopolistic competition only earn normal profits in the long run unless they can suc-

cessfully convince consumers that their product is really different. List as many examples of product differentiation as you can. Do you think the differences are real, imagined, or created? Does product differentiation make any economic difference?

3. Are there any significant differences between the model of pure competition and monopolistic competition? What assumption is different? What differences in the model are created by this changed assumption?

4. What is excess capacity? Is it a good or a bad thing?

SUGGESTIONS FOR FURTHER READING

Chamberlin, Edward H. *The Theory of Monopolistic Competition.* Cambridge, Mass.: Harvard University Press, 1933.

Robinson, Joan. *The Economics of Imperfect Competition.* London: Macmillan & Co., 1933.

Stigler, George J. *Five Lectures on Economic Problems.* New York: The Macmillan Co., 1949.

The Model of Oligopoly

Learning Objectives

After studying the materials found in this chapter, you should be able to do the following:

1. Define:
   (a) oligopoly.
   (b) pure oligopoly.
   (c) differentiated oligopoly.
   (d) Class I oligopoly.
   (e) Class II oligopoly.
   (f) Class III oligopoly.

2. List the characteristics of a cartel and the conditions necessary to assure that a cartel will not break up.

3. Diagram:
   (a) price leadership with a dominant firm and competitive fringe firms.
   (b) the kinked demand curve theory of oligopoly.

At approximately the same time that Professors Chamberlin and Robinson were developing the concept of monopolistic competition, German economist Heinrich von Stackelberg published a book entitled *Market Structure and Equilibrium* (1934), which discussed the idea of interdependence between firms and which formed the basis of the model of oligopoly. *Oligopoly,* the other form of imperfect competition, is the market structure in which there are *few firms.* "Oligopoly" comes from the Greek words *olig* for "few" and *polein* for "sellers." The scarcity of sellers is the key to firm behavior in oligopoly. In oligopoly, firms realize that their small number produces mutual interdependence. As a result, a firm will forecast or expect a certain response from its rivals to any price or output decision that it might initiate.

oligopoly The market structure in which there are few firms. This causes firms to recognize their interdependence.

Because of this mutual interdependence, it is very difficult to develop models that predict the output and pricing behavior of oligopolistic firms. Economists have developed a categorization of different types of oligopoly behavior. This categorization often includes heavy doses of descriptive economics, which stress institutional factors. In this chapter we present a standard description of the types of oligopoly behavior and present examples of that oligopoly behavior.

TYPES OF PRODUCTS PRODUCED BY OLIGOPOLIES

Oligopolies produce a range of products from homogeneous to differentiated, and oligopolistic industries are sometimes categorized by the type of product they produce. An oligopoly which produces a homogeneous product is referred to as a *pure oligopoly*. The distinction is important because pure oligopolies will be characterized as having a single price for the output of all the firms. An example of a pure oligopoly would be the cement industry. As a consumer, you would be indifferent to which firm produced the sack of cement you purchase.

As opposed to a pure oligopoly, a *differentiated oligopoly* produces goods that are different. The auto industry would be a good example. In differentiated oligopolies we get *price clusters,* which are groupings of prices for similar, but not homogeneous, products. The price differentials in these clusters will depend on the amount of product differentiation. The more differentiated the products, the greater the price divergence. Tight price clusters indicate very little differentiation.

OLIGOPOLY COLLUSIVENESS

Perhaps the most useful classification tool for analyzing oligopolies is the system of definitions proposed by Professor Fritz Machlup of New York University.[1]

Professor Machlup divides oligopoly behavior into three classes which are based on the degree of communication, coordination, and collusion among the new firms. *Communication* refers to the firms' ability to signal their intentions to each other; *coordination* refers to the firms' ability to relate their production decisions to the other firms in the industry; and *collusion* refers to agreements between the firms in an industry to set a certain price or to share a market.

It should be obvious that the ability to communicate, coordinate, and collude will depend on the number of firms. As the number of firms increases, the cost of keeping communication open will increase. This point will be stressed as we proceed. In Machlup's scheme, *Class I oligopolies* are characterized by independent action. The firms are both unorganized and uncollusive. *Class II oligopolies* are characterized by perfect joint action. These firms are both organized and collusive. *Class III oligopolies* are those that have imperfect joint action. They are unorganized, but still collusive. We will start by examining Class II, next we will take up Class III oligopolies, and then we will turn to Class I oligopolies.

Class II Oligopolies

Organized, collusive oligopolies are cartels. *Cartels* are groups of independent firms which agree not to compete. Perfect cartels are able to behave as a monopoly behaves. In striving for joint profit maximization, it is necessary for the cartel to set prices, outputs, and marketing areas. However, the cartel can't always set these variables so that each individual firm in the cartel is maximizing its own

pure oligopoly *An oligopoly that produces a homogeneous product.*

differentiated oligopoly *An oligopoly that produces a heterogeneous or differentiated product.*

price clusters *Groupings of prices for similar, but not homogeneous, products.*

communication *Firms' ability to signal their intentions to each other. This is important in oligopoly.*

coordination *Firms' ability to relate their production decisions to the other firms in an industry. This is important in an oligopoly.*

collusion *Agreements between firms in an industry to set certain prices or to share markets in certain ways.*

Class I oligopoly *An oligopoly in which firms are unorganized and uncollusive. Their behavior is characterized by independent action.*

Class II oligopoly *An oligopoly in which firms are organized and collusive. Their behavior can be characterized by perfect joint action.*

Class III oligopoly *An oligopoly in which firms are unorganized, but still collusive. Their behavior is characterized by imperfect joint action.*

---

[1]Fritz Machlup, *The Economics of Sellers' Competition* (Baltimore: John Hopkins Press, 1952).

profits. Examine Figure 25-1 to see this more clearly. In Figure 25-1, we have two firms, A and B, in a cartel which produces a homogeneous product. The marginal cost curves of each firm are MC_A and MC_B, respectively. MC_T is the horizontal summation of MC_A and MC_B. The cartel would maximize profits, behaving exactly as a monopoly, by producing OQ_C at price OP_C because $MR = MC_T$ at OP_C and OQ_C. Now the centralized cartel must enforce this solution by requiring firms A and B to produce OQ_A and OQ_B, respectively. The difficulty is that each firm is not at its individual profit-maximizing output. If each firm could view one half of the market as its own,[2] represented by demand curve d in Figure 25-1, the profit-maximizing outputs would be where $MC_A = mr$ and $MC_B = mr$. Firm A would produce OQ_a and firm B would produce OQ_b.

In short, the profit-maximizing goal of the cartel is not necessarily consistent with the profit-maximizing goals of each individual cartel member. In the exam-

cartel   A group of independent firms which agree not to compete. Perfect cartels behave as monopolies.

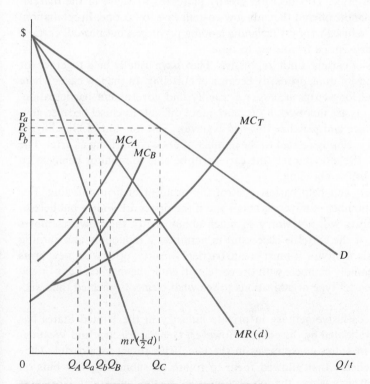

FIGURE 25-1   CARTEL PROFIT MAXIMIZATION

Joint profit maximization by the two firms would occur where $MC_T = MR$. This would establish a price of OP_C and output of OQ_C. The cartel must now force output OQ_A and OQ_B from firms A and B, respectively. The cartel must force this behavior because individual profit maximization, assuming each firm could view one half of the market represented by demand curve (d) as its own, would establish a price of OP_a and output OQ_a for firm A and a price of OP_b and output OQ_b for firm B. The cartel must force firm A to reduce its production and firm B to expand its production relative to their individual maximizing output.

[2]Remember that $MR = \frac{1}{2}D$. See the first figure in the chapter on monopoly for a review.

ple in Figure 25-1, firm *A* would prefer to produce *more* at a *higher* price and firm *B* would prefer to produce *less* at a *lower* price. The example here points out the most important problem faced by cartels. The problem is that joint cartel profit maximization and individual firm profit maximization are often in conflict. As a result, a cartel is very unstable.

Perhaps the greatest danger a cartel faces is that members find it in their own self-interest to cheat on the cartel, a practice known as **chiseling**. If, for example, a cartel agrees on a set price, such as OP_C in the previous example, individual members may attempt to give secret price cuts and capture more of the market. If either firm *A* or firm *B* believes the other is untrustworthy, it will have more of an incentive to chisel. As the number of firms increases, it becomes increasingly likely that individual firms will become suspicious of their fellow cartel members.

chiseling   Cheating on a cartel arrangement by lowering prices in an attempt to capture more of the market.

Some Examples of Cartels.

You may be familiar with the case of Icelandic Airlines. International airline companies have a cartel called IATA (International Air Transport Association). Icelandic refused to join IATA and set fares below the cartel price. This decision greatly increased its share of the market. Before 1978 Icelandic offered the only low-cost air fare to Europe. In retaliation, many countries refused to grant Icelandic landing privileges, but now all carriers chisel on the cartel price from time to time.

The history of cartels is not impressive. They have usually held together for only short periods of time, primarily because of chiseling. In the few cases where cartels have had long-term success, we usually find government participation. Once governments are involved, it becomes more difficult to chisel because government can police and penalize this bad behavior. The amount of chiseling, it should be clear, is closely related to the number of firms comprising a cartel. The fewer the firms, the more closely the cartel will be able to monitor behavior to determine if a firm is chiseling.

Other factors can help cartels control the problem of firm chiseling. For example, if the number of buyers is small and if the prices are widely publicized, the cartel members will not worry so much about one of their own members chiseling. Also, if the cartel is successful in acting as a monopoly and earning higher than normal profits, it must create barriers to entry; otherwise, new firms that might potentially compete with the cartel will enter the market. Let's briefly examine a few cartel-type organizations to see what elements affected their success or failure.

Organized, collusive activity in private industry in the United States has usually been invalidated by the courts. However, General Electric and Westinghouse engaged in secret conspiracies in the late 1950s to act as a cartel. They decided on a scheme that allowed them to rotate on submitting low bids on government contracts where the job was awarded to the low bidder. The most famous scheme depended on the phases of the moon. At every phase of the moon (every two weeks), the firm designated to be the low bidder would gain the right to that contract by the other firm's submitting an uncompetitive, high bid. This plan worked well because there were only two firms dealing with one buyer, the federal government. Each firm would know if the other was cheating because the bids would be made public. In this case the government was inadvertently helping the cartel overcome the chiseling problem.

At the other end of the spectrum of firm numbers is an attempt at cartel formation known as the National Farm Organization (NFO). In 1967 and 1968, the NFO attempted to act as a producer cartel. In two separate actions—one to raise milk prices and the other to raise beef prices—the NFO tried withholding actions. In order to raise prices, cartel members would dump milk and keep cattle away from the market. The farm industry for milk and beef production is composed of large numbers of firms, and the NFO cartel consisted of about 10 percent of these firms. If the NFO members were successful in raising prices, the non-members who continued to produce and sell would be the beneficiaries and would react by expanding output in response to these higher prices. Additionally, as prices begin to rise, there would be tremendous pressure to chisel on the withholding action. In fact, the chiselers would benefit much more than the members who refused to chisel. The realization of this fact resulted in violence. Cattle scales were blown up. Withholding farmers sat in the roads to keep chiselers from taking their products to market. Some chiselers even resorted to taking cows to market in house trailers to avoid detection. The lesson is clear. A cartel with many members will find it very difficult to be successful.

Cartels are much more common in Europe than they are in the United States. In Europe cartels are permitted and often encouraged by governments. In Nazi Germany all the major industries operated as cartels, and in present day Western Europe the Common Market Commission is actively promoting cartels in steel, textiles, and shipbuilding.

As we shall see in the next chapter cartels are, with one exception, illegal in the United States. The one exception, based on the Webb-Pomerene Act of 1918, is the formation of cartels for the purpose of foreign trade. These Webb-Pomerene cartels have not been successful in raising prices, primarily because of the large number of firms participating.[3]

OPEC—Unparalleled Success Story. Without question the most successful cartel in recent years is the Organization of Petroleum Exporting Countries, known as OPEC. In the 1950s international oil companies controlled a major portion of the world's oil supply. These companies, although often attacked for acting as a cartel, frequently engaged in active price competition. In fact, in an attempt to stop such price competition, the Arab governments, along with a few nonArab governments, formed OPEC in 1960. At first OPEC enjoyed little success. But this changed in 1973, as the Arab-Israeli war heated up and the Arab countries came together. As of January 1, 1973, the price of oil was $2.12 per barrel. Of this $2.12, $1.52 went to the governments involved. By January 1, 1974, the price was $7.61 with $7.01 going to the governments. By January, 1975, the price was about $10.50. By 1982, the price had risen to $35.00. The most influential member of the cartel is Saudi Arabia, the major producer.

How did this cartel, which had been in existence since 1960 and which had few members, come to flex its muscles in 1973? At that time, importing governments helped by posting prices and dealing with the OPEC governments in open forums where the individual members could be less fearful of chiseling. More important, however, Saudi Arabia was willing to cut back its production of oil

---

[3]For more on these failures, see Ryan C. Amacher, Richard J. Sweeney, and Robert D. Tollison, "A Note on the Webb-Pomerene Law and the Webb-Cartels," *The Antitrust Bulletin* (Summer, 1978).

to allow other members to sell all they wanted to produce at the high prices set by the cartel.[4]

How stable is OPEC? It is more stable than many observers first believed and more stable than most other cartels. We predicted earlier, however, that successful cartels will meet with two problems. First, there is chiseling. Within OPEC there has been a considerable amount of chiseling, and the real price of oil is now much lower than the 1975 high of $10.50 per barrel. To be sure, the real price of oil is significantly higher than it was prior to 1973, but it is much lower than the 1975 price. Chiseling has weakened OPEC's ability to maintain the real price of oil during the rapid inflation of the late 1970s. This chiseling is increasing as increased cutbacks in production are needed to maintain the high price.

The second problem a successful cartel faces is new entry. Large amounts of new oil are coming on stream from Mexico, the North Sea, and elsewhere. In addition, other sources of energy, such as solar and nuclear, which were uneconomical when oil was $2.00 per barrel, are now economical at the current high price of oil. This new entry has been slow to develop, but the future should prove more difficult for OPEC as new firms producing oil and other competing products enter and challenge the cartel's cohesiveness. OPEC, however, has the great advantage of being run by governments, with each government having the power to police and coerce within its own borders.

Class III Oligopolies

tacit collusion   *Unorganized and unstated attempts to practice joint action. Gentlemen's agreements and price leadership are two forms of tacit collusion.*

Class III oligopolies practice unorganized, collusive activity. Such *tacit collusion* is a much weaker form of collusion than that of Class II oligopolies or cartels. It is weaker because all the incentives to chisel are still present, but organized techniques to guard against chiseling are not. The type of behavior associated with unorganized, collusive oligopolies is found in U.S. industry because Class II oligopolies are clearly illegal under U.S. antitrust laws. Class III oligopolies' behavior can, in part, be viewed as an attempt to form Class II cartels while avoiding antitrust laws. Collusion in Class III oligopolies usually takes the form of gentlemen's agreements to behave in certain ways. Often these agreements arise informally, without any need for clear-cut organization. The most common form of tacit, informal agreement is based on some form of price leadership.

price leadership   *The practice of industry pricing in which other firms follow the pricing initiatives of a particular firm, the price leader.*

dominant firm   *The most influential firm in an industry, usually the price leader. The dominant firm is often the largest firm, but it can be the low-cost firm.*

Price Leadership. *Price leadership* is the practice of industry pricing in which other firms typically follow the initiative of one firm, the price leader. The firm which is the price leader is typically the *dominant firm,* or largest firm, but it can be the *low-cost* firm, which may not be the largest firm in the industry. Price leadership is most effective where firms are few and have clearly similar products (e.g., the auto, cigarette, and steel industries). It helps if the demand for the product is price inelastic since this will further discourage price cutting. When the demand curve for the industry is perfectly inelastic, a firm that chisels on price will gain sales only at the expense of other firms, because a lower price will not bring about additional sales for the industry. Thus, the conflict between firms will be sharper than if demand showed some response to price cuts.

---

[4]An interesting side issue is that much public criticism was leveled on the oil companies rather than the OPEC members. This is odd because the cartel profits are not going to the oil companies but to the governments of the OPEC member countries.

Dominant Firm. In price leadership by the dominant firm, the largest firm which controls a significant share of the market sets a profit-maximizing price and the other firms divide up the market at that same price. The other firms, known as the *competitive fringe* firms, act much like firms in price competition. This can be seen by examining Figure 25-2. The market demand curve for the product is represented by D_m. The marginal cost curve of the dominant firm is MC_d and the summation of all the other fringe firms' marginal cost curves is MC_f. The fringe firms will make production decisions as price takers and will always produce where price is equal to marginal cost. MC_f can thus be viewed as a supply curve. The demand curve that the dominant firm faces can then be derived by horizontally subtracting the amount supplied by the fringe (MC_f) firms from the market demand curve. This subtraction gives the dominant firm's demand curve, D_d, and its marginal revenue curve, MR_d. The dominant firm will now set a profit-maximizing price and output of OP_1 and OQ_d. Once price OP_1 is determined, the fringe firms view this price much as competitive firms view the market price. The fringe firms will, therefore, produce OQ_f units at the market price OP_1 because for them $OP_1 = MR$, and they will, of course, produce where $MR = MC_f$. The production of the dominant firm (OQ_d) and of the fringe firms (OQ_f) satisfies the market demand of OQ_m at price OP_1.

This model of price leadership is applicable to the oil industry, where there is a small group of dominant firms and a large number of small fringe firms.

competitive fringe   In markets with one large, dominant firm, there is sometimes a substantial number of small competitors, which would be referred to as the competitive fringe.

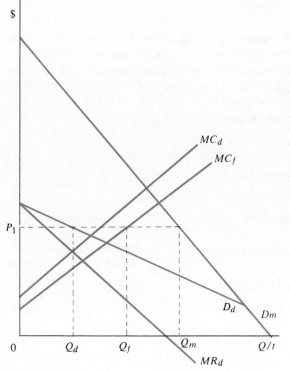

FIGURE 25-2   DOMINANT FIRM WITH COMPETITIVE FRINGE FIRMS.

In the dominant firm model, the dominant firm views a part of the market, D_d, as its own. D_d is determined by subtracting the competitive fringe supply curve, MC_f, from the market demand, D_m. The dominant firm then produces where marginal cost is equal to marginal revenue, setting price OP_1 and producing OQ_d units. The fringe firms then face a perfectly elastic demand at OP_1, thus producing OQ_f units where $MR = MC_f$.

Dominant firm price leadership also appears to prevail in the aluminum, petroleum, and cigarette industries.

Historical Price Leadership. In a few cases, particularly in mature industries, it is possible for a firm to emerge as the price leader because it is convenient for the other firms in the industry to follow the leader and thus coordinate their pricing. This type of price leadership is no different in intent than cartel behavior. Its intent is collusion—to achieve industry-wide profit maximization. Historical price leadership, however, is unorganized and thus not illegal in the United States. This type of price leadership is rampant in U.S. oligopolies. General Motors is the recognized price leader in autos, U.S. Steel in steel, and DuPont in chemicals. It is limited to mature or older oligopolies because it takes time for the firms to trust one another and follow the leader.

Successful Price Leadership. In order to be successful—that is, in order to raise industry profit levels—price leadership must produce a type of cartel but avoid legal sanctions. This means walking a tightrope because, as the tacit collusion embodied in price leadership becomes successful, the incentive to chisel increases. As a result, most successful price leadership situations that are not the dominant firm type occur in industries in which there are only a few firms. The record of such tacit collusion shows that such industries are characterized by rigid prices, and price changes, when they occur, are generally small. Such industries are usually those that blame price increases on rising costs and that can punish firms who do not follow the price increase. The steel and auto industries are two examples. In these industries, potential chiselers know they cannot easily get away with not following the price leader.

Class I Oligopolies

Unorganized, uncollusive oligopolies are characterized by independent action. These are Class I oligopolies by Machlup's classification scheme, which is summarized in Table 25-1. These oligopolists practice profit maximization independently but are affected by the action and response of their rivals; each tries to anticipate the response of its rivals and then takes the predicted response into account when making decisions. Economists tried to develop a model for this

TABLE 25-1 MACHLUP'S OLIGOPOLY CLASSIFICATION

Class	Behavior	Example
Class I	Unorganized, Uncollusive	Hard to distinguish from monopolistic competition.
Class II	Organized, Collusive	OPEC
Class III	Unorganized, Collusive	U.S. firms under anti-trust indictment.

behavior in the early 1800s; and in 1838, A. Augustin Cournot (1801–1877) published a theory of duopoly (two firms). Cournot was an engineer, applied mathematician, and a high-level administrator in the French school system. His work in economics was highly original, and he is considered to be one of the founders of mathematical economics. His theory and the theories that followed up to the post-World War II period, while interesting, are unsatisfactory for our purposes because they assume that the rival firm will not react to the action of the firm under investigation. The post-World War II developments in oligopoly theory rest heavily on mathematical game theory. ***Game theory*** is a relatively new field of mathematics and one which can provide insights into oligopolistic behavior. In game theory, "players" try to reach an optimal position through strategic

game theory A mathematical *technique which can provide insight into oligopolistic behavior. "Players" try to reach an optimal position through strategic behavior that takes into account the anticipated moves of other players.*

Game Theory—The Prisoner's Dilemma

Game theory, a theory of rational decision making under conditions of uncertainty, was first developed by John von Neumann (1903–1957) and Oskar Morgen-

stern (1902–1977) in a book entitled *The Theory of Games and Economic Behavior* (1944).

Standard microeconomics provides a theory of decision making where the outcomes of various decisions are known. Game theory provides rational solutions when the outcomes are uncertain. Game theory has proved very useful in the study of oligopoly markets where each participant must take account of the reactions of its competitors.

Games are usually described as being either zero sum or nonzero sum. Zero-sum games are those where one player's gain is another person's loss. Non-zero-sum games open the door to collusion or cooperative action because all players may gain from a certain course of action.

One of the most famous nonzero-sum games is called the Prisoner's Dilemma. The name comes from a situation where two criminals are interrogated separately. Each criminal knows that if neither confesses, both will go free. However, if one confesses and implicates the other, he or she can go free and the other will be convicted. The rational course of action for the self-interested criminal is to confess and implicate the other. Since both will be motivated in this way, the rational outcome will make both worse off.

	Prisoner *A*	
	Confess	*Not Confess*
Prisoner *B* *Confess*	Both convicted.	*A* convicted; *B* goes free.
Not Confess	*A* goes free; *B* convicted.	Both go free.

behavior that takes into account the anticipated moves of other players. Game theory describes very accurately how oligopolists behave.[5]

The Kinked Demand Curve. One explanation of pricing in oligopoly was formulated by Dr. Paul Sweezy, who was a Stanford University professor and is now editor of *Monthly Review*. Sweezy formulated a model which explained the "fact" that prices in oligopolistic industries tend to be less flexible than prices in other market structures. The model develops a *kinked demand curve* because firms come to believe that if they cut prices, their rivals will follow the price cut and, as a result, the price cut will not produce much of an increase in sales. A price increase, on the other hand, will not be followed and will, therefore, result in a significant loss of sales to the firm raising its price. As a result, once a price is reached (Sweezy said nothing of how or why the original price came about) it tends to remain in effect for long periods.

You can see the effect of a kink in the demand curve by examining Figure 25-3. A kink in the demand curve, *D*, comes about at point *A* (or at price *OP*) because the other oligopoly firms will match any price decrease, making the demand curve below point *A* relatively inelastic; the firm won't increase sales very much by decreasing price. Any increase in price above *OP* will have the opposite effect. Competing firms will not match the increase and, as a result, the demand curve above point *A* will be relatively elastic. Given this kink in the demand curve, the corresponding marginal revenue curve, *MR*, will be discontinuous, meaning it has a break in it from *B* to *C* in Figure 25-3. This break allows a large

kinked demand curve   A model of pricing in oligopoly used to explain price rigidity. The kink comes from the pricing behavior. If firms cut prices, other firms follow suit and there is very little increase in the price-cutters' market share. A price increase, however, is not matched and the price rise will result in loss of a market share.

FIGURE 25-3   THE KINKED DEMAND CURVE

In the kinked demand curve model, the firm faces a kinked demand curve, *D*, because prices above *OP* will not be matched while prices below *OP* will be matched. The kink creates a discontinuity in the marginal revenue curve, which causes the price to be very rigid at the kink (*OP*).

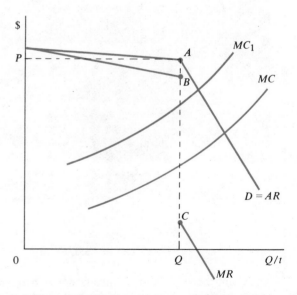

fluctuation in marginal cost, from B to C, with no effect on the profit-maximizing price, OP, or output, OQ. For example, marginal cost could change from MC to MC_1 with no effect on price and output. Sweezy used this result to explain why prices were so rigid in oligopoly.

Sweezy's theory has been devastatingly attacked by Professor George Stigler of the University of Chicago. Stigler attacks the theory on both theoretical and

George Stigler *(1911–   )*

Paul Sweezy *(1910–   )*

George Stigler and *Paul Sweezy* represent polar extremes in economic analysis. Both have written extensively in the field of industrial organization, but the similarities end there.

George Stigler is the personification of the "Chicago School" of free enterprise capitalism. He received a B.B.A. degree from the University of Washington, an M.B.A. degree from Northwestern University, and a Ph.D. from the University of Chicago in 1938. Paul Sweezy is an American Marxist. He was awarded a B.A. degree and a Ph.D. in economics from Harvard University in 1937.

Both economists are coeditors of prestigious journals that are at opposite ends of the ideological spectrum. Stigler is coeditor of the *Journal of Political Econ-*

omy and Sweezy is coeditor of the *Monthly Review.* Stigler's views are best delineated in *The Theory of Price* (1966) and *Organization of Industry* (1968). Sweezy's views can be found in *The Dynamics of U.S. Capitalism* (1972), *Introduction to Socialism* (1968), and *Modern Capitalism and Other Essays* (1972).

Stigler and Sweezy have clashed over Sweezy's development of the kinked demand curve. Sweezy formulated a model which explained the "fact" that prices in oligopolistic industries are more stable than prices in other market structures. This model has been devastatingly attacked by Stigler, who argues that Sweezy's theory is wrong and that his observation that prices in oligopoly are more stable than in other market structures does not stand up to empirical investigation.

empirical grounds.[6] The most telling empirical point is that he finds oligopoly prices to be *less* rigid than monopoly prices. This is one of those areas where there is an ongoing debate between theorists and empiricists.

Non-Price Competition. You should keep in mind that oligopolists compete in dimensions other than just the price dimension. In formulating models, economists tend to treat goods as homogeneous and view competition as occurring primarily through price adjustments. In the real world, however, competition can take other forms. Firms can change the quality, color, texture, design, size, advertising, and a host of other attributes of a product. An oligopolistic firm may resort to this type of non-price competition in an attempt to increase its market share.[7] This non-price competition does not mean that our model is invalid because we can apply the model to these other types of competition. For example, a firm contemplating a new advertising program will need to consider whether the program will increase its market share or prompt a rival to undertake a similar program. In the first instance, the program may be worthwhile. In the second, it would probably only increase costs without creating a larger market share. Thus, even with non-price competition, oligopoly firms are interdependent and need to consider the reactions of rivals.

THE IMPORTANCE OF ENTRY

You will recall that in pure competition entry was free, and in monopolistic competition entry was relatively easy. This contrasted with monopoly, where entry was blocked if the monopoly were to persist and maintain monopoly profits in the long run. In oligopoly, whether there are as few as two firms or as many as a dozen, conditions of entry again play an important role. Regardless of the class of oligopoly, if economic profits are to exist in the long run, it is necessary that the oligopolistic firms prohibit new entry. With new entry, profit-maximization techniques will tend to reduce these profits even if there are just a few firms. A second important point is that potential entry makes cartel formation much more difficult. Why go to the trouble and cost of organizing a cartel if economic profits will be eaten up by new entry? Thus, it is important that cartels or would-be cartels control entry. Consider the following examples.

First, let's examine an oligopolistic industry where entry was easily accomplished. Immediately after World War II, Milton Reynolds formed Reynolds International Pen Company with an investment of $26,000.[8] He was a monopoly producer of ballpoint pens protected by a patent. The pens were marketed by Gimbels department store in New York City and sold for $12.50 each. The first

---

[6]See George J. Stigler, "The Kinky Oligopoly Demand Curve and Rigid Prices," *Journal of Political Economy* (October, 1947), pp. 432–449.

[7]Sometimes quality changes act as inverse price changes. For example, if the price of a candy bar remains at 25 cents but the amount of chocolate or almonds has been decreased, this is equivalent to an increase in price. Oligopolists often engage in this kind of disguised price changing because it seems to provoke less response from rivals.

[8]For a detailed account of this experience, see Richard G. Lipsey and Peter O. Steiner, *Economics* (4h ed.; New York: Harper & Row, Publishers, Inc., 1975), pp. 320–321.

day of sales, Gimbels sold 10,000 pens and by early 1946 Reynolds had earned more than $3 million in net accounting profits. Clearly, above normal profits were being earned. The competition from new entry was fierce. Macy's department store imported a pen to compete with the one Reynolds sold at Gimbels. Eversharp and Sheaffer announced plans to compete. Two totally new pen companies announced products in total disregard of the patent. In October, 1946, the new entry was such that Reynolds had reduced his price from $12.50 to $3.85. Two months later, in December, 1946, about 100 firms were producing ballpoint pens, some priced as low as $2.98. Another two months later, in February, 1947, Gimbels was selling pens produced by another company at $.98. By mid-1948 ballpoint pens were selling for $.39 and by 1951 prices were as low as $.25. In 1975 ballpoint pens were selling at prices starting at $.11.

This experience is a phenomenal one. In a 16-month period, prices fell 96.9 percent! This decline was purely the result of price competition from new entry. If Reynolds or a cartel of Reynolds, Sheaffer, Eversharp, and others could have in some way prevented this new entry, prices would presumably have stayed much higher.

Contrast this experience with the case of the U.S. airline industry prior to 1978 when entry was reasonably well blocked by a few firms. The CAB (Civil Aeronautics Board) acted as an agent in cartelizing the airline industry. In order to fly between states—that is, in interstate commerce—an airline had to receive the permission of the CAB. To fly within a state, or intrastate, no such permission was required. The CAB thus restricted entry into the interstate industry. The result was higher prices than would have existed without CAB regulation. We can see this by comparing intrastate and interstate rates. Theodore Keeler, a Berkeley economist, did just that. He found that before 1978, without CAB regulation, the price of airline travel would have been between 20 and 95 percent lower, depending upon the route examined.[9] When deregulation (of sorts) came in 1978, fares on some routes fell significantly.[10] The interesting question is why doesn't the CAB deregulate even more? One would think that entrepreneurs would be eager to compete for these passengers. The answer is, of course, that some entrepreneurs would, but the CAB doesn't deregulate because certain members of the industry favor the regulation and others (especially new firms) don't.

The domestic airlines tend to favor the CAB because it makes life easy for them by keeping out new entry and enforcing their cartel. How do you suppose Milton Reynolds felt about the competition that reduced the price of his pens from $12.50 to $.11? Most arguments made with respect to the airline industry hold with equal force for the pen industry. You can imagine how the presidents of TWA and Pan American felt about Freddy Laker of Laker Airlines, who wanted to fly his Skytrain between New York and Los Angeles at reduced rates.

The most recent challenge to regulation is coming in the trucking industry. The Interstate Commerce Commission (ICC), the president, and the Senate Antitrust Subcommittee are all proceeding with deregulation plans. True to form,

---

[9] Theodore Keeler, "Airline Regulation and Market Performance," *Bell Journal of Economics* (Autumn, 1972).

[10] To the surprise of many in the airline industry, revenues and profits zoomed. What does this say about the elasticity of demand? What implications might you draw about marginal costs?

large trucking firms are fighting the proposals. Trucking executives, just like airline executives, are arguing that deregulation is not in the public interest.

As we have seen, the restriction of entry by a monopolist or an oligopolist is very difficult in the long run. Entrepreneurs sensing profit will find ways to compete. As a result, it is almost impossible to keep long-run profits above normal rates unless one gets the government to aid in blocking entry. In other words, government sometimes gives would-be cartels aid, and we find the interesting phenomenon of some firms liking regulation. These big firms may talk about free enterprise, but in fact they prefer the regulation. The presidents of the major domestic airlines have historically been opposed to reform and deregulation of their industry through reduction of CAB powers. Even when deregulation comes to an industry, as it did to the airline industry in 1978, vestiges of that regulation and the old ways of doing business continue to get into the way of free market competition.

MARKET STRUCTURES IN REVIEW

This chapter concludes our discussion of the four market structures in the theory of the firm. Table 25-2 summarizes some of the important variables that differentiate the market structures we have examined. The key to understanding the theory of the firm is a solid understanding of monopoly and pure competition. Oligopoly and monopolistic competition expand the theories of monopoly and pure competition, and in effect demonstrate that we can generalize from the pure models to the real-world situations we encounter.

TABLE 25-2   SUMMARY OF MARKET STRUCTURES

Market Type	Number of Firms	Product Differentiation	Control Over Price	Amount of Non-Price Competition	Examples
Pure Competition	Large numbers	Homogeneous product	None	None	Agriculture is reasonably close
Monopolistic Competition	Many	Slightly differentiated	Some	Advertising and product differentiation	Retail trade and service industry
Oligopoly	Few	Homogeneous *or* differentiated product	Some to considerable (it depends)	Advertising and product differentiation	Autos, steel
Monopoly	One	Unique product (no close substitutes)	Considerable	Public relations	Utilities; aluminum before 1945

SUMMARY

1. Oligopoly is the market structure in which there are only a few firms producing goods that are either homogeneous or differentiated.

2. Because there are so few firms, they are interdependent, and they take this interdependence into account in their economic decision making.

3. Oligopolies can be broken down into three classes. Class I oligopolies are characterized by independent action. Class II oligopolies are cartels. Class III oligopolies have imperfect joint action.

4. Cartels are threatened by chiseling behavior on the part of individual members of the cartel.

The larger the number of firms in the cartel, the harder it is for the cartel to hold together.

5. Successful cartels have historically used governments to police the cartel.

6. Price leadership is common in Class III oligopolies. Price leadership can be by a dominant firm or, in mature industries, by a historical leader.

7. Oligopolies are characterized by extensive use of non-price competition.

8. Barriers to entry are important in oligopoly, just as they are in monopoly.

NEW TERMS

oligopoly
pure oligopoly
differentiated oligopoly
price clusters
communication
coordination
collusion
Class I oligopoly
Class II oligopoly

Class III oligopoly
cartel
chiseling
tacit collusion
price leadership
dominant firm
competitive fringe
game theory
kinked demand curve

QUESTIONS FOR DISCUSSION

1. When OPEC meets at its regularly scheduled meetings (usually at very posh resorts), why can't it just set a high price and let all the individual members sell as much as they want at this high price?

2. Is the NCAA (National Collegiate Athletic Association) a cartel? How do some universities (firms) chisel on the cartel? Why do they do this?

3. Explain how the expectation of new entry would limit cartel formation.

4. How would you expect the number of firms in a cartel to affect the probability of its success? Why?

5. Would government policies that require firms to report their sales by quantity and price make it easier or harder for Class III oligopolies?

6. How is Class I oligopoly different from monopolistic competition?

SUGGESTIONS FOR FURTHER READING

Boulding, Kenneth E. *Economic Analysis.* New York: Harper & Brothers, 1955, Chapter 22.

Kamerschen, David R., and Lloyd M. Valentine. *Intermediate Microeconomic Theory,* 2d ed. Cincinnati: South-Western Publishing Co., 1981, Chapter 15.

Machlup, Fritz. *The Economics of Seller's Competition.* Baltimore: Johns Hopkins Press, 1952.

Markham, Jesse W. "The Nature and Significance of Price Leadership." *American Economic Review* (December, 1951).

CHAPTER 26

Theory in the Real World: The Structure of American Industry

Learning Objectives

After studying the materials found in this chapter, you should be able to do the following:

1. Define an industry using the SIC system.

2. Give examples of the arbitrary nature of the definition of an industry.

3. Identify the characteristics of the structure of an industry.

4. Calculate the concentration ratio within an industry.

5. Use concentration ratios as an index of monopoly power.

6. Compare the results of studies of the relationship between concentration and:
   (a) prices.
   (b) profits.

7. Diagram the regulation of monopoly power through:
   (a) price regulation.
   (b) taxation.

8. Identify and discuss the major antitrust laws in the history of antitrust legislation.

9. List the pros and cons of recent developments in antitrust activity and conglomerate mergers.

In the preceding chapters we examined four theoretically distinct types of market structures. In this chapter, we will apply these theories to the real world and examine the extent of monopoly power in American industry. To do this, we need to first determine what constitutes an industry. We can then attempt to determine whether a particular industry is monopolistic and what elements contribute to this monopoly power. Only then can we examine public policy options to address any monopoly power that might exist. This chapter, then, will take you into empirical *industry studies* to develop a real-world appreciation of the monopoly problem. As a separate subfield of economics, this area of investigation is sometimes referred to as *industrial organization.*

Once it is determined that an industry possesses monopoly power, it may be desirable to control or mitigate the worst aspects of that monopoly power. The monopoly power could be destroyed through antitrust action, the monopoly

industry studies *Investigations of particular industries to determine the degree of competitive behavior in the industry.*

industrial organization *A subfield of economics which examines industrial structure in theory and in practice.*

profits could be taxed away, or the monopoly could be regulated and thus forced to behave in some prescribed fashion. Or it might even be better to do nothing about the monopoly power. This chapter will examine the theory and practice of regulation and then the development and record of U.S. antitrust laws. It will conclude with an assessment of the record of regulation and antitrust policy, and will examine recent trends in merger activity in U.S. industry.

WHAT IS AN INDUSTRY?

We have, up to this point, been using the term industry without carefully defining what an industry is. In general, an *industry* is a group of firms producing the same, or at least similar, products. The difficulty with this definition centers on the degree of dissimilarity allowed before the two products are thought of as being produced in different industries. Consider the container industry. Are firms producing glass bottles and aluminum cans similar enough to be included in the same industry? How about including firms making paper cups or even pewter mugs in this industry? Most consumers regard pewter mugs and paper cups as quite different. If you are willing to pay more money for a pewter mug than for a paper cup, you show that you regard them as being distinct products. What about a plastic Ronald McDonald glass? Is it closer to a paper cup or a pewter mug? We raise these questions not because we plan to show you how to obtain a correct answer but rather to demonstrate that whatever answer we reach, it will be arbitrary to some degree and, therefore, some people, even some economists, may disagree with a particular definition.

The problem is even more difficult if we consider that some multi-product firms produce a variety of goods that might be included in different industries. In which industry should we put a firm that produces coffee in addition to soap and cake mixes? Informed judgements and somewhat arbitrary definitions are necessary in order to move from the world of theory into the real world of industry studies.

There is a standard set of data available from the United States Census Bureau where these judgements have already been made. The data are a little more manageable than if each economist made individual judgements and, as a result, industry studies are comparable. The Census Bureau collects and classifies data according to the **Standard Industrial Classification (SIC) system.**[1] The SIC system divides the economy into about 400 four-digit industries. These four-digit groups can then be aggregated into three-digit or two-digit groups, or disaggregated into five-digit (or even seven-digit) product classes. Table 26-1 presents an example of how a product becomes more specific as the industry group is disaggregated. The purpose of such a system is to organize groups of processes, products, and materials into a workable, consistent classification. This SIC system is the basis for studies we will be referring to in the remainder of this chapter.

One of the principles developed earlier, cross elasticity of demand, could be useful in determining whether products belong to the same industry or different

Standard Industrial Classification (SIC) system   *A system devised by the U.S. Census Bureau for classifying industries. The SIC system divides the economy into about 400 four-digit industries.*

---

[1]See U.S. Bureau of the Budget, *Standard Industrial Classification Manual* (Washington: U.S. Government Printing Office, 1967).

TABLE 26-1 SAMPLE SIC CODES

Code Number		Designation	Name
Two-digit	20	Major Industry Group	Food & Kindred Products
Three-digit	201	Industry Group	Meat Products
Four-digit	2011	Industry	Meat Packing Plants
Five-digit	20111	Product Class	Fresh Beef

Source: U.S. Bureau of the Budget, *Standard Industrial Classification Manual* (Washington: U.S. Government Printing Office, 1967).

industries. We saw that if the coefficient of the cross elasticity of demand between two products is positive, the goods are substitutes.[2] Goods that are close substitutes would have a positive and very high cross elasticity of demand coefficient. If we could agree on a cross elasticity coefficient that would represent goods from the same industry, again an arbitrary decision, we could then use this figure in a very mechanical fashion to define an industry.

INDUSTRY STRUCTURE

Once we have overcome the hurdle of defining an industry, we can then determine its market structure. As we saw earlier, this structure will depend critically on a number of elements in that particular industry. Of these elements, degrees of concentration and conditions of entry are especially important. Concentration and entry, of course, interact in such a way that entry barriers make for a more concentrated industry, but for the moment, let's consider them separately.

Loosely speaking, concentration refers to the extent to which a certain number of firms dominate sales in a given market. Measures of concentration have, for many years, been a primary tool of industry studies. The ***concentration ratio*** permits the economist to prepare an index of the relative degree of concentration in an oligopolistic market. To calculate a concentration ratio, the economist uses the SIC codes we just discussed and calculates the percentage of an industry's total sales accounted for by a certain number of firms.[3] For example, a four-firm concentration ratio would calculate the percentage of sales in an industry accounted for by the largest four firms. It is possible to calculate concentration ratios for the largest firm, the three largest firms, the eight largest firms, and so on. Most studies have employed four-firm ratios. Table 26-2 gives concentration ratios for a few selected industries.

It could be argued that the percentage of sales is not the best measure of concentration in an industry. You might instead want to calculate concentration

concentration ratio   An index of the relative degree of concentration in an industry. The one most commonly used is the percentage of sales of an industry accounted for by the four largest firms in that industry.

$$^{2}E_{x,y} = \frac{\text{percentage change in quantity demanded of good } x}{\text{percentage change in price of good } y}.$$

[3] Prelaw students might anticipate a strategy for defense in antitrust cases. The defense, of course, would prefer to have concentration ratios calculated on the basis of the most general category possible in order to insure that any one firm has a small share of the sales in the industry.

TABLE 26-2   CONCENTRATION RATIOS—SELECTED INDUSTRIES

Product	Number of Firms	Concentration Ratio (Sales of Domestically Produced Goods)
Automobiles	4	100%
Telephone Service	4	98%
Chewing Gum	4	97%
Tennis Balls	2	100%
Detergents	3	86%
Soft Drinks	4	65%
Canned Soups	2	90%
Disposable Diapers	4	99%
Sanitary Napkins	2	95%
Air Travel	3	61%
Plywood	4	30%
Wood Furniture	4	14%
Concrete Block and Brick	4	5%

Source: Federal Trade Commission, *The Wall Street Journal, Financial World, Standard & Poor's,* (various issues), and industry sources.

ratios using percentage of assets, percentage of employees, or value of shipments. The various measures of concentration are all statistically highly correlated, however, so it really isn't that crucial which type of ratio you select.

As we discussed earlier, the more concentrated an industry, the more likely it is that there will be a recognized interdependence and joint action of either a collusive or noncollusive nature. When a four-firm concentration ratio exceeds 40–50 percent, the degree of this interdependence is likely to be very high.

Entry is the second element affecting the market structure. Entry conditions have an important effect on concentration. If entry barriers exist and the industry is highly concentrated, it is more likely that joint action can be exploited to earn monopoly profits. We saw earlier that cartels are very unstable and that profits will strongly attract new firms into the industry. But if concentration is high and entry is blocked, the existing firms will in all likelihood be able to exploit their strong market position.

It is important, then, to consider the elements of concentration and entry together. Concentration produces the recognized interdependence that works to make cooperative behavior worthwhile, and entry determines the scope for such cooperative behavior.

CONCENTRATION AND ITS GROWTH OVER TIME

At first glance, it seems that the number of concentrated, oligopolistic industries in the U.S. economy is high. But just how concentrated is U.S. industry? And does concentration make any difference? In other words, would you as a consumer be better off if U.S. industry were generally less concentrated and hence perhaps more competitive? Given the difficulty of defining industries and the fact that any classification scheme requires arbitrary judgements, it is not surprising that studies have reached widely differing conclusions on the degree and trend of concentration in U.S. industry. The studies can be divided roughly into three groups.

One group of studies, which investigated trends in concentration in the first half of the twentieth century, concluded that there had been a pronounced increase in industrial concentration in the United States. This group of studies is associated with and represented by the work of Gardiner Means, who looked at the assets of the 200 largest nonfinancial corporations. Means found (see Group I Studies in Table 26-3) that between 1909 and 1933 the percentage of total assets controlled by the 200 largest nonfinancial corporations increased from 33.3 percent to 54.8 percent.[4]

TABLE 26-3 TRENDS IN CONCENTRATION: GROUP I STUDIES

	1909	1929	1930	1931	1932	1933
Total Assets of All Nonfinancial Corporations: 200 Largest Corporations (Less Taxable Investments; Percent of Total)	33.3	47.9	54.3	55.5	54.8	54.8

	1909	1919	1929	1935	1948	1958
Total Assets of All Manufacturing, Mining, and Distribution Corporations: 100 Largest Corporations (Percent of Total)	17.7	16.6	25.5	28.0	26.7	29.8

	1920	1921	1922	1923	1924	1925
Total Net Income of All Nonfinancial Coporations: 200 Largest Corporations (Percent of Total)	33.4	37.6	32.2	32.8	36.0	37.1
	1926	**1927**	**1928**	**1929**		
	40.0	38.4	40.0	43.2		

Source: Gardiner Means, National Resources Committee, *The Structure of the American Economy* (Washington: U.S. Government Printing Office, 1939), Part 1, p. 107; Norman R. Collins and Lee E. Preston, "The Size Structure of the Largest Industrial Firms," *American Economic Review* (December, 1961); and Adolf A. Berle and Gardiner C. Means, *The Modern Corporation and Private Property* (New York: Macmillan Co., 1933).

[4]Studies by Gardiner C. Means and by Norman R. Collins and Lee E. Preston are representative of such studies. Reference citations to these studies and the others discussed can be found in Table 26-3.

The studies that found increased concentration were challenged by G. Warren Nutter, who argued that between 1901 and 1937 industrial concentration declined in the United States. Nutter's studies were attacked on the grounds that they depended crucially on benchmark figures from 1899, which he took as a starting point, and that these early figures were suspect because of the poor data that existed then. Later, Nutter's figures were updated and extended by Henry A. Einhorn. Einhorn used Nutter's figures for 1939 as a benchmark and sought to determine if concentration had changed between 1939 and 1958. He divided production in the economy, as Nutter had earlier, into three structures: (1) monopolistic, (2) workably competitive, and (3) governmental. He then, like Nutter, sought to determine if the share of production originating in each of the three structures had changed. Einhorn concluded (see Group II Study in Table 26-4) that between 1939 and 1958 roughly three fifths of national income was generated by the workably competitive structure. The monopolistic sector declined only slightly and the governmental sector increased slightly. The conclusion of the Nutter-Einhorn research is that market concentration in the twentieth century has been surprisingly stable. The authors of these studies have to use judgement as to what "monopoly," "workably competitive," and "governmental" mean, and how to determine into which of these three categories a firm fits. If you are interested in these problems of definition, you should consult the original studies.

Two later governmental studies are presented in Table 26-5. These studies seem to indicate that concentration has increased very slightly in the 1950s and 1960s.

Can we draw any conclusions from these seemingly conflicting studies? At one extreme in the debate, we have the position that the level of monopoly power has been stable, and that monopolized production amounts to 15–20 percent of national income. At the other end of the debate we have the position that concentration in American industry increased dramatically in the early part of this century and, since World War II, has also increased but at a much slower pace than in the early 1900s. Regardless of whose data and technique you are most convinced by, it is significant that even the most optimistic figures argue that only about 60 percent of U.S. production can be judged as originating in workably competitive industries.

TABLE 26-4   TRENDS IN CONCENTRATION: GROUP II
             STUDIES

Distribution of National Income by Type of Productive Organization		
	1939	**1958**
Effectively Monopolistic	20.43	15.88
Workably Competitive	59.09	62.02
Governmental	20.16	21.52

Source: G. Warren Nutter and Henry A. Einhorn, *Enterprise Monopoly in the United States: 1899–1958* (New York: Columbia University Press, 1969), pp. 56–57.

TABLE 26-5 TRENDS IN CONCENTRATION: GROUP III STUDIES

Total Manufacturing Assets: 200 Largest Manufacturing Concerns (Percent of Total)	**1929**	**1933**	**1937**	**1941**	**1948**		
	45.8	49.5	49.1	45.1	46.3		
	1950	**1952**	**1954**	**1956**	**1958**		
	46.1	47.7	50.4	52.8	55.2		
	1960	**1962**	**1964**	**1966**	**1968**		
	55.2	55.1	55.8	56.1	60.4		
Value Added by Manufacture: 200 Largest Manufacturers (Percent of Total)	**1947**	**1954**	**1958**	**1962**	**1963**	**1966**	**1967**
	30	37	38	40	41	42	42

Source: Bureau of the Census, Department of Commerce, "Concentration Ratios in Manufacturing, 1967," *Special Reports,* 1970, and Federal Trade Commission Staff, *Economic Report on Corporate Mergers,* 1969, p. 173.

A second thing to keep in mind is that these measures of concentration are all aggregate measures. They may understate the degree of monopoly power in American industry because they ignore or understate the power of local and regional monopolies. The beer industry is a good example. In 1970 the four-firm concentration ratio for beer sales was roughly 40 percent on a national level. However, in some regions the concentration ratio was much higher, approaching 75–80 percent. Thus, the national figures might lead some to conclude that the industry is workably competitive, whereas the regional figures seem to suggest that the industry consists of a series of regional monopolies. One possible way out of the difficulty of agreeing on the measures of economic concentration is to ask whether concentration is really very important.

CONCENTRATION AND PERFORMANCE

We have been discussing concentration and ways to determine the degree of concentration in an industry. Lurking in the background of this discussion is the implicit presumption that concentration, *per se,* is undesirable. This dislike of concentration has become commonplace among industrial organization economists. The reason is that the industrial organization economist typically sees a sequence of events running from (a) the structure of the industry to (b) the behavior of firms in that industry and then to (c) the performance of the industry itself. According to this line of thought, a highly concentrated structure will produce the antisocial behavior we attributed to monopoly. The industrial organization economist, therefore, examines the structure of an industry to determine how the public welfare might be improved. This general structure-conduct-performance chain has been termed the ***Market Concentration Doctrine.***

The Market Concentration Doctrine holds that the degree of concentration is a reliable index of monopoly power. Strict application of this doctrine might

*Market Concentration Doctrine
A hypothesis that holds that the degree of concentration in an industry is a reliable index of the degree of monopoly power in that industry.*

lead policymakers to suggest antitrust action or some other form of control when concentration ratios reach a certain level. Before examining policy action against monopoly, let us first examine the premises behind this doctrine.

Administered Prices

Those who support the Market Concentration Doctrine base their arguments primarily on two empirical points. The first is that prices are more rigid (less flexible) in concentrated industries, and the second is that profit rates and concentration are positively correlated. Supporters of this doctrine believe that both rigid prices and higher profit rates reflect the monopoly power associated with high degrees of concentration.

The lack of price flexibility in concentrated industries was first found by Gardiner Means, and his findings are described in a now famous monograph.[5] He argued, looking at data from 1926–1933, that price movements in different industries varied in frequency. In some industries prices changed very often, and in others prices tended to be constant for relatively long periods of time. He labeled the prices that were relatively rigid, or changed only infrequently, as *administered prices.* Later he demonstrated that these administered prices were related to the degree of concentration in the industry.[6]

administered prices A term coined by Gardiner Means to describe price inflexibility in concentrated industries. Means labeled prices that were relatively rigid or changed only infrequently as administered prices.

This early work by Means has had a significant influence on discussions of public policy toward industry. As might be expected with so significant a study, it was subjected to close scrutiny. As is usually the case with empirical work, the data and methodology used by both sides in the debate have been criticized. Competing researchers claimed that Means's study suffered because his data were gathered from reports submitted by industry to the Bureau of Labor Statistics. Since firms reported at different intervals, his reported price flexibility (or inflexibility) might simply reflect a different frequency of reporting.[7] Other researchers claimed that the Bureau of Labor Statistics' data were composed of prices *asked* by firms and the relevant data are prices *paid* by consumers.[8] Since oligopolists often want to hide their price cuts from their competitors, they often grant buyers secret cuts on posted prices. For this reason, the discrepancies between prices asked and prices paid might be significant.

Even though this question of administered prices has been scrutinized by economists for some time, we do not yet have a scientific conclusion. The standard textbook conclusion is that there is a loose association between concentration and price inflexibility. This conventional wisdom has become part of public policy debates, but the economist, in the capacity of scientist, would be hard put to prove this relationship.

[5]Gardiner Means, *Industrial Prices and Their Relative Inflexibility,* Senate Document 13, 74th Congress, 1st Session (January 17, 1935).

[6]National Resources Committee, *The Structure of the American Economy* (Washington: U.S. Government Printing Office, 1939).

[7]U.S. Congress, Joint Economic Committee, *Government Price Statistics.* Hearings before the Subcommittee on Economic Statistics of the Joint Economic Committee, 87th Congress, 1st Session (1961).

[8]George J. Stigler and James K. Kindahl, *The Behavior of Industrial Prices* (New York: National Bureau of Economic Research, 1970).

John Kenneth Galbraith *(1908–   )*

John Kenneth Galbraith is perhaps the most well-known contemporary critic who happens to be an economist. His fame results from his attempt to write economics in clear English. However, economists, as a group, are not very sympathetic to his economic analysis. Their reservations stem from the fact that Galbraith criticizes in sweeping generalities. His arguments are almost never stated in precise, testable hypotheses. As a result, it is almost impossible for Galbraith to present evidence for his arguments. In a stinging review of Galbraith, Professor Robert Solow of M.I.T. argues that economists are "little thinkers" while Galbraith is a "big thinker." Solow went on to illustrate his criticism of Galbraith by referring to

> . . . the old story of the couple that had achieved an agreeable division of labor. She made the

unimportant decisions: What job he should take, where they should live, how to bring up the children. He made the important decisions: What to do about Jerusalem, who should be admitted to the United Nations, how to deal with crime on the streets.[1]

John Kenneth Galbraith was born in Canada and received a B.S. degree from the University of Toronto. He received a Ph.D. in agricultural economics at the University of California, Berkeley, in 1934. Galbraith went immediately to Harvard as an instructor, where he has been ever since. Galbraith, unlike most economists, is very politically active. He has been chairperson of the Americans for Democratic Action and was an early and outspoken critic of the Vietnam War. President John Kennedy, who knew Galbraith from his days at Harvard, appointed him ambassador to India.

Galbraith has written a large number of books on both economic and noneconomic matters. The most important economics books are *American Capitalism: The Concept of the Countervailing Power* (1956), *The Affluent Society* (1958), and *The New Industrial State* (1967). These books and Galbraith's other works on economics all have a common theme, which has come to be referred to as *Galbraithian economics.* This theme is that monopoly is the dominant force in the American economy and that these monopolies control and manipulate input prices, demand, and governmental policy. The control of the economy is now in the hands of a technostructure rather than the entrepreneur of conventional economic theory. Galbraith also argues that workers are generally exploited by these giant firms.

---

[1] Robert Solow, "Son of Affluence," *Public Interest* (Fall, 1967), p. 100.

Concentration and Profit Levels

The second element of the Concentration Doctrine is that profits and concentration ratios are positively correlated. The theoretical basis for this premise lies in the greater ability for a small number of firms to behave collusively. The empirical link between concentration and profits begins with the work of Joe Bain.[9] Bain

---

[9] Joe S. Bain, "Relation of Profit-Rate to Industry Concentration: American Manufacturing, 1936–1940," *Quarterly Journal of Economics* (August, 1951).

found, although he had some reservations, that profit rates and concentration ratios were positively correlated for a sample of 42 manufacturing industries. Bain also found that when the concentration ratio exceeded 70 percent, there was a significant increase in average profit rates. Economist George Stigler, on the other hand, conducting similar research, found there was no clear-cut relationship between concentration ratios and profit rates.[10] In his study, Stigler defined an industry as concentrated if the four-firm concentration ratio for the value of output exceeded 60 percent. Other studies examining the same hypothesis concluded that there is a weak, but positive, relationship between concentration and profit rates.[11]

There has been some debate about this tendency for profits to be higher in concentrated industries. President Johnson's Task Force on Antitrust Policy concluded that such a correlation exists.

> The adverse effects of persistent concentration on output and price find some confirmation in various studies that have been made of return on capital in major industries. These studies have found a close association between high levels of concentration and persistently high rates of return on capital. . . . It is the persistence of high profits over extended time periods and over whole industries rather than in individual firms that suggest artificial restraints on output and the absence of fully effective competition. The correlation of evidence of this kind with very high levels of concentration appears to be significant.[12]

This conclusion has been challenged by the University of Chicago's Yale Brozen and others.[13] Brozen recalculated many of the older studies using data from later time periods. He found that with the passage of time there was a tendency for rates of profit in concentrated industries to converge with those of less concentrated industries. Rates of profit increased in the industries that previously had below average profit levels and decreased in the industries with above average profit levels. Other economists have pointed out that there are numerous hypotheses that are consistent with the data and that care should be taken before policy is based on any one hypothesis. Thus, the concentration-profit hypothesis, like the concentration-price rigidity hypothesis, has been subject to challenge.

The Market Concentration Doctrine, then, is challenged on two of its most important tenets. There appears to be, at least, debatable evidence to contradict the conventional wisdom that concentration ratios are a good measure of monopoly behavior. Why is this important? It is important because much of present policy discussion concerning the reformulation of antitrust law uses market concentration as a guide. If concentration is illegal, *per se,* in part because concentration is taken as an indicator of monopoly behavior, many industries may be restructured by the courts simply because they are concentrated. If, instead, these industries are concentrated because there are economies of scale, antitrust activity would introduce inefficiencies into the economy.

---

[10]George J. Stigler, *Capital and Rates of Return in Manufacturing* (Princeton, N.J.: Princeton University Press, 1963).

[11]For a review of these studies, see Harold Demsetz, *The Market Concentration Doctrine* (Washington: American Enterprise Institute for Public Policy Research, 1975).

[12]White House Task Force on Antitrust Policy, *Role of the Giant Corporation* (1967), p. 883.

[13]Yale Brozen, "The Antitrust Task Force Deconcentration Recommendation," *Journal of Law and Economics* (October, 1970), pp. 279–292.

In short, the Market Concentration Doctrine has become a conventional tool for policymakers. The challenges to this doctrine, however, are significant enough that it should be examined closely. It is particularly important that economists reach a scientific consensus on this important issue before policymakers take public action to restructure American industry based on the Market Concentration Doctrine.

REGULATION OF MONOPOLY— THEORY

We have seen that monopoly power is present in the American economy, and we have seen that from the point of view of an optimal allocation of resources, monopoly is a bad thing. Society may decide that it is best to regulate a monopoly. Two common ways to do this are price regulation and taxation.

Consider the monopoly represented by Figure 26-1. The monopoly is maximizing its profits by producing OQ_1 at price OP_1. Let us assume that the government wants to force the firm to produce the same amount that would be produced if this were a purely competitive market, that is, to produce where the marginal cost curve intersects the demand curve. If the government would set a price ceiling of OP_2, the monopoly would react by producing OQ_2 units of output, because the demand curve that the monopoly faces is now represented by line P_2AD. The firm, as always, produces where $MC = MR$ and MR up to point

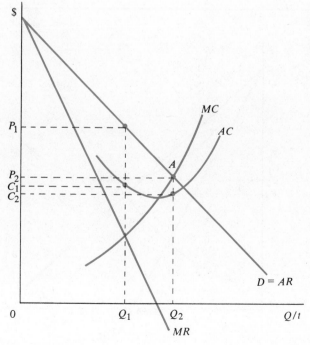

FIGURE 26-1 MARGINAL COST PRICING
If the regulator imposes a price of OP_2, the monopoly would produce OQ_2 units of output. Per-unit profits decrease from C_1P_1 to C_2P_2.

marginal cost pricing   A
theoretical technique for forcing
a monopoly to behave exactly as
a competitive firm by regulating
the monopoly price so that it is
equal to marginal cost and
average revenue.

A is equal to line P_2A because demand is perfectly elastic for segment P_2A. The setting of such a price ceiling is sometimes called **marginal cost pricing.** Note that by regulating this monopoly, per-unit profits decrease from C_1P_1 to C_2P_2. You may be thinking, why not lower the price below OP_2 because every decrease in price between OP_1 and OP_2 will increase output and lower price? The problem is that for output levels greater than OQ_2, every unit produced costs society more than it is willing to pay ($MC > P$), so this is just as bad in its own way as monopoly behavior when $MC < P$ and the cost of an extra unit is less than society is willing to pay.

Consider Figure 26-2. The profit-maximizing monopolist is producing OQ_1 at price OP_1. The monopolist is receiving C_1P_1 profit per unit. Now impose a regulated price of OP_2 on the monopolist. At OP_2 it appears the monopolist would increase output to OQ_2. But note, at price OP_2 and output OQ_2 the monopolist would lose C_2P_2 per unit sold. Price is below average cost so the monopolist would leave the industry. In other words, the optimal output from society's viewpoint is now where $MC = AR$, but this output forces losses on the monopolist. This output could, however, be produced if the government would make up the loss, P_2C_2AB, in Figure 26-2. The monopolist would then produce the desired output, OQ_2, at price OP_2. The problem with this solution is that if the government subsidizes the industry out of general tax revenues, it is transferring income from taxpayers to the consumers of the good. Most people (except consumers of the particular good) would view such a transfer as an inequitable redistribution of income. The trick, then, for the would-be price regulator is to set price equal to MC at the point where the MC curve intersects the demand curve, but only if price is equal to or greater than average cost for that level of output.

FIGURE 26-2   MARGINAL COST PRICING AND LOSSES

If the regulator sets a price of OP_2, the monopolist would lose C_2P_2 per unit of output sold. The monopolist would thus only produce if the regulator subsidizes the monopolist.

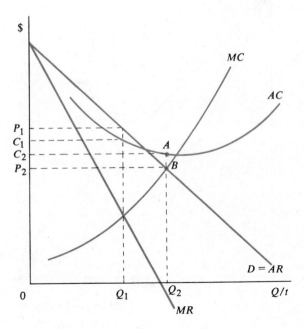

Now let's see how effective taxation is in regulating monopoly power. Suppose we impose a license fee on our monopolist in Figure 26-3. Before the tax, the monopoly, as before, is producing OQ_1 at price OP_1. The monopolist is earning profits of C_1P_1 per unit. If we charge the monopolist a fee for the right to do business, this fee is not related to the level of output, so it represents an increase in the firm's fixed cost. The AC curve thus shifts up by the amount of the fee to AC_1. The monopolist still maximizes profits by producing OQ_1 at price OP_1, but profits have been reduced to C_2P_1 per unit. Note that it is possible to set the tax or fee so as to capture all the monopoly profit. Such a tax shifts average cost to AC_2 in Figure 26-3.

Although there are practical difficulties with both methods of regulating monopoly, they have quite different effects on the industry. Price regulation can cause the monopolist to produce the purely competitive output. Taxation, on the other hand, leaves price and output unchanged. A tax simply captures the monopoly profit for the public coffers. It should be clear, then, that from the viewpoint of the allocation of resources, price regulation is preferred because it increases output and lowers price. The tax only corrects for the effect of monopoly on the distribution of income.

REGULATION OF MONOPOLY—
PRACTICE

We saw in the previous chapter that attempts at regulation often increase the power of oligopolies as the regulatory bodies are "captured" by the industry. There is, however, an additional problem that is relevant to the previous discus-

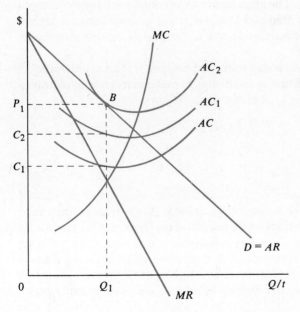

FIGURE 26-3 TAXING THE MONOPOLY
A license fee on the monopolist will be viewed as a fixed cost and will increase average cost but not marginal cost. In this way, the monopoly profit can be taxed away with no effect on output.

sion of setting prices to regulate monopoly output. This problem centers on the fact that regulators may not be able to determine marginal costs and must, therefore, turn to the alternative of regulating the price based on average cost information. The usual practice is to allow a markup on average cost. This is referred to as *cost-plus pricing.* This type of regulation creates some distortions. If the monopolist is allowed to charge a price, say, 10 percent above average cost, we have lessened the incentive of the firm to minimize cost, although consumer demand gives the firm some incentive not to let price get too far out of hand.

cost-plus pricing   The practice in price regulation of allowing firms a markup on average costs of production. This is the most common form of price regulation.

Perhaps the best example of this form of behavior is in our present regulatory environment for the utility industries—electricity, gas, water, and so forth. Since utilities are considered natural monopolies, they are regulated for the public interest. Such regulation is on an average cost-plus markup basis. This markup is often called a *fair rate of return.* As a result, utilities have less real incentive to cut costs than do profit-oriented firms, which directly increase profits by any reduction in costs.

fair rate of return   The idea that a regulated industry must earn a normal profit or it will go out of business.

Try a little experiment to test this conclusion. Contrast the facilities of your local telephone and electric utility to those of a profit-oriented business in your community. If the proposition holds that regulated industries are less cost conscious, you would expect the regulated firm to have much nicer facilities since they need pay less attention to costs. Compare the facilities used by the executives of the two groups in your community.

Some communities have recently been involved in discussions of whether or not utilities should be able to advertise their product. The side against such advertising argues that it simply raises average costs and results in higher prices to consumers. Our analysis supports this argument. Interestingly, our self-interest model of individual behavior would predict that a certain group in the community would support utility advertising. Any guesses? Of course, it would be the news media. The news media have strongly supported utility advertising, often on the grounds of insuring free speech.

Regulation not only makes a firm less cost conscious, but it can also raise the actual cost of doing business. The attendant costs of compliance and noncompliance could mean that less is produced at higher prices because costs are higher. In this sense regulation is counterproductive to the goal of making monopolies produce a larger output.

Regulation, then, is at best a very tricky exercise and is often counterproductive. An alternative to regulation is to attempt to make monopolistic industries more competitive. This is the goal of our antitrust laws.

U.S. ANTITRUST LAWS

Around the turn of the century in the United States, there was a substantial increase in the growth of large business organizations. Legal arrangements such as *trusts,* which were organizations set up to control the stock of other companies through boards of trustees, and *holding companies,* which were single firms set up for the sole purpose of owning and thus controlling other firms, were established. These organizations enabled the *robber barons,* as they have been called by economic historians, to control and coordinate the activities of many previ-

trusts   Legal organizations set up to control the stock of other companies through boards of trustees.

ously independent firms. At first, this new form of business was viewed as a natural outgrowth of the Industrial Revolution in the United States. *Social Darwinism*—a popular social theory at the time—justified such behavior. Social Darwinism applied Charles Darwin's theory of the evolution of the species, often summed up as a belief in the survival of the fittest, to business enterprise. Under that view stronger firms were justified in getting bigger by "gobbling up" the smaller ones.

Eventually the public began to view some of these arrangements with suspicion. One of the earliest organized groups to vigorously oppose the trust movement, and one with which you are probably familiar from courses in American history, was the *National Grange.* The Grange began in 1867 as the Patrons of Husbandry and was opposed to trusts, in particular the railroad trust. The railroad trust was opposed by the Grange because of the high monopoly prices it set and also because it was able to practice price discrimination in the hauling of agricultural produce.

As a result of the Grange and other similar populist political movements against trusts, several states enacted antitrust statutes that regulated businesses chartered in the state. These state statutes failed because corporations were able to seek out less restrictive states in which to seek charters. Two of the more hospitable states were New Jersey and Delaware. Eventually the antitrust sentiment became so widespread and intense that by 1888 both national political parties had an antitrust plank in their presidential platform.

In 1890 Congress passed the *Sherman Antitrust Act.* The Sherman Act had two major provisions. Section 1 of the act declared every contract, combination, or conspiracy in restraint of trade to be illegal. Section 2 made it illegal to monopolize or attempt to monopolize.[14] The language of the law is strong, but it is also vague, and the courts took years to determine its scope. We shall trace some of the important decisions, but first we will examine other antitrust laws.

The *Clayton Act,* passed in 1914, made certain business practices that would lead to monopoly illegal. It prohibited a company from acquiring the stock of a competing company if such an acquisition would "substantially lessen competition."[15] The act also prohibited tying contracts and price discrimination. *Tying contracts* are agreements between producers and retailers whereby a retailer must agree to handle certain items as a prerequisite to handling other items. The Clayton Act, though it prohibited stock acquisition, was circumvented because it did not prohibit asset acquisition. Proposed amendments to strengthen or weaken the bill have become politically popular recently. The *Celler-Kefauver Antimerger Act,* passed in 1950, made it illegal in certain circumstances for a firm to merge with another by purchasing its assets and thereby strengthened the Clayton Act.

---

holding companies *Firms set up for the sole purpose of owning and controlling other firms.*

robber barons *The very successful turn-of-the-century entrepreneurs who amassed fortunes by setting up trusts and holding companies.*

Social Darwinism *Charles Darwin's theory of evolution of the species as applied to business enterprise. Under that view, stronger firms were justified in getting bigger by swallowing up smaller firms.*

Sherman Antitrust Act *Passed in 1890, it was the first antitrust law. Section 1 of the act declared every contract, combination, or conspiracy in restraint of trade to be illegal. Section 2 made it illegal to monopolize or attempt to monopolize.*

Clayton Act *Passed in 1914, it prohibited the acquisition of the stock of a competing company if such an acquisition would "substantially lessen competition."*

tying contracts *Agreements between producers and retailers, whereby a retailer must agree to handle certain items as a prerequisite to handling other items.*

Celler-Kefauver Antimerger Act *Passed in 1950, this act made it illegal in certain circumstances for a firm to merge with another by purchasing its assets. This strengthened the Clayton Act.*

---

[14]"Section 1: Every contract, combination in the form of trust or otherwise, or conspiracy, in restraint of trade or commerce among the several States, or with foreign nations, is declared to be illegal. . . . Section 2: Every person who shall monopolize, or attempt to monopolize, or combine or conspire with any other person or persons, to monopolize any part of the trade or commerce among the several States, or with foreign nations, shall be deemed guilty of a misdemeanor. . . . (Sherman Antitrust Act, Sec. 1, 26 stat. 209 [1890]).

[15]For a publication covering the technical details of all these laws, see J. G. Van Cise, *Understanding the Antitrust Laws* (New York: Practicing Law Institute, 1973).

Federal Trade Commission Act
This act established the Federal
Trade Commission to police
unfair business practices.

In 1914, along with the Clayton Act, Congress passed the **Federal Trade Commission Act**. This act set up the Federal Trade Commission (FTC) to police unfair industrial practices. Initially, the FTC had many powers, but the Supreme Court, in 1919, denied it the power to issue cease and desist orders without judicial review. In recent years, the FTC has worked closely with the Justice Department in antitrust matters.

The History of Antitrust Enforcement

As mentioned earlier, it took some time for the courts to determine the scope of the Sherman Act. In particular, the phrase "in restraint of trade" needed a legal definition. Of course, if we applied a strict economic definition, any firm with monopoly power, that is, power to restrict output or to increase price, would be guilty of restraint of trade. The courts, in two famous 1911 cases against Standard Oil and American Tobacco, enunciated the **rule of reason**. The rule of reason said that monopolies that behaved well were not illegal. In effect, the Supreme Court defined—some might say rewrote—the Sherman Act to make only "unreasonable" restraints of trade illegal. The test of reasonableness was itself difficult to define. The court held that the existence of competitors was sufficient to demonstrate reasonable behavior. In 1920 U.S. Steel, despite its dominance in the steel industry, was found not to be an unreasonable monopoly. The court stated that the law does not make mere size an offense.

rule of reason Indicated that
monopolies which behaved well
did not violate the Sherman Act.
The court held that the existence
of competitors was sufficient to
demonstrate "reasonable
behavior."

In 1945, after 13 years of litigation, this rule of reason was changed. Judge Learned Hand ruled in a case against Alcoa Aluminum that size itself *was* enough to prove the exercise of monopoly power. The change was so fundamental that commentators later referred to the ruling as the "new Sherman Act." The Alcoa case was based on estimates of market power and structural aspects of the industry. In such cases, the way in which an industry is defined is extremely significant and in fact to a large degree determines defense and prosecution strategies. As you might guess, the defense would prefer the industry to be broadly defined, both geographically and by the number of products included, since such a definition tends to reduce the importance of any one firm in any particular industry. The few cases we have mentioned trace major changes in the application of antitrust law and demonstrate the importance of the way the court has changed in its attitude toward the market power of large-scale enterprise.

treble damages A provision
under the Sherman Act that
victims of monopoly can recover
three times the damages they
have sustained.

Another significant change has taken place much more recently. The Sherman Act provides that private parties who are victims of monopoly under Sections 1 and 2 are entitled to sue for **treble damages**. In other words, if a firm is convicted under the Sherman Act, individuals can recover three times the damages they have sustained. This provision was intended to stimulate private suits by firms or individuals who had been victims of price discrimination, but historically it was of very little practical importance. Recently, however, consumer groups have become very active on this front and have brought many recent "class action" suits under the provisions of the antitrust laws. Consumer groups bring action on behalf of the entire class of consumers, and treble damages in these cases could be very large.

The point that there have been very few antitrust cases brought by damaged firms or individuals raises an important question—who brings most antitrust cases? The answer lies in the political process. The courts, as we have seen, have made some significant changes in enforcement, but the courts only rule on cases brought before them. The decision on whether to bring a case or not rests largely with the Antitrust Division of the Department of Justice. This decision is made by a presidential appointee, the assistant attorney general for antitrust. Antitrust policy therefore reflects the desires of the president. Theodore Roosevelt campaigned as the great "trust-buster." He set up the Antitrust Division and his administration brought the first cases against industry. As we saw earlier, this trend was nipped by the Supreme Court and the rule of reason. Franklin Roosevelt's first term saw virtually no activity on the antitrust scene. On the contrary, in the early Depression years of the first Roosevelt administration, the government actually fostered anticompetitive practices through the *National Recovery Administration (NRA)*. The NRA tried to set up cartels in virtually every industry, but they were eventually declared unconstitutional. In 1937 the Roosevelt administration changed its position. Thurman Arnold, the assistant attorney general for antitrust, vigorously brought antitrust cases, including the Alcoa case, which ultimately reversed the rule of reason.

National Recovery Administration (NRA) The NRA was a major New Deal program aimed at business recovery. The NRA was anticompetitive since it allowed and encouraged agreements between firms. It was eventually declared unconstitutional.

Historically, antitrust activity has reflected presidential appointees' and, therefore, presidential desires. Both the Eisenhower and Kennedy administrations pursued active antitrust programs. President Johnson's administration represented, perhaps because of the diversion caused by the Vietnam War, a retreat from vigorous antitrust policy. President Nixon's first appointee, Richard McLaren, vigorously worked to prohibit conglomerate mergers. McLaren ultimately resigned because of political interference by Nixon politicos in the International Telephone and Telegraph case. The interference clearly demonstrated that antitrust prosecution is very much a political decision. Thomas E. Kauper, who served as President Ford's assistant attorney general for antitrust, pursued an active antitrust policy. He launched a major case against AT&T and tripled the number of price-fixing cases filed. He was also instrumental in changing the law to make price fixing a felony instead of a misdemeanor as it had been under the Sherman Act. Kauper, however, also resigned in a political cloud. President Carter appointed John Shenefield as his assistant attorney general for antitrust. Shenefield promised at his confirmation hearings to make an antitrust impact on the concentration of power. Shenefield also promised to attack the notion of *shared monopoly,* in which very few firms control an industry, and to speed up the litigation process so cases would not drag on for dozens of years. We will go into more detail on Reagan's antitrust policy later in this chapter.

shared monopoly A recent term used to describe a highly concentrated industry in which a few firms control the industry. The term is often used by lawyers rather than economists.

It is sometimes argued that in periods of economic slump, politicians are not eager to interfere with the system. Likewise, when the economy is performing well, there are no incentives to tamper. Whatever the economic conditions, there is much room for political influence peddling. All this considered, we might conclude that we shouldn't expect antitrust policy to be extremely effective. Let us turn now to the evidence to see if such a conclusion is warranted.

The Record of Antitrust Enforcement

Economists and lawyers have begun to statistically analyze the case-bringing activity of the Antitrust Division of the Justice Department. The first such study was conducted by Richard Posner and published in 1970.[16] Posner's study offers some statistical evidence concerning some of the propositions we have examined.

Posner found that from 1890, the time of the Sherman Act, to 1969, 1,551 cases were brought by the Justice Department. He found that this activity by the Justice Department does not appear to have been a function of the economic activity in the country. The hypothesis that antitrust activity increased during economic contractions was not supported. You remember, however, that antitrust activity can also be initiated by the Federal Trade Commission (FTC) and even by private citizens. Posner found that contrary to popular belief, the statistics do not bear out the contention that antimonopoly activity of the FTC has increased over time. The number of cases brought by private citizens has increased continuously and significantly since 1949. In the period 1965–1969, 3,136 such cases were initiated as compared to only 399 from 1945 to 1949.

Antitrust enforcement has also been stepped up by the states. This, in part, has resulted from a bill signed into law by President Ford in September, 1976. This law allows state attorneys general to sue suspected price fixers for treble damages on behalf of citizens. Politics enters here also. State attorneys general are often campaigning for reelection or for higher office. They will bring suits for publicity value but will be careful to avoid suits against powerful groups whom they need to count on in future elections. Watch such cases in your state. They are often brought against out-of-state firms. This creates good publicity, but doesn't damage in-state business support for the attorney general who aspires to higher office.

Other statistics show that although the antitrust cases are usually very protracted, with many lasting as long as five and six years, the success rate of the claimant in Justice Department cases is very high. This success rate is much lower in FTC and private cases. Even with high success rates, the problem is far from solved because remedies, the decisions the court imposes, have been far from successful in terms of restoring competition. In civil cases, the remedy has often taken the form of regulation. If we view the goal of antitrust as restoring competition, regulation is in fact an admission that competition cannot be restored. The problems that regulation introduces make the imposition of regulation a very inadequate remedy. On the criminal side, the decisions are notoriously weak. Not until the late 1950s was the first person sentenced to jail for price fixing. In 1960, seven more executives were sentenced to jail. In the few cases where sentences have been imposed, the terms have been very short. In addition, the fines levied have been too small to have much of a deterrent effect. In the post-Watergate environment, we have heard more rhetoric about bigger fines and tougher prison terms for white-collar crimes, but it is still too early to tell if this sentiment will affect antitrust decisions.

Posner's study has spawned some attempts to examine the determinants of antitrust activity. Posner himself pointed out that antitrust activity did not seem to be related to economic conditions in the country. He also examined the influence of politics by looking at the party affiliation of the president. He found

[16]Richard A. Posner, "A Statistical Study of Antitrust Enforcement," *Journal of Law and Economics* (October, 1970).

that the political party in the White House does not seem to affect the number of cases initiated. This, of course, does not mean that politics does not affect the Justice Department's antitrust decisions, only that political interference has not, on average, been too different with one party or the other holding the presidency.

More recently, three economists have attempted to statistically examine the economics that seem important in antitrust activity.[17] They found that the case-bringing decisions of the Justice Department seem to be positively correlated to the size of the industry as measured by sales. Other variables which may more closely represent monopoly power, such as profit rates on sales and concentration, seem to play a less important role in explaining Justice Department case bringing.

The actual record of antitrust activity does not present an encouraging picture. We have seen that even though there is a reasonable success rate for cases brought, the litigation is a long process and civil remedies seldom restore competition. Moreover, the criminal sanctions have been applied with so little vigor that they probably have very little deterrent effect.

Political Activity to Reform Antitrust Law

The 1970s have seen some significant swings in political activity as it relates to antitrust. Beginning in 1972 and until his death in 1976, Senator Philip Hart submitted new antitrust legislation on a yearly basis. The bill, the Industrial Reorganization Act, sought to codify into law the structural position that size, *per se,* should be illegal. We discussed this structuralist position earlier in this chapter. One of the bill's primary goals was to remove the decision to seek antitrust action from the political arena. The bill, which was almost passed after Senator Hart's death, has not been reintroduced.

Political interest in the late 1970s shifted to the oil companies and, specifically, to what these companies were going to do with the huge revenues they were earning in the wake of the OPEC cartel. In 1979, the FTC blocked Exxon from buying Reliance, an electric motor company. This FTC action was, in part, a political response to the uproar generated by Mobil's purchase of Montgomery Ward. Senator Edward Kennedy, in response to these and other suspected takeovers, introduced an amendment to the Clayton Act in 1979. Senator Kennedy's bill would have forbidden large oil companies to merge with any business with assets over $100 million. It should not be forgotten that at the time, Senator Kennedy was vying with President Carter for the 1980 presidential nomination, and public opinion was against big oil.

With the election of Ronald Reagan, antitrust activity changed significantly. These changes were seen on both the academic and the political level.

Academic economists have become more vocal in their questioning of antitrust economics. Even liberal economists have spoken out against antitrust. Lester Thurow has urged that government almost abandon its antitrust system. The arguments are that antitrust laws have contributed to the noncompetitive behavior they were designed to combat.

---

[17]William F. Long, Richard Schramm, and Robert Tollison, "Economic Determinants of Antitrust Activity," *Journal of Law and Economics* (October, 1973).

The Reagan appointees, including Attorney General William French Smith, have stepped into an environment that is growing increasingly more hostile towards antitrust activity. They have made it clear that the Reagan administration does not equate big business with bad business practices.

William Baxter, Reagan's assistant attorney general for antitrust, believes that the purpose of antitrust activity should be to promote efficiency. To this end, Baxter believes that government should not interfere with most *vertical mergers,* mergers in which a company integrates its production backward toward its source of supply or forward in its marketing chain. He also feels that *conglomerate mergers,* mergers in which a company buys a firm unrelated to its business, should be allowed. This is the exact opposite of Senator Kennedy's bill. Baxter argues that vertical mergers and conglomerate mergers seldom foster price fixing and do not reduce competition. On the other hand, Baxter approves of tough action against *horizontal mergers,* where a firm acquires a competitor.

Reagan has appointed James C. Miller III as chairman of the FTC. Miller has been running the government's task force on deregulation and may take action to strip the FTC of much of its antitrust power.

vertical merger   A merger in which a company integrates its production backward toward its source of supply or forward in its marketing chain.

conglomerate merger   A merger in which a company buys a firm unrelated to its business.

horizontal merger   A merger in which a firm buys a competitor.

James C. Miller III *(1942–)*

James C. Miller III is the first chairman of the Federal Trade Commission to be an economist. In the past, the FTC, like most regulatory agencies, was run by lawyers.

Miller brings a fresh and decidedly different approach to regulatory matters. He has stated that he wishes to restrain the zeal of the FTC and keep it from acting as a "national nanny."

Miller is out to reform and drastically alter the mission of the Federal Trade Commission. The next several years will be a test of his success. He hopes to persuade Congress to pare back the FTC's mission in order to reduce its discretionary powers. He hopes to reduce the FTC's interference in the market. Miller says, "Consumers are not as gullible as regulators think they are," and he sees no need for government to act as if consumers were stupid and incapable of making informed decisions.

James C. Miller III received his Ph. D. in economics from the University of Virginia. He was born in Conyers, Georgia, and he attended the University of Georgia where he received his undergraduate degree in economics.

Miller is the author of a number of professional articles and has co-authored or edited five books: *Why the Draft: The Case for a Volunteer Army* (Penguin, 1968); *Economic Regulation of Domestic Air Transport: Theory and Policy* (Brookings, 1974); *Perspectives on Federal Transportation Policy* (American Enterprise Institute, 1975); *Benefit-Cost Analyses of Social Regulation* (American Enterprise Institute, 1979); and *Reforming Regulation* (American Enterprise Institute, 1980).

ALTERNATIVES FOR CONTROLLING INDUSTRY

There is a substantial amount of monopoly power, or at least concentration, in American industry. We explained theoretically why monopoly power is detrimental from society's point of view. Unfortunately our discussion of ways to control monopoly or to restore competition through antitrust enforcement has indicated that it is difficult to control monopoly and that antitrust action has not produced the desired results. What, then, are the alternatives?

First, let's consider the one obvious justification for monopoly power—economies of scale. There have been several empirical studies by economists that have attempted to measure the degree of concentration and relate this concentration to scale economies.[18] Table 26-6 summarizes part of one of these studies. It indicates that there is more concentration than is justified by economies of scale in production. This is calculated by assuming that all four firms in the four-firm concentration ratio are the same size. The actual size can then be compared to the efficient size. This comparison is made in Table 26-6. We take the efficient size and multiply it by four to see how large these four efficient firms would be. We then divide the four-firm ratio by the size of these four efficient firms to get the ratio of firm size to efficient size (column 3). This ratio tells us whether deconcentration would produce inefficiencies. Thus, there could be some decon-

TABLE 26-6   ECONOMIES OF SCALE AND CONCENTRATION

Industry	Efficient Size as a Percentage of Industry Sales	Four-Firm Concentration Ratio	Ratio of Firm Size to Efficient Size
Tractors	12.5%	72%	1.44
Flat Glass	10.0%	91%	2.27
Chewing Gum	6.7%	87%	3.25
Soap	3.9%	88%	5.64
Beer	2.3%	28%	3.05
Steel	1.8%	54%	7.49
Petroleum Refining	1.8%	33%	4.58
Flour	1.0%	39%	9.76
Cement	0.9%	32%	8.89
Shoes	0.3%	29%	24.20

Source: Adapted from H. Michael Mann, "Seller Concentration, Barriers to Entry, and Ratio of Return in Thirty Industries," *Review of Economics and Statistics* (August, 1966).

---

[18]See Roger Sherman and Robert Tollison, "Public Policy Toward Oligopoly: Dissolution and Scale Economies," *Antitrust Law and Economics Review* (Summer, 1971), for a review of several of these studies.

centration without introducing inefficiencies. An interesting fact is that three of the five industries with concentration ratios over 50 percent are not those that are the most oversized; that is, having the highest ratio of firm size to efficient size. In fact, in the tractor industry, deconcentration might come dangerously close to creating less than optimal-size firms. So, again, we must be careful in designing hard and fast rules for deconcentration.

There does, however, seem to be at least one policy action which, if vigorously followed, could increase competitive pressures without endangering the efficiency produced by economies of scale. This policy action takes us back to our earlier discussion of industrial concentration and the threat of new entry. If policy could actually support new entry by actively dismantling *artificial* barriers to entry, competitive pressure would increase. In many cases the threat of new entry alone would be sufficient to alter the behavior of existing oligopolistic industries. We saw in earlier chapters that these artificial barriers are both privately and publicly imposed. Vigorous enforcement of present antitrust law should be sufficient to remove private entry barriers. Deregulation in the airline industry, for example, is necessary in many cases to remove the governmentally sanctioned and imposed barriers. Removal of these barriers would cause market forces to introduce competitive pressure and this would not require the drastic action implied by courtroom interference and restructuring.

SUMMARY

1. Industries are defined by SIC codes which are prepared by the Department of Commerce. These SIC codes can be used to calculate concentration ratios, which are used to measure the degree to which markets are concentrated.

2. There is scientific disagreement on a number of important issues on the concentration trend in American industry. Some researchers have found the concentration level in American industry to be quite stable.

3. An important debate has emerged over the Market Concentration Doctrine. Many economists have long held that the structure of an industry determines its ultimate performance. If this is true, it would simply indicate that concentrated industries should be restructured. We find, however, that there is a good deal of debate concerning the degree to which concentration leads to higher profit rates and more rigid prices. Although most economists still accept the Market Concentration Doctrine, competing evidence warrants more study before we make policy decisions based on the doctrine.

4. Regulation of monopoly leads to cost-plus pricing, which destroys cost-minimizing incentives.

5. Taxation of monopoly is an alternative to regulation. It simply captures monopoly profit without affecting price or output.

6. U.S. antitrust law began with the Sherman Antitrust Act in 1890. The Sherman Act and succeeding laws have been applied with varying vigor and success.

7. The record of antitrust enforcement is not too impressive. Litigation takes a long time and rarely restores competition. Politics plays an important role in antitrust activity.

8. Reform of the antitrust laws has been proposed. This reform could have a significant impact on U.S. industry and, therefore, needs to be carefully studied.

NEW TERMS

industry studies
industrial organization
Standard Industrial Classification (SIC) system
concentration ratio
Market Concentration Doctrine
administered prices
marginal cost pricing
cost-plus pricing
fair rate of return
trusts
holding companies
robber barons
Social Darwinism

Sherman Antitrust Act
Clayton Act
tying contracts
Celler-Kefauver Antimerger Act
Federal Trade Commission Act
rule of reason
treble damages
National Recovery Administration (NRA)
shared monopoly
vertical merger
conglomerate merger
horizontal merger

QUESTIONS FOR DISCUSSION

1. Should profits be used as a measure of monopoly power? Should concentration be used as a measure of monopoly power? Discuss the wisdom of using either or both.

2. What would happen in a regulated industry if price were set so that the firm does not earn a normal rate of return?

3. If all prices in an industry are identical, is this evidence of an antitrust violation?

4. Do concentration ratios tell you anything about changes in conglomerate merger activity?

SUGGESTIONS FOR FURTHER READING

Blair, John M. *Economic Concentration: Structure, Behavior, & Public Policy*. New York: Harcourt Brace Jovanovich, 1972.

Caves, Richard. *American Industry: Structure, Conduct & Performance*, 3d ed. Englewood Cliffs, N.J.: Prentice-Hall, Inc., 1972.

Demsetz, Harold. *The Market Concentration Doctrine: An Examination of Evidence & a Discussion of Policy.* Washington: American Enterprise Institute for Public Policy Research, 1973.

MacAvoy, Paul W. (ed.). *Crisis of Regulatory Commissions.* New York: W. W. Norton and Co., Inc., 1970.

Scherer, Frederick M. *Industrial Pricing.* New York: Rand McNally & Co., 1970.

Sherman, Roger. *The Economics of Industry,* new ed. Boston: Little, Brown & Co., 1974.

Sherman, Roger, and Robert Tollison. "Public Policy Toward Oligopoly: Dissolution and Scale Economies." *Antitrust Law and Economics Review* (Summer, 1971).

PART 6

Factor Markets and Governmental Intervention

Learning Objectives

After studying the materials found in this chapter, you should be able to do the following:

1. Define:
   (a) product market.
   (b) factor market.

2. List and give examples of the three characteristics of the demand for a factor of production, including:
   (a) derived demand.
   (b) joint interdependence.
   (c) technologically determined demand.

3. Define and show the calculation necessary for:
   (a) marginal physical product.
   (b) value of the marginal physical product.
   (c) marginal revenue product.
   (d) marginal resource cost.

4. State the profit-maximizing rule for a firm hiring a resource in terms of *MRP* and *MRC*.

5. Use a factor market diagram including *VMP, MRP, D* (demand for the factor), *MRC,* and *S* (supply of the factor) to illustrate the differences when there is:
   (a) pure competition vs. monopoly in the product market.
   (b) pure competition vs. monopsony in the factor market.

6. Define monopsonistic exploitation in terms of a competitive wage vs. a monopsonistic wage.

7. List the factors which help explain the income of a resource owner.

8. Define:
   (a) economic rent.
   (b) single tax.
   (c) crowding out.

Factor Markets and the Distribution of Income

The distribution of income in a market economy depends on the prices of the factors of production and on the distribution of the ownership of the various factors. In most discussions, much more attention is given to the ultimate distribution of income than to the reasons for this distribution. This chapter discusses factor markets and explains why the distribution of income is what it is. In the next chapter, we will discuss action that can be taken if society doesn't like the distribution of income that is produced by the market process. The following discussion is a theoretical explanation of how incomes are determined in a market system. We will be examining marginal productivity theory, which was first put forward by John Bates Clark in a book entitled *The Distribution of Wealth* published in 1899. Actually, Clark was not the first to explain most of the ideas, but he was the first to put them down in a clear and consistent fashion. Clark made his mark at a very young age and to this day the American Economic Association presents the John Bates Clark Award to economists under the age of 40 who make significant contributions to economic theory.

John Bates Clark *(1847–1938)*

John Bates Clark was the first American-born economist to achieve an international reputation as an economic theorist. He was a reformer and activist who helped form the American Economic Association, later becoming its third president.

Clark was born and raised in Providence, Rhode Island. He graduated from Amherst College in 1872. He gave up the idea of divinity school and instead studied economics from 1872 to 1875 at the University of Heidelberg and the University of Zurich. Upon his return to the United States, Clark taught political economy at Carleton College and then moved to Smith College, Amherst, Johns Hopkins, and finally to Columbia, where he taught political science from 1895 to 1923. After 1911 he became very active in pacifist causes and was the first director of the Carnegie Endowment for International Peace.

Clark's interests in economic theory reflect the times in which he lived. The American Industrial Revolution caused Clark to examine problems of production and distribution. Clark overcame his normative, reformist tendencies and instead concentrated on developing a positive theory based on the competition of rational, self-interested people, as illustrated in his book *The Distribution of Wealth* (1899). This was a radical change from Clark's earlier work, *The Philosophy of Wealth* (1887), in which he attacked the "hedonistic" assumptions of the classical economists. His influence on later economists is in large part due to the analytical tools he developed.

John Bates Clark's status in the American economics profession is recognized in the awarding of a John Bates Clark Prize by the American Economics Association. Every two years this prize is awarded to an economist under the age of 40 who has made a significant contribution to economic theory. The list of winners reads like a *Who's Who* of the American economics profession.

THE DEMAND FOR FACTORS

The demand for factors is, of course, similar to other types of demand that we have studied. In previous chapters we discussed product markets, in which firms or individuals sell the goods and services they produce. We looked at markets in which producers sold to consumers. Now we want to examine factor markets, which are the markets in which firms buy factor inputs—the services of land, labor, and capital—from individuals who are supplying these factor inputs. We are, then, looking at markets in which individual owners of factors are selling services to producers. We can go far in understanding these factor markets by using the same tools we developed to study product markets. There are, however, some differences between factor markets and product markets, and we will concentrate on these differences.

derived demand   A demand that results from the demand for another product. For example, the demand for labor is derived from the demand for the good that the labor is producing.

The demand for a factor of production has three features that make it somewhat different from the demand for a product. The first is that it is a **derived demand.** A firm only demands labor because the labor can be used to produce goods which consumers are demanding. The demand for labor is thus derived from the demand for the product it produces. If there were no consumer demands for milk, there would be no demand for milkers, milking machines, or good dairy cattle grazing land. This holds true for all factors. They are only valuable to a firm if they help produce products that consumers value.

jointly interdependent demand The demand for a factor of production depends on the amount of other factors that the firm plans to use. The demand for a factor is thus interdependent with the demand for other factors of production.

The second feature of the demand for factors is that the demand is **jointly interdependent.** In other words, the amount of one factor that is demanded will depend on the amounts of other factors a firm plans to use. The amount of labor a firm demands depends on the amount of land and capital that will be used with the labor.

technologically determined demand The demand for a factor of production is determined by the techniques of production and the level of technology used.

The third major feature is that the demand for a factor is in part **technologically determined;** that is, the demand will depend on techniques of production and on technological progress. We speak in terms of a production function. The production function tells how much of one factor is needed to produce a certain level of output, given a certain technique of production and the other factors of production used. It is the job of the engineer to help the entrepreneur understand the substitutions that can be made within this production function.

marginal productivity theory A theory originally exposited by John Bates Clark which explains how the distribution of income comes about. Each factor is paid according to its contribution, or its marginal productivity.

You will see these basic elements unfold as we examine **marginal productivity theory.** As we proceed we shall follow John Bates Clark's precedent by developing the theory using labor as an example. The theory holds for all factors of production, but most interest centers on labor and the returns to labor. At the end of the chapter we shall discuss markets for factors other than labor.

THE DEMAND FOR LABOR

You remember that a demand curve graphically depicts the relationship between price and quantity demanded. A demand curve for labor will tell how much labor will be demanded at various wage rates. If we want to develop a theory about the market demand for labor, we start by finding how much labor a firm will employ at various wage rates. Then we aggregate the results across firms in a way very similar to the way we found the market demand for a product in Chapter 3.

The Demand for Labor Under Perfect
Competition in Product and Factor Markets

We shall begin by looking at a firm that is selling its product in a perfectly competitive product market and buying its labor in a perfectly competitive labor market. This means that the firm will take the price of its product *and* the price of labor as given. The firm views itself as having no effect on product prices or on wage rates. Next we need to determine the value of labor to the firm. Suppose the production function is such that, as we vary the amount of labor employed, *ceteris paribus,* the changes in the amount of total product initially become larger and larger but eventually become smaller and smaller. This demonstrates the principle of diminishing marginal productivity, which we discussed earlier when we looked at costs. As we employ more labor with fixed amounts of the other factors, the additional amounts of output per additional unit of labor eventually decline. If this were not the case, we could theoretically grow the entire world's supply of wheat on one acre of land just by employing more workers, and we could do this without having average costs rise. Suppose we hold constant the quantities of the other factors, land and capital, and determine how the firm's output is related to the quantity of labor it uses.

The amount of total physical product for a hypothetical firm is given in column 2 of Table 27-1. Note that this output depends on the technical relationship found in the production function. Once we know the total product, we can determine how much extra product is produced when labor inputs are added; i.e., the marginal physical product (MPP_L) of that unit of labor. It is the marginal physical product because the output is in physical units; e.g., number of autos, pounds of coal, and so on. We can now evaluate this change in physical output to see what it is worth to the firm. To put a value on the output, we simply multiply the amount of the product by the price the firm can sell it for. This produces what we call the *value of the marginal physical product of labor (VMP_L)*; it appears in column 6 of Table 27-1. The VMP_L is a measure of the value that

value of the marginal physical product (VMP)   The value of the marginal physical product is found by multiplying the marginal physical product by the price at which the firm can sell the product.

TABLE 27-1   THE DEMAND FOR LABOR IN PURELY COMPETITIVE PRODUCT MARKETS

(1) Units of Labor	(2) Total Physical Product	(3) Marginal Physical Product (MPP_L)	(4) Product Price	(5) Value of the Physical Product = Total Revenue	(6) Value of the Marginal Physical Product (VMP_L)	(7) Marginal Revenue Product (MRP_L)
1	10	10	$2	$20	$20	$20
2	18	8	2	36	16	16
3	24	6	2	48	12	12
4	28	4	2	56	8	8
5	30	2	2	60	4	4

marginal revenue product (MRP) The amount that an additional unit of the variable factor of production adds to a firm's total revenue.

each unit of labor adds to the firm's product. The ***marginal revenue product of labor* (MRP_L)** is the amount that each unit of labor adds to the firm's total revenue. It is found in column 7 of Table 27-1. You will note that in pure competition in the product market, the $VMP_L = MRP_L$. This is because the product price remains constant. The firm can produce and sell as much as it wants at the market-determined price, which is $2 in this example. In other words, when the firm faces a given price, marginal revenue is exactly equal to price, as we saw in the model of pure competition.

We can plot the VMP_L and the MRP_L on a graph, as in Figure 27-1. The MRP_L is the firm's demand curve for labor. The MRP_L shows the value of the unit of labor to the firm. It thus becomes the demand curve, because it shows how much labor the firm will purchase at various prices (wage rates). If we know the price of labor, we will be able to determine how much labor the firm will purchase. We began by assuming this firm was in a purely competitive factor market. This means the firm can purchase labor at the market wage with no effect on the wage. We see this in Figure 27-2. The market demand for labor (D_L) is the aggregate of all the individual firms' MRP_L curves, since each MRP_L curve indicates the amount of labor each particular firm will hire at any given wage rate. The market supply curve of labor (S_L) is the aggregate of all the individual supply curves, showing how much each worker is willing to work at different wage rates. The equilibrium price OP_W is the wage rate. The firm can now purchase as much labor as it wishes at OP_W. The supply curve the firm faces is thus perfectly elastic at OP_W. This is represented by S_f in Figure 27-2. If the supply curve the firm faces is perfectly elastic, the cost of each additional unit of labor is the same, or constant. We refer to the cost of each additional unit of a resource (in this case, labor) as the ***marginal resource cost* (MRC)**. For a firm in a perfectly competitive labor market, the marginal resource cost of labor, MRC_L, is the same as the labor supply curve. A profit-maximizing firm will employ or purchase a resource until $MRP = MRC$. This makes sense because if a factor adds more to revenue than

marginal resource cost (MRC) The cost of each additional unit of a productive resource.

FIGURE 27-1   THE DEMAND FOR LABOR IN PURELY COMPETITIVE PRODUCT MARKETS

The marginal revenue product of labor curve is the firm's demand curve for labor. When the firm's product market is purely competitive, the marginal revenue product and the value of the marginal product are identical.

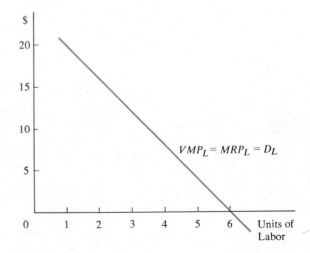

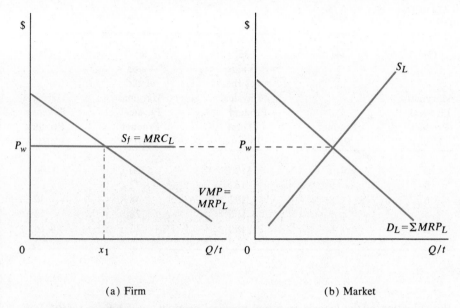

$
P_w \qquad \frac{S_f = MRC_L}{} \qquad\qquad P_w
$

S_L

$VMP = MRP_L$

$D_L = \Sigma MRP_L$

0   x_1 Q/t 0 Q/t

(a) Firm   (b) Market

**FIGURE 27-2   PERFECTLY COMPETITIVE LABOR
                MARKET**

The firm faces a perfectly elastic factor supply curve in a perfectly competitive labor market. If the supply curve is perfectly elastic, the marginal resource cost curve is also perfectly elastic. This means the firm can purchase as much labor as it wants at the market-determined wage rate.

to cost (if $MRP > MRC$), it would be profitable for the firm to purchase more units of the factor. However, if the factor adds more to cost than to revenue (if $MRP < MRC$), the firm should purchase fewer units. In our labor example, the firm will hire laborers until the amount they add to total cost (MRC_L) is exactly equal to the amount they add to revenue (MRP_L). In Figure 27-2, the firm would employ Ox_1 units of labor at wage rate OP_W. In terms of our numerical example in Table 27-1, the firm would employ four units of labor if the market wage was $8 per unit. If the market wage was $4 per unit, five units of labor would be employed.

*The Demand for Labor Under Monopoly in
Product Markets and Pure Competition in
Factor Markets*

We now want to change our example to make the assumption that the firm under consideration is a firm with monopoly power in product markets, rather than a firm selling its product in pure competition. This means that the product price will fall as the firm sells more units of its product. A numerical example is presented in Table 27-2. The difference between this and our first example is that product price (column 4) declines as the firm produces and sells more product. VMP_L and MRP_L are calculated in the same manner as before. VMP_L is simply

**TABLE 27-2   THE DEMAND FOR LABOR IN
MONOPOLISTIC PRODUCT MARKETS**

(1)	(2)	(3)	(4)	(5)	(6)	(7)
Units of Labor	Total Physical Product	Marginal Physical Product (MPP_L)	Product Price	Value of the Physical Product = Total Revenue	Value of the Marginal Physical Product (VMP_L)	Marginal Revenue Product (MRP_L)
1	10	10	$10	$100	$100	$100
2	18	8	9	162	72	62
3	24	6	8	192	48	30
4	28	4	7	196	28	4
5	30	2	6	180	12	−16

the valuation of the labor's marginal physical product, so $VMP_L = MPP_L \cdot P$ (column 3 times column 4). MRP_L is found by multiplying the MPP_L by marginal revenue. MRP_L is shown in column 7. Note that now $VMP_L > MRP_L$. This is because under monopoly, product price is greater than marginal revenue.

We have graphed both a VMP_L curve and an MRP_L curve in Figure 27-3. The MRP_L curve is again the firm's demand curve for labor. This firm, like the previous firm, will employ labor until $MRP_L = MRC_L$. Although the firm is selling its product in a monopolistic product market, it is purchasing labor in a competitive labor market. The firm is thus faced with the situation diagramed in Figure 27-4. The market demand curve is, as before, found by summing the MRP_L

**FIGURE 27-3   THE DEMAND FOR LABOR WITH
MONOPOLY IN PRODUCT MARKETS**

When the firm has monopoly power in the product market, the MRP_L curve will lie below the VMP_L curve. This is because under monopoly, product price is greater than marginal revenue.

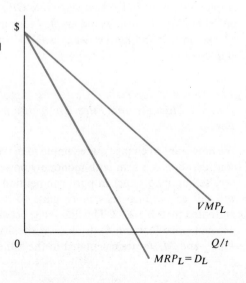

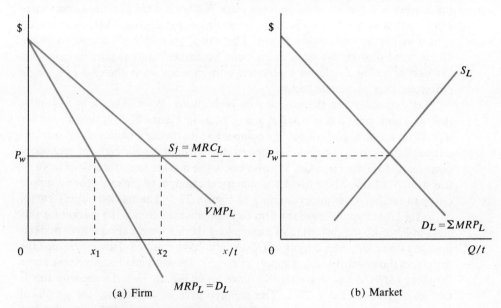

FIGURE 27-4 A MONOPOLISTIC FIRM FACING A PERFECTLY COMPETITIVE LABOR MARKET

A firm with monopoly power in product markets and in a perfectly competitive labor market will face a perfectly elastic supply curve. The firm will hire units of labor until the marginal revenue product of labor is equal to the marginal resource cost of labor.

curves for all firms purchasing this type of labor. The market supply (S_L) depends on individual desires of workers. The market-determined wage is OP_W. This firm can purchase as much labor as it desires at OP_W, so the supply curve facing it, S_f, is perfectly elastic at OP_W. Since S_f is perfectly elastic, MRC_L is also perfectly elastic. The firm maximizes profits where $MRC_L = MRP_L$, so the firm hires Ox_1 units of labor. You will note from Figure 27-4 that the monopolist pays OP_W, the market wage. The fact that $MRP_L < VMP_L$ does not mean the monopolist exploits labor by paying too little—the monopolist has to pay the market wage just like any other employer in this market. Instead, it means that the monopolist employs fewer laborers than similar competitive firms would employ. You remember from the chapter on pure monopoly that the monopolist restricts output to keep price high. The analog of this in the factor market is that the monopolist restricts inputs in order to restrict output. If this were a competitive firm rather than a monopolist, it would want to be on the VMP_L curve (which would then also be the MRP_L curve) and hire Ox_2 workers.

Monopsony

We have looked at competitive and monopolistic firms demanding labor in competitive labor markets, but now we want to consider the case where there is market power in the labor markets. We have assumed to this point that the

monopsony *The case of a single purchaser of a factor of production.*

purchasing firm had no effect on wage rates. But what if the firm does affect wage rates, so that as the firm hires more labor, the wage rate rises? We refer to such a firm as having **monopsony** power. The word "monopsony" comes from the Greek word *monopsonium,* meaning "one purchaser." Just as pure monopoly is the case of a single seller of a product, pure monopsony is the case of a single purchaser of a particular factor.

Let's consider first the case of pure monopsony. We will begin by assuming that we know what a firm's MRP_L curve is, as in Figure 27-5. It doesn't matter if this firm is selling its product in a competitive market or a monopolistic market, although it's hard to imagine a monopsonist without some degree of monopoly power in the product market. We also know the market supply curve of labor to this firm, S_L. Table 27-3 provides a numerical example of the monopsony supply curve to further your understanding of Figure 27-5. The market supply curve, S_L, is the labor supply curve the firm faces because the firm is the market for this class of labor by the definition of monopsony. If this were a competitive market, a wage rate of OP_C and output of OQ_C would have resulted. However, since the firm faces the upward-sloping supply curve, S_L, the marginal resource cost curve for labor (MRC_L) lies above the S_L curve, as in Figure 27-5. To see why this is the case, refer to Table 27-3. The supply curve is, of course, the graphical representation of columns 1 and 2. Since the curve is upward sloping, the firm must pay a higher wage rate as it hires more labor. This is different from a firm hiring in a competitive labor market. The total wage costs go up in this case for two reasons. First, costs rise because more labor is hired. Second, they rise because all laborers receive a higher wage as more workers are hired.

The amount that each additional unit hired adds to wage expenses is the marginal wage expense, or what we generally have been calling the marginal

FIGURE 27-5 MONOPSONY

The monopsony firm faces the market supply curve for labor. Since this curve has a positive slope, the marginal resource cost curve lies above it. The monopsonist thus hires OQ_m units of labor at a wage rate of OP_m.

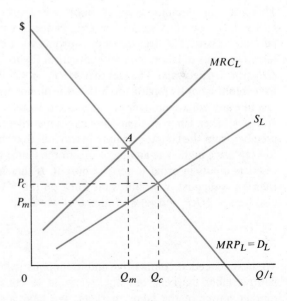

TABLE 27-3 MONOPSONY IN LABOR MARKETS

(1) Units of Labor	(2) Wage Rate	(3) Wage Expense	(4) Marginal Wage Expense (MRC_L)
1	$ 5	$ 5	$ 5
2	6	12	7
3	7	21	9
4	8	32	11
5	9	45	13
6	10	60	15
7	11	77	17
8	12	96	19
9	13	117	21
10	14	140	23

resource cost.[1] You can see by comparing columns 2 and 4 that the curve representing column 4 will lie above the supply curve, as shown in Figure 27-5. The firm, as before, maximizes profits where $MRP_L = MRC_L$. This would be at point A on Figure 27-5. So the firm employs OQ_m units of labor. But what is the wage rate? Remember the supply curve tells you what has to be paid to hire OQ_m units of labor. So the firm will pay OP_m. Note that $OP_m < OP_c$, so the monopsonist is paying a lower wage than would have been paid in a competitive labor market. We refer to this situation as **monopsonistic exploitation** because labor is receiving less than a competitive wage. This does not mean that workers are forced to work at wage rates below what they are willing to work for. Rather, the monopsonist simply restricts input as the monopolist restricts output.

monopsonistic exploitation The underpayment of wages due to monopsony power. Labor receives less than it would receive in competitive markets.

Monopsony in the Real World. Are there any real-world examples of pure labor monopsony? No, because all labor has some alternative employment. Pure monopsony, like pure monopoly, is a theoretical extreme. There are, however, real-world examples of monopsony power. You are probably familiar with the song about the miner who owes his soul to the company store. This song was written about mining companies and how they dominate as the major employer in certain areas. A large university in a small town would be a good example of monopsony power. If you compared university secretarial salaries for similar sized schools in different sized cities, hence varying the size of the labor pool, you would find that where the university dominates, the labor pool salaries would be lower. Why? Monopsony power, of course.

Perhaps the best example of monopsony in our present economy exists in professional sports. Congress has granted sports leagues exemptions from obeying the antitrust laws which we discussed earlier. This allows the leagues to hire as monopsonists by drafting and maintaining their control through reserve clauses.[2]

---

[1] Some other books call this the marginal factor cost.
[2] Reserve clauses have been and are being challenged. Players can now play out their options, thus reducing the monopsony power of the owners.

As a result, wage rates will be lower than if the teams competed for players on an open or at least freer market. Even when there were only two competing leagues, such as the NFL and AFL in football and the NBA and ABA in basketball, salaries were relatively much higher than they are now. A few of you may remember when Joe Namath signed for what seemed like an astronomical salary. A study of the economics of baseball found empirical evidence of this monopsonistic exploitation. Gerald Scully found the *MRP* of star pitchers in 1969 to be $405,300 and their salary to be only $66,800.[3] Think about the case of "Dr. J.," Julius Irving, the basketball player. He receives a very high salary, but consider what he adds to the league in terms of marginal revenue. He fills up the arena for practically every game he plays.[4] His salary is surely under his *MRP*.

Except for these special cases, where we have buyers of very specialized labor skills, there are few instances of significant monopsony power. In general, this is because transportation and communication in U.S. labor markets have increased labor mobility, and with increased labor mobility there is decreased monopsony power. If the miner is aware of job possibilities in other areas and in other jobs, the mine will be forced to pay a competitive wage. Indeed, if only a small percentage of miners are willing to pull up stakes, the mine will be forced to pay competitive wages. This is because we don't need complete labor mobility; it's enough to have mobility only at the margin.

Monopsony Power and Minimum Wages. We saw earlier that minimum wages are price floors set above the market clearing price and, as such, cause surpluses, or unemployment, in these markets. This is not correct 100 percent of the time because a minimum wage that is set in a monopsonistic market can cause employment to increase. Consider the monopsony market in Figure 27-6. The monopsonist would employ OQ_m units of labor at wage rate OP_m. Now suppose a minimum wage of OP_{m1} is imposed. A segment of the market supply curve is replaced by a horizontal line at OP_{m1}, the imposed minimum wage. In effect, the monopsonist is forced to accept the minimum wage. The market supply curve is now represented by the line $P_{m1} AS_L$. The marginal resource cost for labor is now $P_{m1} A$. This is because the supply curve is perfectly elastic in the range $P_{m1}A$. At a wage rate of OP_{m1}, OQ_{m1} would be employed. If the minimum wage selected is OP_{m2} instead of OP_{m1}, the supply curve the firm faces is $P_{m2} BS_L$. The firm would face perfectly elastic supply and *MRC* curves in the relevant range. The firm would in this case employ OQ_m units of labor at wage rate OP_{m2}. You can see that if the minimum wage that is imposed lies between OP_m and OP_{m2}, more employment at a higher wage rate will result.

What we have just analyzed is an exception to the case where minimum wages have antisocial effects. Be careful, though; this result only holds when there is monopsony power in the labor market, and monopsony is very hard to find except in certain very highly skilled situations, such as with basketball players.

---

[3]G. W. Scully, "Pay and Performance in Major League Baseball," *American Economic Review,* Vol. LXIV, No. 6 (December, 1974), pp. 915–930.

[4]Similarly, *Sports Illustrated* reported that the Milwaukee Bucks realized an additional $700,000 profit during Kareem Abdul-Jabbar's first season. His salary was $250,000. So you can see, Abdul-Jabbar's $MRP_L > MRC_L$.

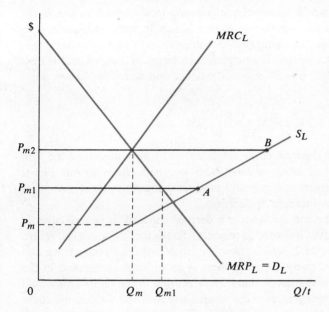

FIGURE 27-6   MONOPSONY POWER AND MINIMUM WAGES

A minimum wage of OP_{m2} in a monopsonistic labor market changes the market supply curve from S_L to $P_{m2}BS_L$. The marginal resource cost curve is the same as the supply curve along $P_{m2}B$, the perfectly elastic portion.

Most empirical studies of the effects of minimum wages show that the monopsony model is not important except as a special case in textbooks.[5]

MARKET COMBINATIONS

We have developed a set of combinations in product and factor markets that you can apply in considering market situations. There can be competition or monopoly in product markets and competition or monopsony in factor markets. The possibilities, when combined, are presented in Table 27-4. We could even expand this list by making further refinements. Just as oligopoly in the product market

TABLE 27-4   MARKET COMBINATIONS

Product Market	Factor Market
Competition	Competition
Competition	Monopsony
Monopoly	Competition
Monopoly	Monopsony

[5]See Jack Hirshleifer, *Price Theory and Applications* (Englewood Cliffs, N.J.: Prentice-Hall, Inc., 1976), pp. 374–377, for a review of these empirical studies.

oligopsony *The market situation in which there are few buyers of a factor of production.*

monopsonistic competition *The market situation that arises when there are relatively large numbers of buyers of a factor of production.*

can be viewed as real-world monopoly, *oligopsony* (few buyers) in the factor market can be viewed as real-world monopsony. Similarly, **monopsonistic competition** might be viewed as real-world perfect competition in factor markets. It is not clear that such an expansion is worthwhile in terms of insights, but it does allow you to complete the classification of product and factor markets.

CHANGES IN FACTOR DEMAND

We have developed the demand curve for labor and determined how the firm decides on the amount of labor to hire. Now we shall return to our earlier discussion of the differences in factor and product demands to determine what causes factor demand to increase or decrease.

We said that the demand for labor is a derived demand. It is derived from the demand for the product it is used to produce. To see this more clearly, return to Table 27-1 and Table 27-2, which show the situations for a competitive and monopolistic firm, respectively. Suppose there is an increase in demand in the product market, with the market demand curve shifting to the right. This would cause the product price to increase for the competitive firm and the demand curve to shift to the right for the monopolistic firm. The figures in column 4 in both tables would be larger. This would mean that the MRP_L for the competitive firm, column 7 in Table 27-1, would increase in proportion to the increase in product price. In most cases, this increase in demand would also cause the monopolist's MRP_L to increase compared to the figures shown in Table 27-2.[6] This would cause the MRP_L curve to shift outward for either kind of firm, representing an increase in the demand for labor. In a competitive labor market, this would result in each firm's wanting to hire more labor at the existing wage rate. This, in turn, would cause the market demand for labor to increase and thus would raise the wage rate. The amount by which the market wage increases will depend on how large this industry is relative to the labor market. If the industry is small, there may be only an imperceptible increase in wages; but if it is large, the wage rate could rise significantly. In a monopsonistic market, the result would be an increase in wages and an increase in employment.[7]

A second important feature of factor demand is that the demands for different factors are mutually interdependent. Refer again to Table 27-1 and Table 27-2. Suppose the capital stock of the firm is doubled. If labor and capital used together are complementary in the sense that an increase in capital makes labor more productive (and we assume they are), each unit of labor will now have a larger total physical product. This will show up in Table 27-1 and Table 27-2 as increases in the figures in column 2. This will cause the MPP_L to increase, which will cause the MRP_L to increase. What has happened is that the MRP_L curve has shifted outward, signifying that the demand for labor has increased. This is what is meant by complementarity; an increase in one factor raises the MRP of the other.

[6]We can create cases where the demand facing the monopolist increases at every price, but marginal revenue and hence marginal revenue product actually fall, so that the demand for labor falls.
[7]You should work through the geometry of such increases.

Increased productivity resulting from an increased capital stock can have several effects. Consider first what happens if the capital stock expands in one firm but has no industry-wide effects. This would cause the firm's demand curve (MRP_L) to increase (shift to the right) in Figures 27-2 and 27-4 without any (noticeable) effect on the aggregate demand curve because the firm is trivial in size relative to the industry. The result would be that the firm would employ more units of labor at the market-determined price. Alternatively, consider the effect of an industry-wide increase in the capital stock. All firms in the industry have an increase in capital, causing their MRP_L curves to increase. The aggregate curve also increases. The result is that more labor is employed at a higher wage rate. Such a situation is graphically depicted in Figure 27-7. Initially we are at equilibrium with the firm employing Ox_1 units of labor at the market wage of OP_w. The industry is employing OQ_1 units of labor. Now let's have an industry-wide increase in capital. The firm's MRP_L curve shifts to MRP_{L1}. Since all the firms in the industry have experienced this increase in MRP_L, the aggregate curve will also increase, as from D_L to D_{L1} in Figure 27-7. This causes the market wage to rise to OP_{w1}. As a result, the supply curve that the individual firm faces shifts from S_f to S_{f1}. The firm now will employ Ox_2 units of labor at wage rate OP_{w1}. Industry employment has risen from OQ_1 to OQ_2. The important point is that the response of the firm to more capital was to hire more workers at higher wages. This was because the increase in the stock of capital increased the marginal productivity of the workers. The demand for the factors, labor and capital, can thus be seen to be interdependent.

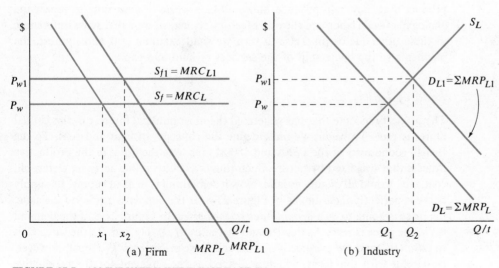

FIGURE 27-7   AN INDUSTRY-WIDE INCREASE IN CAPITAL

An increase in the capital stock will increase the productivity of labor if capital and labor are complementary factors. This increase in productivity will shift the marginal revenue product curve from MRP_L to MRP_{L1} and the market demand for labor from D_L to D_{L1}.

MARGINAL PRODUCTIVITY AND INCOME

This analysis has served to point up an important conclusion of marginal productivity theory. That is, in a competitive factor market, the productivity of the factor determines its price. In turn, the productivity depends on the inherent productive qualities of the factors and the quantity of the factor employed. Labor will receive higher wages the more productive it is. Since wages determine incomes of laborers, more productive laborers will have higher incomes. Laborers that are less productive will have lower incomes. John Bates Clark, the original expositor of this theory, held that it presented a morally correct outcome of economic activity. Whether or not it is morally correct is not the province of economic theory. Theory is positive and says nothing concerning whether the income distribution which results is a good one. Rather, the theory indicates that if markets for factors are competitive, factors will receive returns based on each factor's productivity. If we don't like the outcome, we can then work to change it through political markets (this will be discussed in a later chapter), but theory does indicate that output will be maximized in societies where factors are paid according to their marginal products.

OTHER FACTORS OF PRODUCTION

So far in this chapter we have used labor to illustrate the marginal productivity theory of factor markets. There are, of course, other factors of production which generate income for their owners. Most of the points we have made will hold for these other factors. Firms demand the services of land and capital because land and capital are productive, the demand being derived from the demand for the product that they help produce. It would be a waste of your time to repeat the analogy between labor and the other factors, so instead we will discuss differences in these other factor markets. In turn we shall examine rent and interest, the payments to the ownership of the services of land and capital.

Land and Rent

demand-determined price If supply is perfectly inelastic, the price is determined by changes in demand only.

The property income that has generated the most political interest in the United States is rent. To begin, we must define the concepts of land and rent. To the British economists of the 1700s and 1800s, *land* was the input in the productive process that was fixed by nature. Such things as cultivatable acreage, water, oil, coal, etc., would all qualify as land. Now if something is in fixed supply, its supply curve is perfectly inelastic, as in Figure 27-8. If the supply is perfectly inelastic, the price is going to be a *demand-determined price.* In Figure 27-8, if the demand is D_0, the price is zero. As the demand increases to D_1, D_2, and D_3, the price rises to OP_1, OP_2, and OP_3, respectively. We call these prices *rent.* We must, however, be careful with this term, which is defined as the payment for the productive services of the land. It is not the price of the land. The price of the land would be the capitalized value of the expected flow of these payments. Review the chapter on production and cost, if you have forgotten how to use interest rates to capitalize the value of a stream of payments.

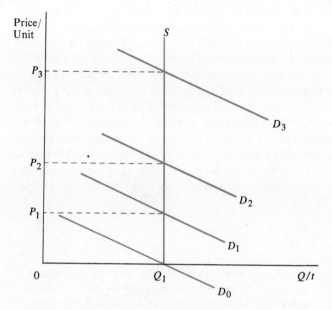

FIGURE 27-8   THE SUPPLY OF LAND

If the supply of land were perfectly inelastic, the price of land would be demand determined.

The idea of rent can be generalized to apply to any factor, and here is where students sometimes go wrong. *Economic rent* is technically a payment greater than the amount necessary to bring the factor into productive use. In other words, in Figure 27-8, all the payments to land are rent because the amount OQ_1 is fixed and the payments don't bring any more land into existence. This idea is distinct from the labor market supply curve in Figure 27-2, where higher wage rates increase the quantity of labor supplied, and the marginal workers entering the market do so only at the higher wage rate. The essential difference between labor and land in this regard is that humans have alternatives to work, such as leisure, which has utility.

The concept of economic rent is important because it is a surplus being paid to the owner of the factor of production. This surplus could be taken away with no change in economic activity. For example, suppose quarterback Ken Anderson's skills are such that he has only two work alternatives: being a bartender and earning $15,000 per year or being a quarterback and earning $500,000 per year. Under such circumstances, he is earning economic rent. If the two occupations are equally attractive to him, he could be paid $15,001 and he would remain a football player.[8] We could then tax away $484,999 of his salary and he would not change his behavior. An idea similar to this was suggested by Henry George as a way to raise money to conduct governmental activity.

In 1879 Henry George (1839–1897) wrote a book entitled *Progress and Poverty,* which suggested a *single tax* on land. George's book was widely read and he may even be the best known American economist of all time (if we measured

economic rent   A payment greater than the amount necessary to bring a factor into productive use.

single tax   A tax on land proposed by Henry George to capture the economic rent on land.

---

[8]Competition for players among NFL teams has kept Anderson's salary above $15,001.

this by the percentage of the population familiar with the book). George ran for mayor of New York City on the idea of his single tax and came very close to winning. He argued that the return to land was a *surplus* of unearned income and should be taxed away by the government. The proposal rested on two basic presumptions. First, the rent was unearned, and landowners were receiving the return simply because they held good land. If you think about this, it has political appeal. Why should someone get rich just because his or her grandfather happened to stake a claim on a piece of land that was located in a future population center? Second, the confiscation of this rent would not affect economic activity because the supply was perfectly inelastic. In other words, the tax wouldn't cause less land to be supplied, as an income tax causes less labor to be supplied. George became a social reformer and argued that this land tax should be the only tax that

Henry George *(1839–1897)*

Henry George may have been the most widely read economist of all time. George's book *Progress and Poverty* (1879) was a best seller—it sold millions of copies. If measured by sales as a percentage of the population, George's book would be the most popular economics book of all time.

Henry George was born in Philadelphia in a lower middle-class environment. He had almost no formal education and went to sea at age 14. He ended up in San Francisco and became a journalist. His interests in

political economy were fueled by his experiences as a journalist. In California, George ran for the legislature but was defeated, in large part because of his strong opposition to state subsidies for railroads.

During this period, George was a devoted reader, and he turned his hand to writing books that combined economics and social commentary. Between 1870 and 1886 he published numerous books and articles, but *Progress and Poverty* brought him international fame. In it, George argued for a single tax on land because landowners contributed nothing to the productivity of the land. Rising land values were explained by general economic growth and westward expansion. George's single tax rested on the proposition that such a tax would not change the allocation of the land and, more importantly, that it was inequitable for landowners to get rich while nonlandowners remained poor. George argued that there was no reason that landowners should get rich by the simple economics of increased demand brought about by the westward expansion of the U.S. population. The increasing value of the land, George argued, was in no way determined or affected by the owners of the land. In this sense, George was arguing that the rising value of land was a "windfall" profit, much in the same way that President Carter argued that deregulation of oil creates "windfall" profits for holders of oil reserves.

George's book and his idea of a single tax made him immensely popular. In 1886 he re-entered politics. This time he ran as the Labor and Socialist parties' candidate for mayor of New York City. George was so popular that it took a major coalition of other parties to defeat him. He ran again in 1897, but died during the campaign.

government collects. His followers became known as the single taxers and some of them are still active today.

The single tax movement died for political reasons (landowners are a strong political force), but also because of some severe theoretical problems. First, one could argue with the proposition that the quantity of land is fixed. Remember, when we draw a demand or a supply curve, we hold quality constant. It is therefore arguable that land can be improved in the quality dimension, thus increasing the quantity of land of a particular quality. Anyone who has seen agriculture in the Arizona or California deserts can attest to this fact. Increasing payments for land causes more land to be irrigated and increases the quantity supplied. If the return to land were taxed away, this incentive to improve land would be gone. Similarly, swamps can be drained and land can be reclaimed from the sea with dikes, as in the Netherlands. For example, several years ago there was a proposal to build a new airport near downtown Chicago. The idea was to build a dike in Lake Michigan, pump out the water, and build an airport at the bottom of the lake. Such projects would not even be contemplated if George's tax were operative.

Secondly, and even more fundamentally, rents serve a very important function even if they don't influence the quantity of land in existence. George argued that the rent the landowner receives plays no part in creating incentives for landowners to supply land. But the other side of the transaction is different. The payment made by the user of the land (the firm) rations the land between competing uses and insures that the land is put to its highest valued economic use. For example, suppose there is a choice acre of vacant land near your school. What should this land be used for—a McDonald's, a massage parlor, a church, or a dump? In a market system the decision will be determined by who is willing to pay the most. In other words, the market rations between competing uses for the land. If payments are not made, a universal planning system would have to be implemented to determine allocation among competing uses of the land.[9]

Thirdly, and perhaps most importantly, if government taxes rents, people will be discouraged from trying to earn them. The quest for these rents, however, is an important economic activity.

Capital and Interest

Firms demand capital because it is productive. We could derive a marginal revenue product curve for capital just as we did for labor. Such a curve is drawn in Figure 27-9. One difference you will note is that the demand for capital is expressed in dollars. It is important to realize that the demand for capital is not a demand for money itself, but rather a demand for physical capital. A demand for money can be used as a proxy, however, because the money is used to purchase the physical capital. In other words, money itself is not productive; the physical capital is productive.

The price of money is the interest rate. Figure 27-9 tells us that at lower rates of interest there will be higher rates of capital formation by firms. You can see

---

[9]The perceptive reader will note that zoning commissions in part play this role in a mixed economy, and to the extent that they don't allow the most economic use of a piece of land, they are taxing the owner's right to the income from that land.

FIGURE 27-9   THE DEMAND FOR CAPITAL

The marginal revenue product curve for capital is the firm's demand curve for capital.

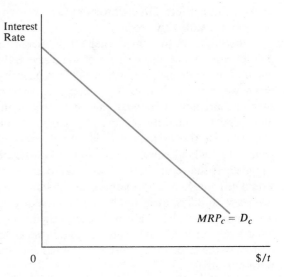

this more clearly by examining Figure 27-10, which shows the market and firm. The market we are talking about is often referred to as the market for loanable funds. The supply of loanable funds comes out of business and personal savings. Firms save out of profits in order to reinvest and individuals save in order to consume more in future periods. At higher interest rates people will save more because the present foregone consumption will allow greater consumption in the

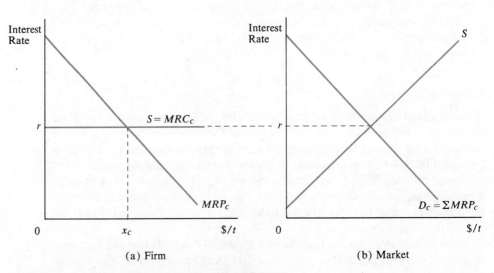

(a) Firm   (b) Market

FIGURE 27-10   THE MARKET FOR LOANABLE FUNDS

The supply of capital to the firm is perfectly elastic at the interest rate set in the market for loanable funds. The firm then invests in capital until the marginal revenue product of capital is equal to the market rate of interest.

future. As a result, we get a normal upward-sloping supply curve. In Figure 27-10, the market demand for capital is the summation of all the individual firm demand curves which are, of course, the marginal revenue product curves for capital. We then get a market rate of interest, Or, which determines, in a competitive capital market, the supply of capital available to a firm. The supply to the firm is perfectly elastic at the market rate of interest, which makes the marginal resource cost curve perfectly elastic. We can then determine the amount of capital formation for the firm, which in this case is Ox_c.

The interest rate allocates loanable funds among competing firms and among competing uses exactly as the wage rate allocates labor services. If we expand on this idea a little we can see why some economists are so concerned with the federal deficit. Consider the fact that there are more than just business firms demanding loanable funds. There are two other important groups in this market for loanable funds. Consumers demand loanable funds to finance the portion of their consumption based on credit. They borrow to buy homes, furniture, automobiles, and more. The other demander of loanable funds is the government. At all levels, federal, state, or local, governments borrow loanable funds. The market for loanable funds is therefore composed of three important segments which might be represented as in Figure 27-11. The market for loanable funds is represented by a supply of S_L and a demand of D_L, which is the summation of the household demand for loanable funds, the business demand for loanable funds, and the governmental demand for loanable funds. The resulting interest rate is Or and a representative firm adds Ox units of capital to its capital stock.

What happens, *ceteris paribus*, when the government increases its borrowing? Government demand increases. This causes aggregate demand to increase to D_{L1},

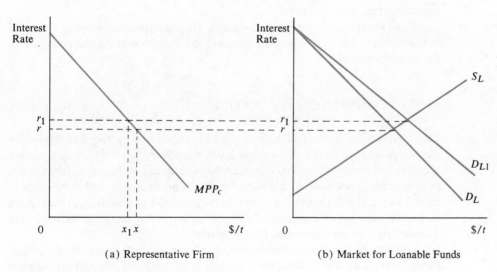

(a) Representative Firm   (b) Market for Loanable Funds

FIGURE 27-11 CROWDING OUT

The market demand for loanable funds is composed of household, business, and governmental demand for funds. An increase in governmental borrowing will cause the market rate of interest to rise. The firm's response to this increased price of capital is to decrease the quantity demanded. We then say firms have been crowded out of capital markets.

which causes the interest rate to rise to Or_1. This means that the supply curve to the firm has shifted up by the amount of the increase from Or to Or_1. The net result is that the firm will decrease its investment from Ox to Ox_1. The government has crowded business (and households) out of capital markets. Interest rates allocate funds among the three uses, and when the government bids them up, households and business will get fewer of these funds.

crowding out   The increased demand for loanable funds by government causes the interest rate to rise; this attracts funds away from business investment, thus crowding out business investment.

Several political and business leaders, perhaps most notably William Simon, former secretary of the treasury, are very worried about such *crowding out.* Simon believes this crowding out is a very real burden of the federal deficit. He argues that the large amounts of borrowing cause the government to bid up the interest rate and compete investment funds away from business. When this happens, business does not grow as much as it would have and the productivity of the economy suffers. Remember the preceding discussion of how increases in the capital stock raise the overall demand for labor. Crowding out would have the effect of keeping the demand for labor from growing as fast as it would have and as a result holds down the wages of workers.

Entrepreneurship and Profits

Profits are a residual. They are what's left for the entrepreneur after the land, labor, and capital have been paid. This is not to say that profits are not important; indeed, as we saw earlier, the quest for profits makes them the prime mover of a market economy. If profits above normal levels are earned, this will be the signal for firms to enter the industry, and if below normal profits are earned, firms will leave the industry. In addition, potential profits are keys to innovative activity and risk taking. The entrepreneur takes chances, and bets on the future because of potential profits. Henry Ford installed the assembly line because he thought it would increase efficiency and lead to higher profits. He was profit motivated and this drove him to be innovative.

Thus, profits play a very important role. They are first and foremost the signal of the market system. Profits also generate the incentive to innovate and strive for greater efficiency.

THE DISTRIBUTION OF INCOME

This chapter has developed a theory which explains why the distribution of income is what it is. At its simplest level, the theory says that, given private property and competitive market conditions, a certain distribution of income will be produced. Labor will be paid according to its productivity, and the owners of capital and land will receive payments according to the productivity of the factors they own. Any event that causes the productivity of a factor to increase will increase the remuneration that factor receives.

distributive justice   Arguments for a fair distribution of income. These are normative arguments for a particular distribution of income.

This theory has received much criticism since it was first exposited by John Bates Clark, who was looking for a natural law to explain how the distribution of income was determined. The criticisms of the theory have almost all been on the grounds of *distributive justice.* Critics argue that such a market system of income distribution is unfair because the old, the sick, the young, and the blind, among others, will not receive a fair share since they are not productive or as productive as others. Another normative criticism of the theory rests on the premise that economic productivity, rather than social productivity, determines remuneration. A writer of pornographic novels earns more than a writer of poetry and some critics say this is also not fair. You should recognize such criticisms for what they are: normative, ethical considerations, and not valid criticisms of the theory. Think back to our early discussion of the role of theory. A theory that is valuable provides a good explanation of some aspect of the real world. According to this test, marginal productivity theory stands up quite well.[10]

SUMMARY

1. The demand for a factor of production is a derived demand. It is determined by the amount of other factors used, as well as technology.

2. A firm demands labor because it is productive. The marginal revenue product curve is the firm's demand curve for labor.

3. In a competitive labor market, the firm faces a perfectly elastic supply curve. When the supply curve is perfectly elastic, the marginal resource cost curve and the supply curve are also perfectly elastic.

4. A monopoly firm in product markets uses less labor than a competitive industry would use. This results because the firm naturally restricts inputs in the process of restricting output.

5. A monopsony is the single purchaser of an input. Monopsony results in fewer units of labor being purchased at less than the perfectly competitive wage. Because the monopsonistic wage is below a competitive wage, we refer to the difference as monopsonistic exploitation. Improved market information and mobility of workers greatly reduce monopsony power.

6. Land is the factor of production that is in fixed supply. Rent is the return to this fixed factor. Economic rent is a payment above the amount necessary to attract an input.

7. Henry George proposed a single tax on land. One important economic difficulty with this proposal is that if rents aren't paid, a planning authority would have to decide among competing uses of the land.

8. Capital, like the other factors, is demanded by firms because it is productive. The payment to capital is interest. As interest rates rise, the quantity of capital that the firm demands will decrease.

9. In cases where the increase in the interest rate is a result of government action, we say that crowding out is taking place in capital markets.

10. Profits are a residual that entrepreneurs receive. In a market economy profits serve as the signal for firms to either enter or leave a particular industry.

11. Marginal productivity theory explains how the distribution of income is determined in a market economy. It says nothing about the normative appropriateness of this distribution.

NEW TERMS

derived demand
jointly interdependent demand

technologically determined demand
marginal productivity theory

---

[10]For a review of empirical studies, see David Kamerschen, "A Reaffirmation of the Marginal Productivity Theory," *Rivista Internazionale Di Scienze Economiche E. Commerciali* (March, 1973).

value of the marginal physical product *(VMP)*

marginal revenue product *(MRP)*

marginal resource cost *(MRC)*

monopsony

monopsonistic exploitation

oligopsony

monopsonistic competition

demand-determined price

economic rent

single tax

crowding out

distributive justice

QUESTIONS FOR DISCUSSION

1. What is economic rent? Have you ever earned economic rent? Would taxation of this rent have caused you to behave differently?

2. Can you think about what might constitute monopsonistic exploitation? What would you recommend as a correction?

3. The demand for accountants has skyrocketed in recent years and the salaries of accountants have increased significantly. Is the demand for accountants a derived demand? If so, from what?

4. Why are professional athletes against reserve clauses?

5. What does it mean to say profits are a residual?

6. Is there any similarity between the concept of economic rent and economic profit?

SUGGESTIONS FOR FURTHER READING

Kamerschen, David R., and Lloyd M. Valentine. *Intermediate Microeconomic Theory,* 2d ed. Cincinnati: South-Western Publishing Co., 1981, Chapters 17, 18, and 19.

Neale, Walter C. "The Peculiar Economics of Professional Sports"; and Simon Rothenberg, "The Baseball Players' Labor Market." Both in *The Daily Economist,* edited by Harvey G. Johnson and Burton A. Weisbrod. Englewood Cliffs, N.J.: Prentice-Hall, Inc., 1973.

Stigler, George J. *The Theory of Price.* New York: Macmillan Co., 1966, Chapters 15, 16, and 17.

CHAPTER 28

The Labor Movement

Learning Objectives

After studying the materials found in this chapter, you should
be able to do the following:

1. List the economic goals of unions and the ways these
   goals might be achieved.

2. Define:
   (a) exclusive union.
   (b) inclusive union.
   (c) featherbedding.
   (d) bilateral monopoly.
   (e) yellow-dog contract.
   (f) secondary boycott.
   (g) closed shop.
   (h) mediation.
   (i) arbitration.
   (j) union shop.

3. Diagram and analyze the economic effects of:
   (a) an exclusive union.
   (b) an inclusive union.
   (c) bilateral monopoly.

4. List the major laws, organizations, dates, and leaders in
   the history of the labor movement.

After looking at factor markets in theory, we can now examine the effect that
unions have on the factor market for labor. Unions in general have goals that are
political as well as economic. American unions have concentrated on economic
goals and have pursued objectives such as good salaries, job security, good pen-
sions, and, of course, good jobs for union leaders. The most important goal has
been to raise wages, and we will concentrate on the effects unions have had on
the wage rate. We will begin with a theoretical look at unions to determine how
they attempt to raise wages. We will then look at the empirical evidence of the
success of unions in raising wages and discuss at whose expense these increased
wages have come. Then we will take a look at the history of the labor movement
in the United States.

THE ECONOMICS OF UNION GOALS

Unions have been formed for all sorts of reasons, many of which are social and political as well as economic. As we shall see later in this chapter, the only lasting American labor unions are those that have concentrated on economic goals. When we speak of economic goals, the bottom line, of course, is the real income of union members. It is largely correct, though oversimplified, to think of unions as existing to increase the wages of their members. Unions, of course, do pursue goals other than wage maximization. Unions have worked for shorter hours and better working conditions, to mention just two goals. These other goals all have the effect, *ceteris paribus,* of increasing the income of workers. If wages are unchanged and working conditions have improved, the worker has received an increase in real income. In order to increase wage rates in a competitive labor market, such as those shown in Figures 28-1 and 28-2, the union must do one of two things. It must either increase the demand for labor (such as to D_{L1} in Figure 28-1) or decrease the supply of labor (such as to S_U in Figure 28-2).

Increasing the demand for labor is very difficult for the union. Remember that D_{L1} in Figure 28-1 depends both on the demand for the product the labor produces and on the productivity of the labor. If the union is to increase the demand for labor, it must increase the demand for the product the firm produces. There have been some attempts at this. Unions have run programs to influence people to "buy union-made" and to decrease imports, thus attempting to increase the demand for domestically produced (union) products. Unions have encouraged educational training programs aimed at increasing productivity and thus increasing demand. The unions have also tried to get government to help by buying union-made goods and also by using macro policy. All things considered,

FIGURE 28-1   UNION GOAL—INCREASE DEMAND FOR UNION LABOR

One way in which a union can raise its members' wages above competitive levels is to increase the demand for union labor. An increase in demand from D_L to D_{L1} would increase wages from OP_c to OP_u. This increase in demand causes employment to increase.

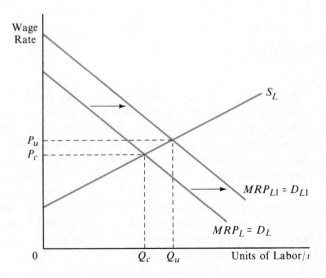

however, it is very difficult for unions to increase the demand for labor. In some instances, unions have been successful in forestalling the elimination of jobs in declining or dying industries. A good example of this is the practice of **featherbedding,** or insisting on required jobs that management claims are unnecessary. A good example of featherbedding is the case of railroad firemen. The advent of diesel and electric power made the fireman obsolete, but unions were successful in maintaining the job. However, even this type of activity may be of only short-run benefit because it speeds the decline of an already dying industry and ultimately weakens the union.

featherbedding The maintenance of jobs that management claims are unnecessary or redundant. Unions often insist on featherbedding in industries that are declining.

The conclusion is that, because of the difficulties of changing demand, unions should work on the supply side of the market, attempting to shift the supply curve, such as from S_L to S_U in Figure 28-2. Historically, many of the "social goals" of unions also have had the effect of restricting the supply of labor. Unions have sought to reduce immigration, limit child labor, encourage compulsory and early retirement, and enforce a shorter workweek. Whatever else you may think of these goals, they all make economic sense for unions if the goal is to increase the union wage rate.

Regardless of whether a union works on demand (Figure 28-1) or supply (Figure 28-2), it has the same effect on wages. In both cases successful union activity will cause the wage rate to rise. The effect on employment is, however, quite different. An attempt to increase demand, as shown in Figure 28-1, will cause employment in the industry to rise. If, however, the union tries to decrease supply, as in Figure 28-2, employment in the industry will decline. Since unions are much more effective at reducing supply than at increasing demand, the first economic implication of unions is that they probably reduce employment in those markets which they successfully organize.

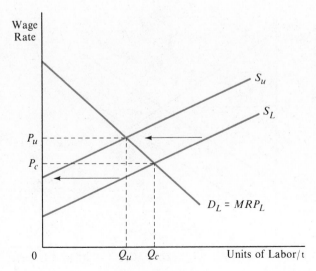

FIGURE 28-2 UNION GOAL—DECREASE SUPPLY OF LABOR

One way in which a union can raise its members' wages above competitive levels is to decrease the supply of labor. A decrease in the labor supply from S_L to S_u will cause wages to rise from OP_c to OP_u. This decrease in supply causes employment to decrease.

TYPES OF UNIONS

exclusive union A union that restricts supply and maintains a higher than competitive wage by excluding workers from the profession. Craft unions are exclusive unions.

In examining unions from a theoretical point of view, we can reduce the different kinds of unions to two basic types, *exclusive* and *inclusive*. An **exclusive union** derives its economic power from the fact that it excludes workers from the work force. Because of this exclusion, the wage rate is higher than it would be in the absence of the union organization. Figure 28-3 represents such a union. Supply curve S_c represents the competitive supply of labor and D_L represents the demand for labor. In the absence of any union organization, the wage rate would be OP_c, and OQ_c units of labor would be employed. The exclusive union attempts to exclude workers from the industry and thus shift the supply curve to S_u. If the union were to succeed in doing this, the wage rate for union workers would be OP_u and the number of labor units hired would be OQ_u.

craft unions Unions composed of skilled workers, such as plumbers and carpenters.

The key, then, to an exclusive union is that it restricts entry into the profession. Examples of exclusive unions are **craft unions,** which are unions composed of skilled laborers such as plumbers and physicians. These unions are very often the type in which workers serve apprenticeships and internships in order to become members.

It should be obvious that a successful exclusive union is very powerful because the wage rate increase results directly from the exclusionary tactics. The union doesn't need to bargain, coerce, or threaten to strike. Its power to exclude competing workers is sufficient to cause the market wage to increase. The power of the union is difficult to challenge once the exclusion has been established.

It is difficult to exclude workers from the union. When wages rise, there will be pressure from other workers to seek employment in these trades. This is a natural economic force and makes it necessary for the union to be able to control

FIGURE 28-3 AN EXCLUSIVE UNION

In an exclusive union, union membership is a precondition for employment. As a result, the union can exclude membership and decrease the supply of labor.

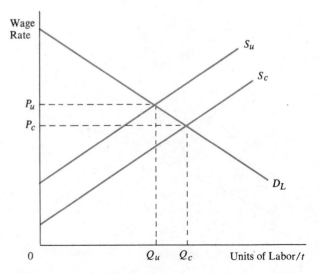

licensure. In particular, many successful exclusive unions find it easier if they can get the government to help them exclude by requiring a worker to earn a license or permit to be a member of the trade. If the union can then gain control of this licensing function, it has an automatic way of excluding labor. This is one way in which plumbers, electricians, and medical doctors have maintained their union power.

The *inclusive union* attempts to organize all the workers in a particular industry. These inclusive unions are sometimes referred to as *industrial unions* and are represented by such unions as the Steelworkers, the Autoworkers, and the Teamsters. The goal of the inclusive union is to bring all workers in an industry into union membership and, as a result, present a strong bargaining position to management. Additionally, it is important that an industrial union organize all workers in that industry, or the nonunionized firms will be at a cost advantage and able to undersell union-organized firms. This will create incentive for unionized firms to try to break the union. As a result, such union organization has been most successful in oligopolistic markets where there are fewer firms in which the labor needs to be organized.

The inclusive union is represented by Figure 28-4. The competitive wage and employment are OP_c and OQ_c, respectively. The union organizes the industry and bargains a wage, OP_u. OP_u is in effect, then, a minimum wage in this industry and employment will be OQ_u. It should be clear that the ability of the inclusive union to raise wages depends on the strength of its bargaining stance, which will, of course, depend on its membership in the particular industry. It is important that an inclusive union have a significant membership in the particular industry in which it operates because its success depends on its ability to threaten the firms in that industry.

inclusive union   A union that attempts to organize all the workers in an industry and maintain a strong bargaining position vis-à-vis management.

industrial unions   Inclusive unions such as the Steelworkers, Autoworkers, and Teamsters which gain power by organizing all (or a large share) of the workers in an industry.

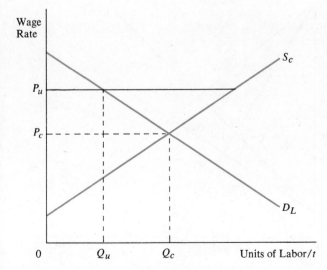

FIGURE 28-4   AN INCLUSIVE UNION
In an inclusive union the union attempts to organize all labor in the industry and then to bargain a wage. This bargained wage then works like a price floor (or minimum wage) in this labor market.

Bilateral Monopoly

bilateral monopoly   Monopolies dealing with each other as buyers and sellers, such as when a monopoly labor union sells labor to a monopsonistic firm.

The inclusive union has been most successful in industries which are very concentrated. The firms in these industries may possess monopsony power in labor markets. What we want to analyze here is a monopoly union selling to a monopsonistic purchaser of labor. Economists call this **bilateral monopoly.** The situation is depicted in Figure 28-5. In the absence of the union, the monopsony firm would employ OQ_f units of labor at a wage rate of OP_f. The competitive wage and employment would have been OP_c and OQ_c. In the absence of monopsony power on the part of the purchaser, the union will press for a wage of OP_L. This is because the monopoly union faces a demand curve for its product (labor supply) of D_L. The marginal revenue of the union is thus represented by MR. The union maximizes where MR is equal to MC or at a wage rate of OP_u and employment level of OQ_u. The result of this process is logically indeterminate; that is, the model will not theoretically explain what the resulting wage will be. All we can say is that the wage will be between OP_f and OP_u. Whether it is closer to OP_f or to OP_u depends on the relative bargaining strengths of the union and the monopsony firm. You should note that if the wage is anywhere between OP_m and OP_f, employment will rise from OP_f with unionization. If, for example, the union is successful in bargaining a wage rate of OQ_c (the competitive rate), employment would rise to OQ_c. You will note that this result is very similar to the effect of a minimum wage in a monopsonistic market, which was discussed in the last chapter.

FIGURE 28-5   BILATERAL MONOPOLY

In bilateral monopoly, a monopolistic seller, the union, sells labor to a monopsony firm. The wage rate will be logically indeterminate, depending on the relative bargaining strengths of the two participants.

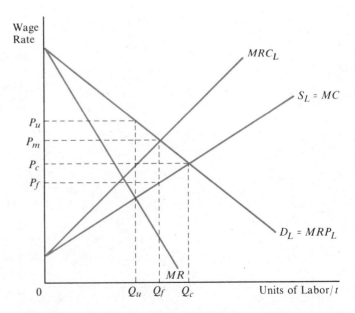

Do Unions Raise Wages?

Regardless of the power of a union, there will be constraints on the degree to which it can influence wages. There will always be competitive pressure from other labor inputs and substitution of other factor inputs for labor inputs. A good example would be a union organizing migrant workers. To compete with the union, the farmer substitutes machinery for labor. A second powerful constraint exists in the product market. If unions raise wages, costs and prices rise. Consumers will react to the increased price and will shift consumption to nonunion products; the demand for union-made products and thus for union labor will then fall. These constraints are always present, and the union can do very little to offset them.

The question at hand, however, is, How successful have unions been in increasing the wages of their members? The path-breaking empirical study in this area was done by Professor H. Gregg Lewis, then of the University of Chicago and now of Duke University. He found that union workers with similar productivity characteristics received on average from 10 to 15 percent higher wages than nonunion workers.[1] The difficulty in this type of research is to separate wage differences based on productivity differences from those based solely on union power. Lewis based his study on data from the 1940s and 1950s. Later studies using Lewis's techniques and more recent data indicate that union salaries are 15 to 25 percent higher for similar productivity characteristics.[2] These same studies indicate that craft unions are more successful in raising wages than are inclusive unions.

If this is true, and most economists would agree with these results, where do these higher wages come from? Your first reaction may be that they come out of business profits, but can this be so? Let's reflect back on the theory we have developed in earlier chapters. Wages are a cost of production. If markets are characterized by competition (pure or monopolistic), the increased cost will result in higher prices because in the long run, with or without unions, the average firm will only be earning normal profits. If the firm possesses some monopoly power, the higher labor costs might reduce profits, but the increased costs will in part be passed forward in higher prices. Additionally, regardless of the firm's market structure, the increased costs of union-made products will cause the quantity demanded of their output to decrease (be less than it would have been without a union). The net result is that there are now more nonunion workers, and wage rates will fall in the nonunion work sector. The supply of nonunion workers increases as the supply of union workers decreases. This analysis indicates that the increased wages of union workers are paid by consumers in terms of higher prices for union-made goods *and* by nonunion workers in terms of lower salaries. Again, Professor Lewis has done empirical research in this area, and concludes that nonunion salaries are 3 to 4 percent lower because of union-increased wages in the organized labor sector.[3]

---

[1]H. Gregg Lewis, *Unionism and Relative Wages in the United States* (Chicago: University of Chicago Press, 1963).
[2]See M. J. Boskin, "Unions and Relative Real Wages," *American Economic Review* (June, 1972); and P. M. Ryscavage, "Measuring Union-Nonunion Earnings Differences," *Monthly Labor Review* (December, 1974).
[3]H. Gregg Lewis, *op. cit.*

Do Unions Cause Inflation?

We have just seen that unions cause wages to be higher in unionized industries and lower in the nonunion sector. We also saw that unions cause prices to be higher in unionized industries. But do unions cause inflation? The answer is *no!* Of course, unions bargain for higher wages and businesses raise prices in inflationary times, but these are responses to the inflation, not causes of the inflation. In fact, the empirical evidence indicates that union wages rise less rapidly during the early part of an inflation than do nonunion wages.[4] This is because the unions are unaware in the early part of the inflation of how high the inflation will be and commit themselves to long-term contracts with wage increases less than the inflation rate. When these contracts expire, the unions try to make up for the inflation in their wage demands, and it sometimes appears as if they are responsible for the inflation, rather than the victims of it who are only trying to catch up.

There are some indirect ways in which union activity can be inflationary. If unions are successful in raising wages above competitive levels in their sector of the economy, less employment in this sector results. If this unemployed labor is unable to find employment in the nonunion sector, unemployment rates will rise. If macro policymakers (the president and Congress) pursue an expansionary monetary and fiscal policy to reduce the unemployment rate, inflation might result. In this sense, then, unions place an inflationary bias on macro policy. A second way unions might have an inflationary influence is if they are successful in raising wages faster than productivity increases. Since real income levels can only increase if productivity increases, the increased wage rates will be dissipated in inflationary pressure.

Keep in mind, though, that unions and businesses do not cause inflation—government policymakers cause inflation through expansionary monetary and fiscal policy. These policymakers may blame unions and businesses, but don't be tricked. It is probably good politics for the president, his advisers, and Congress to try to shift the blame for inflation to businesses and unions, but this is not the case.

A SHORT HISTORY OF THE LABOR MOVEMENT

In the early 1900s the U.S. economy was shifting rapidly from a largely agrarian society to an industrial society. By 1910, employment in industry exceeded employment in agriculture. This industrial labor force grew rapidly, and labor organizers attempted to capitalize on this growth. In 1914, about 7 percent of the work force was unionized. Growth in the labor force and growth in unionization were accompanied by a rapidly rising real wage rate. The real wage rate advancement was largely attributable to rapid growth in technology and in the human capital of the wage earner. This was reflected in the fact that both union and nonunion labor made substantial wage advances during this period.

---

[4]See Albert Rees, "Do Unions Cause Inflation?" *The Journal of Law and Economics* (October, 1959).

The Early Unsuccessful Years

To better understand the labor movement in the United States, it is worthwhile to view it in its historical perspective. In the early 1800s, the labor movement was unsuccessful in organizing significant numbers of workers and was limited to eastern cities in the United States. During this period, the work day changed from the sunup to sundown situation to, for the most part, a 10-hour day. Interestingly, workers still spent 12 hours on the job, but received two 1-hour (mid-morning and mid-afternoon) breaks.

It became apparent by the mid-1800s that a national effort was necessary if unions were to be successful. This was because the transportation network was developing so successfully that local or regional gains by any union would be dissipated by competitive pressures from other geographic areas. In other words, if labor could successfully raise wages above free market equilibrium wage rates in any area, these gains would be short term, because labor from other regions of the country would produce cheaper goods that could be shipped via the rapidly growing, low-cost transportation network. The U.S. Constitution forbids any interference with interstate commerce, so regions or states could not place tariffs on the goods from other regions or states. This meant that all labor in the firms of a particular industry had to be organized if organization was to be successful.

The first successful attempt at organizing a national union was made by William H. Sylvis. Sylvis had been treasurer of the short-lived Iron Molders International Union and in 1867 founded the *National Labor Union.* The National Labor Union was deeply involved politically and espoused the 8-hour day, arbitration, and cooperatives, where union members owned the firms in which they worked. The union published a journal, *The Workingman's Advocate,* as a political voice. The union grew rapidly to a membership of 600,000, but rapidly fell apart after Sylvis's death in 1869. Organizers learned an important lesson from the experience of the National Labor Union. The political environment of the time prevented reform legislation that would lead to labor advancement.

In 1869, the *Knights of Labor* was organized by Uriah Stevens as a secret society. The secrecy was to protect members from reprisals by management. As might be expected, the secrecy led to much suspicion and bad public relations, and, as a result, was dropped in 1879. The Knights' greatest accomplishment was to win the first major strike in U.S. history. The Knights won a strike against the Wabash, Missouri-Kansas-Texas, and Missouri Pacific railroads, which were owned by Jay Gould, the personification of a capitalist robber baron. But by the turn of the century, the Knights had become unimportant as a labor force. The reasons for its demise were important for future labor organizations. The Knights' philosophical goal for political reform was to abolish the wage system and replace it with worker cooperatives. It thus had reformist motivations rather than economic goals. These political reformist goals, coupled with some unsuccessful large strikes and some violent cases of sabotage, contributed to the union's failures.[5]

National Labor Union   The first successful union in the United States that had a national scope. Founded in 1867 by William Sylvis, the union quickly grew to 600,000 members, but fell apart rapidly after Sylvis's death in 1869.

Knights of Labor   Organized by Uriah Stevens in 1869, the Knights of Labor was a secret organization. It won the first major strike in the United States against the railroad industry. The Knights had political reformist goals, which led to its demise.

---

[5]The Knights of Labor were linked to the infamous Haymarket bomb-throwing incident in Chicago in which seven policemen were killed. Eight anarchists were arrested. One was a Knight and the local union refused to expel him because of his involvement. This caused many people to link the Knights with the most radical elements of the labor movement and was politically very costly to the labor movement in general, as well as to the Knights of Labor in particular.

American Federation of Labor (AFL) Founded by Samuel Gompers in 1886, the AFL was the first business union. The AFL was an exclusive union organized for skilled workers.

business union Samuel Gompers's description of a union that worked for economic goals without wanting to change or destroy the business organization in which it worked.

United Mine Workers The industrial union for mine workers.

wildcat strikes Local strikes that are unauthorized by the national union.

International Workers of the World (IWW) An international union that organized American steelworkers after World War I. The IWW was viewed as socialistic in the United States, and this contributed to its demise.

The *American Federation of Labor (AFL)* was founded in 1886 by Samuel Gompers (considered the father of the American labor movement).[6] It was the first *business union,* and it overcame many of the problems the earlier national unions had faced. Gompers was, above all, pragmatic and set a single goal of economic gains for his union members. Importantly, there were no social-reformist goals. Gompers thought it necessary that national labor leaders be supreme and have sole authority to call strikes and control membership dues. This principle has remained in the labor movement to the present day. The Federation was primarily organized for the skilled worker and was an exclusive union movement.

Business and labor are not always at odds. In some cases union organization brings stability to an industry, and in other cases an oligopolistic industry may even use labor power to help monopolize the industry. Before the days of the United Mine Workers, mine operators had a very difficult time with labor, because mine workers were and are a very independent lot. The *United Mine Workers,* under the leadership of John L. Lewis, brought organization *and* discipline to labor. When Lewis ordered the miners back to work, they went back to work! In recent years the United Mine Workers' leadership has not had that sort of control and *wildcat strikes,* which are local strikes unauthorized by the national union, have been frequent. The point is that management is not necessarily hostile to union organization. In recent years, unions and management have often worked together to lobby for reduced pollution control legislation, to curb imports, and even to urge tax cuts for business.

Having briefly examined these early unions, we can now sketch the labor movement in a more general historical framework. Early progress, as we have seen, was not rapid. This can be attributed in large part to the massive immigration of the period. The early hostility of management toward organized labor was understandable, and it was easy to break strikes and even labor organizations with the steady supply of young, healthy, and eager workers who poured in from Europe.

World War I and the accompanying prosperity marked the beginning of success for American unions. Membership increased steadily during this period, and the image of unions started to improve. Much credit for this is due Gompers, who served on President Wilson's Advisory Commission of the National Council of Defense. Unions were, however, flexing their muscles during the war period, and there were many strikes in 1917. This was largely a reflection of the war-generated inflation and the effect this inflation had on long-term union contracts. In 1918 labor was successful in negotiating an eight-hour day and collective bargaining rights in exchange for a no-strike agreement. As a result, labor emerged from World War I stronger than it had ever been.

The postwar period brought increased inflation and more activity to increase wages via strikes. The *International Workers of the World (IWW)* organized the steelworkers, who were unskilled and thus not members of Gompers's Federation. The IWW had been associated with several prominent socialists and was regarded as a radical movement. At this time, the Russian Revolution and the fear of a worldwide Bolshevik revolution gripped the United States. The IWW subsequently went on strike against U.S. Steel and lost. The breaking of the strike

[6]Technically, Gompers founded the Federation of Organized Trades and Labor Unions in 1881, which is regarded as the precursor of the American Federation of Labor.

Samuel Gompers *(1850–1924)*

Samuel Gompers is often called the father of the American labor movement. Gompers was born in a very poor ghetto of East London, England. He quit school after four years and was apprenticed to become a cigar-maker like his father. When he was 13 his family moved to the United States. His home was a two-room tenement next to a cattle slaughterhouse in New York's lower east side. He continued his career as a cigar-maker, leaving home at the age of 17 to get married. His wife and 14 children were to experience much misery and violence because of his devotion to the labor movement.

Gompers joined the Cigar Maker's International Union and aided in the development of the local chapter. In 1874 he was elected president of the local. He was ousted seven years later by socialist opponents.

In December, 1886, Gompers helped found the American Federation of Labor (AFL) and became its first president. By 1904 membership had grown to nearly two million. Much of the union's success was due to Gompers's abilities. Although in his younger days Gompers had been a radical, he realized that to succeed in America the labor movement had to shed its radical-socialist image. Gompers worked hard to overcome the bad publicity for organized labor generated by the management of large corporations and fed by the activities and radical-activist tactics of other unions, such as the International Workers of the World. Gompers joined the National Civic Federation, an association of wealthy eastern capitalists, editors, professional people, and corporation officers. The National Civic Federation particularly emphasized that labor union strength did not undermine American business and that strong business was good for labor.

Perhaps the best evidence of Gompers's success was his acceptance by the political establishment. He proved that labor leaders were respectable members of the establishment, not communist radicals seeking to overthrow American capitalism. During World War I, President Wilson appointed Gompers to the advisory commission to the Council of National Defense, and in 1919, at the Versailles Peace Conference, Gompers served as chairperson of the Commission of International Labor Legislation.

was a major victory for steel companies, who successfully branded the union leaders as socialists attempting to overthrow capitalism. The breaking of the U.S. Steel strike had more significance than one would normally attribute to a single strike. The union's failure, coupled with the recession of 1920–1922, broke what had been a steady rise in union prestige and membership.

The 1920s proved to be a bad time for the labor movement. The Republican presidents, Harding, Coolidge, and Hoover, were probusiness, and business was aggressively opposed to organized labor. The government sanctioned *yellow-dog contracts,* contracts in which the employee had to agree to refrain from union activity as a precondition of employment and which allowed the firm to discharge the worker for violation of the agreement. In addition, the courts were hostile to union activity. This hostility was apparent in the ease with which management

yellow-dog contracts Contracts in which an employee must agree to refrain from union activity as a precondition for employment.

injunctions   *Court orders used
in labor union-management
disputes to order labor back to
work. The Clayton Act (1914)
limited the use of injunctions,
but this section was later
declared unconstitutional.*

Norris-La Guardia Act   *A law
passed in 1932 that (along with
the Wagner Act of 1935) vastly
strengthened the power of labor
unions and set the stage for their
rapid development.*

Wagner Act   *A law passed in
1935 that (along with the
Norris-La Guardia Act of 1932)
vastly strengthened the power of
labor unions and set the stage
for their rapid development.*

secondary boycotts   *Union
actions to stop one employer
from doing business with another
employer. This involves action to
create pressures on third parties.*

National Labor Relations Board
(NLRB)   *Established by the
Wagner Act (1935), the NLRB
was empowered to investigate
unfair business practices and to
determine legitimate bargaining
agents for labor when there were
competing unions.*

Congress of Industrial
Organizations (CIO)   *An
affiliation of industrial unions
that was organized when the
AFL decided not to promote
unions in the mass production
industries.*

was able to receive court *injunctions* requiring labor to return to work. And a section of the Clayton Act (1914), which had been hailed by Samuel Gompers as the Magna Carta of labor because it limited the use of injunctions against labor, was declared unconstitutional.

Success and Power

These bad times for unions were swept away with the election of Franklin D. Roosevelt in 1932. Roosevelt campaigned as the friend of the worker, and the legislation that was proposed and passed during Roosevelt's terms established the bond between organized labor and the Democratic party which still exists today. The two key pieces of legislation were the *Norris-La Guardia Act* (1932) and the *Wagner Act* (1935). These pieces of legislation vastly strengthened unions and set the stage for their rapid development. Jointly, the two acts gave workers the right to organize and made illegal any interference with this right. Yellow-dog contracts were outlawed, and picket lines and *secondary boycotts,* which were union actions to stop one employer from doing business with another employer, were sanctioned. A secondary boycott is more powerful than a picket line because it involves actions against and pressures on third parties. In other words, a union not only boycotts a certain product or firm, which would be a *primary* boycott, but it also boycotts firms (and their products) who do business with the firm the union has an action against. Injunctions against unions and their activities were limited to unlawful acts, and businesses were required to engage in collective bargaining and to bargain in good faith. In addition, the Wagner Act established the *National Labor Relations Board (NLRB).* The NLRB was empowered to investigate unfair labor practices and to determine legitimate bargaining agents for labor when there were competing unions. This act was challenged in the courts and declared to be constitutional by the Supreme Court. Under these laws, private-sector workers were given the right to organize without interference from management. In practice, if organizers can get 30 percent of the work force in a particular place of employment to sign authorization cards, the NLRB steps in and conducts a vote. If the majority of workers support the union, the management of that company must recognize the union and bargain with it.

About this time, a very important debate was going on within the AFL concerning whether or not the AFL should undertake union organization in the mass production industries. The AFL was primarily an organization of exclusive unions, but rapid labor growth had occurred in the mass production industries such as steelworking, automobile manufacturing, and mining. The AFL decided not to promote unions in these industries and, as a result, a number of affiliated unions broke away in 1935 and formed the Committee for Industrial Organization. Shortly thereafter the name was changed to the *Congress of Industrial Organizations (CIO).* John L. Lewis, the colorful, forceful head of the United Mine Workers, became the first president.

World War II and the 1950s

The wartime boom economy brought a number of serious strikes. The Wagner Act had given unions more legal power and the coffers of union treasuries were full. Unions flexed their muscles and a wave of strikes causing substantial work stoppages followed. The unions were successful in achieving sizable settlements. But public sympathy began to shift away from labor and, as a result, Congress passed the *Taft-Hartley Act* in 1947, which was designed to reverse some of the excesses fostered by the Wagner Act. President Truman vetoed the act, but Congress overrode the veto, reflecting the antiunion political atmosphere. The Taft-Hartley Act shifted several legal rights back to employers. *Closed shops,* where workers were forced to become union members before employment, were outlawed. Unions were required to bargain in good faith, and featherbedding and secondary boycotts were outlawed. In certain instances, the president was empowered to call 80-day cooling-off periods before strikes. During this 80-day period, mediation is attempted and the government appoints a fact-finding board. *Mediation* is simply third-party intervention into the strike. The mediator attempts to keep the parties together and talking by offering suggestions and clarifying issues. This is distinct from *arbitration.* In arbitration, a third party hears the arguments of both management and labor, studies their positions, and renders a decision. If the dispute has been submitted to *binding* arbitration, both parties must abide by that decision. Union leaders fought this bill as a "slave labor law" every step of the way, and union leaders continue to campaign to reverse some of its provisions. Despite the Taft-Hartley Act, however, unions have continued to show great strength, which is enhanced by careful and well-organized political activity.

In 1955, the American Federation of Labor and the Congress of Industrial Organizations merged to form the *AFL-CIO.* This gave the labor movement a more unified stance under the leadership of Walter Reuther and George Meany. The *Landrum-Griffin Act,* passed in 1959, was a response to further public concern over union power and practices. The Landrum-Griffin Act was decidedly antiunion and was based on the idea that union practices needed further curbing. The act made unions more democratic, restricted Communist party members and convicted felons from union leadership, and strengthened the Taft-Hartley Act by making picketing illegal under certain circumstances.

The 1960s and 1970s

Recent years have seen a decline in the union membership share of the labor force, partly as a result of the fact that the economy is becoming more service oriented and less manufacturing oriented. Thirty years ago almost 40 percent of the American labor force was unionized. Today, less than 25 percent is unionized. Some observers forecast that by 1990 relative union membership will be at the level it was before the wave of unionization in the mid-1930s. One notable exception has been a dramatic increase in the membership of public unions. The *American Federation of State, County, and Municipal Employees (AFSCME)* is a large and very rapidly growing union. Under the leadership of Jerry Wurf, AFSCME was politically active. However, in 1977 the union lost its first major battle in a confrontation with Mayor Maynard Jackson of Atlanta. The union's garbage workers affiliate struck the city of Atlanta. Much as in 1920, when U.S. Steel broke the IWW, Mayor Jackson refused to bargain with the local AFSCME chapter and hired strikebreakers. Unemployment problems in the city aided the strikebreaking and the jobs were quickly filled. The future should determine if the Atlanta strikebreaking is a minor setback for the public union movement or the

Taft-Hartley Act   Passed in 1947, the act was designed to reverse some of the labor excesses created by the Wagner Act. President Truman vetoed the act but Congress overrode the veto. The Taft-Hartley Act shifted some rights back to the employers.

closed shops   Firms where workers are forced to become union members before employment.

mediation   Third party intervention in a strike. The mediator attempts to keep the parties together and talking by offering suggestions and clarifying issues.

arbitration   A third party hears the arguments of both sides in a labor dispute and renders a decision. In binding arbitration, the sides must abide by the decision.

AFL-CIO   The merged Federation of Labor and Congress of Industrial Organizations. The merger took place in 1955 and gave labor a more unified political stance.

Landrum-Griffin Act   Passed in 1959 and aimed at further curbing union power. The act made unions more democratic and restricted Communist party members and convicted felons from union leadership. It made picketing illegal under certain circumstances.

American Federation of State, County, and Municipal Employees (AFSCME)   One of the few unions that grew in the 1970's; a union of public employees.

first of a series of fatal blows. We should see much in the news in the coming months and years concerning this aspect of the labor movement.

Of course, the real-world operation of labor-management relations does not always run the way a review of the law would indicate. The NLRB is often slow to act and sometimes slow to rule in cases of unfair labor practices. The battleground of labor-management relations has shifted to the South where much of the new industrial growth in this country is taking place. It is also mainly in the South that *right-to-work laws* are found. Right-to-work laws allow people to hold jobs without belonging to unions. This outlaws *union shops,* where union membership is necessary for a worker to remain employed. A union shop law requires that all workers join within a certain period (usually 30 days) of employment. The union shop is allowed under federal law, but the federal law permits individual states to pass right-to-work laws. These laws obviously greatly undermine union power. We saw earlier in this chapter that inclusive unions must organize and present a unified front to be successful in bargaining with management. Right-to-work laws greatly undermine an inclusive union's ability to present this united front.

There has been little in the way of new labor legislation since the Landrum-Griffin Act, except, of course, for frequent increases in the minimum wage. Labor has campaigned vigorously against some aspects of the Taft-Hartley Act, and these campaigns are worth watching. The two most important pieces of legislation that organized labor currently favors are (1) the repeal of right-to-work laws, and (2) the common situs picketing bill, which grants any union the right to picket an entire construction job even when the union represents only a small part of the labor used on the project. In late 1978, however, President Carter signed the ***Humphrey-Hawkins Full Employment Bill*** into law. The original bill was highly praised by organized labor, but the bill that finally passed Congress was viewed by many labor leaders as meaningless. The bill set national goals to reduce unemployment to 4 percent in 1983 and to cut inflation to 3 percent in 1983 and to zero by 1988. The bill defines full employment as the right of full opportunity for useful employment at fair rates of compensation for all individuals able and willing to work. The bill was regarded by labor as merely symbolic because it does not include any means to reach the goals specified, but rather leaves them all to future legislation.

Near the end of his term, President Carter proposed a program of labor legislation that the unions viewed very favorably. The Carter administration claimed that its program was only a reform of the NLRB to make it more responsive. Carter's secretary of labor, Ray Marshall (an economics professor at the University of Texas), argued that the Carter administration only wanted to perfect the implementation of the present law. The National Association of Manufacturers and the U. S. Chamber of Commerce view the bill quite differently and were opposed to the Carter plan.

The 1980s

Of course, with the election of Ronald Reagan, the political environment changed as it relates to unions. Early in his term (August, 1981), Reagan challenged the status of public unions during the Professional Air Traffic Controllers Organization (PATCO) strike.

right-to-work laws State laws that allow people to hold jobs without belonging to unions. Federal law leaves up to the states the choice between right-to-work laws and union shops.

union shops Union membership is necessary for a worker to remain employed. Federal law leaves up to the states the choice between right-to-work laws and union shops.

Humphrey-Hawkins Full Employment Bill A bill passed in 1978 after Senator Humphrey's death. It sets national goals to reduce unemployment to 4 percent by 1983 and to zero by 1988.

PATCO: *The Death of a Union*

PATCO, the Professional Air Traffic Controllers Organization, no longer exists. In 1981, air traffic controllers went on strike, which is against the law for federal employees. President Reagan, through Drew Lewis, his secretary of transportation, challenged the union, ordered workers back to work in 48 hours, and fired those who did not report to work. When the smoke cleared, Robert E. Poli, union president, resigned. By 1982, it appeared as if the union was, in effect, no longer an operating organization.

The government struck with uncharacteristic swiftness, and public opinion was solidly behind the president. Part of the reason for the success of this government strike-breaking behavior can be found in the economics of the situation.

First, the public and members of other unions did not view PATCO members as being underpaid. Salaries of $30,000 per year and more were not uncommon. PATCO negotiators, however, argued that their jobs were high-pressure jobs and "burnout" was a common malady.

This argument was hard to reconcile with market signals. When the government pressed ahead to train new controllers, 45,000 people applied for the course at the FAA Academy in Oklahoma. Thus, if controllers' salaries weren't high enough to compensate for on-the-job pressure, one would have expected a shortfall of applicants. The huge turnout, however, indicated that present salaries were quite adequate for this high-pressure, high-risk occupation.

The implications of this action are potentially far-reaching. As we saw in this chapter, public unions have increased in power in recent years. The action of PATCO and the response of President Reagan may well put a damper on public union power and influence.

This challenge came at a critical juncture in the labor movement. With the exception of public unions, unions had been on the decline. Public unions, however, were growing rapidly in the 1960s and 1970s, as were all levels of government. The Reagan administration seemed prepared to challenge this growth and, therefore, to confront the power of public unions head on. On a local level, the experience of Mayor Maynard Jackson in Atlanta, and on a national level, the experience of President Reagan will not go unnoticed by other public officials as they bargain with local unions in the years ahead. This willingness to confront public unions and to reduce, or at least stop, the growth of government may mean troubled times for public unions.

The Broad Sweep

As the union movement developed in the United States, several motives for unionization were evident. These different motives are reflected in union goals.

welfare unions *Unions that had lofty ideals of social welfare and sought to establish worker cooperatives.*

revolutionary unions *Unions that sought changes in the social order.*

repression phase *The early years of the labor movement in which government and the courts were hostile to union activity.*

encouragement phase *The period (1930–1947) in which government support by legislation greatly increased the power of unions.*

intervention stage *The period since the Taft-Hartley Act (1947) in which the government has intervened in labor disputes and taken away some of labor's earlier gains.*

Some unions were *welfare unions* (the Knights of Labor) that had lofty ideals of social welfare and sought these goals by advocating an end to the wage system and the establishment of worker cooperatives. Other unions were *revolutionary unions* (the International Workers of the World) that sought changes in the social order. Still others were business unions (the American Federation of Labor) that eschewed social and political goals and sought only to better the economic status of their members. History indicates that it is this third type that has been successful and able to survive in the American economic system.

The movement and the struggles of these different types of unions fit into three clearly identifiable periods. The early period from the 1700s until 1930 might be called the *repression phase* because of the hostility of the courts. This was a difficult time for union organization and one in which the successes of unions were few and far between. The period from 1930 to 1947 might be termed the *encouragement phase.* Government support and key labor legislation greatly increased the power and prestige of unions. Unions reached their peak period of influence during this period. The period since 1947 and the Taft-Hartley Act would properly be labeled the *intervention stage,* in which the government has intervened and attempted to put big business and big labor on a more equal footing. It is possible that we are now in a fourth stage where the basic underpinnings of the labor movement are in a state of flux, and are being challenged by government at all levels.

SUMMARY

1. This chapter looks at unions and the labor movement in the United States.

2. Exclusive unions are more likely to be successful than inclusive unions would be at raising wages.

3. Evidence indicates that unions have been successful in raising wages and that this success has come at the expense of consumers and nonunion labor, not at the expense of business profits.

4. Whether unions contribute to inflation and, if so, how, is a volatile question. Politicians blame labor unions for inflation, but the evidence doesn't support this.

5. Early unions had reformist goals and were largely unsuccessful. When Samuel Gompers turned the American Federation of Labor to-

ward strictly economic goals, he was successful. It wasn't until 1932, with the election of Franklin Roosevelt, that unions received active encouragement from government. The Norris-La Guardia Act (1932) and the Wagner Act (1935) greatly enhanced the power of unions. The Taft-Hartley Act (1947) and the Landrum-Griffin Act (1959) diminished this power and put unions and management on a more equal footing.

6. In recent years union membership has declined except in public employee unions, which have grown.

7. A new phase for the union movement may now be taking place and key legislation in the next few years will be important for the labor movement.

NEW TERMS

featherbedding
exclusive union
craft unions
inclusive union
industrial unions
bilateral monopoly
National Labor Union
Knights of Labor
American Federation of Labor (AFL)
business union
United Mine Workers
wildcat strikes
International Workers of the World (IWW)
yellow-dog contracts
injunctions
Norris-La Guardia Act
Wagner Act
secondary boycotts

National Labor Relations Board (NLRB)
Congress of Industrial Organizations (CIO)
Taft-Hartley Act
closed shops
mediation
arbitration
AFL-CIO
Landrum-Griffin Act
American Federation of State, County, and Municipal Employees (AFSCME)
right-to-work laws
union shops
Humphrey-Hawkins Full Employment Bill
welfare unions
revolutionary unions
repression phase
encouragement phase
intervention phase

QUESTIONS FOR DISCUSSION

1. Do unions raise wages? If so, at whose expense?

2. Is there a difference in the way inclusive unions and exclusive unions organize an industry? Which is more difficult?

3. Explain the differences between closed shops, union shops, and right-to-work laws.

4. Suppose that César Chavez is successful in organizing the grape pickers in California. What will be the likely effect on the price of California wine? What will be the likely effect in the number of grape pickers employed? Does the fact that the United States-Mexican border is relatively easy to cross and the supply of undocumented workers is relatively elastic have any impact on Chavez's organizing costs?

5. Has union strength in the North had any impact on business activity in the South?

6. Public unions have increased in strength, yet many states and the federal government forbid public unions from going on strike. Can you think of any reasons why this should be so? Is a police officer in Los Angeles any different than a bank guard in Los Angeles?

SUGGESTIONS FOR FURTHER READING

Dulles, Foster Rhea. *Labor in America: A History.* New York: Thomas Y. Crowell Co., 1966.

CHAPTER 29

Learning Objectives

Governmental Intervention into the Market

After studying the materials found in this chapter, you should be able to do the following:

1. Define:
   (a) natural monopoly.
   (b) externality.
   (c) public good.
   (d) private good.

2. Diagram cases of:
   (a) negative externalities.
   (b) positive externalities.

3. Give the details of the Coase theorem and the conditions under which it holds.

4. Discuss special interest group legislation and the problems in dealing with special interest groups.

5. Define:
   (a) egalitarianism.
   (b) free-riding behavior.
   (c) logrolling.
   (d) risk aversion.
   (e) utility interdependence.

6. List the advantages of a negative income tax as a tool to alter the distribution of income.

7. Use a Lorenz curve to show the relative distribution of income in a society.

8. Define:
   (a) absolute poverty.
   (b) relative poverty.

9. List the major federal government programs designed to alter the distribution of income.

In previous chapters we dealt principally with the operations of a market mechanism free of governmental involvement. When government activity was discussed, it was often shown to have a counterproductive effect on economic efficiency. However, we don't want to give the impression that economic activity undertaken by the government is necessarily always bad. In this chapter we will examine theoretical justifications for governmental activity on grounds of market failure. After examining instances where governmental activity is called for, we will examine how such activity has developed in the United States.

NATURAL MONOPOLY

As we saw in the chapter on pure monopoly, there may be some industries in which economies of scale are such that it makes economic sense to have only one firm. The monopoly that results is called a natural monopoly because efficiency considerations dictate that there be only one firm. When natural monopoly exists, governmental control is justified to prevent the company from abusing its monopoly position. The most common response to this situation is for government to regulate the natural monopoly, and sometimes government ownership is instituted. You can refer to the chapter on the structure of American industry to review the problems associated with regulation and government ownership.

EXTERNALITIES

Where there is interdependence among economic units, and when this interdependence is not reflected in market transactions, externalities may result. *Externalities* are costs or benefits that are imposed on economic units. These units are forced to bear the costs without compensation or are able to gain the benefits without paying for them. An example of an external cost would be air pollution. If you live near a steel mill, you are forced to breathe polluted air without being compensated for the fact that the mill is using the air to dump its debris.

Firms purchase inputs to produce goods and services. A steel mill will purchase iron ore, coal, electricity, and labor, among other inputs. It uses air in much the same way that it uses labor or electricity. In the process of producing steel, it is using clean air. It doesn't pay for this clean air. Instead, society pays, or, more correctly, the people who live in the area near the steel mill pay. They bear this cost in many ways. The area isn't pretty, as you know if you have driven through Gary, Indiana, recently. People cannot hang their clothes outside to dry. They must paint their houses every three years instead of every five years. There is even evidence that in some areas people may die sooner because they breathe bad air. All these are real costs and are borne by the people who live in the affected area.

The economic importance of this is that the firm polluting the area avoids paying these costs. These costs are *external* to the firm using the production process; hence, the term externality. It is quite simple to determine the theoretical effects of these externalities; it is more difficult to determine how to correct them.

Assume we have a competitive industry that is generating a *negative* externality. Smoke, for example, is generally viewed as a negative externality. Smoke causes damage, or what we could call *social costs,* to those in the general area. This situation is represented in Figure 29-1. The demand curve is the normal market-demand curve for the commodity. The supply curve is, of course, the summation of all the individual-firm marginal cost curves (above their average variable-cost curve). Equilibrium is reached at price OP_1 and output OQ_1. Now

externalities   Costs or benefits that are imposed on economic units. These units bear the costs without any compensation, or gain the benefits without paying for them.

social costs   Costs that are borne by society or some group without compensation. Externalities impose damages, or social costs, on groups in the population.

FIGURE 29-1   EXTERNALITIES AND MARKET EQUILIBRIUM

When the social cost of the externality (*SC*) is added to the marginal cost curves of the competitive firms (*S*), the true supply curve (S_t) is found. This true supply curve indicates that too much of the good is produced at too low a price unless the externality is taken into account.

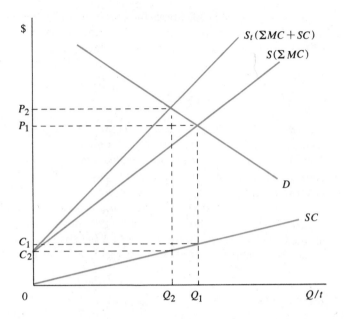

suppose we know what costs are generated by the externality and that these social costs are represented by the curve *SC*. They are zero at zero output, and we assume (to make the graph more simple) that they increase at a constant rate. If we add these social costs to the supply curve, we get the true supply curve, S_t. This curve is the summation of the extra social costs and the private costs embodied in the firms' marginal cost curves. The socially optimal level of production is no longer OQ_1 but the smaller OQ_2. Likewise, the efficient price is OP_2, which is higher than OP_1.

In commonsense terms, when we include the social costs of production, the good becomes more expensive. It wasn't that these costs weren't being borne before, but they weren't being borne by the producers of the commodity; instead, they were being paid by citizens in the area near the production. In failing to take into account the social costs, the firm is producing too much of the good and charging the consumer too low a price because the firm is not paying some of the costs of production. If the set of people who consume this good and the set of people who suffer the externality are different, a subsidy is taking place. The people who bear the externality are subsidizing the people who consume the good.

In the real world, this means that in those areas where significant externalities exist, the people who bear the externalities subsidize consumers of the product. The people who live in Gary, Indiana, pay costs that allow consumers of steel to pay lower prices. If steel producers had to pay for the externality, less steel would be produced, and it would be sold for a higher price. The general theoretical conclusion is that where negative externalities exist, the amount of production will not be optimal. Too much output will be produced at too low a price.

It is very important to understand that accounting for an externality such as pollution does not cause the amount of pollution to fall to zero. In the example in Figure 29-1, the costs associated with the externality fell from OC_1 to OC_2 after the social costs were added in, but some pollution and the costs associated with it continued.

Externality Internalization

In the jargon of economists, the trick is to *internalize* the externality. This simply means that the costs that are borne by society must be taken into account in production decisions. In terms of Figure 29-1, the firms have to bear the social costs SC, so that S_t becomes the supply curve. How can this be done? We must turn these social costs into production costs. It would be a simpler matter if we could easily determine what the social costs were. We can draw general cases, as in Figure 29-1, but in the real world it is very difficult to come up with a dollar value. What is the cost of x number of people dying a year earlier because of respiratory problems? Or, how much is not being able to grow grass worth? If we could determine these costs, we could place a tax on the industry that would shift the supply curve to S_t. The market solution would then result in a price of OP_2 and output of OQ_2.

We could also charge the firms for the amount of externalities they create. We could monitor each firm and charge for amounts on a monthly basis. It would be possible to put a meter on each smokestack and measure the pollutants. In such a way, firms could be charged for the air they use just as for the electricity or labor they use. This would cause costs to rise and move production toward the socially optimal level of output. This problem, however, is similar to the problem with taxation—how to determine the correct charge per pollutant.

These difficulties notwithstanding, we have a legitimate case for government intervention in the market process. When there are externalities, markets don't produce socially optimal results, and it can be argued that government should step in to correct for the market imperfection. The question is, How should the government intervene?

The Coase Theorem and Small-Number Externalities. In an article that has had significant impact on the field of economics, Professor Ronald Coase of the University of Chicago has pointed out that where the number of affected parties is small, individual maximizing behavior will correct for the externality.[1] Coase demonstrates that if property rights are clearly defined, the affected individuals will take action to internalize the externality. Consider, as Coase did in his paper, that there are only two parties involved in a particular dispute, a wheat farmer and a cattle rancher. The externality is the damage done by the cattle roaming on unfenced land. As the rancher increases the size of the herd, the damage done by straying cattle will increase. To account for the externality, it is necessary to cause the rancher to take these costs into account, much as we discussed earlier and depicted in Figure 29-1. If government intervened, it would likely solve the problem by requiring the rancher to pay the farmer for the damage to the farmer's wheat. As a result, the rancher would restrict the number of cattle in the herd until marginal cost equaled marginal revenue (and the marginal cost

internalize   The idea that the cost of an externality that is borne by society should be taken into account in the production process.

---

[1] See Ronald Coase, "The Problem of Social Cost," *Journal of Law and Economics,* Vol. III (October, 1960), pp. 1–44.

includes the damage to the wheat, as we saw in Figure 29-1). Coase shows that even if government did not intervene, the same solution would be obtained. Consider Figure 29-2. D_c and MR_c represent the demand and marginal revenue of raising cattle. MC_c represents the marginal cost of raising cattle and SC_w represents the marginal social cost, or the damage of the externality (the damage to the wheat). Without internalization of the externality, the rancher would raise OQ_1 cattle per year, and the farmer would incur a dollar loss to the wheat crop of OW_1 for the last cow raised. Government intervention would require that, through some tax scheme or direct regulation, the rancher be forced to act on the joint $MC_c + SC_w$ curve and, as a result, the rancher would raise only OQ_2 cattle.

Now consider a Coase solution. All that is necessary is that property rights be defined and enforced. First assume that the farmer has the right *not* to have the wheat harmed. The rancher will then be forced to pay damages, as shown by the SC_w curve, and will add these to production costs. The rancher will then raise OQ_2 cattle. If the rancher has the right to let the cattle roam, the important question then is how much the farmer will be willing to "bribe" the rancher to keep the cattle away. The farmer will be willing to bribe the rancher an amount just slightly less than the cost of the damge done by the cattle, because this makes them both better off than allowing the cattle to damage the wheat. The farmer would pay OW_1 for the last cow not to be raised. The rancher then must include these bribes as opportunity costs, because if the cattle are raised the bribe is foregone. When the foregone bribe is added to the marginal cost curve, the rancher will raise OQ_2 cattle.

The result is that OQ_2 cattle will be raised regardless of who has the property right, as long as the property right is defined and the number of people involved is small. Small numbers are necessary because the farmer and rancher must get

---

FIGURE 29-2   THE COASE THEOREM

The Coase theorem shows how externalities are internalized by the assignment of property rights. The social cost (SC_w) is automatically embodied in the marginal cost curve (MC_c) to form $MC_c + SC_w$, the true cost of raising cattle. The optimal product, OQ_2, will result because a bribe or payment equal to the social cost will automatically come about.

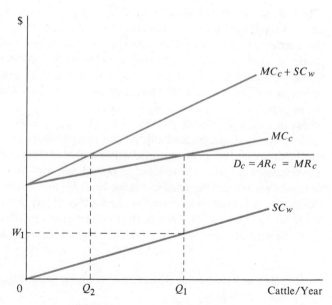

together. Note that the Coase solution says only that allocative results, or the number of cattle produced, will be the same, whoever has the property rights. It says nothing about the distribution of income. The property right assignment does affect who is better off. In one case the farmer's income is higher, in the other the rancher's income is higher.

The importance of the *Coase theorem* is that it draws attention to property-right assignments. Many of our current social problems result from ill-defined or nonexistent property-right assignments. Consider, for example, the case of buffalo and cattle in the Old West. Why were buffalo almost wiped out while cattle thrived? The animals are very similar and roamed the same country. The answer is simple. Nobody owned the buffalo,[2] or rather, everyone had a right to shoot them. Consider air pollution as another example. If a copper mine dumped tailings on your yard, you would sue for damages or expect payment for the use of your land as a dump. Yet when this same mine dumps soot in your air, you are helpless because you don't own the air above your land.

Coase theorem   A solution to externality problems which shows that in the case of small numbers of affected parties, a property right assignment is sufficient to internalize any externality that is present.

Large-Number Externalities. Even if property rights are well defined, there may still be externality problems. If there are large numbers of people sustaining damages or large numbers of firms doing the damage, the results of the Coase theorem may not hold. It may be that the costs of organizing the involved parties prohibit the damaged individuals from suing for damages or organizing a bribe. The individuals damaged would have to mount a door-to-door campaign, advertise in newspapers, and arouse the group for joint action. If the damaging firms are hard to identify, the problem is even greater. In an area with severe air pollution, it would be necessary to determine how each of many firms contributes to this air pollution. It would be necessary to determine who should be sued (or bribed). Because the information and transaction costs increase rapidly as the number of parties increases, it is often argued that the Coase theorem cannot solve the market failure that externalities create.

Governmental Intervention Again

We are, in a sense, back to square one, requiring government intervention to correct the externality. Usually government controls are direct controls, and such controls often lead to unfairness in their own right. Consider the case of the government requiring that all cars have a pollution device that costs $300. The salesperson who drives a lot, and as a result pollutes a great deal, pays very little on a per-unit-of-pollution basis. The person who only drives once a week pays a great deal on a per-unit-of-pollution basis.

In addition, government intervention affects the distribution of income. The incidence of programs can sometimes even impact disproportionately on the poor. For example, as auto prices rise because of pollution equipment, they affect the poor more than the rich. This is because the poor spend a higher proportion of their income on cars than do the rich.

---

[2]For a discussion of how to protect eagles by assigning property rights to them, see Ryan C. Amacher, Robert D. Tollison, and Thomas D. Willett, "The Economics of Fatal Mistakes: Fiscal Mechanisms for Preserving Endangered Predators," *Public Policy,* Vol. XX, No. 1 (Summer, 1972), pp. 411–441.

Since governmental intervention is not without costs, we need to be sure that externality costs are indeed worth worrying about. Sometimes even the government makes mistakes, and these mistakes inflict costs on the economy. Externalities have received much attention in recent years, and this attention may overstate the real costs. We have all seen gruesome pictures of oil spills and fish kills, yet this damage seems to be of an exceedingly short duration. This is not to say that such damage is insignificant. It is only to suggest that the costs of correcting for an externality may exceed the damage it causes, and we need to consider this before racing headlong into governmental regulation of externalities.

The federal government has usually responded to calls to control noxious externalities through regulation. These regulations impose costs on firms, and the regulatory bodies themselves spend large amounts of money. The costs imposed on firms are hard to estimate until the required action is taken. For example, a regulation to keep copper mines from polluting the air may cause them to close because of increased costs of production. In considering the costs of the legislation, one should examine its impact on the affected industry. Production may move to a state (or country) that has less stringent regulation. Some geographic regions may compete for industrial growth by offering fewer environmental or economic regulations.

Each individual call for externality regulation should be carefully considered. Some of these externalities may have already been corrected by market mechanisms. For example, houses near airports sell for lower prices because of airport noise. The people who buy these houses are freely choosing to do so because the lower price compensates for the noise. To change the law because these people don't like the noise would generate a windfall gain to these people. It is not surprising that these residents should lobby for such a change, but it cannot be justified economically. The problem is complicated, however, by the fact that some residents may have purchased their homes before the noise became bad. It might make sense to compensate these individuals.

What we have discovered is that negative externalities cause market solutions to diverge from optimality. We have also seen that government intervention has the potential to correct these externalities. The government, however, does not intervene in a costless fashion, and we must determine if the costs of this intervention are preferred to the original externality cost.

PUBLIC GOODS

public goods *Those goods that generate external benefits that are jointly consumed. It is difficult (impossible) to exclude people from consuming a public good.*

free-riding behavior *Free-riders mask their true demands and indicate they don't want a public good because they know once it is produced they can consume it without paying for it. As a result, less than the optimal amount will be produced.*

Public goods are those goods that generate external benefits, or *positive* externalities that are consumed by more than one person. Public goods are different from private goods since it is very difficult to exclude people from consuming public goods. A pure public good would be a good that the whole country (or world) consumes automatically. A suitable, but not perfect, example at the national level would be national defense. A problem arises because people cannot be excluded from consuming the good, so they will try to consume the good without paying for it. Economists refer to this behavior as *free-riding behavior*. *Free riders* mask their true demands and indicate they don't want the good, or they only want a little of a good because they know once it is produced they can consume it without having to pay for it. When free-riding behavior is prevalent, less than the optimal level of production is attained.

This can be seen clearly by examining Figure 29-3. The demand curve D_P represents a normal demand curve that is based on the private benefits that consumers receive. Suppose the good is produced in a perfectly competitive industry, and the industry's supply curve and marginal cost curve of the good are represented by MC. The consumer or group of consumers will purchase OQ_1 units of the good at the competitive price OP_1. If, however, there are external benefits to others and if the paying consumers can't exclude the others, there are social benefits. In Figure 29-3, the demand curve that includes these social benefits is represented by $D_{P + S}$. The socially efficient level of consumption is no longer OQ_1, but instead is now OQ_2. As a result, we have another legitimate role for government. Government should grant a subsidy to the producing firms in an attempt to induce consumers to consume the socially desirable amount OQ_2. Government is necessary because the free riders can be forced to pay if taxes are levied on them. In terms of Figure 29-3, the government would have to grant a subsidy to producers equal to amount AB. At output OQ_2, consumers pay OP_3, suppliers receive OP_3 plus the subsidy AB, and this gives a price to suppliers of OP_2.

The theoretical justification for supplying public goods can now be seen. Markets don't produce enough of those goods which have external or spill-over benefits, so the government needs to intervene. For example, consider a city building an airport. The argument is that many of the benefits are external to the citizens in the locality. These citizens will build too small an airport because they can't force people from outside the region to help pay for the airport. The federal government can correct for this by taxing all citizens and giving the locality a grant to build an airport of the correct size.

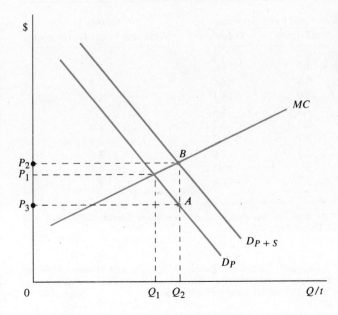

FIGURE 29-3 EXTERNAL BENEFITS
If some of the benefits of a good are public or external benefits, consumers will be unwilling to pay for these benefits that spill over to other consumers. As a result, the private demand curve (D_P) will understate the true demand curve (D_{P+S}), which includes the public benefits.

Imperfections in the Political Process

Externalities and public goods, as we have seen, cause imperfections in markets, and political responses arise to correct for these imperfections. But there are political imperfections as well as market imperfections. One of the best ways to uncover these imperfections is to see how the supply of public goods is actually determined and to compare that with the way the political process works in theory. In theory, voters form a group, or club, or level of government, and vote to supply themselves with a public good. They do this through the political process to overcome the free-riding problem. The government can force all consumers of the good to pay and can thus insure that the correct amount is produced. We need to examine how the desires of voters are translated into the provision of public goods in order to determine how well the political provision of such goods works in practice.

Public Goods and Governmental Budgets[3]

The size of governmental expenditures has grown rapidly in recent years. Table 29-1 depicts some of this growth, while Table 29-2 shows that an increasing share of state and local spending has consisted of *grants* to lower levels of government by the federal government. Much of the federal budget is spent for defense and welfare which are public goods. Local and state spending falls heavily on such public goods as education, airports, and highways. We need, then, to see how effective the political process is in supplying public goods. There are several conflicting theories as to how favorably the political sector reacts to consumer

TABLE 29-1   SELECTED FEDERAL GOVERNMENT
             EXPENDITURES AS A PERCENT OF GNP,
             1939–1980

Year	Purchases of Goods and Services			Grants to State and Local Governments
	Defense	Nondefense	Transfers	
1939	1.7	5.5	1.8	1.4
1945	4.1	0.6	2.6	0.5
1950	5.9	2.0	6.1	1.0
1955	11.7	1.8	4.4	1.0
1960	10.8	2.3	5.7	1.6
1965	8.6	3.1	5.7	1.9
1970	9.1	2.7	7.8	3.0
1975	6.7	3.2	12.0	4.4
1980	6.2	3.2	11.8	4.1

Source: *The National Income and Product Accounts of the United States, 1929–1976* and *Survey of Current Business*, December, 1981.

---

[3]This section draws heavily from Ryan C. Amacher, Robert D. Tollison, and Thomas D. Willett (eds.), "A Menu of Distributional Considerations," *The Economic Approach to Public Policy: Selected Readings* (New York: Cornell University Press, 1976).

TABLE 29-2 U.S. FEDERAL GRANTS AS A PERCENT OF STATE AND LOCAL GOVERNMENT SPENDING

Year	Percent
1927	1.6
1940	10.2
1950	7.4
1960	13.4
1970–71[1]	17.4
1975–76	21.7
1979–80	22.5

Source: *Economic Report of the President,* 1982.
[1]After 1970, data are reported for fiscal years ending in the 12-month period through June 30.

demands. In order to reach an answer, however tentative, it is necessary to examine the systematic forces that operate in the political sector.

There is disagreement among economists, as well as political scientists, as to whether the public sector in the United States is too large or too small, and there may even be a few who would argue that the present public-private mix is the correct one. While different individuals inevitably have different opinions based on their underlying preferences and economic, political, and social positions, one can nevertheless examine the systematic forces at work in the U.S. political and economic systems to determine if they bias the mix of public versus private spending from what the average voter-consumer desires.

Probably the most widely known discussion of the appropriate size of the public sector in the United States is given by John Kenneth Galbraith in his book *The Affluent Society*. Galbraith has argued that there is a systematic imbalance in favor of the private sector and against the public sector, in part because of heavy advertising in the private sector. But it is possible to argue against Galbraith on the grounds that the public sector also advertises. Some of this advertising is concentrated on a few members of Congress and could be more effective than private-sector advertising. In other words, the effective purchasers of some public goods are legislators, and the supplying agency can concentrate on a few purchasers. For example, the Defense Department can concentrate its advertising on the Armed Services Committee of Congress. In addition, many lobby groups tell the public that certain kinds of public spending are good.

Anthony Downs, an economic and political consultant at the Brookings Institution, has arrived at a conclusion similar to Galbraith's; namely, that the government budget in a two-party democracy tends systematically to be too small.[4] He has argued that democratic budgets are not expanded enough in certain directions when vote-maximizing parties compete for the support of utility-maximizing voters. The correct budget, by Downs's benchmark, is the budget

---

[4]Anthony Downs, "Why the Government Budget Is Too Small in a Democracy," *World Politics,* Vol. XII, No. 3 (July, 1960), pp. 541–563.

which would emerge if political parties and voters had perfect information. This benchmark is clearly ethical in character (as Downs stresses), requiring the value judgement that democracy works well under conditions of perfect information. Following this guide, he argues that many potential benefits of governmental action will not be produced in a complex and interdependent democracy where parties must appeal to voters lacking perfect information. Such governmental benefits are remote and uncertain in nature; for example, the benefits of foreign aid expenditures in preventing a future war, or the potential benefits from safety, food, and drug regulation. Voters are simply (and rationally) not aware of the potential returns from governmental activity in such areas and would not recognize such benefits even if political parties invested in an advertising program to make them known. On the other side of the fiscal account, Downs argues that taxes, even indirect ones, are more accurately taken into account by voters than the remote benefits under realistic circumstances.

Professors James Buchanan and Gordon Tullock, both of George Mason University, have mounted arguments counter to those of Downs and Galbraith.[5] They arrived at this position by employing a methodology that is similar, but not identical, to the methodology used by Downs. Buchanan and Tullock argue that majority voting tends to result in overinvestment in the *specific* benefits projects, such as rivers and harbors, at the expense of *general* benefit items, such as defense. They adopted as a benchmark a voter's choice based on the voter's perceived personal costs from collective action. It is a similar benchmark to that of Downs in that it is an ethical criterion. Buchanan and Tullock point out that whether the budget is pushed too far in terms of specific or general benefits depends on the type of taxation that applies. The implication is that general benefit items suffer at the expense of specific benefit items. Under these conditions, the absolute budget size will be too large. What happens is simple to understand. Members of Congress have the power to give projects to their districts and win votes by helping their districts receive projects. Taxes go up by only a small amount due to any one project, but the citizens of an area receive much in benefits. With all members of Congress playing these games, we tend to produce too many projects. The representative from Arizona votes for a bridge in Kentucky in order to get the Kentucky representative to vote for a dam in Arizona. This vote trading is called **logrolling**.

logrolling   Vote trading in a legislative process. Legislators vote for a colleague's program in return for a favorable vote on their program.

Still other approaches to the question have yielded different conclusions. It has been suggested that budgets are too large because of the monopoly character of governmental agencies. Budgets become too large because bureaucrats have incentives to vote for and help politicians who promise still larger budgets because, as budgets grow, bureaucrats become more powerful and receive bigger raises. Furthermore, risk elements, such as the possibility of war, cause us to spend too much on military projects. The conclusions are often mixed, and the arguments concerning the appropriate size of the budget are surrounded by a great deal of confusion.

A very important point emerges from all this confusion. We have seen that the market breaks down with regard to public goods, but the political process also diverges from the theoretical ideal. What we need to determine is which of these

[5]James Buchanan and Gordon Tullock, *Calculus of Consent: Logical Foundations of Constitutional Democracy* (Ann Arbor: University of Michigan Press, 1962).

two imperfect mechanisms does a better job of providing goods that are more or less public in nature. In some cases, such as national defense, it is likely that government will do the best job. In others, such as tennis courts, the market process may do a better job. It is clear that we should not always presume that market failure implies the need for governmental intervention. What we have suggested is that market failure and government failure are *both* possible in the real world.

Special Interest Groups: The Problems of Changing the Direction of Governmental Growth

The election of Ronald Reagan in November, 1980, made it clear that voters thought that government intervention was too extensive.

Some important insights into the growth of government and the budget process can be found by examining the difficulty of dealing with special interest groups. Economist George Schultz, Secretary of State in the Reagan administration, has pointed out that 46 percent of American families receive significant governmental transfers, and these transfers are difficult to tamper with.

President Reagan gained much publicity in 1981 by engineering a significant budget cut. But one must be careful in calling this a budget cut. It wasn't an actual cut in spending, but a cut in increased levels of future spending. In forecasting governmental growth, it is worth examining some of the special interest groups with which any Congress and any president must contend. Similar groups exist on the state and local levels.

Business. Business lobbies have become more numerous in recent years. In the 1950s and 1960s, business was not very active politically, but in the mid-1970s, business Political Action Committees (PACs) and business-oriented lobbies mushroomed. These groups often support legislation aimed at deregulation of markets; in some cases, they have sponsored and advocated specific special interest legislation aimed at their own industry. Favorable tax treatment for oil companies is just one example of business special interest.

Labor. Labor unions have been actively involved in politics for many years. Labor unions generally support the liberal Democratic party. This support originated with President Franklin Delano Roosevelt, who supported labor goals and labor growth.

Consumers. Consumer groups arose in the 1970s. The consumer movement, exemplified by Ralph Nader, prompted governmental legislation of a regulatory nature. Consumer groups are often against the free market and in conflict with business lobbies.

Environmentalists. Groups such as Friends of the Earth and the Sierra Club have a large and well-organized membership. These groups are often antigrowth and advocate restrictive use of government land. They often are at odds with both business and labor groups.

The Elderly. Elderly, retired groups have a very special interest in government, particularly in social security.

Women. Women's groups have their own agenda of governmental causes. In recent years, they have concentrated on the passage of the Equal Rights Amendment (ERA).

Blacks. The National Association for the Advancement of Colored People (NAACP) and the National Urban League are probably the most familiar and active political groups for Blacks. These organizations have their own agenda of social programs that they advocate.

Abortion Activists. Abortion activists, on both sides of the issue, have been very vocal in recent years. Their agenda has been credited with defeating some United States senators in some areas of the country.

Local Officials. Local governments receive large amounts of federal money. Federal agencies collect the money and return it to local governments for projects such as building airports and operating schools. These local governments have a vested interest in seeing that federal spending favors them.

Farmers. The American Farm Bureau and the militant American Agriculture Movement are just two of the lobbies representing farmers. For years, farmers have enjoyed huge subsidies from both the state and the federal government. These subsidies run the gamut from grants to build farm ponds to price supports and subsidized loans.

Disarming Special Interest Groups

The above listing is incomplete. We are all members of one special interest group or another. Perhaps you belong to more than one. The difficulty in doing something about the size of government, if one concludes it is too large, is that while each of us attacks legislation for one special interest, we can rarely admit that our own special interest is similar to the one we bemoan. The farmer deplores the welfare going to the unemployed worker, but fails to see the welfare in his or her government-funded stock pond. The environmentalist attacks the leasing of public land for petroleum exploration, but fails to see the economic subsidy in supplying recreational areas. We could go on, but the point is simple: Special interest groups ask for more government, and they get it. Voters often complain about the size of government, but they are usually members of at least one special interest group. Therein lies the problem; special interest groups are so powerful, it is difficult to tamper with them.

INCOME DISTRIBUTION AS A PUBLIC GOOD

It could be argued that redistribution of income is a public good. However, some members of society will free ride on private redistributive efforts, and, as a result, less than the optimal amount of redistribution of income will take place. This will happen because the free riders will think that there is no need to help the poor because others will give. The electorate, as a result, may decide to redistribute income and tax all citizens to achieve a better outcome than the market-produced outcome.

The need for this redistribution comes from the normative conclusion that we don't like the distribution of income the market produces. This distribution was discussed in detail in the chapter on factor markets, and at that time we said that the theory only explained how the distribution came to be what it was, and that later we would examine how and why it could be changed. However, first we need to measure the distribution of income to determine just what we mean by an unsatisfactory distribution of income. Then we can examine governmental redistribution programs to see why they have or haven't worked.

Does the Market Produce Equitable Outcomes?

Assuming a perfectly competitive market for the factors of production (land, labor, capital, and entrepreneurship), what determines the *laissez-faire* distribution of income, and is this a just or equitable solution? Economic theory gives us an unambiguous answer to the first of these two questions. The second is much more difficult to answer. In this discussion, the marginal productivity theory of income distribution, which we examined in detail in a previous chapter, will serve as a useful benchmark as we consider some additional *normative* and *positive* questions concerning the distribution of income. This marginal productivity theory is an important cornerstone of positive economics. It enables economists to analyze many problems concerning factor movements and changes in factor shares in the face of changed market conditions. As we shall see, many of the normative questions about income distribution arise because the market is not the only institution affecting the distribution of income in most societies. The discussion that follows will consider how other factors might affect the market-produced distribution of income in such a way as to make it unacceptable.

As we saw when we discussed factor markets, the return to the factors of production (rent, wages, interest, and profits), hence, the distribution of income, is determined by the supply of and demand for factors of different kinds and qualities. This functional distribution of income is treated in economic theory as a reflection of choices made by individuals in the marketplace. The demand for factors of production, including labor, is a demand derived from the demand for the good the factors are combined to produce. A factor's value is derived from what it produces. Differences in income are a result of a combination of influences, including differences in the productivity of factors and in the demand for the final products they produce.

Given factor inputs of equal physical productivity, the highest reward will go to the factor unit employed in the industry producing products most highly valued in the market. Also, labor inputs of different skills employed in the same industry will be rewarded with respect to their physical productivity, with the more productive factor receiving the greater remuneration at the margin. Additionally, the return to the factor will be affected by the physical productivity of the other factor units it is combined with and by the relative amounts of each factor employed. Thus, it is possible that factors of equal quality receive different remuneration when combined with different factors of production. A good example of this point is the return to the management of General Motors versus the return to the management of a small hometown plant. The managers of General Motors receive a higher return for one reason—because they are combined with larger amounts of capital, making the value of these units of managerial decision making higher.

An important aspect of this determination of income distribution is that it is associated with efficiency in resource allocation. *Ceteris paribus,* factors flow to those employments with the highest remuneration; that is, those in which their productivity is most highly valued. Such a system has value by contrast to some other ethical, nonmarket determination of factor remuneration, because it rewards productivity. In freely operating markets, the return to factors of equal productivity will tend toward equality and, over time, factors will tend to transfer to their highest valued use.

The Role of Chance

risk aversion   Most individuals will, ceteris paribus, *avoid risk unless they are compensated for assuming risk.*

egalitarian   Programs and individuals that are concerned with promoting a more equal distribution of income.

The market-determined distribution of income may be unsatisfactory because there are substantial elements of chance associated with this distribution. Most economists view risk as an unattractive situation which individuals will avoid unless they can be compensated for assuming this risk. We say people have *risk aversion.* An individual's future income is subject to a considerable degree of uncertainty. To a great extent this uncertainty may not be avoidable privately; hence, government programs of an *egalitarian* nature (programs aimed at creating a more equal distribution of income) that affect either the income distribution or the distribution of specific commodities appear. Thus, privately uninsurable risk may lead to income redistribution as a valid function of the state. Government may respond to such risks either by acting to reduce the risk itself or by implementing various types of insurance plans. In the former case, there are many examples of preventive public programs, such as public health and education programs, and programs designed to regulate product safety. In the latter case, institutions such as Social Security, unemployment insurance, progressive income taxation, and macroeconomic stabilization policy are examples of governmental policies that respond to some extent to risk-aversion among voters.

Should Distribution Be Completely Separated from Market Outcomes?

As we have seen, economists are reluctant to make interpersonal comparisons of utility. This restricts their analysis of distributional problems. The basic reason for this reluctance on the part of economists is that value judgements are necessary to judge alternative distributions of income, and value judgements are not scientific data. However, various economists and philosophers have developed general distributional schemes which depend in one way or another on interpersonal comparisons.

For example, a utilitarian would argue that income should be distributed to maximize society's satisfaction. Of course, this would be a difficult criterion to agree upon since there is no scientific way to compare satisfaction. Operationally, it would be difficult, if not impossible, to obtain reliable measures of satisfaction since each individual would have a clear incentive to lie. As stated above, economists have long argued that there is simply no way to make interpersonal comparisons of satisfaction, even if there were a way to operationally measure individual satisfaction. For example, say we wish to tax a rich student $100 and redistribute the $100 to a poor teacher. It is impossible for us to conclude that the satisfaction the rich student gave up by consuming $100 less champagne is less than the satisfaction the poor teacher received by consuming $100 more of Coors beer.

Since general schemes such as "maximizing society's satisfaction" are both theoretically and operationally impossible to implement, it might make sense to distribute income on some computed egalitarian basis as an approximation of the desire to make income more equal. The Greek philosopher, Plato, was explicit on such a rule. He argued that no one in society should be more than four times richer than the poorest member of society. Once such a normative decision to redistribute is made, the problem then becomes one of determining an operational basis. Again, economists have done little work in this area because of their unwillingness to make the necessary value judgements.

A Negative Income Tax

One operational rule that could be applied would be for everyone in a jurisdiction to be guaranteed at least some minimum income. This suggests that a guaranteed annual income is probably the best operational way to change the market-determined income distribution. Assuming that this idea is accepted, the problem is then to decide what the minimum income should be. Again, this has to be a strictly normative decision; economic theory can give us no clue as to what this level should be. The most workable approach would seem to be that of calculating a typical poverty level budget at current prices.

Professor Milton Friedman has suggested a *negative income tax* to replace the costly, inefficient, and incentive-destroying "present grab-bag" system of redistribution.[6] A negative income tax is a transfer to people from the government, rather than a transfer to the government from citizens; hence, the term *negative income tax*. A negative income tax has two components: an income guarantee and a negative tax rate. In Friedman's plan the basic income guarantee varies with family size. Say a family of four would have a guaranteed income of $3,000. The negative tax is, say, 50 percent. This means that for each dollar the family earns, it loses 50¢ of welfare payments. This is argued to be more conducive to work incentives because the family keeps part of its earned income rather than losing 100 percent in welfare reductions. Table 29-3 gives a hypothetical example for four families, assuming a $3,000 income guarantee and a 50 percent negative tax. The transfer received by a family is $3,000 minus 50 percent of any income earned that is less than $6,000. The amount of welfare that a family receives can be determined by the formula

$$T = IG - t_n (EI),$$

where T is the welfare payment, IG is the income guarantee, t_n is the negative tax rate, and EI is the earned income. At some point the family reaches the break-even point, which is the point at which no more income is transferred, and the family starts paying normal, positive taxes. With an income guarantee of $3,000 and a negative tax of 50 percent, this break-even point would occur at

negative income tax   A transfer from the government to the poor based on a formula similar to the present income tax system. A negative income tax has two components: an income guarantee and a negative tax rate.

---

[6]See Milton Friedman, "The Case for the Negative Income Tax," *Republican Papers,* edited by M. R. Laird (New York: Praeger, 1968).

TABLE 29-3   A NEGATIVE INCOME TAX[1]

Family:	A	B	C	D
Earned Income	$ 0	$2,000	$4,000	$6,000
Transfer	3,000	2,000	1,000	0
Disposable Income	3,000	4,000	5,000	6,000
Increase in Income of $100	100	100	100	100
Earned Income Becomes	100	2,100	4,100	6,100
Tax Rate	(−50%)	(−50%)	(−50%)	Normal Tax Rate
Welfare Payment	2,950	1,950	950	0
Disposable Income	3,050	4,050	5,050	6,100 (less normal tax on income over $6,000)

[1]Assumes a $3,000 guaranteed income and a 50 percent negative tax rate.

$6,000. Table 29-3 represents a numerical example and shows how an additional $100 of income would benefit the welfare recipient.

The major benefits of the negative income tax system are easy to see. In the first place, it concentrates public funds on the poor rather than on a large welfare bureaucracy through which funds must trickle down to those in need. It would therefore cost less for the same amount of redistribution because it is directed specifically at poverty, eliminating the need for intermediary agencies. And, instead of cutting off funds to those whose income is just above the poverty level, it provides aid to the near poor as well. Perhaps most importantly, however, the negative income tax does not eliminate work incentives. Most present systems reduce transfers by 100 percent of any earned income; if a person on welfare earns $1,000, benefits fall by $1,000. A system that allows individuals to keep a portion of what they earn would be favorable to work incentives. Another argument for such a system is that it would greatly reduce the cost of administering welfare programs. Then the welfare bureaucracy could be largely dismantled and the function of redistribution carried out by the Internal Revenue Service. The negative income tax is an objective and impersonal vehicle, thus allowing recipients to maintain a sense of dignity, instead of forcing welfare recipients to deal with a bureaucracy that at times is arrogant and demeaning. Furthermore, many programs, such as minimum wage legislation and agricultural subsidies, are justified on distribution grounds. It might be possible to eliminate some of these if the negative tax system were operative.

As long as a negative income tax is not merely superimposed on the current system so that it does not become simply another "rag in the bag" but, instead, replaces all direct public-assistance programs (if not all welfare programs in general) it is considered by most authorities to possess a decided advantage over other welfare-reform proposals. The main obstacle to its adoption is the entrenched vested interests of the present welfare bureaucracy.

Should Strings Be Attached?

A question basic to discussions of income redistribution is, What should be redistributed? In other words, should general money grants such as a guaranteed income be given or should the redistribution be in the form of goods (in kind)? If money is redistributed, a related question is whether or not conditions should be attached to the transfer.

The argument that money should be given instead of certain goods is part of the argument that lump-sum transfers of general purchasing power are the optimal form of transfer. A transfer of money allows more options and maximizes the freedom of the recipient; that is, it places the individual on the highest possible indifference curve. This is the traditional welfare analysis of transfers of money and is based solely on the idea of maximizing the utility of welfare recipients. It assumes we should transfer money and let the welfare recipients maximize their own well-being.

Professor James Buchanan has argued that maximizing the utility of welfare recipients by allowing them freedom is not relevant; one should instead consider maximizing the freedom of the welfare donor. This implies money or in-kind transfers, depending on what the donor specifies. This argument applies if we are discussing negative externalities (such as the poor) or positive externalities (such as faculty members or citizens' groups deciding what is best for students to read).

The conditional granting of transfers is likely to be an important factor when the motivation for the transfer is *not* concern for the welfare of the recipient, per se. The motivation may stem from a distaste for a particularly noxious externality, or it may stem from a desire to influence behavior in a certain way. That is, it may stem from a desire to reduce the cost of policing against a certain action or a fear that unless some redistribution takes place the poor will become unruly. These are distinctly separate motivations, but they produce the same distributional response, and they both imply that it is the freedom of the donor that should be maximized. When these motivations are important to the donor, it is likely that strings will be attached to the transfer. Probably the best example of such conditional granting of transfers is the often-cited example of the welfare requirement that able-bodied males must be willing to accept work if offered. In effect, the argument here is that transfers to reduce specific externalities may be quite rational from the point of view of the donor-voter. This is supported in a positive sense by the observation of the large amounts of such specific transfers in practice.

Basic Needs

Many of the transfers that we observe are in-kind transfers of specific commodities; for example, the surplus-commodity food program and Salvation Army soup kitchens. Grants and transfers of this kind may result when the concerns of those initiating the transfer are aimed at what they consider basic needs. The transfer is not so much based on the desire to reduce income inequality as on the desire to insure that basic needs, such as food and shelter, are provided. Professor James Tobin of Yale University has pointed out this distinction by referring to it as *specific egalitarianism.* Tobin believes that most economists are *general* egalitarians (to the extent they are egalitarian), because they recognize the inefficiencies introduced by in-kind transfers. The majority of the electorate, however, are *specific* egalitarians. They are concerned with ill-clothed and ill-fed people, not with poverty, per se. If this observation is correct, one can expect most public transfers to be transfers in kind, or with strings attached.

Redistribution Through Jobs

An exception to the argument that recipients prefer the money transfer to the in-kind or strings-attached transfer is the argument that the poor do not want welfare, but rather, meaningful jobs. This is, in essence, a call for in-kind transfers in the form of jobs, sometimes publicly provided. This argument can often be added, in a subtle fashion, to arguments concerning monetary and fiscal policy. Labor leaders often argue in Washington that publicly provided jobs are needed to cushion the harshness of contractionary monetary and fiscal policy.

Redistribution to Special Interests

An interesting case of redistribution occurs when the recipients attempt to conceal the fact from themselves and others that a transfer is being made. This case constitutes back-door welfare; that is, transfers from the general public to special interest groups via some form of trade-restricting legislation. Arguments for such legislation, as you will see in the next chapter, appear frequently in international trade literature, but arguments for tariffs and quotas are by no means the only arguments used by special interest groups for back-door welfare. Each of the special interest groups just discussed has a lobby in Washington. Each believes the others seek back-door welfare, but rarely attribute those motives to their own actions. An example of such an argument would be the mink-breeder's association arguing that they need protection from cheap mink being imported from Eastern Europe. In effect, the mink breeders are asking for an income transfer from consumers of mink. It is an income transfer because the tariff or quota will allow the price of mink to be higher than it would be in the absence of any import restrictions. This means the consumers of mink pelts, or people who buy mink coats, are transferring income to the mink producers. Some of you may think this is all right, because people who buy mink coats are rich, but what if we change the example to one where the people who want the tariff are producers of cotton shirts, or beef, or shoes. The transfer is well-camouflaged, and many industry leaders and producing firms would strongly object to putting the protection argument in these terms. Nevertheless, the protection represents a transfer to the protected industry.

In fact, it might well be argued that every lobbyist in Washington is really asking for back-door welfare. In addition to promoting these transfers, one could say that these lobbyists help produce unproductive entrepreneurial activity. An example here would be investment in tax avoidance through the hiring of tax lawyers and accountants who are employed solely to avoid taxes.

Private Versus Public Mechanisms for Redistributing Income

There are many ways that the types of general or specific transfers we have been discussing can be carried out. The manner in which redistribution is accomplished can influence the type and amount of the ultimate transfer.

Private redistribution through charity takes place voluntarily. Such transfers can spring from a variety of motivations, all linked to some form of concern by an individual about other individuals in society. The analytical term for such concern is **utility interdependence.** Interdependence of utility functions exists for any one of a number of reasons, ranging from a sense of social justice to finding offensive the life-style of those who are poor. The important point about such transfers is that they are voluntary and, hence, may be presumed to be optimal in the sense that both parties benefit. However, as we argued before, there is a problem with relying upon private redistribution alone. If the income equality achieved via private charity can be characterized as a public good, the private charity might produce too little redistribution. This would happen because the individuals in a large group would recognize that they do not have to contribute since others will. In large groups there is a tendency to free ride in this way and, in practice, give very little to charity. The reason, as Professor Tullock has so aptly said, is that the two drives of consuming and helping the poor are in conflict. The result is that people generally talk as if they are charitable but in practice demonstrate that they are not as charitable as they profess. Of course, if all followed this strategy, there would be no private redistribution or at least not enough redistribution. Such an argument provides a basis for collectivizing the function of income redistribution. The person who gives to others because of the personal satisfaction gained from the act does not present a free-rider problem. However, if the personal gain the giver receives is seeing less poverty in the world, the act of others' giving diminishes the need to give, and the free-rider problem can arise.

An important variable in determining the amount of private redistribution is the size of the group in which the distribution takes place. If we are dealing with a relatively small, homogeneous group of givers and receivers, the amount of private redistribution increases. This is observable in such groups as the Mormon church and certain Amish sects. It is consistent with the view that the externalities associated with poverty are more significant (i.e., observable) the smaller the group size. Thus, one might predict that in a collective context, a small country with a relatively homogeneous population, such as Sweden, would likely practice more redistribution than a large melting pot country like the United States.

We have up to this point been discussing the theory that those who are relatively rich use the state as a mechanism in transferring income to the poor. There is, however, another theory: that the poor use the state as a means of extracting transfers from the rich. This view is grounded on some empirical evidence, since the poor do vote and the amount of redistribution does seem to be a function of the degree to which they vote.

utility interdependence The fact that some individuals gain satisfaction from the consumption of goods by other parties.

Positive Theories of Income Redistribution

The preceding discussion has centered on a consideration of some basic motivations that lie behind various arguments for income redistribution. The result has been a conclusion that redistribution follows from any of a number of benign and nonbenign motivations. There have been very few attempts to distill these arguments into a positive theory of income redistribution based on the usual self-interest models employed by economists. Two exceptions have been positive theories exposited by Professor George Stigler of the University of Chicago and Professor Gordon Tullock, who consider why people might try to redistribute to themselves rather than to others.

Stigler theorizes that the government will use its coercive power to extract resources which would not be forthcoming by voluntary agreement in the society. Any group that can gain control of the government machinery can then use this power to its own benefit. Stigler argues that the group that controls government is the middle class; hence, most public expenditures are made for the benefit of the middle class.

Along similar lines, Tullock argues that only a small portion of the massive amounts of government transfers go to the poor. He argues that in the nature of the voting process, resources will be taken from the rich, but it is not entirely clear how they will be distributed. Since the middle-income groups will be crucial in obtaining the authority needed to take resources from other members of society, he expects that money will flow from both ends of the income ladder toward the middle.

Both Tullock and Stigler argue that the state is used primarily for the taking of resources and that political power will be used to advance these ends. As a result, income distribution will, in reality, be a method by which the dominant political group, the middle class, extends its power. Both Tullock and Stigler present examples, such as farm policy, education, and so on, where examination of the incidence of the benefits supports this hypothesis. The lesson that should be drawn here is that the real reason for income redistribution and the expressed political intent are often quite different. Of course, these arguments are closely related to some of the arguments that were treated earlier. In fact, they are forms of special-interest redistribution or redistribution via bureaucracy. Tullock's contention that in most cases transfers do not reach the poor is particularly telling.

A Complex System

We have considered some of the normative and positive arguments concerning the distribution of income. As one would expect, the discussion was complex. There are many ways of looking at the question of the distribution of income and obviously many trade-offs to be considered in determining an optimal or acceptable answer to the question of what is the proper distribution. Our approach has been only to sketch the relevant questions and trade-offs. We have followed this approach because the resolution of distribution questions is something that we cannot pronounce upon as economists. Rather, we hope that the discussion of distribution considerations that we have presented will be helpful in coming to grips with the basic trade-offs involved in understanding distribution policy, which by necessity can only be determined in the political arena.

MEASURING THE DISTRIBUTION OF INCOME

Lorenz curve A geometric construction which traces the cumulative percentage of income that households receive, ranked from the lowest to the highest.

If we are going to design programs to redistribute income, we must first determine what the distribution of income is and identify the poor. A traditional way to measure the distribution of income is with a **Lorenz curve.** A Lorenz curve traces the cumulative percentage of income that households receive, ranked from lowest to highest. In Figure 29-4, we have Lorenz curves for three hypothetical economies. A perfectly egalitarian society would have a Lorenz curve represented by

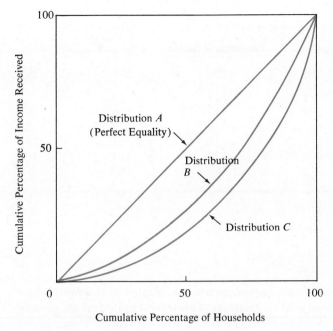

FIGURE 29-4   LORENZ CURVES

A Lorenz curve traces the cumulative percentage of income households receive, ranked from lowest to highest. A perfectly egalitarian society would have a Lorenz curve represented by Distribution *A*. *B* and *C* represent more unequal distributions of income.

Distribution *A*. If incomes were absolutely uniformly distributed, the lowest 10 percent of the households would have 10 percent of the income, the highest 20 percent would have 20 percent, and so on. When we get a distribution in which everyone does not have the same income, the Lorenz curve diverges from the 45-degree line of perfect equality. Distribution *B* in Figure 29-4 represents a less than perfectly egalitarian society. The greater the difference between the 45-degree line and the Lorenz curve, the greater the inequality in the cumulative distribution. In terms of Figure 29-4, Distribution *C* represents a more unequal distribution of income than Distribution *B*.

We can draw Lorenz curves for countries to compare them to the level of egalitarianism among other countries. If we did that, we would find Sweden's Lorenz curve to be closest to the 45-degree line, and the countries in the under-developed world to be the most skewed from the 45-degree line. Another useful exercise is to examine how the distribution of income changes over time. The data in Table 29-4 allow us to draw Lorenz curves like those of Figure 29-5. Both the table and the figure indicate that our society has become more egalitarian since 1929.

Lorenz curves tell us about the *relative* distribution of income. A particular Lorenz curve might indicate that the lower 20 percent of the households have only 5 percent of the income, but it doesn't say if this income is high or low in an absolute sense. This 5 percent could be high enough so that everyone is well fed, well housed, and well clothed. Being in the lowest 5 percent in the United States, for example, may be better than being in the middle 5 percent of some other country.

TABLE 29-4   INCOME DISTRIBUTION IN THE UNITED STATES, 1929–1979

Family	Income Class	Percentage of Income				
		1929	1947	1960	1972	1979
Lowest	5th	3.5	5.1	4.8	5.4	5.3
Second	5th	9.0	11.8	12.2	11.9	11.6
Middle	5th	13.8	16.7	17.8	17.5	17.5
Fourth	5th	19.3	23.2	24.0	23.9	24.1
Highest	5th	54.4	43.3	41.3	41.4	41.6
Highest	5%	30.0	17.5	15.9	15.9	15.7

Source: *Statistical Abstract of the United States,* 1981, and previous issues.

The Absolute Level of Income

We need to somehow determine how much income, or more appropriately, how little income, defines poverty in an economy. This is hard to do because poverty is both an absolute and a relative concept. People who are relatively poor in one country may be well off by another country's standard, or in the same country in different decades or centuries. These problems notwithstanding, we need to attempt to measure poverty. The U.S. government makes such definitions and

FIGURE 29-5   INCOME DISTRIBUTION IN THE UNITED STATES, 1929–1980

Plotting Lorenz curves for the United States for 1929 and 1980 shows that the distribution of income has become more equal.

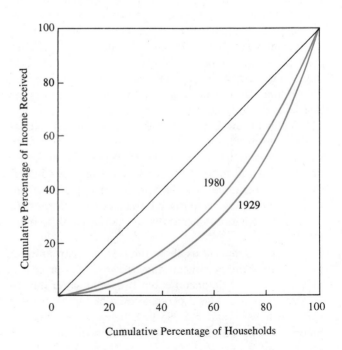

updates them from time to time. In 1978, the official poverty level ranged from $2,650 for a single female on a farm to $11,038 for a two-parent family of seven in an urban area. The average nonfarm family of four had a poverty threshold of $6,665. Of course, these figures are higher now due to inflation. Table 29-5 shows that in recent years, the number of people below the poverty level has decreased. The next relevant question is, Who are these poor? The answer, of course, is difficult to determine. The poor come from everywhere and from every age group. However, it may be possible to pinpoint certain social, geographic, and racial characteristics of the poor. Geographically, for example, the poor tend to live in the rural south and northern cities. Table 29-6 points out some other important characteristics of people below the poverty line. If we take 12 percent as the standard, because approximately 12 percent of all persons fell below the poverty line in 1980, we can see that the incidence is higher than 12 percent for certain segments of the population. Nonwhites have a much higher incidence of poverty. Age is an important variable, with the young and old representing a sizable percentage of the group below the poverty level. Education is important, with high school and college graduates being under-represented. This, of course, makes good sense if we view education as an investment in human capital. It also suggests that education is one way to deal with the problem of poverty. Marital status is important also; as you can see, widowers and divorced women who are heads of households have a high incidence of poverty.

Nonwhite Poverty

Nonwhites have a much higher incidence of poverty. Of course, a major reason for this is that the nonwhite population has a much higher representation of the characteristics associated with poverty listed in Table 29-6. Another reason is racial discrimination. Whatever the cause of this race-related poverty, the effects have not diminished in recent years despite programs to overcome nonwhite poverty. Table 29-7 shows that the nonwhite-white income differential has remained surprisingly stable. Perhaps the most hopeful sign is that the educational achievement of nonwhites has been increasing significantly, and this achievement should translate into higher income levels. UCLA Professor Thomas Sowell, for example, has argued that the return to education is much higher for minority individuals than it is for nonminority individuals.[7]

TABLE 29-5 PERCENTAGE OF POPULATION
CONSIDERED POOR

1959	22.4
1966	14.7
1972	11.9
1976	11.8
1979	11.6

Source: *Statistical Abstract of the United States,* 1981.

[7]See Thomas Sowell, *Race and Economics* (New York: David McKay Co., 1975).

TABLE 29-6 POVERTY INCIDENCE—1980

Characteristic	Percentage Who Fall Below Poverty Line
All Families	11.6
Race	
White	8.9
Black	30.9
Spanish Surname	21.6
Age	
Children Under 18	17.0
White	8.9
Black	30.9
65 and Older	15.1
Employment Status	
Employed	5.1
Unemployed	24.0
Not in Labor Force	22.3
Education of Family Head	
Elementary	23.8
1–3 Years of High School	13.8
4 Years of High School	6.6
Some College	3.1
Marital Status (head of household)	
Married—Spouse Present	11.6
Widowed	41.3
Divorced—Women	31.9

Source: U.S. Bureau of the Census, *U.S. Census of Population, 1980.*

PROGRAMS TO REDISTRIBUTE INCOME

Regardless of how one feels about the theoretical arguments concerning whether or not redistribution should be publicly or privately provided, it is unmistakably clear that redistribution of income has become a public activity. The public share of welfare has increased dramatically in recent years. The governmental programs are varied and have varied constituencies. Yet there is a basic philosophy that has run through the welfare program. This philosophy calls for jobs for those who are able to work, social insurance for the elderly and those temporarily unemployed, and direct assistance for children and the infirm.

Employment opportunities are provided through macroeconomic policies and programs. The Humphrey-Hawkins Bill further advocates this aspect of governmental responsibility by codifying into law the proposition that every

TABLE 29-7   NONWHITE-WHITE INCOME DIFFERENTIALS

Year	Mean Incomes of Nonwhites as a Percentage of Mean White Income
1964	56
1965	55
1966	60
1967	62
1968	63
1969	63
1970	64
1971	63
1972	60
1973	62
1974	65
1975	66
1976	68
1977	66
1978	63
1979	64

Source: *Statistical Abstract of the United States,* 1981.

American has a right to a job and that it is the government's responsibility to provide jobs as the employer of last resort.

Old Age, Survivors and Disability Insurance (Social Security) is the government's program to provide social insurance. The Social Security Act was passed in 1935 and pays retirement subsidies to the aged and to widows and children of workers who are covered under the law. Medicare and Medicaid are other examples of governmental social insurance. Unemployment benefits are also paid to those temporarily out of work.

Direct assistance programs are designed to help the poor who are not covered by social insurance. The largest of such programs are the AFDC (Aid to Families with Dependent Children) and OAA (Old Age Assistance) programs. These programs are targeted to the categories with high incidences of poverty, as we saw in Table 29-6. In addition to these programs, there are many other direct assistance programs such as food stamps, rent supplements, Head Start, and so on.

Problems in Governmental Transfers

There has been much frustration recently with the inability of governmental welfare programs to alleviate poverty. Senator Daniel P. Moynihan, who was President Nixon's welfare adviser, believes the problem is that many of the governmental programs simply don't reach the poor. He says, "This money did not go to poor people, but to the new class of professionals who manage the

Thomas Sowell *(1930–)*

Thomas Sowell is currently a professor of economics at U.C.L.A. He has a B.A. from Harvard, an M.A. from Columbia, and a Ph.D. in economics from the University of Chicago. Professor Sowell has used positive economic theory and analysis to examine some politically explosive problems of race and income distribution in the United States. These problems have often been examined only in a very normative fashion.

In one study, Professor Sowell examined the need for affirmative action employment plans in higher education. He demonstrated that the administration of affirmative action programs has run counter to the intent of the Civil Rights Act of 1964. The law rejected quotas and placed the burden of proving discrimination on the government. In reality, the burden of proof has been shifted to the employer. This has resulted in a tremendous increase in the costs of higher education. Sowell found in a statistical comparison that salaries of black academics with comparable training and credentials equaled or surpassed salaries of white academics before the application of the law in 1971. Sowell also statistically demonstrated that male-female career differentials are not the result of employer discrimination but are more likely explained by social mores that place family responsibilities disproportionately on women. This explanation suggests that government intervention aimed at reducing these differentials simply won't work.

In his most recent work *Ethnic America: A History* (1981), Sowell examines each wave of immigrants to determine what caused their success. His message is that disciplined hard work and entrepreneurial ability can surmount poverty and bigotry. He cites the impressive record of West Indian Blacks as evidence that being black is not a fatal handicap in America.

In all his work, Sowell has used the logic of economics to examine social policy questions of considerable interest. In doing so, he does not shy away from very sensitive questions of race and claims of discrimination. To examine Sowell's ideas and arguments, you should read his *Affirmative Action Reconsidered* (1975); *Black Education: Myths and Tragedies* (1970); *Race and Economics* (1975); *Knowledge and Decisions* (1980); and *Ethnic America: A History* (1981).

programs."[8] This view of the system from someone who tried to change it fits very closely with the theories of Stigler and Tullock, which we discussed earlier in this chapter.

The inability of government programs to substantially affect poverty has led to a so-called welfare crisis. Many citizens are frustrated by what is perceived as a large group of welfare cheats and by the belief that, for many individuals,

---

[8]*Newsweek* (November 7, 1977), p. 42.

welfare has become a way of life. One reason for this view is that present welfare practices have had the effect of destroying work incentives and in some cases have even created incentives for family dissolution. AFDC is a case in point. Fathers have been known to leave home so the family could become eligible for AFDC payments. Work incentives are destroyed because an increase in earnings usually means an equivalent loss of welfare benefits. The negative income tax which we discussed in detail earlier in this chapter could help to overcome this problem.

The difficult policy decisions and conflicting social goals among which policy-makers must choose are inescapable under a negative income tax program. But it is important to remember that virtually none of the major problems or objections to the negative income tax are limited only to this proposal. They are to be found in any welfare program, particularly with respect to the work-incentive question.

Social Security: A Chain Letter?

Social Security is in the news, and it's big news. For many years, workers viewed Social Security as a retirement program with associated insurance aspects for disabled workers. But it never really was a retirement program in the sense of a private retirement program. In a private program, workers contribute to a fund while they work. The fund is invested, causing it to increase, and the workers draw on the fund when they retire.

The Social Security program is, and always was, a tax and transfer program. Workers were taxed, and those taxes went into a trust fund that paid the retired members of the system. Those who paid taxes would receive transfers when they retired. This is very similar to the workings of a chain letter. Chain letter participants pay now to receive money from those who later join the chain.

A funny thing happened in the 1960s. The age distribution of the population changed. In 1950, there were 16 workers paying Social Security taxes for every beneficiary of the system. In 1960, this ratio shrunk to three workers for each beneficiary. By the year 2025, there will be only two workers for each beneficiary. The result of this trend is clear. There will be an increasing burden on workers whose taxes keep the fund solvent.

We have already experienced some implications of this change in age distribution of the population. Between 1965 and 1981, there was a 900 percent increase in Social Security taxes. At present, the system is spending $12,400 more a minute than it is taking in.

The solutions are painful for all. Benefits must be reduced. At least the automatic raise component that is tied to the Consumer Price Index must be changed. Taxes will have to rise. Eventually, the system, if it is to be maintained, must be supported out of general tax revenue. This will end, once and for all, the charade that the system is a retirement system, and it will clearly label the system as a tax-transfer mechanism from working taxpayers to the retired.

The War on Poverty: Two Views [9]

The War on Poverty started in the United States in 1960. President Kennedy asked his Council of Economic Advisers for data and background information on the problems of poverty. It is reported that, in part, his motivation for asking was the result of the poverty he encountered during the West Virginia primary. Robert Lampman, an economist working for the Council, reported that the gradual decline in the incidence of poverty that had been taking place since the end of the Great Depression had slowed in the 1950s, and that full employment and economic growth alone were not enough to solve the problem. As a result of the Council's report, President Kennedy started to attack some of the causes of poverty in America.

After Kennedy's assassination, President Johnson continued this interest in poverty. In 1964, in his first State of the Union Address, Johnson declared war on poverty and launched his Great Society programs. The Johnson administration was so concerned with eradicating poverty that all government programs were scrutinized and evaluated in terms of what they did for the poor. [10]

We now have more than 20 years of experience in the War on Poverty. What has been accomplished? There are two polar answers to the question.

The War Was Lost. [11] The argument that the war was lost is based in large part on the fact that there is still a great deal of poverty in the United States. As we saw earlier, the distribution of income, as measured by a Lorenz curve, is relatively stable. In the late 1970s, the feeling emerged that the huge rise in social spending didn't accomplish very much, and that throwing money at problems didn't solve them. Some of the most radical reformers argue that the war on poverty failed because it didn't restructure capitalism.

The War Was Won. [12] Another politically popular argument is that the War on Poverty was won. Thus, the massive social programs that were implemented are no longer needed. Martin Anderson, President Reagan's former domestic policy adviser, advocates this view. He argues that poverty in America has virtually been eliminated by the growth in governmental programs.

Reconciling the Extremes. Professor Sheldon Danziger of the University of Wisconsin and Robert Plotnick of Dartmouth College have examined the empirical evidence supporting these two views. [13] They have found that the level of absolute poverty has declined, but that the relative level of poverty has not. In other words, the basic needs of the poor have been better met, but the incomes of the bottom group have not increased relative to the average level of income in the United States. Danziger and Plotnick have concluded that cutbacks of transfer payments, such as those advocated by President Reagan, will increase the

---

[9]Sheldon Danziger and Robert Plotnick, "The War on Income Poverty: Achievements and Failures," *Welfare Reform in America: Perspectives and Prospects,* edited by Paul Sommers (Hingham, Mass.: Martinus Nijhoff Publishers, 1981).

[10]Robert Lampman, "What Does It Do for the Poor? A New Test for National Policy," *Public Interest,* No. 34 (Winter, 1974), pp. 66–82.

[11]Marc Pilisuk and Phyllis Pilisuk (eds.), *How We Lost the War on Poverty* (Brunswick, N.J.: Transaction Books, 1973).

[12]Martin Anderson, *Welfare* (Palo Alto: Hoover Institution Press, 1978).

[13]Danziger and Plotnick, *op. cit.*

absolute level of poverty in America. They do not recommend the expansion of transfer payments, because they believe that that would only increase transfers to those above the poverty line. However, they do argue against decreasing these programs, because the reduction will increase poverty.

Prospects for Reform

Welfare reform is, of course, high on the political agenda. The prospects for meaningful reform dim, however, when one examines the bureaucratic vested interests involved. We will have to wait to see how any of the various proposed welfare reforms fare in the political arena. Choosing between different welfare programs requires value judgements. Economic theory can help us analyze the effects of different programs, but it cannot tell us which is the correct reform. Such questions require political solutions.

SUMMARY

1. This chapter has examined various arguments for and against government intervention into the market.

2. Externalities exist when there is interdependence between economic units and when this interdependence is not reflected in market transactions. As a result of negative externalities, competitive firms will produce too much output at too low a price.

3. The government *may* be able to internalize the externalities and move the market closer to a social optimum.

4. The Coase theorem suggests that, where few parties are affected by externalities, the government may not need to intervene; that is, the market will automatically internalize the externalities.

5. The provision of public goods is another area where government intervention may be necessary.

6. Public goods may be underproduced because individuals free ride on the provision of the goods. As a result, the government may need to provide for the goods out of general tax revenue if the correct amount is to be provided.

7. It is necessary to weigh carefully the costs of government intervention in providing public goods or correcting externalities. It is easy to show that markets do not always produce optimal outputs, but government intervention is not cost-free. The choice is between two imperfect mechanisms, and we must be sure that the benefits of intervention outweigh the costs.

8. One of the debates surrounding government provision of certain goods is how to determine the correct amount of public goods that government should provide. Economists have different ideas about whether government produces too large or too small an amount of public goods.

9. Special interest groups are, in effect, lobbies for the provision of public goods.

10. It can be argued that one of the primary public goods that government produces is income redistribution. The motivations for income redistribution are varied, but we should begin from the assumption that the market produces a less than desirable distribution of income.

11. The Lorenz curve is the most common technique for measuring the relative distribution of income in a society. But income distribution is an absolute as well as a relative concept.

12. Different means of measuring the absolute levels of poverty and the social characteristics associated with poverty are necessary to paint an accurate picture of poverty in America.

13. The American response to poverty has taken three distinct forms: to provide jobs, to provide social insurance, and to provide direct assistance to children and those who are unable to work because of age and health problems.

14. Actual government programs are beset by a number of problems. One of the most formidable is that very little money filters down to the most needy in our society.

15. The measure of success in dealing with poverty depends on whether one is concerned with relative or absolute poverty. America has achieved some success in dealing with absolute poverty, but the level of relative poverty has not declined.

NEW TERMS

externalities
social costs
internalize
Coase theorem
public goods
free-riding behavior

logrolling
risk aversion
egalitarian
negative income tax
utility interdependence
Lorenz curve

QUESTIONS FOR DISCUSSION

1. Should the government intervene in every case where an externality exists?

2. Is there air or water pollution where you live? What should be done about it? Should the pollution be entirely done away with? How much more in taxes or higher prices for goods would you be willing to pay in order to have less pollution?

3. What factors determine wages? What causes some people with equal skills to receive different wages? Would a competitive economy reduce or increase these differentials?

4. Who is responsible for the fact that some people are poor? What would you do about it if you were in a position to take some action?

5. Do you think a negative income tax would solve the U.S. poverty problem? Why or why not?

6. Should we be concerned with relative or absolute poverty? How would dealing with absolute poverty differ from programs dealing with relative poverty?

7. Is education a public good? If not, why should taxes help pay for the college education of some individuals?

SUGGESTIONS FOR FURTHER READING

Amacher, Ryan C., Robert D. Tollison, and Thomas D. Willett. "Budget Size in a Democracy: A Review of the Arguments." *Public Finance Quarterly* (April, 1975).

———(eds.). "A Menu of Distributional Considerations." *The Economic Approach to Public Policy: Selected Readings.* New York: Cornell University Press, 1976.

Anderson, Martin. *Welfare.* Palo Alto: Hoover Institution Press, 1978.

Bethell, Tom. "Treating Poverty: Wherein the Cure Gives Rise to the Disease," *Harper's,* Vol. 260, No. 1557 (February, 1980), pp. 16–24.

Danziger, Sheldon and Robert Plotnick, "The War on Income Poverty: Achievements and Failures," *Welfare Reform in America: Perspectives and Prospects,* edited by Paul Sommers. Hingham, Mass: Martinus Nijhoff Publishers, 1981.

Oates, Wallace. *Fiscal Federalism.* New York: Harcourt Brace Jovanovich, Inc., 1972. Chapters 3 and 4.

Weil, Gordon L. *The Welfare Debate of 1978.* White Plains: The Institute for Socioeconomic Studies, 1978.

PART 7

International
Influences

International Economics

Learning Objectives

After studying the materials found in this chapter, you should be able to do the following:

1. Contrast absolute advantage to comparative advantage.

2. Diagram the supply curve adjustment necessitated by a:
   (a) quota.
   (b) tariff.

3. List the arguments for protectionism.

4. Outline the reasons why the arguments used in favor of protectionism are incorrect.

5. Describe the trade policy referred to as beggar-thy-neighbor.

6. Define and contrast:
   (a) voluntary export restraints (VERs).
   (b) orderly marketing agreements (OMAs).
   (c) the General Agreement on Tariffs and Trade (GATT).

7. Define:
   (a) clean floating.
   (b) dirty floating.
   (c) pegged exchange rates.
   (d) flexible exchange rates.
   (e) fixed, but adjustable, exchange rates.
   (f) tariffs.
   (g) quotas.

8. Diagram and explain the effect of government intervention in the form of either a price floor or a price ceiling on the exchange market.

Until this chapter, we've discussed a closed economy; that is, one that isn't open to international influences. Neglecting these international influences made the analysis less complicated. For an economy such as that of the United States, which exports less than 10 percent of its total GNP, this neglect may not be too serious; but for an economy such as that of the Netherlands, which exports more than half of its GNP, a great deal of attention must be directed to international developments. In fact, it has become increasingly clear in recent years that the

United States must also carefully watch international developments; we are not as isolated from foreign economies as we once were.

This chapter has several purposes. First, we will discuss why nations engage in trade—the incentives to import and export goods and services. Second, we will examine arguments for protection and techniques of protection. Third, we will discuss the role of changes in exchange rates in bringing about equilibrium in foreign exchange markets. (Foreign exchange markets are those in which people with various currencies trade them; the price of one currency in terms of another is the exchange rate of the two currencies.)

WHY COUNTRIES ENGAGE IN FOREIGN TRADE

Countries engage in trade for the same reasons individuals do. In fact, in countries where private enterprise plays a role, most of a country's trades are made by individuals.

Trade Between Individuals

One evening, Freddy Foghorn trades two car washes to Suzy Sizzle for three apple pies. They do so because it looks like a good deal; both of them believe they'll be better off from the trade. Voluntary exchanges are mutually beneficial, or they wouldn't be entered into. It works the same way with nations if Freddy and Suzy are nationals of different countries.

Even with the simple example of Suzy and Freddy, there are problems of misinterpretation. First, Suzy may decide that while the deal looked good in advance, she's sorry afterwards. Trade is always based on *expected gains,* and we can sometimes be wrong in our estimates. But if we observe that Suzy and Freddy go on trading week after week, we have to believe that their estimates are pretty close to what actually happens and that they keep trading because both feel better off with trade than without.

Second, Freddy may feel that Suzy is getting the better deal even though both are better off with trade than without. Both of them gain from trade, but the *gains from trade* may not be evenly split in the eyes of one (or both) partners.

Third, before Suzy came on the scene, Freddy was trading with Jerry Jock. Suzy offers a better deal, so Freddy reduces his trade with Jerry, and Jerry feels injured by Suzy's "unfair" competition in trade. Of course, no one likes to fight competition, so it's easy to understand Jerry's feelings. It's still true, though, that all three of them are better off with some trade than they would be if they couldn't trade at all. As compared to the old days when only Jerry and Freddy traded, the new arrangement makes Suzy better off (otherwise she wouldn't trade), makes Freddy better off (or he would be trading only with Jerry), and makes Jerry worse off—he wishes Suzy would get lost! However, Jerry is better off competing with Suzy than not trading at all.

Differences Between Nations and Individuals

Trade makes individuals better off or they wouldn't do it. International trade makes individuals in nations better off in the same way; they give up something

expected gains *The anticipated utility a consumer foresees when engaging in trade. Trade and consumption are based on expected rather than actual gains.*

gains from trade *The extra satisfaction an individual anticipates when voluntarily engaging in trade.*

they have for something they want more than what they give up. The problem is, while the nation as a whole is better off with trade, usually some individuals are worse off. Those who are hurt naturally don't like the trade that causes the damage and seek some protection from the government against this damage from foreign trade.

Economists say that countries are better off with free trade than with no trade, but we have to clarify what this means. After trade starts, some people will gain from it while some will lose. It would be possible to take funds from the gainers and give them to the losers until the losers are just compensated for their losses, and the gainers would still be better off. With this sort of compensation, nobody loses and some people gain, so it is clear that the people of the nation as a whole are better off. However, since this kind of compensation is seldom carried out, the losers can't be blamed for being upset.

The losers are people who are hurt by competition from imports. This is just like Jerry's competition with Suzy, only now Jerry can think of his competitor as a foreigner, and when foreigners are involved, it is easier to get the government to interfere in the process. The gainers are those who can buy more cheaply from abroad than at home or those who can sell their output abroad at a better price than they could at home. Consumers of goods generally gain, and so do the factors of production engaged in the export industries, as well as businesses that import raw materials or semifinished goods from abroad.

Productivity as a Basis for Trade

So far, we have explained trade as simply being due to a natural desire to trade what you have for something you would prefer to have. It's important to have gone this far because we can see that if you are forbidden to trade, your level of satisfaction and number of options would both be reduced. But we have to ask why trade can boost satisfaction. What is it that makes you (and nations) willing to trade? We want to go behind the desire to trade and ask what causes this desire.

In the early 1800s, David Ricardo and other economists offered an explanation of trade based on different levels of productivity of nations in different industries. Ricardo's example dealt with trade between England and Portugal. He considered two goods: wool, which England exported, and port wine which Portugal exported.

Let us look at his example, supposing that each country has only one factor of production, labor. Table 30-1 shows that one English worker could produce either 6 bales of wool or 3 casks of port. In England, then, the opportunity cost of one more cask of port is 2 bales of wool. In Portugal, however, one worker

TABLE 30-1   WOOL AND PORT WINE AS PRODUCED
             BY ENGLAND AND PORTUGAL

	One English Worker	One Portuguese Worker
Wool	6 bales	1 bale
Port	3 casks	1 cask

David Ricardo *(1772–1823)*

David Ricardo may have been the most influential of all the classical economists. Born in London to Dutch-Jewish parents, he entered his father's stock-brokerage firm at the age of 14. Seven years later he married a Quaker and became a Christian. He did this against the wishes of his family, and, as a result of their disapproval of his wife, he started his own business. By age 25 he had amassed a sizable fortune.

In 1799, while he was on vacation, Ricardo picked up a copy of Adam Smith's *Wealth of Nations* because he was bored. He was immediately attracted to economic theory by the power of Smith's analysis. Despite his lack of formal education, he quickly became a leading intellectual of his time. His experience is in contrast to almost all the other classical economists who had pursued rigorous programs of formal education. In 1814 Ricardo retired to devote his time to political economy. In 1819 he became a member of Parliament and, with the help of James Mill (father of the great economist John Stuart Mill), founded the Political Economy Club of London. This club became the forum in which the classical economists discussed their ideas.

Ricardo was a prolific writer of letters and pamphlets intended to influence policy discussions on economic matters. His chief formal work, *On the Principles of Political Economy and Taxation,* was published in 1817. He is best remembered for his statements on the principles of comparative advantage and his support of free trade, which are only a part of his comprehensive work. In fact, much of his early interest in economics was generated by his interest in international trade and by his interest in showing the benefits of such trade. Ricardo also developed a labor theory of value which greatly impressed Karl Marx, who extended and radicalized Ricardo's theory.

can produce 1 bale of wool or 1 cask of port. Thus, in Portugal the opportunity cost of one more cask of port is 1 bale of wool. Or, to get one more bale of wool, the Portuguese must sacrifice 1 cask of port. Table 30-2 shows how the opportunity cost is determined for production in each country.

TABLE 30-2 OPPORTUNITY COSTS OF PRODUCTION

England

6 bales of wool cost 3 casks of port, so
1 bale of wool costs ½ cask of port.
3 casks of port cost 6 bales of wool, so
1 cask of port costs 2 bales of wool.

Portugal

1 bale of wool costs 1 cask of port.
1 cask of port costs 1 bale of wool.

This is the perfect opportunity for a sharp entrepreneur. The entrepreneur could buy 1 cask of port in Portugal for 1 bale of wool. Thus, 1 bale of wool could be shipped to Portugal, traded for 1 cask of wine, which could be sold in England for 2 bales of wool. Thus, differences in prices in two countries which arise from differences in productivity can explain the motives for international trade.

Absolute Advantage Vs. Comparative Advantage

Look again at Table 30-1. It was designed to show that a worker in England is more productive in both industries than a worker in Portugal. How can Portuguese workers hope to compete? The answer lies in the difference between **absolute advantage** and **comparative advantage.**

absolute advantage *The absolute difference in productivity between countries.*

In absolute terms, the English worker is at an advantage (more productive) compared to the Portuguese worker in both industries. But notice that while an English worker is six times more productive than a Portuguese worker in the wool industry (producing 6 bales while the Portuguese worker can produce only 1 bale), the English worker is only three times more productive in the port industry (producing 3 casks while the Portuguese worker can produce only 1 cask). Thus, if we compare industries, the English worker is relatively more productive in the wool industry than in the port industry. We would thus say that England has a *comparative advantage* in the wool industry (though an *absolute advantage* in both industries).

comparative advantage *The relative difference in productivity between countries which allows them to trade regardless of absolute levels of efficiency.*

If England has a comparative advantage in the wool industry, it must mean that it has a *comparative disadvantage* in port. This means that England's absolute advantage in wool is proportionately greater than its absolute advantage in port.

England's comparative advantage in wool means Portugal has a comparative disadvantage in wool. But England's comparative disadvantage in port corresponds to Portugal's comparative advantage in port. Portugal is less productive than England in both industries, but it is at less of a disadvantage in port production; this is where its comparative advantage lies. Looked at this way, the least skilled and least productive nation must have a comparative advantage in something, because there will be some industry in which it is least disadvantaged. But if England is better at producing port than Portugal, why doesn't England produce its own wine rather than import it? The reason is that England finds it cheaper to concentrate on producing what it's really good at—wool—and trading this wool for port.

This principle of comparative advantage is really a simple one but one which people sometimes don't grasp. Consider yourself as an example. Suppose when you graduate from college you are the world's best tennis player and also the world's best wheat farmer. Should you grow your own wheat *and* play your own tennis? Of course not. The time spent growing wheat would be time away from tennis. Assuming you could earn more playing tennis than growing wheat, you would play tennis and buy wheat from some wheat farmer who isn't as good a wheat farmer as you, but who isn't as good a tennis player either. This farmer would then have a comparative advantage in growing wheat.

Prices and the Gains from Trade

The price of goods in the two countries will determine if trade takes place. Let's assume that wool and wine are produced in competitive markets in both countries and that, as a result, prices reflect the opportunity costs of production as stated in Table 30-2. We can thus see what prices are necessary for trade to be beneficial. Examine Table 30-3, which is derived from Table 30-2. The table shows what the world prices of wool and port have to be in order for England and Portugal to engage in trade. Let us begin by assuming that 1 bale of wool sells for .8 of a cask of port. The price of a cask of port is thus 1.25 bales of wool. A quick check of Table 30-3 shows that the prices of wool and port fall in the range that makes trade beneficial to both countries.

TABLE 30-3 PRICES AT WHICH TRADE TAKES PLACE

England

    If 1 bale of wool sells for more than ½ cask of port, England gains by selling wool.

    If 1 cask of port sells for less than 2 bales of wool, England gains by buying port.

Portugal

    If 1 bale of wool sells for less than 1 cask of port, Portugal gains by buying wool.

    If 1 cask of port sells for more than 1 bale of wool, Portugal gains by selling port.

Therefore:

    If the price of port on world markets is between 1 bale of wool and 2 bales of wool, and if the price of wool on world markets is between ½ cask of port and 1 cask of port, trade will be mutually beneficial.

Table 30-4 shows how the total output of wool and port will increase if firms in each country reallocate laborers to the product in which the country has a comparative advantage. The English wool industry hires a laborer away from the port industry, and the Portuguese port industry hires four workers away from the wool industry. The world output of port has increased by 1 cask, and the world output of wool has increased by 2 bales.

Now assume that the English firm exports 3 bales of wool to Portugal. Since the price of a bale of wool is .8 casks of port, the trade yields England 2.4 casks

TABLE 30-4 GAINS FROM THE TRANSFER OF ONE WORKER IN ENGLAND AND FOUR WORKERS IN PORTUGAL

	One English Worker	Four Portuguese Workers	Total Output
Wool	+6	−4	+2
Port	−3	+4	+1

of port. By referring to Table 30-1, we can see that before international trade occurred, the English firm could have obtained only 1.5 casks of port for its 3 bales. Now it can get 2.4 casks. Before trade, the Portuguese could have obtained only 2.4 bales of wool for their 2.4 casks of port. Now they can get 3 bales. Both countries have gained from the exchange, and world output is greater than it was before specialization and exchange. To return to an earlier point, however, this example says nothing about how the gains from exchange are distributed between the two countries. A different set of prices, say 1 bale of wool equal to .7 casks of port, would have been more beneficial to Portugal, while a price of 1 bale of wool equal to .9 casks of port would have been more beneficial to England. But the important point is that as long as the world price falls in the range established in Table 30-3, both countries gain from specialization and exchange.

If constant costs prevailed in the production of port and wool, eventually all the wool would be produced in England, and all the port would be produced in Portugal. However, since increasing costs will likely occur at some point, the cost of producing port in Portugal and wool in England will rise, and trade will thus eventually be curtailed. This happens automatically, and, as a result, it is seldom the case that one country produces all of one commodity.

PROTECTIONISM

When England starts trading with Portugal and exports wool to obtain port, it cuts back on producing port and expands its wool industry. Given a price of port of somewhat less than 2 bales per cask, England, as a nation, is better off from the trade. However, some people in the English port industry are hurt by trade with Portugal. At the very least, some workers will be forced to leave the port industry to find new jobs in the wool industry. In realistic terms, this may involve moving hundreds of miles and being unemployed for a certain period. Older workers may find it difficult to get new jobs. People specialized in the industries that are hurt may find their skills are worthless elsewhere, or valued less than before. Similarly, plants and equipment may be highly specialized. A small, one-industry town can be devastated when subjected to import competition. How would you like to be a grocer in such a town when half the work force is thrown out of work?

On the other hand, consumers benefit from lower import prices. People in the United States buy Volvos, Toyotas, and Volkswagens because they think they are getting a better deal. The factors of production in the exporting industries also benefit because of expanded employment and lower prices for imported raw materials and semifinished goods. In fact, as pointed out above, those who benefit from trade could compensate the losers and still be better off.

Such compensation doesn't just happen, however. Those who are hurt by trade resort to the political process to gain either compensation or protection from foreign competition. The federal government's program for *trade adjustment assistance* is designed to retrain workers and to temporarily provide funds to those workers and businesses injured by trade to help them adjust. This program is in part geared to be fair, but it also allows further liberalization of trade by compensating the losers from trade to some extent. The program does not, however, provide complete compensation, nor does it automatically help all

trade adjustment assistance
Programs to help workers and industries adjust to the effects of foreign competition.

those who are hurt. You must apply for the aid, and, as with all such programs, some who deserve aid will not qualify, while some will qualify who are less deserving. No wonder, then, that threatened industries prefer protection to adjustment assistance.[1]

Firms can seek two different types of **protection**. One way is to attempt to get the government to establish a *quota*. Quotas are limits on the number of units of an item that can be imported. For example, the government might say that 1,000 casks of port can be imported from Portugal, and that is the limit. This type of protection shields the domestic industry from the foreign competition. Its economic impact is that it reduces the gains from specialization. Alternatively, the firm could attempt to have a *tariff* placed on the importation of the foreign good. You can easily see how a tariff can stop the flow of trade. In our earlier example we had a world price of 1 cask of port equal to 1.25 bales of wool. If the port-producing firm in England could get the government to enact a tariff of .76 bales of wool for each cask of port imported, it would transform the price of a cask of port to 2.01 bales of wool. Return to Table 30-3. At a price of 2.01 bales of wool, port will no longer be imported into England. The tariff is, therefore, prohibiting the flow of trade.

Economists as a group strongly favor free trade and oppose the use of tariffs and quotas that interfere with the free exchange of goods and services. Nevertheless, powerful political forces exist that favor increasing protection of U.S. industry. Because of these political pressures, it is worthwhile to examine some of the arguments for protection through either tariffs or quotas.

protectionism   The desire to limit imports into a country in order to protect national firms from foreign competitors.

quota   Physical limits on the amount of a commodity that may be imported.

tariff   Taxes that are placed on the importation of goods into a country. A tariff can be a fixed amount per item or it can be a percentage of the value of the item.

The Effects of Tariffs and Quotas

We can see the effects of tariffs and quotas by examining Figures 30-1 and 30-2. In Figure 30-1, D represents the home country's demand for a good that is homogeneous (e.g., wheat, oil, copper, steel, etc.) while S_D represents the domestic supply curve. The world market price is OP_W so citizens of the country can import as much of the good as they want at OP_W. In other words, the supply curve is perfectly elastic at OP_W (as drawn in Figure 30-1). OQ_1 units will be consumed at price OP_W. Now assume the government imposes a quota of OQ_3 units per time period. The supply faced by domestic consumers is no longer perfectly elastic at OP_W. Instead, it is represented by the curve $P_W ABS_D$. The price in domestic markets will rise to OP_1 and consumption will fall to OQ_2.

An interesting question once the quota is enacted is, Who benefits and who loses from the quota? Clearly, consumers of this good lose. Its price has risen, and less of the good is available for consumption. Who gains? Remember our earlier discussion about the need to prohibit entry into monopolized markets? This is one way to prohibit entry. A monopolist who can persuade the government to keep foreign competition out has a very effective artificial barrier to entry. Additionally, those importers who have the good fortune (or have made the payoffs) to be the ones importing OQ_3 can make huge profits. Foreign suppliers

[1]See the chapters by Malcolm D. Bale, "Adjustment Assistance: Dealing with Import-Displaced Workers," and Rachel McCulloch, "Determinants and Implications of U.S. Trade Performance," in *Tariffs, Quotas, and Trade: The Politics of Protectionism* (San Francisco: Institute for Contemporary Studies, 1979).

FIGURE 30-1   THE EFFECTS OF A QUOTA

The supply curve of a homogeneous good is perfectly elastic at the price on world markets (OP_W). If D represents domestic demand, OQ_1 units will be consumed at price OP_W. OQ_1–OQ_4 units are imported. A quota of OQ_3 units causes price paid by domestic consumers to rise to OP_1 and the home consumption to fall to OQ_2 units.

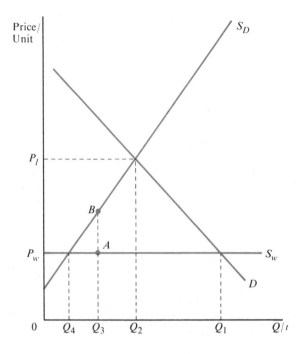

will supply OQ_3 at a price OP_W but domestic consumers will pay OP_1. The difference is a profit to the importer who has the right to import OQ_3. You can see how import licenses can be very valuable when quotas are being used. If the government auctioned off permits to import the good, the profit would be captured as revenue for the federal Treasury rather than as a gain for a fortunate importer. Of course, it's not done this way. In addition, domestic producers can charge OP_1 rather than OP_W for their output.

Figure 30-2 shows the effect of a tariff. The demand for the foreign good is D_F and the supply of the foreign good is S_F. For purposes of this example, assume that this is a good that is not produced at home (e.g., Scotch or a Mercedes-Benz). In the absence of any government interference, OQ_1 of the good would be imported at price OP_1. Now assume the government imposes a tariff of t per unit of the good imported. This shifts back the supply curve, exactly as a tax would. The price rises to OP_2 and imports fall to OQ_2. There are two effects. First, there is a ***revenue effect*** of the tariff. This is the amount of revenue generated for the government. The revenue is the amount of the tariff times the amount imported. In Figure 30-2 the revenue effect is $(OP_2 - OP_3)OQ_2$, which is the shaded area in the diagram. Second, there is a ***protective effect*** of the tariff. This is similar to a quota in that it keeps foreign competition out of domestic markets. Domestic firms are now able to sell at a higher price because some output, in this case $OQ_1 - OQ_2$, has been kept out of the market. In colonial American history, and even today in some less developed countries, the revenue generated by tariffs was and is an important source of government revenue. Since income taxation and other forms of taxation may prove to be difficult to collect because of inadequate

revenue effect   The revenue effect of a tariff is the amount of tax revenue it raises for the government.

protective effect   The protective effect of a tariff is the degree to which it limits imports, thus protecting national industry from foreign competition.

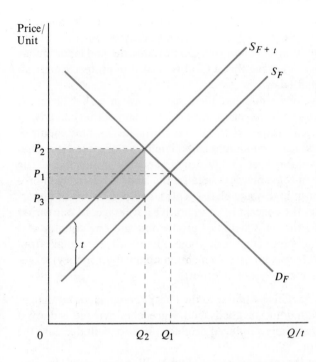

Price/Unit

S_{F+t}

S_F

P_2

P_1

P_3

t

D_F

0   Q_2 Q_1 Q/t

FIGURE 30-2   THE EFFECTS OF A TARIFF
A tariff per unit of output causes the price paid by consumers to rise and the price received by suppliers to fall. This decreases the amount of the good that is imported.

---

record keeping, tariffs can play a large role. At the present time, however, tariffs generate an insignificant portion of federal revenue in the United States.

Arguments for Protection

There are several arguments for the use of tariffs and quotas. Some of them are nonsensical from an economic viewpoint, but they often are used as reasons to decrease trade and should be seen for what they are.

Keep the Money at Home. It is reported that Abraham Lincoln once remarked: "I do not know much about the tariff, but I know this much, when we buy manufactured goods abroad we get the goods and the foreigner gets the money. When we buy the manufactured goods at home we get both the goods and the money."[2] Many economists have pointed out that the only thing correct in the statement is the first eight words. The problem is that many people would accept this argument. Do you? An economist wouldn't. Foreign countries and their citizens export goods because they want to buy goods of other countries. They don't want money. Think how great it would be if all they wanted was our currency. We could print money, send it to foreigners, and get cars, television sets, and caviar in return. But, of course, foreigners want to spend that money on our goods or on the goods of other countries, who in turn spend it on our goods. The argument confuses money as a *measure* of wealth with money as wealth. Money is desired because it represents the ability to buy goods and services.

---

[2]Cited in Asher Isaacs, *International Trade* (Homewood, Ill.: Richard D. Irwin, Inc., 1948), p. 229.

The Cheap Foreign Labor Argument. It is obvious to anyone who has traveled outside the United States that wages vary significantly between countries. (They even vary considerably within countries.) Some industries and labor unions use this differential in wages to argue that a tariff is needed to protect American workers from cheap foreign labor.

This is clearly a fallacious argument. First, as we saw in earlier chapters, labor is only one of the factors of production. As a result, commodities embodying a lot of labor can be produced cheaply where labor is cheap, just as some countries will be able to cheaply produce commodities embodying a lot of capital if capital is cheap, or land, if land is cheap. Second, low wages imply low productivity. The reason wage rates are low in some places is because the labor is relatively unproductive compared to labor in high-wage places. Third, and perhaps most important, this argument ignores the concept of comparative advantage. In our earlier example, where labor was the only factor of production and one country was absolutely more efficient at producing both goods, there still were gains from trade. And, notice that there was no need to mention nominal (or money) wages for the argument. They are simply not relevant.

Employment Protection. This is similar to the cheap foreign labor argument. Foreign goods compete with domestic goods, and, since labor demand is derived from the demand for domestically produced products, imports will decrease the demand for domestic labor.

This argument ignores the two-way nature of trade. We export goods because foreigners demand our goods. This creates a derived demand for labor that is used to produce these exported goods. These goods wouldn't be demanded if we didn't import goods from the countries to which we now export.

The Infant Industry Argument. This may be one of the oldest protectionist arguments and was a favorite of Alexander Hamilton, the first secretary of the U.S. Treasury. The argument is that in a country where industry is just beginning to develop, production costs may be high and protection is therefore necessary for it to survive. On a more sophisticated level, the argument is that there are potential economies of scale in an industry that can't be realized because the industry is being undersold by a mature foreign industry that has already reached these economies of scale. It is thus argued that the industry should be protected until it grows and can compete with the foreign industry.

There is some economic sense to this argument. The problem is that it is impossible to determine *a priori* which industries will be able to compete when they mature and which ones won't be able to compete. There is no magic theory or formula to determine when an industry is no longer in need of protection, and it has been observed time and time again that tariffs, once enacted, are hard to get rid of.

Further, and this is an important point regarding all tariffs and quotas, the tariff is the same thing as a subsidy to the infant industry. In other words, consumers of the good are subsidizing domestic producers of that good by not being allowed to purchase the good at a lower price. So, if an argument can be made that an industry should be helped to reach maturity because it is in the interest of the country to have such an industry, it is much more equitable that such a subsidy should be paid out of general tax revenues. This would insure that all citizens pay the subsidy, not just the consumers of a particular product.

National Defense. "No price is too high to pay for the defense of our country." How can anyone disagree with such a statement? So, imagine yourself as a monopolist seeking to keep foreign competition out of your industry. Think of the impact of going to Congress and arguing that if foreign competition destroys your industry, the country could be cut off from its source of supply in a time of national crisis. This politically powerful argument is the refuge of almost every industry pleading its case before Congress.

The argument, while politically sound, has several problems. First, how is one to decide what is essential for national defense? Prior to World War II we thought a cut-off of natural rubber would be a disaster. However, if we had had a domestic natural rubber industry, we may not have had the rapid development of synthetic rubber. The second problem is similar to one that we discussed above. The national defense argument is an argument for a subsidy. If an argument can be made that it is essential to protect an industry for defense reasons, it should be done through a very visible subsidy rather than a hidden subsidy paid via a tariff or a quota. For many years it was argued that we should have a tariff on imported oil for national defense reasons. The argument was that if we didn't protect the domestic industry we could be caught in time of war without a domestic oil industry. The result of the tariff was that we used our own oil instead of cheap foreign oil. The program might well have been labeled "Drain America First." The net result is that we have larger national defense problems now than we would have had if we had heeded some sage economic advice: "Buy where the goods are cheapest."

Beggar-Thy-Neighbor Policies

A high level of domestic unemployment has frequently been used as an argument for protection. Keynesian economics demonstrates that an increase in exports relative to imports stimulates output. Income rises because the increase in exports means a larger demand for the country's output, and when output rises, so does income. This extra income stimulates domestic spending; thus, income rises even further through the multiplier process.

In the Great Depression of the 1930s, many countries adopted trade policies that attempted to raise their own level of national income by increasing their exports and reducing their imports. The problem with this is that if one country reduces its imports, the exports of the country from which the goods came must fall. If a country increases its exports, there must be an accompanying increase in the imports of the countries to which it sells. When a country tries to help itself in this way it is doing so at the expense of its trading partners. Such policies are called ***beggar-thy-neighbor policies.*** It is easy to see why these policies are counter-productive. If all countries adopted beggar-thy-neighbor policies, world trade would shrink.

beggar-thy-neighbor policies Trade policies designed to improve a country's macroeconomic performance at the expense of its trade partners' economies.

Quasi-Tariffs and Quotas

Industries sometimes find it difficult to obtain tariffs and quotas because they smack of blatant appeals for government aid. That is why we often hear arguments for back-door tariffs and quotas.

There are many ways to reduce imports. For one thing, a country can impose stringent health requirements on imported foodstuffs. While you wouldn't want

Fair Trade Vs. Free Trade

A political challenge to the principles of free trade and comparative advantage is being mounted in some industries. The proponents of these arguments advocate "fair trade" as an alternative to free trade.

Fair trade proponents argue that industries in countries which produce U.S. imports should have to meet the same standards that U.S. firms must meet. Consider copper mining. A fair trade argument would concentrate on the unfairness of U.S. firms having to meet clean air standards and land reclamation regulations while foreign firms in, for instance, Zaire don't have these same costs imposed on them. To make it fair to U.S. producers, there should be a tariff on copper equal to the cost of the standards imposed on the U.S. firm.

The other fair trade argument concerns tariff and nontariff barriers in other countries. The automobile industry argues for tariffs on Japanese automobiles. The argument centers on the "unfairness" of the policy that other countries set on excluding U.S. exports. Japan places a 22.5 percent indirect commodity tax on foreign cars sold in Japan. As a result, the price of an American-made automobile in Japan is noncompetitive. In addition, the Japanese give a tax break to automobile producers for cars sold in the United States. Therefore, Japanese cars sell for a lower price in Los Angeles than they do in Tokyo.

This seems grossly unfair to most Americans. Thus, the fair trade arguments make a great deal of political sense. Remember, however, that the arguments for free trade don't say anything about fairness or equity. Instead, they relate to economic efficiency.

---

voluntary export restraints (VERs) *Restraints that one country places on its exports to avoid harming trade partners.*

orderly marketing agreements (OMAs) *Agreements by one country to restrict exports to another so as not to cause "disorderly" conditions in the latter's import-competing industries.*

subsidy payments *In international trade, payments to exporters to encourage exports.*

to eat an unhealthy candy bar from abroad, health regulations can be abused to reduce imports. In the 1960s and 1970s, *voluntary export restraints (VERs)* and *orderly marketing agreements (OMAs)* were widely used. These are agreements between one country and its foreign suppliers to voluntarily reduce exports to the country in order to provide orderly market conditions; that is, an agreement to avoid disrupting domestic markets. The foreign countries are forced to agree to these arrangements to prevent outright tariffs or quotas.

Exports can be stimulated in a number of ways. Most governments have offices for export promotion designed to encourage exports by helping domestic suppliers sell abroad and by enticing foreigners to buy. Exports are also subsidized in other ways, sometimes by straight *subsidy payments* from the government to producers for units of their output sold abroad. Another technique is used by the United States Export-Import Bank (a federal government agency). The Export-Import Bank will often lend money for purchases to foreigners at low interest rates if they will buy only from the United States. Other countries, of course, do the same thing, and there is a good deal of competition to see who can give the biggest subsidy.

Current Status of Protectionism

During World War II, when western nations were planning a new international system to make the coming peace better than the prewar period, they remembered the disastrous fall in trade in the Depression, the tariffs and quotas, and the retaliation. It was widely believed that such episodes should be avoided in the future. For this purpose, countries signed the **General Agreement on Tariffs and Trade (GATT).** The purpose of GATT was to ban the competitive, retaliatory trade actions of the 1930s and to work for increasingly freer trade. GATT is headquartered in Geneva, Switzerland. It has been instrumental in promoting international negotiations that have lowered trade barriers.

General Agreements on Tariffs and Trade (GATT) Administered by a Geneva-based organization; designed to help negotiate freer trade.

Nevertheless, powerful forces still favor increasing trade protection.[3] For example, the dominant force in the U.S. labor movement, the AFL-CIO, favors protection in order to preserve jobs. Further, new forms of protection have been used, such as the VERs and OMAs discussed above. Economists as a group are very strongly in favor of free trade. Many economists would advocate temporary adjustment assistance to reduce the hardships of those people injured by trade. However, few are in favor of using trade policy to affect national income. They would instead rely on monetary and fiscal policy to stabilize the economy's output.

THE BALANCE OF PAYMENTS

International financial matters often seem very mysterious, and among the more confusing topics in this area is the balance of payments. The newspapers report figures for the balance of payments deficit (or surplus) and, there is a whole list of possible meanings for the deficit or surplus. Often you hear references to the balance of trade or the current account. The balance of payments (BOP) is not really so mysterious once some of the basic ideas involved are spelled out.

Table 30-5 is useful in answering questions about the balance of payments. In studying it, you should remember two points. First, the easiest way to understand the balance of payments is to understand that it is simply a matter of accounting. Second, the approach taken in BOP accounting is that what Americans as a whole buy from foreigners in a month, quarter, or year has to be paid for with something that foreigners buy from Americans in the same period.

The first entry in Table 30-5 is **merchandise exports,** meaning such things as cars, food, and so on. These are sales of American-produced goods to foreigners, for which U.S. residents acquire claims on foreigners in return. The second entry is **merchandise imports,** which are simply tangible goods imported by U.S. residents. The difference between merchandise exports and imports is defined as the **merchandise trade balance,** entry (3). This balance is what people often mean when they refer to the "balance of trade."

merchandise exports and imports Exports and imports of physical goods such as autos, grain, etc., but not services such as tourism and the provision of insurance.

merchandise trade balance The difference between the values of merchandise exports and imports.

---

[3]See the chapters by John T. Cuddington and Ronald I. McKinnon, "Free Trade Versus Protectionism: A Perspective"; Ryan C. Amacher, Robert D. Tollison, and Thomas D. Willett, "The Divergence Between Theory and Practice"; and Alan V. Deardorff and Robert M. Stern, "American Labor's Stake in International Trade," in *Tariffs, Quotas, and Trade: The Politics of Protectionism* (San Francisco: Institute for Contemporary Studies, 1979).

TABLE 30-5   U.S. BALANCE OF PAYMENTS, THIRD QUARTER, 1981 (millions of dollars)

(1) Merchandise exports	$ 58,037	
(2) Merchandise imports	65,079	
(3) Merchandise trade balance $=(1)-(2)$		$ -7,042
(4) Service transactions, net[1]	1,618	
(5) Military transactions, net	-72	
(6) Investment income, net	9,490	
(7) Balance on goods and services $=(3)+(4)+(5)+(6)$		3,994
(8) Unilateral transfers, net	-1,894	
(9) Balance on current account $=(7)+(8)$		2,100
(10) Change in U.S. assets abroad, net (minus sign means increase in these assets)	-18,004	
(11) Change in foreign assets in the U.S., net	15,056	
(12) Increase in foreign assets in the U.S. minus increase in U.S. assets abroad $=(11)+(10)$	-2,948	
(13) Statistical discrepancy $=(9)+(12)$		848

Source: *Economic Indicators,* January, 1982
[1]Includes net travel and transportation receipts.

service transactions *In the balance of payments, imports and exports of services, such as tourism, insurance, and investment income.*

military transactions *In the balance of payments, imports and exports of military items are entered separately.*

net investment income *In the balance of payments, investment income payments are treated as payments for the services of capital that one nation allows others to use. They are entered on a net basis.*

balance on goods and services The difference between the values of exports of goods and services and imports of goods and services.

So far this is a relatively narrow view of trade, because it neglects services, or intangible, nonphysical exports and imports. Examples of these would be the banking and insurance services the United States provides foreigners, the shipping services foreigners provide us, and the tourism that nations provide each other.

Entry (4) states the value of *service transactions* in net terms; that is, the differences between the value of services provided *by* American residents and the value provided *to* them. Entries (5) and (6) are also shown in net terms. *Military transactions* are customarily shown as separate entries. One reason for this is so we can see how important they are relative to other transactions, and another reason is that many of them are based on government policy rather than being market-determined.

Net investment income acknowledges that U.S. residents own foreign stocks, bonds, and shares in foreign businesses, as well as that foreigners own assets in the United States. These assets pay returns (interest, dividends, profits), and net investment income is the difference between the amount earned by American-owned assets abroad and the amount earned by foreign-owned assets in the United States. The reason for including such entries under services is that one country's residents allow foreigners to use the services from the capital they provide, and the value of these services is measured by the earnings (investment income) of this capital. Entry (7), the *balance on goods and services,* can be looked at as providing earnings to finance imports (entry [2]).

Unilateral transfers represent gifts from one government to another and from individuals. For example, if you sent money to a relative or friend overseas, it would be a unilateral transfer. If the government gives a grant or gift to another country, it is called a unilateral transfer. In Table 30-5, unilateral transfers have a negative sign which means that the U.S. government and its citizens gave more gifts in 1981 than they received.

The *balance on current account* represents the sum of all the export categories (including unilateral transfers) minus the sum of the import categories. The U.S. ran a current account surplus of $2,100 billion in the third quarter of 1981. This means that it earned $2,100 billion more on merchandise exports, service transactions, military transactions, and investment income than it spent on merchandise imports and unilateral transfers. This raises two questions: First, where did the foreigners get the funds to pay for this surplus? The U.S. merchants who sold these goods and services have to be paid somehow. Second, what is the economic meaning of such surpluses (and deficits)?

On the accounting level, the current account surplus must be paid for by *net changes in U.S. assets held abroad* or by *net changes in foreign assets held in the United States*. Net changes in U.S. assets held abroad, entry (10), is the difference between U.S. assets held abroad at the start of the period and at the end of the period. For example, if a private American citizen owns $1 million of bonds issued in France, these count as U.S. assets held abroad. If an American citizen buys $1 million more of the French bonds, this increases U.S. assets held abroad by +$1,000,000. This is why increases in U.S. assets held abroad are entered with a minus sign in the balance of payments.

Suppose foreigners buy $5 million of General Motors stock during this period. This shows up as a positive entry (11), since foreigners have increased their holdings of assets in the United States. This $5 million purchase must somehow be paid for by foreigners, just as they must somehow pay for U.S. exports sold to them. From entries (10) and (11), we can see that in 1981, foreigners bought more than $15 billion of U.S. assets (net), while U.S. residents bought more than $18 billion of foreign assets (net). Entry (12), then, shows that U.S. residents spent $3 billion more on net asset purchases than did foreign residents. This $3 billion represents funds that foreigners can use to help pay the current account surplus.

In fact, if all transactions for goods, services, transfers, and assets were accurately measured, entry (12) would exactly equal the current account surplus in entry (9). Since measurement is never perfect, there is a *statistical discrepancy* reported in entry (13). This might mean that there were more imports from abroad measured (so entry [9] should be a larger number) or that U.S. residents bought more foreign assets than were measured (so entry [10] should be a larger negative number).

What is the economic sense of the fact that without the statistical discrepancy, entries (9) and (12) would have to balance exactly? To answer this, ask what U.S. citizens who get the extra $2 billion represented by the current account surplus do with these funds. If they buy goods or services, they are already included in the import or net services figures. Aside from this, they can hold checking or savings deposits abroad, buy foreign stocks and bonds, and so on. Sometimes, the choice of assets purchased by U.S. exporters is part of the export deal. For example, suppose goods are delivered to Spain but the Spanish importer

unilateral transfers   In the balance of payments, transfers to foreigners that bring no matching import or ownership of a foreign asset.

balance on current account   The difference between the values of exports of goods and services and imports of goods and services minus net unilateral transfers abroad.

net changes in U.S. assets held abroad   Over a period of time there is a net change in the assets held in foreign countries by all U.S. residents.

net changes in foreign assets held in the United States   Over a period of time there is a net change in the assets held in the United States by all foreign residents.

statistical discrepancy in the balance of payments   Net changes in asset holdings must exactly balance the current account deficit or surplus; but since the deficit and the net changes in asset holdings are both estimates, they are seldom equal to each other, and the difference is called the statistical discrepancy.

trade credit   In the balance of payments, credit that an exporter grants an importer as part of a deal.

is not required to pay for three months. This is **trade credit,** or credit granted in the process of trade. For the quarter in which such exports occur, they are financed by U.S. citizens acquiring a capital claim on the Spanish importer. So, the answer is simple, if U.S. citizens don't buy goods and services, they must be holding assets.

Sometimes a sizable deficit in the balance of payments is perceived as a bad thing or as a sign that the country is in trouble. Perhaps this is because we use a minus sign to designate a situation where imports exceed exports. The negative sign does not, however, denote a bad thing. There is no one account in the balance of payments, or size of deficit in an account, that can automatically be used to judge how well a country is doing. After the Civil War and into the 1900s, the United States ran current account and merchandise trade balance deficits by importing more than it exported. These imports, however, were used to build up American agriculture and industry. The deficits were financed by foreign loans, but these loans could later be paid back by the larger, more productive economy that the foreign loans helped finance. Thus, these deficits were really healthy. Sometimes a nation will run deficits simply to import more goods that are used solely for consumption. The foreign loans used to finance these deficits are then difficult to pay back, and the country is in international difficulties. The trick, then, is not to view entries in the balance of payments as good or bad, but to ask whether they reflect good or bad developments in the overall economy.

From the point of view of an accounting balance in the balance of payments, it doesn't matter whether these net changes in U.S. assets held abroad and foreign assets held in the United States refer to the actions of private citizens or governments. If a foreigner puts $1 million in a savings account in New York City, it doesn't matter if the depositor is a private citizen in Bonn, West Germany, or the West German government; the $1 million is still there. However, when private citizens make transactions, they are usually doing so in their own self-interest rather than to further a policy goal of their country. Governments, on the other hand, make many of their exchange market transactions to affect the foreign exchange value of their currency, an issue we will now explore.

DETERMINATION OF THE EXCHANGE RATE

exchange rate   The price at which one currency sells for another.

So far, we have not discussed the *exchange rate,* or the rate at which two currencies trade for each other. In examining the law of comparative advantage and the basis for mutually beneficial trade, we didn't need to consider exchange rate and money to see the main points concerning the benefits of trade. However, the exchange rate plays a major role in international trade and must be considered because disequilibrium exchange rates can impede trade flows.

Let's look at demand and supply in an exchange market where U.S. dollars are exchanged for British pounds. For example, if you spend the summer traveling in Great Britain, you will have to make your transactions there in pounds, so you want to buy pounds at a bank, either here or in Great Britain, with your dollars. Figure 30-3 shows that the greater the number of dollars required to buy one pound, the smaller the quantity of pounds people want to buy; the demand curve has a negative slope. This makes sense. If it becomes more expensive to buy

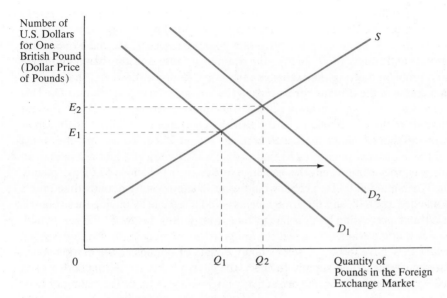

FIGURE 30-3   DEMAND AND SUPPLY IN THE FOREIGN EXCHANGE MARKET FOR U.S. DOLLARS AND BRITISH POUNDS

A floating exchange rate is determined by the underlying conditions of supply and demand for the currency. An equilibrium price emerges as the exchange rate. If demand for the currency increases, as from D to D_1, the exchange rate will rise from OE_1 to OE_2.

pounds, you'll cut short your stay, buy fewer gifts for the folks back home, or just not go at all. We also see that the supply curve has a positive slope. The equilibrium exchange rate is OE_1, where the demand and supply curves intersect and the quantity demanded equals the quantity supplied, OQ_1.

Governments naturally are very interested in the exchange rate of their currency versus foreign currencies. At one extreme, they may adopt a hands-off attitude and allow the rate to be determined by the forces of demand and supply, as in Figure 30-3. When governments allow demand and supply to determine the exchange rate, it is said to be a *floating exchange rate* or *flexible exchange rate*. At the other extreme, they may attempt to keep the exchange rate in a tight zone or band.

If the exchange rate is flexible or floating, the basic forces of supply and demand will determine the exchange rate, which is simply the price of one currency in terms of another. Suppose, for example, that travel to Great Britain becomes the popular thing to do. This means that tastes change in favor of vacations to Great Britain and against vacations in the United States and other countries. This, in turn, means that U.S. citizens will demand more pounds. In terms of Figure 30-3, the demand for pounds shifts from D to D_1. If rates are floating, the dollar price of pounds rises from OE_1 to OE_2. It now takes more dollars to buy a pound. Another way of saying the same thing is to say that the dollar has depreciated relative to the pound or that the pound has appreciated relative to the dollar.

floating, or flexible, exchange rate   An exchange rate that is determined solely by the underlying forces of supply and demand.

pegged, or fixed, exchange rate
An exchange rate that is fixed at
a predetermined level by
intervening governments.

Figure 30-4 shows a case of a ***pegged exchange rate*** or ***fixed exchange rate*** in the band of $2.02 to $1.98 for each British pound. That is, one or both of the governments want to keep the price of a pound between $2.02 and $1.98. With demand and supply of D_1 and S_1, the equilibrium rate is in this band, and there is no problem meeting the exchange rate target. Suppose, however, that there is an increase in the demand for pounds in the foreign exchange market to D_2. This would lead to an equilibrium exchange rate above $2.02 per pound. To prevent this, either the United States or the British government (or both) can ***intervene*** in the foreign exchange market to keep the rate at $2.02. To do this, they must sell the additional pounds (AB) that people want to buy at $2.02 per pound. In this way, they can prevent the exchange rate from rising above $2.02 per pound. Or, if demand fell to D_3, people would want to supply more pounds than others demanded at $1.98, and the governments could intervene by buying these pounds (CE) and preventing the exchange rate from falling below $1.98 per pound. Notice that governments can set the limits to the exchange rate, but this pegging means they have to buy or sell as many dollars or pounds as the market wants based on demand and supply. In effect, the governments are setting both a price ceiling and a price floor and are actively intervening to make the ceiling or floor effective.

exchange market intervention
The action taken by government
to establish an exchange rate
other than the
market-determined rate.

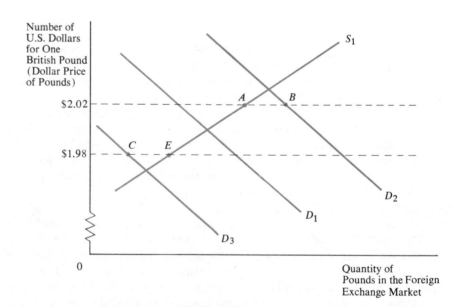

**FIGURE 30-4   EXCHANGE MARKET INTERVENTION
TO PEG THE EXCHANGE RATE**

Pegging an exchange rate establishes a band in which the rate is allowed to fluctuate. If the rate exceeds $2.02 per pound, the central authority intervenes by selling pounds and buying dollars. If the rate falls below $1.98 per pound, the central authority intervenes by buying pounds and selling dollars.

From the point of view of governments, both freely floating exchange rates as well as pegged or fixed exchange rates can cause problems. For example, suppose the exchange rate is floating and there is an increase in demand, as when demand shifted from D_1 to D_2 in Figure 30-3. This will cause the dollar price of a pound to rise. Since pounds are now more expensive, Americans will tend to cut back on their trips to Great Britain, on their purchases of British Fords and Rolls Royces, on their purchases of Scotch and of other goods. This is damaging to British exporters. Depending on the political power of exporters, the British government may want to pay attention to the exchange rate and may be tempted to intervene in the exchange market to keep the rate from going up.

However, intervention to peg or control the exchange rate has its own problems. Assume the British government wants to peg the dollar price of the pound between $2.02 and $1.98, as in Figure 30-4. First, suppose that demand is D_3, so that with a floating exchange rate the dollar price will fall below $1.98 per pound. Britain can prevent this by buying up the extra pounds (distance CE in Figure 30-4) that represent the difference between the number of pounds people are willing to demand and supply at $1.98. To buy these pounds, Great Britain uses its **international reserves,** which are its stocks of assets that are liquid and readily acceptable internationally. Its international reserves include its holdings of gold, dollar deposits, and its deposits and credit lines with the International Monetary Fund (IMF) in Washington, D.C., as well as other assets. Further, it may be able to mobilize extra reserves quickly by borrowing from foreign central banks. If Great Britain must keep buying up pounds with its international reserves day after day and month after month, it will sooner or later run out of reserves. As reserves fall, Great Britain eventually has to give up and **devalue** the pound (let it *depreciate*), resulting in a new, lower dollar price of the pound. Thus, while the intervention may be able to work for a time, often the country has to give up in the end. In the meantime, the government wastes the reserves it uses up. Further, if you are engaged in trade, you have a good deal of uncertainty about when, or if, devaluation will occur.

Suppose that demand is D_2 in Figure 30-4. To keep the dollar price of a pound at $2.02, the British government would have to supply the extra pounds (distance AB) beyond what the private market will supply. One way for the government to supply these pounds is simply to print them. Thus, intervention to keep the dollar price of the pound from rising would expand the British money supply. Monetarists and many Keynesians would argue that this would eventually lead to higher inflation for Great Britain. Thus, intervention to keep the price of currency from rising can lead to loss of control of the money supply, excessive monetary expansion, and inflation.

Note that while Great Britain is selling AB pounds in the previous example, it is using them to buy dollars, and this increases British international reserves. If the exchange market sometimes has demand of D_3 and at other times D_2, the reserves lost in one period can be rebuilt in the next, and government intervention would keep the rate in the target band. However, if demand permanently rises to D_2, the country can be dragged into inflation; or if demand permanently falls to D_3, it can engage in a futile and costly struggle to stop devaluation. The problem is, how do governments know which are permanent changes and which are only temporary?

international reserves Stocks of assets that are liquid and readily acceptable as international payment.

devaluation Occurs when a country allows a fixed or pegged exchange rate to depreciate closer to its equilibrium level.

FROM FIXED TO FLOATING RATES

fixed, but adjustable, exchange rates The exchange rate system that existed from 1945 until the early 1970s. This system consisted of a pegged rate that could be adjusted when demand and supply moved permanently out of balance.

After World War II, a system of *fixed, but adjustable, exchange rates* was adopted. The idea was to peg rates, but if demand and supply became permanently unbalanced at the target rate (say D_2 or D_3 in Figure 30-4), the exchange rate would be adjusted. The system seemed to work satisfactorily up through the mid- and late 1960s.

The 1970s were much more turbulent. The pegged but adjustable rate system was abandoned during the early 1970s. Thereafter, sharp movements in exchange rates occurred, and massive shifts of funds became commonplace. Most economists agree that the pegged rate system could not have been maintained in these turbulent times, and there was no alternative but to go to floating rates. However, many countries continued to peg their rates. A great many less developed countries pegged their rates to the dollar, while some European countries floated against the dollar but pegged against each other (for example, Germany and the Netherlands). In addition, even countries that didn't peg all the time would often intervene on occasion, sometimes significantly. Because of the extent of pegging and intervention, the float (or the floating exchange rate) was referred to as *dirty floating*, with *clean floating* meaning no intervention in the exchange market.

dirty float A floating exchange rate system in which there is some intervention to move the rate adjustment in a certain direction or at a certain speed that is different from the market rate.

clean float A floating exchange rate system in which there is absolutely no intervention by governments.

Economists have mixed views on the success of the dirty float. Most argue that pegged rates couldn't have been maintained. However, some argue that floating has not worked well, with exchange rate movements that are too large, erratic, and unrelated to underlying economic fundamentals. They urge greater fixity of rates and an attempt to move toward a system with more pegging. Other economists argue that the float worked about as well as could be expected. The large and frequent changes in exchange rates were often justified, in their view, and they doubt the ability of government intervention in financial markets to bring about better performance. Those who think markets work pretty well would like the governments to stay out of them, while others think that government actions can improve market performances.

SUMMARY

1. We have extended our discussion of the market mechanism to include trade across national borders.

2. The motivations for such trade and the benefits of such trade are no different than those for trade between two individuals who are residents of the same country.

3. The principle of comparative advantage shows that in order to gain from trade there must be different relative costs in each country. Absolute advantage in all goods does not mean there can be no gains from trade. Countries with an absolute disadvantage should produce and trade those goods they are least inefficient

in producing; those countries with an absolute advantage in all goods should produce and sell those goods that they are most efficient in producing.

4. Not all parties gain from trade. Some firms and the labor within these firms will be hurt. This is no different than inefficient domestic firms being hurt by domestic trade. However, when foreign nations are involved, the damaged parties often call on the government to keep the foreign competition out by the use of tariffs and quotas.

5. There are many arguments for protection through tariffs and/or quotas. A few of them

make sense, but they must be recognized as arguments for a subsidy to a particular industry.

6. The balance of payments is really a system of accounting focused on foreign transactions. It must balance in every period in the sense that purchases from foreigners have to be paid for in some manner.

7. Exchange rates, or the price of one currency in terms of another, are determined by the forces of supply and demand just as prices of other commodities are determined.

8. If the government stays out of exchange markets and allows currency to reach market clearing prices, we say we have a flexible, or floating, exchange rate. If the government intervenes by establishing price floors or ceilings, we have a fixed, or pegged, exchange rate.

NEW TERMS

expected gains
gains from trade
absolute advantage
comparative advantage
trade adjustment assistance
protectionism
quota
tariff
revenue effect
protective effect
beggar-thy-neighbor policies
voluntary export restraints (VERs)
orderly marketing agreements (OMAs)
subsidy payments
General Agreement on Tariffs and Trade (GATT)
merchandise exports and imports
merchandise trade balance
service transactions
military transactions

net investment income
balance on goods and services
unilateral transfers
balance on current account
net changes in U.S. assets held abroad
net changes in foreign assets held in the United States
statistical discrepancy in the balance of payments
trade credit
exchange rate
floating, or flexible, exchange rate
pegged, or fixed, exchange rate
exchange market intervention
international reserves
devaluation
fixed, but adjustable, exchange rates
dirty float
clean float

QUESTIONS FOR DISCUSSION

1. Suppose Arizona labor is more productive than California labor in the production of every good and service. Explain why the two states may still find it mutually profitable to engage in trade.

2. Diagram the effect of each of the following events on the pound-dollar exchange rate and on the dollar-pound exchange rate. (Hint: Use two markets, the market for pounds and the market for dollars.)

   (a) Bourbon becomes more popular in the United States and Great Britain than Scotch.

   (b) Because of the increased cost of gasoline, Americans begin buying motorcycles produced in Great Britain.

   (c) You marry a British citizen and send a $500 Christmas present to your new in-laws.

3. "If we trade with the Japanese we will lose our jobs to the Japanese because they don't allow American goods into their country." Do you agree with this statement? Analyze it.

4. Why might a U.S. monopoly seek a tariff on the good it produces? Might organized labor support this plea? Who gains and who loses?

5. Suppose there are freely floating exchange rates. What would happen to the value of the pound, as measured in terms of the number of dollars it takes to buy one pound, if:

(a) more Americans decide to vacation in Great Britain?

(b) more Americans decide to buy Rolls Royces?

(c) Britons decide to buy more Oldsmobiles?

(d) Americans decide to buy more British stocks and bonds?

SUGGESTIONS FOR FURTHER READING

Amacher, Ryan C., Gottfried Haberler, and Thomas D. Willett (eds.). *Challenges to Liberal International Order.* Washington: American Enterprise Institute, 1979.

Heller, H. Robert. *International Trade: Theory and Empirical Evidence,* 2d ed. Englewood Cliffs, N.J.: Prentice-Hall, Inc., 1973.

Institute for Contemporary Studies. *Tariffs, Quotas, and Trade: The Politics of Protectionism.* San Francisco: Institute for Contemporary Studies, 1979.

Kindleberger, Charles P., and Peter H. Lindert. *International Economics,* 6h ed. Homewood, Ill.: Richard D. Irwin, Inc., 1978.

Root, Franklin R. *International Trade and Investment,* 4h ed. Cincinnati: South-Western Publishing Co., 1978.

Willett, Thomas D. *Floating Exchange Rates and International Monetary Reform.* Washington: American Enterprise Institute, 1977.

Economic Development and Social Change

Learning Objectives

After studying the materials found in this chapter, you should be able to do the following:

1. List and discuss the characteristics common to less developed countries.

2. Define:
   (a) the crude birth rate.
   (b) the crude death rate.
   (c) human capital.

3. Explain what development economists call the vicious circle of poverty.

4. Compare and critically evaluate the economic development theories of Marx and Rostow.

5. Contrast the following economic development strategies:
   (a) big push vs. backward/forward linkages.
   (b) *laissez-faire* vs. forced development.

In this chapter we use the economic principles we have discussed in the previous chapters to compare relative rates of development among countries and to examine some of the reasons for the differences in the levels of development. Development economists spend a great deal of time trying to solve practical problems in poor countries and trying to design and implement programs that will aid in the economic development of particular economies. Development economics is based on statistical evidence rather than theoretical models.

SIMILAR CHARACTERISTICS OF LESS DEVELOPED COUNTRIES

More than twenty years ago, the general manager of the United Nations Special Fund, a program to fund development projects, painted a concise, yet very illuminating, picture of what was, at that time, referred to as an underdeveloped country:[1]

> Everyone knows an underdeveloped country when he sees one. It is a country characterized by poverty, with beggars in the cities, and villagers eking out a bare subsistence in the rural areas. It is a country lacking in factories of its own, usually with inadequate supplies of power and light. It usually has insufficient roads and railroads, insufficient government services, poor communication. It has few hospitals, and few institutions of higher learning. Most of its people cannot read or write. In spite of the generally prevailing poverty of the people, it may have isolated islands of wealth, with a few persons living in luxury. Its banking system is poor; small loans have to be obtained through money lenders who are often little better than extortionists. Another striking characteristic of an underdeveloped country is that its exports to other countries usually consist almost entirely of raw materials, ores, or fruits, or some staple product with possibly a small admixture of luxury handicrafts. Often the extraction or cultivation of these raw material exports is in the hands of foreign companies.[2]

Low Per Capita Income Levels

The United Nations now considers any country with a gross national product of less than $360 per capita as a low-income country. This $360 per capita figure is in current 1978 U.S. dollars, so an adjustment to account for inflation since 1978 has to be made. There are 38 countries in this category. Using per capita income or per capita GNP is not very precise because of the problems associated with statistical measures of income and production. We discussed these problems earlier and they apply with even greater force when we are talking about less developed countries, since these countries have very unsophisticated methods of gathering and processing data, and much of the income is in-kind, so it doesn't enter the statistics. For example, the food a family grows for itself is not included.

Table 31-1 presents the latest World Bank data for selected, representative countries. The most obvious measure of low levels of development is, of course, low-income levels per capita, and Table 31-1 gives you the best available relative breakdown of per capita income. The category "Capital Surplus Oil Exporters" includes three rich countries whose wealth is based on their oil resources rather than on development. They export more than they import and so are called capital surplus countries. The communist countries are also listed separately as "Centrally Planned Economies"; they rely less on the market system than most other countries, and often the quality of their statistics is poor compared to other countries at similar levels of development.

---

[1]In the jargon of development economists, the name for the less developed countries has changed frequently, in part reflecting the increased political power of these countries. In the 1950s and 1960s the term "underdeveloped countries" was most commonly used. (Before that, they were often called "backward" countries.) In the late 1960s and early 1970s the term "less developed countries" emerged. In the late 1970s the term "Third World" was in vogue, and the latest United Nations' publications use the terms "low-income countries," "middle-income countries," and "industrialized countries" to designate the level of development.

[2]Paul G. Hoffman, *One Hundred Countries—One and One Quarter Billion People* (Washington: Committee for International Economic Growth, 1960), p. 14.

TABLE 31-1 BASIC INDICATORS OF ECONOMIC DEVELOPMENT

	Population (millions)	Area (thousand square kilometers)	GNP Per Capita (in current U.S. dollars)	Average Annual Growth (percent)	Average Annual Rate of Inflation (percent)	
	mid-1978		1978	1960–78	1960–70	1970–78
Low-Income Countries	1,293.9	26,313	200	1.6	3.1	10.6
Bangladesh	84.7	144	90	−0.4	3.7	17.9
India	643.9	3,288	180	1.4	7.1	8.2
Afghanistan	14.6	647	240	0.4	11.9	4.4
Sierra Leone	5.1	72	210	0.5	2.9	10.8
Indonesia	136.0	2,027	630	4.1	180.0	20.0
Middle-Income Countries	872.8	32,998	1,250	3.7	3.7	13.1
Egypt	38.1	1,001	280	1.9	3.5	5.2
Philippines	45.6	300	510	2.6	5.8	13.4
Paraguay	2.9	407	850	2.6	3.0	12.3
Chile	10.7	757	1,410	1.0	32.9	242.6
Mexico	65.4	1,973	1,219	2.7	3.5	17.5
Spain	37.1	505	3,470	5.0	6.3	15.0
Industrialized Countries	667.8	30,424	8,070	3.7	4.2	9.4
United Kingdom	55.8	224	5,030	2.1	4.1	14.1
Japan	114.9	372	7,280	7.6	4.8	9.6
France	53.3	547	8,260	4.0	4.1	9.3
Federal Republic of Germany (West)	61.3	249	9,580	3.3	3.2	5.9
United States	221.9	9,363	9,590	2.4	2.8	6.8
Capital Surplus Oil Exporters	60.1	6,011	3,340	7.1	1.2	22.2
Saudi Arabia	8.2	2,150	7,690	6.2	—	28.4
Libya	2.7	1,760	6,910	6.2	5.2	20.7
Kuwait	1.2	18	14,890	−2.3	0.6	19.8
Centrally Planned Economies	1,352.4	34,826	1,190	4.0	—	—
People's Republic of China	952.0	9,597	230	3.7	—	—
Hungary	10.7	93	3,450	5.0	—	—
USSR	261.0	22,402	3,700	4.3	—	—
Poland	35.0	313	3,670	5.9	—	—
German Democratic Republic (East)	16.7	108	5,710	4.8	—	—

Source: Adapted from *World Development Report, 1980* (New York: Oxford University Press, 1980). Copyright © 1980 by the International Bank for Reconstruction and Development/The World Bank. Published by Oxford University Press, Inc.

Agriculture

Agriculture predominates in less developed countries. It is basically subsistence agriculture or agriculture designed to provide food for the individual family rather than crops sold for cash. Rural overcrowding, small land holdings which prevent modern economical cultivation, and low agricultural yields per acre predominate. An examination of Tables 31-2, 31-3, and 31-4 confirms this. In the low- and middle-income countries, more than half the labor force is engaged in agriculture, almost half the GDP (gross domestic product) is attributed to agriculture in the low-income countries, and the growth in the agricultural sector is lower than in other sectors of the economy in these countries. To a large degree, the extent to which a country devotes itself to agriculture indicates its level of poverty. No country is poor if it is easily able to feed itself by producing its own food or by exporting nonfood items and importing food. Today, less than 5 percent of the U.S. labor force can feed the entire United States well, with a surplus left for export; the vast bulk of the labor forces of the 38 poorest countries are in agriculture, and even then their peoples are poorly fed.

Climate

A surprising fact is that almost all the poorest of the low-income countries are in tropical climates. Conversely, all the industrialized countries are north of 35 degrees latitude or south of 20 degrees latitude. Also, the pockets of low levels of development in the industrialized countries are in the southern regions. This holds for such countries as Italy and, to some extent, at least historically, even the United States. This relationship between climate and development is so strong that it seems to many people that it could hardly be a coincidence. It is sometimes referred to by development economists as the *North-South problem*. Some development economists have suggested that warmer climates produce lower human effort, more diseases, and unfavorable agricultural conditions. On the other hand, Hong Kong, Singapore, and Saudi Arabia are doing rather well.

TABLE 31-2 GROWTH OF PRODUCTION (average annual growth rates—percent)

	GDP*		Agriculture		Industry		Services	
	1960–70	1970–78	1960–70	1970–78	1960–70	1970–78	1960–70	1970–78
Low-Income Countries	3.9	3.6	2.5	2.0	6.1	4.5	4.4	4.3
Middle-Income Countries	6.0	5.7	3.4	3.1	7.8	7.1	5.7	5.8
Industrialized Countries	5.1	3.2	1.2	1.0	6.1	3.4	4.8	3.7

Source: Adapted from *World Development Report, 1980* (New York: Oxford University Press, 1980). Copyright © 1980 by the International Bank for Reconstruction and Development/The World Bank. Published by Oxford University Press, Inc.
*GDP (Gross Domestic Product) is a concept very close to GNP.

TABLE 31-3   STRUCTURE OF POPULATION

| | Percentage of Population | | | | | | Percentage of Labor Force in Agriculture | |
| | In Urban Areas | | Below Age 15 | | Of Working Age (15–64 years) | | | |
	1960	1980	1960	1978	1960	1978	1960	1978
Low-Income Countries	17	21	43	44	56	55	77	72
Middle-Income Countries	37	51	44	44	55	55	58	45
Industrialized Countries	67	77	26	24	63	65	17	6

Source: Adapted from *World Development Report, 1980* (New York: Oxford University Press 1980). Copyright © 1980 by the International Bank for Reconstruction and Development/The World Bank. Published by Oxford University Press, Inc.

TABLE 31-4   STRUCTURE OF PRODUCTION

| | Distribution of Gross Domestic Product* (percent) | | | | | |
| | Agriculture | | Industry | | Services | |
	1960	1978	1960	1978	1960	1978
Low-Income Countries	50	38	17	24	33	38
Middle-Income Countries	22	16	31	34	47	50
Industrialized Countries	6	4	40	37	54	59

Source: Adapted from World Development Report, 1980 (New York: Oxford University Press, 1980). Copyright © 1980 by the International Bank for Reconstruction and Development/The World Bank. Published by Oxford University Press, Inc.
*Gross domestic product (GDP) is a concept very close to GNP.

Population

Perhaps the most striking features of less developed countries are their demographic characteristics. (*Demography* is the study of populations.) As Table 31-5 indicates, all poor countries have high birth rates. The ***crude birth rate*** is demographics jargon for the number of births per thousand of population. As Table 31-5 shows, there is a significant difference between the crude birth rates in poor and industrialized countries. The median birth rate in the low-income countries is 39 per thousand; in the middle-income countries it is 35 per thousand, compared to a median crude birth rate of 14 per thousand in the industrialized

crude birth rate   Number of births per one thousand of population.

TABLE 31-5   DEMOGRAPHIC INDICATORS

	Crude Birth Rate per Thousand Population		Crude Death Rate per Thousand Population		Percentage Change in:	
					Crude Birth Rate 1960–78*	Crude Death Rate 1960–78*
	1960	1978	1960	1978		
Low-Income Countries	48	39	24	15	−14.4	−31.5
Middle-Income Countries	40	35	14	11	−17.4	−29.9
Industrialized Countries	20	14	10	9	−31.3	−6.0

Source: Adapted from *World Development Report, 1980* (New York: Oxford University Press, 1980). Copyright, © 1980 by the International Bank for Reconstruction and Development/The World Bank. Published by Oxford University Press, Inc.
*Weighted average

median   If a series of observations are arranged from the lowest to the highest value, the median is the observation where there are as many higher values as lower values.

countries. The ***median*** is the statistic which is the middle number in a distribution arrayed from highest to lowest.

There are many reasons for these high birth rates. Perhaps the most obvious is that women marry soon after puberty in many poor regions. But why do they marry so early? The reasons may be cultural as well as economic. On the economic side, they marry early because they have few economic alternatives except marriage, and they may produce children early because children, especially sons, are useful as labor and old-age insurance. On the cultural side, they may marry and have children early because of social stigmas that may result if they don't. In most poor countries, for example, there are few worse social stigmas for a woman than to be barren, and a man's worth is often measured by the number of children and grandchildren he has.

The most important consequence of this high birth rate is that a very large proportion of the population is unproductive. As Table 31-3 indicates, almost half of the population of low-income countries is younger than 15 years of age, compared to less than 25 percent under 15 years of age in the industrialized world. These children have to be fed and clothed but produce very little output. In this sense they are a drag on the productive capacity of the country. Additionally, people in poorer countries have a shorter life expectancy. This can be seen in Table 31-6. The median life expectancy at birth is 50 years in the low-income countries compared to 74 years in the industrialized world. This means that the productive work life of any adult is much shorter in the less developed countries. The consequence of the short life expectancy and the high birth rate is large numbers of children with relatively few adults to support them. This is a very uneconomic age distribution from the point of view of the society's ability to accumulate wealth.

Still another significant statistic is that recent health techniques have substantially lowered the death rate in most poorer countries. As Table 31-5 indicates,

TABLE 31-6   HEALTH-RELATED INDICATORS

| | Life Expectancy at Birth | | Mortality Rates per Thousand | | | | Population per: | | | | Percentage of Population with Access to Safe Water |
| | | | Infants Aged 0–1 | | Children Aged 1–4 | | Physician | | Nursing Person | | |
	1960	1978	1960	1975	1960	1978	1960	1977	1960	1977	1975
Low-Income Countries	42	50	N.A.		30	20	18,020	9,900	9,050	8,790	28
Middle-Income Countries	54	61	N.A.		18	10	8,960	4,310	2,235	1,860	60
Industrialized Countries	69	74	29	13	1	1	820	630	390	220	—

Source: Adapted from *World Development Report, 1980* (New York: Oxford University Press, 1980). Copyright © 1980 by the International Bank for Reconstruction and Development/The World Bank. Published by Oxford University Press, Inc.

the *crude death rate* fell significantly from 1960 to 1978 in the low-income and middle-income countries. The crude death rate is the absolute number of deaths per one thousand of population. It remained almost constant in the industrialized countries. The consequence of this declining death rate and high and stable birth rate has been a population explosion in low-income countries. This population explosion means that these countries must grow rapidly in productive capacity just to stay *even* in per capita income. The effect of this is easily seen by comparing Tables 31-1 and 31-2. In Table 31-2 we see that the average annual growth rates of production in the low-income and middle-income countries were in some cases higher than the rates in the industrial countries. Even the median growth rates for the middle-income countries are higher in all three sectors than the rates in the industrial countries. But we get a different picture when we examine per capita GNP growth in Table 31-1. The high rates of population growth have meant that the poor countries have fallen further behind on a per capita basis even though their growth has been more rapid in terms of aggregate GNP.

crude death rate   Number of deaths per one thousand of population.

Low Investment in Human Capital

Most low-income countries invest very little in what economists call **human capital,** or the health, education, and skills of their citizens. Labor that is healthy and well educated is more productive, so investment in humans can be as productive as investment in machines, bridges, and tractors. Of course, one reason that low-income countries invest little in human capital is that they have little to invest, and one of the reasons they have little to invest is that they have such low levels of investment in human capital and other kinds of capital. This is the *vicious circle of poverty.* There is little investment because there is a low level of income, and there is a low level of income because there is little investment.

The very low level of investment in human capital is easily seen in Tables 31-6 and 31-7. In Table 31-6 we see median population per physician and nursing

human capital   Investment in the education, health, skills, and training of a population.

vicious circle of poverty   Little investment because of a low level of income, and a low level of income because of little investment.

persons. There are more than double the number of persons per physician in low-income countries than in the middle-income countries, and more than 30 times more people per physician in the low-income countries compared to the industrialized countries. The relationship with nursing persons per population is even more pronounced. The percentage of the population having access to safe water follows this pattern. In the middle-income countries, 60 percent of the population has safe water compared to 28 percent in the low-income countries. These data indicate the very important point that the population in the low-income countries is less healthy, less vigorous, and, as a result, less productive.

Turn now to Table 31-7, which presents data on the educational levels in the world. We see that the median literacy rate is 38 percent in the low-income countries, 71 percent in the middle-income countries, and 99 percent in the industrialized countries. The reasons for this can easily be found by examining the data in Table 31-7, which shows the numbers enrolled in school. The reasons for the low enrollments in the low- and middle-income countries are easy to understand. In a subsistence economy, everyone must work to support the family. Education is a luxury that the family cannot afford. The effects are obvious. An uneducated work force is a less productive work force.

Culture

Another characteristic of less developed countries is the fact that they all have what might be termed "uneconomic" cultures. Many of these countries cling to old ways of life which are in conflict with industrialization and economic development. This is not to say that these cultural traits are bad in any normative or moral sense, but only that they hinder economic development. Economic development may not be a society's primary goal.

TABLE 31-7   EDUCATIONAL LEVELS

	Numbers Enrolled in Primary School as Percentage of Age Group				Numbers Enrolled in Secondary School as Percentage of Age Group		Numbers Enrolled in Higher Education as Percentage of Population Aged 20–24		Adult Literacy Rate (percent)	
	Total		Female							
	1960	1977	1960	1977	1960	1977	1960	1976	1960	1975
Low-Income Countries	54	77	37	64	14	24	2	4	29	38
Middle-Income Countries	81	97	74	93	17	40	4	11	54	71
Industrialized Countries[1]	114	98	108	102	68	87	17	36	N.A.	99

Source: Adapted from *World Development Report, 1980* (New York: Oxford University Press, 1980). Copyright, © 1980 by the International Bank for Reconstruction and Development/The World Bank. Published by Oxford University Press, Inc.
[1]For countries with universal primary education, the gross enrollment ratios exceed 100 percent since some pupils are below or above the official primary school age.

In many countries, this manifests itself in an acceptance of the status quo. In some countries, particularly in Asia, consumption and wealth are considered vulgar, and Hinduism and Buddhism both consider self-denial virtuous. Even begging, which flourishes in these poor countries, is not looked down upon. This is in stark contrast to the western ideal and particularly to the so-called "Protestant Ethic" which holds that economic success and its trappings are a sign of goodness.

In many low-income countries, superstition plays a key role. Success in business or in agriculture is thought to depend heavily on spirits. These spirits are invoked to insure success. Even in Latin America, where the population is predominantly Catholic, people in many areas solicit the help of pre-Christian deities. All this activity works against the development of modern industrial and agricultural techniques and slows the course of economic development.

Upward *im*mobility is a characteristic of low-income countries. The intelligent, vigorous individual is often blocked from advancement by a caste system, or suspicions or sanctions against such advancement. As a result, entrepreneurial talents are often given an opportunity only in the military or government service. The private sector and manufacturing suffer. Many talented individuals emigrate from less developed countries to countries with greater opportunity.

The grip of custom strangles many less developed economies. Much is done in a prescribed manner because it is dictated by custom. This grip of custom makes it very difficult to emerge from a state of constant per capita income in real terms. Economic growth and development require the acceptance of technological changes and innovations. Custom works against such change. A number of writers have argued that, in part, the success of the Industrial Revolution may be the result of the radical changes that took place during this period that touched and challenged the basic customs of the population. Indeed, industrial revolutions have often occurred after social upheavals that changed and challenged entrenched power structures.

THEORIES AND MODELS OF DEVELOPMENT

The theories and models of economic development are not elegant economic theories; indeed, the field of economic development has attracted practitioners and field economists rather than theorists. There are, however, several models or theories (theory used in a loose sense) of various aspects of the development process. These models have at times been the basis of policies aimed at helping the development process along.

Historical Theories of Development

There are two basic theories of development that are historical in nature in that they try to examine history and draw from it guidelines for development. The first is the theory of Karl Marx as expressed in *Das Kapital.* The second is the theory of W. W. Rostow, presently a professor at the University of Texas and formerly adviser to President Lyndon Johnson.

Das Kapital. Marx saw all society passing through the historical stages of: (1) primitive society (tribal communism), (2) slavery, (3) feudalism, (4) capitalism, (5) socialism, and, finally, (6) communism. At this final stage, Marx argued, scarcity would not exist and workers would produce without material incentives. To Marx, the important stage was the decay of capitalism and the transition to socialism. Marx felt that the transition would come about because of fundamental weaknesses inherent in capitalism. One of the major weaknesses Marx saw was based on his view of the *labor theory of value* and the class struggle that would emerge between the proletariat and the capitalists. To Marx, all value in produced goods was derived from labor. The machines that were used in the production process were simply embodied or congealed labor from earlier production. All commodities were valued in terms of the common denominator of the labor time embodied in them. The relative prices of goods were thus determined by the labor time embodied in them. If a wagon took five times longer to produce than a harness, it would sell for five times the price of the harness.

labor theory of value A central theme in the writings of Karl Marx. All commodities were reduced to a common denominator of the labor time embodied in the product.

This labor theory of value produced a struggle based on Marx's observation that capitalists only pay workers the minimum amount necessary to survive. He argued that wages always tend toward subsistence because capitalists, seeking profits, only pay the lowest amount necessary. The difference between the labor value of the goods produced and the subsistence wage the workers received was labeled *surplus value* by Marx. This surplus value represented capitalistic exploitation of workers.

surplus value The difference between the labor value of goods produced and the subsistence wages received by the workers.

Marx also believed that there would be an eventual decline of profits as capitalists accumulated more and more capital. The private economy would become very monopolized, and business cycles would increase in severity. As a result of all these forces, a large group of unemployed laborers would result, called the *reserve army of the unemployed.* These unemployed workers would unite and socialism would ultimately develop.

reserve army of the unemployed The large group of unemployed laborers that Marx predicted would unite, ultimately developing socialism.

Marx does not win high grades as an economist. His economic reasoning was primitive even in his own day. His labor theory of value is not a particularly good theory. As we saw earlier, price is determined by the interaction of supply and demand. It is true that labor costs play a large role in determining supply, but other costs of production also play a role, as does demand.

Marx's prognosis for the future did not fare much better than his economics. It is true that industrialization spread throughout the world as the Industrial Revolution occurred, particularly throughout the western world, but the Industrial Revolution did not result in just a few industrialists acquiring all the wealth at the expense of the working masses. In fact, the material well-being of workers increased rapidly with spreading industrialization.

A Non-Communist Manifesto. W. W. Rostow, in a book entitled *Stages of Economic Growth,* responded to Marx's theory in the same historical tradition.[3] Rostow, in fact, subtitled his book *A Non-Communist Manifesto,* making clear that it was intended as an anti-Marxist statement.

Rostow argues that all countries go through five stages of economic growth. He believes that it is possible to classify countries according to the stage they are

---

[3]W. W. Rostow, *Stages of Economic Growth* (2d ed.; New York: Cambridge University Press, 1971).

in and that we can then investigate why some countries have not advanced into the next stage in their development process.

The first stage is the *traditional society*. Rostow characterizes this stage as *pre-Newtonian*. By pre-Newtonian he means that the scientific age and advanced technology have not yet arrived. Countries in this stage would exhibit the characteristics of underdevelopment we discussed earlier, including the noneconomic culture. The second stage develops the *preconditions for takeoff*. In this stage, the uneconomic culture is overcome, advances in agriculture take place, and an entrepreneurial class of risk-takers begins to emerge. *Takeoff*, the third stage, follows. During *takeoff into sustained growth*, there is a significant increase in the rate of saving and *leading sectors* develop; increased saving finances investment in capital goods in the leading sectors. These leading sectors grow rapidly and their growth pulls other sectors along. The takeoff is, of course, the key to emerging as an industrial country. The Industrial Revolution in Western Europe and the United States would date the takeoff in these countries. Some of the countries in the middle income range in Table 31-6 would presently be in the takeoff stage.

The final two stages are the *drive to maturity* and the stage of *high mass consumption*. The drive to maturity is the stage when lagging sectors of the economy catch up to the leading sectors and the industrial revolution is consolidated into sustained growth. The fifth stage, high mass consumption, is characterized by the level of development in the United States and Western Europe at the present time.

Rostow's stage theory implies that all countries follow a (roughly) similar path to development. Criticisms of the theory have centered on the contention that while the stages might usefully categorize how the present industrialized nations have developed, the present low-income countries cannot be so easily categorized. The pre-Newtonian stage, while perhaps characteristic of pre-Industrial Revolution England, does not categorize today's low-income countries where very modern technology exists next to urban squalor. Professor Simon Kuznets, a Nobel prizewinning economist, has pointed out that there are significant differences between today's less developed countries and the pre-industrial phase of the now developed countries.[4] Among the most important of these is the fact that per capita agricultural production in today's less developed countries is about one fourth the level it was in pre-industrial stages of the present developed countries, and social and political obstacles are more formidable in today's less developed world. Indeed, it can be argued that pre-Industrial Revolution England was not an underdeveloped country at all compared to today's less developed countries.[5]

traditional society A society largely governed by tradition and including a traditional economy.

preconditions for takeoff The stage where "uneconomic" culture is overcome, advances in agriculture take place, and an entrepreneurial class of risk-takers begins to emerge; the next stage is takeoff.

takeoff The stage at which there is a significant increase in the rate of saving. Leading sectors develop and pull others along, and sustained growth is achieved.

drive to maturity The stage where the lagging sectors of the economy catch up and the industrial revolution is consolidated into sustained growth.

high mass consumption The stage where growth settles into high mass consumption, such as in the United States and Western Europe.

Push Strategies

All the less developed economies have low saving rates, but it has seemed clear to a number of practitioners that these low saving rates are not the primary cause of low growth. As a result, a number of strategies have emerged on ways in which

---

[4]See Simon Kuznets, *Economic Growth and Structure* (New York: W. W. Norton & Co., Inc., 1965).
[5]See Ryan C. Amacher, "Economic Growth and Structural Change in Pre-Industrial Revolution England: Where Are the Lessons for Growth?" *Journal of European Economic History* (1983).

The New International Economic Order

Third world nations have increasingly mounted a drive for what they call the "New International Economic Order." This movement demands a fundamental and significant revision of the institutions that govern world trade. These countries attack the present system, which is based on market exchange, on the grounds of inequality and inequity, two terms used synonymously. The market system is seen by these countries as a tool of exploitation that is used by the developed countries to foster economic growth at the expense of developing countries.

The New International Economic Order has existed since 1974. In 1955, the United Nations had 59 members; by 1975, the United Nations had 141 members. One hundred ten of these members belong to a group of nonaligned, less developed countries that are referred to as the Group of 77 (the original members totaled 77). The Group of 77 has increasingly voiced displeasure with the existing economic order, calling for a better deal for themselves.

The New International Economic Order calls for a superstructure as part of the United Nations to determine trade flow and aid on a more equitable basis. The difficulty from an economic viewpoint is that the New Order expands the economic power of nonmarket participants and decreases the political power of market participants. If the decisions as to who trades with whom, and how much trade occurs, are to be made in a bureaucratic, political framework in which normative political and social criteria determine trade flows and prices, the result will be easy to predict. There will be less trade and more political conflict.

---

big push *The development strategy calling for one major thrust on all fronts in the economy by government, or induced by government through private enterprise.*

leading sectors *The development theory calling for concentration on a number of leading sectors that will pull along other sectors in the development process.*

to break the cycle and cause a spurt in economic growth. Although there are a number of such strategies, there are only two basic variants, the *big push* and *leading sectors.* The big push calls for one major thrust on all fronts in the economy by government or induced by government through private enterprise.[6] This idea is based on the classical notion that growth in the output of an industry is limited by the extent of the market. As a result of the low level of development, it is futile for any one industry to expand its output to a larger scale because it would be unable to sell its product. But if all industries expand in a big push, the inputs needed for the production of one commodity become the demands for other industries' output, and the incomes generated will create a demand for the final product. This must be done by the government, the proponents of the big push argue, because no single entrepreneur or group of entrepreneurs has the incentive to expand production without the simultaneous expansion in other industries. The argument comes down to a call for government action to stimulate the growth process. The main challenge to this approach would rest on the fact

---

[6] Paul Rosenstein-Rodan, "Notes on the Theory of the 'Big Push,'" in *Economic Development for Latin America,* edited by H. S. Ellis (New York: St. Martin's Press, Inc., 1963).

that the industrialized countries, the now developed world, did not have such a government-sponsored big push.

Professor Albert O. Hirschman of the Institute for Advanced Studies in Princeton, New Jersey, a development economist with a great deal of field experience, takes a different track from the push strategy.[7] Hirschman argues that a country does not need a big push on all fronts or in all sectors of the economy. Instead, Hirschman argues that a country should concentrate on developing backward and forward *linkages* from and to successful industries. For example, if there is a successful sardine-fishing industry, it could be linked forward to a canning operation, which in turn could move forward to a packing and shipping industry. Backward linkages could develop effective demand for cans, stimulating a mining industry for metal for cans and a paper industry for shipping cartons. In this view, if the government is to be involved in the development process, it should concentrate its efforts on certain products that maximize the number of linkages. Private entrepreneurs would then take over in response to the demand created through the linkages.

linkages In development economics, the idea of concentrating on the encouragement of a particular sector that will then influence other sectors in the chain of production.

Laissez-Faire Vs. Forced Development

The area of development economics does not have much of a theoretical core of literature. Instead, most economists in the field of development concentrate on institutional and cultural problems. It is interesting to note that no single comprehensive theory of development has emerged that has superseded the original work by Adam Smith in 1776. The complete title of Smith's *Wealth of Nations* was *An Inquiry into the Nature and Causes of the Wealth of Nations.* In this book, which most economists view as marking the beginning of classical economics, Smith exposited the classical principles of economic development. These principles rested on a governmental policy of *laissez-faire*—nonintervention—toward private industry and commerce. The division of labor and the increased productivity brought on by the division of labor were only limited by the extent of the market. As a result, free trade was advocated as a way to promote this division of labor by exploiting each nation's comparative advantage in production.

Recent actions by less developed countries and policies advocated by some development economists are at odds with this *laissez-faire* approach. The argument is that government must force the development process. Many of these opinions grew out of the experience of the 1930s and 1940s when the Soviet Union was able to grow very rapidly by applying severe authoritarian development techniques.[8] As a result of the Soviet development success, economists began to argue that:

> No policy of economic development can be carried out unless the government has the capacity to adhere to it. . . . Quite often, however, democratic governments lose equanimity and determination in the face of opposition. . . . This is the dilemma of most democratic governments. It is here that socialist countries . . . have an immense advantage: their totalitarian structure shields the government from the rigorous and

---

[7]Albert O. Hirschman, *The Strategy of Economic Development* (New Haven: Yale University Press, 1958).

[8]This severe planning technique is sometimes called the Stalinist model. For a more complete analysis, see the next chapter.

reactionary judgments of the electorate. . . . Another advantage of the socialist countries is their passionate conviction and dedication to the objective of economic growth—which contrasts visibly with the halting and hesitant beliefs and actions of most democracies. The firm and purposive sense of direction . . . is in pointed contrast to the extensive revisions and changes in policies and methods which are prompted by minor setbacks in most democratic governments and which produce a sense of drift and helplessness. The political economy of development poses, in this respect, a cruel choice between rapid (self-sustained) expansion and democratic processes.[9]

This idea that development requires authoritarian leadership has been challenged in an empirical study by Dr. G. William Dick, an economist with the federal government.[10] He divided the independent less developed countries of the world into three classifications: authoritarian, semicompetitive, and competitive. An authoritarian government was headed by one political party, and a competitive government had two or more political parties competing for power with free elections at regular intervals. A semicompetitive government was defined as one with one majority party and several minority parties or one political party which conducts legitimizing elections. In any case, there was no extensive control of the population in a semicompetitive country. He then examined the growth of real gross domestic product per capita. The results of the comparison are interesting because they indicate that authoritarian governments fare worse than competitive governments when such growth rates are compared. The main lesson of this empirical study is that the conventional wisdom that rapid growth and democracy are incompatible does not bear close scrutiny.

U.S. Assistance for Development

Agency for International Development (AID) The U.S. agency that is part of the State Department, and is in charge of U.S. aid to foreign countries.

The United States concentrates its official development assistance through the **Agency for International Development (AID),** which is part of the State Department. A recent publication of AID states that:

Programs to assist these people reflect an American tradition of sharing and helping the needy as well as enlightened national self-interest. In part, foreign aid is an expression of the American people's sense of justice and compassion. It also plays an important role in the continuing effort to achieve an enduring structure of world peace. This role is essential to the quest for global tranquility, freedom and progress. There are some things, however, that foreign aid cannot do. Experience has shown that it cannot right all social wrongs or solve every economic problem in a developing country. It cannot bring about instant progress. Nor is it designed to accomplish alone what diplomacy cannot. It must be considered as a complement to other elements of foreign policy.[11]

The United States is a major contributor to the development programs of low-income countries. In 1981, the latest year for which figures are available, the United States contributed almost 30 percent of all the aid funds given by western

---

[9]Jagdish Bhagwati, *The Economies of Underdeveloped Countries* (New York: McGraw-Hill Book Co., 1966), pp. 203–204.
[10]G. William Dick, "Authoritarian Versus Nonauthoritarian Approaches to Economic Development," *Journal of Political Economy* (July/August, 1974).
[11]Agency for International Development. *AID's Challenge in an Interdependent World.* (Washington: Office of Public Affairs [AID, DN-RIA-119, 90/78], 1978), p. 3.

Development Assistance

In 1981, leaders from the United States and Western Europe met with the leaders of 14 less developed countries in Cancun, Mexico, to discuss development needs. President Reagan delivered a tough message indicating that the era of massive U.S. aid was over. Instead, the United States would concentrate on trade with developing countries. Most importantly, President Reagan indicated the U.S. aid was going to go to countries favorable to the United States.

The United States has long given aid to developing countries. The first table presented here shows that the United States gives more than any other country in absolute dollars. As a percent of GNP (or of similar measures such as industrial production), the United States ranks far below some countries of Western Europe. In addition to development assistance, the United States contributes more than 25 percent of the annual budget of the United Nations.

Many poorer nations, including those attending the Cancun meeting, feel that the developed countries should give more economic aid to Third World countries. They have set a target of .7 percent of GNP as the amount that developed nations should contribute. The table shows that only the Netherlands, Norway, Sweden, and Denmark are presently at or above this target level of giving. President Reagan does not agree with the demands of these Third World representatives.

As the second table shows, in 1981, the ten countries receiving the most economic aid from the United

States were countries not always friendly in world forums. It will be interesting to watch the flow of U.S. aid to see if it responds to President Reagan's rhetoric.

DEVELOPMENT ASSISTANCE

Country	1980 (millions of dollars)	Percentage of Total Output (GNP or GDP)
Netherlands	$ 1,577	.99
Norway	473	.82
Sweden	923	.76
Denmark	464	.72
France	4,041	.62
Australia	657	.48
Belgium	575	.48
West Germany	3,518	.43
Canada	1,036	.42
Britain	1,785	.34
Japan	3,304	.32
New Zealand	60	.27
United States	7,091	.27
Switzerland	246	.24
Austria	174	.23
Finland	106	.22
Italy	678	.17
Soviet Union	1,580	.14
Eastern Europe	237	.06

Source: Organization for Economic Cooperation and Development, *National Accounts of OECD Countries,* 1981.

RECIPIENTS OF UNITED STATES AID IN 1981

Country	Millions of Dollars
1. Egypt	$ 1,189
2. Israel	785
3. India	244
4. Turkey	200
5. Bangladesh	155
6. Indonesia	128
7. Sudan	105
8. Nicaragua	95
9. Philippines	92
10. Peru	81

Source: Organization for Economic Cooperation and Development, *National Accounts of OECD Countries,* 1981.

industrialized countries and gave far more than any one of these countries. However, if we look at that giving as a percentage of GNP, the figures tell another story. Some of these countries gave a much larger share of their GNP to low-income countries than did the United States; on this basis, for example, France gave more than twice as much, and Norway more than three times as much as the United States. See the inset in this chapter for more information on country-to-country economic assistance.

IS ECONOMIC DEVELOPMENT GOOD OR BAD?

Of course, development is neither wholly good nor wholly bad. The appropriate question is, What policies can be adopted to minimize the bad aspects of economic growth and encourage the good aspects?

In the 1940s, Los Angeles was surrounded by orange groves. Now its suburbs stretch for more than 60 miles inland from the Pacific Ocean. In the 1950s, smog was not a problem in Phoenix, but population and economic growth have both contributed to make smog a serious problem. Some of these problems and their causes can be remedied, at least in part. Antipollution regulations have improved the smog situations in Arizona and in southern California, in spite of continued high growth.

What can be done about economic development? Many Americans are uneasy about adopting official policies on population growth because they feel this is a private matter. Economic growth is condemned by some, praised by others. It is clear there are costs to growth. However, it is also clear that growth is virtually the only way for standards of living to rise. This is true for the average family and also true for poorer families. It simply isn't true that redistributing wealth would do much to improve the lot of the poor. When we see the vast gulfs of wealth between the very rich and the very poor in less developed countries, we have to realize that only a small segment of the population is rich. Even if all wealth were distributed equally in a poor country, everyone would be poor. The only hope for poor people everywhere is economic development.

SUMMARY

1. Development economics is often concerned with specific, detailed policies for improving the development of a particular country.

2. Less developed countries have similar characteristics that can be easily recognized when countries are grouped by level of income. Agriculture dominates in less developed countries and is usually of a subsistence nature. Many of these same countries lie in tropical and subtropical climates. A poor harvest means disaster for the countries' populations.

3. The demographic characteristics of less developed countries also exhibit a common structure. Birth rates are high, which means that a significant share of the population consumes but doesn't produce. The crude death rate in low-income countries is falling. This, coupled with the high birth rates, produces the population explosion which causes per capita income to fall or to rise at a slow rate.

4. Low-income countries invest little in human capital; that is, in the health, vigor, and educa-

tion of the population. An unhealthy and uneducated labor force is relatively unproductive.

5. Cultural factors play a significant role in the development process. Economic growth requires a progressive economic attitude. This attitude is slow to develop in some cultural environments.

6. There are two basic historical models of economic development. The first is Marx's theory in which countries advance through stages from primitive society to communism. This transition comes about because of a fundamental weakness in capitalism that forces all workers to a subsistence level of income. Many workers would be thrown out of work as the economy became more monopolized and business cycles became increasingly severe. These unemployed workers, the reserve army of the unemployed, would unite, and socialism, the stage before communism, would develop. Marx's prognosis has not fared well. As industrialization spread in the world, the standard of living of the work force improved dramatically.

7. W. W. Rostow has also developed a theory based on stages of growth, but it is quite distinct from Marx's. In Rostow's theory, each country proceeds in stages from traditional to high mass consumption. Rostow argues that every country proceeds through a similar growth path.

8. The big push strategy suggests that government can speed the process through a major thrust on all fronts of the economy.

9. The leading sectors strategy strongly suggests that if growth is concentrated on some key sectors and if linkages are developed, these sectors will create demand on other sectors to grow.

10. Both strategies suggest an active role for government in the development process. A key question is the extent to which government should play a role. Some economists argue that government should play an active role, even to the detriment of democratic policy. Others argue that development does not require authoritarian leadership.

11. The United States has traditionally aided less developed countries. This aid is primarily channeled through the Agency for International Development. U.S. aid is large in an absolute sense, but other western nations contribute a larger share of the GNP than does the United States.

NEW TERMS

crude birth rate
median
crude death rate
human capital
vicious circle of poverty
labor theory of value
surplus value
reserve army of the unemployed
traditional society

preconditions for takeoff
takeoff
drive to maturity
high mass consumption
big push
leading sectors
linkages
Agency for International Development (AID)

QUESTIONS FOR DISCUSSION

1. What effect will the worldwide energy crises and the high price of oil have on world development?

2. Does development change the cultural environment or does the cultural environment cause economic development?

3. What role do you think the United States should play in world development?

4. What effect do "no growth" policies have on different economic levels of society?

5. Should the U.S. government try to limit population growth in less developed countries? Do you foresee any problems with such a policy?

SUGGESTIONS FOR FURTHER READING

Amacher, Ryan C., Gottfried Haberler, and Thomas D. Willett (eds.). *Challenges to a Liberal International Order.* Washington: American Enterprise Institute, 1979.

Enke, Stephen. *Economics for Development.* Englewood Cliffs, N.J.: Prentice-Hall, Inc., 1963.

Kindleberger, Charles P., and Bruce Herrick. *Economic Development,* 3d ed. New York: McGraw-Hill Book Co., 1977.

Mishan, Ezra J. *Technology and Growth: The Price We Pay.* New York: Praeger Publishers, 1970.

Schumacher, Ernest Friedrich. *Small Is Beautiful: Economics as If People Mattered.* New York: Harper & Row Publishers, Inc., 1973.

CHAPTER 32

Comparative Economic Systems and Ideologies

Learning Objectives

After studying the materials found in this chapter, you should be able to do the following:

1. Define:
   (a) capitalism.
   (b) socialism.
   (c) communism.
   (d) fascism.

2. Describe the major features of the types of, and differences in, the economic systems found in:
   (a) Russia.
   (b) China.
   (c) Cuba.
   (d) Yugoslavia.

3. Calculate input coefficients given physical data in an input-output table.

4. Define:
   (a) shadow prices.
   (b) the socialist controversy.
   (c) the competitive solution.

We often talk about and refer to other economic systems without really knowing how to define such terms as *capitalism, socialism,* and *communism.* What are the key differences among these systems and to what degree do these differences affect economic outcomes? In Chapter 2 we began our study by saying that all economic systems are mixed systems and that the material we would cover in the intervening chapters would serve to allow us to analyze any economic system. We still stand by that statement. You might ask, If the economics we have already learned is good for all systems, why include a chapter on alternative systems? The answer is that politics and ideology mix with economics to create widely differing economic-political systems. It is enlightening to examine the political, economic, and historical settings of the various institutions that comprise the different economies we may wish to analyze.

In order to introduce you to the subject of comparative economics, we will begin with an attempt to define ideological systems. We will then examine some of the dominant, but different, forms of communism. We will next present a decision-making approach to the analysis of differing systems, and then conclude with a treatment of the advantages and disadvantages of economic planning.

IDEOLOGIES

In Chapter 2 we divided economic systems into three major groups, which we labeled *traditional, planned,* and *market.* The field of comparative economic systems breaks this categorization into smaller parts so classification of economies can be made more easily. A very common approach, and perhaps the oldest, is to classify systems according to the underlying political philosophy *and* the basis of ownership of the factors of production. This might be called the *isms* approach because it concentrates on four major *isms:* capitalism, socialism, communism, and fascism.

This approach makes it difficult to be specific when we talk about alternative economic systems because we are used to thinking in terms of communism, socialism, and capitalism as if these three systems were the only alternatives of economic organization. There are, however, a myriad of economic systems in the world. The term capitalism is often applied to the economic systems found in western democracies, but the differences among economic institutions in the United States, Great Britain, France, and Sweden are significant. Likewise, we may refer to the economic organization in Eastern Europe and the USSR as communism, but there are significant differences among the institutions in the USSR, Yugoslavia, and Romania. In this complexity lies the difficulty of separating the critical elements of difference between and among various economic systems. We must determine the differences in institutions and then determine if these differences cause economic behavior to be different among the systems. In doing so, the *isms* approach focuses primarily on the ownership of the factors of production.

Capitalism

capitalism *An economic system based on the idea of private ownership of the means of production.*

Capitalism is a system based on the idea of private ownership by individuals (or groups of individuals) of the factors of production. These individuals must be free to use the property as they see fit. Any limitations on the use of the property diminishes its value. These private-property holders are the center of the decision-making process in capitalism.

The system that evolves is one where individuals maximize their own well-being, whether in terms of profit or utility. This categorization can be and is viewed very broadly to allow for a great deal of government intervention. It thus is possible for systems as divergent as the U.S. economy and the British economy to be labeled by some observers as capitalism.

Socialism

socialism *An economic system in which the nonhuman means of production are owned by society, or the state.*

Under a system of **socialism,** the nonhuman means of production are owned by society, or the state. Socialism is seen by its advocates as a way of shifting the decision-making structure, or the authority, from individual entrepreneurial agents to a central authority. This central authority then makes the major economic decisions. Socialism is advocated as a way of promoting equality and/or economic development. The key to understanding socialism is the central authority concept. Utopian socialists see this central authority as promoting the "common good," however that may be defined. Writers who are critical of socialism point out that this authority may be perverted into a centralist, personal dictatorship, as in the case of Stalin, and perhaps best exemplified in present day Eastern Europe by Romania's President Nicolae Ceausescu.

As with capitalism, there are many types of socialism. There is utopian socialism and its variants, including some, such as the Fourier movement, that were actually practiced in the United States. Other variations, particularly those espoused by the Social Democrats, have become forceful political movements in Western Europe. For instance, Francois Mitterand, a socialist, was elected president of France in 1981. Today it is almost meaningless to label someone a socialist or a set of institutions as being socialistic.

Communism

To Karl Marx, *communism* was the final stage of the progression from capitalism, with socialism representing the middle stage of the transition. Under communism, Marx saw the end of scarcity, the end of conflict among the classes, and the creation of a new social order. A member of this new order might be viewed as the antithesis of the self-interested individual on which we based much of the preceding analysis. In the final stage, each individual would receive goods and services according to his or her needs and the state would wither away to a point where all it did was administer the economy. The organizational structure which Marx foresaw under communism is not at all clear. One must presume that everyone would contribute labor in exchange for goods and services needed. A major problem would be the definition and determination of needs. The motivation driving the system and creating incentives would have to lie in the development of this new noneconomic order.

communism The final stage in the theory of Karl Marx, in which the state has withered away and economic goods are equitably distributed.

Fascism

In the countries in which it has been practiced, which include Spain, Portugal, and pre-World War II Germany and Italy, *fascism* combines monopoly capitalism, private property, and a strong authoritarian central government personified by a dictator. Fascism is, in essence, an authoritarian state imposed upon a capitalistic system. As a result, it is a strange permutation that promotes monopoly and then imposes "national interests" on that monopoly structure. This destroys the large degree of personal freedom that is a characteristic of free-enterprise capitalism. There are very few real-world examples of fascism.

fascism An economic system that combines monopoly capitalism, private property, and a strong authoritarian central government.

Weakness of Isms Approach

The problem of the *isms* approach to systems analysis is that it is often too simplistic and does not include many of the keys to determining control over resources. The *isms* approach equates ownership with control and control with decision-making power over the factors of production. This distinction is becoming less clear over time. Consider just a few examples. In the Soviet Union, the leaders of the government do not own much of anything, yet they unmistakably control the system. In the United States, many people own land, but they cannot use it as they please because of local zoning regulations, state land use planning, or federal environmental regulations. So, all in all, the *isms* approach, while often used in political-economic classification schemes (and political rhetoric), is not very useful. In fact, to apply this classification scheme across countries would likely produce just two sets of systems, capitalism and socialism. Yet no serious analyst would consider the United States, France, and Great Britain in one classification that revealed anything significant. Likewise, the Soviet Union, Yugoslavia, and China are too diverse to be labeled socialist and still have the term contain any meaning.

MARX, MARXISTS, AND MARXISM

Perhaps no other economist has had more effect on the political shaping of the world than Karl Marx who, with Friedrich Engels, published the *Communist Manifesto* in 1848. This book, along with Marx's magnum opus, *Das Kapital,* published in three volumes in 1867, 1885, and 1894, form the philosophical basis for a widely divergent group of socialistic-communistic, economic-political systems. Since such a diverse group of communists lay claim to being the true Marxists, it is necessary to distinguish between Marx and Marxism (or Marxists). The central ideas of Marx's economic theory were outlined in the previous chapter. He believed that every society evolved through the historical stages of tribal communism, slavery, feudalism, capitalism, socialism, and finally, communism. The most important transition came when capitalism decayed because of internal contradictions and was succeeded by communism. Under communism, scarcity would disappear and workers would produce without material incentives.

What, then, is the significance of Marx's writings? It is curious that in the countries where communism has spread, the level of industrialization has been very low, the exact opposite of what Marx predicted. The significance is not in Marx himself, nor, for that matter, in his writings, but rather in the rhetorical, philosophical movement his work has spawned. A widely divergent group of communist parties consider themselves Marxists and appeal to the writings of Marx to justify their views on various issues. In some respects they have similar roots. They all condemn the exploitation of workers by monopoly capitalism and eschew the use of the term profit. They all claim to have full-employment economies and claim to have overcome the problem of the capitalistic army of unemployed workers. But once these simplistic notions are out of the way, wide differences come into focus. Countries as diverse as China, Yugoslavia, the Soviet Union, Albania, Romania, and Cuba all claim to be the true Marxists. The significance of Marx is that he is the father of a political, rather than an economic, movement.

LEADER-*ISMS*

Socialism was Marx's intermediate stage between capitalism and communism. Under a system of socialism the decision-making authority is shifted from individual entrepreneurs to a central authority. These central authorities have historically almost always been personified by strong, dominant individuals. It is thus possible to view many of the offshoots of Marxism as the products of these strong-willed leaders.

Leninism

Vladimir Lenin (1870–1924) was active in developing the Communist party of Russia and led the successful Bolshevik Revolution in Russia. He claimed to be a follower of Marx but developed new directions for the achievement of communism. Lenin refused to wait for the maturation of capitalism and instead developed a different formula for revolution based on four essential ingredients: (1) a small, revolutionary elite; (2) economic underdevelopment (the opposite of Marx's industrialization); (3) an estranged peasantry; and (4) war against an outside force. Lenin's formula worked in Russia and has worked in Yugoslavia, China, Vietnam, and Cuba. In fact, Lenin's formula is the way communism has almost always taken root. The exceptions are those countries of Eastern Europe where communism was imposed by the Soviet Union following World War II.

Lenin, who engineered and led the Bolshevik Revolution, became the first communist to be faced with the task of setting up an economic system after the political system was secure. The first system that was implanted in Russia by Lenin is often referred to as *War Communism* because the Communist party was engaged in civil war with the non-Communist White Russians throughout the period. This system substituted rigid administrative control of the economy for the previous market economy in an attempt to marshal the requisite resources to engage in war. Widespread nationalization took place throughout this period, and all private trading was outlawed. All labor mobility was rigidly controlled, and money as an exchange mechanism virtually disappeared. This period is difficult to evaluate, and some economic historians claim that Lenin instituted War Communism only because of the pragmatic concern of carrying out a war.[1] In any event, in 1921 Lenin abandoned War Communism and instituted a program referred to as the *New Economic Policy (NEP),* which was an attempt at *market* socialism with rigid plans for only the key industries in the economy. The remainder of the economy was to be organized under basic market principles. There was very rapid economic growth during this period, and the Soviet economy quickly recovered from the protracted civil war. Lenin died in 1924, and in 1926 the New Economic Policy came to an end for a variety of reasons. A major cause was that the re-marketization of the economy during NEP greatly reduced the power of the Communist party to channel and direct the course of economic development.

War Communism The economic system that was imposed by Lenin in Russia immediately after the Bolshevik Revolution. It is called War Communism because there was continuing civil war.

New Economic Policy (NEP) An attempt at market socialism from 1921 to 1926 in the Soviet Union.

Stalinism

From 1924 to 1928, open debate took place in the Soviet Communist party. It is referred to as the *Great Industrialization Debate.*[2] The debate consisted of differing views on how the Soviet economy should develop. The left wing, led by

Great Industrialization Debate An open debate that took place in the Soviet Union from 1924 to 1928 concerning the correct way to industrialize the economy.

---

[1]Others claim Lenin instituted War Communism out of a desire to see such a system evolve as the economic application of communism. For this view, see Paul Craig Roberts, *Alienation and the Soviet Economy* (Albuquerque: University of New Mexico Press, 1971).

[2]See Alexander Erlich, *Soviet Industrialization Debate, 1924–1928* (Cambridge: Harvard University Press, 1960).

economist E. A. Preobrazhensky, argued that the country should make a big push and pursue rapid industrialization of key sectors of the economy. This would be carried out by the central allocation of investment expenditures. N. I. Bukharin, who was the spokesperson for the right wing, disagreed with this position and stressed balanced growth of the economy. Bukharin argued that all sectors of the economy must grow together because they all support and feed one another.

Joseph Stalin (1879–1953) was both an observer and a participant in the debate. Stalin played one side against the other while consolidating his own power base. At the time of Lenin's death, Stalin allied himself with the right wing of the party in order to counteract the power of Leon Trotsky and the left wing of the party. This allowed him to discredit and weaken the left wing, a task he accomplished by 1927. He then turned on the right wing, and by 1928, had the leaders of the right wing denounced by the party. Stalin was then in complete control, since he had purged any dissidents.[3] The planning system that Stalin adopted was centrally directed and was set up in five-year increments. The five-year time increment was chosen since most investment projects can be completed in such a period. Stalin's first five-year plan was an extreme version of the left-wing superindustrialization plan. Its achievement required very centralized planning, investment in heavy industry, and extreme measures in the agricultural sector, which was expected to supply food and raw materials. The costs of this policy were great in human terms. Millions of people were purged or starved to death. Industrialization was very rapid, however. By the 1960s the Soviet Union had become the second most powerful country in the world, second only to the United States.

The Soviet Union and its rigid central planning is the legacy of Stalin. Today, Stalinism signifies a ruthless dictatorship as well as an extreme, severe, and highly centralized planning structure. However, Stalinism is not openly practiced in any communist country today. Romania perhaps comes the closest by combining the rigid, very centralized planning of Stalinism with a strong leader in the person of its president, Nicolae Ceausescu. Ceausescu has not, however, demonstrated the bloody ruthlessness that characterized Stalinism.

Titoism

Josip Broz Tito, president of Yugoslavia, broke with Stalin in 1948 over Soviet interference in Yugoslavia's internal affairs. Tito was not a puppet of Stalin, since he had carried out his own revolution in Yugoslavia rather than having been installed by the Soviets, as had happened in the other Eastern European communist countries in the post-World War II period. Tito formulated his own "road to socialism," which began as a Stalinist-prototype centrally planned economy, but has become a market-planned economy with less central control than some western market economies (France, for example). A key element, and one that is unique in the world, is the Yugoslav concept of *workers' self-management.* The concept is that all the workers, including what we would call blue-collar and white-collar workers, help direct the firm for which they work and have a financial stake in its outcome. Such a system could only have economic meaning if the

workers' self-management The system in Yugoslavia in which workers direct and have a financial stake in the firm in which they work.

---

[3]For an excellent economic history of the Soviet Union, including this period, see Alec Nove, *An Economic History of the USSR* (London: Penguin, 1975).

firm were autonomous; as a result, a great deal of central authority has withered away in Yugoslavia. Yugoslav communists claim that such self-management by the workers is the true Marxist ideal because it removes the alienation of the worker.

Titoism is unique in the world and owes much to the strength and personality of one man, Tito. In planning for his own death, Tito fashioned an elaborate, collective leadership, consisting of a 23-member presidium with rotating membership. After his death in the spring of 1980, the collective leadership promised to continue Tito's policies. What will follow is impossible to forecast.

Maoism

In China, the Communist party came to full power in October, 1949, after decades of struggle. Mao Tse-tung was the revolutionary leader who had taken command, just as Lenin's formula for communist revolutionaries had dictated. In the early years of Chinese communism, the goal was industrialization, much as it had been in the Soviet Union, but this policy was formulated without the help of Moscow. The Chinese Communist party, from the very beginning, was fiercely independent of the Soviet Union.

In 1958, the *Great Leap Forward* took place. The Great Leap Forward was an impossibly overambitious plan to increase per capita income in China by 25 percent in five years. Many of the programs were foolishly conceived, such as the production of steel on a small scale in backyard furnaces. The result was a worthless product. The regime then took a strange twist in the *Cultural Revolution* that took place in 1966 through 1969. This period represents the high point in the adulation of Mao. We see the essence of Maoism in this time span. The Cultural Revolution embraced revolutionary values. Mao saw a completely classless society, organized as a collective operation rather than as a state enterprise as in the Soviet Union. The motivation for the society was to be completely altruistic. Here we have the concept of the "new man" who responds to social rather than material incentives. The system used moral and honorific rewards to motivate the labor force. To some degree, this technique has had some influence, but it is not clear to what degree this new man has been motivated by indoctrination and coercive administrative controls.

The Chinese economy has changed often and in radically different directions. There is at present not enough information to get any real feel for the success of Maoism relative to economic development. Several economists have traveled to China, and give strikingly different reports. For example, Professor John Gurley of Stanford argues that China has made great strides and has eradicated poverty, while Professor James Tobin of Yale University argues that there was not much economic progress under Mao.[4]

Interesting developments in China are occurring. Since Mao's death in 1976, the new leaders have pursued a very pragmatic development strategy that often seems openly hostile to Mao. The new leaders openly attacked the "Gang of Four," consisting of Mao's widow and three other radicals. In attacking the Gang

Great Leap Forward
Communist China's highly overambitious modernization plan that was launched in 1958.

Cultural Revolution *The revolutionary reevaluation of the Chinese economy that took place from 1966 through 1969. This period represents the high point in the adulation of Mao Tse-tung.*

---

[4]John Gurley, "Maoist Economic Development," and James Tobin, "The Economy of China: A Tourist's View," in Edwin Mansfield, *Economics: Readings, Issues, and Cases* (New York: W.W. Norton & Co., Inc., 1977).

of Four, the leaders attacked the ideas of the Cultural Revolution and, in fact, Mao himself, although they have been very careful not to attack Mao by name. *Newsweek* reports that Chinese officials argue that "Chairman Mao was deceived by the Gang of Four."[5] The attack on the Gang of Four culminated in the trials of 1981.

The Chinese have considered worker's self-management as used in Yugoslavia. As we have seen, this requires decentralization. Chinese leadership is quickly cementing relationships with the West. These movements represent significant breaks with Mao's policy of self-reliance and self-development.

The present regime seems to be moving still further away from Mao. The new party chairman, Hu Yaobang, replaced Mao's handpicked successor, Hua Guofeng. The real source of power in China is Deng Xiaoping, who is committed to modernizing China. This westernization will bring with it the influence and ideas of western capitalism, as has already happened in the communist countries of Eastern Europe.

At the sixtieth anniversary of the Communist party in 1981, Hu and Deng went further than ever in attacking Mao. The party blamed Mao for the present low level of economic development because he persecuted intellectuals and listened to the Gang of Four.

It appears that Deng is in control of the party organization, and that economic development is the primary commitment of the party leadership. It will be interesting to observe the course of Chinese communism over the next decade.

Castroism

Fidel Castro learned the lesson of Lenin's formula for revolution very well. He had a small group of committed revolutionaries, a large, estranged peasant class, an undeveloped economy, and the United States, which he could use as an outside enemy. In many ways the Cuban system is most like Chinese communism in that Castro has placed heavy emphasis on the creation of a "new man."[6] The goal is to remove all social inequities and motivate workers by moral incentives rather than material incentives. This is very close to Marx's view of the final stage of communism. In Cuba, this policy was in large part the work of Che Guevara and was received skeptically by the Soviets, who were financially underwriting the Cuban economy and, therefore, had a large economic interest in Cuba.

The Cuban experience also relies heavily on agriculture. Rather than attempting to rapidly industrialize the Cuban economy, Castro concentrated on agriculture and sought to exploit the export potential of the sugarcane industry. This required the transfer of labor from cities to rural areas, the exact opposite of the experience of the European communist regimes. Planning in Cuba is carried out in a system referred to as the System of Budgetary Finance. This is an extreme central-planning system that views the economy as a single firm to be rigidly controlled by the central authority.

As in many other communist countries, Cuban communism is uniquely the product of one man, Castro. Like Stalin in the Soviet Union, Tito in Yugoslavia,

---

[5] *Newsweek* (October 30, 1978), p. 50.
[6] For a good view of Castro's Cuba, see Carmelo Mesa-Lago (ed.), *Revolutionary Change in Cuba* (Pittsburgh: University of Pittsburgh Press, 1971).

and Mao in China, Castro is a strong leader. We may not see the true face of communism in Cuba during his lifetime. That is why it is perhaps most correct to refer to communism in Cuba as Castroism, at least for the present.

ORGANIZATION AND DECISION-MAKING APPROACH TO THE STUDY OF SYSTEMS

We have been looking at alternative economic systems in terms of how their ideology affects the organization of the system. In many cases this resulted in the study of how a dominant personality shaped an entire system. Some of you may have found this an exciting and useful way to categorize the world. Others may have found it frustrating to study each individual system or country, rather than general principles of how differing systems are organized and how they affect behavior. This approach has been the dominant way economists have historically examined alternative systems. In recent years, however, a new approach has been developed. This newer approach, instead of looking at individual countries, attempts to formulate organizational principles using the economic theory we developed in previous chapters as a coherent analytical framework.[7]

The System

To understand the system, it is necessary to examine both the organizational setting for the production of goods and services *and* the institutional setting for the distribution of those goods and services. The important questions concern the structure of decision making in production and distribution. Perhaps the most important question concerns which individuals, and at which levels, make the important decisions concerning production and distribution. In the United States, production decisions would be made at the entrepreneurial level; in the Soviet Union, these same decisions would be made at the planning level. At this stage of analysis we would determine at which level in the planning hierarchy the decisions are made.

Once the level of decision making is determined, it is necessary to examine the motivational structure at this level of decision making. How do the decision makers bear the costs of wrong decisions or reap the rewards of correct decisions? Additionally, it is necessary to determine how one person influences another. This is different than individual rewards and punishments to the extent that it is possible to change another individual's internal values. In other words, do institutions affect individuals' value systems?

Once these two aspects of the decision-making structure are determined, we can turn to the informational structure in the system. This concerns the way in which individuals learn about their options so they can act on these options. In the U.S. economy, prices are an important source of information; but in the Soviet economy, the plan plays this role. As the decision making becomes centralized,

---

[7]For a comprehensive development of this path-breaking approach, see Egon Neuberger and William J. Duffy, *Comparative Economic Systems: A Decision Making Approach* (Boston: Allyn & Bacon, Inc., 1976).

more and better information is critical because the costs of wrong decisions are so much larger. System questions are predominantly microeconomic in nature.

The Environment

After examining the system, we turn to a country's environment; that is, its social structure, physical conditions, and international situation. Some of the more critical aspects of the environment in terms of possible impact on the system are: the level of economic development; the size of the country in area and population; the availability of natural resources from within and from safe allies; the values of the people (religious, cultural, and so on); the political system; the size of the country relative to its near neighbors; the level of development relative to the rest of the world and relative to near neighbors; and the sphere of influence the country is in (United States, Soviet, or Chinese, for example). These are only a few of the considerations that can influence a system, but they are representative of the concept of environmental influence.

Performance

The way in which an economy performs can have a powerful effect on the environment and the system. Economists usually focus on the performance of gross national product and examine per capita growth in production, stability of production (cycles can be socially destabilizing), and equity in the distribution of this production. These are predominately macroeconomic questions.

Policy

Policy changes can be made within a system without changing the underlying fabric of the system. Policy refers to marginal changes in the system and its environment in order to affect performance. Policy changes can influence the system in a positive or negative way. A "good" system might develop "bad" policies that produce "bad" performance and in turn result in a negative change in the "good" system.

Interactions of Systems, Environment, Performance, and Policy

Of course, all these organizational elements interact in a simultaneous fashion. But using this terminology can help in understanding the slippery concept of why economic systems differ and why they are similar. For example, consider a small country having the USSR or the United States as a close neighbor. How would this affect the development of the system? It has had a profound effect on the communist countries of Eastern Europe. Likewise, being close to the United States has had effects on Canada, Mexico, and Cuba. What environmental factors caused the Industrial Revolution to spread from England to the United States, but not to Russia? How might performance influence an economic system? It's part of Lenin's formula: If things get bad enough, there might be a revolution. On the other hand, if they start to get good enough in communist countries, there might be a move toward capitalism or market socialism. We can't begin to answer all these complex questions, but this approach may give you a start in finding the answers and in organizing your thoughts.

PLANNING

Throughout this chapter, whether we were using the *isms* approach to systems or a more structured organizational approach, we continually flirted with the question of planning. Such questions as who directs production, who makes decisions, and who bears the costs for wrong decisions or receives the rewards for correct decisions kept coming to the forefront. This is the essence of the problem of understanding systems. The question is not whether planning should take place, but rather who should do the planning. General Motors plans, home-builders plan, wheat farmers plan—and so do you. The question is the degree of centralization of planning and control. At extremes, the market position would be that individual consumers and entrepreneurs should plan, and at the command end of the spectrum, the position would be that the central authority should plan.

The Socialist Controversy[8]

Marx had little to say about the actual workings of the economic system under socialism. Instead, Marx criticized capitalism and left the development of the economics of socialism to his followers. In 1922 a professor at the University of Vienna, Ludwig von Mises, wrote a famous article, "Economic Calculation in the Socialist Commonwealth."[9] This article purported to show that national economic calculations were impossible under socialism. Ludwig von Mises based his argument on a number of factors, but the essence of the argument was quite simple. If the state owned the factors of production (other than labor), it would have to allocate them between competing uses. Without a market to determine prices, this would be an impossible task. A simulated market with **shadow prices** could not supply correct prices because of the absence of the profit motive. In fact, von Mises argued that "the most serious menace to socialist economic organization" was the lack of reward for correct managerial decisions and penalty for incorrect managerial decisions. This article kicked off a debate known as the **socialist controversy**.

Professor Oskar Lange, a famous Polish economist who at the time was on the faculty at the University of Chicago, responded to von Mises by developing a model sometimes referred to as the **competitive solution**. In the model, Lange tried to prove that a socialist economy with central *and* local decision making can arrive at the same efficiency standards as the model of pure competition we developed earlier. Prices are arbitrarily set by the central authority. Local managers are told to maximize profits, although they cannot keep these profits. They are solely accounting profits. If shortages or surpluses develop, the price is changed, and in this way an equilibrium price is finally reached. One of the most

shadow prices *Simulated market prices used by economic planners.*

socialist controversy *A debate started by Ludwig von Mises and Oskar Lange concerning the feasibility of planning without markets.*

competitive solution *The name given to the model developed by Oskar Lange to show that a planned economy could, theoretically, reach the same efficiency solutions as a market economy.*

[8]For a thorough discussion of the socialist controversy, see Paul R. Gregory and Robert C. Stuart, *Soviet Economic Structure and Performance* (New York: Harper & Row, Publishers, Inc., 1974).
[9]Ludwig von Mises, "Economic Calculation in the Socialist Commonwealth," in F.A. Hayek (ed.), *Collectivist Economic Planning* (Clifton, N.J.: Augustus M. Kelley Publishers, 1967), p. 103.

telling criticisms of Lange's solution is that if equilibrium prices are sought, why not use a market in the first place?[10]

The debate has never been resolved as to the technical feasibility of centralized planning. Is it possible for a central authority to make the necessary calculations to produce efficiently? In an article that might be considered a continuation of this debate, F. A. Hayek, Nobel prizewinning economist, says no.[11] Hayek argues that information is the friction in the system that causes economic models

Solidarity: Death of the Polish Union Movement

In the late 1970s, the Solidarity movement in Poland began a power struggle that broke into world headlines in 1980. Solidarity, led by Lech Walesa, a shipyard worker, gained a worldwide following by extracting important concessions from the Polish government. By the end of 1981, martial law had been imposed and the concessions gained by Solidarity were lost. The union was in disarray, and Lech Walesa was under house arrest. The reasons for the martial law are easy to understand if one examines the threat that an independent labor movement posed to the communist leadership in Poland and in the Soviet Union.

Solidarity's early success with the Polish government bolstered the confidence of the union and made them almost ache for a confrontation with the Soviet Union. Even Walesa, who had been an early moderating influence, was puffed up with confidence and talk of a showdown. He said: "We must explain to the people what is at stake, that the stakes are very high, that we are changing the present order, and that the game cannot end in any other way. No system can be changed without hand-to-hand fighting."[1]

Older, more experienced hands were more cautious. But the young ruled the day, bragging that if the government called out 6,000 troops, Solidarity would call out 200,000 workers. They forgot that the state controlled the phones, the mail, the printing shops, the factories, all the means of communications and production. When the government moved, it moved rapidly and it crushed Solidarity. The Soviet Union simply could not permit such action in Poland and it could not tolerate the possibility that it could spread to other client states.

Thus, the only real surprise was not that the Soviet Union pressured the Polish government to act, but that it waited so long to act.

---

[1]*Newsweek*, December 21, 1981, p.27.

---

[10]Paul Craig Roberts, "Oskar Lange's Theory of Socialist Planning," *Journal of Political Economy,* Vol. 79, No. 3 (May-June, 1971), pp. 562–568.

[11]F.A. Hayek, "The Use of Knowledge in Society," *American Economic Review,* Vol. XXXV, No. 4 (September, 1945), pp. 519–528.

to diverge from the textbook ideal of either von Mises or Lange. We must, therefore, examine which type of system needs less information because economizing on costly information is necessary for efficient production. Hayek goes on to argue that market systems need less information than do centrally planned systems.

An earthquake destroys a copper mine in the United States and a copper mine in the USSR. In both countries, copper is now more scarce and needs to be used more sparingly. What happens in each economy? In the United States, the price of copper will rise, reflecting its increased scarcity (decrease in supply). Profit-minded entrepreneurs will substitute cheaper metals in order to minimize costs. The entrepreneur does not need any information other than the fact that the price of copper has risen. In the Soviet Union, the planner must first be informed of the disaster. The planner must then make some estimate of the severity of the scarcity. Each user of copper must be informed that in the future less copper will be supplied and that other metals should be substituted. Producers of other metals will also need to be contacted and told to ship to the enterprises which had been using copper. Additionally, the planner will have to set priorities as to how the available copper is to be utilized. In the market system this priority setting was done by the increase in price. So Hayek's position is quite simple—central planning can never be as efficient as a market system because it requires too much information in order to work. The market system, on the other hand, economizes on the amount of information needed.

How to Plan

Whether central planning is efficient or not does not change the fact that it is undertaken. Most socialist countries rely heavily on central planning in order to move production in the desired direction. We should, therefore, examine how planning takes place in the Soviet Union, the command economy with the longest experience in planning.

First, priorities must be established; the decision has to be made as to what to produce. In the early years of Soviet planning, this was only done at the most aggregate level. The first plan was, in fact, called the State Plan for the Electrification of Russia. Today this planning is done in the State Planning Commission, commonly called the *Gosplan*. At the most aggregate level, the decision can be made on whether to produce consumer or investment goods. This was one of the early uses of planning in the Soviet Union. The goal of the leaders was rapid economic growth. They therefore made the decision to produce investment goods at the expense of consumer goods. As a result, very few consumer goods were available, and consumers were forced to save. This permitted heavy investment and very rapid rates of economic growth. Yet there were, and still are, significant shortages of consumer goods in the Soviet Union. Tourists traveling in the Soviet Union are well aware of these shortages and are familiar with Soviet citizens' attempts to buy items from them.

Once the decision of what to produce is made, the planners must turn their attention to how much to produce. This is a difficult planning problem because the amount depends on the productive capacity of the existing industry and on the resources that will be available during the period. Production uses up resources; therefore, the planners must plan for the production of the resources that will be used for the final output. At this stage of planning, the various industries

Gosplan   The State Planning Commission in the Soviet Union.

are brought into the picture, and the ministries, one for each major industry, make their plans based on the overall plan. Once these plans are finalized, they must be communicated to all the productive enterprises so they can take the necessary action to put the plan into operation. This is an ongoing process, and even though the planning period is usually expressed in five-year increments, it is a continuous exercise in revision and implementation.

This process in itself uses up a great deal of productive capacity. The individuals engaged in this planning are highly trained engineers and economists, people who are taken out of their productive capacities in order to plan. It is not, therefore, difficult to understand the burden that planning places on the economy. Many of the poorest countries, where most communist revolutions have taken place, are the very ones that can least afford to plan because of the opportunity cost of the personnel used in the planning process.

Input-Output Analysis

input-output analysis   An attempt to quantify the flows between different sectors of the economy. Input-output analysis is useful in economic planning.

The complexity of planning can easily be seen by examining an input-output table for a small, fictitious economy in which there are only a few industries to control. **Input-output analysis** was developed by Nobel prizewinning economist Wassily Leontief and shows that everything depends on everything else. These interrelationships are what make planning so difficult, because specific plans must be made as to how much of each good is to be produced, by whom, and for whom.

To begin, we look at an aggregate economy in Table 32-1 that has only three industries—electricity, trucks, and steel. In addition, these individual industries supply inputs to the other industries. We also show a labor sector and a corresponding category of consumption. The input to labor is consumption. Reading across the rows of Table 32-1 gives us the output of each industry and the labor sector, as well as showing how that output is distributed. One of the reasons that input-output tables are especially useful in the communist economies is that the units are expressed in physical units, and prices of these outputs and inputs are not needed for the analysis.

TABLE 32-1   INPUT-OUTPUT TABLE FOR A SIMPLE THREE-INDUSTRY ECONOMY

Input↓	Output→ Electricity	Trucks	Steel	Consumption	Total Output
Electricity (Kilowatts)	1,000	500	6,000	1,500	9,000 Kilowatts
Trucks (Number of Trucks)	1,000	1,000	2,000	1,000	5,000 Trucks
Steel (Tons)	5,000	3,000	8,500	3,500	20,000 Tons
Labor (Person-Days)	2,000	500	3,500	0	6,000 Person-Days

Wassily Leontief *(1906–)*

Wassily Leontief was born in Russia and received an M.A. degree at the University of Leningrad in 1925. In 1928 he received a Ph.D. from the Free University of Berlin. Later he emigrated to the United States and taught at Harvard University. At Harvard he established the Harvard Economic Research Project on the structure of the American economy. He was director of the project for more than 20 years until 1975 when, citing his unhappiness with the Harvard economics department, he accepted an appointment at New York University.

While at Harvard, Leontief completed his earlier work on input-output analysis. His ideas were first published in his book, *The Structure of the American Economy, 1919–1929* (1941). In 1973 Professor Leontief was awarded the Nobel Prize in Economics for his work on input-output analysis.

As we have seen in this chapter, the essence of input-output analysis is the recognition of the many interdependencies throughout the economy. This concept, however, was certainly not new with Leontief. As early as 1758 in his *Tableau Economique,* François Quesnay (1694–1774), personal physician to Louis XV, drew upon his understanding of the interrelated flows in the body to hypothesize interrelated flows in the economy. Quesnay's work was extended by many other economists, but Leontief was the first to develop a system that could quantify these interrelationships and simulate the economy based on extensive data sets.

Input-output analysis is an extremely important tool of planners, whether these planners be central government planners in the Soviet Union or economists in the planning department of a capitalist corporation. The technique is so necessary in socialist economies that the Soviets are fond of noting that the technique was developed by a Russian, without noting that he is now a U.S. citizen.

To interpret our input-output table, read across the row. For example, the steel industry had an output of 20,000 tons, which was sold or allocated by the central authority to the following sectors: 5,000 tons to the electricity industry, 3,000 tons to the truck industry, 8,500 tons to the steel industry, and 3,500 tons to the labor sector. Reading down a column tells us the inputs that were needed to produce the output. Take steel as an example again. In order to produce the 20,000 tons of steel, the steel industry used inputs. These inputs were: 6,000 kilowatts of electricity; 2,000 trucks; 8,500 tons of steel; and 3,500 person-days of labor. Once we understand the simple arithmetic of input-output, we can use it to plan future output.

The key assumption used in input-output analysis is that production takes place in all industries at *constant* costs. There are no economies or diseconomies of scale. This means that if we want to double the production of the steel industry, all we need to do is double the inputs. Regardless of the level of output planned, the amount of inputs required per unit of output remains the same. However, for large increases in output this is a very unrealistic assumption.

We can use Table 32-1 to calculate the input needed to produce additional units of output. The numbers we calculate are referred to as *input coefficients* in the jargon of input-output analysis. An input coefficient signifies the ratio of a particular input to the total outputs in that industry. Each input coefficient in Table 32-1 can be calculated by dividing each cell in a column by the total output of that industry. For example, the input coefficient of electricity in the truck industry is .10 kilowatts/truck (= 500/5,000). Table 32-2 reproduces a part of Table 32-1 with input coefficients instead of physical units. Each input coefficient represents the amount of input needed per unit of output.

We can then use the input coefficients to plan increases in output. Reading Table 32-2 gives us a clue to the use of the input-output technique. Examine the column for trucks. The input coefficient tells us what increase we need from each supplying industry to get an increase in output in the truck industry.

We can use our input-output system in Tables 32-1 and 32-2 to plan our economy. Suppose we want to expand the output of the electricity industry by 2,000 kilowatts. A 2,000-kilowatt expansion in output would require 220 kilowatts of electricity, 220 trucks, 1,120 tons of steel, and 440 person-days of labor. These needed inputs are found by multiplying the input coefficient by the desired increase in output. We would, therefore, know how to direct these industries to deliver the required inputs to produce the planned output. You should note that there are feedback effects in this simultaneous system. In order to produce more electricity, more electricity must be consumed in the production of the additional output. This happens throughout this interdependent system. The example assumes that there are no bottlenecks in the capacity of any sector of the economy. In fact, however, this may not be the case. In order to produce more electricity, it may be necessary to build new power generators. This may require time and, as a result, may disrupt the plan.

The problems encountered in actually using input-output analysis for planning stem from the fact that the coefficients are constant and are calculated on the basis of the historical record. In other words, the required inputs are cal-

input coefficients   In input-output analysis, the ratio of a particular input to the total outputs in that industry.

TABLE 32-2 INPUT COEFFICIENTS

Input↓	Output→ Electricity	Trucks	Steel
Electricity	.11	.10	.30
Trucks	.11	.20	.10
Steel	.56	.60	.425
Labor	.22	.10	.175

culated on the assumption that the input mix is constant and the same as that used when the data for the table were compiled.

Problems of Central Planning

We can see that the technique of planning is conceptually simple. The actual calculations for a realistic economy can soon become overwhelming, however. Consider an input-output table for an economy with 100 industries, 1,000 industries, or maybe 5,000 industries. The interdependencies between the industries become mind-boggling, not to mention computer-boggling.

Perhaps more significantly, the problems of planning really begin after the plan has been created. These are the problems of implementing the plan, as well as the problems of creating and maintaining incentives that get workers and managers behind the plan. It is not surprising that plans are often announced with a great deal of publicity and fanfare, while the results are often played down.

The more an economy grows, the more sophisticated it becomes and the more difficult it is to control the complexity of the interrelationships between the sectors. This increased complexity explains, in part, the trend in several of the communist countries to introduce market forces to replace some aspects of the plans.

SUMMARY

1. The study of comparative systems allows the economist to analyze different institutions and how they can affect economic outcomes.

2. The most common approach to this study of systems is to classify the systems according to the dominant ideology. This approach is not too useful because almost all systems must be labeled as capitalism or socialism. Since systems can differ considerably within these general labels, the approach is limited.

3. Marx's writings form the basic political framework on which all the communist countries are based. The economic systems of these countries are, however, widely divergent.

4. The development of these varying systems has been, in many cases, the result of very significant and dominant political leaders. As a result, it is possible to distinguish among Leninism, Stalinism, Titoism, Castroism, and Maoism as separate variants of communism.

5. Another way to analyze different systems is to examine their organizational and decision-making differences. This approach looks at the levels at which decisions are made as well as the informational requirements and motivation of the decision-making units. This approach also examines the interaction of systems, environment, performance, and policy to determine how each affects the other.

6. Planning is carried out in all economies; the key difference between systems is the level at which the planning is carried out. The higher the level of planning, the greater the informational requirements of the system.

7. Central planning requires the determination of what to produce. In the Soviet Union such planning resulted in rapid growth, because the central authority decided not to produce many consumer goods. This forced the population to save and generated high rates of investment.

8. The planning technique is exemplified in input-output analysis. Input-output analysis presents the historical experience of the inputs necessary to produce a given output. The experience can then be used to determine what inputs are necessary to produce a desired

output. Input-output analysis assumes that this historical production record will hold in the next period.

9. After all the technical problems of planning are worked out, it is necessary to put the plan into operation. This requires the transmitting of the plan to the production units and the creation of the proper incentives to bring about the desired production.

NEW TERMS

capitalism
socialism
communism
fascism
War Communism
New Economic Policy (NEP)
Great Industrialization Debate
workers' self-management

Great Leap Forward
Cultural Revolution
shadow prices
socialist controversy
competitive solution
Gosplan
input-output analysis
input coefficients

QUESTIONS FOR DISCUSSION

1. How does a union such as Solidarity in Poland threaten the Communist party? Why is the Soviet Union so interested in developments in Poland?

2. How did Lenin change the theories of Marx? Which of the two appears more important as the inspiration of communist revolutions?

3. Is planning an important function in all economies? Is it more important in market or in command economies?

4. How would allowing the input coefficient to vary complicate input-output analysis? Is the assumption of fixed coefficients a damaging one?

5. Try to list as many problems of maintaining proper incentives under a central planning system as you can. Do these problems exist only in centrally planned economies?

SUGGESTIONS FOR FURTHER READING

Gregory, Paul, and Robert C. Stuart. *Soviet Economic Structure and Performance*. New York: Harper & Row Publishers, Inc., 1974.

Grossman, Gregory. *Economic Systems,* 2d ed. Englewood Cliffs, N.J.: Prentice-Hall, Inc., 1974.

Laidler, Harry W. *History of Socialism*. New York: Thomas Y. Crowell Co., 1968.

Neuberger, Egon, and William J. Duffy. *Comparative Economic Systems: A Decision-Making Approach.* Boston: Allyn & Bacon, Inc., 1976.

Schnitzer, Martin C., and James W. Nordyke. *Comparative Economic Systems,* 2d ed. Cincinnati: South-Western Publishing Co., 1977.

PART 8

The Economics of Being an Economist

Learning Objectives

After studying the materials found in this chapter, you should be able to do the following:

1. List reasons why one would major in economics.

2. List reasons why some students avoid studying economics.

3. Describe the benefits of an economics major.

4. Become familiar with some of the career opportunities for economists.

5. Prepare an undergraduate curriculum in economics.

An Economist: To Be or Not to Be?

Now that you have completed your first course in economics, it is appropriate to reflect on what you have learned, to consider the possibility of other economics courses, and perhaps even to consider economics as a major field of study. In this chapter we will discuss a potpourri of material related to majoring in economics, career opportunities for economists, and graduate study in economics. We will also present a guide to material that can help you stay current in economics.

WHY MAJOR IN ECONOMICS?[1]

The great English economist Alfred Marshall (see Chapter 3 for a biographical sketch) wrote that, "Economics is a study of mankind in the ordinary business of life."[2] You will find that an economics major prepares you for almost any professional career, because economics offers a way of thinking that is clear, concise, and rigorous. As a result, job recruiters and graduate school admissions' counselors alike are attracted to economics majors.

In choosing a major in college, it is helpful to consider a number of important and related questions. First, what profession(s) do you have in mind? Second, does the major offer flexibility in the sense that if your originally chosen profession

---

[1]This entire chapter draws very heavily from a handbook prepared by Dr. Laurence E. Leamer and the Center for Economic Education and Public Policy of the State University of New York at Binghamton. Dr. Leamer graciously permitted us to use his ideas, his format, and in many cases his exact words.

[2]Alfred Marshall, *Principles of Economics* (8h ed.; Don Mills, Ontario: The Macmillan Co. of Canada, Ltd., 1920), p. 332.

suddenly becomes unattractive, you will still have sufficient opportunities within the field without having to switch majors? Third, if you have selected a profession that can be approached through a number of different avenues, are there distinct advantages in choosing one major over another? Lastly, will the major be useful in everyday life as well as providing the necessary training for your life's work? With these questions in mind, why choose economics?

The most basic and enduring strength of economics is that it provides a logical, ordered way of looking at various problems and issues. It draws upon history, philosophy, and mathematics to confront topics ranging from how an individual household or business can make sound decisions, to societal issues such as how to fight unemployment, inflation, and environmental decay. As a result, economics is widely recognized as a solid background for many jobs and professions.

An undergraduate major in economics can be ideal preparation for work on a Master of Business Administration (M.B.A.) degree at a graduate business school. In many organizations, an M.B.A. is an important credential for getting a desirable job. Most business graduate schools (but not all) prefer their students to have a broad, liberal arts background, which an economics major provides. Most business graduate schools don't require an undergraduate economics major, but they encourage students to take at least some economics courses, and they certainly don't have a prejudice against admitting students with economics majors.

If you can get into an M.B.A. program without a major in economics, why bother with economics? One reason is that a fair portion of the content of an M.B.A. program is based on economics. In the competition to see who does well in the program, you are at an advantage if you are already familiar with the central ideas in economics. Furthermore, an M.B.A. program exposes you to different ways of looking at business and policy problems, and one way that is stressed is economic reasoning. It is certainly not harmful to have experienced this sort of thinking as an undergraduate.

If your goal is to become a lawyer, economics offers excellent preparation. Many law schools believe that economics represents one of the best backgrounds for success because of its logical, ordered approach to problems. Specific courses recommended for the prelaw student include the major economics requirements, industrial organization, and antitrust economics. Public administration, such as jobs with the government and other nonprofit organizations, provides many job openings to those with economics degrees. Specific economics courses recommended for this area include public finance, economics of human resources, economics of state and local government, and urban economics. Private business also employs many economists. Business firms (banks and other financial institutions included) employ economists to undertake specialized economic analysis in evaluating their market positions and profit possibilities, the federal government's domestic economic policies that have important implications for their businesses, and international economic events that affect the operations of their firms. Business firms also employ economics graduates to do nonspecialized work in sales and management because business officials believe economic training to be very desirable for these positions. For these positions, the economics major is well trained to compete with majors in the other business or liberal arts fields. Many economists are employed in colleges and universities, both as professors and administrators. In general, graduate degrees are required for such positions. Economists are involved in community, state, and regional planning. Also, a large number of economists are employed in planning positions in foreign countries by the Agency for International Development, the United Nations, and the U.S. State Department. Finally, economists engage in private research and act as consultants to both large corporations and government agencies.

As this listing demonstrates, economics majors have a wide range of choices and a great deal of flexibility when deciding on an interesting and challenging profession. To repeat a point made earlier, the reason for this flexibility is that the logical and encompassing approach of economics enables an individual to analyze many diverse topics, both in a professional capacity and in private, day-to-day living. We will discuss career opportunities for economists in more detail after we examine economics as a major field of study.

WHY STUDENTS CHOOSE ECONOMICS —WHY STUDENTS AVOID ECONOMICS

Choosing a major is one of your most important academic decisions. It is a choice among several desirable alternative future courses for your life. An economics major is chosen at the cost of one in humanities, in science, in another social science, or in a professional area such as business, and it strongly influences the type of person you might become.

You have learned in economics that intelligent choices require a knowledge of one's alternatives. The purpose of this section is to make you more knowledgeable of some of the benefits and costs of majoring in economics. We hope you can then compare an economics major with other majors and apply the economic principles of choice to your own decision.

Benefits of an Economics Major: Reasons for Studying Economics

You are already aware, from your study of introductory economics, of some of the reasons why many students find economics a challenging area for undergraduate study, while others choose to avoid it. Here are some reasons for studying economics.

Economics Deals with Vital Current Problems. Inflation, unemployment, monopoly, economic growth, pollution, free enterprise versus planning, poverty, income distribution, and so forth, are all covered in the study of economics. Economics is a problem-based social science, and the problems with which it is especially concerned are among the most disturbing of our age. They fill our newspapers and pervade our politics. Not only is economics relevant to the big problems of society, but it also relates to personal problems, such as one's job, wages, unemployment, the cost of living, taxes, voting, and so on.

Probably more than any other reason, its relevance attracts students to economics. We like to be knowledgeable of a subject that so many feel is important. Even a person with only a little knowledge of economics is rapidly considered an authority because so many people feel economic events are baffling.

Economics Is a Successful and Prestigious Social Science. The accomplishments of economics have established it as perhaps the most successful social science. For example, yours is the first generation in decades never to have experienced a major depression, thanks in part to economists. No other social science has had equivalent success in applying reason and science to the shaping of our social destiny. Our nation has a Council of Economic Advisers; no such permanent agency exists for any other social science. Indeed, few scientists of any kind have as wide a following as such economists as Galbraith, Samuelson, or Friedman.

Economics has had many notable successes. Past successes alone do not assure great future developments; but since science is cumulative, it is probable that in your lifetime, past successes of economics will be dramatically overshadowed by future breakthroughs. Students may therefore choose to major in economics out of a desire to participate in these breakthroughs.

Economics Consists of Theoretical Structure, Models, and the Scientific Method. Some students become impatient with the seemingly endless world of fact and conjecture which characterizes much of the social sciences. Economics is often their refuge, because it is a social science which has developed models, or simplifying constructs, for organizing facts and for thinking about policy alternatives. Economics has a highly theoretical content. Development of theory is crucial to any science. Because economics deals with prices and numbers, because so many of its magnitudes are measurable, economic theory is more fully developed than most social theory. Many students find this attractive.

Murray C. Weidenbaum *(1927–)*

Murray Weidenbaum served as the first chairman of President Reagan's Council of Economic Advisers. Weidenbaum is now director of the Center for the Study of American Business at Washington University in St. Louis, Missouri. He received a Ph. D. in economics from Princeton University in 1958, a Master's degree from Columbia University, and his undergraduate degree at City College of the City University of New York.

Professor Weidenbaum is a specialist on the impact of government regulations on business. His textbook, *Business, Government, and the Public* (1981), details how government impacts on the business sector. He is now in a public position that allows him to develop policy to reduce that impact.

Weidenbaum believes that government should stay out of a wide range of economic activities. He believes economic development is a task for the private sector, and that government should only maintain the environment conducive to private enterprise.

Economics Provides an Opportunity to Put Math to Use. Sometimes students view math as a fascinating game or language but are impatient at not being able to use it for human problems. While mathematics is increasingly used by all the social sciences, economics has long been in the forefront in its usage. A student with a background in algebra, geometry, calculus, and statistics finds a place to use these skills in economics.

Economics Majors Have Options. Some majors are dead-ends, one-ended, or lead to relatively few alternative futures. An economics major, like other majors, may lead to graduate study and therefore possibly to the development of a professional scholar or teacher. For the nation as a whole, approximately ten out of every 100 economics majors complete an M.A. in the subject, and one of these ten continues to complete a Ph.D. Most graduates use their economics as a stepping stone to other occupations.

Alternatives for economics students are unusually varied. These include business, law, journalism, teaching, educational administration, politics, finance and banking, government service, public and private overseas service, labor leadership, or graduate study in a second discipline or another professional area. But there are other employment advantages of an economics major. Employers looking for liberal arts graduates, due to their broad backgrounds, often favor economics majors because the students have already shown an interest related to the employment being sought. This is particularly true of business employers. One great advantage of an economics major is that, in the eyes of many employers, an economics graduate is a preferred employment risk. The demands of the economics major itself tend to drive away those looking for an easy major; the less ambitious avoid economics, and many better minds are attracted to it. Thus, to be an economics major may be a valuable credential. A good grade point average in economics speaks for itself.

As a result, the salaries of economists, both academic and nonacademic, tend to be higher than those of other social scientists. This has been fostered by the accelerated growth in the use of economists in an increasing variety of roles. Indeed, economists often rise to pivotal positions; for example, David Rockefeller and Arthur Burns in finance; James C. Miller III and Phil Gramm in government; Clark Kerr in education; Gabriel Hauge of Manufacturers Hanover Trust, Jane Pfeiffer Cahill of IBM, and Carl Madden of the Chamber of Commerce in business; Leonard Silk of the *New York Times* in journalism.

An Economics Major Prepares Students for a Vocation or Avocation in Which a Knowledge of Economics Is Vital. Some disciplines are easily learned on the job or in one's spare time. But if you are ever to develop a basic background in economics, it will probably be in college, not later. A knowledge of economics and an understanding of current economic institutions and problems is essential in certain occupations. For example, business leaders are usually expected by the general public, and often by colleagues, to be knowledgeable of economic phenomena.

Economics and economic issues may be your avocation. As a person knowledgeable of the subject, you may play a leading role in a local or national political party, on a civic club committee concerned with the local economy, as a bargaining agent for a union or teacher's association, or as an informed commentator on current issues at your club or at home. With the media so full of economic matters, few disciplines are equal to economics for preparing one to be an interested, interesting, and understanding observer of passing events.

Costs of an Economics Major: Reasons for Avoiding Economics

There are many reasons why students may want to avoid economics. Another discipline may simply be more attractive; something else may interest you more. Some students may be disenchanted by the nature of economics itself. Here are some reasons for avoiding economics.

Economics Is a Quantitative Social Science Which Employs Algebra, Geometry, and Calculus.   Perhaps mathematical thinking is difficult for you, or you have an aversion to it, or you simply lack a mathematical background or interest. Possibly you should look for a major elsewhere. While it is true that much of economics (probably most of undergraduate economics) is presented in a narrative-descriptive form, mathematics is still frequently employed as a way to understand economic phenomena because of its greater precision and clairty. Yet it is possible for a student who does not plan to go on to graduate study of economics, but who is really interested in the subject, to major successfully in economics with only a basic knowledge of algebra, geometry, and calculus.

Economics Involves Abstract Thinking and Theory.   Some students have an aversion to theoretical thinking. They may defend their aversion by saying theory is impractical or useless. Their minds thrive on the concrete, the real, but are closed to the theoretical. If that is you, you'd better look elsewhere for a major.

Still, there is some validity to that belief. Teachers of a science that has developed an extensive theoretical system, like economics, sometimes make theory the prime goal of their teaching, rather than a tool for understanding real problems. Thus, students may legitimately complain that while economics is potentially the most relevant of the social sciences, it is sometimes taught as if it is hardly related to the real world. You can overcome this problem by mixing theory courses and policy courses.

Economics Utilizes Scientific Methods.   Science, even social science, is a bore to some students and a threat to others. They come to the study of economics with preconceived ideas and with closed minds. Their aim is not to learn or to scrutinize ideas, but to convert others and to argue. They are sure the teachings of economics are wrong, and they are therefore unwilling to study the subject to see what economists think they know and why. They are unwilling to employ a method which begins with careful observation, proceeds to hypotheses, then to testing and possible verification, and finally to a tentative conclusion. If you are unwilling to work with scientific methods, you had better look elsewhere.

Economics Is Difficult.   Economics has a long tradition of being a difficult subject. To study the world in terms of the infinite trade-offs and complexities we find in economics is much more difficult than a simple world of cause and effect. To study the economic world, in which there is often no cause or effect, but rather more intricate patterns of mutual or reciprocal causation, is challenging. Simple answers are lacking. To understand takes real effort. And what one eventually learns is not a final truth, but only an approximation. If you thrive best in a simpler world that is largely descriptive, and in an environment of students you can easily surpass, avoid economics.

Economics Is a Narrowly Focused Discipline. Other social sciences often study society or societies as a whole, including their economic aspect (for example, anthropology, history, or sociology). But economics tends to exclude many very important subjects. It usually takes as givens the wants, the politics, and the goals of society, and leaves those questions to other fields of study. Economics is usually regarded as a science of means toward given or accepted ends.

If social science or social philosophy are what you really want to study, then you should consider another major. Or, if the economic side of life really fascinates you, and you want the fullest understanding of economics courses, use your electives outside of economics to broaden this sometimes narrowly focused discipline.

Economic Reasoning Can Be Stifling. Economics has been called the "dismal science," and not without reason. It is always counting costs; that is, it is constantly reminding us that choices are usually made at the cost of other things. It is a conservative science; it may make one afraid of the possible costs of change. The economic way of thinking may make one obsessed with efficiency, with improving the organizations of society for attaining whatever society values. In its defense, Alfred Marshall said that economics is a science concerned with the "material means to a refined and noble life." Before we can be creative, we must learn to be productive.

You might try to design a major to combine both the economic and the creative worlds. As a result, you might become an intellectual leader in the effort to define a new, more appropriate scope for economics, or develop new applications of old methods for old or new purposes. Remember, economics is an evolving social science.

CAREER OPPORTUNITIES FOR ECONOMISTS

Jacob Viner, one of the greatest economics educators and the teacher of many great economists, was reported to have remarked that, "Economics is what economists do." The truth in this statement is demonstrated by the wide range of job opportunities open to economists.

But what is an economist? According to the National Science Foundation, an economist is someone who has had professional training in economics at the graduate level and is identifiable as a member of a professional group, such as the American Economic Association or the National Association of Business Economists. Let's not worry too much about classifying people as economists. Rather, let's examine some of the opportunities for economists.

Most jobs for undergraduate economics majors are not classified as jobs for economists. Instead, they are jobs that make use of training in economics as a background for positions in personnel, management, marketing, education, or some other field. This is not surprising, since very few undergraduate degrees lead to jobs where the job classification is the same as the student's major. Accounting and engineering are two exceptions to this principle. In other words, if you want to be an *economist,* you will need graduate training in economics in most cases. But before we discuss graduate studies, let's examine the three major career paths of economists.

The Academic Economist

Almost one half of all professional economists are engaged in college teaching. This will likely change as college enrollments decline, and people with graduate economic degrees shift to government and business employment. In order to teach at the college level, it is now virtually essential to have a Ph.D. Junior college instructors usually have an M.A. in economics, but a Ph.D. or work toward a Ph.D. may be required.

A new Ph.D. generally begins an academic career at the assistant professor level. Starting salaries in 1983 ranged from about $18,000 to $25,000 for nine months. The salary, of course, depends on the type of school and the area of the country in which it is located. Responsibilities include teaching from two to four courses, which constitutes a 6 to 12 credit hour load on a semester basis. Promotion to associate professor usually occurs from five to seven years after the original appointment. As the job market tightens, more schools are becoming "publish or perish" institutions, meaning the faculty member must publish books and articles in order to be promoted. Promotion to the full professor rank usually occurs from five to fifteen years after the promotion to associate professor. The elapsed time depends in large part on the research record, publications, and teaching ability of the faculty member. Mobility in large part depends on publications, and mobility speeds up promotion by giving the faculty member more options.

Academic economists supplement their income writing textbooks and other educational materials, and by consulting. Consulting opportunities for the academic economist are numerous, the most common being economic analysis for government, business, and the legal profession. Most organizations which employ economists on a full-time basis also provide consulting opportunities for academic economists. In many cases, academic economists are sought out by government and the legal profession because of their objectivity and impartiality.

The Business Economist

Undergraduate economics majors are recruited by business firms in all size ranges, from small, local companies to the very largest multinational corporations. An economics degree prepares students to compete with students from marketing, management, and finance, as well as students with liberal arts majors such as history and political science. These jobs are general-purpose jobs for which employers are interested in bright, highly-motivated students who can learn a specific business through on-the-job training.

The Growth of Economics as a Business Tool. The profession of business economist sometimes requires graduate training in economics. This is a rapidly growing professional field and reflects the rising prominence of economics as a business tool. It is a fairly recent phenomenon, because for many years the business community disdained academic training and expressed a preference for practical experience. In fact, the Wharton School of Business and the Harvard

Citibank

Among the places economists work are *Citibank* (headquarters in New York City), the United States *Department of the Treasury* (headquarters in Washington, D.C.), the *National Association of Manufacturers* (headquarters in Washington, D.C.), and the *United Automobile Workers* union (headquarters in Detroit, Michigan). These represent merely a few of the kinds of jobs economists are qualified for and the thousands of organizations for which they work.

Economists work in government and industry, for unions and for management, for banks and for manu-

The Department of the Treasury

facturers. Some economists at Citibank and the Treasury follow developments in the foreign exchange markets and in particular foreign countries (economic *and* political developments). Other economists—for example, at the UAW and NAM—follow national macro policies, their development, and results. Some economists are deeply involved with particular industries; for example, the steel industry would be of concern to economists in the UAW, NAM, and the Treasury. Thus, a single, large organization can have economists involved in a wide range of activities.

Graduate School of Business did not open their doors until 1884 and 1908, respectively. So business education is only about 100 years old.[3] Additionally, business schools have, until very recently, looked upon economics as too theoretical. The image of the economist was that of the ivory-tower dreamer. Bernard Baruch, the famous industrialist, was reported to have defined an economist as a man with a Phi Beta Kappa key on his chain, but no watch! This attitude toward economics is in large part explained by the role that these early business schools played. They were largely a training ground for middle managers and were founded to teach accounting and management skills. Any contact that these early business students had with economics was accidental and usually unsatisfactory.

---

[3]See Robert A. Gordon and James E. Howell, *Higher Education for Business* (New York: Columbia University Press, 1959).

National Association of Manufacturers

Economists can be generalists working on many kinds of topics over a year. Or they can specialize, knowing almost everything there is to know about the market for housing mortgages in California, for example, but neglecting much of the rest of the economy.

Many people with backgrounds in economics spend their entire careers in jobs that are recognizably "economics." Others use their training in economics to get their first job in corporations, government agencies, or other organizations, and then move on to more gen-

UAW Headquarters

eral, administrative jobs. Others with backgrounds in economics never do formal work as "economists." People who sooner or later move away from being strictly economists usually find their background to be valuable in whatever they are doing. We've heard this from lawyers, presidents of banks and savings and loan associations, executives of manufacturing firms, officers of nonprofit organizations, government officials, etc. It's still surprising to us where people with economics degrees or backgrounds turn up!

This has all changed today. Emphasis is placed on economics in the training of general business majors. More importantly, it is reflected in the ever-increasing role that graduate-trained economists play in the business community and on the faculty of business schools. In the 1950s economists were only to be found in the research departments of large banks and manufacturing firms, but the economists of the 1980s are found throughout the business community from top management positions down through the company hierarchy. This rapid growth of the economist's roles has come from the awareness that economic reasoning can help solve business problems, as well as help formulate business policy in a complex and changing environment.

Jobs for the Business Economist. It is impossible to list all the individual jobs that are performed by the business economist, but it is most likely that an economist would begin a career with business in the firm's "think-tank" or economics department. These organizational divisions undertake a variety of tasks, including forecasting the general business environment and how it might affect the particular firm in question, interpreting the effects of governmental policy, and gathering and processing economic data and intelligence. From this beginning, there is room for upward mobility. The economist may remain in the role of the economist, or may move into the management side of the business organization. In this role the economist is following the earlier lead of the professional engineer, accountant, and lawyer in moving into the top management positions in both large and small business firms.

Business economists receive excellent salaries because the demand for professional economists is great. The largest employers of economists, according to the National Association of Business Economists (NABE), are firms engaged in manufacturing, banking, business services, and securities and investments.

The future market for economists in business will likely expand. More and more business firms are coming to appreciate the skills and abilities of professional economists. Economists are being asked to join lawyers, accountants, engineers, and other business professionals in solving business problems. In addition, the business economist is increasingly being drawn into top management positions. All these demands for intelligent economic thinking make the profession of a business economist a career with great potential.

The Government Economist

Since the New Deal era of Franklin Roosevelt, economists have moved into the forefront of governmental policy analysis. In recent years economists have begun to displace political scientists and lawyers in the top administrative posts in government. Recent presidential cabinets have had more economists than any other identifiable profession.[4]

Economists in the Federal Government. This area of employment for economists is growing because economists have displayed the tools necessary for analysis of public issues. In the federal government there are positions for economists in every governmental agency. A few positions are available at junior grades for undergraduate economists, but most governmental positions in which one works as an economist require a master's or a doctorate degree in economics. A wide spectrum of jobs is open, many in the traditional areas of economics. There are jobs for labor economists, international economists, development economists, and population economists, as well as macro and microeconomists. The duties of a governmental economist are very diverse and in large part depend on the particular governmental agency. For example, an economist for the State Department or the CIA might become an expert on the economy of a particular country, while an economist at the Office of Management and Budget may be an expert in cost-benefit analysis.

The governmental economist sometimes takes on the role of being an advocate for a particular agency. This is a change for the economist, *qua* scientist, who

---

[4]For an interesting view of the economist as a policy adviser from a professional economist with extensive high-level governmental experience, see George P. Shultz and Kenneth W. Dam, *Economic Policy Beyond the Headlines* (New York: W. W. Norton and Co., Inc., 1978).

has been trained to use positive, scientific analysis. Governmental economists often take on duties that turn the role of the economic analyst into that of an administrator. In this sense, as in opportunities in business and academics, economics can lead to high-level administrative jobs in government.

Working for Congress is a relatively new area of opportunity for economists. Until very recently, except for the Joint Economic Committee, very few congressional committees or individual congressional staffs hired economists. This is changing rapidly. Legislation and issues facing Congress are becoming increasingly complex and economic in nature. As a result, Congress is turning to economists for expert advice on these issues.

The economist in Washington, whether a permanent career economist or a business or academic economist on temporary duty in Washington, must operate in a political environment. This is one of the problems for the many academic economists who move into short-term Washington jobs. The professional bureaucrat looks with derision on the analyst who cannot operate in the political environment. In Washington, "good economists" and "academic economists" are not necessarily synonymous. This does not mean that academics cannot be viewed as good economists, but this is a label that has to be earned in the bureaucratic environment.

The economist in government is well paid. In 1982 an individual with a B.A. or B.S. degree and at least 21 semester hours in economics could get a job as a GS5 or GS7 which paid a starting salary of $12,854 and $15,922, respectively. An M.A. degree in economics qualified one to start work as a GS9 at $19,477 per year, and a Ph.D. qualified an individual to start work as a GS13 at $33,586 per year.

Economists in State and Local Government. Perhaps the fastest growing area of employment for economists is in state and local government. This, of course, follows the very rapid growth of state and local governments in the last decade. State economists play a wide variety of roles, just as they do in the federal government, but there are a few differences. State economists are more likely to be involved with microeconomic problems and issues because states do not carry out independent monetary and fiscal policy. At the state and local level of analysis, the primary areas of research by economists are labor market analysis, school finance issues, state and local taxation and tax reform, environmental issues, and budgetary expenditure analysis. Economists are moving into important administrative responsibilities in state and local government, as in all the other areas we discussed.

GRADUATE SCHOOL IN ECONOMICS

All the career positions that we have discussed place emphasis on graduate training. It is never too early to plan your career education goals, so we will now turn to a discussion of graduate education in economics.

Graduate schools in economics currently award about 800 Ph.D. degrees and about 2,000 master's degrees annually. Many of the jobs we discussed in the previous sections require a Ph.D. or a master's degree. In fact, holding a job with the designation of "economist" usually requires graduate work. This section will introduce you to some of the items you should consider in preparing yourself for graduate study in economics.

There are over 100 graduate schools in the United States offering Ph.D.'s in economics and a number of others offering a master's only. Which ones would you like to attend? To which ones should you apply? What should you do as an undergraduate to prepare for graduate school and to increase the likelihood of being admitted to the schools of your choice?

Your Undergraduate Preparation

If you aspire to graduate study in economics (or if you are unsure but want to keep that possibility open), there are certain guidelines you should keep in mind.

Mathematics. Most graduate departments require a background in mathematics. You should, as a minimum, take calculus. Some schools offer a course called *Mathematical Analysis for Economists*. Some graduate departments allow you to make up deficiencies in mathematics after entrance, but this is less than satisfactory; you should begin graduate study with your "tools" ready for use.

Theory. Macro and micro theory are the foundations on which most graduate study is based. Your first graduate courses will probably be in micro and macro theory, but with the assumption that you already have a firm foundation in basic theory. Economics is a science based on theory; there is no more important part of your undergraduate economics study than your theory courses for preparing you for graduate study.

Grades. If you are to go on to graduate school, your undergraduate grades really matter. A C or even a $C+$ average, especially in economics courses, usually means that you will not be admitted; an A average or close to it is indispensable. An upward-moving grade average may indicate blooming promise; a falling grade average may spell disaster for graduate school admission.

Product Differentiation. Graduate study of economics is usually very specialized. You have little time for broadening your education. Thus, whether or not you become any more than a narrowly trained technical economist is probably determined by what you have done with your undergraduate electives.

For example, your knowledge of foreign languages may be a major determinant of how you later use your economics. An economist with a working knowledge of Chinese, Russian, or Arabic may have an indispensible product differentiation (for research, for government service, for a multinational corporation, or for other international agencies). Likewise, an economist with a strong foundation in accounting, in law, or in politics may well have a combination of talents of unusual value. An economist who is skilled in communication—in listening and understanding, in writing and speaking—has one of the scarcest talents in the profession. With the expansion of knowledge and with economics alienating itself from the average citizen by its use of a specialized vocabulary and language, the synthesizer or communicator of knowledge is becoming indispensable.

The foundations of all these skills (language skills, knowledge of related disciplines, communication skills) must be laid in undergraduate school. Indeed, your undergraduate education is likely more important than your graduate training for determining whether you become any more than a technically competent economist. Give some thought to your personal product differentiation.

Determining Your Goals

By the time you are a senior, your past is an unchangeable prologue to graduate study. Before trying to select a school, review and possibly revise your goals, for they may influence the school you should select. The following tabulation is meant to remind you of possible goals. Which do you now value? You might check your choices (or determine tentative priorities).

Professional Goals (that is, toward what professional roles do you aspire?).

		In a— Prestigious University Graduate School
ACADEMIC	Teaching Research and Writing Administration	State College Small Private College Junior College Secondary School

RESEARCH: In a Private Economic Research Organization
In a Public Economic Research Organization

BUSINESS: Economic Adviser to
a Business Firm
Finance and Banking
Economic Consulting Agency
International Business

SPECIAL INTEREST
GROUPS (e.g.,
business, labor,
agriculture): Economic Adviser, Interpreter, Defender

GOVERNMENT: International, Federal, State, Local, Political Parties

COMMUNICATIONS: Economic Journalism, TV, Freelance Writer

Personal Intellectual Goals.

AREA OF KNOWLEDGE—Is there some aspect of economics, some area of knowledge, which you would like to develop as a specialty (something about which you want to know as much as any other economist)?

AREAS OF SKILL—Are there particular personal skills which you hope to develop to a very high level of proficiency? For example:
Application of mathematical methods in economics.
Teaching of economics.
Clear writing, oral explanation, or argument.
Interpreting economic ideas, synthesizing and clarifying professional and/or political issues.

Personal Status Goals (that is, from whom do you seek deference and recognition for your professional accomplishments?)

FROM PROFESSIONAL ECONOMISTS GENERALLY—You should apply to as prestigious an institution as will admit you.

FROM GOVERNMENT, BUSINESS, AND OTHER NON-ECONOMIST LEADERS—Similar to the above, but since there is prestige in being an economist, you may be judged by your proficiency in serving leaders' objectives. Thus, less prestigious schools may serve as well or better.

FROM THE PUBLIC—Here your status may depend on your ability to relate to the public and to articulate their unformulated desires. The status of your school will count for little.

FROM YOURSELF—This is for you to answer. What kind of school is necessary to give you a sense of self-confidence and personal pride?

Enough, then, on goals. There are no doubt others we have overlooked. These are for you to formulate and relate to criteria for the choice of a graduate school.

Constraints on Your Choice

One more preliminary before looking at graduate schools: What constraints are likely to limit or influence your choice? Here are several that may apply. You should determine whether they are relevant to you.

Money. Do you have the financial resources to attend any school (up to $7,000–$15,000 a year for a minimum of three years)? If not, are you able and willing to work? Do you have any salable talent? What about fellowships, assistantships, borrowing, and so forth?

Your Academic Qualifications.

GRADES

STATUS OF YOUR COLLEGE—Being a college graduate is a good credential, but you will be competing with graduates of other, perhaps better known, colleges and universities.

ACADEMIC PREREQUISITES—Do you have the math and the economic theory to qualify you?

Geographic Location.

LOCATION OF STUDY—Are there constraints on you personally, or personal preferences, to study in one part of the country or another?

LOCATION OF FUTURE EMPLOYMENT—Where would you like to be employed upon graduation? Some graduate schools have a national reputation and placement market. Others are regional, and if you are interested in a particular geographic area, you may be better off going to school in that area, particularly if you are interested in business or state government.

Schools Offering Ph.D.'s in Economics

With your goals and constraints in mind, you are ready to survey your options for graduate study. Table 33-1 presents a list of all universities offering Ph.D.'s in economics, with the top ten ranked in order of the quality of their faculty.

This ranking is based upon a survey by the American Council on Education regarding the quality of each school's graduate faculty as judged by representative

**TABLE 33-1 ECONOMICS DEPARTMENTS OFFERING
PH.D.'s (Listed by Rated Quality of Graduate
Faculty)**

Top 10 by Rank

1–2	Harvard, M.I.T.
3	Chicago
4	Yale
5	University of California (Berkeley)
6	Princeton
7–10	Michigan, Minnesota, Pennsylvania, Stanford

Other Schools Offering Ph.D.'s

(by region)

Northeast	North Central	South	West
Brown	Case	Alabama	Arizona
*Bryn Mawr	Catholic	*Arkansas	*Arizona State
Carnegie-Mellon	Cincinnati	Duke	Claremont
Columbia	Illinois	Florida	Colorado
Connecticut	Indiana	*Florida State	*Colorado State
Cornell	Iowa	Georgia State	Davis (U. of CA)
Johns Hopkins	Iowa State	Houston	Los Angeles (U. of CA)
Massachusetts	Kansas	Kentucky	*New Mexico
New York University	Kansas State	L.S.U.	Oregon
Penn State	Michigan State	Maryland	Riverside (U. of CA)
Pittsburgh	Missouri	Miami	*San Diego (U. of CA)
Rochester	Nebraska	*Mississippi	Santa Barbara (U. of CA)
*R.P.I.	*Northern Illinois	*Mississippi State	Southern California
*SUNY-Albany	Northwestern	North Carolina	Utah
*SUNY-Binghamton	Notre Dame	North Carolina State	*Utah State
SUNY-Buffalo	*Ohio	Oklahoma	Washington (Seattle)
SUNY-Forestry	Ohio State	Oklahoma State	Washington State
Syracuse	Purdue	Rice	*Wyoming
	*St. Louis	*South Carolina	
	Southern Illinois	Southern Methodist	
	Washington (St. Louis)	Tennessee	
	*Wayne State	Texas	
	Wisconsin	Texas A & M	
	*Wisconsin (Milwaukee)	Tulane	
		Vanderbilt	
		Virginia	
		Virginia Polytechnic	
		*West Virginia	

Metropolitan Areas

New York	Washington	Boston	Other
*Fordham	American	Boston College	Hawaii
*Hunter	Catholic	Clark	*Temple
New School	Georgetown	Tufts	
Rutgers	George Washington		
*SUNY-Stony Brook			

*New degree programs since 1965

economists from institutions that award 2 percent or more of all Ph.D.'s in economics. This procedure favors the larger departments because they are more likely to have graduates in positions to be known. For similar reasons, it favors long-established departments and departments with faculty that are highly visible due to their publications. In this sense, the survey suffers from many of the same problems as college football polls. It tends to overlook the new programs, those with few graduates, those serving primarily a regional area, and those whose primary aim has been something other than educating economic scholars (for example, teachers, public servants, business). Also, none of the departments offering only an M.A. degree have been listed.

How, then, may this table be used to identify departments for further study? Following is a list of criteria which you may want to employ in evaluating departments. Note that individual criteria are not listed in order of their importance, but in order of the introduction of relevant information. You determine what is important.

Professional Status of the Department (that is, how each department is viewed in the eyes of the profession nationally). Would you prefer to attend one of the more prestigious departments (and do you have the qualifications)? If yes, then Table 33-1 is your guide.

Keep in mind that in the past, economics, especially academic, has been a very stratified community. To be a graduate of one of the more prestigious departments may be an important credential for your future employment. Your academic-social mobility may be horizontal or downward, but is usually not upward. A graduate of a prestigious department may be employed by another prestigious one and may avidly be sought by lower rated ones, while a graduate of a little known department is likely to move to another little known one, or possibly into government or business, or into some employment in which one is judged more by what one can do than by what school one graduated from. Of course, with the recent increase of new Ph.D.'s, it is possible that this academic stratification will decrease in the future.

Location of the Department. If you have a preference as to the part of the country in which you want to study, Table 33-1 should assist you in identifying schools in your preferred region. Also, as mentioned earlier, the location of schools, particularly of the less prestigious, may determine the part of the country in which you are most likely to find employment.

Recency of Development of the Doctoral Program. You may prefer one of the older and thus more mature departments or one of the newer programs. The newer departments may try harder. Being smaller, and knowing that the reputation which they have yet to build will be through their products, they may invest more time in the development of individual students. Or, being insecure, they may be more conservative and traditional; they may seek to copy the prestigious programs rather than to strike out innovatively on their own. The asterisks in Table 33-1 enable you to identify the newer programs; that is, those Ph.D. programs which did not exist in 1965 when an earlier study was made by the American Economic Association. Recently established graduate programs in economics have much to offer; study them to be sure they have what you want.

Effectiveness of Doctoral Programs. The economists whose views are summarized in Table 33-1 were also asked to rate the effectiveness of doctoral programs. The resulting ratings were approximately the same as the ratings of faculty. Therefore, they are not repeated. You might, however, like to inspect them. See Roose and Anderson, *A Rating of Graduate Programs,* American Council on Education, 1970. When the same economists rate a department's program differently than the quality of its faculty, it may be important. In any case, remember the limitations of this manner of securing ratings.

Survey of Departmental Flyers

The list of all economics departments should enable you to select some to investigate more thoroughly. Take a look at the advertising flyers that are likely posted in your department; others are included in the latest Peterson's *Annual Guides to Graduate Study—Economics,* or the American Economic Association's *Graduate Study in Economics.* These have varied summaries (usually one page or less) of each department and its program. While you should perhaps focus on your selected schools, browsing is really in order, for you may discover possibilities you have not previously considered. What are some of the criteria to watch?

Curriculum Design. Largely prescribed or elective? Narrow in focus or broad? Confined to economics courses or permitting others? Prerequisites? Math requirements? Traditional in design, innovative, or experimental? Adequate course alternatives? Adequate areas of specialization? (For example, can you study labor economics, if you wish?)

Departmental Product Differentiations. Is there any evidence that the department is trying to make anything special of itself? Beware of the aim of general or all-round excellence; this may merely be a cover for trying nothing. Are the specialties of the department of real interest to you? Are they marketable?

The Department's Real Values. Watch for clues as to what the department really values. What is stressed about its faculty members or its graduates—their scholarship, their teaching, their status, their number of publications? What is stressed about its view of economics—its rigor, its relevance, the place of applied or institutional economics? In the description of the goals of the department's Ph.D., what seems of primary or of secondary importance? How does the department seem to value teaching, research, and public service?

Department Size. A class of around 50 graduate students has been suggested as a minimum size for efficient and effective operation, which should be large enough to permit a reasonable variety of courses and to foster an effective intellectual community of students. In very large departments, one's choices and contacts may be increased, but possibly at the expense of impersonalization. The reverse may occur in very small departments.

Costs, Assistantships, Student Aid, and the Cost of Living. If these are important to you, get information from flyers and department guides.

Student Body. Full-time, part-time? Foreign, and from where? Percent supported by assistantships?

Study of Graduate Catalogs and Materials

From your survey of departmental flyers and national guides to economics graduate departments, you have narrowed and focused your choice to several which meet your goals and fit your constraints. You are ready to write to the departments for information and application blanks, or inspect catalogs found in the library. In addition to the above criteria, here are others to which the catalog may relate.

Departmental Efficiency, Courtesy, and Imaginativeness. A department may reveal itself to you by the way it responds to your interest. Promptness? Has it been imaginative and really helpful in designing materials to aid your choice? Beware of all sales but no substance.

Teaching. How seriously does the department take its teaching? For example, are new graduate students just out of undergraduate school immediately assigned to teaching? This may be a clue to a department which really does not take teaching seriously and exploits cheap student labor to free faculty time for research. Is there a teaching seminar for graduate students who are being trained to teach? Is there a carefully planned teaching apprenticeship as part of the Ph.D. program? Or does the department let these things take care of themselves?

Quality of Faculty. By inspecting the list of faculty, or perhaps brief biographies the department may provide, you can see where faculty members have been granted their degrees, what their scholarly interests are, and where and how recently they have been published. How many faculty members really seem to have a currently vital professional specialty?

Employment Market. Where are its graduates placed? Does it have contacts with markets for the kind of employment you want?

Special Facilities and Programs. Library, computers, data banks, lecture programs, outside guests, visiting professors, outside funding and grants?

Finally. As you study catalogs and flyers, watch for the unusual. Also watch for what is *not* said. Remember, sometimes a catalog bears little relation to what you will find; it may give an idealized picture. Be alert.

Calendar for Graduate School Applicants

SOPHOMORE AND JUNIOR YEARS—Prepare (see above for suggestions).

EARLY SENIOR YEAR—Review your goals and constraints.

FALL SEMESTER, SENIOR YEAR—Survey flyers, write for information, register for Graduate Record Exam (GRE) and take it. The GRE is like the College Boards, only harder. Many schools require it for you to be considered.

JANUARY, FEBRUARY—Apply to several schools (including a sure one).

MARCH, APRIL—Await the results.

ECONOMICS AS AN AVOCATION

After all our discussion of economics careers and graduate schools, the truth of the matter is that most of you finishing this course will not major in economics.

And even those majoring in economics will not be employed as economists. For the majority of you, economics will be, at most, an avocation. The avocation of economics will make you a more informed citizen. Some of the economics you have learned in this course will be superseded by new theories, new institutions, and even new problems. Ten years ago no economic textbooks devoted space to the energy problems that now face all of us. You have, however, learned principles that will allow you to sort through new problems if you continue to be informed. The course you have just finished and this book will have been successful if they opened your eyes to the economy and activated your interest in it!

To aid you in your continued study of economics, we offer the following calendar of recurring economic events. Economics as a hobby is facilitated by the fact that many economic events and the reporting of them occur at regular times. They usually set off reactions in the form of interpretive news articles, editorials, comment by columnists, and TV reporting and commentary. The following calendar should alert you to the monthly cycle and yearly patterns of recurring economic events.

MONTHLY

First Week—Unemployment for prior month, both actual rate and seasonally corrected rate.

Second Week—Producer prices (wholesale price index) for prior month, both actual and seasonally corrected index.

Third Week—Consumer price index for prior month, both actual and seasonally corrected index.

—Industrial production index for prior month.

—Personal income for prior month. This is the only monthly national income figure and thus a monthly measure of aggregate output.

Fourth Week—Balance of payments for prior month.

—Index of leading indicators for prior month. This is an index of variables that tend to lead real output; that is, tend to indicate when booms or recessions are likely to be coming.

ANNUALLY

January:

Early in month—Annual economic review of the prior year and forecasts for current year abound in newspapers and periodicals; for example, the *New York Times.* After mid-month—Gross national product for the October-December quarter. Revised figures are often issued one month later. Last week—President's annual economic message and annual *Economic Report of the President.*

February:

Hearings by the Joint Committee on the Economic Report. Prominent economists usually appear. Their views are reported in the press.

March:

Final report of the Joint Committee on the Economic Report. Around the 20th —Balance of payments for the prior year.

April:

Fourth week—Balance of payments for the first quarter. After mid-month—First quarter gross national product.

May:

June:

Late in month—Mid-year report of Council of Economic Advisers.

July:

After mid-month—Second quarter gross national product.

August:

September:

Third week—Second quarter balance of payments.

October:

After mid-month—Third quarter gross national product.

November:

December:

Last week—American Economic Association annual meeting.

SUMMARY

1. This chapter was a potpourri of information for those interested in economics as a career or as an avocation.

2. An undergraduate major can open the door to a wide range of professional careers.

3. The job classification of economist usually requires graduate training in economics.

SUGGESTIONS FOR FURTHER READING

Business Economics Careers. Washington: National Association of Business Economists, 1974.

Cartter, Allan. *An Assessment of Quality in Graduate Education.* Washington: American Council on Education, 1966.

Norton, Hugh S. *The World of the Economist.* Columbia: University of South Carolina Press, 1973.

ability to pay principle   The idea that people should pay taxes in relation to their ability to pay such taxes.

absolute advantage   The absolute difference in productivity between countries.

accelerationist theory   Theory that states that the government can maintain unemployment below the natural rate only at the cost of ever-increasing rates of inflation.

acreage allotment   A farm program that sets a limit on the total number of acres that can be placed in production.

administered prices   A term coined by Gardiner Means to describe price inflexibility in concentrated industries. Means labeled prices that were relatively inflexible, or which changed only infrequently, as administered prices.

advances   Direct loans from the Fed to its members.

AFL-CIO   The merged American Federation of Labor and Congress of Industrial Organizations. The merger took place in 1955 and gave labor a more unified political stance.

Agency for International Development (AID)   The U.S. agency that is part of the State Department and which is in charge of U.S. aid to foreign countries.

agricultural support program   The political response to pressure to increase farm incomes. Most programs in agricultural support are aimed at decreasing supply or increasing demand for raw agricultural production.

allocation function   The government's effect on the mix of goods and services that is produced.

allocative efficiency   When price is equal to marginal cost, firms expand production to the exact level that consumers desire, as measured by the market price.

American Federation of Labor (AFL)   The first business union, founded by Samuel Gompers in 1886. The AFL was an exclusive union organized for skilled workers.

American Federation of State, County, and Municipal Employees (AFSCME)   One of the few unions that grew in the 1970s; a union of public employees.

arbitration   A situation where a third party hears the arguments of both sides in a labor dispute and renders a decision. In binding arbitration, the sides must abide by the decision.

arc elasticity   Average elasticity over the space between two points.

ATS accounts   Automatic transfer system accounts. Accounts that allow an individual to electronically transfer funds from one account to another or to pay bills automatically.

average fixed cost   Total fixed cost divided by output. Average fixed cost declines as production is increased.

average physical product   The total physical product (output) divided by the number of units of a factor used.

average revenue   Total revenue divided by the quantity sold. A demand curve is an average revenue curve.

average total cost   Total costs of production divided by the number of units of output.

average variable cost   Total variable costs divided by the number of units of output.

balanced budget multiplier   The multiplier that shows the change in national income when government expenditures and tax receipts both increase by the same amount. The value of the balanced budget multiplier is unity.

balance on current account   The difference between the values of exports of goods and services and imports of goods and services minus net unilateral transfers abroad.

balance on goods and services   The difference between the values of exports of goods and services and imports of goods and services.

bank panics   Sudden waves of fear that banks will not be able to pay off their depositors.

banks of deposit   In the Middle Ages, organizations that took in precious metal, evaluated it, and promised to return metal of equal value.

barriers to entry   Natural or artificial obstacles that keep new firms from entering an industry.

barter   Exchange of one good for another without intermediation of money.

base year   The year relative to which other years' prices, gross national products, etc., are measured.

beggar-thy-neighbor policies   Trade policies designed to improve a country's macroeconomic performance at the expense of its trade partners' economies.

benefits principle   The idea that people should pay taxes in relation to the benefits they receive from public programs.

big push   The development strategy calling for one major thrust on all fronts in the economy by government, or induced by government through private enterprise.

bilateral monopoly   Monopolies dealing with each other as buyers and sellers, such as when a monopoly labor union sells labor to a monopsonistic firm.

bills of exchange   An order by one person requiring a second person to give a certain payment to a third person.

bimetallism   The use of both gold and silver as parts of the money stock.

black markets   Markets in which people buy and sell goods or services illegally at prices above imposed price ceilings.

board of directors   The individuals elected by the stockholders of a corporation to select the managers and oversee the management of a corporation.

Board of Governors   The central governing body of the Federal Reserve System.

bonds   Interest-earning certificates issued by governments or corporations as a way of borrowing money.

bracket creep   A situation that arises when individuals move into higher tax brackets as a result of inflation. Bracket creep can only occur in a progressive tax system.

budget constraint   A given level of income that limits the amount of goods that may be purchased by an individual.

budget line   The graphical representation of the budget constraint indicating achievable levels of consumption given the prices of goods and the consumer's income.

business cycle   The irregular ups and downs of business activity along general trend lines.

business firm   An organization formed by an entrepreneur to transform inputs into marketable outputs.

business inventories   Stocks of goods held by business from which it can make sales to meet demand.

business union   Samuel Gompers's description of a union that worked for economic goals without wanting to change or destroy the business organization in which it worked.

Cambridge k   The constant that relates a country's nominal income to the stock of money that it desires to hold.

capital   The durable, but depreciable, input in the production process. Machines, tools, and buildings are capital.

capital consumption allowances and adjustments (depreciation)   An entry in the national income accounts that reflects depreciation. It is equal to the difference between gross and net national product, and between gross and net private domestic investment.

capitalism   An economic system based on the idea of private ownership of the means of production.

cartel   A group of independent firms which agree not to compete. Perfect cartels behave as monopolies.

Celler-Kefauver Antimerger Act   This act, passed in 1950, made it illegal in certain circumstances for a firm to merge with another by purchasing its assets. This strengthened the Clayton Act.

certificates of deposit (CDs)   Certificates showing that the owner has deposited a certain sum, at a specified interest rate, for a given period of time.

ceteris paribus   A Latin term that means "holding everything else constant."

chiseling   Cheating on a cartel arrangement by lowering prices in an attempt to capture more of the market.

circular flow of income   The idea that the expenditures of one group are income for other groups.

The income is then spent to create income for still other groups.

Class I oligopoly An oligopoly in which firms are unorganized and uncollusive. Their behavior is characterized by independent action.

Class II oligopoly An oligopoly in which firms are organized and collusive. Their behavior can be characterized as perfect joint action.

Class III oligopoly An oligopoly in which firms are unorganized, but still collusive. Their behavior is characterized by imperfect joint action.

Clayton Act This act, passed in 1914, prohibited the acquisition of the stock of a competing company if such an acquisition would "substantially lessen competition."

clean float A floating exchange rate system in which there is absolutely no intervention by governments.

closed shop A firm where workers are forced to become union members as a condition of employment.

Coase theorem A solution to the externality problem which shows that, in the case of small numbers of affected parties, a property right assignment is sufficient to internalize any externality that is present.

coefficient of price elasticity of demand (E_d) The numerical measure of price elasticity of demand. The percentage change in quantity demanded divided by the percentage change in price.

coefficient of price elasticity of supply (E_s) The numerical measure of price elasticity of supply. The percentage change in quantity supplied divided by the percentage change in price.

collusion Agreements between firms in an industry to set certain prices or to share markets in certain ways.

communication Firms' ability to signal their intentions to each other. This is important in oligopoly.

communism The final stage in the theory of Karl Marx, in which the state has withered away and economic goods are equitably distributed.

comparative advantage The relative difference in productivity between countries which allows them to trade regardless of absolute levels of efficiency.

competitive fringe In markets with one large dominant firm, there is sometimes a substantial number of small competitors which would be referred to as the competitive fringe.

competitive solution The name given to the model developed by Oskar Lange to show that a planned economy could theoretically reach the same efficiency solutions as a market economy.

complements Goods which are jointly consumed. The consumption of one good enhances the con-

sumption of the other good. Complements have a negative cross elasticity of demand.

Comptroller of the Currency The regulator of some aspects of national banks; grants charters to national banks.

concentration ratio An index of relative degree of concentration in an industry. The index most commonly used is the percentage of sales of an industry accounted for by the four largest firms in that industry.

conglomerate merger A merger in which a company buys another firm that is unrelated to its business.

Congress of Industrial Organizations (CIO) An affiliation of industrial unions that was organized when the AFL decided not to promote unions in the mass production industries.

constant cost industry An industry in which expansion of output does not cause average costs to rise. The long-run supply curve is perfectly elastic.

constrained sales maximization The situation that occurs when a manager's primary goal is to increase the sales of the firm because managers are rewarded by stockholders for increasing the firm's share of the market.

consumer durable goods Goods that last, on average, a substantial length of time; for example, automobiles.

consumer nondurable goods Goods that last, on average, only a short period of time; for example, bread.

consumer price index (CPI) An index showing changes in the average price of a basket of goods purchased by consumers.

consumer surplus The extra utility gained from the fact that some consumers pay less for an item than they would be willing to pay for the item.

consumption expenditures Expenditures by the household sector on currently produced final output.

consumption function The relationship between the level of consumption demand and the economy's real disposable income.

coordination Firms' ability to relate their production decisions to the other firms in the industry. This is important in an oligopoly.

corporation The form of business enterprise where stockholders are the legal owners of the firm. The stockholders' legal liability is limited.

cost The dollar value of the factors of production used by a firm in producing and distributing goods or services.

cost-plus pricing In price regulation, the practice of allowing firms a markup on average costs of production. This is the most common form of price regulation.

countercyclical policy   Government policy designed to offset the cyclical fluctuations of the macro economy.

craft unions   Unions composed of skilled workers, such as plumbers and carpenters.

credit market   Financial institutions of all sorts that channel the savings of households to business firms that want to invest.

cross elasticity of demand   A measure of the responsiveness of changes in the quantity demanded of one product to changes in the price of another product.

crowding out   The increased demand for loanable funds by government causes the interest rate to rise. This attracts funds away from business investment, thus crowding out business investment.

crude birth rate   Number of births per one thousand of population.

crude death rate   Number of deaths per one thousand of population.

Cultural Revolution   The revolutionary reevaluation of the Chinese economy that took place from 1966 through 1969. This period represents the high point in the adulation of Mao Tse-tung.

currency drain   An increase in currency holdings by the public causes a dollar-for-dollar decline in reserves available to the banking system.

debasement of money   The practice of reminting coins while adding base metals. This practice increased the number of coins in circulation, reducing the value of each coin and driving up the price of goods.

decrease in demand   A shift in the demand curve indicating that at every price consumers demand a smaller quantity than before.

decrease in supply   A shift in the supply curve indicating that at every price suppliers will supply a smaller quantity than before.

decreasing cost industry   An industry in which expansion of output causes average costs to fall in the long run. The long-run supply curve has a negative slope.

deficit   The situation which occurs when government or an individual spends more than is taken in as income.

deflationary gap   If there is a deflationary gap, aggregate demand is less than the output that can be supplied at full employment, so output and prices fall.

demand   The desire and ability to consume certain quantities at certain prices.

demand curve   A graphical representation of a demand schedule showing the quantity demanded at various prices.

demand-determined price   If supply is perfectly inelastic, the price is determined by changes in demand only.

demand schedule   A tabular listing which shows the quantity demanded at various prices.

dependent variable   The variable that changes in response to the independent variables in an equation.

depreciation   A reduction in the value or usefulness of an asset, such as a machine or factory, over time.

derived demand   A demand that results from the demand for another product. For example, the demand for labor is derived from the demand for the good that the labor is producing.

devaluation   The situation that occurs when a country allows a fixed or pegged exchange rate to depreciate toward its equilibrium level.

diamond-water paradox   The problem that classical economists faced when they argued that value in use could not determine price (demand) because diamonds, while less useful than water, were more expensive than water.

differentiated oligopoly   An oligopoly that produces a heterogeneous or differentiated product.

differentiated product   A good that has real or imagined identifiable characteristics that are different from other goods.

diminishing marginal utility   The fact that marginal utility declines as consumption increases; less satisfaction is obtained per additional unit as more units are consumed.

dirty float   A floating exchange rate system in which there is some intervention to move the rate adjustment in a certain direction or at a certain speed that is different from the market rate.

discount   A loan on which the interest is taken in advance.

discounting   The practice of taking interest on a loan in advance. Also, the term given to the technique of calculating present values.

discount rate   The interest rate which the Fed charges its members on loans it makes to them.

discount window   The Fed is said to make loans to financial institutions at the "discount window."

diseconomies of scale   Increases in average cost that are due to increased plant size. Increasing long-run average costs.

disposable income   Personal income after subtracting personal taxes and nontax payments (such as license fees).

distributive function The government's involvement in changing the distribution of income. This usually involves transfer payments to the poor.

distributive justice Arguments for a fair distribution of income. These are normative arguments for a particular distribution of income.

dominant firm The most influential firm in an industry, usually the price leader. The dominant firm is often the largest firm, but it can be the low-cost firm.

double coincidence of wants In barter, the requirement that a trader find someone wanting to trade what the first trader wants for what the first trader has.

drive to maturity The stage where the lagging sectors of the economy catch up and the industrial revolution is consolidated into sustained growth.

dumping The practice of selling in foreign markets at lower prices than in domestic markets. This is a form of price discrimination.

earning assets Assets that pay a return, as opposed to reserves held with the Fed which pay no interest.

econometrics The use of mathematics, statistics, economic models, and data to test economic theory and forecast developments in the economy.

economic approach A way of thinking about and analyzing problems that relies heavily on the basic tools of economic theory.

economic efficiency The least-cost method of production.

economic profit The return to the firm in excess of the explicit and implicit costs of production.

economic rent A payment greater than the amount necessary to bring a factor into productive use.

economics The scientific study of people and their institutions from the point of view of how they go about producing and consuming goods and services and how they face the problem of making choices in a world of scarce resources.

economies of scale Declines in average cost that are due to increased plant size. Declining long-run average costs.

economize Since wants are insatiable and resources are scarce, individuals must make choices; they must economize.

egalitarian Programs and individuals that are concerned with promoting a more equal distribution of income.

elasticity A measure of the sensitivity or responsiveness of quantity demanded or quantity supplied to changes in price (or other factors).

eminent domain The right of government to condemn certain land for use in the public interest.

encouragement phase The period (1930–1947) in which government support by legislation greatly increased the power of unions.

entrepreneurship The input to the production process which represents management, innovation, and risk-taking.

equation of exchange An identity stating that the money stock multiplied by velocity must equal the price level multiplied by real output.

equity A measure of fairness.

ex ante A Latin phrase meaning "before the event."

excess capacity Underutilization of existing plant size. In monopolistic competition, the firm produces less than the efficient capacity of the plant.

excess reserves Reserves held in excess of those which are required.

exchange market intervention The action taken by government to establish an exchange rate other than the market-determined rate.

exchange rate The price at which one currency sells for another.

excise tax A tax that is placed on the sale of a particular item, such as liquor, cigarettes, or electricity.

exclusive union A union that restricts supply and maintains a higher than competitive wage by excluding workers from the profession. Craft unions are exclusive unions.

expectations Individual forecasts of the state of the future.

expected gains The anticipated utility a consumer foresees when engaging in trade. Trade and consumption are based on expected rather than actual gains.

expected yield The expected rate of return on an asset.

expenditure multiplier A concept used to determine the amount of final change in equilibrium national income brought on by a change in aggregate demand.

explicit cost Bookkeeping cost or money outlay.

exports Goods and services sold to foreign buyers.

externalities Costs or benefits that are imposed on economic units. These units bear the costs without any compensation, or gain the benefits without paying for them.

face value The amount printed on a bond's face that the issuer promises to pay when the bond matures.

factor markets Markets in which owners of factors of production sell these factors' services to producers or consumers.

factors of production The inputs of land, labor, capital, and entrepreneurship that a firm uses to produce outputs.

fair rate of return   The idea that a regulated industry must earn a normal profit or it will go out of business.

fascism   An economic system that combines monopoly, capitalism, private property, and a strong authoritarian central government.

featherbedding   The maintenance of jobs that management claims are unnecessary or redundant. Unions often insist on featherbedding in industries that are declining.

Fed   The nickname of the Federal Reserve System.

federal budget deficit   The situation which occurs when federal government expenditures exceed tax revenues.

federal budget surplus   The situation which occurs when federal government tax receipts exceed expenditures.

federal funds market   The market in which banks borrow and lend reserves.

federal funds rate   The rate of interest that banks pay when they borrow funds from each other. The interest rate charged in the federal funds market.

Federal Open Market Committee (FOMC)   The Fed committee that sets general monetary policy.

Federal Power Commission (FPC)   An independent agency that controls hydroelectric projects and regulates the interstate sale of electricity and natural gas.

Federal Reserve districts   The United States is divided into 12 Federal Reserve districts, each with its own district bank and board of directors.

Federal Reserve System   The central bank and monetary authority of the United States.

Federal Trade Commission Act   The act which established the Federal Trade Commission to police unfair business practices.

fiat money   Money that is not a commodity and is not redeemable in any commodity.

final goods   Goods that do not have to be further processed before final sale.

fiscal federalism   The system of economic relationships that exists between various levels of government in the United States.

fiscal policy   The use of government spending and taxation policies to influence the level of economic activity, inflation, and economic growth.

fixed, but adjustable, exchange rate   The exchange rate system that existed from 1945 until the early 1970s. This system consisted of a pegged rate that could be adjusted when demand and supply moved permanently out of balance.

fixed factors   The factors of production that cannot be varied in the short run, such as the size of the plant.

fixed investment   That part of investment which does not add to inventories.

floating, or flexible, exchange rate   An exchange rate that is determined solely by the underlying forces of supply and demand.

flow variable   The rate at which consumption, production, sales, etc., take place over time.

Ford Tax Rebate   A fiscal policy designed by the Ford administration that featured tax cuts in the form of a rebate to individual taxpayers and tax incentives for buying a new home.

foreign investment   Investments by residents of one country in the economy of another country.

fractional reserves   Reserves equal to only a fraction of the total obligations outstanding.

free ride   The consumption of a public good with avoidance of a fee. Since public goods are nonexcludable, people will attempt to free ride on their provision.

free-riding behavior   Free riders mask their true demands and indicate that they do not want a public good. This is because they know that, once it is produced, they can consume it without paying for it. As a result, less than the optimal amount will be produced.

frictional unemployment   Unemployment due to friction in the economy, such as the time it takes to move from one job to the next, to select a job out of the number of offers available, and so on.

Friedman-Meiselman tests   Tests carried out by Milton Friedman and David Meiselman from which they concluded that the MQT outperformed the simple Keynesian model.

gains from trade   The extra satisfaction an individual anticipates when voluntarily engaging in trade.

game theory   A mathematical technique which can provide insight into oligopolistic behavior. "Players" try to reach an optimal position through strategic behavior that takes into account the anticipated moves of other players.

General Agreement on Tariffs and Trade (GATT)   A system, administered by a Geneva-based organization, designed to help negotiate freer trade.

goldsmiths   People who work gold. In their roles of accepting deposits and making loans, goldsmiths were the forerunners of banks.

Gosplan   The State Planning Commission in the Soviet Union.

government saving   Tax collections minus government expenditures; the government budget surplus (or, if negative, the deficit).

Great Depression   The severe downturn in real U.S. economic activity from 1929 to 1941.

Great Industrialization Debate   An open debate that took place in the Soviet Union from 1924 to 1928 concerning the correct way to industrialize the economy.

Great Leap Forward   Communist China's highly overambitious modernization plan that was launched in 1958.

greenbacks   Paper money issued by the federal government during the Civil War that was not backed by gold and not traded at its face value in gold.

gross national product (GNP)   The value, at market prices, of all final goods and services produced in the economy during a given time period.

gross national product price deflator   Money gross national product divided by real gross national product. It is used to measure how average prices of final goods change over time.

gross private domestic investment   New capital equipment or inventories added to the domestic economy without adjustment for depreciation.

high mass consumption   The stage where growth settles into high mass consumption, such as in the United States and Western Europe.

holding companies   Firms set up for the sole purpose of owning and controlling other firms.

horizontal equity   A situation that is achieved when all taxpayers in a certain economic category pay the same tax.

horizontal merger   A merger in which a firm buys a competitor.

human capital   Investment in the education, health, skills, and training of a population.

Humphrey-Hawkins Full Employment Bill   A bill passed in 1978 after Senator Humphrey's death. It sets national goals of reducing unemployment to 4 percent by 1983 and to zero by 1988.

impact lag   Time lapse between the implementation of a fiscal policy and the time when it begins to influence economic activity.

imperfect competition   The market structures of oligopoly and monopolistic competition.

implementation lag   Once an economic problem is identified, there is a lapse of time that passes while appropriate action is formulated and moved through legislative channels.

implicit cost   The cost implied by the alternatives given up. The opportunity cost of production.

imports   Purchases from foreign firms.

impounded funds   After Congress has approved expenditures for a project, the funds are not spent. In this way, the president can circumvent Congress and use restrictive fiscal policy without the approval of Congress.

inclusive union   A union that attempts to organize all the workers in an industry and maintains a strong bargaining position relative to management.

income-consumption curve   A curve that shows how the consumption of two goods changes as income changes.

income effect   As the price of a good falls (rises), the consumer's real income rises (falls), and the consumer buys more (less) of all normal goods.

income elasticity of demand   A measure of the way in which quantity demanded responds to changes in income.

increase in demand   A shift in the demand curve indicating that at every price consumers demand a larger quantity than before.

increase in supply   A shift in the supply curve indicating that at every price a larger quantity will be supplied than before.

increasing cost industry   An industry in which expansion of output causes average costs to rise in the long run. The long-run supply curve has a positive slope.

increasing opportunity cost   To produce more and more units of one good, larger and larger sacrifices of another good are required. These sacrifices represent the opportunity cost of producing the first good.

independent variable   The variable or variables in an equation which are determined outside the equation.

indifference curve   The graphical representation of an indifference set. An indifference curve shows all combinations of two commodities among which the consumer is indifferent.

indifference curve analysis   A technique of analyzing consumer behavior that does not require the concept of measurable utility.

indifference map   A series of indifference curves representing different levels of satisfaction for a consumer.

indifference set   Bundles of goods among which the consumer is indifferent. The bundles yield equal satisfaction.

industrial organization   A subfield of economics which examines industrial structure in theory and in practice.

industrial unions   Inclusive unions, such as the Steelworkers, Autoworkers, and Teamsters, which gain power by organizing all (or a large share) of the workers of an industry.

industry   A group of firms producing similar or related products.

industry studies   Investigations of particular industries to determine the degree of competitive behavior in the industry.

inferior good A good for which demand decreases as income increases.

inflation A rise in the general level of prices, particularly an ongoing increase in prices rather than a single increase.

inflationary gap If there is an inflationary gap, then at full-employment output, aggregate demand is larger than output and prices will be rising.

injections Fresh spending in the circular flow of income; investment, government expenditures, and exports.

injunctions Court orders used in labor union-management disputes to order labor back to work. The Clayton Act (1914) limited the use of injunctions, but this section was later declared unconstitutional.

input coefficient In input-output analysis, the ratio of a particular input to the total outputs in that industry.

input-output analysis An attempt to quantify the flows between different sectors of the economy. Input-output analysis is useful in economic planning.

insatiable wants There can never be enough of everything to satisfy everyone's wants for all goods and services.

interest The return to the capital factor of production.

interest rate targets Targets where the monetary authorities would like interest rates to be. Sometimes targets are designed to control money supply growth.

intermediate goods Goods that are to be further processed before being sold as final goods.

internalize The idea that the cost of an externality that is borne by society should be taken into account in the production process.

international reserves Stocks of assets that are liquid and readily acceptable in international trade.

International Workers of the World (IWW) An international union that organized American steelworkers after World War I. The IWW was viewed as socialistic in the United States and this contributed to its demise.

interpersonal utility comparisons Attempts to compare levels or amounts of utility between consumers. This is impossible because utility is subjectively determined.

intervention phase The period since the Taft-Hartley Act (1947) in which government has intervened in labor disputes, taking away some of labor's earlier gains.

inventories The stocks of goods that have been produced by businesses but which have not yet been sold.

invest When a business purchases real, tangible assets such as machines, factories, or stocks of inventories.

investment demand schedule A ranking of all possible investment projects in declining order of their expected rates of profit.

Investment Tax Credit (ITC) A tax write-off or credit given to business for undertaking investment spending.

Johnson Tax Surcharge A fiscal policy designed by the Johnson administration to reduce inflation. The program included a 10 percent tax surcharge on individual and corporate income effective for one year, with a presidential option to extend it for another year. It also included the elimination of the investment tax credit and a decrease in the rate of government spending.

jointly interdependent demand The demand for a factor of production depends on the amounts of other factors that the firm plans to use. The demand for a factor is thus interdependent with the demand for other factors of production.

Kennedy Tax Cut A fiscal policy designed by the Kennedy administration to close the deflationary gap through a decrease in personal and corporate taxes and an increase in government spending.

Keynesian Cross A graph that illustrates the intersection of the *AD* and *AS* lines. This intersection determines the equilibrium level of national income.

Keynesian fiscal policy Fiscal policy that manipulates government expenditures and taxation in order to move the economy toward a socially desirable level of income and output.

kinked demand curve A model of pricing in oligopoly used to explain price rigidity. The kink comes from the pricing behavior. If firms cut prices, other firms follow suit, and there is very little increase in the price-cutters' market share. A price increase, however, is not matched and the price rise will result in a loss of market share.

Knights of Labor Organized by Uriah Stevens in 1869, the Knights of Labor was a secret organization. It won the first major strike in the United States against the railroad industry. The Knights had political reformist goals which led to its demise.

labor The factor of production which represents the

human element in the production process.

labor theory of value   A central theme in the writing of Karl Marx. All commodities were reduced to a common denominator of the labor time embodied in the product.

Laffer curve   Curve illustrating the fact that, as taxes rise, the revenue generated increases up to a certain point at which revenues start to decline. This is because, as taxes increase, disincentives to work and invest become more significant.

land   The factor of production which represents resources which are fixed or nonrenewable.

Landrum-Griffin Act   An act passed in 1959 which was aimed at further curbing union power. The act made unions more democratic and restricted Communist party members and convicted felons from union leadership. It made picketing illegal under certain circumstances.

law of demand   The quantity demanded of a good is an inverse function of its price, *ceteris paribus*.

law of supply (not quite)   The quantity supplied of a good or service is usually a positive function of price, *ceteris paribus*.

leading sectors   The development theory calling for concentration on a number of leading sectors that will pull along other sectors in the development process.

least-cost combination   The lowest attainable per-unit cost for a fixed plant size. It is represented by the minimum point on the average cost curve.

legal reserves   Those assets of banks that count as reserves; the actual amount of reserves as opposed to the required amount.

legal tender   Money that must be accepted by private parties and governments in payment of debts and obligations.

lender of last resort   A lender for banks that were sound but which couldn't pay off sudden large demands during runs on banks.

limited liability   The fact that the stockholders of a corporation cannot be sued for failure of the corporation to pay its debts; only the corporation itself can be sued.

linkages   In development economics, the idea of concentrating on the encouragement of a particular sector that will then influence other sectors in the chain of production.

liquid assets   Assets that can be quickly converted into cash with little or no loss in value.

local monopoly   A firm which has monopoly power in a geographic region. Even though close substitutes exist, the distance between sources of supply creates monopolies.

logrolling   Vote trading in a legislative process. Legislators vote for a colleague's program in return for a favorable vote on their program.

long and variable lags   The time span between a change in monetary policy and a resulting change in income and prices.

long run   A period of time in which all inputs, including plant and equipment, can be varied.

long-run average cost curve   The lowest attainable average cost of producing any given output. A curve tangent to all the possible short-run cost curves.

long-run profit maximization   The argument that even if managers follow satisficing behavior or constrained sales maximization, they do this only because it leads to higher profits in the long run.

Lorenz curve   A geometric construction which traces the cumulative percentage of income that households receive, ranked from the lowest to the highest.

lumpy   Indivisibilities in consumption. Consumption of houses is lumpy, for example, because 10 percent of a house cannot be purchased and consumed.

M_1 The amount of demand deposits at commercial banks plus currency, the traveler's checks of nonbank issuers, NOW accounts, and ATS accounts. It also includes credit union share drafts and demand deposits at mutual savings banks.

M_2 The total of M_1 plus small-denomination time and savings deposits at all financial institutions plus minor entries.

M_3 The total of M_2 plus large time deposits and repurchase agreements.

macroeconomics   The study of the economy as a whole. Macroeconomics is concerned with policy issues such as the level of employment and the overall price level.

marginal cost   The change in total cost of producing one more (or one less) unit of output.

marginal cost pricing   A theoretical technique for forcing a monopoly to behave exactly as a competitive firm by regulating the monopoly price so that it is equal to marginal cost and average revenue.

marginal efficiency of investment schedule   A ranking of all of society's investment possibilities according to their expected rate of profit or their marginal efficiency.

marginalism   A technique used to analyze economic problems. The results of small changes in economic variables are examined.

marginal physical product   The change in physical output that is produced by a unit change in a factor of production.

marginal productivity theory   A theory originally developed by John Bates Clark which explains how the distribution of income comes about. Each factor is paid according to its contribution, or its marginal productivity.

marginal propensity to consume (MPC)   The fraction of any change in income that is consumed. The MPC is greater than zero and less than one, and $MPC + MPS = 1$.

marginal propensity to save (MPS)   The fraction of any change in income that is saved. The MPS is greater than zero and less than one, and $MPC + MPS = 1$.

marginal rate of substitution   The consumer's trade-off between two goods represented on an indifference curve. The slope of the indifference curve represents this trade-off.

marginal resource cost (MRC)   The cost of each additional unit of a productive resource.

marginal revenue   The change in total revenue from selling one more (or one less) unit of output.

marginal revenue product (MRP)   The amount that an additional unit of a variable factor of production adds to a firm's total revenue.

marginal utility   The amount of utility added by an additional unit of consumption.

market clearing price   The price at which supply and demand are equal—the equilibrium price. It is a market clearing price because there are no frustrated purchasers or suppliers.

Market Concentration Doctrine   A hypothesis that holds that the degree of concentration in an industry is a reliable index of the degree of monopoly power in that industry.

market demand   The summation of all individual consumer demand curves. A market demand curve shows what quantity will be demanded by all consumers at various prices.

market economy   An economy in which fundamental economic questions are answered by the forces of supply and demand.

market equilibrium   The price and quantity that will exist if no impediments are placed on the free working of the market.

marketing quota system   A farm program which specifies how much output a farmer can bring to market.

market power   The ability of firms or buyers to affect price. Large numbers of buyers and sellers insure that no one buyer or seller can affect price.

market supply   The summation of all the individual firm supply curves. A market supply curve shows what quantity will be supplied by all firms at various prices.

maturity date   The point at which a bond matures and is paid off.

median   If a series of observations are arranged from the lowest to the highest value, the median is the observation where there are as many higher values as lower values.

mediation   Third party intervention in a strike. The mediator attempts to keep the parties together and talking by offering suggestions and clarifying issues.

medium of exchange   Money in its function of facilitating the exchange of goods by allowing people to exchange their services for money and then exchange the money for the goods they want.

merchandise exports and imports   Exports and imports of physical goods such as autos, grain, etc., but not services such as tourism and the provision of insurance.

merchandise trade balance   The difference between the values of merchandise exports and imports.

merit goods   Goods that are considered to be inherently beneficial but which will not be consumed by individuals in great enough volume unless government supplies them; e.g., free education.

microeconomics   The study of interactions in individual markets. Microeconomics concentrates on the individual unit—the consumer, the firm, the industry.

military transactions   In the balance of payments, imports and exports of military items are entered separately.

minimum wage   A price floor imposed by a governmental unit in labor markets.

modern quantity theory (MQT)   A modern reformulation of the quantity theory of money intended to remove the older theory's shortcomings. It tries to explain shorter run changes in the price level and real output and income, as well as the determination of the long-run price level.

monetary base (B)   Currency in the hands of the public plus reserves held by banks; the funds available to support the money supply.

monetary disturbance   A change in monetary conditions that disturbs the economy but that does not change the capital stock, labor supply, or productive capacity of the economy.

money   An item (thing) that people accept as payment for a good or service.

money expansion multiplier   The maximum increase in the money supply for a given increase in reserves.

money (nominal) gross national product   The value of gross national product in current dollars.

money market mutual funds   Accounts which invest deposits in the money market and on which checks can be written.

money multiplier (m)   The money stock divided by the monetary base.

money supply target zone   The band within which the monetary authorities want money supply growth rates to fall.

monopolistic competition   The market structure in which a large number of firms produce differentiated products. Entry into the industry is relatively easy.

monopoly   The market structure in which there is a single seller of a product that has no close substitutes.

monopoly power   The ability to exercise some of the economic effects as predicted in the model of pure monopoly.

monopsonistic competition   A market situation that arises when there are relatively large numbers of buyers of a factor of production.

monopsonistic exploitation   The underpayment of wages due to monopsony power. Labor receives less than it would in competitive markets.

monopsony   The case of a single purchaser of a factor of production.

moral suasion   Attempts by the Fed to convince banks to do what the Fed thinks is right.

multiplier effect   The ability of a given initial change in aggregate demand to cause a larger final change in equilibrium national income.

National Banking System   Chartered and regulated national banks during the latter half of the nineteenth century; preceded the Federal Reserve System.

national banks   Those banks that are chartered by the federal government and are subject to its rules and regulations.

national debt   The debt of the U.S. federal government.

national income (NI)   The sum of income payments to labor, land, capital, and entrepreneurship.

national income accounts   A system of accounting at the national level that focuses on overall output and income of the economy.

National Labor Relations Board (NLRB)   Established by the Wagner Act (1935), the NLRB was empowered to investigate unfair business practices and to determine legitimate bargaining agents for labor when there were competing unions.

National Labor Union   The first successful union in the United States with national scope. Founded in 1867 by William Sylvis, the union grew quickly to 600,000 members, but fell apart rapidly after Sylvis's death in 1869.

National Recovery Administration (NRA)   The NRA was a major New Deal program aimed at business recovery. The NRA was anticompetitive since it allowed and encouraged agreements between firms. It was eventually declared to be unconstitutional.

natural monopoly   A monopoly that emerges because of economies of scale. The size of the market is such that there is room for only one optimally sized firm.

natural rate of unemployment   The idea that there is some level of unemployment to which the economy naturally tends to move and which is not affected in the long run by the inflation rate or by government monetary and fiscal policies.

near money   Assets that are relatively close and similar to the kinds of assets included in the money stock being considered.

negative income tax   A transfer from the government to the poor based on a formula similar to the present income tax system. A negative income tax has two components: an income guarantee and a negative tax rate.

net changes in foreign assets held in the United States   Over a period of time, there is a net change in the assets held in the United States by all foreign residents.

net changes in U.S. assets held abroad   Over a period of time, there is a net change in the assets held in foreign countries by all U.S. residents.

net foreign investment   Exports of goods and services minus imports. This difference equals the accumulation of domestically held foreign assets.

net investment income   In the balance of payments, investment income payments are treated as payments for the services of capital that one nation allows others to use. They are entered on a net basis.

net national product (NNP)   Gross national product less capital consumption allowances and adjustments (depreciation).

net private domestic investment   Gross private domestic investment less capital consumption allowances and adjustments (depreciation).

neutral tax   A tax that causes no distortion in economic activity.

New Economic Policy (NEP) An attempt at market socialism from 1921 to 1926 in the Soviet Union.

nominal (market) interest rate The rate of interest established in the market but not adjusted for inflation as the real rate of interest is.

non-price competition Competing with rivals through advertising, style changes, color changes, and techniques other than lowering price.

normal good A good for which demand increases as income increases.

normal profit The opportunity cost of capital and entrepreneurship. It is the level of profit that is necessary for a firm to remain in a competitive industry.

normative economics A set of propositions about what ought to be. These propositions embody value judgements about the world.

Norris-LaGuardia Act A law passed in 1932 that vastly strengthened the power of labor unions and set the stage for their rapid development.

note A promise of payment.

NOW accounts Negotiable order of withdrawal accounts. Checking accounts that pay interest.

oligopoly The market structure in which there are few firms. This causes firms to recognize their interdependence.

oligopsony The market situation in which there are few buyers of a factor of production.

100 percent reserves Reserves equal to 100 percent of the obligation outstanding.

open market desk The part of the Fed that engages in open market operations.

open market operations Purchases and sales of securities on the open market by the Fed.

opportunity cost Because of scarcity, every decision to produce or to consume means that we forego producing or consuming something else. The cost is the production or consumption foregone.

optimal-size plant The plant represented by the short-run average cost curve with the lowest attainable per-unit costs.

orderly marketing agreements (OMAs) Agreements by one country to restrict exports to another so as not to cause "disorderly" conditions in the latter's import-competing industries.

paradox of thrift The paradoxical result in the simple Keynesian model that when planned saving rises (the saving function shifts up), income falls, and actual saving is no higher than before.

parity Parity prices are an attempt to define fair prices —those which establish agricultural purchasing power at some past level. The period of 1910–1914 is usually viewed as the golden age of agriculture, and parity is often linked to this period.

partnership The form of business enterprise where there is more than one owner, and these owners are not legally distinguishable from the firm itself.

pegged, or fixed, exchange rate An exchange rate that is fixed at a predetermined level by intervening governments.

perfectly elastic A price elasticity coefficient of infinity. The quantity demanded responds in an infinite way to a change in price. The demand curve is a horizontal line.

perfectly inelastic A price elasticity of demand coefficient of zero. There is no response in quantity demanded to changes in price. The demand curve is vertical.

permanent income hypothesis The idea that people do not base their consumption decisions on their current income but on some longer-run average of the level of income they can expect.

personal income (PI) National income after subtraction of corporate profits taxes and undistributed corporate profits and after addition of net transfer payments.

Phillips curve A curve which seems to illustrate a short-run trade-off between the level of unemployment and the rate of inflation.

planned (command) economy An economy in which fundamental economic questions are answered through central command and control.

planning curve The long-run average cost curve. In the planning stage, any short-run curve tangent to the long-run curve can be selected.

point elasticity The responsiveness of quantity to price at a particular point on a curve.

positive economics A set of propositions which describes the world as it is, rather than as it ought to be.

positive theory A theory that leads to implications and hypotheses about the consequences of certain actions. Such a theory makes no judgements about the moral correctness of these implications.

precautionary motive Holding money as a precaution against unexpected requirements for using it.

preconditions for takeoff The stage where "uneconomic" culture is overcome, advances in agriculture take place, and an entrepreneurial class begins to emerge.

present value The capitalized value of an item to be paid for or sold in the future. A future value discounted to the present.

price The value, usually in money terms, for which goods and services are exchanged.

price ceilings Prices imposed by a governmental unit that are set as a limit. The ceiling is a price that cannot be exceeded.

price clusters Groupings of prices for similar, but not homogeneous, products.

price-consumption curve A curve that shows how the consumption of two goods changes as the price of one of the goods changes.

price discrimination The practice of charging different consumers different prices or a particular consumer different prices for different quantities purchased.

price elasticity of demand A measure of the responsiveness of the quantity demanded to changes in price.

price elasticity of supply A measure of the responsiveness of the quantity supplied to changes in price.

price floors Prices established as minimum prices. A governmental unit sets a price which cannot be undercut.

price index An index intended to show how the average price of a basket of goods changes over time.

price leadership The practice of industry pricing in which other firms follow the pricing initiatives of a particular firm, the price leader.

price searcher A firm that sets price in order to maximize profits. A price-searching firm has monopoly power.

price taker A firm in pure competition is a price taker because the firm views itself as having no influence on price. It can sell any amount at the market clearing price.

principle of diminishing marginal rates of substitution As a consumer receives more and more of a particular good, its value in terms of other goods declines. This is represented by the changing slope of the indifference curve.

principle of diminishing returns As more and more units of a variable factor are added to a set of fixed factors, the resulting increments of output will eventually become increasingly smaller.

producer price index (PPI) An index showing changes in the average price of goods that are of particular interest to producers.

product group A market for a good that is differentiated but which has a large number of close substitutes.

production The transformation of inputs into marketable outputs.

production function A description of the technical relationships that transform inputs into outputs. Production functions can generally be described by mathematical relationships.

production possibilities curve A graph which depicts the concept of opportunity cost by showing production trade-offs between two goods in a hypothetical economy.

production possibilities schedule A tabular representation of the production possibilities curve.

product markets Markets for the goods and services produced by firms or individuals.

profit The return to the entrepreneurship factor of production. Profit is the residual after all other factors have been paid.

progressive income tax An income tax which applies a higher tax rate to taxpayers with higher levels of income. The tax rate and income level are positively correlated.

property rights The legal rights to specific property. Markets and exchange can occur only if individuals have property rights to goods, services, and labor.

proportional income tax An income tax which applies the same tax rate to all taxpayers regardless of their level of income.

protectionism The desire to limit imports into a country in order to protect national firms from foreign competitors.

protective effect The protective effect of a tariff is the degree to which it limits imports, thus protecting national industry from foreign competition.

public goods Those goods that generate external benefits and which are jointly consumed. It is difficult to exclude people from consuming a public good. Goods for which consumption is nonrivalrous and nonexcludable; e.g., national defense.

pure competition The market structure in which there are many buyers and sellers. The firms produce a homogeneous product and there is free entry and exit of these firms to and from the industry.

pure oligopoly An oligopoly that produces a homogeneous product.

quantity theory of money The dominant macroeconomic theory until the Keynesian revolution of the 1930s. It focused on the determination of the overall price level in the long run and viewed the quantity of money as the primary influence on the long-run price level.

quota A physical limit on the amount of a commodity that may be imported.

ratifying price increases The idea that if either businesses or unions manage to raise prices, government will use expansionary policy so that the price increases won't reduce aggregate demand, output, and employment.

rationing   Limiting the amounts of various goods that people are allowed to buy.

Reaganomics   Economic policy as advocated by President Reagan. It emphasizes deregulation and tax cuts to spur investment and production.

real disturbance   A disturbance which affects some real aspect of the economy and thus changes the productive capacity of the economy.

real gross national product   Gross national product adjusted for price level changes (inflation).

real rate of interest   The nominal rate of interest minus the expected rate of inflation.

real wages   An index of wages, adjusted by a price index, showing how wage rate changes compare to price level changes.

recession   A decline in real GNP which lasts two quarters or longer.

reciprocity   A system of performing tasks and services for others in the expectation that others will recompense you by acting similarly.

recognition lag   The time lapse between when an economic disturbance occurs and when it is recognized by government policymakers.

redeemable paper money   Paper money that would be redeemed at face value in terms of some other money, usually precious metal.

rediscount   Using a discounted loan as collateral for borrowing, with the interest on this loan paid in advance.

regressive tax   A tax that takes a smaller percentage of income as income rises.

rent   The return to the capital factor of production.

rent control   Price ceilings that are imposed by governmental units on apartment rentals.

representative firm   A firm used to represent the firms in an industry; an average firm.

representative money   Money redeemable in a particular commodity.

repression phase   The early years of the labor movement during which government and the courts were hostile to union activity.

required reserves   The amount of reserves that a bank is required to hold on its various deposits.

reserve army of the unemployed   The large group of unemployed laborers that Marx predicted would unite, ultimately developing socialism.

reserve leakage   When a bank makes a loan, it expects that some of the loan will eventually be deposited elsewhere causing its reserves to fall.

reserve requirements   Requirements that certain percentages of Fed members' deposits be held as reserves.

revenue effect   The revenue effect of a tariff is the amount of tax revenue it raises for the government.

revenue sharing   The sharing of tax revenues among various levels of government. In the United States, the federal government usually shares revenue with state and local governments.

revolutionary unions   Unions that sought changes in the social order.

right-to-work laws   State laws that allow people to hold jobs without belonging to unions. Federal law leaves up to the states the choice between right-to-work laws and union shops.

risk   The idea that an actual outcome may be better or worse than expected.

risk aversion   Most individuals will, *ceteris paribus*, avoid risk unless they are compensated for assuming it.

robber barons   The very successful turn-of-the-century entrepreneurs who amassed fortunes by setting up trusts and holding companies.

rule of reason   The idea that industries which behaved well did not violate the Sherman Act. The court held that the existence of competitors was sufficient to demonstrate "reasonable behavior."

rules vs. discretion   The argument over whether monetary policy should be dictated by a set of simple rules or should be left to the discretion of the monetary authority.

runs on banks   Attempts by large numbers of people to withdraw their money all at once from the banks.

St. Louis Fed model   A model of the U.S. economy that took into account some of the earlier Keynesian criticisms of the Friedman-Meiselman tests.

satisficing   The situation that occurs when management does not seek to maximize profits, but rather seeks target levels of output and profits that are satisfactory to the interests of ownership.

save   The act of not spending an income flow for a particular period on goods and services.

Say's Law   Jean-Baptiste Say's theory which states that supply creates its own demand.

scarcity   The fact that there are not sufficient resources to produce everything that individuals want.

secondary boycotts   Union actions to stop one employer from doing business with another employer. This involves action to create pressures on third parties.

self-interest   A basic assumption of economic theory according to which individual decision makers act in a selfish manner. They do what is best for themselves.

self-regulating markets   Markets which quickly eliminate problems of shortage or surplus through price changes.

separation of ownership and control   Corporations are run by hired managers, not owners. These managers might operate by some principle other than profit maximization. This behavior results if managers have goals different than the owners' and if the owners cannot control the managers.

services   That part of consumption composed of such activities as those provided by gardeners, service personnel at restaurants, stock brokers, and so forth.

service transactions   In the balance of payments, imports and exports of services, such as tourism, insurance, and investment income.

shadow prices   Simulated market prices used by economic planners.

shared monopoly   A term used to describe a highly concentrated industry in which a few firms control the industry. The term is often used by lawyers rather than economists.

Sherman Antitrust Act   The first antitrust law, passed in 1890. Section 1 of the act declared every contract, combination, or conspiracy in restraint of trade to be illegal. Section 2 made it illegal to monopolize or attempt to monopolize.

shortage   The amount that consumers wish to purchase at some price exceeds the amount that suppliers wish to supply. A shortage can occur on a lasting basis only when a price ceiling is in effect.

short run   The period of time too short to vary all the factors of production. Short-run decisions are those concerned with using the existing plant more or less intensively.

short-run supply curve   The supply curve in the short run—the period in which the size of the plant cannot be varied. In pure competition, the short-run marginal cost curve is the short-run supply curve.

shutdown point   The level of output at which the firm minimizes its losses by ceasing operation.

single tax   A tax on land proposed by Henry George to capture the economic rent on land.

sluggish price and wage behavior   Prices and wages may respond slowly to some economic changes.

social costs   Costs that are borne by society or by some group without compensation. Externalities impose damages, or social costs, on groups in the population.

Social Darwinism   Charles Darwin's theory of the evolution of species as applied to business enterprise. Under that view, stronger firms were justified in getting bigger by swallowing up smaller firms.

socialism   An economic system in which the nonhuman means of production are owned by society, or the state.

socialist controversy   A debate started by Ludwig von Mises and Oskar Lange concerning the feasibility of planning without markets.

soil bank program   A program which attempts to raise farm income by paying farmers who allow their land to lay idle.

sole proprietorship   The form of business enterprise where no legal distinction is made between the firm and its owner.

speculative motive   The factor that makes people want to hold money as a hedge against the uncertain yields on securities.

stabilization function   The government's involvement in promoting full employment and stable prices.

stabilization policy   Government policy designed to stabilize the macro economy and smooth out fluctuations.

stages of production   Stage I is where increasing returns to the variable factor are experienced. Stage II is the area of diminishing returns. Stage III is the area of negative returns.

stagflation   A stagnant economy, combining recession or low economic growth with inflation.

Standard Industrial Classification (SIC) system   A system devised by the U.S. Census Bureau for classifying industries. The SIC system divides the economy into about 400 industries.

standard of debt   Money in its function of allowing borrowers and lenders to specify how a debt can be repaid in a generalized form of purchasing power rather than in specific goods.

standard of value   Money in its function of providing a standard for valuing goods, and thus readily comparing the value of different goods.

state banks   Banks chartered and regulated by individual states.

statistical discrepancy in the balance of payments   Net changes in asset holdings must exactly balance the current account deficit or surplus. However, since the deficit and the net changes in asset holdings are both estimates, they are seldom equal, and the difference is called the statistical discrepancy.

sticky downward   The downward inflexibility of prices and wages.

stockholders   The owners of a corporation.

stock market crash　The large, swift fall of the U.S. stock market in October, 1929.

stocks　Certificates of ownership in a corporation.

stock variable　An amount of some commodity in existence at a given point in time.

store of generalized purchasing power　Money in its function of providing purchasing power in a general form that can be used to purchase any particular good the holder desires.

structural unemployment　Unemployment due to structural shifts in the economy; for example, skills not matching job openings, workers being located in one area and their jobs in another, and so on.

subsidy payments　In international trade, payments made to exporters to encourage exports.

substitutes　Goods that replace the consumption of other goods. Substitutes have a positive cross elasticity of demand.

substitution effect　When the price of a good falls, it becomes less expensive relative to all other goods and more of it is consumed, substituting for other goods.

sunspot theory　A theory which states that business cycles are closely related to activity on the surface of the sun, or sunspots.

supply　The quantity of goods offered for sale at a particular place and a particular time.

supply curve　A graphical representation of a supply schedule showing the quantity supplied at various prices.

supply schedule　A tabular listing which shows quantity supplied at various prices.

supply-side economics　An economic theory which holds that if expectations of an environment conducive to business are created, business will see a potential for costs to be lowered, and supply will increase.

support prices　Price floors in agriculture that were used before 1973.

surplus　The amount that suppliers wish to supply at some price exceeds the amount that consumers wish to purchase. A surplus can only occur on a lasting basis when a price floor is in effect.

surplus value　The difference between the labor value of goods produced and the subsistence wages received by the workers.

tacit collusion　Unorganized and unstated attempts to practice joint action. Gentlemen's agreements and price leadership are two forms of tacit collusion.

Taft-Hartley Act　An act, passed in 1947, to reverse some of the excesses created by the Wagner Act.

President Truman vetoed the act but Congress overrode the veto. The act shifted some rights back to employers.

takeoff　The stage of development at which there is a significant increase in the rate of saving. Leading sectors develop and pull others along, and sustained growth is achieved.

target prices　Prices that the government determines are fair to farmers. After the market clearing price is determined, the government pays each farmer the difference between the target price and the market price.

tariff　A tax that is placed on the importation of goods into a country. A tariff can be a fixed amount per item or it can be a percentage of the value of the item.

tax-based incomes policy (TIP)　An incentive system under which a firm that granted any wage increase in excess of that allowed under wage-price controls would be penalized by the corporate income tax it pays.

tax efficiency　A measure of how a tax affects economic activity.

tax incidence　The place where the burden of a tax actually rests; those who pay the tax after all shifting has occurred.

tax wedge　Taxes are treated by businesses as costs of production which are then passed on to consumers in the form of higher prices.

technical efficiency　A method of production which minimizes physical usage of inputs according to some rule.

technologically determined demand　The demand for a factor of production is determined by the techniques of production and the level of technology used.

testable hypothesis　An inference from economic theory which is capable of being empirically tested.

theory　A set of principles which can be used to make inferences about the world.

total cost　The sum of all the costs of production.

total fixed cost　The cost of the fixed factors of production. Total fixed cost does not vary in the short run.

total physical product　The amount that a firm produces in physical units.

total revenue　The quantity of a good or service that a firm sells multiplied by the price of the good or service.

total variable cost　The total of costs that vary directly with output, increasing as more output is produced.

trade adjustment assistance   Programs to help workers and industries adjust to the effects of foreign competition.

trade credit   In the balance of payments, credit that an exporter grants an importer as part of a deal.

traditional (subsistence) economy   An economy in which fundamental economic questions are answered by appeals to tradition.

traditional society   A society largely governed by tradition and including a traditional economy.

transfer payments   Income payments to households not based on services performed. Transfers can be made by any sector, but the most important in the national income accounts are business and government transfer payments.

Treasury bills   Shorter term Treasury securities which pay no interest. The investor earns a return by buying the bill at an amount less than the Treasury pays when the bill matures.

treble damages   A provision under the Sherman Act that victims of monopoly can recover three times the damages they have sustained.

trusts   Legal organizations set up to control the stock of other companies through boards of trustees.

tying contracts   Agreements between producers and retailers whereby a retailer must agree to handle certain items as a prerequisite to handling other items.

unilateral transfers   Transfers to foreigners that bring no matching import or ownership of a foreign asset.

unintended business inventory changes   Changes that occur when the inventory level rises above, or falls below, that desired by the firm because the production level is inconsistent with the trend in sales.

union shops   Situations where union membership is necessary for a worker to remain employed. Federal law leaves up to the states the choice between right-to-work laws and union shops.

United Mine Workers   An industrial union for mine workers.

unit elastic   A price elasticity of demand coefficient of one. The change in quantity demanded responds at the same rate as any change in price. The demand curve is a rectangular hyperbola.

user charge   A fee charged by a governmental unit to consumers of certain publically supplied outputs.

util   An arbitrary unit used to measure utility.

utility   The satisfaction that an individual receives from consuming a good or service.

utility function   A preference function ordering a consumer's desire to consume differing amounts of goods.

utility interdependence   The fact that some individuals gain satisfaction from the consumption of goods by other parties.

utility maximization   The way a consumer adjusts consumption, given a budget constraint and a set of prices, in order to maximize the total amount of satisfaction.

value in exchange   Price, or value in exchange, is determined by marginal utility. Scarcity is related to value through utility.

value in use   Usefulness, or value in use, is often thought of as the total utility an item supplies. Water is thus very valuable in use, but not very valuable in exchange (price) because it has a low marginal utility.

value of the marginal physical product (VMP)   The value of the marginal physical product is found by multiplying it by the price at which the firm can sell its output.

variable factors   The factors of production that can be varied in the short run.

vault cash   Cash held in bank vaults.

velocity of money   The number of times the average dollar must "turn over" (be used) to purchase the period's final output (gross national product).

vertical equity   A situation that is achieved when taxpayers of different economic categories are treated differently.

vertical merger   A merger in which a company integrates its production backwards toward its source of supply or forward in its marketing chain.

vicious circle of poverty   Little investment because of a low level of income, and a low level of income because of little investment.

voluntary export restraints (VERs)   Restraints that one country places on its exports to avoid harming trade partners.

wages   The return to the labor factor of production.

Wagner Act   A law passed in 1935 that vastly strengthened the power of labor unions and set the stage for their rapid development.

Wagner's Law   A law, named for Adolph Wagner, which states that government tends to grow in a democracy.

War Communism   An economic system that was imposed by Lenin in Russia immediately after the Bolshevik Revolution. It is called War Communism because there was a continuing civil war at the time.

welfare economics   A branch of economics which evaluates the economic order from an ethical perspective.

welfare unions   Unions that had lofty ideals of social welfare and sought to establish worker cooperatives.

wildcat strikes   Local strikes that are not authorized by the national union.

withdrawals   Flows out of the circular flow of income, such as savings, taxes, and imports.

workers' self-management   The system in Yugoslavia in which workers direct and have a financial stake in the firm in which they work.

yellow-dog contracts   Contracts in which an employee must agree to refrain from union activity as a precondition for employment.

yield   The rate of return on funds invested in an asset.

INDEX

A

Abdul-Jabbar, Kareem, 550n
Ability to pay principle, defined, 107
Abortion activists, as a special interest group, 592
Absolute advantage, 616; comparative advantage vs., 616
Absolute level of income, 602–603
Accelerated cost recovery system depreciation, 112
Accelerationist theory, 281–283; defined, 278
Acceptability: as a desirable property of money, 62; of money, 68–69
Acreage allotment, defined, 380
Adjustable, but fixed, exchange rates, 632
Adjustment process, speeding up the, 310
Administered prices, defined, 522
Administration, in judging a tax structure, 109–110
Administrative Behavior, 484
Advances, defined, 82
Advertising: a possible decline in price and, 494; product differentiation and, 494–496
Assets, earning, 84
Affirmative Action Reconsidered, 606
Affluent Society, The, 523, 589
AFL-CIO, 625; defined, 575
Agency for International Development (AID), defined, 648
Aggregate demand, 122–123; formula for, 180; the Keynesian multiplier and changes in, 192
Aggregate demand schedule, 180, 185; planning the, 183–184
Aggregate prices, quantities and, 121
Aggregates, 4
Aggregate supply, 122–123
Aggregate supply schedule, 186–187
Agricultural support program, defined, 379
Agriculture: the economics of, 378–381;

the role of, in economic development, 638
Aid to Families with Dependent Children, 605, 609
Alchian, Armen, 484
Algebra, of the balanced budget multiplier, 223–224
Allocation function of government, defined, 99–100
Allocative efficiency, defined, 461
American Agriculture Movement, 592
American Capitalism: The Concept of the Countervailing Power, 523
American Farm Bureau, 592
American Federation of Labor (AFL), defined, 572
American Federation of State, County, and Municipal Employees (AFSCME), defined, 575
Anderson, Ken, 555
Anderson, Martin, 608
Antitrust enforcement in the United States: history of, 530–531; record of, 531–533
Antitrust laws in the United States, 528–534; political activity to reform, 533–535
Antitrust policy, President Johnson's Task Force on, 524
Arbitration, defined, 575
Arc elasticity, defined, 345
Arnold, Thurman, 531
Artificial barrier to entry, 471
Assets held abroad, net changes in United States, 627
Assets held in the United States, net changes in foreign, 627
Automatic transfer system accounts (ATS accounts), defined, 68
Automobiles, the market for, 339
Average cost curve: long-run, 434; marginal and, 432
Average fixed cost, defined, 430
Average physical product: defined, 427; marginal physical product and, 427–428

Average revenue, defined, 448
Average total cost, defined, 430
Average variable cost, defined, 430
Aversion to risk, 594

B

Backward countries, 636n.1
Bain, Joe, 523–524
Balanced budget multiplier, 208–209; algebra of the, 223–224
Balance of payments, 625–628; statistical discrepancy in the, 627; in the United States, third quarter of 1981, 626
Balance on current account, defined, 627
Balance on goods and services, defined, 626
Bank notes: checking accounts, other forms of money and, 67–68
Bank panics, defined, 76
Banks: as creators of money, 66–67; national, 78; runs on, 76; services of, 67; state, 78
Bank services, 67
Banks of deposit, defined, 67
Barriers to entry: artificial, 471; defined, 471; government and, 472; natural, 471
Barter: defined, 57; and the invention of money, 57–61
Baruch, Bernard, 680
Base year, defined, 130
Basic needs, provision of, 597
Battalio, Ray, 395
Baumol, William, 483
Baxter, William, 534
Beer: an excise tax on, 365; utility schedule for, 386
Beer industry, as an oligopoly, 495
Beggar-thy-neighbor policies, defined, 202n, 623
Behavior, taxes and, 109
Benefit-Cost Analyses of Social Regulation, 534
Benefits, external, 587

McLaren, Richard, 531
Macro, 3
Macroeconomic and microeconomic topics: defending the dollar, 11; economic security, 10–11; environmental standards, 11
Macroeconomic goals and policies, 10: curing inflation, 10; economic growth, 10; unemployment—full employment, 10
Macroeconomic policy: does government's, make things worse, 298–301; economic performance and, 295–321
Macroeconomic problems, 25
Macroeconomics, 137–336; classical, 138–157; defined, 4; the demise of classical, 167; Keynes's criticism of classical, 167–172
Macroeconomic theory, concepts and definitions in, 115–120
Macroeconomic topics, microeconomic topics and, 10–11
Macro economy: crucial role of unintended business inventory changes and equilibrium in the, 189–190; equilibrium in the, 188–198; a model of the, 120–122
Madden, Carl, 676
Maoism, 659–660
Mao Tse-tung, 659, 661
Marginal, 9n
Marginal analysis, 9
Marginal cost, defined, 430
Marginal cost curves, average and, 432
Marginal cost pricing: defined, 526; losses and, 526
Marginal efficiency of investment schedule, defined, 249
Marginalism, defined, 9
Marginal physical product: average physical product and, 427–428; defined, 427; value of (VMP), 543
Marginal productivity, income and, 554
Marginal productivity theory, defined, 542
Marginal propensity to consume (MPC): defined, 182; marginal propensity to save and, 182–183
Marginal propensity to save (MPS): defined, 182; marginal propensity to consume and, 182–183
Marginal rate of substitution: defined, 404; diminishing, 404
Marginal resource cost (MRC), defined, 544
Marginal revenue: defined, 438; demand and, 467–469; demand relationships with, 468
Marginal revenue product (MRP), defined, 544
Marginal revenue product of labor, 544
Marginal utility: defined, 306; diminishing, 386; the law of demand and, 392–393; principle of diminishing, 387–388; total, 387
Market clearing price, defined, 49
Market combinations, 551–552
Market Concentration Doctrine, defined, 521
Market demand, defined, 37
Market demand curve, 38, 467
Market economy, defined, 19

Market equilibrium, 47–49; defined, 47; externalities and, 582
Marketing quota system, defined, 380
Market intervention, exchange, 630
Market outcomes, completely separated from income distribution, 594–595
Market power, defined, 447
Market resolution, 20–22
Markets: black, 368, 369–370; demand for labor in monopolistic product, 546; demand for labor with monopoly in product, 546; the demand for labor under monopoly in product markets and pure competition in factor, 545–547; demand for labor under perfect competition in product and factor, 543–545; demand for labor in purely competitive product, 543–544; the distribution of income and factor, 540–562; factor, 22; governmental intervention into the, 580–610; intervention in, 367–372; for loanable funds, 558; a monopolistic firm facing a perfectly competitive labor, 547; monopsony in labor, 549; perfectly competitive labor, 545; product, 22; role of, in producing equitable incomes, 593–594
Market Structure and Equilibrium, 499
Market structures, 446, 512; summary of, 512
Market structures continuum, 488
Market supply, 44–45; defined, 44
Market supply curve, 455
Marshall, Alfred, 3, 142, 143, 145, 148, 170, 227n, 385, 672, 678; biography, 36
Marshall, Ray, 576
Marx, Karl, 154, 615, 643–644, 660, 663; Marxists, Marxism, and, 656
Mass consumption, high, 645
Maturity, drive to, 645
Maximization: consumer, 408; profit, 438–440, 449; utility, 391
Maximization of satisfaction, 407–411
Means, Gardiner, 519, 522
Meany, George, 575
Median, defined, 640
Mediation, defined, 575
Medicaid, 605
Medicare, 605
Medium of exchange, defined, 61
Meltzer, Allan H., 228, 261; biography, 230
Merchandise exports and imports, defined, 625
Merchandise trade balance, defined, 625
Merger: conglomerate, 534; horizontal, 534; vertical, 534
Merit goods, defined, 100
Meyer, Stephen A., 333
Micro, 3
Microeconomic issues, 11–12: activity of government, 11; energy policy, 11; labor unions, 11
Microeconomic problems, 19–20
Microeconomic questions, basic, 19
Microeconomics: defined, 3; the basics of, 337–417
Microeconomic topics, macroeconomic topics and, 10–11
Micro tools, some applications of basic, 361–383

Middle-income countries, 636n.1; demographic indicators of, 640; educational levels of, 642; growth of production in, 638; health-related indicators of, 641; structure of population in, 639; structure of production in, 639
Military transactions, defined, 626
Mill, James, 615
Mill, John Stuart, 615
Miller, James C., III, 676; biography, 534
Minimum wage, 371–372; defined, 371; monopsony power and the, 550–551
Mixed economy, 19; modern government in a, 99–102
Mixed economy resolution, 25–26
Model of pure competition, 446–465; characteristics of, 447; competitive adjustment in the long run and the, 455–461; competitive adjustment in the short run and the, 447–455; equilibrium in the, 461–462; examples of, 463–464; profits in the, 462–463
Modern Capitalism and Other Essays, 509
Modern quantity theory of money, 225–245; defined, 225; inflation and the interest rate and, 254–259; Keynesian views of the world vs., 297–303; origins of the Keynesian revolution and the, 226–227; from the quantity theory to the, 228–229; stagflation as viewed by, 308–310; views on inflation and the interest rate, 254–259
Monetarists, on stopping inflation, 266. *See also* Modern quantity theory of money
Monetary base, defined, 260
Monetary disturbance: defined, 122; real vs., 122
Monetary policy: the appropriate role of, in the Keynesian view, 254; bond prices and bond yields in, 247–248; bond yields and, 248–249; economic performance and, 246–269; the effects of, in the Keynesian analysis, 247; fiscal policy vs., 254; investment spending and the rate of interest and, 249; Keynesian views on the influence of, 247–254; problems Keynesians see with, 251–254; the status of the debate on, 296–297
Monetary system, evolution of United States', 64–68
Money: acceptability of, 62, 68–69; bank notes, checking accounts, and other forms of, 67–68; banks as creators of, 66–67; barter and the invention of, 57–61; the behavior of k and V and the demand for, 231–235; a bookkeeping alternative to using, 59–60; creation of, 74–76; debasement of, 63; defined, 56; desirable properties of, 62–64; divisibility of, 62; durability of, 62; expected yields, risk, and the demand for, 232–234; fiat, 68; the functions of, 61–62; homogeneity of, 62; inflation and the creation of, 210; Keynes and the quantity theory of, 170–171; as a medium of exchange, 61; modern quantity theory of, 225–245; motives for holding, 232; ongoing inflation and, 289–290; price level changes and the demand for,

ACKNOWLEDGEMENTS

For permission to reproduce the photographs on the pages indicated, acknowledgement is made to the following:

COVER

Photograph by Sarah Baehr, Photographer, New York, New York.

PART 1

p. 6: Historical Picture Service, Inc., Chicago. p. 7: University of Chicago/Office of News and Information. p. 7: Massachusetts Institute of Technology, News Office. p. 21: BBC Hulton Picture Library. p. 24: The Bettmann Archive, Inc. p. 36: Historical Picture Service Inc., Chicago. p. 42: S. McElhinney/NEWSWEEK.

PART 2

p. 58: Rick Browne. p. 63: National Museum of Natural History, Smithsonian Institution. p. 80: The Bettmann Archive, Inc. p. 84: Bruce Hoertel. p. 132: Herman Kokajan/Black Star. p. 134: Harvard University News Office.

PART 3

p. 146: Wide World Photos. p. 151: Historical Picture Service, Inc., Chicago. p. 168: Library of Congress. p. 169: BBC Hulton Picture Library. p. 188: Tennessee-Tombigbee Waterway Development Authority. p. 195: Harvard University News Office. p. 214: Tom Foley/University Relations, University of Minnesota. p. 214: Paul Conklin/The Brookings Institution. p. 218: BYTE Publications, Inc. p. 230: James S. Peck/University of Rochester. p. 230: Carnegie-Mellon University. p. 238: Board of Governors of the Federal Reserve System. p. 255: Charles Erickson/Yale University Office of Public Information. p. 261: Werner Wolff/Black Star. p. 283: Indiana University News Bureau. p. 283: University of Chicago/Office of News and Information. p. 289: Sipa Press/Black Star. p. 300: Cambridge University Library. p. 300: Aran Patinkin. p. 313: Dennis Brack/Black Star. p. 328: Faith Kattenbach/Grant Heilman. p. 331: University of Southern California Finance and Business Economics Department.

PART 4

p. 352: Historical Picture Service, Inc., Chicago. p. 358: Ken Love/Black Star. p. 369: Sipa Press/Black Star. p. 378: Robert Barclay/Grant Heilman. p. 388: BBC Hulton Picture Library. p. 395: Bruce Coleman, Inc. p. 399: Wide World Photos.

PART 5

p. 442: Lane Stewart/SPORTS ILLUSTRATED. p. 454: Leslie Goldman/Black Star. p. 463: Paul V. Thomas/Black Star. p. 476: Chrysler Corporation. p. 484: Carnegie-Mellon University Public Relations Department. p. 489: Nicholas Lee/Ramsey & Muspratt, Cambridge, England. p. 489: Harvard University News Office. p. 507: Tom O'Brien/Tri-Con Photos. p. 509: University of Chicago/Office of News and Information. p. 509: Sam Sweezy. p. 523: Rick Stafford/Harvard University News Office. p. 534: Federal Trade Commission.

PART 6

p. 541: Brown Brothers. p. 556: The Robert Schalkenbach Foundation. p. 573: AFL-CIO News. p. 577: Martin Levik/Black Star. p. 606: Thomas Sowell.

PART 7

p. 615: Brown Brothers. p. 624: James Mason. p. 646: United Nations. p. 649: Rick Reinhard/Black Star. p. 664: Sipa Press/Black Star. p. 667: New York University

PART 8

p. 675: Council of Economic Advisers. p. 680: Lois Wadler. p. 680: Uniphoto. p. 681: N.E.W.S. Photo News. p. 681: The Archives of Labor and Urban Affairs/Wayne State University.